The Incarnation

The Incarnation

An Interdisciplinary Symposium on the
Incarnation of the Son of God

Edited by

Stephen T. Davis
Daniel Kendall, SJ
Gerald O'Collins, SJ

OXFORD

UNIVERSITY PRESS

Great Clarendon Street, Oxford OX2 6DP

Oxford University Press is a department of the University of Oxford.
It furthers the University's objective of excellence in research, scholarship,
and education by publishing worldwide in

Oxford New York

Athens Auckland Bangkok Bogotá Buenos Aires Cape Town
Chennai Dar es Salaam Delhi Florence Hong Kong Istanbul Karachi
Kolkata Kuala Lumpur Madrid Melbourne Mexico City Mumbai Nairobi
Paris São Paulo Shanghai Singapore Taipei Tokyo Toronto Warsaw

with associated companies in Berlin Ibadan

Oxford is a registered trade mark of Oxford University Press
in the UK and in certain other countries

Published in the United States
by Oxford University Press Inc., New York

British Library Cataloguing in Publication Data

Data available

Library of Congress Cataloging in Publication Data

The Incarnation: an interdisciplinary symposium on the Incarnation of the Son of God /
edited by Stephen T. Davis, Daniel Kendall, Gerald O'Collins.
p. cm.
Proceedings of the Incarnation Summit, held Apr. 23–26, 2000
at Dunwoodie, Yonkers, N.Y.
Includes index.
1. Incarnation–Congresses. I. Davis, Stephen T., 1940– II. Kendall, Daniel.
III. O'Collins, Gerald. IV. Incarnation Summit
(2000: Dunwoodie, Yonkers, N.Y.)
BT220.I5 2002 232'.1–dc21 2001033839

ISBN 0-19-924845-1

1 3 5 7 9 10 8 6 4 2

Typeset in Photina
by Joshua Associates Ltd., Oxford
Printed in Great Britain
on acid-free paper by
Biddles Ltd., Guildford and King's Lynn

Preface

From the beginning of the twentieth century monographs on the incarnation, or belief that the Son/Word of God personally assumed a fully human existence at the time of Emperor Augustus, have appeared at regular intervals. In particular, since the Second World War ended in 1945, this central Christian doctrine has been examined and expounded by Hans Urs von Balthasar, Karl Barth, G. S. Hendry, John Hick, Bernard Lonergan, W. R. Matthews, Jürgen Moltmann, T. V. Morris, Wolfhart Pannenberg, Norman Pittenger, Karl Rahner, Paul Tillich, T. F. Torrance, and others. Biblical and historical studies by such writers as J. D. G. Dunn, Alois Grillmeier, Richard Hanson, J. N. D. Kelly, C. F. D. Moule, Jaroslav Pelikan, and Rowan Williams have enriched scholarly appreciation of the origins and development of belief in the incarnation.

Theological reflection on the incarnation could be enhanced by more symposia, especially those of an interdisciplinary character. But, to say the least, there have not been many such symposia. A collaborative work edited by John Hick, *The Myth of God Incarnate* (London: SCM Press, 1977) was a welcome exception. Its sequel, edited by Michael Goulder, *Incarnation and Myth: The Debate Continued* (London: SCM Press, 1979) proved an even more fruitful and stringent interchange. Over twenty years later, at the start of the third millennium, it seemed worthwhile gathering experts in a variety of disciplines (biblical studies, ancient Christian writers, ancient Jewish writers, theology, philosophy, preaching, literature, and the fine arts) from three continents to explore collaboratively the incarnation. Hence we brought together twenty-one other specialists, many of whom have already published works on different aspects of the specific Christian belief in the incarnation. We managed to secure papers, sometimes more than one paper, in all these fields.

To promote advance discussion and establish stronger connecting threads between the different contributions, we encouraged those presenting papers to circulate them in advance to all members of the symposium. In almost every case drafts had been sent out (and often also made available by e-mail) for feedback before we met at Dunwoodie (23–6 April 2000) for the Incarnation Summit itself. An article by Gerald O'Collins (*Furrow*, July 2000) tells the story of the meeting.

In *Incarnation and Myth: The Debate Continued* Maurice Wiles named five issues concerning the incarnation as being of major importance: the logical coherence of the belief in itself, its coherence with other Christian doctrines, the evidence for the incarnation from foundational Christian literature, the uniqueness and universality of Jesus, and the impact of cultural conditioning on forming belief in the incarnation (pp. 5–12). All these issues have maintained their importance and are addressed in the book we are editing. But our collaborative project takes up a number of further questions such as: could the incarnation have occurred more than once? What sense would it make to imagine the incarnation of the first or third person of the Trinity? How should the doctrine of the incarnation be expressed in art and preaching? What influence should it have on ethics?

After a critical survey of the issues (O'Collins), this collection moves from biblical questions and milieu (Dearman, Wright, Fee, Aletti, and Segal) through some classical teaching and reflection on the incarnation (Coakley, Daley, and Stump), and on to theological and philosophical debates (Davis, Evans, and Leftow). It ends with some 'practical' applications of incarnation faith to writing, art, ethics, and preaching (Norris, Zagzebski, Brown, and Shuster). This volume proposes approaching the multi-faceted incarnation faith in an organized and coherent way: namely, by reflecting on biblical, historical, foundational, systematic, and practical data and questions. What now follows in this preface will unfold the movement of the book as a whole and the interrelationship between the particular papers. To achieve even further unity, Chapter 1 will also point out links with later chapters and their place in the landscape of incarnation studies. That chapter, along with those to follow, recognizes how various issues connected with the incarnation cannot be solved with relative ease. Here, as elsewhere, orthodox Christian faith must face serious and difficult challenges.

In Chapter 1, Gerald O'Collins outlines twelve issues: the particular, historical truth of the union of divinity and humanity in the one person of Jesus Christ; his personal pre-existence; the paradox in holding the Chalcedonian teaching of Jesus being truly divine and fully human; the objection that the incarnation entails unfairness on the part of God; the divine and human wills and minds of Christ in their sinless harmony; the virginal conception as the way the incarnation actually happened; God's reasons for the incarnation; its revelatory and redemptive impact; the relationship of the incarnation to the crucifixion and resurrection; the incarnation being possible only for the Word of God; the incarnation as a once and for all occurrence; the credibility of the incarnation.

In Chapter 2, Andrew Dearman examines two elements in the OT: the anthropomorphic presentation of God in theophany and the creation of humankind in the *imago Dei*. Anthropomorphism was a way that divine presence could be apprehended by people, and theomorphism indicated both a basis on which humankind understood its divinely mandated tasks and one way in which the divine-human relationship could be represented. In spite of anti-anthropomorphic traditions elsewhere in the OT, these two elements influenced the presentation of Christ in the early church and both may contribute to a modern understanding of the incarnation.

In Chapter 3, Tom Wright challenges the view that no first-century Jew could think of incarnation, let alone believe himself to be the incarnate Son of God. Wright argues that Jesus understood his own journey to Jerusalem and what he would do and suffer there as the long-awaited coming of YHWH to his Temple. Jesus believed himself called to do and be things which Israel's God was to do and be. This self-understanding provides the deepest historical root for the growth of NT faith.

In Chapters 4 and 5, Gordon Fee and Jean-Noël Aletti provide complementary studies on St Paul. Fee offers an exegetical/historical re-examination of Paul's Christology on the question of Christ's incarnation (and pre-existence) over against those who either reject or offer a diminished view of these ideas in the Apostle's letters. Fee examines four groups of Pauline passages: those that explicitly presuppose the pre-existence of Christ as the mediator of creation; texts that speak of his 'impoverishment' in becoming human; texts that speak of God's sending his Son into the world so as to redeem it; and several passages that emphasize Christ's humanity in a way that seems to presuppose an incarnational Christology. Since

Wisdom Christology plays a major role in most versions of Pauline Christology—in support of both traditional and reductive views—a section of this chapter offers a critique of this wisdom analysis.

Aletti takes up a specific passage, Romans 8: 3–4, and argues that, despite its spare and precise style, these verses do allude to the incarnation. His chapter also draws out the redemptive consequences Paul sees in the incarnation.

In Chapter 6, Alan Segal starts by observing that incarnation is not an easy category to fit into native Jewish categories for talking about God. Casting around for adequate precedents, he first examines Plato's conceptions of matter and spirit (along with mortality and immortality). Philo was to use Platonic thought and vocabulary significantly, although he did not breach the line between spiritual and material objects. Philo looked askance at incarnation. Segal then recalls various angelic theophanies and mediation scenes, where precedents for the Christian conception of incarnation seem better grounded in Jewish literature.

Beginning with Chapter 7, the book moves to the patristic and medieval periods with the contributions of Sarah Coakley, Brian Daley, and Eleonore Stump. In Chapter 7, Sarah Coakley challenges three versions of the meaning of the Chalcedonian Definition of 451: that the Definition merely regulates the use of language about Christ without making any direct affirmations; that the Definition is 'metaphorical' in a non-cognitive sense; that the Definition is 'literally' true, even to the point of producing specific, univocal, and empirical assertions that were alien to the fifth-century authors of the text. She then expounds a fourth position that treats the Definition as a 'horizon' which sets boundaries about what can and cannot be said of Christ, while remaining open-ended and apophatic about the mystery of his person.

In Chapter 8, Brian Daley observes how contemporary theologians are often puzzled by the language and concepts of later patristic discussions about the person of Christ, especially by the Council of Chalcedon's teaching that he is one hypostasis or persona subsisting 'in two natures, without confusion, without change, without division, without separation'. This chapter looks again at the significance of this classical christological vocabulary, in the light of an assertion made by the sixth-century Leontius of Byzantium and echoed by Maximus Confessor and John of Damascus in the centuries that followed: that it is 'the mode of union, rather than the intelligible structure of nature, which contains the great Mystery of our religion'. After sketching the background and apparent implications of the ancient language of 'modality' and of 'union', the chapter looks more closely at the Christology of these three post-Chalcedonian writers to argue that for classical Greek Christology in its later stages the unity and distinctiveness of Christ as a person, who is at once human and divine, are grounded in the unique way in which the divine and human realities condition and express each other in the historical Jesus of Nazareth. In the light of this 'relational' or 'modal' Christology, these late patristic authors also present human salvation as the beginning of a new mode of our own natural existence, and a new relationship with the triune God modelled on that of God the Son.

In Chapter 9, Eleonore Stump presents Aquinas' interpretation of the metaphysics of the incarnation—his attempt to make sense out of a theological doctrine bequeathed to him as a traditional and central part of Christian belief. This chapter aims to clarify and support both his understanding of doctrine and his metaphysics. Stump begins by laying out the parts of Aquinas' metaphysics which are particularly important for the doctrine of the incarnation. Then she turns to his interpretation of the doctrine itself. She is concerned particularly with the way in which Aquinas understands the Chalcedonian formula, the resources which his interpretation of the formula has for handling familiar objections to the doctrine of the incarnation, and the view of the mind(s) of Christ to which his interpretation is committed.

In Chapter 10, Stephen Davis explores the rationality of belief in the incarnation by analysing the argument used by C. S. Lewis and others that Jesus was either 'mad, bad, or God'. He concludes that this argument does establish the rationality of incarnational faith.

In Chapter 11, Stephen Evans defends as religiously powerful and theologically legitimate a 'kenotic' theory of the incarnation, arguing that some kind of divine 'self-emptying' or 'self-limitation' does justice to the NT accounts of Jesus and the claims of Chalcedonian orthodoxy. In particular, the chapter defends recent work by Stephen Davis and Ronald Feenstra, who hold that Jesus may be fully divine even if he divests himself, perhaps only temporarily, of such qualities as omnipotence and omniscience. The possibility of such divesting is implied by a plausible account of the nature of omnipotence developed by Richard Swinburne.

Evans also proposes that a decision by God to become incarnated, literally embodied, is best understood as a decision to assume such limitations. In conclusion, the chapter discusses the implications of a kenotic theory for the exalted and glorified Christ, and the question whether Jesus, understood kenotically as the incarnate Word, can be personally identical with the pre-existent second person of the Trinity.

In Chapter 12, Brian Leftow argues that divine timelessness and the incarnation are compatible. He first sketches what it means to say that God is timeless. He then presents two major arguments for holding that divine timelessness is incompatible with the incarnation. With this done he sets out enough of the orthodox doctrine of the incarnation to let him address the arguments and show how they fail. He concludes that it is *prima facie* plausible that God can be both timeless and incarnate.

The fourth and concluding section of the book ('The Incarnation Practised and Proclaimed') begins, in Chapter 13, with Kathleen Norris who deals with incarnational language (in a literary rather than an exclusively theological sense) and the task of writers.

In Chapter 14, Linda Zagzebski proposes a formal framework for an ethical theory in which the incarnation is central and the imitation of Christ the basic normative idea. Her formal framework of exemplarism makes it possible to utilize the advantages of narrative ethics within a formal theory. She then sketches a practical form of exemplarist virtue theory that she calls Divine Motivation (DM) theory. In this theory all evaluative concepts are derived from the concept of a good motive, and God's motives are the metaphysical ground for all value. Zagzebski argues that DM theory is more distinctively Christian than such law-based theories as Divine Command theory and Natural Law theory.

In Chapter 15, David Brown discusses how the humanity and divinity of Christ have been presented in twentieth-century art. Some representative artists are examined: for painting, Bacon, Chagall, Dalí, Ernst, Magritte, O'Keeffe, Picasso, Rouault, Spencer, and Warhol; for sculpture, Epstein, Gill, and Moore. Brown concludes not only that the religious and incarnational impulse in modern art is healthier than is commonly supposed, but also that certain non-Christians have been highly effective in conveying the truth of a doctrine in which they themselves do not believe. Even where this is not so, sometimes the implicit critique that they offer still requires careful consideration on the part of Christian believers. Brown also notes the wide range of means that have been employed to indicate divinity.

In Chapter 16, Marguerite Shuster explores the handling of the incarnation in Christmas sermons from seven twentieth-century preachers: four Roman Catholic and three Protestant. Her analysis is structured by the issues O'Collins's chapter identified as critical for contemporary discussion. Perhaps surprisingly, almost all his key questions are treated by these preachers in their sermons. Furthermore, the doctrinal material is most often handled in a moving and homiletically satisfying manner. Thus, these examples may prove encouraging for preachers concerned with the viability of doctrinal preaching.

As the summaries offered above indicate, this volume contains sixteen presentations from the Incarnation Summit. In fact, each of the presentations was followed by a response that initiated the discussion of the particular paper. To avoid making this volume too long, we did not include the responses.

We are most grateful to the McCarthy Family foundation and, specifically, to Dr Eugene and the late Maureen McCarthy, for their most generous and prayerful support of our Incarnation Summit. Our special thanks go to Monsignor Francis J. McAree, Rector of St Joseph's Seminary, Dunwoodie (Yonkers, NY), for his gracious hospitality and help. We wish to thank warmly the Catholic Archbishop of New York, the late Cardinal John O'Connor, for his continuing encouragement. Fr. Gerard R. Rafferty and other members of the Dunwoodie staff provided us once again with extraordinarily efficient assistance. Claudia Devaux of Hewlett-Packard generously set up a web page so that the Summit participants could keep in touch with one another. The lavish generosity of the Rudin family (in particular, Jack and Susan Rudin) and the untiring work of Monsignor Gregory Mustaciuolo and the staff of Cardinal O'Connor's office made possible the memorable lecture on 'Christ and Twentieth-Century Art' at the Metropolitan Museum by Professor David Brown and the reception which followed. We also wish to thank Joseph Zwilling and various representatives of the media for their vivid interest and sincere support. Lastly, we are particularly grateful to Hilary O'Shea, Lucy Qureshi, and Jenny Wagstaffe of Oxford University Press, to all the scholars who participated in and contributed to our symposium, to the seven hundred guests who attended David Brown's lecture, to those who shared in the open seminar on 27 April which followed the Incarnation Summit, and to Sarah Coakley who once again joined us in running that seminar.

As world history moves into the third millennium, we offer the results of this interdisciplinary and international symposium to all interested readers. We dedicate our book with deep love and affection to the late Charis Davis, Maureen McCarthy, and Cardinal John O'Connor. May this volume offer some help towards understanding that faith in the incarnate Son of God which was the heart of their human existence and worship. As have millions of other Christians, they directed their hearts and minds constantly towards the figure whom Ben Jonson (1572–1637) in 'A Hymn on the Nativity of My Saviour' called 'the author both of life and light'.

STEPHEN T. DAVIS, DANIEL KENDALL, SJ, and GERALD O'COLLINS, SJ
31 July 2000

Contents

Plates   XV

Abbreviations   XVI

Participants in the Incarnation Summit (Easter, 2000, New York) xviii

1. The Incarnation: The Critical Issues   I
   GERALD O'COLLINS, SJ

BIBLICAL WITNESS

2. Theophany, Anthropomorphism, and the *Imago Dei*:
   Some Observations about the Incarnation in the Light
   of the Old Testament   31
   J. ANDREW DEARMAN
3. Jesus' Self-Understanding   47
   N. T. WRIGHT
4. St Paul and the Incarnation: A Reassessment of the
   Data   62
   GORDON D. FEE
5. Romans 8: The Incarnation and its Redemptive Impact   93
   JEAN-NOËL ALETTI, SJ
6. The Incarnation: The Jewish Milieu   116
   ALAN F. SEGAL

PATRISTIC AND MEDIEVAL WITNESS

7. What Does Chalcedon Solve and What Does it Not?
   Some Reflections on the Status and Meaning of the
   Chalcedonian 'Definition'   143
   SARAH COAKLEY

8. Nature and the 'Mode of Union': Late Patristic Models for the Personal Unity of Christ 164
   BRIAN E. DALEY, SJ
9. Aquinas' Metaphysics of the Incarnation 197
   ELEONORE STUMP

FOUNDATIONAL AND SYSTEMATIC ISSUES

10. Was Jesus Mad, Bad, or God? 221
    STEPHEN T. DAVIS
11. The Self-Emptying of Love: Some Thoughts on Kenotic Christology 246
    C. STEPHEN EVANS
12. A Timeless God Incarnate 273
    BRIAN LEFTOW

THE INCARNATION PRACTISED AND PROCLAIMED

13. A Word Made Flesh: Incarnational Language and the Writer 303
    KATHLEEN NORRIS
14. The Incarnation and Virtue Ethics 313
    LINDA ZAGZEBSKI
15. The Incarnation in Twentieth-Century Art 332
    DAVID BROWN
16. The Incarnation in Selected Christmas Sermons 373
    MARGUERITE SHUSTER

Index of Names 397

List of Plates

The plates appear on pp. 365–72

1. George Rouault, *Nazareth* (1948). Vatican Museum.

2. Stanley Spencer, *The Last Supper* (1920). Stanley Spencer gallery, Cookham, Berkshire. © Estate of Stanley Spencer 2002. All Rights Reserved, DACS.

3. Salvador Dalí, *Christ of St John of the Cross* (1951). St Mungo Museum of Religious Life and Art, Glasgow Galleries. Glasgow.

4. Max Ernst, *The Infant Jesus Chastised by the Virgin Mary before Witnesses* (1926). Museum Ludwig, Cologne. © ADAGP, Paris and DACS, London 2002.

5. Francis Bacon, *Fragment of a Crucifixion* (1950). Stedelijk van Abbe Museum, Eindhoven, Netherlands. © Estate of Francis Bacon / ARS, NY and DACS, London 2002.

6. Marc Chagall, *White Crucifixion* (1938). Art Institute of Chicago. © ADAGP, Paris and DACS, London 2002.

7. Eric Gill, *The Holy Face of Christ* (1925). Manchester City Art Gallery.

8. Jacob Epstein, *Consummatum Est* (1936). Scottish National Gallery of Modern Art, Edinburgh.

Abbreviations

ACO	E. Schwartz *et al.*, *Acta conciliorum oecumenicorum* (Berlin: de Gruyter, 1914–)
BAGD	W. Bauer, W. F. Arndt, F. W. Gingrich, and F. W. Danker, *Greek–English Lexicon of the New Testament* (2nd edn., Chicago: University of Chicago Press, 1979)
BCE	Before Common Era
CAG	*Commentaria in Aristotelem Graeca*
CD	*Church Dogmatics*
CE	Common Era
ETL	*Ephemerides theologicae lovanienses*
GCS	Die griechischen christlichen Schriftsteller der ersten Jahrhunderte
GNO	Werner Jaeger *et al.*, *Gregorii Nysseni Opera*, 10 vols. (Leiden: Brill, 1960–90)
JETS	*Journal of the Evangelical Theological Society*
JSJ	*Journal for the Study of Judaism in the Persian, Hellenistic, and Roman Period*
JSNTSS	Journal for the Study of the New Testament. Supplement Series
JSOT	*Journal for the Study of the Old Testament*
JSOTSS	Journal for the Study of the Old Testament. Supplement Series
JTC	*Journal for Theology and the Church*
JTS	*Journal of Theological Studies*
KJV	King James Version
LXX	Septuagint
NEB	New English Bible
NICNT	New International Commentary on the New Testament
NJB	New Jerusalem Bible
NovTSup	Novum Testamentum. Supplement Series
NRSV	New Revised Standard Version

NT	New Testament
NTS	*New Testament Studies*
OT	Old Testament
PG	Patrologia Graeca (J.-P. Migne)
QDV	Questiones Disputatae de Veritate (St Thomas Aquinas)
RB	*Revue biblique*
RSV	Revised Standard Version
SBL	Society of Biblical Literature
SC	Sources chrétiennes
SCG	*Summa contra Gentiles*
ST	*Summa Theologica*
TOB	Traduction œcuménique de la Bible
TrinJ	*Trinity Journal*
TS	*Theological Studies*
TU	A. von Harnack, *et al.*, *Texte und Untersuchungen zur Geschichte der altchristlichen Literatur* (Berlin: Akademie-Verlag, 1882–)
VTSup	Vetus Testamentum. Supplement Series
WBC	Word Biblical Commentary
WUNT	Wissenschaftliche Untersuchungen zum Neuen Testament
ZNW	*Zeitschrift für die neutestamentliche Wissenschaft*

Participants in the Incarnation Summit
(Easter, 2000, New York)

JEAN-NOËL ALETTI   Born in Groslay, France, he received his Master's in Philosophy and Mathematics (Paris, Sorbonne); licentiates in theology at the Seminaire des Missions (Lyon) in 1973 and in scripture at the Pontifical Biblical Institute (Rome) in 1975, and a doctorate in scripture (Pontifical Biblical Institute) in 1981. Currently he is Professor of New Testament Exegesis at the Pontifical Biblical Institute. Recent publications include: *Israël et la Loi dans la lettre aux Romains* (Paris: Cerf, 1998), *Il racconto come teologia. Studio narrativo del terzo Vangelo e del libro degli Atti degli Apostoli* (Rome: Dehoniane, 1996), and *Jésus Christ fait-il l'unité du Nouveau Testament?* (Paris: Desclée, 1994).

WILLIAM P. ALSTON   Born in Shreveport, Louisiana, he earned his Bachelor's degree from Centenary College of Louisiana, and his Ph.D. from the University of Chicago in 1951. Currently he is Professor Emeritus of Philosophy at Syracuse University. Recent books by him include *Illocutionary Acts and Sentence Meaning* (2000), *A Realist Conception of Truth* (1996), *The Reliability of Sense Perception* (1993), and *Perceiving God: The Epistemology of Religious Experience* (1991), *Epistemic Justification* (1989), and *Divine Nature and Human Language* (1989), all published by Cornell University Press (Ithaca, NY).

DAVID BROWN   Born in Galashiels, Scotland, he obtained an MA (in Classics) at Edinburgh and a second MA (in Philosophy and Theology) at Oxford, and his Ph.D. (in Moral Philosophy) from Cambridge. Formerly a Fellow of Oriel College, Oxford, he is currently Van Mildert Professor of Divinity in the University of Durham. Publications by him include: (with David Fuller) *Signs of Grace: Sacraments in Poetry and Prose* (London: Continuum, 2000), *Discipleship and Imagination: Christian Tradition and Truth* (Oxford:

Oxford University Press, 2000), *Tradition and Imagination: Revelation and Change* (Oxford: Oxford University Press, 1999), and *The Word To Set You Free* (London: SPCK, 1995)

SARAH COAKLEY   Born in London, she obtained her undergraduate degree (1973) as well as her doctoral degree (1982) from the University of Cambridge. Currently she is Edward Mallinckrodt, Jr., Professor of Divinity, Harvard University. Writings by her include: (editor) *Religion and the Body* (Cambridge: Cambridge University Press, 1997), *God, Sexuality and the Self: an Essay 'On the Trinity'* (Cambridge: Cambridge University Press, forthcoming), (coedited) *The Making and Remaking of Christian Doctrine: Essays in Honour of Maurice Wiles* (Oxford: Clarendon Press, 1993), and *Christ Without Absolutes: A Study of the Christology of Ernst Troeltsch* (Oxford: Oxford University Press, 1988).

BRIAN E. DALEY   Born in Orange, New Jersey, he obtained his Bachelor's degree at Fordham University in 1961, and a BA (MA) in Classics and Philosophy at Merton College, Oxford, in 1964. After entering the Society of Jesus in that year, he obtained a Ph.L. at Loyola Seminary, Shrub Oak, New York, in 1966, and an STL at the Hochschule Sankt Georgen, Frankfurt-am-Main, in 1972. He received a D.Phil. in theology from Oxford University in 1978. He is currently the Catherine F. Huisking Professor of Theology at the University of Notre Dame. Books by him include: *The Dormition of Mary: Early Greek Homilies* (Yonkers, NY: St Vladimir's Press, 1998), *The Hope of the Early Church: A Handbook of Patristic Eschatology* (Cambridge and New York: Cambridge University Press, 1991), and a translation of Hans Urs von Balthasar's *Cosmic Liturgy. The Universe According to Maximus Confessor* (San Francisco: Ignatius Press, forthcoming). He expects to publish soon a critical edition of the works of Leontius of Byzantium, in the Greek series of the *Corpus Christianorum*, and is working on a book on Gregory of Nazianzus (for Routledge) and a commentary on the Psalms drawn from Patristic sources (for Eerdmans).

STEPHEN T. DAVIS   Born in Lincoln, Nebraska, he obtained his Bachelor's degree from Whitworth College in 1962, his M.Div. from Princeton Theological Seminary in 1965, and his Ph.D. from the Claremont Graduate School in Philosophy in 1970. Currently he is Professor of Philosophy of Religion at Claremont McKenna College. Books by him include: *God, Reason, and Theistic Proofs*

(Edinburgh: Edinburgh University Press, 1997), *Risen Indeed: Making Sense of the Resurrection* (Grand Rapids, Mich.: Eerdmans, 1993), *Death and Afterlife* (New York: St. Martin's Press, 1989), and *Encountering Jesus* (Atlanta: John Knox Press, 1988).

J. ANDREW DEARMAN Born in Columbia, South Carolina, he obtained his Bachelor's degree from the University of North Carolina, his M.Div. from Princeton Theological Seminary, and his Ph.D. from Emory University in 1981. Though he is Professor of Old Testament and Academic Dean at Austin Presbyterian Theological Seminary in Austin, Texas, currently he is Visiting Professor of Old Testament at the University of Stellenbosch. His publications include: *Religion and Culture in Ancient Israel* (Peabody, Mass.: Hendrickson, 1992), *Studies in the Mesha Inscription and Moab* (Atlanta: Scholars Press, 1989), *Property Rights in the Eighth-Century Prophets. The Conflict and its Background* (Atlanta: Scholars Press, 1988). He is currently working on commentaries on Jeremiah (Zondervan) and Hosea (Eerdmans).

C. STEPHEN EVANS Born in Atlanta, Georgia, he received his Bachelor's degree from Wheaton College in 1969 and his Ph.D. in Philosophy from Yale University in 1974. He is currently Professor of Philosophy and Dean for Research and Scholarship at Calvin College in Grand Rapids, Michigan. His published works include fifteen books, of which the most recent are *Faith Beyond Reason* (Edinburgh: Edinburgh University Press, 1998), *The Historical Christ and the Jesus of Faith: The Incarnational Narrative as History* (Oxford: Oxford University Press, 1996), and *Why Believe? Reason and Mystery as Pointers to God* (Grand Rapids, Mich.: Eerdmans, 1996).

GORDON D. FEE Born in Ashland, Oregon, he received his BA and MA from Seattle Pacific University (1956, 1958) and his Ph.D. from the University of Southern California in 1966. He currently teaches New Testament studies at Regent College, Vancouver, British Columbia. Books by him include: *Paul, the Spirit and the People of God* (Peabody, Mass.: Hendrickson, 1996), *Paul's Letter to the Philippians* (Grand Rapids, Mich.: Eerdmans, 1995), *God's Empowering Presence* (Peabody, Mass.: Hendrickson, 1994), and *Commentary on the First Epistle to the Corinthians* (Grand Rapids, Mich.: Eerdmans, 1987).

BRIAN HEBBLETHWAITE Born in Bristol, England, he obtained undergraduate degrees from Magdalen College, Oxford (Literae

Humaniores) in 1961, and from Magdalene College, Cambridge (Theology) in 1963, and his BD from Cambridge University in 1984. Currently he is a Life Fellow of Queens' College, Cambridge. From 1973 to 2000 he was University Lecturer in the Philosophy of Religion at the University of Cambridge. Books by him include: *Ethics and Religion in a Pluralistic Age* (Edinburgh: T. & T. Clark, 1997), *The Essence of Christianity* (London: SPCK, 1996), *The Ocean of Truth* (Cambridge: Cambridge University Press, 1988), and *The Incarnation* (Cambridge: Cambridge University Press, 1987).

DANIEL HOWARD-SNYDER Born in Tonasket, Washington, he obtained his Bachelor's degree from Seattle Pacific University in 1983 and his Ph.D. from Syracuse University in 1992. Currently he is Associate Professor in the Department of Philosophy at Western Washington University. Books edited by him include: (with Paul Moser) *New Essays on Divine Hiddenness* (New York: Cambridge University Press, 2000), *The Evidential Argument from Evil* (Bloomington: University of Indiana Press, 1996), and *Faith, Freedom, and Rationality* (Lanham, Md.: Rowman & Littlefield, 1996). Recent articles have appeared in *American Philosophical Quarterly*, *Canadian Journal of Philosophy*, *Faith and Philosophy*, *International Journal for the Philosophy of Religion*, *Philosophia Christi*, *Philosophy and Phenomenological Research*, *Religious Studies*, and *Southern Journal of Philosophy*.

DANIEL KENDALL Born in Miami, Arizona, he obtained his Bachelor's degree from Gonzaga University in 1962, his STM from Santa Clara University in 1971, and his STD from the Gregorian University in Rome in 1975. Currently he teaches theology at the University of San Francisco. Publications by him include: (with Stephen T. Davis and Gerald O'Collins) *Trinity* (Oxford: Oxford University Press, 1999), (with Stephen T. Davis and Gerald O'Collins) *Resurrection* (Oxford: Oxford University Press, 1997), (with Gerald O'Collins) *The Bible for Theology* (Mahwah, NJ: Paulist Press, 1997), and (with Gerald O'Collins) *Focus on Jesus* (Leominster: Gracewing, 1996).

BRIAN LEFTOW Born in Brooklyn, New York, he obtained his BA from Grove City College in 1977, his MA from Yale University in 1978, his M.Phil. from Yale in 1981, and his Ph.D. from Yale in 1984. Currently he is Professor of Philosophy at Fordham University. He has published *Time and Eternity* (Ithaca, NY: Cornell, 1991), *Divine Ideas* (Ithaca, NY: Cornell, forthcoming), and *Aquinas on Metaphysics: Matter, Parts and Number* (Oxford: Oxford University Press, forthcoming).

JOSEPH LIENHARD   Born in the Bronx, he received his BA and MA from Fordham University, Ph.L., BD, and STM from Woodstock College, and the Dr. Theol. Habil. from the University of Freiburg im Breisgau (Germany). He is Professor of Theology at Fordham University. His most recent books are *Contra Marcellum: Marcellus of Ancyra and Fourth-Century Theology* (Washington, DC: Catholic University of America Press, 1999), his translation: *Origen: Homilies on Luke; Fragments on Luke* (Washington, DC: The Catholic University of America Press, 1996), *The Bible, the Church, and Authority: The Canon of the Christian Bible in History and Theology* (Collegeville, Minn.: Liturgical Press, 1995), and *Augustine: Presbyter Factus Sum*, of which he was the coeditor (New York: Peter Lang, 1993).

CAREY NEWMAN   Born in Florida, he has earned degrees from the University of South Florida (BA, 1980), Southwestern Baptist Seminary, the University of Aberdeen, and Baylor University (Ph.D., 1989). He is currently the Executive Director of the Institute for the Study of Christian Origins. Recent publications include: *Jesus and the Restoration of Israel: A Critical Assessment of N. T. Wright's Jesus and the Victory of God* (Downers Grove, Ill.: InterVarsity Press, 1999), 'Resurrection as Glory: Divine Presence and Christian Origins' (in *Resurrection* (Oxford: Oxford University Press, 1997)) and *Paul's Glory-Christology* (Leiden: Brill, 1992).

KATHLEEN NORRIS   Born in Washington, DC, she obtained a Bachelor's degree from Bennington College in 1969. A self-employed writer since 1974, her books of non-fiction are *The Quotidian Mysteries: Laundry, Liturgy, and Women's Work* (New York: Paulist Press, 1998), *Amazing Grace: A Vocabulary of Faith* (New York: Riverhead Books, 1998), *The Cloister Walk* (New York: Riverhead Books, 1996), *Dakota: A Spiritual Geography* (New York: Houghton Mifflin, 1993), and a volume of poetry, *Little Girls in Church* (Pittsburgh: University of Pittsburgh Press, 1995).

GERALD O'COLLINS   Born in Melbourne, Victoria, he obtained his undergraduate degree from Melbourne University in 1957 and his Ph.D. from Cambridge University in 1968. Since 1974 he has taught theology at the Gregorian University in Rome. Publications by him include: *The Tripersonal God* (Mahwah, NJ: Paulist Press, 1999), (with others) *The Trinity* (Oxford: Oxford University Press, 1999), (with others) *The Resurrection* (Oxford: Oxford University Press, 1997), (with Daniel Kendall) *The Bible for Theology* (Mahwah, NJ: Paulist Press, 1997), and *Christology* (Oxford: Oxford University Press, 1995).

ALAN PADGETT Born in Washington, DC, he earned his BA from Southern California College (1977), M.Div. from Drew University (1981), and D.Phil. from Oxford University (1990). Currently he is Professor of Theology and Philosophy of Science at Azusa Pacific University (California). Books by him include: (with Steve Wilkens) *Christianity and Western Thought*, vol. ii (Downers Grove, Ill.: InterVarsity Press, 2000), (ed.) *Reason and the Christian Religion: Essays in Honour of Richard Swinburne* (Oxford: Oxford University Press, 1994), and *God, Eternity and the Nature of Time* (London: Macmillan, 1992).

GERARD RAFFERTY Born in New York City, he received his Bachelor's degree from Columbia University in the City of New York, and studied at Harvard Divinity School before entering St Joseph's Seminary (Dunwoodie) in Yonkers, NY. He received his M.Div. degree in 1978 and was ordained for the Archdiocese of New York in 1979. He studied at the Pontifical Biblical Institute (Rome) and received his Licentiate in Sacred Scripture (SSL) in 1987. He has taught at St Joseph's Seminary for over ten years. Currently he is Chair of the Scripture Department and holds the Cardinal John O'Connor Distinguished Chair in Hebrew and Sacred Scripture. He has been the co-ordinator of all three theological Summits which have met at St Joseph's, Easter 1996, 1998, 2000.

ALAN F. SEGAL Born in Worcester, Massachusetts, he earned his Bachelor's degree at Amherst College in 1967 and his Ph.D. at Yale University in 1975. Currently he is Professor of Religion at Barnard College, Columbia University. Publications by him include: *The Messiah: Developments in Earliest Judaism and Christianity* (Minneapolis: Fortress, 1992), *Paul the Convert: The Apostleship and Apostasy of Paul the Pharisee* (New Haven: Yale University Press, 1990), and *Rebecca's Children* (Cambridge, Mass.: Harvard University Press, 1988).

MARGUERITE SHUSTER Born in Santa Paula, California, she obtained her Bachelor's degree at Stanford in 1968, M.Div. from Fuller Theological Seminary in 1975, and her Ph.D. from the Fuller Theological Seminary Graduate School of Psychology in 1977.

She served as a Presbyterian pastor for nearly twelve years. Currently she teaches Preaching and Theology at Fuller Theological Seminary. Her writings include (editor) *Who We Are: Our Dignity as Human* (Grand Rapids, Mich.: Eerdmans, 1996), (coedited) *Perspectives on Christology: Essays in Honor of Paul K. Jewett* (Grand Rapids, Mich.: Zondervan, 1991), doctrinal sermons in *God, Creation, and Revelation* (Grand Rapids, Mich.: Eerdmans, 1991), and *Power, Pathology, Paradox: The Dynamics of Evil and Good* (Grand Rapids, Mich.: Zondervan, 1987).

ELEONORE STUMP   Born in Germany, she obtained her Bachelor's degree from Grinnell College in 1969, her Master's degrees from Harvard University in 1971 and Cornell University in 1973, and her Ph.D. from Cornell University in 1975. Currently she is the Robert J. Henle, SJ, Professor of Philosophy at St. Louis University. Her writings include *The Cambridge Companion to Augustine*, edited with Norman Kretzmann (Cambridge: Cambridge University Press, 2001), *Philosophy of Religion: The Big Questions*, edited with Michael Murray (Oxford: Blackwell Publishers, 1999), *Aquinas's Moral Theory: Essays in Honor of Norman Kretzmann*, edited with Scott MacDonald (Ithaca, NY: Cornell University Press, 1998), and *Reasoned Faith* (Ithaca, NY: Cornell University Press, 1993).

N. T. WRIGHT   Born in Morpeth, Northumberland, England, he received his BA from Exeter College, Oxford, 1971, his MA from Exeter College, Oxford, 1975, and his D.Phil. from Exeter College, Oxford, 1981. Currently he is Canon Theologian at Westminster Abbey. Recent publications include *The Challenge of Jesus* (Downers Grove, Ill.: InterVarsity Press, 1999), *The Way of the Lord* (Grand Rapids, Mich.: Eerdmans, 1999), *The Millennium Myth* (Louisville, Ky.: Westminster/John Knox, 1999), *The Meaning of Jesus: Two Visions* (with Marcus J. Borg) (London: SPCK, 1997), and *Jesus and the Victory of God* (Philadelphia: Fortress, 1996).

LINDA ZAGZEBSKI   Born in Glendale, California, she obtained her Bachelor's degree from Stanford University in 1968, and her Ph.D. from the University of California at Los Angeles in 1979. She taught for twenty years at Loyola Marymount University. Currently she is Kingfisher College Chair in Philosophy of Religion and Ethics at the University of Oklahoma. Her books include: *Virtues of the Mind* (New York: Cambridge University Press, 1966), and *The Dilemma of*

Freedom and Foreknowledge (New York: Oxford University Press, 1991). She is currently working on divine motivation theory.

Note: William Alston, Brian Hebblethwaite, Daniel Howard-Snyder, Daniel Kendall, Joseph Lienhard, Carey Newman, Alan Padgett, and Gerard Rafferty were all active and valuable participants in the Incarnation Summit, but this volume does not include contributions from them.

1

The Incarnation: The Critical Issues

GERALD O'COLLINS, SJ

Far from merely surveying recent literature in the area, this opening chapter aims to identify critical issues concerning the incarnation. Obviously not all the issues raised here can be addressed by the chapters which follow. That would mean doubling the size of this book. Yet a wide-ranging account will enable the reader to place the other contributions in the landscape of incarnation studies. At least twelve issues call for attention.

(1) Any study of 'incarnation' must begin by asking: what kind of truth does 'the incarnation' embody? Does it refer to a unique event: namely, the second person of the Trinity being born into history to live, teach, die, and then rise gloriously from the dead—all with a view to inaugurating a radical new relationship between human beings and God? Some argue that the 'incarnation' claims from the New Testament and such subsequent Christian confessions as the Nicene-Constantinopolitan Creed of 381 should be understood as 'myth', in the sense of being merely a non-historical, religious truth about ourselves which has been communicated under the form of talk about a divine being coming among us. Stephen Evans chooses David Friedrich Strauss and Joseph Campbell among others to exemplify this non-historical interpretation of 'the incarnation' as being only a universal truth about the general human condition.[1]

St Paul writes of God 'sending his own Son' (Rom. 8: 3), or of Christ Jesus being 'in the form of God' and then 'being born in human likeness and being found in human form' (Phil. 2: 6–8). The Letter to the Hebrews opens by declaring that 'in these last days'

---

[1] See C. S. Evans, *The Historical Christ and the Jesus of Faith* (Oxford: Oxford University Press, 1996), 43–4, 51, 73–4. One might add D. H. Lawrence to this list. In 'The Body of God' he finds 'incarnation' in 'any lovely and generous woman' and in 'any clear and fearless man'.

God has 'spoken to us by his Son' (Heb. 1: 2). John's prologue announces that 'the Word became flesh and lived among us, and we have seen his glory' (John 1: 14). The Nicene-Constantinopolitan Creed hinged around the confession that 'the only-begotten Son of God . . . for us and for our salvation came down from the heavens, was incarnate from the Holy Spirit and the Virgin Mary, became man, and was crucified under Pontius Pilate'. The revisionists expound such statements that clearly seem to be in some ways informative about the Word or Son of God—ways to be explored in this chapter and subsequently in this book—as *simply* statements expressing deep truths about ourselves. Paul, John, the anonymous author of Hebrews, and the bishops at the First Council of Constantinople in 381 appeared to have been referring to what the Son of God did, suffered, and was, but they were 'really' talking only about themselves. This way of 'interpreting' incarnational language means that those ancient writers were either deliberately deceptive or else extraordinarily incompetent. They used a variety of expressions that millions of people subsequently understood to refer to the Son of God 'being sent', 'coming', 'being born', 'becoming flesh', and so forth. But they were *merely* expressing general truths about themselves. This line of interpretation constructs its own meaning for 'incarnation' in ways that do not match the New Testament testimony.[2] It develops that low Christology, for which Jesus differs from other Spirit-filled or saintly persons only in degree and not in kind. At best he is merely the highest human example of someone motivated by the divine Spirit. In a 'Letter to the Editors: Incarnation' John Hick endorsed this line of argument: 'Incarnation . . . becomes a matter of degree: God is incarnate in all men insofar as they are Spirit-filled, or Christ-like, or truly saintly.'[3] Years later Hick added the obvious conclusion: 'Incarnation in this sense has occurred and is occurring in many different ways and degrees in

---

[2] It is also a 'version' of a central Christian belief which robs it of any hard challenge. 'Incarnation' is simply reduced to a truth, in Joseph Campbell's account a rather flattering truth, about each of us and our innate possibilities. As Alan Padgett pointed out to me, Strauss was deeply influenced by G. W. F. Hegel, who also exemplifies a non-historical interpretation of the incarnation. On Hegel's 'universalist' interpretation of the incarnation see D. P. Jamros, 'Hegel on the Incarnation: Unique or Universal?', *TS* 56 (1995), 276–300. Strauss's radical reinterpretation of the meaning of 'incarnation' should be distinguished from the approach of contemporary revisionists. In reducing the 'incarnation' to a matter of degree, they frequently want, however, to speak of God's special, or even unique, presence and action in Jesus.

[3] *Theology*, 80 (1977), 205.

many different persons.'[4] Strauss, Campbell, and Hick (in some of his works) differ strikingly from Trypho, Celsus, and their modern successors (of whom more anon). The latter all recognized what Christians claimed with their incarnation language, but in the name of monotheistic faith, sensitivity to the divine transcendence, and other religious or philosophical convictions, deemed the Christian claim to be incredible.

In what follows in this and later chapters the incarnation will be understood not only realistically—as a belief about a specific and unique event that happened only once in human history—but also in the strong sense of the union between true divinity and full humanity in the person of Jesus Christ. I am not then taking 'incarnation' in the broad or 'soft' sense of any kind of spiritual being (e.g. a created soul) assuming (in an 'incarnation') or returning to (in a 'reincarnation') a physical body.[5] For the incarnation conceived as an event in the realistic and strong sense, the first major issue concerns its point of departure.

(2) The personal pre-existence of the Word, Wisdom, or Son of God is a necessary element in any orthodox affirmation of the incarnation or 'the Word becoming flesh' (John 1: 14). By personally pre-existing 'before becoming flesh', the Word can mediate creation (see Gordon Fee's chapter below), be 'sent by the Father', become incarnate, 'be impoverished' (see the chapters below by Fee and Stephen Evans), and take on the human condition through the power of the Holy Spirit. Belief in Jesus' divinity stands or falls with accepting his *personal* pre-existence within the eternal life of the Trinity. This belief is not to be confused with false ideas about some pre-existence of his created humanity.[6]

The personal distinctions within the eternal life of God affirmed by trinitarian faith are rejected, of course, by many of our contemporaries: for instance, millions of Muslims and Jews. Within Christian history, the ancient Modalists, Unitarians (from the sixteenth century and later), and others have diverged from traditional trinitarian

---

[4] *The Metaphor of God Incarnate* (London: SCM Press, 1993), 111.

[5] See Ch. 6 below, where Alan Segal treats 'the simple meaning' of 'incarnation' that describes the interaction of matter and spirit, and Ch. 8 below, where Brian Daley examines the patristic use of the body/soul analogy to illuminate the hypostatic union of the incarnate word.

[6] Unfortunately such ideas are endorsed by Pierre Benoit, 'Préexistence et incarnation', *Revue biblique*, 77 (1970), 5–29; and Louis Bouyer, *Le Fils éternel* (Paris: Cerf, 1974), 486.

faith in a way that logically rules out the incarnation. John Hick, for instance, writes: 'God is humanly known—as creator, as trans-former, and as inner spirit [all in lower case]. We do not need to reify these ways as three distinct persons.'[7] If there are no distinct persons within God, there can at best be only a 'metaphorical' incarnation— 'metaphorical' in Hick's sense of the term.[8]

These positions differ from that of St Augustine of Hippo, St Anselm of Canterbury, and other mainstream Christian writers. While appreciating the difficulty of applying to the tripersonal God our human concepts and language of persons,[9] they decided that they must still do so. At least in some respects the Father, Son, and Holy Spirit are like human persons, even if the dissimilarity remains infinitely greater. So long as we respect this dissimilarity, we can avoid anthropomorphism when acknowledging three persons in God.

Within the Trinity (and not just between the Trinity and human persons) there is also the challenge, which Karl Rahner stressed almost to the point of exaggeration. So far from being a 'univocal conception with regard to the three divine persons', there exists an 'unbridgeable difference between the way each divine person is person'. Since they are persons in different ways, it is 'only the loosest of analogies that allows us to apply the same notion of person to all three'.[10] Nevertheless, even in the face of the looseness of the analogy and massive developments in the concept of person since its use by the Council of Chalcedon, Rahner accepted its continuing place in trinitarian discourse: 'there is no other word which would be really better, more generally understandable and less exposed to misconceptions'.[11]

Some who have problems with the personal pre-existence of the Word (and the Spirit) represent latterday variants on Tertullian's progressive view of the personal generation of the Word (*Adversus Praxean*, 7). They argue for the Word being fully personalized only at the incarnation itself. Thus Piet Schoonenberg will not characterize 'the word' and 'the spirit' as persons 'prior to' the unfolding of

[7] Hick, *Metaphor of God Incarnate*, 153.

[8] On Hick's use of 'metaphorical' and other items in his anti-incarnational argument, see G. O'Collins and D. Kendall, *Focus on Jesus* (Leominster: Gracewing, 1996), 30–46.

[9] See St Augustine, *De Trinitate*, 5. 10.

[10] K. Rahner, 'Remarks on the Dogmatic Treatise "De Trinitate"', *Theological Investigations*, iv (London: Darton, Longman & Todd, 1966), 77–102, at 91.

[11] Ibid. 101.

salvation history. He maintains that the Logos first becomes person in the human person of Jesus at the incarnation. He argues similarly for the Holy Spirit becoming a person only at the glorification of Jesus. Prior to the incarnation and the glorification, respectively, the Logos and the Holy Spirit are only extensions of God's simple personhood.[12]

This position must face serious questions: if it takes the incarnation to constitute the divine Logos as fully personal, how can God be and be recognized as Father 'prior' to the incarnation? If there is 'not yet' a second divine person, there can be no 'first' person. Any who would respond that 'prior' to the incarnation the first person is at least potentially 'the Father' of the Logos/Son posits at the heart of God a remarkable actualization of a potentiality. One might be tempted to parody the old Arian saying and declare: 'there was a time when the Father was not, or at least not yet Father.' Furthermore, how could the assumption of a finite human existence at the incarnation have an infinite effect: namely, the full constitution of a divine person? A strange asymmetry between cause and effect seems to open up here. Those who take Schoonenberg's line face even more problems than Tertullian.[13] After all, he proposed in *Adversus Praxean* that the Son comes into existence before and in view of creation—not that his 'complete birth' as divine person takes place only 'later', at the incarnation.

On the exegetical front James Dunn's *Christology in the Making*[14] has encouraged a healthy debate about the emergence of the Christian notion of incarnation: that is to say, the real 'taking flesh' of a personally pre-existent divine being. Whether we find this belief clearly expressed for the first time in the prologue of the Fourth Gospel or already present, at least implicitly, in Paul's letters, Dunn rightly observes that the Apostle primarily focuses on Christ's death and resurrection. Paul offers a functional Christology in which 'the ontological corollaries' are 'not yet clear'.[15] Should we follow Jean-Noël Aletti (see below) and find in Romans 8: 3 at least

---

[12] See P. Schoonenberg, *The Christ* (New York: Herder & Herder, 1971); id., 'Spirit Christology and Logos Christology', *Bijdragen* 38 (1977), 350–75.

[13] Alan Padgett has brought to my attention another difficulty for Schoonenberg: if the Logos *comes into being* at any time, he cannot share the same divine being as the Father, who exists necessarily and eternally.

[14] 2nd edn.; London: SCM Press, 1989.

[15] J. D. G. Dunn, *The Theology of Paul the Apostle* (Grand Rapids, Mich.: Eerdmans, 1998), 292–3. It seems more accurate to say 'not yet fully clear', since some ontological corollaries, e.g. about the Son's creative power (e.g. 1 Cor. 8: 6), are already beginning to show through.

an allusion to pre-existence and incarnation? However we interpret Paul's thought in Romans 8: 3 and other texts (Gal. 4: 4; Phil. 2: 6–7), mainstream Christianity, in attempting to ponder the personal, pre-incarnational existence of the Word, has always grappled with the majestic statement from John, 'the Word became flesh and dwelt amongst us' (John 1: 14). What then does it mean for the eternal Word to take on personally the experience of being a human individual?

(3) In itself the incarnation confronts us with a unique relationship between the uncreated and the created: divinity and humanity in a personal or hypostatic union. This claim goes far beyond the general action and presence of God in creating and maintaining in existence all non-divine realities. The claim also leaves far behind such special divine actions as God's 'taking possession' of a piece of ground, 'being enthroned' on Zion, 'filling' the Temple with his glory, 'speaking through' the prophets, 'guiding' the people across the desert, or working miracles.[16] The incarnation involves a divine being who is by definition eternal, without a body, and unlimited in power, knowledge, and presence (i.e. omnipotent, omniscient, and omnipresent) personally taking up an existence that is temporal, partly material, and thoroughly limited in power, knowledge, and presence. Through the incarnation God, who is pure Spirit, assumes (and not merely creates and conserves) matter; the eternal God personally enters time.[17] Whatever side we take in the debate about God existing or not existing 'in time', the incarnation entails an immortal, unchanging divine person becoming subject to change and, above all, to death. The eternal Word, who necessarily exists and whose divine life is immune from suffering, becomes contingent, experiences suffering, and dies on a cross. In holding one and the same individual to be both fully divine and fully human, we seem to claim something that is logically inconceivable: an individual who has mutually exclusive sets of characteristics, being simultaneously eternal, incorruptible, immutable, and a-spatial on the one hand,

---

[16] See e.g. Num. 24: 2–24; 1 Kgs. 8: 11–13; Ps. 84: 1; 132: 12–14; Ezek. 10: 3–4; 43: 1–4. In their chapters Andrew Dearman, Alan Segal, and Tom Wright ask about possible OT 'precedents' for Christian belief in the incarnation.

[17] Some like Nicholas Everitt, in 'Interpretations of God's Eternity', *Religious Studies* 34 (1998), 25–32, argue against divine a-temporality and maintain that God is in time. Brian Leftow's chapter below argues that divine timelessness and incarnation are compatible; it is *prima facie* plausible that the Son of God can be both timeless and incarnate.

and temporal, corruptible, changeable, and spatially determined on the other.

From the beginning we come across numerous Christians who frankly admitted the paradox of simultaneously attributing properties of divinity and humanity to the incarnate Word. In his homily 'On the Pasch' St Melito of Sardis in the second century spoke of Christ as the divine creator who suffered a shameful human death: 'he who hung up the earth is himself hung up; he who fixed the heavens is himself fixed [on the cross]; he who fastened everything is fastened on the wood; the Master is reviled; God has been killed' (nr. 96). Such a belief could not go unchallenged. St Justin Martyr (d. *c.*165) recorded the baffled reaction of cultured Jews of his time. Their monotheistic faith and sense of the intrinsic otherness of God made them judge it quite 'incredible' and 'impossible' to think of God deigning to be born a human being and end up dying on the cross (*Dialogue with Trypho*, 68). A few years later Origen (d. *c.*254) responded to similar scepticism over the incarnation coming from Celsus, a learned pagan who had declared God to be 'incapable' of incarnation; divinity (being immortal and immutable) and humanity could not be united in the one Christ (*Contra Celsum*, 4. 14). The very notion of incarnation appeared to embody logically contradictory ideas.

The charge that faith in the incarnate Word involves such an incoherent claim has flared up right down to our own day. In the nineteenth century F. D. E. Schleiermacher framed the issue this way: 'one individual cannot share in two quite different natures.'[18] In the twentieth century Don Cupitt put the same objection even more vigorously: 'the eternal God and an historical man are two beings of quite different ontological status. It is quite unintelligible to declare them identical.'[19] One could multiply examples of those who detect in the notion of incarnation mutually exclusive predicates and conclude that the incarnation is simply impossible in itself.

In a 1995 book I offered one response to this difficulty:

It would be a blatant contradiction in terms to attribute to the same subject at the same time *and under the same aspect* mutually incompatible properties. But that is not being done here. With respect to his divinity Christ is omniscient, but with respect to his humanity he is limited in knowledge.

[18] *The Christian Faith* (Edinburgh: T. & T. Clark, 1928), 393.
[19] D. Cupitt, 'The Finality of Christ', *Theology*, 78 (1975), 618–28, at 625.

Mutually exclusive characteristics are being simultaneously attributed to him but not within the same frame of reference.[20]

Distinguishing between the incarnate Son of God *qua* divine and *qua* human seems to deliver belief in the incarnation from falling under a ban from the principle of contradiction. My aim then was not to establish positively the possibility of incarnation, but only to rebut a long-standing argument about the doctrine being incoherent. The incarnation is a paradox but not a blatant logical contradiction. This belief has not been shown to be metaphysically impossible or logically incoherent like talk of a married bachelor or a square circle.[21]

A defender of the Schleiermacher–Cupitt objection might declare me open to a *tu quoque*-type of rejoinder and say: 'Your position on the incarnation solves nothing because one could play the same sort of tricks with square circles: namely, claim that they are four-sided *qua* squares and have all their points equidistant from the centre *qua* circles.' Against such a rejoinder I want to insist that you cannot predicate of the same object at the same time and *within the same frame of reference* mutually exclusive properties. Circles and squares find themselves within exactly the same frame of reference: geometrical figures. My protagonist, in pressing the rejoinder, would have to make an impossible claim: the square circles are four-sided as geometrical figures, but simultaneously and also as geometrical figures all their points are equidistant from the centre. In the case of the incarnation the frames of reference, divinity and humanity, differ and that saves the situation at least from blatant incoherence.

In this context one can add two further arguments from Stephen Evans's 1996 book, *The Historical Christ and the Jesus of Faith*. First, basing himself on the work of Peter Geach and Richard Swinburne, Evans recalls that in general 'a proof of coherence or non-contra-dictoriness is often extraordinarily difficult to achieve'. In particular, no direct proof for the coherence of the concept of God can be offered. If that is so, it is 'certainly unreasonable to expect such a proof of the coherence of the claim that God became incarnate'.

---

[20] *Christology* (Oxford: Oxford University Press, 1995), 234. Alan Padgett has offered me a good analogy from physics. The same *event* is given mutually exclusive characteristics (past, simultaneous, and future) in *different* inertial frames of reference, according to the Special Theory of Relativity. The same distant event can be *future* for me, but *simultaneous* for an observer moving near the speed of light relative to me.

[21] See also the reduplicative strategy adopted below in Eleonore Stump's chapter.

Since we cannot directly prove the non-contradictoriness of the concept of God, we cannot be expected to prove directly the non-contradictoriness of the concept of the God-man.[22]

Second, Evans draws on Brian Hebblethwaite to argue that 'prior to any special revelation', we may know something about God and ourselves but we lack 'a clear understanding of which properties are essential to being God and which are essential to being human'. *A priori* we have only a limited sense of what God and we ourselves are like.[23] Hence, Evans continues, *a priori* 'we do not know enough about God' to say whether an incarnation is possible or not. *A posteriori* (at least for those who accept the incarnation) we know that 'it is possible for God to do this'. Once we 'have good reason to believe that the incarnation has occurred, we also have good reason to believe that it is possible for God almighty to become incarnate'.[24] In that sense the fact of the incarnation (which is under dispute) positively establishes the possibility of the incarnation—at least for believers.

This second argument from Evans presupposes, on the one hand, that prior to any knowledge of the incarnation as such we already know *something* about divine and human properties. Otherwise how could we recognize an incarnation in the case of Jesus? But, on the other hand, the argument also presupposes that before acknowledging this incarnation, we do not enjoy a *sufficiently clear understanding* of divine and human properties to declare positively that incarnation is possible or impossible.[25] How can we establish this 'knowing something' but not yet 'sufficiently clearly'? One might appeal to the traditional Christian belief that, being a divine

---

[22] Evans, *Historical Christ and the Jesus of Faith*, 125–6.

[23] In *Christology* I made a similar point about Christ's revelation revising and even transforming our notions of what it is to be divine and what it is to be human (pp. 229, 232). Karl Rahner went even further by arguing that human nature is '*ultimately* explained' only 'on the basis of the self-exteriorizing self-expression of the Logos himself' ('Remarks on the Dogmatic Treatise "De Trinitate"', 92 n. 21). We know human beings are possible and understandable (i.e. our anthropology) only because we now know the self-expression of the Logos in the incarnation to have happened (and therefore to have been possible). As Rahner put it: 'Christology is the end and beginning of anthropology.' He defined human beings as 'that which ensues when God's self-utterance, his Word, is given out lovingly into the void of god-less nothing' ('On the Theology of the Incarnation', *Theological Investigations*, iv (London: Darton, Longman & Todd, 1966), 105–20, at 116, 117).

[24] Evans, *Historical Christ and the Jesus of Faith*, 124–5.

[25] Believers should also agree that our understanding of divinity and humanity will reach final clarity only at the eschaton.

mystery, the incarnation, even after it is revealed and known, surpasses the powers of human understanding. Or else one might cite great thinkers like Aristotle or Confucius who appreciated some of the major human and divine properties but never raised the possibility of a genuine incarnation of God.

As regards the ontology of the incarnation, it found classical expression at the Council of Chalcedon (451): one person or subsistence in two natures. Later chapters of this book discuss the intelligibility and ongoing validity of the Chalcedonian teaching.[26] Richard Sturch has responded well to the first of two common objections against that teaching: the language of 'two natures' is obsolete, and the notion of 'person' has so changed its meaning as to be confusingly useless. We still use the word 'nature' in 'much the same sense as Chalcedon used it': the essential characteristics that we have in common establish our human nature.[27] What I missed in Sturch's argument was a good case for there being some continuity, along with much discontinuity, in the way the language of 'person' is used.

A feature of recent Western scholarly literature that is worth remarking on here is the new interest in the Eastern christological debates *after* Chalcedon. The West has long tended to assume that 451 is the culmination, indeed end, of patristic christological discussion. But vital debates on the relation between Christ's divine and human natures, reflected in conciliar decisions, continued until 787, the last of the ecumenical councils (see Brian Daley's chapter below). Once this longer trajectory is opened up, many of the philosophical sticking-points associated with Chalcedon take on a new light. Further, there has been a tendency of late to re-evaluate the status of Chalcedon itself as not so much 'defining' Christ' or even giving 'definitive' (final) expression to his personal existence, but seeing Chalcedon rather as establishing a regulatory linguistic code for *talking* about Christ that remains open to different further explications (see Sarah Coakley's chapter below). This not only leaves more room for an 'apophatic' reading of Chalcedon, but has obvious implications for ecumenical endeavours between churches divided on the issue of Christology.

---

[26] In particular, Eleonore Stump's chapter argues that Aquinas' interpretation of the metaphysics of the incarnation is a plausible version of the Chalcedonian definition.

[27] R. Sturch, *The Word and the Christ* (Oxford: Clarendon Press, 1991), 142.

Let me mention one ecumenical agreement which concerns Chalcedon's specific teaching of 'one person in two natures (*phuseis*)'. Appropriate religious and cultural sensitivities may well call for other terminology. Thus the May 1973 christological declaration signed by the (Oriental Orthodox) Coptic Pope, Shenouda III of Egypt, and Pope Paul VI of Rome officially set at rest one cause of a schism that went back to 451 when some Christians in Egypt and elsewhere refused to accept the two-natures terminology. The 1973 declaration avoided that language, but said what is functionally the equivalent by confessing Jesus as 'perfect God with respect to his divinity, perfect man with respect to his humanity. . . . In him are preserved all the properties of the divinity and all the properties of humanity together in a real, perfect, indivisible and inseparable union.'[28]

Before leaving the ontology of the incarnation, let me draw attention to two further issues: special divine action and special divine presence. Those who for various reasons reject in principle all special divine actions will logically rule out the possibility of an incarnation, an event *par excellence* that cannot be causally explained in a completely 'normal' way through the regular 'laws of nature'. The incarnation discloses divine activity that is distinct from the normal intentions and power that 'God manifests in creating and conserving the universe'.[29] The objections to special divine activity that have been repeated or have come up for the first time in the last thirty years are summarized, classified, and—I believe—satisfactorily answered by Paul Gwynne, who concludes that the concept of special divine action 'emerges somewhat battered but intact'. It 'seems to be far from collapsing and there are good reasons for affirming its coherence and credibility.'[30]

As Evans's chapter in *The Historical Christ and the Jesus of Faith* and, even more, the whole work by Gwynne show, the literature on special divine actions is extensive. This is not the case, however, with the themes of presence and the special divine presence entailed by the incarnation. In *The Dream of Gerontius* John Henry Newman

---

[28] See J. Neuner and J. Dupuis (eds), *The Christian Faith* (6th edn.; New York: Alba House, 1996), 246.

[29] Evans, *Historical Christ and the Jesus of Faith*, 143. Evans dedicates a whole chapter to the possibility and knowability of miracles and other special acts of God (pp. 137–69).

[30] P. Gwynne, *Special Divine Action: Key Issues in the Contemporary Debate (1965–1995)* (Rome: Gregorian University Press, 1996), 326.

expressed the incarnation in terms of presence: 'Praise to the Holiest in the height | And in the depth be praise . . . And that a higher gift than grace | Should flesh and blood refine | God's *presence* and His very Self, | And essence all-divine' (italics mine). When we move from the story of God's chosen people to that of Jesus, we see that salvation is made possible not merely by God's activity in history but now by God's personal presence in history. To elaborate Newman's choice of language we need not only to study the theme of presence biblically but also to reflect on it philosophically. The divine presence pervades the biblical story that reaches its climax in the life of Jesus. Philosophically speaking, we need careful analyses of 'presence', its nature, its conditions, its impact, and its variety—something which is singularly lacking in Western literature but which a clear account of the doctrine of the incarnation calls for.[31] A fully deployed theology of the incarnation invites much more reflection on presence and the special divine presence in the person and activity of Jesus. Such reflection might also help to undercut an objection to incarnational faith that John Hick (in *The Metaphor of God Incarnate*) and other writers have pressed.

(4) Like Rousseau[32] and others, Hick deems traditional incarnation faith to be religiously and morally objectionable. It represents God as being non-egalitarian in extending an unfair advantage to those who know about and believe in the incarnation. Christians enjoy a crucial opportunity, a headstart in salvation, not extended to others. Apropos of those who have never had the chance of learning about Jesus or have learned about him in a distorted fashion, Evans draws on Kierkegaard to articulate the difficulty: 'it seems unjust to allow accidents of history and geography to decide the eternal destiny of an individual.'[33] Evans rightly challenges strictly egalitarian versions of God. Jonah, Second Isaiah, and further major voices of the biblical revelation attest God to be the One who treats all people fairly, albeit in very different ways, and is not to be judged by our merely human standards of equality. In

---

[31] On this lacuna see O'Collins, *Christology*, 306–23; and id., 'The Risen Jesus: Analogies and Presence', in S. E. Porter *et al.* (eds.), *Resurrection*, JSNTSS 186 (Sheffield: Sheffield Academic Press, 1999), 195–217, at 211–17.

[32] J. J. Rousseau, *Émile or On Education*, trans. Alan Bloom (New York: Basic Books, 1979), 304–5. This passage comes from the profession of faith of the Savoyard Vicar in Bk. 4 of *Émile*.

[33] Evans, *Historical Christ and the Jesus of Faith*, 103. Aquinas reported and replied to much the same objection in *SCG*, 4. 53. 10, 11; 4. 55. 12, 13.

general, inequalities *vis-à-vis* information leading to salvation seem no more 'problematic than the disparities that already exist in human intelligence, happiness, health, moral and religious sensitivity, and so on'.[34] In particular, those who know of the incarnation, far from triumphalistically asserting their 'special privileges' and advantages in the business of salvation, should be humbled by what they know in faith. Believers have a 'special task' for the whole human race.[35] Further, the fact that God did/does something in Christ that was/is not done elsewhere should not be construed to mean that God is inactive and absent elsewhere. People who have not been in the position to know and accept the message of the incarnation can be saved through some awareness of the Word, even without knowing of his historical, incarnated existence as Jesus of Nazareth, just as they can be open to the Spirit without knowing about Pentecost and the Spirit's visible manifestation in the church.[36]

(5) The Council of Chalcedon's teaching about the incarnate Christ's one person and two natures figured in (3) above. That whole section looked at matters ontologically. Apart from explicitly affirming his 'rational soul and body', Chalcedon did not spell out the properties of the humanity the Son of God assumed. More than two centuries later, the Third Council of Constantinople (680–1) drew a conclusion from Chalcedon: the two natures of Christ enjoy a distinct will appropriate to each nature, with his human and divine wills operating together in perfect harmony. This conciliar concern to uphold Christ's two wills has been complemented, in medieval and modern times, by a serious interest in his two minds: the divine mind shared (distinctly but not separately) with the other two divine persons, and Jesus' human mind which the incarnate Word claims as his own. Issues abound for those interested in the psychology of the incarnate Word. Here I can do no more than insert several observations.

First, somehow the inaccurate notion has crept in that talk of Christ's two minds *replaces* a theology of his two natures. Perhaps some intend to do just that and reduce to 'mind' everything denoted

---

[34] Evans, *Historical Christ and the Jesus of Faith*, 113.

[35] Ibid. 114; see O'Collins and Kendall, *Focus on Jesus*, 46.

[36] In an address to the Roman Curia of 22 Dec. 1986, Pope John Paul II developed the teaching of the Second Vatican Council to say: 'Every authentic prayer is called forth by the Holy Spirit, who is mysteriously present in the heart of every person' (nr. 11) (*Acta Apostolicae Sedis* 79 (1987), 1082–90, at 1089; trans. mine).

by 'nature'. But I would argue against any such reduction. Human nature refers to all the essential characteristics that we have in common; they include but go beyond our being 'minded'. Second, when writing about Christ's two minds, some seem to overlook the fact that these minds exist at infinitely different levels. Can we be truly helped, for instance, by analogies between his two consciousnesses (divine and human) and cases of 'divided minds' and multiple personality disorders, given the infinite qualitative difference between the uncreated and the created mind of the incarnate Word?[37] The relationship between these two minds was and is radically unsymmetrical. During the earthly life of Jesus, the person of the Word (through his divine mind) knew the human mind (of Jesus) as his own human mind, but not vice versa.[38]

Third, as regards the free operation of Christ's human will, the primary issue concerns his sinlessness. The New Testament and mainstream tradition has maintained that right through his earthly life Jesus was *de facto* without sin and morally flawless. But there remains the *de iure* question: was he necessarily impeccable? Was he in principle immune from the possibility of sinning under any imaginable circumstances? For any positive answer an obvious difficulty arises from the way the Gospels and the Letter to the Hebrews attest the fact of Jesus' having been tempted. Surely genuine temptations presuppose at least the possibility of moral failure? No one wants to suggest that Jesus' temptations were a mere charade, as if he simply went through the motions of being tempted to give us a good example, without feeling any pull whatsoever from temptation. How then could he have been subject to temptation and yet incapable of moral error?

Tom Morris has made the interesting suggestion that in his human consciousness Jesus did not know that he was necessarily good; he thought sin to be possible for him, even if this possibility was never actualized. In other words, the metaphysical impossibility of sinning did not rule out the psychological or epistemological possibility of being tempted. Hence we can praise and honour Christ for not sinning, because, although he could not possibly have sinned, he did not know this at the time. Whether one sides with

---

[37] What Aquinas observed about Christ's two natures, 'the divine nature exceeds the human by infinity' (*SCG* 5. 35. 8) applies equally to Christ's two minds.

[38] See T. V. Morris, *The Logic of God Incarnate* (Ithaca, NY: Cornell University Press, 1986), 153–62; O'Collins, *Christology*, 246–8; O'Collins and Kendall, *Focus on Jesus*, 41.

Morris or his critics,[39] I would urge the need to recognize that it is persons (rather than their consciousness and nature) who sin, refrain from sin, or are immune from sin. Hence we should avoid such expressions as this: 'the decision arrived at by his [Christ's] earthly *consciousness* not to sin was not causally imposed on him by his divine *nature*'.[40] Acknowledging that sin is to be attributed to the person and is a personal offence against God (and not 'merely' a moral failure of my nature or a wrong decision of my consciousness) should lead us to rephrase the question of the incarnate Word's sinlessness: could a divine person, in his incarnate state, have possibly sinned? If God is necessarily and *de iure* impeccable, the same should hold true of the Logos incarnate as Jesus of Nazareth. Otherwise we must contemplate the possibility of a moral fissure within the Trinity: the (incarnate) Son possibly sinning against the Father.[41]

(6) Despite the difference between their ontological and psychological concerns, under (3) and (5) we have been examining debates concerned with the 'what?' of the incarnation. Let us now turn to face the 'how?' and the 'why?' Traditional Christianity has followed Matthew and Luke in explaining *how* the incarnation took place: through a virginal conception.[42] By the power of the Holy Spirit, Mary conceived Jesus without normal sexual intercourse providing a male sperm from a biological father. Here almost everyone follows the language of some early creeds ('by the power of the Holy Spirit he was born of the Virgin Mary') and speaks or writes of 'virgin birth' when they mean the virginal conception. The Nicene-Constantinopolitan Creed of 381 confesses more precisely, however, that the Son of God 'became flesh from the Holy Spirit and the Virgin Mary and was made man'. The late Raymond Brown and myself seem to have been nearly alone in insisting on the accurate terminology: virginal conception. After having earlier used the term 'virginal conception', even Joseph Fitzmyer slipped back into the language of 'virgin birth' when writing about 'the story of the

[39] For details see D. Werther, 'The Temptation of God Incarnate', *Religious Studies*, 29 (1993), 47–50.

[40] Morris, *Logic of God Incarnate*, 150; italics mine.

[41] We might usefully distinguish here betwen Jesus *qua* human and *qua* divine. *Qua* human Jesus was capable of sinning, but *qua* divine that possibility was ruled out.

[42] The incarnation and the virginal conception are quite distinct. The incarnation is possible without a virginal conception, and vice versa a virginal conception does not mean automatically an incarnation.

virgin birth', although he agreed that it 'would be better [more accurate?] to speak of the virginal conception of Jesus'.[43]

Whatever the terminology, many dismiss the virginal conception as peripheral, inessential, impossible, a mistake in biblical interpretation, an insult to married love, or 'merely' a symbolic way of expressing Jesus' divine identity that parallels ancient stories of gods impregnating women and producing remarkable offspring. Space allows two observations here. First, I believe that the objections to the factuality of the virginal conception can be rebutted one by one. But, second, it seems to me more important to reflect positively and theologically on the virginal conception. A mere defence of its factual character is not sufficient; the theological richness of this truth calls for much more attention.[44]

(7) The virginal conception, as a miraculous event between God and Mary of Nazareth, has a mysterious, private sense to it. The finality of this event, however, has a universal and eminently public character. Why would God will the incarnation (which as a matter of fact took place through a virginal conception)? In his *Cur Deus Homo* of 1098, St Anselm of Canterbury magisterially spoke for all those who interpret the incarnation primarily (or even solely) as *the* divine means for remedying the sinfulness of men and women everywhere. We can now be saved through sharing in what the God-man did by 'satisfying' for (others would say 'expiating' or 'overcoming') all-pervasive moral evil. Left to our own devices, we could not have delivered ourselves from bondage to sin and its tragic consequences; we could not even have discovered the full truth of our fallen condition. We needed the incarnation because we are sinners, as St Athanasius, for instance, also stressed in his *De Incarnatione*.

Other such voices from the great tradition as St Irenaeus (d. *c.*200) and Blessed Duns Scotus (d. 1308) go beyond any talk of remedying sin to interpret the incarnation primarily in the light of God's self-communicating love. The Word became flesh in order to complete a project more than to heal something that had gone terribly wrong. The three stages that make up the one great drama

---

[43] See J. A. Fitzmyer, *A Christological Catechism: New Testament Answers* (2nd edn., New York and Mahwah, NJ: Paulist Press, 1991), 32–6, at 32.

[44] For more material on the virginal conception see R. E. Brown, *The Birth of the Messiah* (2nd edn., New York: Doubleday, 1993), 298–309, 517–33, 635–9, 697–712; O'Collins, *Christology*, 273–8.

of divine self-giving see God creating, personally coming among us, and then bringing all things home at the final consummation. Certain writers (like Karl Rahner when developing systematically some impulses from Pierre Teilhard de Chardin[45]) expound the incarnation within an evolutionary perspective. Granted that God 'reaches down' to us when the Word 'comes from heaven' to assume a human existence, the incarnation should also be recognized as the highest conceivable development for humanity, 'the unique, *supreme* case of the total actualization of human reality'.[46] An individual, created human nature is taken up into the very life of God. Interestingly, St Thomas Aquinas (d. 1274), while understanding the primary motive for the incarnation to be a remedy for human sin, also appreciates both the place of God's self-communicating goodness and the rise of human nature to its highest possible perfection.[47] In passing, Aquinas thus makes room for the perspectives of Irenaeus, Scotus, Teilhard de Chardin, and Rahner that enrich a theology of the incarnation.

But not even Aquinas' openness could make room for the perspective of those who take an Hegelian line and explain the incarnation (followed by the crucifixion, resurrection, and outpouring of the Spirit) as the tripersonal God's necessary destiny. This confuses the intradivine life with the story of human salvation to the point of 'limiting' God to the world's becoming. If one follows Schoonenberg, for instance, in pushing matters to an extreme and arguing that the incarnation and glorification of the crucified Jesus establish the personhood of the Word and the Spirit, as if God somehow needed this historical process in order to become actually trinitarian, then an odd conclusion follows: the divine persons cannot share in that incarnation and glorification inasmuch as the Word and the Spirit, respectively, were not yet truly persons 'prior' to those events. Quite apart from strange consequences for trinitarian doctrine, taking the incarnation to be a necessary divine act flies in the face of mainstream Christian testimony from the time of the New Testament: the incarnation was a free act motivated by God's gratuitous love (John 3: 16; Rom. 5: 6–11; 8: 3, 31–9).

[45] See K. Rahner, 'Christology within an Evolutionary View of the World', *Theological Investigations*, v (London: Darton, Longman & Todd, 1966), 157–92; id., *Foundations of Christian Faith* (London: Darton, Longman & Todd, 1978), 178–202.

[46] Rahner, 'On the Theology of the Incarnation', 110. See also id., *Foundations of Christian Faith*, 218.

[47] See *ST* 3a. 1. 1, 3; 3a. 3. 8.

Aquinas, following Anselm, had the weight of the great tradition behind him when he wrote of the incarnation being 'fitting' but not strictly necessary (*ST* 3. 1. 1 and 2).[48]

(8) Our last section has already adumbrated the issue of the relationship (for divine self-revelation and human salvation) between the incarnation and the Easter mystery. But before summarizing that issue we should ask: what must be said about the revelatory and redemptive impact of the incarnation itself upon the world and human beings? First, we can take a cue from Matthew's Gospel and acknowledge that the incarnation reveals and guarantees that, besides creating, conserving, and guiding the world, God is now irrevocably 'with us' (Matt. 1: 23). Second, the personal sign of God's desire to be one of us, the 'last Adam' (1 Cor. 15: 45) exists 'for us' as *the* visible head, focal point, and principle of unity that 'recapitulates' the created cosmos and human society—to echo Irenaeus.[49] Third, the very fact of Emmanuel and the Last Adam being present has changed irrevocably humanity and the whole material world; through the event of the incarnation matter is now and will forever remain united to the person of the Word. Fourth, the enhanced nature of matter brought by the incarnation points forward to the church's sacramental system. Water, bread, wine, and oil will be raised to a new level in bringing the Holy Spirit and life in Christ. Fifth, the transformed status of the whole material universe entails massive moral consequences for believers: in responsible sensitivity towards their natural environment, respect for other bodily human beings, and regard for their own bodily nature. The incarnation's impact on the world and humankind should transform one's moral vision and behaviour (see Linda Zagzebski's chapter below).

(9) The immediately preceding section, while it focused on the religious, material, sacramental, and moral repercussions of the incarnation, did not intend to isolate it from the whole christological story that follows: in the life, death, and resurrection of Jesus, with the coming of the Holy Spirit, the emergence of the church, and the glorious consummation to come. Such an inclusive meaning

---

[48] See D. Brown, '"Necessary" and "Fitting" Reasons in Christian Theology', in W. J. Abraham and S. W. Holtzer (eds.), *The Rationality of Religious Belief* (Oxford: Clarendon Press, 1987), 211–30.

[49] In *Gaudium et spes* (the Pastoral Constitution on the Church in the Modern World), the Second Vatican Council (1962–5) called the incarnate and risen Son of God 'the key, the centre, and the purpose of all human life' (nr. 10).

attaches to the theme of the 'incarnational narrative' that recurs in Stephen Evans's *The Historical Christ and the Jesus of Faith*. Such an inclusive meaning also surfaces in Aquinas' *Summa contra gentiles* (4. 53, 55), but has not always been respected. His struggle against Gnostic undervaluing of matter led Irenaeus to insist on the Word's true enfleshment and make John 1: 14 the primary text: 'the Word became flesh.' The incarnation tended to displace the resurrection of the crucified One as the central christological mystery.[50] Despite the liturgical centrality of Easter, the feast of Christmas grew in importance at the expense of Good Friday, Easter Sunday, and Pentecost— a shift reflected in the fact that the hymns and carols for Christmas still outnumber Good Friday and Easter Sunday hymns.

Poets and spiritual writers can help us here. In 'The Coming of the Magi' T. S. Eliot has one of the wise men wonder whether they 'were led all that way for Birth or Death'. He recalls how they journeyed through winter nights and eventually arrived 'not a moment too soon' in Bethlehem. There they found 'this Birth' to be 'hard and bitter agony for us, like Death, our death'. For the contemplation on the nativity in his *Spiritual Exercises* St Ignatius of Loyola invites the retreatant to behold and consider 'Jesus being born in greatest poverty, so that after so many hardships and insults, he may die on the cross, and all this for me' (nr. 116). What will unfold in the life and death of Jesus reveals the radicality of the divine love embodied in the incarnation; the cross to come gives meaning and purpose to the birth of Christ. In the many essays on the incarnation which came from Karl Rahner, different pressures may have been at work to encourage a more dynamic view. But his Jesuit familiarity with the *Spiritual Exercises* and Ignatius' thought undoubtedly played a role in the way Rahner increasingly linked the incarnation with what was to come—in Christ's life, crucifixion, and resurrection.[51] Rahner leads us to a further question.

(10) When reflecting on the incarnation, Rahner took up a question that has recurred in speculative theology since the

---

[50] See J.-P. Jossua, *Le Salut, Incarnation ou Mystère Pascal: chez les Pères de l'Église de saint Irénée à saint Léon le Grand* (Paris: Cerf, 1968).

[51] In his *Theological Investigations* (London: Darton, Longman & Todd, 1961–92) Rahner kept taking up the incarnation and linking it more clearly with the christological events to come. On the Ignatian roots of his thought and the links he drew between the incarnation and the Easter mystery, see I. Sanna, *Teologia come esperienza di Dio: la prospettiva cristologica di Karl Rahner* (Brescia: Queriniana, 1997), 49–53, 167–77.

Middle Ages: could any of the three divine persons have become incarnate? Why was it only the Logos who assumed a human existence and not one of the other two persons? Rahner argued that 'the Word of God . . . alone is the one who begins and can begin a human history'.[52] A few years later Rahner repeated this position:

> it is contained in the meaning and essence of the Word of God that only *he* and he alone is the one who begins and can begin a human history in case God makes the world his own in such a way that this world is not only his work, a work distinct from himself, but [that] it also becomes his reality.[53]

This was to rule out an incarnation for the Father and the Holy Spirit. Their incarnation would have entailed changing personal relations within God and these relations are not interchangeable. It is the unoriginated Father who generates the Son within the eternal life of God, and 'then' sends him on a mission of salvation. An incarnated Father, sent by the Son (and the Spirit) would *per impossibile* reverse the eternal relationship of generation. Rahner put this impossibility in terms of the Father uttering the Word:

> The Father is by definition the unoriginated who is essentially invisible and who shows and reveals himself only by uttering his Word to the world. And the Word, by definition, is both immanently and in the economy of salvation the revelation of the Father, so that the revelation of the Father without the Logos and his incarnation would be the same as a wordless utterance.[54]

Some years later Rahner repeated his conviction that only the Word of God could become man. Being 'the immanent self-expression of God in its eternal fullness', the Logos 'makes possible God's self-expression outwards and outside himself'.[55] In brief, without the Logos and the incarnation of the Logos there could be no divine self-revelation in human history.

Rahner did not offer such a detailed argument against the Holy Spirit 'entering into a hypostatic union' with a created human being. He was content to observe that those who entertain the possibility of the Father and the Holy Spirit becoming incarnate falsely reject 'any real and intrinsic connexion between the mission

---

[52] 'On the Theology of the Incarnation', 106.
[53] Rahner, *Foundations of Christian Faith*, 215. See also K. Barth, *Church Dogmatics* (hereafter *CD*), trans. G. W. Bromiley, IV/1 (Edinburgh: T. & T. Clark, 1956), 66.
[54] 'Remarks on the Dogmatic Treatise "De Trinitate"', 91.
[55] *Foundations of Christian Faith*, 223.

of a divine person and the immanent life of the Trinity'. In doing that, they are 'quite contrary to the inner movement of Sacred Scripture'.[56] If we base ourselves on the immanent divine relations, however, it does not seem totally clear that we would likewise need to rule out *a priori* a historical sending of the Holy Spirit that would take the form of an incarnation. Within the life of the Trinity the Spirit 'proceeds' from the Father and (or through) the Son; they jointly send the Spirit into the world, the Church, and individuals. The 'breathing' of the Spirit within the eternal life of God stands behind the Spirit's being sent into the world. If the Spirit can be so sent and become indirectly visible (e.g. through the church and the Scriptures), why could not the Spirit even become incarnate and be directly visible? Can we then rule out the possibility of the Spirit's incarnation?[57]

Some features from the history of salvation may help us here. Although St Paul speaks of both the Son and the Spirit being 'sent' by the Father (Gal. 4: 4–6), the verb must be understood analogically; the two cases may be similar but are not precisely the same. The sending of the Son involves being 'born of a woman' and life as a Jew that ends on a cross (Gal. 3: 1, 13; 4: 4; 6: 14). The Spirit is sent 'into our hearts' (Gal. 4: 6), as a self-effacing, interior Helper and not a public figure. We receive and *have* the Spirit, whereas incorporated into our brother Jesus we *are* sons and daughters in the Son, with the Spirit always referring us to the Son and transforming us into the likeness of the Son. What Paul, in particular, says of our participation in salvation precludes the visible incarnation of the Spirit. Such an incarnation would have the Spirit functioning as a rival figure over against the incarnate Son—an image of things in the history of salvation that would imply strange rivalry (between the second and third persons) within God. What would it say about the inner life of the Trinity if among the believing community, instead of divisions over Peter, Paul, Apollos, or other human leaders (1 Cor 1: 10–17), there were some who proclaimed, 'we belong to the Son', and others who

---

[56] 'Remarks on the Dogmatic Treatise "De Trinitate"', 91–2. See Rahner, *The Trinity* (2nd edn., New York: Crossroad, 1997), 11.

[57] In the second century AD, Montanus believed that prophets (above all himself) and prophetesses (above all Prisca and Maximilla) were the 'mouth' of the Holy Spirit, the first manifestation of a striking outpouring of the Spirit on the church in her final years—almost an incarnation of the Spirit. See W. H. C. Frend, 'Montanismus', *Theologische Realenzyklopädie*, xxiii. 271–9.

proclaimed, 'we belong to the Spirit'? In short, where inner-trinitarian relations undoubtedly rule out the possible incarnation of the Father, the economy of salvation succeeds better in ruling out the possible incarnation of the Spirit.

(11) A related speculative question takes up the possibility of the Logos being incarnated more than once. Could one and the same Logos have also been embodied in many select individuals (men or women)[58] down through the ages in different cultures and continents? Could such multiple incarnations also include becoming incarnate in such non-persons and hypostases as horses and dogs? (After all, if the Word of God creates and conserves such animals, why could not the Word take them into his personal existence?[59]) For many people (egalitarian philosophers like Rousseau, some feminists, Hindus, and some Christian theologians in dialogue with non-Christians) one solitary incarnation of the Word in a first-century Jewish male seems scandalously particular and even particularly scandalous. Why should we accept just one incarnation and then attribute universal saving significance to the solitary figure of Jesus of Nazareth?

The reflections of St John of the Cross (1542–91) on the prologue of John's Gospel and the opening verses of Hebrews form the classical response to the thesis of multiple incarnations. In uttering and sending his Son into our history, God has said it all and has nothing (or no one) more to say.[60] The once-for-all character of the incarnation corresponded to the single uttering or generating of the Son within the eternal life of God. Here we reach the heart of the Christian challenge. Nathan Söderblom wrote almost a century ago: 'the conception of one solitary incarnation of deity is peculiar to Christianity.'[61] Other religions tell of immortal gods assuming human form, but these are at best shadowy 'incarnations' and no real parallel to the Word becoming flesh to live among us and die 'under Pontius Pilate'. Inasmuch as

[58] The Shakers believed that Mother Ann Lee (1736–84) was the female incarnate Logos; see L. A. Mercadante, *Gender, Doctrine, and God: The Shakers and Contemporary Theology* (Nashville: Abingdon, 1990).

[59] Through knowing and loving the human spirit is open to the infinite—something that is not true of any animals. Hence, as Aquinas put it (*SCG* 4. 55. 6), it was 'fitting' for the Word of God to assume a rational and not a lesser nature.

[60] *Ascent of Mount Carmel*, 2. 22. 4–5; trans. E. Allison Peers (Tunbridge Wells: Burns & Oates, 1983), 163–4.

[61] N. Söderblom *et al.*, 'Incarnation', in J. Hastings (ed.), *Encyclopedia of Religion and Ethics* (Edinburgh: T.& T. Clark, 1908–26), vii 183–201, at 184.

God eternally speaks the one Word or generates the only-begotten Son, we can find a parallel between the divine life *ad intra* and *ad extra* that can justify a unique incarnation which happens once and for all.

But this still leaves the feminist question insufficiently addressed, it could be argued. Even if the scandal of particularity *per se* is faced, what of the scandal of Jesus' maleness? Does Jesus' maleness implicitly subordinate or devalue the role of women in the church, specifically in relation to their potential for ordained ministry? Clearly this (implicitly christological) question is one of enormous contentiousness in our day.

The answer of feminist theologians to date has tended to be twofold. Either a 'message Christology' is adopted, which turns attention to the option Jesus made for the dispossessed and underrated (including women), and averts attention *away* from his maleness, or a high Christology is adopted which rises beyond gender differentiation or claims to include both (so-called) 'feminine' and 'masculine' characteristics. A more subtle, and third, approach, however, can argue that Jesus' very particularity as male (a male cruelly executed for failing to conform to patriarchal expectations of messianic triumphalism) *exposes* patriarchy for what it is. Yet meanwhile the churches that still rule out women's ordination continue to ruminate on the question of whether Jesus' maleness presents a bar to a woman celebrating the Eucharist as 'alter Christus'.

(12) Whatever conclusions one draws from Jesus' maleness, how do we know that the incarnation has taken place and that we relate to reality when we accept it? Any answer obviously presupposes some stand on the character of knowledge and religious knowledge. Those who refuse to go beyond the scrutiny of empirical evidence find it unreasonable, prescientific, and downright superstitious to accept the incarnation. At best they are agnostic about the existence of God. Hence before we can investigate the incarnation, we need to justify or at least presuppose both the existence of God and the possibility of our knowing that in particular historical contexts God has acted in special ways and communicated some special truth over and above what might be gleaned from God's normal activity in conserving and guiding the created universe.

Accepting the incarnation, it seems to me, engages the total person (with his or her intellect, will, and imagination)[62] in life and worship with others. Both in first acquiring and then living one's faith in the incarnate Word, much more than a mere appeal to appropriate evidence is involved. We do not, for instance, establish and confirm belief in the incarnation *simply* by marshalling the biblical data and reaching some well-argued historical conclusion: 'yes, it certainly looks as if Jesus of Nazareth, at least implicitly, claimed a divine identity and then what happened in his resurrection showed that he was/is the incarnate Son of God.' To be sure, *pace* Rudolf Bultmann, historical evidence does matter for faith in the incarnate and risen Christ; *pace* various neo-Arians, biblical scholarship can responsibly support a high Christology. Yet it would be illusory to think that we might test belief in the incarnation by 'impartially' appealing to allegedly 'objective' facts that we suppose 'anyone of good will' can and should recognize. Neither this belief nor any other belief can be demonstrated by pretending to set aside our 'biases' and follow a neutral, unprejudiced procedure.[63]

Belief in the incarnation emerges from the interplay of factors 'from the outside' and 'on the inside'. 'From the outside' we receive testimony to the incarnation that reaches back through many generations in the church to the first Christians,[64] and, as Tom Wright in his chapter on Jesus' self-understanding rightly insists, back to Jesus himself and the Jewish categories he thematized. We can hear and test what the NT witnesses say about Jesus' words, deeds, and destiny after crucifixion: we see the fruits of their message in the ways incarnational faith has affected and even radically transformed many lives. 'On the inside' the activity of the Holy Spirit opens us up to hear the external witness and agree: 'yes, the

---

[62] See the chapters by David Brown, Kathleen Norris, and Marguerite Shuster in this book, as well as Carol Harrison's reflections on the drawing power which St Augustine found in the beauty of the incarnation: see 'Incarnation' in her *Beauty and Revelation in the Thought of Saint Augustine* (Oxford: Clarendon Press, 1992), 192–238. In the 20th cent. Hans Urs von Balthasar developed at length the theme of divine glory revealed in the incarnate, crucified, and resurrected Christ. For an excellent account of Balthasar's understanding of Christ as the epiphany of the Father's glory, see G. Marchesi, *La Cristologia trinitaria di Hans Urs von Balthasar* (Brescia: Queriniana, 1997), 191–321.

[63] See A. G. Padgett's 'Advice for Religious Historians: The Myth of a Purely Historical Jesus', in S. Davis, D. Kendall, and G. O'Collins (eds.), *The Resurrection* (Oxford: Oxford University Press, 1997), 287–307.

[64] We can reasonably assess their account of what Jesus said and did by applying Stephen Davis's argument. That account leaves us with a choice between three conclusions: Jesus was either mad, or bad, or truly Son of God.

story of Jesus is indeed the story of the incarnate Son of God.' We are enabled to know this story and know it to be true by living in its truth and letting its truth change our lives. In short, triggers of incarnational faith work cumulatively—from the outside and on the inside.

As regards the testimony 'from the outside', our education and available time will shape the scrutiny we can give to the testimony and the historical evidence to which it points. Impressed by a sense of God's self-communicating goodness deployed in creation and human history, some may be predisposed to greet that testimony. Others may join Kierkegaard in judging the claim that the Son of God became man in our sinful world to be a bizarre offence to rational human thought. The paradoxical, unparalleled character of this claim elicits the conclusion: we could not have invented such an incarnational belief by ourselves.[65] In the spirit of Tertullian one might say: this tale is so strange and seemingly impossible that it must be true. The apologetic for the incarnation developed by St Gregory of Nyssa (d. *c.*395) in his *Great Catechetical Discourse* takes both forms. Although he appealed much more to what was known of the cosmos and of human existence in pressing the plausibility of the incarnational narrative, he also argued that the story of a human life which did not begin after sexual intercourse and did not end with decomposition in the grave was so extraordinary and incredible that it had to be true (13. 1).

'On the inside' the witness of the Spirit, who also operates 'out there' in the church and the world, works on fertile ground. Incarnational belief speaks to the deepest needs and spiritual hungers of human beings. Why does it matter for us and to us that the incarnation took place? From the first centuries Christians have pondered our need for the coming among us of One who was/ is truly divine and human. Generally they articulated the vital importance of the incarnation in terms of salvation. On the one hand, if Christ were not truly divine and only another human figure chosen and sent by God, he would not have had the power to redeem us, nor would his saving work have been valid for everyone and for the whole cosmos. As we might put it today, a merely human figure like a successful guru or superior social worker could not have saved us. On the other hand, if he were not genuinely

[65] On this argument from Kierkegaard, see Evans, *Historical Christ and the Jesus of Faith*, 53–4.

human, we would not have been saved from the inside—by one of ourselves. In that sense every denial of the (full) humanity of Jesus was seen to deny our redemption. It is through his being truly and fully human that he could heal us and make possible a new relationship with God and with one another.[66]

Along with redemption, revelation forms the other face of the divine self-communication. Without the personal self-manifestation of God that the incarnation brings, God could seem remote and distantly other, even separated from us by an infinite gulf.[67] The incarnation personally reveals the astonishing concern and merciful love of God towards all men and women. It also illuminates the human condition: not only our sinfulness but also the meaning and purpose of our life. By assuming a particular, and in many ways a very ordinary, human existence, the eternal Word sheds light on the significance and lasting importance of the particular and often unspectacular lives we all live. We receive our eternal salvation not by escaping from the specifics of our embodied and everyday existence but by working through them.

Let the last word on this issue belong to Myles Connolly and the story he originally published in 1928, *Mr Blue*. After sunset one clear evening in New York, the narrator found himself on a rooftop with Blue, four hundred feet above Broadway. Blue asked: 'did it ever occur to you that it was Christ who humanized infinitude, so to speak? When God became man, he made you and me and the rest of us pretty important people. He not only redeemed us. He saved us from the terrible burden of infinity.' With his eyes glowing in the dark, Blue threw his hands up towards the stars and continued: 'my hands, my feet, my poor little brain, my eyes, my ears, all matter more than the whole sweep of these constellations! . . . God himself, the God to whom this whole universe-specked display is as nothing, God himself had hands like mine and feet like mine, and eyes, and brain, and ears.' Blue looked at the narrator intently and went on: 'without Christ we would be little more than bacteria breeding on a pebble in space, or glints of ideas in a whirling void of abstractions. Because of him, I can stand here out under this cold immensity and

---

[66] For some patristic material on this and the next point see O'Collins, *Christology*, 155–8.

[67] See e.g. Aristotle's noble and sophisticated vision of God in *Metaphysics*, 1. 27; yet the 'God' of this great philosopher remains tragically distant from personal involvement in the human scene.

know that my infinitesimal pulse-beats and acts and thoughts are of more importance than this whole show of a universe.'[68]

To conclude. We have outlined and briefly evaluated twelve issues that concern the doctrine of the incarnation: (1) the particular truth of the historical union of divinity and humanity in the one person of Jesus Christ; (2) the Word's personal pre-existence within the Trinity as an essential part of incarnation faith; (3) the paradox (but not contradiction) of holding the Chalcedonian teaching of Jesus being truly divine and fully human; (4) the objection to the incarnation as entailing unfairness on the part of God; (5) the divine and human wills and minds of Christ in their sinless harmony; (6) the virginal conception as the way the incarnation actually happened; (7) God's reasons for the incarnation; (8) the revelatory and redemptive impact of the incarnation; (9) the relationship of the incarnation to the resurrection; (10) the incarnation being possible only for the Word of God; (11) the incarnation as a once-and-for-all occurrence; (12) the credibility of the incarnation. Indisputably other questions can be raised. But these twelve issues should be enough to give a reasonably clear view of the current landscape of serious Christian reflection on the incarnation.[69]

---

[68] Myles Connolly, *Mr Blue* (Albany, NY: Richelieu Court Publications, 1990), 25. A perspective shaped by a Teilhardian sense of the universe's development would insist more on humanity being the crown of evolution rather than on its being set somewhat over against 'this whole show of a universe'. Shortly after writing and publishing *Mr Blue*, Connolly, who was born in 1897 and had been a Boston journalist, married and moved to Hollywood, where he was a writer and producer of many notable films for the next 35 years. In particular, he collaborated frequently with Frank Capra. He died in 1964.

[69] For some valuable criticisms and comments on this chapter, I want to thank David Brown, Sarah Coakley, Stephen Davis, Daniel Howard-Snyder, Brian Leftow, Alan Padgett, and the members of a study circle which met at the Alphonsianum in Rome.

BIBLICAL WITNESS

2

Theophany, Anthropomorphism, and the *Imago Dei*: Some Observations about the Incarnation in the Light of the Old Testament

J. ANDREW DEARMAN

The Old Testament itself does not often play a significant role in modern scholarship when interpreting the origins of the Christian doctrine of the incarnation.[1] This may seem understandable in historical-critical analysis. When read historically, the OT is a collection of pre-Christian documents and primarily concerned with 'monotheizing in a polytheistic context', to use an interesting phrase of J. Sanders,[2] whereas the crucial steps in the formation of incarnational belief come in the first four centuries CE. Nevertheless, the OT (or parts thereof), especially in Greek translation, was the Bible of early Christianity. Thus it is really early Christian readings of the OT that have received intensive study in reconstructing the origins of the doctrine, readings with exegetical and philosophical presuppositions that differ considerably from those of historical-critical analysis.[3]

[1] For some attention to the matter, see D. J. Reimer, 'Old Testament Christology', in J. Day (ed.), *King and Messiah in Israel and the Ancient Near East*, JSOTSS 270 (Sheffield: Sheffield Academic Press, 1998), 380–400; R. H. Fuller, 'The *Vestigia Trinitatis* in the Old Testament', in C. A. Evans (ed.), *The Quest for Meaning and Context: Studies in Biblical Intertextuality in Honor of James A. Sanders* (Leiden and New York: Brill, 1997), 499–508; F. C. Holmgren, *The Old Testament & the Significance of Jesus Christ* (2nd edn.; London: SCM Press, 1989), esp. 139–91.

[2] See his collected essays, *From Sacred Story to Sacred Text* (Philadelphia: Fortress, 1987), 7, 21, 166, 187.

[3] The bibliography just on the interpretation of the OT in the New Testament is immense. For a study of the historical origins of the doctrine of the incarnation, where the NT's interpretation of the OT is a significant part of the analysis, see J. D. G. Dunn, *Christology in the Making: A New Testament Inquiry into the Origins of the Doctrine of the Incarnation* (Grand Rapids, Mich.: Eerdmans, 1996). His work contains an extensive bibliography. For subsequent studies of the NT interpretation of the OT, see C. A. Evans, *Early Christian Interpretation of the Scriptures of Israel: Investigations and*

As is well known, patristic interpreters found references in the OT to the pre-incarnate Logos. For them this validated the OT as a preparation for the coming of Christ and as a support for the confession of Christ's uniqueness.[4] Justin Martyr is an early case in point.[5] In searching the OT for instruction in Christian faith, the patristic writers followed the precedent of the New Testament writers. John's affirmation that the divine word became flesh (John 1: 1–3, 14),[6] Paul's adaptation of an early hymn celebrating the *kenosis* and exaltation of the Messiah (Phil. 2: 6–11),[7] and the confession in the letter to the Hebrews that the Son is an 'imprint/ stamp' of God (1: 3)[8] are examples of NT precursors to the later, creedal doctrine of the incarnation, where in each instance the author is also influenced by the OT. The hermeneutical approaches of the NT writers and those of the church Fathers, while diverse

---

Proposals (Sheffield: Sheffield Academic Press, 1997); id., *The Function of Scripture in Early Jewish and Christian Tradition* (Sheffield: Sheffield Academic Press, 1998); and W. Horbury, *Jewish Messianism and the Cult of Christ* (London: SCM Press, 1998). For the patristic period, see M. Simonetti, *Biblical Interpretation in the Early Church: An Historical Introduction to Patristic Exegesis* (Edinburgh: T & T Clark, 1994); P. Blowers (ed.), *The Bible in Greek Christian Antiquity* (Notre Dame, Ind.: University of Notre Dame Press, 1997); and C. Hall, *Reading Scripture with the Church Fathers* (Downers Grove, Ill.: InterVarsity Press, 1998).

[4] According to A. von Harnack, *History of Dogma* (New York: Dover, 1961), iii. 30, the OT and its presentation of theophanies played a key role in the early church's struggle over adoptionist Christologies. OT theophanies, often interpreted as appearances of the pre-incarnate Logos, served as confirmation of the Son's pre-existence.

[5] Justin argued that the appearances of the angel of the Lord (see below) in the OT were appearances of the pre-incarnate Christ (*Dialogue*, 56. 4, 10; 58. 3; 59. 1; 62. 5; 128. 4). See further, B. Kominiak, *The Theophanies of the Old Testament in the Writings of St Justin* (Washington, DC: Catholic University Press, 1948); and D. C. Trakatellis, *The Pre-existence of Christ in the Writings of Justin Martyr* (Missoula, Mont.: Scholars Press, 1976). A. T. Hanson, *Jesus Christ in the Old Testament* (London: SPCK, 1965) proposes similar beliefs among certain NT writers. He concludes that they believed in a 'real presence' of the pre-incarnate Jesus in ancient Israel.

[6] The personal nature of the Greek term for 'word' (*logos*) has history-of-tradition roots in the OT where the agency of the 'word' (Hebrew: *dabar*) of God is understood as an extension of God's activity in the world (e.g. Isa. 55: 10–11). See n. 19 below. The history-of-tradition root of the verb 'dwell' in John 1: 14 is brought out in the Authorized Version's rendering 'tabernacled'.

[7] The exaltation of Jesus as Lord (Greek: *Kurios*) is portrayed in language taken from Isa. 45: 22–5, where 'every knee shall bow and tongue confess' is praise given to God the Lord (LXX = *Kurios*; Hebrew = *YHWH*). On the issue of using texts addressing YHWH in the OT and applying them to Jesus, see D. Capes, *Old Testament Yahweh Texts in Paul's Christology* (Tübingen: Mohr/Siebeck, 1992).

[8] See the description of wisdom in Wis. 7: 25–6. In Heb. 1: 1–3 the Son is the eschatological culmination of God's revelation begun through the prophets (i.e. the OT scriptures).

among themselves, are indeed different enough from those of modern, historical-critical analysis, that a mere 'repeating' of their claims regarding the OT is inadequate. For modern appropriation it is better to reformulate their reading strategies on historical/developmental grounds, to make discriminating use of typological analysis, and to affirm that what God began in and through Israel reaches culmination in Christ, the word made flesh.

In what follows, therefore, I will propose that two elements in the OT concerned with anthropomorphism, namely accounts of theophanies and texts concerning the *imago Dei*, can still contribute to the understanding of the incarnation. A long history of discussion in Christian thought exists regarding both of these, since both were frequently cited by pre-modern interpreters as scriptural sources for a 'high Christology'. Although I will concentrate on interpreting both of them historically in the context of their pre-Christian origins, I hope to show that points of contact remain with views expressed by early Christians.

I Theophany as God's Anthropomorphic Self-Presentation

Accounts of theophanies in the OT fall in two broad categories.[9] The first depicts revelation as God's personal self-manifestation to an individual or company of people (e.g. Gen. 26: 24–5; Exod. 24: 9–11). A theophany may occur in a cult-place, but this is not required. Anthropomorphic imagery of the Lord and/or of his messenger/representative is often a distinguishing feature (e.g. Exod. 3: 1–15; 33: 12–23; Judg. 6: 11–24; Amos 7: 7–9). It is this first category, and particularly those accounts of God and/or messenger in anthropomorphic form, which concern us. The second describes divine manifestation through natural phenomena (e.g. Exod. 24: 16–17; Deut. 4: 11: 1 Kgs. 19: 11–18). On occasion, divine warrior symbolism is portrayed through depiction of weather-related phenomena (e.g. Exod. 15: 4–10; Ps. 78: 13–14;

---

[9] J. Jeremias, *Theophanie* (Neukirchen-Vluyn: Neukirchener Verlag, 1965); J. K. Kuntz, *The Self-Revelation of God* (Philadelphia: Westminster, 1967); W. Eichrodt, *Theology of the Old Testament* (Philadelphia: Westminster Press, 1961, 1967), i. 206–27; ii. 15–45, are basic studies.

Hab. 3: 3–15). The fine study by Jeremias concentrates on this second category.

Modern scholars have suggested that those accounts in which God 'appears' can be assessed through a broad chronological and religious development. The earliest texts are sometimes judged naive in their depiction, and the later ones, where a sense of divine transcendence and otherness grows more pronounced, demonstrate greater reserve in describing God anthropomorphically. Later texts also attribute more to mediatorial figures such as angels or to the active presence of God's spirit and glory and less to unmediated speech from God. Thus in the early text of Genesis 18, God and two travelling companions come to the tent of Abraham and Sarah, are served a meal (!),[10] and engage in conversations about the birth of Isaac and the fate of neighbouring cities. Isaiah's vision of the enthroned Lord in chapter 6 refrains from direct mention of physical attributes, although it assumes a human form of gigantic proportions. Ezekiel's vision in chapter 1 combines stormy wind and fire with surrealistic creatures, a wheeled chariot-throne for locomotion, and the appearance of God as 'something like a human form' (1: 26).[11] Daniel's dream in chapter 7 also describes a scene with beasts, fire, and angelic attendants around an enthroned 'Ancient of Days',[12] whose clothing is white and whose hair is like wool, and who grants sovereignty and an everlasting kingdom to one 'like a Son of Man'. Not all the accounts of theophany give an indication of bodily form in their reference to God 'appearing', but when they do, it is human form rather than animal form that is indicated. All accounts, whether early or late in composition, are reticent about description of the divine form itself.

Several accounts of theophany/divine revelation include a

[10] The Palestinian Targum on Genesis holds that the three visitors only seemed to eat. See Tobit 12: 19 for similar reticence regarding angels partaking of food.

[11] 1: 28b describes the scene in summary as: 'This was the appearance of the likeness of the glory of the Lord'; see n. 29 below.

[12] The symbolism of Dan. 7 contains a fundamental contrast between the theriomorphic forces of rebellion and the anthropomorphic figures who comprise the eternal kingdom. The latter include one 'like a son of man' (7: 13) and the 'holy ones' (7: 22, 25) gathered around the throne. In Rev. 1: 13–20 the Christophany of the one 'like a Son of Man has history-of-tradition roots in Dan. 7 and 10, combining descriptions of the 'Ancient of Days' (hair, 7: 9) and the anthropomorphic figure(s) in 7: 13; 10: 5–6, 16, 18. The figure in Dan. 10 is an angel. See n. 21 below on angelomorphic figures.

'messenger' sent by God to deliver a communication or to complete
a task (e.g. Gen. 16: 7–14; 18: 1–19: 23; 21: 15–19; 22: 9–19;
32: 1–2, 22–32; Exod. 3: 1–15; 14: 19–20; Num. 22: 22–35;
Josh. 5: 13–15; Judg. 6: 11–24; Zech. 1: 7–6: 8; Dan. 8: 15–26;
10: 5–17). Some of these accounts are not theophanies in the strict
sense (i.e. those where God is absent), but because the anthropomorphic divine messenger manifests himself to work with or to
speak on behalf of God, they require some consideration in this
context. The two common Hebrew terms for messenger are *mal'ak*
often translated by the LXX as angel, and *'ish*, elsewhere a typical
term for man, human being or person.[13] Human form is common
in reference to these individuals (although it is not their only
form), who comprise part of the 'heavenly host' or 'heavenly
council' of God (1 Kgs. 22: 19–23).[14] More specifically, they are
part of the genus 'sons of God', i.e. created beings who serve
YHWH, the divine King and Lord of Hosts (4QDeut. 32: 8–9 (cf.
LXX); Isa. 6: 5; Ps. 29: 1; Job 1: 6; cf. 1 Enoch 13: 8; 106: 5). As
part of the genus they may bear the title 'divine' (*'elohim*), which
may be better understood as 'supernatural' or 'otherworldly'. It is
probable that some in Israel regarded these beings from the divine
world as deities in their own right.[15] By the time the book of

[13] Most English translations use 'angel' in these accounts for the Hebrew term
mal'ak. Both Hebrew terms for 'messenger' occur in the singular and plural.
Approximately half of the occurrences of *mal'ak* in the OT refer to human
messengers. The three figures who visit Abraham in Gen. 18: 2 are called 'men'
and the two figures distinct from the Lord are called 'messengers' (19: 1). In
Josh. 5: 13–15, the man (*'ish*) met by Joshua further defines himself as 'captain of
the army/host of YHWH'. In Dan. 8: 15 and 10: 18 the angel is described 'as in
appearance like a man'.

[14] For further explanation of these terms and bibliography, see C. A. Newsom,
'Angels', *Anchor Bible Dictionary* (Garden City, NY: Doubleday, 1992), i. 248–53. The
older work of W. Heidt, *Angelology of the Old Testament: A Study in Biblical Theology*
(Washington, DC: Catholic University of America, 1949) is also helpful. The host of
heaven who gather around the enthroned YHWH are masculine in human form. In
the heavenly throne-scene of 1 Kgs. 22: 19–23, the 'spirit' (*ruah*) who is commissioned by the Lord to be a 'lying spirit' in the mouth of Ahab's prophets is probably
one of the heavenly host. This implies that human form designates function for host
members, but not ontology. Even though the Hebrew word for spirit (*ruah*) is
grammatically feminine, it is rendered as grammatically masculine in 1 Kgs. 22: 21–
2. The cherubim of Gen. 3: 24 and the seraphim of Isa. 6: 2 are created beings who
serve YHWH, but it is unclear if they too are members of the genus 'sons of God'. They
have animal characteristics. There are figures in Ancient Near Eastern iconography
which provide parallels to these creatures.

[15] For further discussion, see L. K. Handy, *Among the Host of Heaven: The Syro-
Palestinian Pantheon as Bureaucracy* (Winona Lake, Ind.: Eisenbrauns, 1994); and D. V.

Daniel reaches its final form in the second century BCE, Judaism had developed a sophisticated angelology. Two angels are named in Daniel (Gabriel, 8: 16; Michael, 10: 13), and in addition to bearing information, these angels are involved in such activities as advocacy and intercession. Other, second-temple documents provide the names of additional angels and presuppose an involved hierarchy among them.[16]

As noted above, the appearance of one of God's messengers (without God in accompaniment) is not a theophany in the strict sense, even if the account has similarities with those of the appearance of God. The issue of theophany becomes quite complicated, however, in certain accounts where the messenger acts/speaks with the authority of God and his (literary) appearance cannot be distinguished from that of God. In particular this is true of the anthropomorphic messenger called the 'angel (*mal'ak*) of the Lord/God'. This intertwining of *divine/angelic* roles can be seen in such accounts as the appearance to Hagar in Genesis 16: 7–14, the instruction to Abraham in Genesis 22: 9–19, and the sign of divine presence in Exodus 3: 1–15, among several others.[17] For example, in the appearance to Hagar the angel of the Lord speaks a word of blessing; at the conclusion of their encounter Hagar confesses that she has seen God (Gen. 16: 13). So close is the identification of the figure with God in these early accounts that some interpreters have concluded the figure is actually intended to describe the presence of God himself in anthropomorphic form. Others think that the term 'angel of the Lord' has been interpolated in some of the accounts as a way to soften the naive anthropomorphism of YHWH's direct appearance. And yet others have seen the 'angel of the Lord' figure as a way to refer to a divinely commissioned messenger who serves the Lord in a specific capacity.[18] Whatever the author's intention (and it may vary

Edelman (ed.), *The Triumph of Elohim: From Yahwisms to Judaisms* (Kampen: Kok Pharos Publishing House, 1995).

[16] M. Mach, *Entwicklungsstadien des jüdischen Engelglaubens in vorrabbinischer Zeit* (Tübingen: Mohr/Siebeck, 1992); and S. M. Olyan, *A Thousand Thousands Served Him: Exegesis and the Naming of Angels in Ancient Judaism* (Tübingen: Mohr/Siebeck, 1993).

[17] See Newsom, 'Angels', 250; and for a fuller discussion, S. Meier, 'Angel of the Lord', in K. van der Toorn *et al.*, *Dictionary of Deities and Demons in the Bible* (Grand Rapids, Mich.: Eerdmans, 1999), 53–9.

[18] In later, second-temple texts (e.g. Zech. 3: 1–10) the 'angel of the Lord' is

among accounts), the portrayal of deity and messenger is perplexingly similar in the earlier accounts; the figure personally represents God, acts on/with divine authority, and can speak as God. In a strange way he serves as an anthropomorphic extension of the Lord's presence in the world. In second-temple texts, there are parallels to this personal extension of divine presence where even attributes of the Lord are personified (e.g. wisdom, word, spirit, and glory).[19] The NT is heir to all this; in the canonical Gospels, the post-resurrection appearance stories of Jesus have their decisive history-of-tradition roots in the OT divine appearance stories,[20]

probably a reference to a particular angel (Gabriel?) who bears a message from God, since in these texts his appearance and activity can be distinguished from that of the Lord. In the NT cf. Matt. 1: 20; Luke 1: 11; 2: 9. J. Borland, *Christ in the Old Testament* (Chicago: Moody Press, 1978), continues to maintain that the OT 'angel of the Lord' is Christ pre-incarnate. W. G. MacDonald, 'Christology and "The Angel of the Lord" ', in G. Hawthorne (ed.), *Current Issues in Biblical and Patristic Interpretation* (Grand Rapids, Mich.: Eerdmans, 1975), 324–35, sees the OT angel of the Lord as a typological prefigurement of Christ.

[19] Personified attributes in second-temple Judaism are a conceptual key to the incarnation of the word in John 1: 14. See n. 6 above and C. A. Evans, *Word and Glory: On the Exegetical and Theological Background of John's Prologue* (Sheffield: JSOT Press, 1993). Of these attributes-in-action, that of wisdom probably contributes the most to early christological formulations; see Prov. 8: 22–31; Wis. 7: 22; 9: 1–2, 9–10; Sir. 1: 1; 34: 8. According to M. Hengel, 'Jesus as Messianic Teacher of Wisdom and the Beginnings of Christology', in his *Studies in Early Christology* (Edinburgh: T & T Clark, 1995), 116, wisdom is the 'mother of high Christology'.
   For further discussion of personified attributes, see W. Eichrodt, *Theology of the Old Testament* (Philadelphia: Westminster, 1967), 15–92; A. R. Johnson, *The One and the Many in the Israelite Conception of God* (Cardiff: Universiy of Wales Press, 1961); J. Habermann, *Präexistenzaussagen im Neuen Testament* (New York: Peter Lang, 1990); A. Chester, 'Jewish Messianic Expectations and Mediatorial Figures and Pauline Christology', in M. Hengel and U. Heckel (eds.), *Paulus und das antike Judentum* (Tübingen: Mohr/Siebeck, 1991), 17–89; and C. Gieschen, *Angelomorphic Christology: Antecedents and Early Evidence* (Leiden and Boston: Brill, 1998).
[20] See J. E. Alsup, *The Post Resurrection Appearance Stories of the Gospel Tradition* (Stuttgart: Calwer Verlag, 1975), esp. 239–74, for the influence of the OT theophanies in depicting the resurrected Lord. In a later address, 'Resurrection and Historicity', *Austin Presbyterian Theological Seminary Bulletin*, 103 (1988), 17, Alsup writes concerning the Gospel appearance stories: 'Within the quest for adequate expression, integration, and understanding, the Old Testament theophany genre emerged within the reflective consciousness and conversations of those earliest participants and they returned to this analogy of approximation again and again. Perhaps they did so because it had the capacity to interpret to them with adequacy and power what had, in fact, happened to them: they had been encountered in history by the God of their Old Testament frame of reference who, of old, had met their people in human form, in self-disclosure to save, to restore, to make new. It was a typological way of thinking rooted in scripture itself.'

and the complex world of divine messengers (angels) influenced the shape of christological development.[21]

By way of summary it can be said that anthropomorphic appearance is a significant part of the theophanic traditions in the OT, both in the guarded way that God is said to 'appear' and in the way that his messengers appear. If there is an intrinsic link between anthropomorphism and divine appearing in these accounts, it is assumed rather than explicit. Moreover, there are other claims in the biblical tradition that discourage thinking of God in human form (see below). Nevertheless, a unique relationship of form between God and humankind is explicitly claimed in the first account of the creation of humankind (Gen. 1: 26–8), and to this and related texts we turn next for commentary on the significance of anthropomorphism in the OT.

II Divine Image, Anthropomorphism, and Theophany

According to the first creation account (Gen. 1: 27), God created humankind (Hebrew: *'adam*; Greek: *anthropos*) in his image (Hebrew: *šelem*; Greek: *eikon*). Early Christian authors found in this unique[22] claim both a way to understand the significance of Jesus and that of humanity.[23] Modern analysis, however, has been

---

[21] The study of Gieschen, *Angelomorphic Christology*, goes beyond the question of whether early Christians thought of Jesus as an angel to the more fundamental question: 'Where and how did early Christians use the variegated angelomorphic traditions from the OT and other sources to express their Christology?' (p. 349). He concludes, *contra* Dunn, *Christology in the Making*, that angelomorphic traditions exerted considerable influence on early Christian confessions of Jesus' unique identity.

[22] According to the OT only humankind is created in the divine image. These are the only direct references: in Gen. 1: 26 God proposes to create humankind in 'our image' and 'according to our likeness'. The LXX translation does not have the possessive pronoun 'our'. In Gen. 5: 1–3 the narrator reports that God made humankind in the 'likeness' of God, and that Seth, the first child of Adam, is in the 'image' of Adam his father. In Gen. 9: 6 the possibility of capital punishment for murder is enjoined because humankind is created in the 'image' of God.

[23] e.g. in 2 Cor. 4: 4 and Col. 1: 15–20 Christ *is* the image (*eikon*) of the invisible God. Dunn, *Christology in the Making*, 105, describes Paul's view of salvation 'as the fashioning or reshaping of the believer into the image of God'.

The following sampling will demonstrate the importance of the *imago Dei* in early Christianity: R. Leys, *L'Image de Dieu chez Grégoire de Nysse: Esquisse d'une doctrine* (Bruxelles: Desclée, 1951); W. J. Burghardt, *The Image of God in Man According to Cyril*

preoccupied with establishing the meaning of the claim as part of Hebrew anthropology. For the purposes at hand it is not crucial to review all the options for interpretation or provide an exhaustive exegesis of the text.[24] In what follows I shall put the subject of the *imago Dei* in Genesis in historical-critical dialogue with that of theophany and anthropomorphism.

In spite of the labour expended on the subject, it is not at all clear what the (priestly?) writer intended by the claim that humankind is created in the divine image. The primary contextual clue is God's blessing in 1: 28–9, a blessing that humankind should procreate and rule over other creatures (cf. Ps. 8). Ancient Near Eastern parallels offer additional perspective to complement this interpretation. In surrounding cultures the concept of divine image is typically associated with the person of the king and royal ideology.[25] Royal overtones have been democratized in the Genesis version, but they fit well with the tasks assigned in 1: 28–9. Moreover, the famous 'let us' and 'our' in Genesis 1: 26 are plausibly interpreted as speech to the heavenly court by the cosmic king.[26] Another reinforcement of the functional interpretation comes with the discovery in 1979 of a statue of an Aramean king with a bilingual inscription (Assyrian, Aramaic), where the statue is referred to as the 'image' and 'likeness' of the king. According to the inscription, King Hadad-Yithi placed this statue of himself in a city to remind his subjects of him and his rule when he is physically absent from them.[27] Thus literary and cultural

of Alexandria (Washington, DC: Catholic University of America Press, 1957), R. Wilson, 'The Early History of the Exegesis of Genesis 1: 26', *Studia Patristica*, 1 (1957), 420–37; H. Crouzel, *Théologie de l'image de Dieu chez Origène* (Paris: Aubier, 1957); J. Fantino, *L'Homme image de Dieu chez saint Irénée de Lyon* (Paris: Cerf, 1986); and F. G. McLeod, *The Image of God in the Antiochene Tradition* (Washington, DC: Catholic University of America Press, 1999).

[24] G. A. Jónsson, *The Image of God. Genesis 1: 26–28 in a Century of Old Testament Research* (Stockholm: Almqvist & Wiksell, 1988).

[25] See further A. Angerstorfer, 'Ebenbild eines Gottes in babylonischen und assyrischen Keilschrifttexten', *Biblische Notizen*, 88 (1997), 47–58. For the Egyptian materials, see B. Ockinga, *Die Gottesebenbildlichkeit im Alten Ägypten und im Alten Testament* (Wiesbaden: Harrassowitz, 1984).

[26] The best parallels in the OT to the 'let us' and 'our' of 1: 26 occur in Isa. 6: 1–8 and 1 Kgs. 22: 19–23. Both texts concern a vision of YHWH enthroned and elements of the heavenly court around him. Isa. 6: 8 has the Lord say: 'who will go for us?' The Lord's words in 1 Kgs. 22: 20, 22, do not contain a first-person plural pronoun, but they are addressed to the assembly.

[27] The statue was discovered at *Tell Fekheriyeh* in northern Syria. See A. Millard

contexts combine to suggest that the *imago Dei* is a blessing extended to humankind, a functional status through which the creator is represented in the world.

Exegetes often call attention to the fact that the Hebrew term for image (*šelem*) in Genesis 1: 26–7, 5: 3, and 9: 6 refers elsewhere to something material and concrete rather than something more abstract.[28] The Hebrew term for 'likeness' (*demut*) in 1: 26 and 5: 1 can have more abstract range to it, indicating approximation and similarity and not just copy or physical model. It is not clear from either the syntax or context whether 'likeness' is intended as a qualifier of 'image' in Genesis 1: 26 or essentially as a synonym.[29] The interchange of 'likeness' and 'image' in Genesis 5: 1 and 9: 6 implies that the two words are used synonymously with reference to the *imago Dei*. Does this indicate that a human is a direct physical copy of the deity? For at least two reasons the answer is negative. First, the claim is that humankind is created 'in' the image and 'according to' divine likeness, not that humankind *is* the image of God. Form and function are related and important to the concept, but there is no formal identity of humankind as *the* image of God. Procreation and rule are functional consequences of the *imago Dei* for humankind, but procreation in the human sense is not constitutive for deity (or the heavenly court?). Second, the qualification of humankind as 'male and female' in 1: 27 indicates that it is the species itself, not a gender-specific man, which is created in the image of God.[30] And

and P. Bordreuil, 'A Statue from Syria with Assyrian and Aramaic Inscriptions', *Biblical Archaeologist*, 45 (1982), 135–41. A 9th-cent. BCE date for the statue is probable. The Aramaic terms for 'image' (line 12) and 'likeness' (line 1) are cognate terms with those in the Hebrew of Gen. 1: 26–7. Both Aramaic terms refer to the statue itself.

[28] In addition to the commentaries, see G. von Rad, *Old Testament Theology* (New York: Harper & Row, 1962), i. 144–7.

[29] 'Likeness' is intended to qualify or 'soften' a theophany in Ezek. 1: 26, 28. In the *Tell Fekheriyeh* inscription (n. 27 above), the Aramaic cognate terms for 'image' and 'likeness' are apparently used as synonyms.

[30] Some exegetes conclude that *'adam* as male and female in Gen. 1: 27 is an editorial addition to supplement the earlier claim that man himself is the image of God. Similarly, others propose that the claim is not explicative but additive, i.e., God first created a gender-specific man in his image but then also the human species as male and female. There is no textual basis for the first proposal. The second founders on the relationship between the image in 1: 26–7 and the commission in 1: 28. It is more consistent with the context of Gen. 1: 26–31 to see both male and female as reflective of the image of God, since both are also blessed to procreate and to rule.

here again a rigid application of the physical model breaks down; nowhere else in the OT is sexuality attributed to God, either as male or as androgynous/hermaphrodite. Nevertheless, bodily form and function are integral to the claim that humankind is created in God's image. There is nothing in the literary context or in the semantic range of the Hebrew terms 'image' and 'likeness' to suggest that the emphasis lies on spiritual perception, rational faculties, or the possession of a soul, even though these have often been suggested as the spiritual meaning of the *imago Dei* for humankind. Hebrew anthropology assumes the integrity of personhood through form and function rather than in the analysis of constituent elements.

Surprisingly, the rest of the OT is silent regarding the *imago Dei*. Psalm 8 gives a poetic presentation[31] of its significance, but there is no further reference to it until the Hellenistic period and later, when elaboration upon its significance by Jews and Christians goes in several directions. What the early church[32] did with the concept is part of a wider rethinking of the *imago Dei*.

The *imago Dei* concept in the OT, therefore, is relevant to the link between theophany and anthropomorphism. Genesis 1: 26–8 provides an etiology for anthropomorphism as a means to understand the divine–human relationship, rooting the significance of the relationship in creation itself. Whatever else is intended by or consistent with the *imago Dei* concept in Genesis, human form is primary. God, some members of the heavenly court, and humankind have bodily form, although not material identity. Stated differently, the *imago Dei* is not understood in ontological categories in the OT period, but in functional terms. According to the first creation account, what it means to be human is directly related to what it means to be created in the divine image. Also, what it means to be a member of the heavenly host is related to the function of (human) bodily form. And finally for the Genesis account, what it means to be God, and thus the creator of both humankind and the heavenly host, is that his 'appearance' and their forms have 'likeness'.

When imagining the work and will of the divine, it is constitutive of the human mind to employ anthropomorphic analogy. This

---

[31] See the christological reading of the Psalm in Heb. 2: 5–9.
[32] The Adam–Christ typology in the early church also brings with it some assumptions about the nature of the *imago Dei*.

is recognized by anthropologist and theologian alike. One should not, however, lose sight of a fundamental claim of the account when taken on its own terms. As von Rad perceptively put it: 'Israel conceived even Jahweh himself as having human form. But the way of putting it which we use runs in precisely the wrong direction according to Old Testament ideas, for, according to the ideas of Jahwism, it cannot be said that Israel regarded God anthropomorphically, but the reverse, that she considered man as theomorphic'.[33] One may want to resist this claim philosophically and thus insist that a theological anthropology can only proceed 'from below'. On the basis of other biblical traditions (cf. below), one will want immediately to qualify it; yet the implications of von Rad's claim assist one in seeing not only a connection in the OT between anthropomorphism, theophany, and the *imago Dei*, but also possibly a preparation for the later claim that Jesus was uniquely the 'image' of God, the 'stamp/imprint' of God, or 'in the form' of God. What remained linked but mysteriously unexplored in the OT—that is, the correspondence between divine and human form—emerges in the early church as a way to understand the claim that 'God was in Christ'.

In his study of theophany and anthropomorphism, Barr[34] proposes that the divine appearance accounts have more significance for the OT understanding of God than other anthropomorphic speech about God (e.g. God's 'hand'; God's 'whistling'). 'It is in the theophanies where God lets himself be seen that there is a real attempt to grapple with the form of his appearance. Indeed, for Hebrew thought, "form" and "appearance" may be taken as correlative, and where there is no "appearance" a passage is of only secondary importance for the idea of form.'[35] On first reaction it might seem that one need go no further than the broader biblical tradition to counter this point about the significance of anthropomorphism and the corollary proposed by von Rad. There are OT texts which indicate that God is neither human nor fleshly (Hos. 11: 9b; Num. 23: 19; Isa. 31: 3), and perhaps more importantly, those which prohibit the making of divine images of any form (Exod. 20: 4–6/Deut. 5: 8–10; cf. Deut. 4: 12). The

---

[33] G. von Rad, *Old Testament Theology*, i. 145.
[34] J. Barr, 'Theophany and Anthropomorphism in the Old Testament', VTSup 7 (1960), 31–8.
[35] Ibid. 31–2.

prohibition of images has a long and complicated history in the OT. Its impact, however, was profound, for aniconism set Israel and second-temple Judaism apart as decisively in cultural and theological terms as did the monotheizing trend noted by Sanders.[36]

One sees the anti-anthropomorphic influences clearly in Philo of Alexandria, who spoke for many when he declared that 'neither is God in human form nor is the human body God-like'.[37] And the New Testament continues in this vein with claims that no one has actually seen God (who is 'spirit') and that God is invisible or veiled from human sight (John 1: 18; 4: 24; 1 Tim. 6: 16; Col. 1: 15). To be sure, second-temple Judaism did not intend to deny the revelatory significance of the OT theophanies, but their anthropomorphic aspects are understood in a spiritual and highly symbolic sense. The NT writers apparently accept this qualification of the theophanies, but then proceed in various other ways to reinterpret divine presence in christological terms.

Since the anti-anthropomorphic traditions are also congenial to modern sensibilities, it is common in the Judaeo-Christian tradition to emphasize their primacy over and against the more naive anthropomorphic elements in the OT.[38] Barr cites H. H. Rowley as a representative figure who writes: 'in the OT God is nowhere conceived of as essentially in human form. Rather is he conceived of as pure spirit, able to assume a form rather than having in himself physical form.'[39] The question is whether this summary is fair to the various biblical traditions about how God 'appears'. For example, Rowley's view must assume a spiritual interpretation of

---

[36] See n. 2 above. For a study of Israelite aniconism see C. Dohmen, *Das Bilderverbot: Seine Entstehung und seine Entwicklung im Alten Testament* (Frankfurt: Athenäum, 1986); T. Mettinger, *No Graven Image? Israelite Aniconism in its Ancient Near Eastern Context* (Stockholm: Almquist & Wiksell, 1995). Aniconism means 'without the worship of images (icons), esp. images of the human form'.

[37] *On the Creation of the World*, 69.

[38] In my own theological tradition God has been defined as 'a most pure spirit, invisible, without body, parts or passions . . .' in *The Westminster Confession of Faith*, II. 1. Maimonides would agree with this part of the confession about incorporeality (cf. his third article of faith). I think that a plausible case can be made from the various scriptural traditions that God is a spirit but also that (to coin a term) *metacorporeality* is a significant aspect of who God is. By *metacorporeality* I mean that using or possessing form is not alien to God's divine being as spirit, or inconsequential to God's purposes in creating human beings in his image, in revealing himself through anthropomorphic form, and ultimately in self-revelation through the incarnation.

[39] *The Faith of Israel: Aspects of Old Testament Thought* (Philadelphia: Westminster Press, 1957), 75.

the *imago Dei* in the Genesis account and also that anthropomorphism essentially reflects human conceptual limitation. In reply Barr states:

I think the central truth in this is the ability of God to assume a form, and to let this form be seen by men. The question whether we can go on usefully to say that he is conceived as pure spirit I would rather leave alone, because I am not sure if it is either fully meaningful or if there is good evidence on which to decide it. The most important question which remains is perhaps better phrased thus: not 'Is God conceived of as essentially in human form?', but 'when he does appear in a form at all, is it thought that the human form is the natural or characteristic one for him to assume?' To the question put in this way it seems to me that we are entitled to answer in the affirmative.[40]

Barr's reflection on the significance of anthropomorphism complements that of von Rad on the significance of the *imago Dei*. Something profound is at stake in Israel's grappling to express the mystery of divine appearance. The question is more than that of the best way to represent the disparate biblical traditions, some of which represent God anthropomorphically and some of which either avoid such representation or radically reinterpret it: It is whether Israel's effort to depict God anthropomorphically is also a way that the invisible God has chosen to reveal himself, and if so, to what end? If, indeed, such was the way of divine revelation, the incarnation can be seen as the ultimate 'fleshing out' of Israel's 'portrait' of God and a goal for which anthropomorphism and the *imago Dei* in humankind were preparation. Although naive and limiting in some respects, the anthropomorphism of the OT can be understood as divine preparation, pointing forward to a Christophany/theophany in which the difficulty of 'seeing' God has given way to the Lord who appears in the fulness of time.[41]

---

[40] Barr, 'Theophany', 32–3.

[41] See U. Mauser, *Gottesbild und Menschwerdung* (Tübingen: Mohr/Siebeck, 1971), 18–115, for related and constructive discussions of anthropomorphic language about God and about the prophetic figures Hosea and Jeremiah, who image God as messengers of his word. The book concludes with a study of Pauline theology as it is influenced by these OT traditions.

III SOME CONCLUDING REFLECTIONS

There is no line of thought which leads inevitably from the OT to the Christian doctrine of the incarnation. The material presented above suggests some of the connections that can be made between OT text and Christian belief, connections which are mediated through second-temple Judaism. Certainly much more should be said about the fascinating ways in which second-temple Judaism, the NT, and patristic Christianity read the OT texts. I have tried to provide something of this in the notes, particularly regarding the NT, but the notes do little more than indicate where the OT connections appear in later documents. I am conscious of the fact that major issues remain untouched in examining the conceptual world in which the connections were made, issues such as the nature of monotheistic belief in second-temple Judaism,[42] or the difficulties of transmitting a Hebrew anthropology to a Hellenistic setting which thought in ontological terms and of personhood more as a soul with a body.[43] When all is said, however, about reading strategies, cultural contexts, and conceptual limitations, the most important connection between the OT and the doctrine of the incarnation is finally the person of Jesus Christ himself. In his pre- and post-resurrection life he embodies the metacorporeal[44] mysteries to which the *imago Dei* and the theophanies of the OT give authoritative witness. The correspondence between OT theophany, *imago Dei*, and incarnation is theological typology and a gift from God. The earliest Christian communities began with faith in the

[42] For one side of the debate, which affirms that a 'high Christology' did emerge from the monotheistic seed-bed of Hellenistic Judaism, see L. Hurtado, 'What Do We Mean by "First Century Jewish Monotheism?"', in E. H. Lovering (ed.), *SBL Seminar Papers* (Chico, Calif.: Scholars Press, 1993), 348–68; and J. D. G. Dunn, 'The Making of Christology—Evolutionary or Unfolding?', in J. B. Green and Max Turner (eds.), *Jesus of Nazareth: Lord and Christ* (Grand Rapids, Mich.: Eerdmans, 1994), 437–52. For the other side, which claims Gentile Christianity is the decisive impulse for 'high Christology', see P. M. Casey, 'The Deification of Jesus', in E. H. Lovering (ed.), *SBL Seminar Papers* (Chico, Calif.: Scholars Press, 1994), 697–714; and id., *Is John's Gospel True?* (New York: Routledge, 1996).

[43] G. J. Warne, *Hebrew Perspectives on the Human Person in the Hellenistic Era: Philo and Paul* (Lewiston, NY: Mellon Biblical Press, 1995). On the conceptual difficulties for modern understanding, see the introduction by C. Schwöbel, in Schwöbel and C. Gunton (eds.), *Persons, Divine and Human* (Edinburgh: T. & T. Clark, 1991), 1–29.

[44] See n. 38 above for the term *metacorporeality*. In essence it means that God's 'appearance' in visible form is consistent with a definition of God as spirit, and not antithetical to it.

person of Jesus and they worked back in the authoritative tradition of the OT to provide vocabulary and conceptual underpinning for their Christology. And although no line of thought in the OT leads inevitably to the doctrine of the incarnation[45] (because of the difference between anticipation and reality, seed-bed and flower), when interpreters work back to the OT from the claim that 'whoever has seen me has seen the Father' (John 14: 9), they find themselves in mysteriously familiar territory.

---

[45] In this context I should call attention to the stimulating work of J. Neusner, *The Incarnation of God: The Character of Divinity in Formative Judaism* (Philadelphia: Fortress, 1988). 'When we talk about the incarnation of God, we are talking about a very specific thing. It is the representation of God as a human being who walks and talks, cares and acts, a God who not only makes general rules but also by personal choice transcends them and who therefore exhibits a particular personality. True, that way of framing the direct encounter with the living God found its canonical place and hearing only at the end of the history of the formative stage of the Judaism of the dual Torah. But from then to the present, God as personality . . . endured' (p. 21).

3

Jesus' Self-Understanding

N. T. WRIGHT

I INTRODUCTION (A): TODAY'S *SITZ IM LEBEN*

As I prepared to write this short chapter on Jesus' self-understanding, three things happened to sharpen up in my mind both why it is necessary and what it is I want to say.

The first was a review of my book *The Challenge of Jesus*.[1] Amongst some generally encouraging remarks, the reviewer gave as his chief area of disagreement the following: 'I believe that Jesus had a much more developed self-awareness as the Son of God than Wright seems to indicate. I think Jesus' sense of oneness with the Father and sense of transcendent experience comes through in the Gospels whereas Wright depicts Jesus more as a man struggling to work out His own beliefs.' This is typical of the reaction I have had in some quarters to the thesis I proposed in *Jesus and the Victory of God*, chapter 13, and in the fifth chapter of *Challenge*, which develops the same points in other ways and which forms more of the backdrop for the present paper.[2] My brief comment here is that, though one gets inured to these things, it is frustrating to be misunderstood at the very point where one had struggled to be clear.

The second incident was the arrival of a feature article in a major national newspaper in which the Roman Catholic writer gave a warm welcome to Geza Vermes' fourth book on Jesus.[3] The writer

[1] Downers Grove, Ill.: InterVarsity Press, 1999; London: SPCK, 2000. The review is by J. T. Morrison in the InterVarsity Christian Fellowship *Faculty Newsletter* for Spring 2000.

[2] *Jesus and the Victory of God* (hereafter *JVG*): *Christian Origins and the Question of God* (London: SPCK; Minneapolis, Minn.: Fortress, 1996), vol. ii. See too my 'The Divinity of Jesus', in M. J. Borg and N. T. Wright, *The Meaning of Jesus: Two Visions* (San Francisco: HarperSanFrancisco, 1998; London: SPCK, 1999), 157–68.

[3] G. Vermes, *The Changing Faces of Jesus* (London: Penguin, 2000). The review: Daniel Johnson, 'In Search of the Jewish Jesus', *Daily Telegraph*, 15 April 2000. [For a

declares that there is now 'a consensus in favour of the Jewish Jesus'. Without noticing that this simply raises the question 'Yes, but which Jewish Jesus?', he then summarizes Vermes' (by now well-known) view. The 'real' Jesus, Vermes argues, was nothing like John's incarnate Word, Paul's cosmic drama of redemption, or the risen Christ of the Acts and the Synoptics. The 'real' Jesus

saw Himself and, in His lifetime at least, was seen by His disciples as a devout Jewish rabbi, firmly in the prophetic tradition, obedient to the Torah though liberal in his interpretation. He was a son of God, not the Son of God, and He wanted His followers to have the same intimate relationship with the Father. He could not even have understood, much less taught or believed in, the Hellenistic mystery religion that had become recognisable as Christianity by the early second century.[4]

The book, says the review, 'is a compelling interpretation of the facts, supported by formidable scholarship'. And it fits, of course, with the new *rapprochement* of Christianity and Judaism that recently saw a Polish Pope visit Yad Vashem and leave a prayer of contrition at the Western Wall. Again, my only comment at this stage is to note that there are multiple misunderstandings in both the book and the review, and that unless we address them there is a vacuum at the heart of all our christological deliberations.

The third incident came hot on the heels of the second, and indeed belongs with it in terms of contemporary (mis)understandings. A phone call from the BBC's flagship 'Today' programme: would I go on air on Good Friday morning to debate with the authors of a new book, *The Jesus Mysteries*? The book claims (so they told me) that everything in the Gospels reflects, because it was in fact borrowed from, much older pagan myths; that Jesus never existed; that the early church knew it was propagating a new version of an old myth, and that the developed church covered this up in the interests of its own power and control. The producer was friendly, and took my point when I said that this was like asking a professional astronomer to debate with the authors of a book claiming the moon was made of green cheese. Just as I refused to debate Robert Funk when he came to England recently—why should I give the now moribund Jesus

different assessment of Vermes' book see G. O'Collins' review in the *Tablet*, 1 July 2000, 895–7. Eds.]

[4] It is wryly amusing to note that the *Daily Telegraph*, though it can shock its conservative readers with views like this, cannot slap them in the face by printing He, His and Himself in lower case.

Seminar more publicity than it has generated for itself?—so I refused this invitation. But it speaks volumes about what the world 'out there' beyond our seminars and seminaries is prepared to swallow.

It is for this reason that, when I received the initial invitation to give this paper, I proposed a topic which had not been on the (long) original list. The list included, it seemed, everything in sight: Jesus in the Old Testament, pre-existence, Jesus' birth/conception, the hypostatic union, redemption, patristic teaching, the creeds, Aquinas, and so on, finishing with Paul, Mark, Hebrews, John, and the Trinity. All wonderful topics, but unless we can say something about Jesus himself we are missing the point. We are pumping up the tyres of a car that has no engine. That is perhaps a shade too strong, but it draws attention to the point.[5]

I understand, of course, why this situation has come about. Systematicians, and indeed Pauline and Johannine scholars, have looked across the fence to see what the Historical Jesus scholars have been up to, and have decided against venturing into a jungle where so many poisonous snakes and wild beasts roam unchecked. They select, for their own farm, one or two animals that seems to be reasonably tame—and that seem to offer what they themselves want—and they import them. Thus, for instance, Macquarrie's heavy reliance on James Dunn.[6] The situation we now face is not just the fragmentation of our disciplines, which we all bemoan but which we seem powerless to avoid. It is a double assumption producing a double bind: first, that 'history' was always supposed to come up with 'results' that would be handed over to the systematician for incorporation in a larger scheme; second, that we all now know that history has done nothing of the kind. If the systematician waits for history to produce consensus-based 'facts', he or she may wait in vain. In any case, the idea of the historian as the neutral,

---

[5] A parallel phenomenon nearly occurred in the 1980s when InterVarsity Press drafted the *New Dictionary of Theology* (1988) which had articles on everything under the sun—except Jesus. I pointed this out at a late stage (I was writing the article on Paul), and wrote an article which they printed. This protest anticipates the fuller statement in *Challenge*, ch. 1: it seems to be one of my missions in life to get the question of Jesus back on the agenda when people are talking about Christology.

[6] J. Macquarrie, *Jesus Christ in Modern Thought* (London: SCM Press; Philadelphia: Trinity Press International, 1990). Similar things could be said about J. Moltmann, *The Way of Jesus Christ: Christology in Messianic Dimensions* (London: SCM; Philadelphia: Trinity Press International, 1990), which manages to avoid almost all contact with NT scholarship, despite the fact that it could have offered him substantial help in mounting and shaping his own thesis.

objective observer simply discovering facts is of course hopelessly
outdated. The historian is every bit as much influenced by shifting
philosophical and cultural opinion as the philosopher or systematician. Indeed, when the systematician goes in search of a historian
who can be used within his project, one fears that what he is really
looking for is the reflection of his own face in a mirror at the other
end of the library stacks.

In particular, systematicians have been implicitly warned off
looking for actual material about Jesus, in particular about his
self-understanding, not simply by the perceived difficulties in discovering anyone's self-understanding (are we to psychoanalyse
them? how?), but by the power of what is said again and again,
not only in newspaper articles but in the academy: no first-century
Jew could think of a human being, far less than himself, as the
incarnation of God. Jewish monotheism prohibits it; and even if it
didn't (if we take Alan Segal's point about pluriformity within early
Jewish God-talk), there is no actual model for it within Judaism.
Hence Vermes, who is after all only saying what two generations of
history-of-religions scholarship had presupposed (not usually
argued). Hence, too, on the one hand, the airport-bookstall
blockbusters which say that Jesus was a back-projection of mys-
tery-religion mythology; and, on the other, J. D. G. Dunn's well-
known *Christology in the Making*, which seems to be taken more
seriously by systematicians than by other New Testament scholars.[7]
We still live in a climate of thought in which two propositions are
assumed as axiomatic: *(a)* no first-century Jew could think of
incarnation, let alone believe it, let alone believe it of himself;
(b) no sane people (and we hope Jesus was sane, though even his
family said he was mad!) could think of themselves as the incarnate
Sons of God.

II INTRODUCTION (B): JOHN, PAUL, AND BEYOND

It is basic to New Testament Christology that the human Jesus
discloses in himself the being and nature of the true God. 'No one
has ever seen God', declares John at the climax of the Prologue; 'God
the only-begotten, who is in the bosom of the Father, has unveiled

---

[7] J. D. G. Dunn, *Christology in the Making: A New Testament Inquiry into the Origins of
the Doctrine of the Incarnation* (2nd edn.; London: SCM Press, 1989).

him' (1: 18). The well-known textual variants in the verse, and the difficulty of translating *exegesato* at the end, should not divert our attention from what is being claimed. Human beings are not granted immediate, that is, unmediated, knowledge of God, but in Jesus we see, truly and undistortedly, who God is.

Paul agrees (again we should not be distracted by questions of authorship): 'He is the image of the invisible God' (Col. 1: 15). We don't see God; Jesus discloses him. Paul and John, of course, develop the thought to insist that the most complete and radical disclosure of the true and living God is accomplished on the cross, revealing God's glory (John), God's justice (Paul), and God's love (Paul and John in unison).

This is well known, though not in my view sufficiently pondered either by New Testament exegetes or by systematic theologians. I regard most of the debate about, for instance, Pauline Christology, as unduly defensive in the face of Dunn and other similar writers. As I have argued at length elsewhere, it is not only in one or two debatable verses, but throughout his writings, that Paul presupposes and regularly states that the human being Jesus of Nazareth is to be identified as the *kyrios* of the Septuagint, and that this identification was not something to which Jesus attained at the end of a successful, human-only career but something which made sense in terms of the identity of this human being.[8] He was *already* 'in the form of God'; he already possessed 'equality with God', and did not abandon that equality nor regard it as something not his own at which he could not snatch. The proper translation of *ouch harpagmon hegesato* in Philippians 2: 6, now happily adopted by the NRSV, is 'he did not regard his equality with God as something to exploit', something to take advantage of.[9] In other words, he already possessed it, but did not regard it as an opportunity for self-aggrandizement after the fashion of pagan rulers. When Paul speaks of the death of Jesus as the full revelation of the love of God (Rom. 5: 6–11), this of course only makes sense if the one who dies is in some way or other the embodiment of this God. When Paul draws on various Jewish traditions to say more or less exactly that in Romans 8: 3–4, 31–9, we should allow him to mean what he says, and not try to evacuate his statements because they do not

---

[8] See *The Climax of the Covenant: Christ and the Law in Pauline Theology* (Edinburgh: T. & T. Clark: Minneapolis: Fortress, 1991), esp. chs. 2–6.
[9] See *Climax*, ch. 4.

cohere with a particular post-enlightenment view of what he could and could not have thought.[10]

But all this means that John and Paul themselves should press us back to the central issue: if it is in the human life of Jesus of Nazareth that the living, saving God is revealed, that means that John and Paul themselves would urge us to consider Jesus himself—not merely by asking about the hypostatic union and the like (we can be sure that Jesus of Nazareth would have found that puzzling!), or by cleaning up the categories of Aquinas, Calvin, or anyone else, but by enquiring once more about the worldview and mindset of a first-century Jew possessed of a particular vocation. That is what I tried to do in *JVG*, chapter 13 (and *Challenge*, ch. 5), and I now want to highlight some aspects of the case.

III INTRODUCTION (c): OTHER NECESSARY NOTES

Four other brief preliminary comments.

1. John and the Synoptics have traditionally been held apart in Jesus-scholarship. My own Jesus-work so far has deliberately been on the Synoptics rather than on John; not because I am committed to giving John a low historical value but because I am taking part in a complex debate, not least with writers like Sanders and Crossan, that has been conducted in an almost exclusively Synoptic frame of reference. It seems to me clear, though, that the Synoptics have, in their own way, just as high a Christology as John; see below. If I am right about Jesus himself, and about the Synoptics, this will do something towards bridging the notorious gap between the Gospels.

2. 'Messiah', or 'Christ', does not mean 'the/a divine one'. It is very misleading to use the words as shorthands for the divine nature or being of Jesus. It is comparatively easy to argue that Jesus (like several other first-century Jews) believed he was the Messiah (see *JVG*, ch. 11). It is much harder, and a very different thing, to argue that he thought he was in some sense identified with Israel's God. In this context, the phrase 'son of God' is systematically misleading, because in pre- and non-Christian Judaism its primary referent is either Israel or the Messiah, and it retains these meanings in early

[10] I am not attempting here to engage with J.-N. Aletti's fascinating and subtle chapter, but merely responding to a range of scholarship of which Dunn's work is typical.

Christianity (e.g. Rom. 1: 3–4) while also picking up the overtones of Paul's early, high Christology. It seems to me, in fact, that the title was perceived very early on in Christianity—within the first decade or so at least—as an ideal one for Jesus because it enabled one to say *both* 'Messiah' *and* 'the incarnate one'. However, its subsequent use simply for the latter meaning, coupled with its too-ready identification with the virginal conception story,[11] make it in my view difficult to use without constant qualification in contemporary systematic discussions.

3. The question of what precisely we mean by self-understanding must be left open for the moment. Here of all places we need a label that can then function heuristically, being eventually defined more precisely by its content. That is to say, I am engaging in a process neither of psychoanalysis, nor of romantic fiction, but of history. History seeks, among other things, to answer the question: why did this character act in this way? And among the characteristic answers such questions receive is: he believed, at the core of his being, that it was his duty, his destiny, his vocation, to do so. The study of people's belief about their own vocation has not been made sufficiently explicit. I think it offers a way through the impasse between saying either 'Jesus knew he was the second person of the Trinity' or 'Jesus was just a human being who had no thought of being divine'. But to pursue this further we must come to the substantial topic.

4. Can you have a serious Christology without having Jesus aware of it? This sounds like the sort of question one might set in a final degree examination, but it is actually a serious question facing our whole enterprise. One might suppose that the lower one's Christology, the less Jesus' awareness of it matters, but this is illusory: if Jesus was a human being and nothing more, part of the picture will precisely be that he was aware of being a human being and nothing more. Unless we can give some sort of account of Jesus' own self-understanding, I simply don't think it's good enough to talk about two minds (or one), two natures (or one), or about the various combinations and permutations of persons and substances. Any such discussions should be grounded in Jesus himself. But when we try to talk about Jesus himself we may find that, in the first instance at least, our enquiry leads in quite a different direction.

[11] Luke 1: 32 indicates a connection, but of course most NT uses of 'son of God' shows no such interest.

IV THE GOD WHO COMES

With all due respect to colleagues who have argued at length for other views—I think in particular of my good friend Alan Segal—the reason scholars have not noticed the Jewish roots of very early and high Christology is that they have been looking in the wrong places. With the exception of the figure of Wisdom (see below), they have been examining models of mediators such as angels, the figure of Melchizedek, and so forth, none of which have more than an occasional or tangential relationship to New Testament Christology, and none of which seem to have figured in Jesus' self-understanding. Nor is it relevant to the origins of New Testament Christology to examine how Jews at the time reflected on the body/soul problem. That is not the sort of thing that early Christology *is*. There are, however, two major topics and one major theme which, though conspicuous by their absence from most relevant discussions, ought to be moved at once into the centre of the stage. The topics are Temple and Torah; the theme is that of the coming, or the return, of Israel's God, YHWH.

Take the latter first. That is, of course, the primary subject of *JVG*, chapter 13, which participants in the Incarnation Summit have read. It has recently been argued that the theme of YHWH's return to Zion is a major topic, perhaps *the* major topic of Mark.[12] Though this of course provides an easy let-out for those who want to be cautious ('it may be a theme in Mark, but surely it doesn't go back to Jesus?'), I have come to regard it as central in the thinking, the vocational self-understanding, of Jesus himself. 'The glory of YHWH shall be revealed', says Isaiah, 'and all flesh shall see it together'. Yes, says Mark: and that is what happened in and through the ministry and death of Jesus.

It appears, I think, that just as the study of christological *titles* was too wooden and limiting (to take an obvious example, 'the son of man' needs to be understood, not in terms of the title alone, but in terms of the ways in which the narrative of Daniel 7 was being read, and freshly understood, in first-century Judaism), so the study of potential christological *models* has been too influenced by the abstract, dehistoricized mode in which much systematic theology has been conducted. If we want to get into the minds of first-century

---

[12] In Rikki Watts, *Isaiah's New Exodus and Mark* (Tübingen: Mohr, 1994).

Jews, we should not look so much for idealized figures as for characters in a narrative.[13] The crucial narrative, as I have argued at length (*ad nauseam*, say some of my critics), is that of the long-awaited return from exile, not only Israel's return, but above all that of YHWH himself.[14] This offers a basis for a historical understanding of Jesus' self-understanding, not simply in that it enables us to say 'this happened in history', but in the sense that what Israel was awaiting was something that her God had promised to do, personally, within her history. Isaiah again: 'In all their affliction he was afflicted; it was no angel, but his own presence, that saved them.'[15] This is not, then, a matter of an idealized figure, but of a story in which YHWH himself, in person, plays the leading role. And the burden of my song in *JVG*, chapter 13, was that Jesus understood his own vocation in these terms; that he would embody in his own actions, his own journey to Jerusalem and what he would do there, and supremely in his own death, this long-promised and long-awaited action of YHWH.

What can we say about such a self-understanding? Shocking? Yes. Striking? Very much so. Worrying, then and now? Of course. Believable in the mindset of a first-century Jew? Certainly. The proposal, which I have spelt out in that chapter is no doubt itself controversial, and needs discussion (remarkably, reviewers have managed so far to avoid it). To the suggestion, already noted, that it might be yet another projection of Synoptic or Johannine Christology back on to Jesus, I make the response I made in *JVG*, and note, in line with what my teacher at Oxford, George Caird, said about the use of 'son of man': what was thinkable for the early Jewish church must have been thinkable for the early Jewish Jesus.

If I am anything like on target this creates a context not only for understanding Jesus within his historical framework, not only for discerning the real roots of New Testament Christology (the reason, for instance, why Paul so quickly took to using the LXX

---

[13] On the search for 'Jewish divine mediator figures', see C. C. Newman, J. R. Davila, and G. S. Lewis (eds.), *The Jewish Roots of Christological Monotheism* (Supplements to *JSJ* 63; Leiden: Brill, 2000).

[14] On the controversial subject of the still-awaited 'return', see my 'comments' in C. C. Newman (ed.), *Jesus and the Restoration of Israel: A Critical Assessment of N. T. Wright's Jesus and the Victory of God* (Downers Grove, Ill.: InterVarsity Press, 1999), 252–61; and the essay of C. A. Evans in the same volume, 77–100.

[15] Isa. 63: 8–9. The translation is difficult, but the overall meaning—that it is YHWH's own presence that saves, not that of some lesser being—is clear.

kyrios-passages for Jesus), but also for rethinking traditional systematic debates. What would it do, for instance, to questions about hypostatic union? How might it affect the use of words like nature, person, substance, and so forth? I think it might open up a flood of new possibilities; it might even slice through the denser thickets of theological definitions and enable us to talk more crisply, dare I say more Jewishly, and for that matter more intelligibly, about Jesus and about God.

Of course—and Paul already saw this—what is at stake here is not just a way of talking about Jesus, but a way of talking, and thinking, about God. Back to first principles: nobody has seen God, but Jesus—this human Jesus—has unveiled him. I think it is a particular view of God that has stopped more (apparently) conservative Christians from embracing this kind of Christology.[16] But what I think I see in this way of telling the story is precisely a more believable *first-century Jewish* view of God. The roots of the incarnation lie, not in speculation about angels, not in subtle pre-Christian use of certain titles for certain figures, but in long-held Jewish beliefs about what God would one day do in person.

V THE TABERNACLING PRESENCE

For me, the way in to a fresh understanding of Synoptic Christology was through puzzling over Jewish understandings of the Temple.[17] To the normal charge that first-century Jews had no idea of incarnation, I have been accustomed to respond: of course they did; think of the Temple. The Temple, from the beginning, had as its whole *raison d'être* the dwelling of Israel's God in the midst of his people, and the daily and yearly sacrifices through which fellowship with this God, and forgiveness from this God, were assured. The Temple has for too long been the forgotten factor in New Testament Christology. Omit it, and you will spend a lifetime in titles, 'figures', and other unsatisfying by-paths. Make it central, and the whole picture will come into focus.

And what has been clear, since at least the writings of Borg and

---

[16] See my 'In Grateful Dialogue', in Newman (ed.), *Jesus and the Restoration of Israel*, 276–7, finishing with a warning against implicitly learning the meaning of the word 'God' from somewhere other than Jesus himself.

[17] I made this more explicitly thematic in *Challenge*, ch. 5.

Sanders in the 1980s, is that the Temple was one of the main focal points of Jesus' public career. Not so much in the sense that he was always going there or always speaking about it; even if we give a high historical value to John, that is not necessarily the case. No: in the sense that it represented, on the one hand, all that had gone wrong in Judaism, all that he opposed in the name of the in-breaking Kingdom of God. It had come to stand for that failure to find its true vocation for which Jesus, with sorrow, rebuked his contemporaries. But it represented, on the other hand, in promise and hope, all that Jesus was then himself offering in his own work and actions. Forgiveness of sins, restoration into fellowship with God: Jesus was offering them to all and sundry who would believe and follow him. He was acting as a one-man Temple-substitute. If the ministry of John the Baptist was implicitly at least a counter-Temple movement, as many scholars now agree, how much more was that of Jesus. Thus, as I have often said, when Jesus came to Jerusalem the place wasn't big enough for both of them, himself and the Temple side by side. The opening charge at Jesus' 'trial' is that he had spoken against the Temple, threatening it in some way with imminent destruction. I regard it as absolutely certain that he had in fact spoken this way; though the charge is put in the mouth of 'false witnesses'; the evangelists who tell us this also tell us, at some length, that Jesus did indeed predict the destruction of the Temple. And John, differently of course but with deep underlying similarity, has Jesus say 'destroy this Temple, and in three days I will build it again'.

This, in fact, is what one might call the deep Synoptic root of full-orbed Johannine Christology. 'The Word became flesh, and tabernacled in our midst'; *eskenosen* is of course a Temple-image, and if we understand John 1: 1–18 in terms of its Jewish roots, and its parallels in, for example, Sirach 24, this should not surprise us. Word, Wisdom, Spirit and ultimately Temple and Torah—these are the themes which, in Judaism, speak of the one, true and living God active within the world in general and Israel in particular, promising future decisive personal action to save Israel and the world. These are the themes of the Prologue, and of the whole Gospel; and I suggest that they are also major themes in the Synoptics. They point forward, not backward, to Paul's Temple-pneumatology (e.g. Romans 8, where the 'indwelling' of the Spirit is to be understood as a Temple-theme). And I insist that they are common to these traditions because they go back to Jesus himself.

What might it do to our systematic Christologies to make the Temple, rather than theories about natures, persons, and substance, central to our reflection? I do not know. But I do know that if we were even to try we might find all kinds of new avenues opening up before us. There would, of course, be various political repercussions: only last month I saw, on a Tel Aviv airport bookstall (next to a copy of Borg and Wright!), a book by two American fundamentalist Christians writing enthusiastically about the preparations now being made for the Third Temple, the breeding of red heifers in mid-Western farms ready for the recommencement of the Old Testament sacrificial system, and telling of how, since the Muslims regarded Mecca, not Jerusalem, as their real Holy City, there would not actually be much of a problem about Jews re-occupying the Temple Mount. We may smile at the naivety, and frown at the worrying consequences. But what we cannot do, if I am right, is address such issues without recognizing that they are essentially christological—or address Christology without recognizing that it is essentially bound up with the redemptive dwelling of Israel's God in the midst not only of Israel but also of the world.

VI Torah, Wisdom, and Jesus

It has long been recognized that the Torah plays a role in Paul's Christology, though the way in which this is so is not usually, in my view, sufficiently carefully explored. What we have not so normally done is to see how Torah already represented an incarnational symbol within Judaism, and to explore how Jesus himself understood his vocation in relation to it. I have already said what I want to say about this, and here merely point up some consequences.[18]

Jesus, I have argued, took upon himself the role not merely of a new Moses, or a new Torah (though both of these are true), but a new Torah-*giver*. If we are to take this theme seriously we will again be confronted with quite new christological possibilities. Again, we must not flatten this out into an abstract or timeless 'role'; we must speak of the story in which Jesus and his contemporaries were living, of the role of Torah within that story, and of Jesus' self-understanding and mission in relation to that role. What might this

---

[18] See *JVG*, 646–7; *Challenge*, 84–5.

do to our normal categories of christological discussion? How would it give us a new perspective on Christology and (what we please to call) 'ethics'?

The same is true for the figure of Wisdom. I do not think this figure is so prominent in the Gospels as has sometimes been suggested.[19] Wisdom is undoubtedly part of New Testament Christology, and from this perspective those Fathers who endlessly debated Proverbs 8 were not far from the topic. One wishes they had devoted similar energy to Temple and Torah. And the same is true also for those other often neglected themes, Spirit and Word.

VIII CONCLUSION: FROM JESUS TO CHRISTOLOGY

My case has been, and remains, that Jesus believed himself called to do and be things which, in the traditions to which he fell heir, only Israel's God, YHWH, was to do and be. I think he held this belief both with passionate and firm conviction and with the knowledge that he could be making a terrible, lunatic mistake. I do not think this in any way downplays the signals of transcendence within the Gospel narratives. It is, I believe, consonant both with a full and high Christology and with the recognition that Jesus was a human figure who can be studied historically in the same way that any other human figure can be.[20] Indeed, I have come to regard such historical study not just as a possibly helpful source for theology but a vital and non-negotiable resource: not just part of the possible *bene esse*, but of the *esse* itself. Partial proof of this drastic proposal lies in observing what happens if we ignore the history: we condemn ourselves to talking about abstractions, even perhaps to making Jesus himself an abstraction. Fuller proof could only come if and when systematicians are prepared to work with the first-century Jewish categories which are there in the historical accounts of Jesus and which shaped and formed his own mindset.

[19] See e.g. B. Witherington, *Jesus the Sage: The Pilgrimage of Wisdom* (Minneapolis: Fortress, 1994); E. Schüssler Fiorenza, *Jesus: Miriam's Child, Sophia's Prophet: Critical Issues in Feminist Christology* (London: SCM Press, 1994).

[20] I have spelt out what I mean by 'studied historically' in e.g. *The New Testament and the People of God* (London: SPCK; and Minneapolis: Fortress, 1992), part II; *The Meaning of Jesus: Two Visions* (with Marcus J. Borg) (London: SPCK, 1997), ch. 2; and most recently in 'In Grateful Dialogue', in Newman (ed.), *Jesus and the Restoration of Israel*, 245–52.

It will also enable other topics in New Testament theology, notably the Christology of Paul, John, Hebrews, and indeed the Synoptics, to fall into a more appropriate place and shape. The ultimate origins of that very early, very Jewish, very high Christology which we find not only in Paul but in the (hypothetically) pre-Pauline passages are to be found, I suggest, not in an explosion of creative thought which took place after the resurrection—though there certainly was an explosion of creative thought at that point—but in the mindset of Jesus himself. And this mindset is discovered not by probing individual sayings in isolation, but in the whole tenor and aim of Jesus' public career and teachings.

It will be noted that I have come as far as the last paragraph without mentioning the resurrection. Despite a long tradition, I do not regard the resurrection as instantly 'proving Jesus' divinity'. In such Jewish thought as cherished the notion of resurrection, it was what would happen to everybody, or at least all the righteous. It would not constitute those raised as divine beings. Nor would the 'glorification' of Jesus, his ascension to God's right hand, have that effect; Jesus had, in New Testament theology, thereby attained the place marked out from the beginning not for an incarnate being but for the truly human one (note the use of Psalm 8 in e.g. 1 Cor. 15: 27). But this is *not* to say that the resurrection and ascension have nothing to do with the early church's belief in Jesus' divinity. We must not short-circuit their thought-processes, even though the time involved for such thinking may have been very short.

My own reading of the process goes like this. The resurrection and ascension proved, first and foremost, that Jesus was indeed the Messiah. This meant, at once, that his death had to be regarded in some fashion as a victory, not a defeat, whereupon all Jesus' cryptic sayings about the meaning of his death fell into place. Within that, again very quickly, the earliest Christians came to see that what had been accomplished in Jesus' death and resurrection, as the decisive climax to his public career of kingdom-inauguration, was indeed the victory of YHWH over the last enemies, sin and death. And with that they could no longer resist the sense, backed up again by Jesus' cryptic sayings, that in dealing with him they were dealing with the living—and dying—embodiment of YHWH himself, Israel's God in person. From that it is a short step—not a long haul, involving abandoning Jewish categories and embracing those of the pagan world!—to speaking of 'that which was from the beginning, which we heard, which we saw with our eyes, which we beheld, and which our hands touched, concerning the word of life' (1 John 1: 1). The worship of Jesus in early Jewish Christianity, a worship which was not perceived as flouting monotheism but as discerning its inner heart, was indeed, as is now more regularly seen, the beginnings of Christian thinking about Jesus. But that worship was simply discerning, in the Jewish categories that he had himself made thematic, what lay at the heart of the vocation and self-understanding of Jesus himself.

4

St Paul and the Incarnation: A Reassessment of the Data

GORDON D. FEE

It is fair to say that the theological term 'incarnation' fits the Johannine corpus more readily than it does the rest of the New Testament.[1] Nothing elsewhere sounds quite like John 1: 14 ('and the Word became flesh and "tabernacled" among us, and we beheld his glory, the glory of the Only Son, who came from the Father, full of grace and truth'[2]) or 1 John 4: 2 ('every spirit that acknowledges that Jesus Christ has come in the flesh is from God'), where the pre-existent Son of God is 'en-fleshed' historically in Jesus of Nazareth.

Although there are understandable differences among scholars about many issues in Johannine theology, most would agree that John's view of Christ as the Incarnate One lies at the very centre of his theological enterprise. Here is how the eternal Father has made himself known, finally and fully (John 1: 18; 14: 7; etc.)—by 'sending his Only Son', who does nothing except what he 'sees the Father doing' (5: 19; 10: 36–8). And here is how the Father has made his own life—'eternal life', the 'life of the age to come'—available to those who are his own. Thus for John the incarnation is an explicit theological construct whereby both knowledge of God and salvation from God have been manifested in the present fallen world.

But it is precisely such bold and explicitly incarnational theology at the end of the New Testament era that has sometimes led to a diminution of such theology in its earlier documents, especially in

---

[1] There is, for example (and understandably), no article on 'incarnation' in G. F. Hawthorne and R. P. Martin (eds.), *Dictionary of Paul and his Letters* (hereafter *DPL*) (Downers Grove, Ill.: InterVarsity Press, 1993), although there is an excellent one on 'pre-existence' (L. W. Hurtado).

[2] Unless otherwise noted, this and subsequent 'translations' are my own, in which I try to gloss into English something more woodenly like the Greek.

the letters of Paul. This is done either by denying pre-existence altogether or by downplaying its role in Paul's admittedly central concern for 'salvation in Christ'.[3] Such an attenuation is also often the handmaiden of attempts to see 'development' in New Testament Christology, so that John, at the end of the first Christian century, makes boldly explicit what is at best only hinted at earlier—which also therefore makes John's Christology suspect as a later development.[4]

The purpose of this chapter is to overview the relevant data in Paul against the backdrop of this diminished view of his Christology,[5] especially regarding Christ's pre-existence and therefore of the concept of incarnation.[6] Although my aim is primarily exegetical— to look at the data afresh on the basis of what Paul says in given historical and literary contexts—the ultimate goal is theological, to assess what is explicit or presuppositional regarding his understanding of Jesus as the Christ, the Son of the Father.[7] At the

---

[3] See *inter alios* J. D. G. Dunn, *Christology in the Making: A New Testament Inquiry into the Original of the Doctrine of the Incarnation* (2nd edn.; London: SCM Press, 1989), whose views have been moderated somewhat in *The Theology of Paul the Apostle* (Grand Rapids, Mich.: Eerdmans, 1998); J. Murphy-O'Connor, 'Christological Anthropology in Phil. 2. 6–11', *RB* 83 (1976), 25–50; K.-J. Kuschel, *Born before All Time? The Dispute over Christ's Origins* (trans. J. Bowden; London: SCM Press, 1992 (German original, 1990)).

[4] This is especially evident in Dunn's *Christology*.

[5] For a similar recent study, whose interests are likewise theological but whose survey of the data more limited in scope, see B. Byrne, 'Christ's Pre-existence in Pauline Soteriology', *TS* 58 (1997), 308–30.

[6] In some ways this chapter reflects interests similar to those in my contribution to the Trinity Summit. At issue then was whether 'Trinity' is the proper term to use for the kind of clearly triadic data regarding God that appear in the Apostle, even though the ontological questions that such data demand are never addressed (see 'Paul and the Trinity: The Experience of Christ and the Spirit for Paul's Understanding of God', in S. Davis, D. Kendall, and G. O'Collins (eds.), *The Trinity* (Oxford University Press, 1999), 49 n. 3). At issue in this chapter is whether 'incarnation' is a proper model for Pauline Christology, given that Paul asserts and presupposes both the pre-existence of the Son and his full humanity, but never asks questions about 'two natures'. As with 'trinity' I shall argue not only that 'incarnation' is proper terminology, but also that to speak otherwise would be theologically misleading.

[7] At issue ultimately in the matter of pre-existence *per se* is whether the One who came to be known among his earliest followers as 'the Son' had prior personal existence before he became 'manifest in the flesh' (1 Tim. 3: 16); and at issue in the matter of 'personal existence' is whether the incarnation involved deliberate choice on the part of the Son (cf. 'I have come', (Mark 2: 17; Matt. 11: 19; Luke 12: 47), even though the New Testament speaks of the Father as 'sending' the Son, (Gal. 4: 4; Rom. 8: 3; John 3: 16; 1 John 4: 9; cf. Heb. 1: 2; 2 : 9)). Cf. Byrne, 'Christ's Pre-existence', 311–14. The larger theological issue, of course—whether the Son is eternal and coexisted with the Father—lies beyond the Pauline data as such, although

same time, the relationship of Paul's theology to that of John will also be pointed out.

Four groups of passages will be examined:[8] (1) those that explicitly presuppose the pre-existence of Christ as the mediator of creation; (2) texts that speak of Christ's 'impoverishment' in becoming human; (3) texts found in soteriological constructs that speak of God's 'sending his Son' into the world to redeem; and (4) several passages that emphasize Christ's humanity, and therefore seem to presuppose incarnational Christology. Since Wisdom Christology plays a major role in most analyses of Pauline Christology—in support of both traditional and diminished views—a section of this chapter also offers a critique of this point of view.

But before that, two preliminary matters related to exegetical-theological method: First, although Pauline theology must first of all be based on *explicit* theological data, one must also pay close attention to what is *presuppositional* for Paul, to which, because it is presupposed by both himself and his readers, he can refer without the need of full explication. The most obvious illustration of this is his own uncompromising monotheism, which finds explicit expression only four times in the corpus (Rom. 3: 30; 1 Cor. 8: 4, 6; Eph. 4: 6; 1 Tim. 2: 5). But who would gainsay that it lies as the presupposition behind not only scores of texts (e.g., 1 Thess. 1: 9–10; 1 Cor. 1: 9), but in fact his entire theological enterprise? Paul's understanding of Christ as pre-existent, it will be argued, seems likewise to belong to this presupposed symbolic universe, and is occasionally made explicit.

Second, it is of some interest that many of the texts under purview in this exercise appear in material that is admitted by all to be

---

his data contribute in part to such a formulation. A further christological issue, the subordination of the Son to the Father, is likewise omitted from this discussion, since it does not impact on the issue of pre-existence *per se* (some orthodox Christians, for example, believe in the eternal subordination of the Son). And in any case, the Pauline texts involved in this discussion (e.g. 1 Cor. 15: 28; 3: 23) are soteriological passages, having to do with the 'history of salvation'. See my commentary, next note.

[8] Missing from this exercise are two texts that have traditionally been looked upon as expressing incarnational theology: 2 Cor. 5: 16 ('God was in Christ reconciling the world to himself', a translation that probably misses Paul's own concerns, which could better be expressed as 'in Christ, God was reconciling the world to himself'; thus making this primarily a soteriological text); and 1 Cor. 15: 47, which in the KJV was rendered 'the second man is the Lord from heaven', but which has nothing to do with incarnation (see the discussion in G. D. Fee, *The First Epistle to the Corinthians* (Grand Rapids, Mich.: Eerdmans, 1987), 791–3).

'creedal' or 'hymnic' in nature. For many scholars this has served as evidence for the prior existence of 'incarnational theology' as part of the early church's common faith;[9] for others it has served as part of the argument for its non-Pauline character.[10] But it would seem to be an expression of methodological nihilism to argue that what Paul 'cites' by incorporation into his own dictated sentences he does not thereby also affirm! In this chapter therefore I shall assume that Paul is the 'author' of his own sentences, even if they incorporate material that did not originate from his own fertile mind at the moment of dictation.[11]

I CHRIST AS AGENT OF CREATION AND REDEMPTION

At the beginning of John's prologue, he asserts both that the Word had prior existence as God and that the Word was the mediator of the whole created order: 'In the beginning was the Word . . . and the Word was God; all things [$\pi\acute{a}\nu\tau a$] came into being *through* him [$\delta\iota'$ $a\mathring{v}\tauo\mathring{v}$]'. Such a view had already found earlier expression in the prologue of Hebrews: 'In these last days God has spoken to us in his Son, . . . through whom [$\delta\iota'$ $o\mathring{v}$] also he made the worlds'. But its earliest moment in the New Testament appears in one of its oldest documents (1 Cor. 8: 6) and does so in such an off-handed way—not as something to be proved but as something to be argued from—that it can scarcely be other than the common stock of early Christian belief. When it finds fuller expression in a later letter (Col. 1: 15–17), it functions explicitly as part of Paul's argument against some false teaching. Both of these texts need closer scrutiny.

1 Corinthians 8: 4–6. At issue in this section of 1 Corinthians is an ongoing argument between Paul and the Corinthians over their

---

[9] See e.g. A. M. Hunter, *Paul and his Predecessors* (2nd edn.; London: SCM, 1961).

[10] See especially the debate over whether Phil. 2: 6–11 is pre-Pauline and how that affects what may be said about the passage as reflecting Paul's theology. By cutting it from its Pauline moorings, some have felt free to make it go in a variety of interesting directions. See, *inter alios*, E. Käsemann, 'A Critical Analysis of Philippians 2: 5–11', *JTC* 5 (1968), 45–88; Murphy-O'Connor, 'Christological Anthropology'.

[11] I should also add that for similar reasons I will treat all the canonical letters of Paul letters as 'Pauline' in the sense that they reflect what is a genuinely Pauline point of view. Although I happen also to believe that one can make best sense of the so-called deutero-Paulines as stemming from the Apostle himself, my reason for including passages from these letters here is that they stand in a clear theological line with passages from the undoubted letters, and therefore 'Pauline' in any reasonable sense of that term.

insistence on the right to attend festive meals in pagan temples.[12] Apparently he has already forbidden such practice (5: 9), but in their return letter, they have argued vigorously for their right (ἐξουσία) to continue to do so (8: 9). Their argument can be reconstructed with a measure of confidence from Paul's citations from their letter: 'We all have knowledge' (8: 1) that 'an idol has no reality' since 'there is only one God' (v. 4); therefore since food is a matter of indifference to God (v. 8), it matters not either what we eat or where we eat it (v. 10).

Paul's response to this is remarkable indeed. For even though he will eventually condemn their stance as a misunderstanding of the demonic nature of idolatry (10: 14–22), he begins by appealing to the nature of Christian love that should forbid the casual destroying of the faith of others (8: 2–3, 9–13). Early on, however, he also offers a preliminary correction to their theology *per se* (vv. 5–6). In doing so, he acknowledges the 'subjective reality'[13] of idolatry in the form of the 'gods many and lords many' of the Graeco-Roman pantheon and the mystery cults (v. 5). But before spelling out in verse 7 the consequences for 'weaker' believers, for whom the subjective reality of idolatry still outweighs the objective reality being affirmed by those 'in the know', Paul does an even more remarkable thing: He insists that their understanding of the 'one God' needs to be broadened to include Christ as well (v. 6), and does so, because at the end of the day the attitudes and actions of the 'knowing ones' who assert their 'rights' serve potentially to destroy the work of Christ in others (vv. 10–13).

---

[12] For the full argumentation for this perspective see G. D. Fee, 'Εἰδωλόθυτα Once Again—An Interpretation of 1 Corinthians 8–10', *Biblica*, 61 (1980), 172–97; cf. *First Corinthians*, 357–63. The objection to this point of view presented by Bruce Fisk ('Eating Meat Offered to Idols: Corinthian Behavior and Pauline Response in 1 Corinthians 8–10', *TrinJ* 10, 1989, 49–70) is flawed at several key points both in his lexical analysis and theological presuppositions about Corinth and Paul.

[13] This is my own term for the nature of Paul's argumentation. In 10: 14–22 he asserts that despite 'idols being nothing' they nonetheless have an 'objective' reality as the habitation of demons. In the present argument, besides v. 5 where he affirms that for pagans there are 'gods many and lords many', in his application in v. 7 he acknowledges that some with weak consciences do not have the 'knowledge' of the others. This surely does not mean that they do not understand the truth that God is one and therefore that idols have no reality as gods; rather, because they had long attributed reality to the idols, when the 'weak' became believers they were unable to shake themselves free from these former associations—which is why returning to the temples for festive meals that honoured a 'god' would be so deadly for them (vv. 11–12).

Our interest lies in verse 6, where in nicely balanced clauses Paul affirms:

(1) ἀλλ' ἡμῖν   εἷς θεὸς   ὁ πατὴρ
    ἐξ οὗ τὰ πάντα καὶ   ἡμεῖς εἰς αὐτόν,
(2) καὶ εἷς κύριος Ἰησοῦς Χριστός,
    δι' οὗ τὰ πάντα καὶ ἡμεῖς δι' αὐτοῦ.

(1) But for us one God the Father
    From whom all things and we *for* him
(2) and One Lord Jesus Christ
    through whom all things and we *through* him.

Over and against the 'gods many' of paganism, the *shema* rightly asserts—as the Corinthians themselves have caught on—that there is only one God; furthermore, the one God stands ἐκ/εἰς in relation to everything that exists, as its source and goal/purpose of being—although the final word, noticeably and very Pauline, is not about creation as such but about God as the goal of his people in particular.[14] The surprising word is the second one (line 2). Over against the 'lords many' of paganism, there is only *one* Lord, Jesus Christ, whose relation to creation is that of mediator. Thus the Father has created all things through the agency of the Son,[15] who is also—and now Paul's second point is being established—the agent of their redemption. The whole, therefore, in typically Pauline

[14] Because of this, and because he is enamoured with the text as a pre-Pauline creed, Kuschel (*Born before All Time?*, 285–91) argues that this passage has only to do with soteriology (as did Murphy-O'Connor before him ('I Cor. VIII, 6: Cosmology or Soteriology?', *RB* 85 (1978), 253–67); Byrne finds the argumentation compelling enough to omit discussion of the text in his 'Christ's Pre-existence'). But that is to misread the passage in context; the analogy for Pauline usage here is Rom. 11: 36, not 2 Cor. 5: 18. What seems to make this certain is the identical use of τὰ πάντα δι' αὐτοῦ in Col. 1: 16—which Kuschel gets around by denying Pauline authorship to Colossians (a circular argument that assumes what is questionable—see n. 20 below). Moreover, the καί joins the two parts of each line; and in each case the ἡμεῖς is on the 'for us' side of the line only. Cf. the critique in Dunn, *Theology*, 268, n. 5.

[15] To be sure, Paul does not here use 'Son' language in referring to Christ. But this is one of those certain places where Paul's presuppositions allow us to associate Christ as 'Son', when Paul speaks of the Father, just as he assumes God as Father when he speaks only of 'the Son'. The evidence for this is writ large in his letters; in the present letter, see 1: 3 and 9, where in v. 3 'God' is 'our Father', while in v. 9 the God who has already been so designated has called believers 'into fellowship with his Son, Jesus Christ'. It is sophistry of the worst kind that would eliminate that relationship as in view here, simply because Paul does not use 'Son' language. Of the large literature on this matter, see esp. L. W. Hurtado, 'Son of God', *DPL* 900–6; cf. id., 'Jesus' Divine Sonship in Paul's Epistle to the Romans', in S. K. Soderlund, and N. T. Wright (eds.), *Romans and the People of God* (Grand Rapids, Mich.: Eerdmans, 1999), 217–33.

fashion, encloses the work of the Son within that of the Father: ἐκ – διά – διά – εἰς (all things are 'from' God the Father (as ultimate source); they are 'through' the Son, 'through' whom also comes our redemption, all with God the Father as their ultimate goal (cf. 1 Cor. 15: 28)).

What is most striking about this christological assertion is that at one level it is unnecessary to the present argument, since nothing *christological* is at stake here; and in Romans 11: 36, in a doxology directed toward God alone, the full phrase ἐξ αὐτοῦ καὶ δι' αὐτοῦ καὶ εἰς αὐτόν ('*from* him and *through* him and *for* him') appears without this christological modification. Nonetheless, at a deeper level this is precisely the assertion that will make both the ethical and theological dimensions of the argument work. By naming Christ as the 'one Lord' through whom both creation and redemption were effected, Paul not only broadens the Corinthians' narrow perspective on the *shema*, but at the same time anticipates the role Christ is to play in the argument that follows (esp. 8: 11–12; 10: 4, 9, 16–22), where everything hinges on their ongoing relationship to Christ himself. What is important for our present purposes is (1) Paul's deliberate use of κύριος ('Lord') for Christ, language that in the Septuagint was substituted for the divine name of the one God, and (2) the *presuppositional* nature of Christ's pre–existence as personally present at the creation itself. Thus the one who at his exaltation is granted the right to be called 'Lord', thus assuming full divine prerogatives (Phil. 2: 9–11), is understood by Paul already to be present at creation as its mediating agent.

1 Corinthians 10: 4, 9. Although this passage does not reflect the motif of Christ as the pre-existent agent of creation, I bring it forward in the discussion because what is said about Christ in 8: 6 is what helps to make sense of the unusual assertions in 10: 4 and 9, about Christ as present with Israel in the desert. It is important to note that 10: 1–22, despite the long 'digression' in 9: 1–27,[16] is a

---

[16] At issue, as I understand 9: 1–27 in context, is Paul's ἐξουσία as an apostle, which includes his 'rights' to their material support (vv. 3–12a, 13–14), as well as his right to refuse it (vv. 12b, 15–18), precisely so that he may model both 'becoming all things to all people' for their sakes (vv. 19–23) and proper self-restraint when the occasion calls for it (vv. 24–7). Thus, even though it is digressive in terms of the actual argument that began in 8: 1–13, the whole of ch. 9, by which he kills several birds with one stone, is absolutely crucial to the overall argument both of chs. 8–10 and of 1 Cor. as a whole. After all, at stake ultimately in 1 Cor. is the Corinthians' ongoing relationship with Christ as the Crucified One, which carries with it their

continuation of the argument begun in 8: 1–13. At issue for Paul right along is the matter of idolatry, that the Corinthians' insistence on attendance at the temple meals amounts to engaging in idolatrous practices (which he will go on to describe as κοινωνία with demons in 10: 14–22, esp. vv. 20–1).

But before moving directly to the prohibition of 10: 14, Paul resumes the argument in 10: 1 by picking up on the theme of self-control as applied to himself in 9: 26–7, which at the same time served as implicit warning to those who fail to live so. That warning is now pursued vigorously in 10: 1–13, using as his example Israel's being 'overthrown' in the desert (v. 5), primarily because they 'tested' God through idolatry and sexual immorality both at Mount Sinai and with the Moabites (vv. 6–11). And this, despite their 'salvation' with its prefiguration of the sacraments of baptism and eucharist (vv. 1–4).

What is most striking about this argument, and now the role of 8: 6 in the larger context comes into perspective, is Paul's insistence in verse 4 that 'the rock that followed them was Christ', and thus it was 'Christ' whom they were testing in the desert (v. 9). Whereas on its own this could be simply an interesting piece of rabbinic typology, in this argument it is not on its own. The reason for bringing the *pre-existent* Christ into the picture in 8: 6 now comes into full view. Not only are the 'knowing' Corinthians destroying others by insisting on their ἐξουσία ('rights') to attend temple meals (8: 11), but in so doing they are also sinning against Christ himself (v. 12). Now Paul brings the picture full circle. For Christ was already present in the exodus with 'our fathers',[17] who thus tested *Christ* when they turned to idolatrous practices (v. 9).[18] Paul's point

relationship with Christ's apostle whom 'God has put on display at the end of the procession as one condemned to die in the arena' (4: 9).

[17] One needs to take Paul's ἦν in v. 4 with full seriousness. There is a considerable difference between this past tense of the verb and Paul's use of the present tense in passages like 2 Cor. 3: 17; Gal. 4: 25; and Eph. 4: 9, where he interprets a word or event from the past and gives it additional meaning. What does not seem possible in this argument, therefore, is that Paul is dealing only with the Corinthians and cares nothing for Israel at all, as e.g. Dunn claims: 'He is simply saying Christ is the source of *our* spiritual sustenance' (*Baptism in the Holy Spirit* (London: SCM Press, 1970), 125). That may be so as well, but the 'typology' carries its clout only if Paul understood it first of all to be true of Israel.

[18] There is, of course, a very significant body of textual witnesses who have substituted κύριος for Χριστός in this passage (including ℵ B C *et al.*); but despite this support, 'Lord' is clearly the secondary reading here. See the full argumentation in C. D. Osburn, 'The Text of 1 Corinthians 10: 9', in E. J. Epp and G. D. Fee (eds.), *New*

in all of this is for the sake of the Corinthians, who live in continuity with Israel as the people of God—a continuity that for Paul included Christ as already present with God's ancient people! His present concern is that the Corinthians not follow Israel's example and 'test Christ' as most of Israel did, whose 'bodies lie scattered all over the desert' (v. 5).

This further passage in the same argument thus adds to the significance in 8: 6 of Paul's declaring our saviour Jesus Christ to be the 'one Lord', who as pre-existent was the agent of creation and who in history was the agent of redemption.

Colossians 1: 15–17.[19] The second instance where Paul asserts Christ's pre-existence as the divine agent of creation occurs in a deliberately programmatic way at the beginning of a letter[20] to a church where some false teaching has emerged that has had the effect of diminishing both the person and work of Christ.[21] Thus a sentence that began as thanksgiving to God for redemption in 'the Son of his love' (vv. 12–14) now proceeds—in what appears to be a two-stanza hymn[22] (vv. 15–20)—to exalt the Son, by picking up the two sides of his agency in creation and redemption expressed in

Testament Textual Criticism: Its Significance for Exegesis. Essays in Honour of Bruce M. Metzger (Oxford: Oxford University Press, 1981), 201–12; cf. B. M. Metzger, *A Textual Commentary on the Greek New Testament* (2nd edn.; Stuttgart: United Bible Societies, 1994), 494; and G. Zuntz, *The Text of the Epistles* (London: Oxford University Press, 1953), 126–7.

[19] As with most of the passages in this paper, there is a considerable bibliography here; in this case, see *inter alia*: P. Beasley-Murray, 'Colossians 1: 15–20: An Early Christian Hymn Celebrating the Lordship of Christ', in D. A. Hagner and M. J. Harris (eds.), *Pauline Studies* (Exeter: Paternoster, 1980), 169–83; N. T. Wright, 'Poetry and Theology in Colossians 1. 15–20', *NTS* 36 (1990), 445–58; and several articles by L. L. Helyer: 'Colossians 1: 15–20: Pre-Pauline or Pauline?' *JETS* 26 (1983), 167–79; 'Arius Revisited: The Firstborn Over All Creation (Col 1: 15)', *JETS* 31 (1988), 59–67; 'Recent Research on Col 1: 15–20 (1980–1990)', *Grace Theological Journal* 12 (1992), 61–7; 'Cosmic Christology and Col 1: 15–20', *JETS* 37 (1994), 235–46, this latter especially in response to Dunn's treatment of this passage, and of others, in his *Christology*.

[20] I will not labour here the historical difficulties I have with the rejection of the Pauline authorship of Colossians. One wonders how a pseudepigrapher would have had access only to the semi-private letter to Philemon among the letters of Paul and used only its incidental data as the basis for a letter like this written in Paul's name. To accept Philemon as by Paul and reject Colossians seems historically illogical. See further G. D. Fee, *God's Empowering Presence* (Peabody, Mass.: Hendrickson, 1994), 636, n. 4.

[21] For a convincing presentation that the 'false teaching' was a syncretism of the gospel with folk religion (including magic and belief in intermediate beings), see C. E. Arnold, *The Colossian Syncretism* (Grand Rapids, Mich.: Baker Book House, 1996).

[22] But see Wright, 'Poetry', who prefers to see it simply as a poem.

creed-like fashion in 1 Corinthians 8: 6. Our interest lies in the first strophe (vv. 15–17), which in effect is a considerable elaboration on the δι᾽ οὗ τὰ πάντα ('through whom are all things') of line 2 in 1 Corinthians 8: 6.[23]

(a)	ὅς ἐστιν	εἰκὼν	τοῦ θεοῦ τοῦ ἀοράτου
(a')		πρωτότοκος	πάσης κτίσεως,
(b)	ὅτι	ἐν αὐτῷ	τὰ πάντα
(b¹)			ἐν τοῖς οὐρανοῖς καὶ ἐπὶ τῆς γῆς
(b²)			τὰ ὁρατὰ καὶ τὰ ἀόρατα
(b³)			εἴτε θρόνοι εἴτε κυριότητες
(b⁴)			εἴτε ἀρχαὶ εἴτε ἐξουσίαι.
(b')	τὰ πάντα	δι᾽ αὐτοῦ καὶ	εἰς αὐτὸν ἔκτισται.
(c)	καὶ αὐτός ἐστιν	πρὸ πάντων	
(c')	καὶ τὰ πάντα ἐν αὐτῷ συνέστηκεν		

The strophe is expressed in three pairs of parallels, with a considerable expansion between the two lines of the second pair. Together they emphasize the Son's supremacy over the whole created order, especially over the powers. The first doublet affirms the two essential matters: 'the Son' as the εἰκών ('image') of the otherwise invisible God, thus using *Pauline* language to emphasize Christ as the revealer of God (cf. 2 Cor. 4: 4–6); the Son as the πρωτότοκος of every created thing, which points to his holding the privileged position of 'first-born' over the whole of creation.

The ὅτι that begins the *b* lines, typical of many Psalms, gives reasons for exulting in the one who is the 'image' of God and holds primacy over creation. The two lines are synonymous and together emphasize that 'all things' were created 'in him',[24] which is elaborated in the second line to mean both 'through him' and 'for him'. The *b'* line begins as a direct echo of 1 Corinthians 8: 6; its second half, however, now asserts that the Son, who is the 'image' of the Father, is as well the goal of creation, the one for whom all

---

[23] While not all agree with my structural arrangement, my concern here is simply to have a convenient display of the whole passage so as to comment briefly on its relevant parts.

[24] This phrase has been the subject of some debate, whether it is instrumental (E. Lohse, *Colossians and Philemon*, Hermeneia (Philadelphia: Fortress, 1971)) or sphere (F. F. Bruce, *The Epistles to the Colossians, to Philemon, and to the Ephesians*, NICNT (Grand Rapids, Mich: Eerdmans, 1984); P. T. O'Brien, *Colossians, Philemon*, WBC 44 (Waco: Word, 1982)); most likely it is the latter, having the same force as the 'in him' of Eph. 1: 4: 'God's creation, like his election, takes place "in Christ" and not apart from him' (O'Brien, 45).

creation exists and toward whom it points. Thus two (διά, εἰς) of the all-encompassing prepositions in Romans 11: 36 are found here; the ἐκ that belongs to the Father alone is here moderated by asserting that all things were created 'in him'.

Finally, the *c* lines re-emphasize what was said in lines *a'*, *b*, and *b'*, that the Son *is*—not 'was'—*before* all things, where the Greek preposition bears the same ambiguity (temporal and spatial) found in the English 'before', thus emphasizing both his existence prior to the created order and his having the position of primacy over it because he is the agent of its existence. In the final line (*c'*) his role as the pre-existent creator of all things is furthered by emphasizing that they are currently 'held together' in and through him.

The linguistic ties between this passage and 1 Corinthians 8: 6, not to mention 2 Corinthians 4: 4, suggest that something very much like this present hymn lies behind the creedal passage in 1 Corinthians, especially so since the next stanza (vv. 18–20) spells out in similar detail the καὶ ἡμεῖς δι' αὐτοῦ ('and we through him') of the earlier passage. It would seem more natural, of course, to speak of the later passage as an expansion of the former; but my point is not that the Colossians 'hymn' existed before the Corinthians 'creed', but that both passages assert the same theology of Christ as personally pre-existent and the agent of creation. The Colossians passage only spells out in greater detail what is altogether presupposed in 1 Corinthians.

Before leaving this passage, we should note how much this hymn has theologically in common with the Prologue of John, in that both assert Christ's full deity, including his pre-existence, both assert his revelatory role, and both assert his role as the divine agent of the creation of 'all things'.

II A WISDOM CHRISTOLOGY IN PAUL?

Up to this point I have purposely avoided any reference to a possible Wisdom motif as present in the preceding passages. This motif has often been urged as the source of Paul's view of Christ's pre-existence, especially so in light of 1 Corinthians 1: 24 and 30 and Colossians 2: 3. Such a motif has also been found in a slightly different way as lying behind 1 Corinthians 10: 4 and the 'sending' language of Galatians 4: 4 and Romans 8: 3 (based on an alleged 'formula' from Wisdom 9: 10 and 17, where the verb ἐξαποστέλλω appears in a context of God's 'sending' personified Wisdom). Interestingly, the view that a personified Wisdom tradition lies behind Paul's understanding of Christ's pre-existence has been urged as both supporting[25] and diminishing the concept of *personal* pre-existence.[26] My reason for not bringing it forward earlier is that I have considerable doubts as to whether it is a Pauline construct at all, or if so, whether it is a truly christological one. This is not the venue to argue the matter in full; so let me here sketch the reasons for my doubts—and concerns.[27]

1. The argument that Paul has personified Wisdom in mind in 1 Corinthians 8: 6 goes something like this:

> *Major premise*: in the Jewish wisdom tradition personified Wisdom is pictured as the mediator of creation;
> *Minor premise*: the Jewish Paul specifically calls Christ the Wisdom of God (1 Cor. 1: 24) and sees him as the mediator of creation (8: 6);
> *Conclusion*: therefore when Paul speaks of Christ as the agent of creation, he is both relying on this tradition and putting Christ in the role of Wisdom.

As with many such syllogisms, however, when there are questions about how one reaches a given conclusion, the problem often lies with one or other of the premises. And so it is in this case. The minor premise is especially suspect; but there are flaws in the major premise as well, which makes the whole argument seem tenuous.

[25] Again the literature is large here; see *inter alia*: M. Hengel, *The Son of God* (Philadelphia: Fortress, 1976 (German original, 1975)), 48–51; S. Kim, *The Origin of Paul's Gospel*, WUNT 2/4 (Tübingen: Mohr/Siebeck, 1981), 114–23; B. Witherington III, *Jesus the Sage: The Pilgrimage of Wisdom* (Minneapolis, Minn.: Fortress, 1994), 295–333; and E. J. Schnabel, 'Wisdom', *DPL*, 967–71. It has also become an especially crucial construct in the Roman Catholic feminist theology of Elizabeth Johnson (see 'Jesus, the Wisdom of God: A Biblical Basis for Non-Androcentric Christology', *ETL* 61 (1985), 261–94 (esp. 276–89)).

[26] Most recently, Dunn, *Theology*, 267–81; see e.g. on 1 Cor. 8: 6: 'Is there then a thought of preexistence in 1 Cor. 8. 6, . . .? Of course there is. But it is the preexistence of divine Wisdom. That is, the preexistence of God. . . . Whether the subtlety of the theology is best expressed as "the preexistence of Christ" *simpliciter* is another question' (pp. 274–5).

[27] I take on the matter of Wisdom Christology in Paul with a bit of fear and trembling, since one has a sense of bucking an entire tradition that is quite captivated by what at first was a possibility, but has recently become a matter of 'clearly' (see esp. Kim, *Origin*, and Witherington, *Jesus the Sage*). This material has now been expanded considerably and appears as Fee, 'Wisdom Christology in Paul: A Dissenting View', in J. I. Packer and S. Soderlund (eds.), *The Way of Wisdom: Essays in Honor of Bruce K. Waltke* (Grand Rapids: Mich.: Zondervan, 2000), 251–79.

2. I begin with the 'minor premise', since by starting with Wisdom there is the inherent danger of reading too much into Paul and, as is often the case, of not paying close enough attention to his argumentation in context.[28] It is especially doubtful in fact whether 'wisdom' is a truly *Pauline* word, and whether therefore he ever thinks of Christ as the historical embodiment of personified Wisdom.[29] The linguistic data tell much of the story: The noun *sophia* and its cognate adjective *sophos* occur 44 times in the Pauline corpus—28 in 1 Corinthians, 26 of these in chapters 1–3,[30] and most of them pejorative! Of the remaining 17, one occurs in a similarly pejorative way in 2 Corinthians 1: 12, while 10 occur in Colossians and Ephesians, where the 'heady' nature of the false teaching being addressed again calls forth this language. This means that in the rest of the corpus this word group appears only 5 times, only one of which is the noun (Rom. 11: 33), where it echoes Old Testament usage referring to God's inherent wisdom. These statistics indicate that 'wisdom' is a *Corinthian* thing, and that Paul is trying to counter it by appealing to God's foolishness[31] as the certain evidence that the gospel which saved them is *not* to be confused with *sophia* in any form![32]

Indeed, Christ as 'God's power' and 'God's wisdom' in 1: 24 (note Paul's order) are not christological pronouncements at all, as though Paul were reflecting either a Dynamis or Sophia Christology.

[28] See also Wright, 'Poetry', 452, whose concern is slightly different, but who also questions whether starting with Wisdom is the best procedure. Wright does, however, finally subsume the whole of Col. 1: 15–20 under 'Wisdom', but with what seems to me to be a somewhat questionable methodology. On the question of method, see my 'Wisdom Christology in Paul'.

[29] Witherington is bold here: '[Paul] saw Christ as Wisdom come in the flesh (cf. 1 Cor. 1: 24)' ('Christology', *DPL* 103).

[30] And the remaining two (6: 5; 12: 8) seem clearly to hark back to the issue raised here. 'Can it be that there is no one *wise* enough to adjudicate between brothers?' in 6: 5 is straight irony, predicated on the Corinthians' own position as it has emerged in chs. 1–3; while in 12: 8, in his listing of Spirit manifestations in the community, Paul begins with the two that played high court in Corinth (λόγος σοφίας, λόγος γνώσεως) so as to recapture them for the vital life of the Spirit within the community ('for the common good', v. 7).

[31] First, by saving through a crucified Messiah (1: 18–25); second, by choosing the Corinthian 'nobodies' to be among his new eschatological people (1: 26–31); third, by calling them through Paul's preaching in personal weakness (2: 1–5). For details see Fee, *First Corinthians*, ad loc.

[32] In fact Paul asserts categorically that 'in the wisdom of God' (as attribute) the world through wisdom (διὰ τῆς σοφίας) did *not* know God; it seems altogether unlikely that he then turns about and says that Christ is 'wisdom' and therefore one can know God through Wisdom after all.

Rather, he is taking the Corinthians' word, however they understood it, and 'demythologizing' it by anchoring it firmly in *history*—
in a crucified Messiah, God's 'foolishness' and 'weakness' whereby
he turned the tables on all human schemes and wisdom that try to
'find out God'. Christ 'the wisdom of God' is thus shorthand for:
'God's true wisdom and power, that belong to him alone, are to be
found in the foolishness and weakness of redeeming humankind by
means of the cross', which by God's own design is intended to nullify
the wisdom of the wise (hence the citation of Isa. 29: 14 in v. 19).
Thus the use of *dunamis* and *sophia* here more likely echo a passage
like Job 12: 13,[33] having to do with God's attributes of 'power and
wisdom' being put on full display in the ultimate oxymoron of a
'crucified Messiah'.

This understanding is further confirmed by verse 30. Having
reaffirmed that God has made Christ to be 'wisdom for us', Paul
immediately qualifies it in such a way that they could not have
imagined that he had personified Wisdom in mind. 'Wisdom for us'
is again clarified in terms of Christ's saving work—righteousness/
justification, sanctification, redemption,[34] three nouns which appear
later as 'saving verbs' (6: 11) or as metaphor (6: 20).

Finally, in 2: 7 Paul argues again that there is wisdom indeed to
be found in the gospel he preached; but it is (formally) 'hidden
wisdom', which is so contradictory to merely human wisdom that it
can only be known by the revelation of the Spirit (v. 10), which the
whole context and verse 12 in particular (by use of χαρίζομαι)
indicate is to be found in the cross.

This means that when Paul refers to Christ in 8: 6 as our 'one
Lord, Jesus Christ, through whom are all things and we through
him', it is altogether unlikely that he is now thinking christologically

[33] LXX παρ' αὐτῷ σοφία καὶ δύναμις, αὐτῷ βουλὴ καὶ σύνεσις. The importance of this
text is not that Paul is so much echoing it directly, as that it occurs in an expression of
Jewish Wisdom in which Wisdom is not personified—very much the same way it is
found in Prov. 3: 19–20 ('The Lord in wisdom laid the earth's foundations', etc.).

[34] Witherington (*Jesus the Sage*, 310–11) tries to circumvent this by (1) making the
ἐν Χριστῷ Ἰησοῦ instrumental (a possible, but unusual sense for this phrase), (2)
making the relative clause, towards which the whole sentence is pointing, a
parenthesis (!), and (3) thus turning the three nouns which sit in apposition with
σοφία into predicate nouns with 'you are'. Thus, 'But from God *you* are through Christ
(who was made Wisdom for us by God), righteousness and sanctification and
redemption' (both italics and comma (!) in the original). This is hardly the 'natural
sense of the grammar' as Witherington further asserts. And in any case, Wisdom in
this passage is related to the Greeks/gentiles who seek wisdom and therefore has
nothing to do with the Jewish Wisdom tradition.

of something that he historicized in 1: 18–31. To argue so would require significant *linguistic and conceptual* evidence, which is exactly what is lacking in this passage. Not Christ as 'wisdom' was present with God at creation, but the 'one Lord' whom they know historically as Jesus the Christ was present. This is made certain by the fact that the designation for the 'one God' is 'Father', which thus presupposes the 'one Lord' to be his 'Son', Jesus Christ, who became present among us as God's agent of redemption.

Similarly the association of Christ with 'wisdom' in Colossians 2: 3 hardly reflects the personified wisdom of the Jewish wisdom tradition. In this case Paul does *not* refer to Christ as 'wisdom', but, *vis-à-vis* all lesser 'powers', as God's (now revealed) 'mystery', in whom the divine attributes of 'wisdom and knowledge' are found as treasures. This is several leagues short of referring to Christ as personified Wisdom, present at creation as agent.

3. When one examines the wisdom tradition itself more closely (the 'major premise'), one is surprised to find how much mileage is made on what appears to be more vapour than petrol. First, despite constant assertions to the contrary, nowhere in the tradition is it *explicitly* stated that personified Wisdom was the *divine agent* of creation. The passages most often brought forward are Proverbs 8: 22–31 (in light of 3: 19); Sirach 24: 3–12; and Wisdom 7: 12, 22; 9: 1–9; 14: 2. But none of these texts uses language similar to that found in Paul and John; that is, they do *not* say that διὰ σοφίας (*through* Wisdom) God created τὰ πάντα (all things).[35] Rather, Wisdom is 'personified' as present in another sense, as the attribute inherent in God by which he ordained all things. In fact, Proverbs 8: 22–6 asserts in a variety of ways that 'wisdom' was the first of God's 'creation', emphasizing her priority in time—not so that she could *mediate* the rest of creation but so that as *present* with God the whole creation thus reflects God's wise design.

Thus Proverbs 3: 19 affirms that 'in wisdom the Lord laid the earth's foundations'; that this does not mean *personified* Wisdom is made plain by the rest of the quatrain: 'by understanding he set the heavens in place; by his knowledge the deeps were divided, and the

---

[35] The closest thing to it in the LXX in fact is Ps. 103(104): 24, πάντα ἐν σοφίᾳ ἐποίησας ('in wisdom you created all things'), which is not only in a non-wisdom passage, but in fact reflects what the wisdom tradition does indeed affirm, that 'God in his own wisdom created' things so that they reflect his wisdom of design and purpose—which scarcely amounts to mediation.

clouds let drop the dew'. When Wisdom is later personified in the marvellous poetry of 8: 22–31, not as a hypostasis but in a literary way only,[36] she is pictured as present at creation, but not as its creator: 'I was there when he set the heavens in place, when he marked out the horizon on the face of the deep.'

So also in 'the Praise of Wisdom' in Sirach 24: 1–22. When Wisdom says, 'I came forth from the mouth of the Most High, and covered the earth like a mist' (v. 3), this refers not to her creative agency, but to her having 'sought a resting place' (v. 5), which took place historically *not* in creation, but in her being present with Israel in the exodus! And in verse 8 again, God alone is 'the Creator of all things'.

Likewise in the Wisdom of Solomon. Even though the personification may move in a more hypostatic direction here,[37] wisdom is never given a mediatorial role at creation. As with Proverbs, not only is this never explicitly stated,[38] but in fact in the key text (Wisd. 9: 1–2) the author says, 'O God of our fathers and Lord of mercy, who *created all things by your word*, and *in your wisdom* fashioned humankind to have dominion over the creatures *you have made*'. It takes several leaps to move from this to an assertion that personified Wisdom lies behind 1 Corinthians 8: 6 and Colossians 1: 16 as *mediator* of creation.

What is lacking in all this material is a verbal or conceptual

---

[36] A point made by Dunn (*Christology*, 168–76; cf. *Theology*, 270–2) that has seemed to fall on deaf ears. My disagreement with Dunn is in his finding a wisdom motif as present at all in the Pauline texts, when there does not appear to be one. The evidence he posits based on Col. 1: 15–20, which to him offers 'a sequence of correlation [that] can hardly be a matter of coincidence' (*Christology*, 269), seems to be in need of reconsideration. For example, Wisdom is not 'the image [εἰκών] of God' in Wisd. 7: 26, but is merely 'an image of his goodness' (the only such use of εἰκών in the biblical Wisdom literature); nor is she the ' "firstborn" in creation', since the word πρωτότοκος does not occur in this sense at all in the tradition (the texts brought forward, Prov. 8: 22 and 25, have quite different words in the LXX, which mean something considerably different from Paul's use of πρωτότοκος here); and that she is the agent of creation is precisely what the evidence does *not* say. Such questionable evidence hardly constitutes the kind of 'correlation of coincidences' asserted in the literature. For a full refutation see Fee, 'Wisdom Christology in Paul'.

[37] As Witherington (*Jesus the Sage*, 109) suggests; but see the cautions in Dunn, *Christology*, 272.

[38] Passages like Wisd. 7: 12 ('I rejoiced in them all [all good things], because wisdom is leader among them; but I did not know that she was their mother') have nothing to do with creation, but with her primacy among all the other gifts that 'Solomon' had received at God's hand in asking for wisdom; so also in 14: 2, which deals not with personified wisdom at all, but 'wisdom' as the 'artisan' who built a sailing vessel.

linkage between personified Wisdom and creation of the kind explicitly found in Paul and John with reference to Christ. On the contrary, Wisdom is regularly referred to as 'created' before all other things (Prov. 8: 22; Sir. 24: 9), a motif never applied to Christ; and quite in keeping with the Genesis narrative—and its later echoes in the Old Testament[39]—God created by *speaking* 'all things' into existence (or by fashioning everything with 'his hands').

When we turn from this material to 1 Corinthians 8: 6, what we see is not similarity but contrast. Here Paul asserts that along with the one θεός, 'the Father', there is a one (uncreated) κύριος, who is distinguished in *strictly personal terms based on his incarnation in human history*, 'Jesus the Christ'. Thus it is not in some nebulous way akin to Wisdom's presence with God at creation that Paul understands Christ as agent of creation; rather it is Jesus Christ, the Son of God himself, who is not simply present at creation but the actual agent of creation. 'All things' came to be 'through him'. This understanding is made certain by the fact that in the final phrase about the 'one Lord' (καὶ ἡμεῖς δι᾽ αὐτοῦ, 'and we through him'), Paul uses the same preposition to refer to Christ's historical work of redemption.[40]

I recognize that some would see this exercise as undercutting the concept of pre-existence in Paul's view of Christ. But not so; my point is first to call into question personified Wisdom as the *source* of Paul's understanding, and thus to undercut the use of terms like 'transferring, adopting, adapting' from Wisdom, when referring to Paul's Christology—because of the highly suspect nature of the data themselves. Second, I want to point out that the use of Wisdom to *diminish* the aspect of pre-existence in Paul's theology is equally suspect. Wisdom is virtually of no—or very little—help in understanding Paul's view of the pre-existent Christ; and if hypostatic personified Wisdom must be barred from the front door, it does no good to bring a diminished view of 'pre-existent Wisdom' in through the back door, as Dunn and others try to do.

4. We need also to look, finally, and now in anticipation of Part IV below, at the other way Jewish wisdom has been brought forward

---

[39] Thus in Ps. 33: 6, 'By the word of the Lord were the heavens made, their starry host by the breath of his mouth'. Here is the more certain tie to John's Christology.

[40] Some (e.g. Schnabel, 'Wisdom', *DPL* 970) see here a second 'transfer' to Christ of personified Wisdom's role in the Wisdom tradition, namely a soteriological one. But this rests on an even shakier understanding of the relevant texts.

as background to Paul's way of speaking of Christ's pre-existence. In an article that has had considerable influence, Eduard Schweizer argued for a double 'sending' formula in Wisdom 9: 10–17.[41] The texts read as follows:

10 ἐξαπόστειλον αὐτὴν ἐξ ἁγίων οὐρανῶν,
καὶ ἀπὸ θρόνου δόξης σου πέμψον αὐτήν.
17 βουλὴν δέ σου τίς ἔγνω, εἰ μὴ σὺ ἔδωκας σοφίαν
καὶ ἔπεμψας τὸ ἅγιον σου πνεῦμα ἀπὸ ὑψίστου;

The alleged 'formula' is found in the request for wisdom (v. 10) and the gift of *pneuma* (v. 17), which is argued to 'parallel' Paul's words in Galatians 4: 4 and 6 about the Father having sent the Son and the Spirit. The linguistic tie is asserted to be in verse 10, where 'Solomon' prays for wisdom to be 'sent' (ἐξαποστέλλω), the same verb Paul uses in a *heilsgeschichtliche* way to refer to the set time when God 'sent forth' first his Son to redeem and then the Spirit of his Son for the actualization of redemption 'in our hearts'.

But finding a 'sending formula' in this passage is especially suspect. First, the author of Wisdom does not in fact speak of a double sending. In the first instance, where the use of the verb is the only 'parallel'—indeed the only clue of any kind—it comes in the form of a prayer, namely, Solomon's prayer to receive wisdom so that he might rule wisely and justly. But in verse 17 the sending of the 'spirit' is expressed in the past tense, with a different verb, and is obviously not a second 'sending', but refers to the Spirit of God who provides wisdom. In between is a considerable exposition of the need for wisdom, which mortals could not have at all, had God not (previously) sent his Spirit. To find here a 'double sending *formula*', even in Schweizer's watered-down version of 'thought pattern in the tradition', as though the author had historical moments of sending in mind upon which Paul himself is *dependent* (or even reflecting in an independent way), is suspect in the highest degree. 'Borrowing' and 'influence' must be made of sterner stuff!

---

[41] 'Zum religionsgeschichtlichen Hintergrund der "Sendungsformel" Gal 4, 4f., Rm 8, 3f., Joh 3, 16f., 1 Joh 4, 9', ZNW 57 (1966), 199–210, who bases his study on an alleged 'sending formula' regarding Wisdom and πνεῦμα in Wis. 9: 10 and 17. I have had occasion to call much of this study into question, regarding both the 'formula' itself as well as the way Schweizer (and others following him) uses the Spirit material, some of which is repeated here (see Fee, *God's Empowering Presence*, 911–13).

III CHRIST AS 'IMPOVERISHED' REDEEMER

The texts discussed in Part I serve as a proper starting-point for the discussion of pre-existence in Paul, since 1 Corinthians 8: 6 is the earliest certain expression of Christ's pre-existence in Christian history. It is in light of such certainties that one should approach the second and third set of texts, which assert respectively (*i*) that Christ became 'impoverished' in joining our human race to redeem us (Phil. 2: 6–8; 2 Cor. 8: 9), and (*ii*) that God 'sent' his (own) Son for that same purpose (Gal. 4: 4–5 and Rom. 8: 3). In both cases, these texts not only assume or assert pre-existence but also affirm 'incarnation' in a variety of off-handed ways.

Philippians 2: 6–8. Without going into detail on the various issues that surround this important passage,[42] I simply point out what a plain reading of this text seems to make clear:[43] that the one who as a man humbled himself to the point of death on the cross had previous existence as God, and as such 'poured himself out' by becoming human. Both the structure and the language tell the story. Thus the poetry of verses 6–8 is expressed in two similarly structured sentences, which may be displayed as follows:

I. *a* ὃς ἐν μορφῇ θεοῦ ὑπάρχων
    b οὐχ ἁρπαγμὸν ἡγήσατο τὸ εἶναι ἴσα θεῷ.
    c ἀλλὰ ἑαυτὸν ἐκένωσεν
    d μορφὴν δούλον λαβών,
    e ἐν ὁμοιώματι ἀνθρώπων γενόμενος·

[42] For extended discussions see G. D. Fee, *Paul's Letter to the Philippians*, NICNT (Grand Rapids, Mich.: Eerdmans, 1995), 39–46, 191–7.

[43] Even Dunn (*Christology*, 114) begins his discussion by admitting that the passage 'certainly seems on the face of it to be a straightforward statement contrasting Christ's pre-existent glory and post-crucifixion exaltation with his earthly humiliation'. Given that, a large part of his argument in *Theology* (pp. 282–8) about the nature of 'allusive' art and poetry seems to be a form of special pleading. Paul's use of allusion and echo is well-known, but in most cases such echoes help us further to understand what Paul has said, or to fathom what is otherwise a mystery. Here Dunn must argue that what is 'on the face of it' be disregarded for what is merely allusive, and at times questionably so at that. The problems with Dunn's interpretation remain: he must find ways around the plain sense of words and sentences (nothing in the Genesis account suggests either that Adam was 'equal with God' or desired to 'enhance' that equality), and then offer what is sometimes obtuse at best (e.g. that 'not content with being like God, what God had intended, [Adam] became like men [!], what men now are', *Christology*, 116). Dunn has now moderated some of this in his *Theology*, and tries to leave the question more open-ended; but in the end he still settles for a rather diminished view of pre-existence.

II. *f*   καὶ σχήματι εὑρεθεὶς ὡς ἄνθρωπος
   g   ἐταπείνωσεν ἑαυτὸν
   h   γενόμενος ὑπήκοος μέχρι θανάτου,
   i   θανάτου δὲ σταυροῦ.

Note the following: (1) that both sentences begin with a participial phrase (lines *a* and *f*) about Christ's two 'forms' of existence, as God and as a man; (2) that in each case these are followed (lines *c* and *g*) by the main verb in the sentence, along with the reflexive pronoun, spelling out what Christ did by personal choice and action as God and man—with the important difference in the first instance that the positive action is set off by a 'not/but' contrast; (3) that the main clause in each case is followed by at least one modal participial phrase (lines *d/e* and *h*) indicating the way in which he 'emptied himself' and 'humbled himself'.

What this means, then, is that whatever the degree of Adam–Christ analogy might be present in the first stanza, the analogy breaks down precisely at the point of the main verb and its twin modifiers ('He emptied himself, by taking the "form" of a slave, by coming in the likeness of human beings'), where the second modifier (*e*) elaborates the first (*d*) by emphasizing Christ's 'becoming' human. Thus those who turn a *possible* Adam–Christ analogy into a *full-blown* one, and thereby dismiss or diminish pre-existence and incarnation in this passage, must overcome one linguistic and conceptual difficulty after another. I briefly note the following.

First, despite constant avowal to the contrary, that μορφή ('form') has semantic overlap with εἰκών ('image') of a kind necessary for this analogy to work is scholarly mythology based on untenable semantics;[44] whatever else, εἰκών does not carry the sense of being 'equal with God'. Second, even more tenuous is the assertion that, when Adam desires to be 'like God' (Gen. 3: 5), this is equal to Christ's *not* grasping at 'equality with God'; Paul's sentence can scarcely bear that meaning, since Christ's 'being μορφῇ θεοῦ' is equated with 'to be like God', which is what he always was, not something he desired to obtain.[45] Third, the metaphor inherent in ἐκένωσεν ('he emptied

---

[44] See Fee, *Philippians*, 209 n. 73 and the sources cited there.

[45] The structure of Paul's sentence rather demands this interpretation. The basic clause states, 'Being in the form of God, he emptied himself by taking on the form of a slave.' But before the main verb, Paul in typical fashion inserts a 'not/but' contrast; the 'not' side of which both clarifies 'being in the form of God' and sets out in stark contrast the clear 'choice' being made. Glossed 'literally' Paul's Greek reads: 'not ἁρπαγμὸν [something to be exploited] did he consider the "to be equal with God".' The

himself') seems strikingly inappropriate to refer to one who is already human, but makes perfectly good sense as a metaphor for the 'impoverishment' of one who had prior existence as God and had become human. Fourth, the one described in the opening participle (v. 6) as 'being in the form of God', which is then elaborated as being 'equal with God', is later said to 'be made/born in human likeness' and is then 'found in human appearance'—an especially strange thing to say of one who was human from the start. Fifth, this view ultimately divests the narrative of its essential power, which rests in the pointed contrast between the opening participle ('being in the form of God') and the final coda ('death of the cross').

Paul's nicely balanced sentences are written precisely to counter the two negative attitudes expressed in v. 3 ('selfish ambition' and 'vain glory'), so that Christ as God 'emptied himself by taking the form of a slave' and as man 'humbled himself by becoming obedient to the point of death on the cross'. All of this makes perfectly good sense in terms of Paul's understanding of Christ as pre-existent and fully divine, but very little sense *in this context* as emphasizing his role in contrast to Adam and assuming a view of Christ that begins from below.

It needs only be pointed out that the twin emphases in the first stanza make the very points being pressed in this study: (1) that Christ was both in the 'form' of God and equal with God, and therefore personally pre-existent, when he chose to 'empty himself' by taking the 'form' of a slave; (2) that he took the 'form' of a slave by coming to be ($\gamma\epsilon\nu\acute{o}\mu\epsilon\nu os$) in the likeness ($\acute{o}\mu o\acute{\iota}\omega\mu a$) of human beings.

A final note about the sometimes troubling word 'likeness', since it occurs again in Romans 8: 3 discussed below. Paul's choice of $\acute{o}\mu o\acute{\iota}\omega\mu a$ in both instances seems deliberate and is used because of his belief (in common with the rest of the early church) that in becoming human Christ did not thereby cease to be divine.[46] This word allows for the ambiguity, emphasizing that he is similar to our humanity in some respects and dissimilar in others. The similarity lies with his full humanity; in his incarnation he was 'like' in the sense of 'the same as'. The dissimilarity in this case has to do with

---

article before 'to be equal with God' is anaphoric, picking up what it means for him to be $\acute{\epsilon}\nu$ $\mu o\rho\phi\hat{\eta}$ $\theta\epsilon o\hat{\nu}$. The point of it all lies with v. 3: in contrast to doing anything from 'selfish ambition' or 'empty conceit', the Philippians should 'consider' the needs of others ahead of their own—Christ now being the paradigm for them to follow.

[46] Cf. n. 59 below.

his never ceasing to be 'equal with God'. Thus he came in the 'likeness' of human beings, because on the one hand he has fully identified with us, and because on the other hand in becoming human he was not only human. He was God living out a truly human life, all of which is safeguarded by this expression.[47]

2 Corinthians 8: 9. We turn now to an earlier passage, where the 'impoverishment' expressed in full in Philippians 2: 6–7 had found similar expression in a metaphorical way. The contrasts are stark and the metaphor pregnant with meaning: 'being rich, for your sakes he became poor, in order that you by means of his poverty might become rich'.

It is often stated, indeed sometimes argued, that this metaphor does not require us to think in terms of personal pre-existence. But that is to read texts in isolation from one another, as though the author of this text did not also write Philippians 2: 6–8.[48] Let us grant that we must always use caution when looking at one passage in light of another and that on its own this passage does not necessarily lead to a view of personal pre-existence. But the plain sense of the metaphor in this case carries all the freight in a presuppositional way of the normal sense of the language and theology of Philippians 2: 6–7.

The modifying participle with which the sentence begins in this case is followed by a predicate adjective, thus creating a metaphor ('being rich') that expresses the glory inherent in Christ's pre-existent state. As in the prior passage, the main verb again expresses the enormity of his grace: for your sakes he 'became poor'—from the 'richness' of eternity to the 'impoverishment' of our humanity. The reason for this 'impoverishment' is redemptive, to elevate us to his 'richness'. The power of the metaphor, as a way of expressing Christ's grace, lies precisely in the presupposition of pre-existence and incarnation, which again implies choice on the part of the pre-existent One. Moreover, it would seem to be a metaphor that would never come to mind in speaking of one who was merely human from the beginning.

---

[47] Even so, one should not miss that this phrase is also part of the powerful contrasts being set up in the passage. Christ 'made himself of no reputation' in becoming human—whether we humans like that or not!

[48] The hidden supposition is that the use of a passage from another letter by the same author to elucidate a given text is somehow to play unfair with the integrity of both texts.

IV   CHRIST AS THE 'SENT ONE' FROM THE FATHER

Another place where Paul's theology of pre-existence is in common
with John is his understanding of Christ's having been 'sent' by the
Father in order to redeem. Two passages are significant here
(Gal. 4: 4–6; Rom. 8: 3),[49] both of which are set in contexts
where Paul's concern is that Christ and the Spirit have made
Torah observance obsolete. Both passages are therefore altogether
soteriological in their scope; in both Paul asserts that God 'sent his
(own) Son' to free humankind from enslavement to both Torah and
death.

Galatians 4: 4–6. This sentence offers the christological-soteriological
basis for Paul's singular interest throughout the letter—that
because they are in Christ, the Galatian Gentiles do not need to
come 'under Torah'. The sentence begins with language that ties
what is about to be said to the preceding analogy (vv. 1–2) and its
application (v. 3). In contrast to a former time when God's people
were no better off than 'a minor', still under the tutelage of a slave-
pedagogue, God's time for them to reach their maturity has now
arrived. As Paul has argued in a variety of ways throughout, God's
time came with Christ, especially through his redemptive work on
the cross.

In the rest of the sentence, and in language that seems deliberately chosen so as to tie together the work of Christ and the Spirit,
Paul says that 'God ἐξαπέστειλεν his Son'. Despite a few voices to the
contrary,[50] two matters indicate that this is an assertion of Christ's

---

[49] Cf. also 1 Tim. 1: 15, 'This is a faithful saying and worthy of all acceptance, that
"Jesus Christ came into the world to save sinners".' I have omitted this passage
because of constraints of space; in my commentary on the Pastoral letters I note: 'To
say that he came into the world, of course, does not in itself necessarily imply pre-
existence, but such an understanding would almost certainly have been intended' (*1
and 2 Timothy, Titus* (Peabody, Mass.: Hendrickson, 1988), 53).

[50] See especially Dunn, *Christology*, 38–44, whose case builds on a series of
(correct) observations that on its own such language neither argues for (which is
certainly true) nor necessarily presupposes pre-existence. Thus he points to messenger
and commissioning formulas which use this word, including Jesus' use of it in his
parable of the wicked tenants, etc. But this seems to be a case of 'divide and conquer',
which fails to take into account the cumulative effect of what is here said, and
neglects altogether the significance of the parallel language of the Spirit in v. 6. It is
certainly true that the concern for Paul is not in fact Jesus' origins; but the cumulative
weight of the evidence and the way all of this is expressed certainly *presupposes* pre-
existence. Cf. W. Kasper, *Jesus the Christ* (New York: Paulist, 1976), 173, and most
commentaries.

pre-existence, that Christ is himself divine and came from God to effect redemption: the linguistic evidence itself and especially the parallel in verse 6 about *sending forth* the Spirit; and the otherwise unnecessary clause 'born of a woman'. Each of these needs further comment.

First, it is true that the compound ἐξαποστέλλω on its own does not necessarily imply the sending forth of a pre-existent being.[51] For example, it appears regularly in Acts for the 'sending away' of people (9: 30; 17: 14) or of 'sending' someone on a mission (11: 22); and on the divine side, it is used without concern for 'origins' in God's 'commissioning' of human servants (Acts 7: 12; 22: 21). But it is also true that in other contexts God 'sends forth' angels as his divine messengers on earth (e.g. Gen. 24: 40; Acts 12: 11) or his own wisdom, now personified, to Solomon (Wisd. 9: 10). At issue, then, is not what the verb *could* possibly mean, but what Paul himself was presupposing and what the Galatians were expected to pick up by this terminology.

It is at this point that the twin usage in verse 6 about the Spirit becomes relevant. Using language reminiscent of Psalm 104: 30, and in a clause that is both parallel with and intimately related to what is said in verses 4–5, Paul says that 'God sent forth *the Spirit of his Son*' into our hearts with the *Abba*-cry, thus verifying the 'sonship' secured by the Son whom God had previously 'sent forth'. It is this double sending, where in the second instance God's sending forth the Spirit of his Son can only refer to the pre-existence of *the Spirit of God* now understood equally as the Spirit of the Son, that makes certain that in the first instance Paul is also speaking presuppositionally about Christ's pre-existence.[52] It need only be noted finally that this way of speaking of God's 'sending his Son' is also common to John's theology (John 3: 16–17; 1 John 4: 9).

Second, in keeping with his whole argument to this point, for Paul the work of Christ is a historical and objective reality. At one point

[51] As Dunn, *Christology*, 39, points out; indeed much of his case rests on his scouring the literature to find evidence for this reality, to which all will readily accede. But what one must be careful not to imply, as Dunn seems to, is that because it does *not necessarily* refer to such a sending forth, it therefore *probably* does not. The overall evidence of the passage suggests exactly the opposite: Since it *may* refer to a sending forth of a heavenly being, the overall context and language of this passage suggests that here *it does indeed*.

[52] Cf. F. F. Bruce, *Commentary on Galatians* (Grand Rapids, Mich.: Eerdmans, 1982), 195: 'If the Spirit was the Spirit before God sent him, the Son was presumably the Son before God sent *him*'.

in human history, when God's set time had arrived, Christ entered our human history (born of a woman) within the context of God's own people (born under the Law), so as to free people from Torah observance by giving them 'adoption as "sons".' What is striking about the phrase 'born of a woman' is how unnecessary it is to the argument as a whole.[53] Paul's concern lies precisely in the next two members of his sentence ('born under the Law in order to redeem those under the Law'). His first mentioning Christ as γενόμενον ἐκ γυναικός seems understandable only if one recognizes the presuppositional nature of Christ's pre-existence that is the predicate of the whole sentence. Paul's emphasis here, 'in passing' though it seems to be, is on Christ's incarnation, who thereby stands in stark contrast to the ahistorical, atemporal *stoicheía tou kosmou* (v. 3) to which these former pagans had been subject.

Romans 8: 3–4.[54] It is important always to read this sentence in the context of the present argument in Romans, since it is an elucidation of 7: 5–6, but now by way of the lengthy 'digression' over the question of whether or not Torah itself is evil. This explanation is finally necessary, not only because so much that has preceded comes down hard on the Law, but especially now because in 7: 4–5 Paul—remarkably indeed—has placed it on the same side of such things as sin, the flesh, and death. Thus, his primary objective in the present sentence (8: 3–4) is to elaborate the 'third law' (v. 2; cf. 7: 22–3), that of the Spirit who gives life, predicated on the redemptive work of Christ. It is in referring to Christ's role in making Torah observance obsolete that Paul speaks once more in terms of God's sending his Son to redeem.

The work of Christ is the obvious central concern of the sentence, whose basic subject and predicate assert that 'God condemned sin in the flesh', which probably has a double referent: that in Christ's own death 'in the flesh' God condemned the sin that resides in our 'flesh'. How God did this is the point of the central modifier, 'having sent his own Son in the likeness of the flesh of sin and as a sin-offering'.

On the matter of Christ's pre-existence and incarnation, Paul

---

[53] The fact that nothing in the argument is picked up from this phrase, and thus its apparent lack of necessity in the argument in context, is one of the factors that have led many to think that Paul is here using a pre-Pauline 'sending formulation'. See n. 41 above.

[54] See now esp. the ch. by J.-N. Aletti below, who independently argues for a position similar to the one taken here, but argues it in much greater detail.

neither argues for such, nor, as has often been pointed out,[55] is such an understanding essential to his present point. Nonetheless, such realities seem to be the natural *presupposition* of Paul's language. Despite some occasional demurrers to the contrary,[56] the threefold combination of 'having sent', 'his *own* Son', and 'in the likeness of sinful flesh', which assumes that Christ had not experienced 'flesh' before he was sent, seems to bear witness in its own way to this theological perspective.[57] To put all of this in another way, given Paul's belief in Christ's pre-existence and incarnation from other passages, that such a presupposition lies behind the present language makes far more sense of the language than otherwise.

First, to combine the first two matters, the sending language here is reflective of that which appears later in John, the aorist participle ($\pi\acute{\epsilon}\mu\psi\alpha\varsigma$) in this case implying an action that preceded the action of God's condemning sin in the flesh. What catches one's eye is the unique phrase 'his *own* Son' ($\tau\grave{o}\nu$ $\acute{\epsilon}\alpha\upsilon\tau\hat{o}\hat{\upsilon}$ $\upsilon\acute{\iota}\acute{o}\nu$), with 'his own' in the emphatic position.[58] This emphasis probably points to the pre-existent Son as having been sent to deal with the very sin that the Law was unable to deal with in God's 'son', Israel.

Second, the phrase 'in the likeness of the flesh of sin' harks back to this combination that began in 7: 14 ('I am *fleshly*, sold under *sin*'), picked up again in verses 18–20. In 7: 18 'in me' is defined as 'in my flesh', which in verse 20 is expressed in terms of 'the *sin* that dwells *in me* (= "in my flesh").' Paul now says of Christ that he came 'in the *likeness*' ($\acute{o}\mu\omega\acute{\omega}\mu\alpha\tau\iota$; cf. Phil. 2: 7 above) of such, meaning that he was similar to our 'flesh' in some respects but dissimilar in others.[59] That this is Paul's intent seems certain from the use of this word at all. Had Paul intended a more complete identification with us in our

---

[55] e.g. Käsemann, *Commentary on Romans* (Grand Rapids, Midi.: Eerdmans, 1980), 217, D. Moo, *The Epistle to the Romans*, NICNT (Grand Rapids, Mich.: Eerdmans, 1996), 510–11.

[56] See esp. J. D. G. Dunn, *Romans 1–8*, WBC 38C (Dallas: Word Books, 1988), 420–1, who thinks the 'Adam-christology' latent in some of this language rules against such a view; cf. his *Christology*, 38–40, 44–5, where this is argued in greater detail. Why one could not have an Adam-Christology with a presuppositional understanding of Christ as the incarnate one remains a singular mystery to me.

[57] So most commentators; cf. Käsemann, *Romans*, 216: '. . . a liturgical statement which describes the incarnation of the pre-existent Son of God as the salvation of the world'.

[58] Cf. $\tau\hat{o}\hat{\upsilon}$ $\acute{\iota}\delta\acute{\iota}o\upsilon$ $\upsilon\acute{\iota}o\hat{\upsilon}$ later in the same chapter (v. 32).

[59] Cf. BAGD (on $\acute{o}\mu\omega\acute{\iota}\omega\mu\alpha$): 'It is safe to assert that [Paul's] use of our word is to bring out both that Jesus in his earthly career was similar to sinful men yet not absolutely like them'.

sinfulness itself, he could easily have said simply 'in sinful flesh'. All the words of this phrase are necessary (i.e. 'likeness', 'flesh', 'of sin') because of the preceding argument. Christ must effectively deal with sin, thus come in 'our flesh' (which in our case is full of sin), but only in the 'likeness' of such, because though 'in the flesh' he was not in sin (as 2 Cor. 5: 21 makes clear). Thus, despite our common use of the adjective 'sinful' to translate the genitive ἁμαρτίας, Paul did not in fact do so. Because he is speaking of Christ's incarnation, it is 'flesh' characterized (in our case) by sin, but not in his. The similarity in this case is to be found in the flexibility of the word 'flesh', which now has a slightly altered nuance from that in 7: 14–20; that is, Christ came 'in the flesh', to be sure, and therefore identified with us in our flesh, our humanness, even though ours was riddled with sin. But his was not 'flesh' of this latter kind, the flesh now understood as fallen and opposed to God. Thus he came 'in the likeness of the flesh *of sin*', meaning that he shared 'flesh' with us all, but only in the 'likeness' of our 'flesh' which was laden with sin.

Again, as with the preceding passage, the sentence makes most sense if Paul's presuppositional Christology found elsewhere is what lies behind it. Moreover, as with all the passages in Parts III and IV of this chapter, the language at once presupposes pre-existence and incarnation. The latter is especially in view in this text, with its emphasis on Christ's having been sent 'in the likeness of the flesh of sin'.

V PAUL AND INCARNATION: CHRIST AS TRULY HUMAN

We come finally to a series of passages where Paul affirms Christ's true humanity, which, given the presuppositional nature of his understanding of Christ as the pre-existent one who 'was sent by God' for our redemption, in turn become references to the incarnation. There are several such texts.[60] I begin by recalling three that

[60] I have included here only those texts in which incarnation seems to be the corollary of pre-existence, which excludes several other passages where Christ's humanity is alluded to in some way (e.g. 2 Cor. 4: 6; 10: 1; 13: 4). Also excluded are 2 Cor. 5: 16, where κατὰ σάρκα carries all of Paul's special theological freight and is not a reference to Christ's own 'flesh' (see Fee, *God's Empowering Presence*, 330–2), and the Adam–Christ analogies in 1 Cor. 15 and Rom. 5, which play such a large role in Dunn's *Christology*. Moreover, because of space limitations, I have

have already been discussed: Galatians 4: 4; Romans 8: 3; Philippians 2: 7–8. Each of these in its own way has expressions that affirm Christ's humanity, precisely because in each case they have also presupposed his prior divine existence. That is, it is because in each of these passages the beginning point is 'from above' that something further is said, often in unusual ways, about his genuine humanity.

What that produces, therefore, are remarkable phrases like 'born of a woman' (Gal. 4: 4—are not all human beings 'born of a woman'?) or 'sent in the likeness of the flesh of sin' (Rom. 8: 3—as a way of both identifying Christ with and distinguishing him from the rest of us). Even more remarkable are the two participial clauses in Philippians 2: 7, that (1) his taking the 'form of a slave' came about by his 'coming to be in the likeness of human beings', and (2) that it was as he 'was found in appearance as a (specific) human being' that he humbled himself to the point of dying on the cross. Again, both of these clauses clearly imply that human existence was assumed by one who had not known it previously.

Colossians 2: 9. This is the most significant passage in Paul that emphasizes Christ's incarnation:[61] 'Because in him dwells bodily all the fullness of the divine nature.' Here is another passage which on its own does not necessarily refer to the incarnation. That is, it could simply mean that Jesus the Messiah embodied in his earthly life what God was truly like. But as before, the text is not on its own; rather, it comes at a crucial place in the argument which began by asserting that Christ as the pre-existent one was the agent of creation, including all lesser beings and powers. Now Paul asserts that the same pre-existent Son is the full revelation of the fullness of God's being and character, precisely *in his earthly life* in which he also secured redemption for us. As before, Paul's concern is with the absolute supremacy of Christ over all other beings (v. 10) and as Saviour from all merely human regulations that such powers would impose on God's people (vv. 13–15).

1 Timothy 2: 5 and 3: 16. These passages are seldom brought into these discussions because of the suspicions about authorship. But however one resolves that difficulty,[62] these two passages both

had to deal 'once over lightly' with the texts that are included; much more could be said in each case.

[61] So also Dunn, *Theology*, 204–5.

[62] Whose answer most likely lies in the broader arena of our very narrow view

reflect what is clearly Pauline elsewhere. In the first instance it is asserted: 'There is one God and one mediator between God and humans, Christ Jesus himself human, who gave himself a ransom for all.' The very fact that Christ's humanity, and therefore identity with human beings, is emphasized in a phrase of its own again indicates that the presupposition is with his deity, so that special note needs to be made of his humanity.

The second passage makes much the same point. In a hymn of six lines[63] the point of the whole emphasizes his genuine humanity, which is made clear in the first line: 'He was manifested in the flesh.' Most likely the hymn exists at this point in the argument as a response in anticipation to the false teachers described in 4: 1–5, whose asceticism denies the physical dimensions of present human life (forbidding marriage and the eating of certain foods). In any case, this line clearly indicates that Christ came to be seen 'in the flesh', thus implying that he became incarnate.

Romans 1: 3–4 and 9: 5. My interest in these passages lies with the phrase κατὰ σάρκα (according to the flesh) common to both, and used with regard to Jesus' human lineage. Granted that in neither instance is pre-existence or incarnation mentioned; but given what we have shown to be presuppositional in Paul, the use of this phrase in both contexts makes best sense if it is emphasizing the human ancestry involved in his incarnation. In the first instance, Paul asserts that God's Son 'came to be from the seed of David according to the flesh', meaning according to his earthly, human descent.[64]

That this is the implication in 1: 3 seems to be made certain by its reappearance later in the noted crux of 9: 5 (ἐξ ὧν ὁ Χριστὸς τὸ κατὰ σάρκα ὁ ὢν ἐπὶ πάντων θεὸς εὐλογητὸς εἰς τοὺς αἰῶνας). However one finally punctuates this sentence—and I lean toward the view argued

of 'authorship' fostered by the Enlightenment. While forgery was well understood in antiquity, 'authorship' as such was more broadly conceived, so that Cicero, for example, notes two different ways—with two different amanuenses—he 'authored' his letters, in one of which the concerns and thoughts were his own and given to the secretary, who in turn actually composed the letter for him which he signed off.

[63] There is much ink spilled over this passage in terms of both its structure and the meaning of some of the lines; for the view that lies behind the present discussion, see Fee, *1 and 2 Timothy, Titus*, 92–5.

[64] Dunn has argued for a pejorative sense to κατὰ σάρκα (see esp. 'Jesus—Flesh and Spirit: An Exposition of Romans 1. 3–4', *JTS* 21 (1970), 309–20), but he has been rightly refuted on this matter by several critics.

for by Metzger[65] that the whole is a description of Christ—at least the 'who is over all' almost certainly goes with Christ, not with the θεός that follows as independent of Christ.[66] This means that the phrase 'from whom is Christ according to the flesh' is deliberately set in contrast to his being the one who is also 'over all things'. Again the phrase seems to point to his humanity in the sense of his becoming incarnate 'according to the flesh' within the context of Judaism and in the lineage of David.

Although there are not many such texts in Paul, this is only evidence for the fact that christological issues of this kind, with the possible exception of Colossians and Ephesians, seldom emerged within the context of his churches—or at least not in ways that called forth responses by letter. But what does emerge in his letters, most often in ways that are somewhat off-hand with regard to another issue that is being addressed, indicates that the personal pre-existence of the Christ who became incarnate in order to redeem us is fully presuppositional to Paul's theology, even if the 'ontological corollaries' are 'not yet clear'.[67]

What all this suggests, therefore, is that the explicit incarnational theology of John has its *theological* predecessor in Paul, both in terms of Christ's personal pre-existence with the Father and in the ways they express the role of the pre-existent One and his 'being sent' in order to redeem.

What, then, of Dunn's remonstrance that views like this seem to be 'content . . . without asking what that would have meant to Paul and his generation'?[68] But how important is this question, one wonders, in the end. Surely the beginning point for them was the resurrection and exaltation of Christ to his place 'at the right hand of God' (Rom. 8: 34; 1 Cor. 15: 25 echoing Ps. 110: 1)—the events that gave them their revelatory 'Aha, so this is who he was, this uncommon man who lived and died among us'! Here is the most likely source of his being called 'Lord', which in turn led them to use

---

[65] See B. M. Metzger, 'The Punctuation of Rom. 9: 5', in B. Lindars and S. S. Smalley (eds.), *Christ and Spirit in the New Testament* (Cambridge: Cambridge University Press, 1973), 95–112.

[66] That is, *pace* many commentators, all other analogies of Pauline grammar, both for the participle ὁ ὤν and the doxologic formulation 'blessed be God', make the rendering 'of whom is Christ according to the flesh', followed by 'Blessed be God who is over all', extremely difficult to negotiate.

[67] Dunn, *Theology*, 292–3.

[68] Ibid. 292 n. 125.

all manner of κύριος passages from the LXX as now pertaining to Christ. Since those believed events, plus the subsequent gift of the Spirit, are what gave them the clue as to his divine status at all, wherein lies the difficulty, one wants to ask, with their believing that the one who had been 'exalted to the highest place' (Phil. 2: 9), following his 'humiliation in death', had also come from the Father in the first place? That they make such statements with presuppositional regularity suggests that the difficulty is perhaps an Enlightenment one that we have read back into Paul and the early church. Indeed, perhaps there is a place yet for *revelation* in Pauline theology, since he himself is not adverse to such an idea!

In any case, some tend to put too much confidence in the idea that if we could ferret out the 'source' of such believing, we might somehow better understand how Paul and his generation understood things. An even greater misfortune is the assumption that if Paul does not articulate the inherent difficulties in his affirmations, therefore the 'affirmations' should be moderated to mean something less than they seem certainly to mean. We may not be able fully to understand the mystery of incarnation, but to deny that Paul had such a theology because of our own difficulty with mystery seems unfortunate indeed.

Better, it would seem, to follow the lead of the early church, found already in the author of Hebrews and John, and take Paul for what he says. It will always be the task of the later church to try to understand how these affirmations cohere with our understandings of 'reality'.

5

Romans 8:
The Incarnation and its Redemptive Impact

I have been asked to examine the impact of the incarnation in Romans
8. But since not all exegetes admit that Paul speaks of the incarnation
in Romans 8: 3–4, it is important that we first examine very critically
these verses. If Paul does not allude here to the 'becoming-human' of
the Son of God, then all our reflections on the incarnation and its
impact would be simply out of place. After situating the verses in their
context, we will see if Paul makes an allusion to the incarnation, and if
he does, what importance he gives to such an allusion.

I THE PASSAGE AND ITS CONTEXT

To understand the formulation of Romans 8: 3–4 we should not
forget the manner in which the Apostle's reflections progress in
Romans 5–8. In an earlier publication I have presented the
composition of Romans 5–8, and shown that Romans 5 must be
attached to Romans 6–8. Whoever wants to have exhaustive
information on this question can consult what I have already
defended at length elsewhere.[1] Let me recall here the outline of
this subsection of Romans, and comment very briefly on it.

1. Outline of Romans 5–8[2]

5: 1–11: introduction to the section;
5: 12–21: preparation for the 'argument', by a comparison *(synk-*

[1] J.-N. Aletti, *Comment Dieu est-il juste?* (Paris: Seuil, 1991); *Israël et la Loi dans la
lettre aux Romains* (Paris: Cerf, 1998).
[2] I use here the scheme that can be found in my 'Romans', *International Biblical
Commentary* (Collegeville, Minn.: Liturgical Press 1998), 1571.

risis) of two contrasted figures and systems: Adam and Christ, the economy of sin and that of grace;

> *5: 20–21*: the comparison ends with a thesis stating the questions to be explored and defined (between grace and sin, law and grace, law and sin):
>> The Mosaic Law has caused sin to abound;
>>> Grace has abounded all the more (apart from the Law) through Jesus Christ.

6: 1–8: 30 a series of proofs ('argument') in three stages:

> (A) 6: 1–7: 6 (with a 'sub-thesis' in 6: 1, reprised in 6: 15): those in Christ cannot remain in sin because they have died to sin with Christ.
> 6: 1–14; 6: 15–23;
> 7: 1–6 ('sub-peroration' or partial conclusion, also preparatory to the following units).

> (B) 7: 7–25 (with a 'sub-thesis' in 7: 7): *the* Law is holy but it is *at* the service of sin and cannot release its subjects from their radical weakness,
> 7: 7–13 (v. 13 is a transition); 7:(13) 14–25

> (A′) 8: 1–30 ('sub-thesis' in 8: 1): what the Law could not do, *God has* done in Christ. Believers have received the Spirit and, with it, adoption and inheritance.
> 8: 1–17: the gift of the Spirit and its consequences;
> 8: 18–30: present sufferings and future glory.
> 8: 31–9: 'peroration' (with hymnic accents).

If the logic is seamless from Romans 5 to 8, we must ask: what is the function of Romans 7, wedged between two positive descriptions of the believers who are in and with Christ?[3] It appears that Romans 5: 12–19 has developed a comparison between the two figures who inaugurated the two completely opposed regimes of sin leading to death, on the one hand, and grace leading to life, on the other. Their respective posterities are described in a comparable manner (technically, that of *synkrisis*) in Romans 6–8, since Adam and Christ are not contrasted except as a basis for the opposition between the old humanity (Romans 7) and the new humanity (Romans 6 and 8):

---

[3] The subsequent paragraphs are from my 'Romans', 1585–6.

Adam	Christ
(Rom 5: 12–14,15–19, 20a, 21a)	(Rom 5: 15–19, 20b, 21b)
those without Christ	*those in/with Christ*
(Romans 7: 7–25)	(Romans 6 and 8).

2. Outline of Romans 8[4]

The composition is primarily argumentative in nature. Two 'sub-theses' (vv. 1–2 and 18) respectively introduce two units, vv. 1–17 and 18–30. We should not forget that Romans 8 is the culmination of the section (see the outline above of Romans 5–8) and recapitulates many themes of the preceding chapters, emphasizing in particular the gift of the Spirit which allows the believers to live and to hope. It is especially important to note that the comparison between the two types of humanity continues up to 8: 17:

Romans 7	Romans 8
indwelling of sin	indwelling of Christ and the Spirit
inability to practice the divine Law	accomplishing the commandment of the Law
living according to/in the flesh	living according to/in the Spirit
death	life
slavery	son/daughtership and inheritance.

The contrast is extended still further in vv. 18–22, to the extent that creation is associated with the liberation of the children of God and waits for that liberation with them.

The composition of Romans 8 can be outlined as follows:

vv. 1–17
  vv. 1–2: 'sub-thesis' followed by its 'proof';
  vv. 3–17: the believers are guided by the Spirit;
  (*a*) past: the sending of the Son and its purpose (vv. 3–4);
  (*b*) present: the believers are made alive by the Spirit (vv. 5–13);
  vv. 5–8: exposition of general principles (flesh vs. spirit);
  vv. 9–11: application of these principles to those in Christ because

---

[4] Ibid. 1586–7.

they have the Spirit of life, and are therefore (vv. 12–13)
capable of ethical conduct that leads to life;
(c) the Spirit of sons/daughters and their glorification (vv. 14–17).

A. Keys for Reading and Questions (8: 1–17)

These verses confirm the interpretation given to Romans 7 (the 'I'
does not describe a Christian), to the extent that Paul repeats to his
readers in Romans 8: 5–11: 'you are not in [or under the control of]
the flesh; you are in the Spirit'. The Spirit will give them the power
to do what is good and to carry out the will of God. Indeed, the
believers bear in their bodies the marks and wounds of sin (they
cannot escape physical death: v. 10), but the Spirit who lives in
them is life and the promise of resurrection: they share in the glory
of Christ with whom they are now united (v. 11).

The description Romans 6 and 8 give of the believers seems
unreal, too ideal to be true, because they are not sinless (far from
it!), and many forget the vital link that has united them with Christ.
Nevertheless, Paul does not forget the problem, for he adds: 'if you
live according to the flesh, you will die'. The Christian can live like a
sinner and will be rewarded as such. The Apostle simply emphasizes
the status of the baptized and the moral attitude that should
normally follow from it: how can the Spirit dwelling in them not
give them power and cause them to bear spiritual fruit? The life of
faith cannot fail to develop in that way, since the Spirit has been
poured into their hearts. And the ethical life is a necessary witness to
the power of the Gospel (cf. Rom. 1: 16).

B. Progress of the Argument (8: 1–17)

8: 1–2. The 'sub-thesis' and its 'proof'. 'There is therefore now no
condemnation for those who are in Christ Jesus' means that, not
being in the ranks of sinners (in the desperate situation described in
Romans 7: 7–25), the believers cannot incur condemnation. The
first reason given (called the ratio (or 'proof') by the manuals of the
time) is the Spirit of life who, living in and guiding believers, delivers
them from sin. Paul again proceeds here by means of *antanaclasis*,[5]
as in 7: 21–23 (q.v.).

8: 3–4. First explanation of the 'proof'. We note that here again

---

[5] A form of speech in which a key word is used again, but in a different, and
sometimes contrary, sense: for instance, 'the craft of a politician is to appear before the
public without craft.'

the first argument invoked is christological. It is in the super-abundance of the event of Jesus Christ that the present situation of the baptized finds its explanation.

Verse 3 begins by recalling the paradox of a holy and good Law that is powerless. For it is precisely in taking our impotent flesh, marked by sin, suffering, temptation, and death, that the Son of God has been able to condemn sin in the very place of its domination, the flesh. As with most of his paradoxical expressions, Paul does not attempt to explain or justify what he says. Was it necessary to take that route? Why the passage through the wounded flesh in order that the victory over sin be obtained in that same flesh? And so on.

After mentioning the One sent, Paul speaks of his purpose (v. 4). He does not say that God sent the Son to uphold the Law or to give it a power it had lost. The Law remains holy and good (as it always had been), but people themselves are transformed—by the work of God in Christ, and not by the Law! From the beginning, the righteousness required by the Law had been accomplished in them. Many see in this verse a slightly veiled reference to Jeremiah 31: 31–3 and/or Ezekiel 36–7, and that is indeed probable.

As already indicated with regard to the composition of Romans 8: 4 (life in the Spirit) will be expanded in three stages: vv. 5–8 expound general principles (opposition between flesh and Spirit); vv. 9–11 apply those principles to the believers who have received the Spirit of life, and are therefore (vv. 12–13) capable of ethical action leading to life.

The conclusion of the 'argument' (vv. 14–17) returns to the moving force in the life of the baptized: having received the Spirit of adoption, they should act as children of God and heirs (of glory) with Christ, to the extent that they suffer with him. But why should the baptized share in the sufferings of Christ? And which sufferings are those? As so often, Paul does not explain himself, but the following verse (v. 18) makes us understand that it is a question of the trials related to the human condition—marked by the effects of sin—that the Son of God himself underwent in this world (v. 3). The last end is glory with Christ: that seems to be the point at which Paul was aiming all along.

In order to understand the utterances concerning the problem under discussion, that is, the affirmation of the incarnation and its impact, we needed to see the progression of the entire section (Rom. 5–8) and of Romans 8 in particular.

II A Hint at the Incarnation in Romans 8: 3?

Translation by Dunn: [1]So now, there is no condemnation for those in Christ Jesus. [2]For the law of the Spirit of life in Christ Jesus has set you free from the law of sin and death. [3]For what the law was unable to do in that it was weak through the flesh, God sent his own Son in the very likeness of sinful flesh and as a sin offering and condemned sin in the flesh, [4]in order that the requirement of the law might be fulfilled in us who walk not in accordance with the flesh but in accordance with the Spirit.[6]

Translation in RSV: [3]For God has done what the law, weakened by the flesh, could not do: sending his own Son in the likeness of sinful flesh and for sin, he condemned sin in the flesh, [4]in order that the just requirement of the law might be fulfilled in us, who walk not according to the flesh but according to the Spirit.

The question can be simply formulated thus: is there an allusion to the incarnation in Romans 8: 3? In other words, does Paul think that God sent a heavenly or spiritual, pre-existent Being who would have been from all time his Son, so that he may become man among humanity? In responding to such important theological questions on the basis of grammatical, linguistic, and rhetorical data, we exegetes apparently have no interests at stake but can, nevertheless, confirm or do harm to the most beautiful and daring theological hypotheses. Conscious then of the impact of the exegesis on theological and christological questions, we examine a possible allusion to the incarnation in Romans 8: 3–4.

1. *Galatians 4: 4 and Romans 8: 3*

Romans 8: 3–4 is usually analysed along the lines of Galatians 4: 4, because the two texts have in common

— the movement of thought, that is, (*a*) the initiative of God, and (*b*) its soteriological purpose—the redemption and blessing of all, Jews and Gentiles;
— the theme of *the sending of the Son*, with its concrete modalities, in particular his humanity.

---

[6] J. D. G . Dunn, *Romans 1–8* (Dallas: Word Books, 1998).

If we recognize that Romans 8: 3 and Galatians 4: 4 have many common traits, the latter passage will help us to know if Paul ever alludes to the incarnation of the Son of God. According to a certain number of exegetes, Galatians 4: 4 does not necessarily imply pre-existence. Without lingering much over reasons given for this position, we note only that neither the tense nor the mood of the verbs—the participles and the indicatives are in the aorist—allow us to determine with ease the sequence of events. According to some, *the sending of the Son* is prior—at least logically—to the becoming human and becoming a Jew (they suppose then a real heavenly pre-existence); according to others, there is a concomitance;[7] according to others again, *the sending* would have been posterior[8] (it corresponds to the beginning of the ministry of Jesus,[9] or even to his entry into the passion).

The Christian reader is without doubt inclined to think that Paul alludes here to the incarnation. But before we come to a decision, we should carefully analyse the different phrases, because this interpretation has been criticized for being anachronistic[10]—a weighty

---

[7] *The sending* would then be that of a Son *fully human and Jew*. The idea of a divine choice right from the maternal womb, before birth, is expressed (certainly with other words) by many of the prophets and equally by Paul; see Jer. 1: 5; Isa. 49: 1–5; Gal. 1: 15.

[8] *The sending* will be paraphrased as: 'God sent his Son, previously born of a woman and born subject to the Law, in order to redeem . . .', or more briefly, 'who was man and Jew'. It is indeed the humanity and Jewishness of the Son of God that is stressed.

[9] The episode which follows the baptism in the Synoptics (Matt. 3: 17 par.), would then be a narrative equivalent of the affirmation of Gal. 4: 4, with the difference being however that the Synoptics do not mention *the sending* but only the declaration of sonship.

[10] The remark holds also for Rom. 8: 3. It suffices to mention here the reflections of J. D. G . Dunn, *Christology in the Making: A New Testament Inquiry into the Origins of the Doctrine of the Incarnation* (2nd edn.; London, SCM Press, 1989), 42: 'Indeed we would be hard pressed to find any real parallel in this period for language which speaks both of a divine sending and of a divine begetting *in the same breath*, since in fact there are alternative ways of saying the same thing, of describing the divine origin of the individual in question or of his commission. So far as we can tell, such language only appears in Christian writings of the second century subsequent to the ideas of virginal conception in Matthew and Luke and *the sending* of the pre-existent Logos in John and as the harmonization of them (Ignatius, *Eph* 7. 2; Aristides, *Apology* 15. 1; and especially Justin, *Apol.* I. 21. 1; 32. 10–14; 63. 15f; *Dial* 45. 4; 84. 2; 85. 2; 127. 4). It follows that if Paul intended to imply what we now call the doctrine of incarnation in Gal 4. 4 he would have been taking *a radically new step*, something his readers could hardly have expected to come from a Jew. And if he did intend to take that step we would have expected his earliest recorded intimation of it to be a much more explicit and careful exposition (cf. the care he takes to expound his understanding of who the seed of Abraham really are—Gal 3).'

objection but one which is not directly based on the phraseology of the verse, the completely unusual syntactic construction of which is intriguing. The least that can be said is that commentaries on Galatians often fail to consider carefully the different linguistic phenomena. Commentators generally observe that the expression *born of woman* is equivalent to another very common usage, γεννητὸς γυναικός, which designates simply the human origin of someone.[11] But why then does Paul not follow a usage that he would have known very well? Before speaking of simple equivalence, let us examine the entire linguistic phenomena of the verse. In effect, the sequence (aorist indicative + complement + aorist participle (in the same case, gender and number as the complement)) is found elsewhere in the two Testaments. But the Veterotestamental examples that could be referred to are not appropriate, because the participle, preceded each time by an article, is equivalent to a defining or explanatory relative clause.[12]

For this reason the sequence has to be treated as noun + article + participle (the three being in the same case, gender, and number), which occurs many times elsewhere, particularly in Paul.[13] If the two occurrences of *born* were preceded by the article, they would be equivalent to explanatory relative clauses,[14] and so insufficient to allow us to determine with certitude the temporal relation existing between the Son's human being, Jewishness, and *sending* by God.[15]

[11] See Job 11: 2, 12; 14: 1; 15: 14; 25: 4; also Matt. 11: 11; Luke 7: 28.

[12] A clause is said to be *defining*, when it is used to distinguish one category of objects from another, and in a way that it cannot be removed without distorting the meaning. It is *explanatory* if it contains only a useful explanation but is not indispensable for the meaning. In our languages unlike a defining clause an explanatory clause has to be inserted between two commas. See e.g. Deut. 32: 15, 1 Sam. 13: 15, Isa. 51: 13, and Jer. 48: 10, where the participle is defining, and 2 Kgs. 8: 21, where the participle is explanatory.

[13] See Rom. 1: 3, an interesting verse because the first participle is the same as in Gal. 4: 4 ([the Gospel] concerning his Son, born [τοῦ γενομένου] of the seed of David according to the flesh, designated [τοῦ ὁρισθέντος] son of God in power). See also Rom. 2: 9; 3: 5; 4: 17; 5: 5; 8: 33,34; 12: 3, 6, 15; 16: 22; 1 Cor. 12: 6; 15: 37, 54, 57; 2 Cor. 1: 6, 8, 9; 4: 6; 5: 5, 18; 8: 16, 19, 20; Gal. 1: 1, 4, 11; 2: 9, 20; 3: 21.

[14] The phrase 'his Son' already designates Jesus unequivocally; for this reason the participles contain very useful explanations but are not indispensable for knowing which son we are dealing with. Having said this, we must admit that it is not always easy to specify to what type, defining or explanatory, these participles belong. Thus in Rom. 1: 3–4 the two participles 'born' and 'designated', seem to be explanatory. But since they are followed by the name 'Jesus', it could be that they prepare this designation and are defining.

[15] The explanatory clauses would thus be differently translated, according to the point of view chosen. Those for whom it is anterior to *the sending*, would render it:

The Old and the New Testaments use another phrase (article + *ek* + noun) to indicate the origin in space (such as a person from such and such a region or town), in time (since the beginning, since his youth, or always), or again, as in Paul, in derivation (2 Cor. 5: 2, 'our dwelling, the one [coming] from heaven'). The phrase 'the one [coming] from heaven' has a *distinct designative function*, by stressing that it is the heavenly dwelling and not the other, the earthly one. We can see also Romans 9: 30 and Philippians 3: 9 where we find an opposition: between the two justices: 'the one [coming] from the Law' [and therefore not from God], and 'the one coming from God or from faith' [and therefore not from the Law]. But we never find, as far as I know, the following sequence, 'Human being + article + 'of woman'. Thus, in Galatians 4: 4, the participle 'born' (*genomenos*) serves to indicate the birth in a non equivocal manner. But the participles of Galatians 4: 4 are not preceded by an article.[16] How then are we to understand them?

The participle without an article could be a circumstantial complement or an attribute.[17] Should one interpret those of Galatians 4: 4 as attributes, or perhaps as circumstantial complements in reference to the noun 'Son' (τόν υἱόν)? If the participles were circumstantial complements, only the temporal meaning would fit them: 'God sent his Son, after he was born of a woman, after he was born under the Law, in order to redeem . . .'[18] But the

---

'God sent his Son, who was (already) born of a woman and was born under the Law'. Those for whom these events are posterior to *the sending*, would read it: 'God sent his Son, who was born of a woman, born under the Law'. The participle 'born' is used because *ginomai* is here a substitute for *gennaō*.

[16] When the two participles are not separated by a co-ordinating conjunction, that often means, as elsewhere in Gal. 4: 4, that the second is subordinate to the first: to be a Jew (under the Law), the Son must evidently first be born and belong to our human race! One sees immediately the semantic consequence of this subordination: the two purposes touch all humanity.

[17] As a circumstantial complement or attribute, the participle refers to the subject or to the complement. Apart from Gal. 4: 4 and 6, see e.g. Acts 3: 26; 8: 31; 9: 12, 38; 15: 27.

[18] The reason ('because he was born of a woman . . .'), the condition ('if he were born of a woman . . .'), and the concession ('though he was born of a woman . . .') are obviously excluded, because they do not respect the logic of the statement. As regards the purpose ('so that he may be born of a woman . . .'), it would be better expressed with the help of a future participle (*genēsomenos*). If the construction is the same in Gal. 4: 6, the temporal relation of the verbs in this verse is more easily interpreted because the present participle 'calling out' refers to the present time of believers.

order of the sentence is articulated according to the law of the 'inversion':[19]

I (a) God sent his son,
        born of a woman (*a*),
   (b) born under the Law (*a*),

II (b') in order to redeem those under the Law (*β*),
   (a') so that we might receive adoption-as-sons (*β*).

This order shows that Paul did not intend *a fortiori* to stress the anteriority of birth over the being-sent, but rather the *purpose* of such a birth: if the Son is man and Jew, it is in order that the subjects of the Law may be redeemed, and that all humanity might receive adoption as sons and daughters. What we have in the repeated participle 'born' is an attributive participle, which is ordinarily used with verbs that can be followed by a substantival clause.[20] But, even if the participles had been preceded by the article τόν and so had enjoyed an explanatory value, would this change the meaning? In reality, if the two occurrences of 'born' had such an explanatory value, they would have determined exclusively the noun 'Son', whereas their primary function is to prepare the two purposes (in ἵνα) which follow it: it is *in order that* we may be redeemed from the curse of the Law and obtain adoption as children that the Son of God became man and Jew. It may be difficult to determine with certitude an allusion to the incarnation in Galatians 4: 4, but the soteriological function and importance of the two phrases 'born of a woman'and 'born under the Law' cannot be denied.

---

[19] A *reversio* is not always a chiasm (which is to the *reversio* what the species is to the gender), because it does not necessarily form a literary unit. Thus in Gal. 4: 4, the initial adverbial phrase ('when the time had fully come') does not belong to the *reversio*. Having said this, we must add that the *reversio* (*aββ'a'*) is not the only principle of composition; one should not forget the syntactic repetitions (two participles followed by two purposes: *aaββ*) and the two dominant constituents: (I) *the sending* of the Son, and (II) its double purpose (God is the subject of the principal verb and of the verb in the two final clauses). Does the parallelism *aaββ* allow us to relate 'born of a woman' (equivalent to a statement of human sonship) to the second purpose, 'so that we might receive adoption as sons (or the divine sonship)'? The two expressions would thus be opposed, the first preparing paradoxically the second. The passage from one to the other has been diversely interpreted and there is no need here to take up again the discussion. We note only that this composition (*aaββ*) is internal to the *reversio* and that our adoption as sons (a') is explicitly, that is to say lexically, placed in relation to *the sending* of the Son of God (a).

[20] Such are the verbs that mean *see*, or *hear, learn, understand, know, show*, and so forth.

Whatever of the incarnation, the arrangement of the passage—in other words, the 'inversion'—shows at least that the divine sonship of the Son accompanies the process which goes with his *sending*—from (before) his birth as man and as a Jew[21]—to the reception of adoption as children by humans. The same 'inversion' highlights the difference that exists between *the being-son* of the Son and our adoption as sons.[22] Certainly Paul does not want to say that we became sons in a weak sense, but the contiguity of the words 'God' and 'Son' stresses the same point as the personal pronoun αὐτοῦ *(him,* translated above into a possessive adjective '*his* [Son]'): the closeness to and the unique relation of the Son with God.

1. Romans 8: 3 and the Incarnation of the Son of God

If the phraseology of Galatians 4: 4 does not allow the reader to arrive at a firm conclusion about the incarnation of the Son of God, is Romans 8: 3 more explicit? Of itself, any temporal relationship between the aorist participle 'having sent' (πέμψας) and the principal verb 'condemned' (κατέκρινεν) does not decide matters. The history of exegesis, from the church Fathers to our own times, shows that the verse has been interpreted in diverse ways: as *the sending* of the eternal Son in our mortal flesh (the incarnation), or as *the sending* of Jesus by God, at the beginning of his ministry—a Jesus similar to us in all things, fully a member of a humanity wounded by the effects of sin.[23] On what arguments do the different interpretations base themselves?

A. No Allusion to the Incarnation?

Among scholars who hesitate to see an allusion to the incarnation in Romans 8: 3, J. D. G. Dunn is doubtless the one who has developed most reasons.[24] To those who base themselves on the

---

[21] Those who reject here the idea of preexistence must at least admit that Gal. 4: 4 expresses, with other words, the idea of a choice operated well before the birth in view of a given mission, as e.g. in Jer. 1: 5; Isa. 49: 1–5 and Gal. 1: 15.

[22] It is enough to compare the first and the last line.

[23] The two actions (*the sending* and the condemnation) could not be concomitant: as the principal verb manifestly indicates the beneficial effect of the death of Christ (that is the condemnation of sin), the phrase *pempsas ktl* must designate this (prior) death and the form it took (the torture of criminals and sinful people). The formulation would then be equivalent, more or less, to one used elsewhere by Paul: 'God gave up his Son' (Rom. 8: 32).

[24] Dunn, *Christology*, 44–6.

verb πέμπειν, used four times in the Book of Wisdom with God as subject to describe the sending of a heavenly being,[25] it must be observed that

> [p]empein is clearly more or less synonymous with *exapostellein*—as Wisd. 9. 10 and the Johannine parallel to Mark 9. 37 and Luke 10. 16 suggest (John 13. 20). In particular, we might note that Luke uses *pempein* both in speaking of Elijah's divine commissioning (Luke 4. 26) and in the parable of the dishonest tenants for the father's sending of his son (Luke 20. 13). It may also be significant that just as Rom. 8. 3 speaks of God sending 'his own Son', so the Markan and Lukan versions of the parable of the dishonest tenants speak of the father sending his 'beloved Son', and that the thought of others participating in the son's inheritance is central in both contexts (Mark 12. 7–9 pars.; Rom. 8. 1–17). So here too the Synoptic tradition, particularly the parable of the dishonest tenants, probably provides a closer parallel to and explanation of Paul's language in Romans 8. 3 than the sending of Wisdom.[26]

Without any doubt, the verb 'to send' by itself is not enough either to annul or to confirm the one or other interpretation. Further clues are necessary, in particular the syntactic organization, that is very interesting here. In effect, not only by putting together the words 'God' and 'Son' as in Galatians 4: 4, but also by using the reflexive ἑαυτοῦ, the verse highlights *the being-son* of the Son, who is the *proper* son of God. Without specifying further who this Son is,[27] the formulation invites the reader to conclude that this Son should not be confused with any other being and is unique. Furthermore, if one compares the order of the words of Galatians 4: 4 and those of Romans 8: 3, it is difficult to say with Dunn that

> [t]he phrase 'in the (precise) likeness of sinful flesh' probably has the same function in Rom. 8. 3f. as the phrase 'born of woman, born under the law' had in Gal. 4. 4f. For the thrust of Paul's thought is as clearly soteriological in Rom. 8. 3f as it is in Gal. 4. 4f. *In other words, 'in the precise likeness of sinful flesh' describes the character of Jesus' sonship*. . . .[28]

In effect, by placing the two occurrences of 'born' with the noun 'Son', Galatians 4: 4 describes well the two components[29] of the

[25] Wisd. 9: 10, 17; 12: 25; 16: 20.

[26] Dunn, *Christology*, 44–5. The arguments are the same in his commentary on *Romans 1–8*, 420.

[27] By a defining participle, as we already saw above, or by giving a name ('Jesus').

[28] Dunn, *Christology*, 45. The italics are mine.

[29] The formulation of Dunn implies that these characteristics are the only ones. Yet it is better to be prudent and admit that even if these characteristics are decisive here,

sonship of Jesus. On the other hand, Romans 8: 3 does not authorize the same conclusion, since the prepositional phrase 'in the likeness of sinful flesh' does not follow the noun 'Son', but the participle 'having sent', which it determines and specifies. Against Dunn, we must also maintain that 'in the likeness of sinful flesh' constitutes a modality of *the sending* by God and not primarily a component of *the becoming-son* of the Son. We cannot conclude immediately with certainty that the πέμψας of Romans 8: 3 designates the incarnation, but only that the prepositional phrases 'in the likeness of sinful flesh and for sin' are components or modalities of this participle.[30]

Dunn adds that if Paul wanted to refer to the incarnation, he would have done so in an unambiguous way:

Not incarnation seems to be in view here, for that would probably have required a much more careful statement than the ambiguous language Rom. 8. 3 uses, but an affirmation of the complete oneness of Christ with sinful man making his death effective for the condemnation of sin by the destruction of its power base (the flesh). In short, Rom. 8. 3 like Gal. 4. 4 probably belongs together with the other passages where Paul associates Jesus' sonship with his death, rather than in a separate category.[31]

But Romans 8: 3 does not associate directly the sonship of Jesus with his death on the cross. The beginning of the verse insists on the relationship of the Son to God—he is his *own* Son. Moreover, strictly speaking, the sonship of Jesus is not associated here with his death, which Paul simply does not mention. It can be objected that Jesus' death is implied. Maybe, but we have just been told that Paul knows how to choose words and to order them intentionally. Let us therefore respect his silence! Dunn claims that the incarnation 'would probably have required a much more careful statement than the ambiguous language Rm, 8: 3 uses', but he does not offer any suggestion about the words which the Apostle could have used to this effect. In brief, the linguistic arguments provided by Dunn and others against any allusion to the incarnation are far from being decisive.

because of their soteriological weight, they do not exhaust *the being-son* of the Son of God—in other words, they could not be the only ones.

[30] This point was well made by Douglas Moo (*Romans* (Grand Rapids, Mich: Eerdmans, 1996), 479), who without denying the soteriological meaning of the verse, speaks of the two prepositional phrases as 'Paul's description of the way in which God sent the Son'.

[31] Dunn, *Christology*, 45.

B. An Allusion to the Incarnation?

Those who are inclined to see an allusion to the incarnation in Romans 8: 3 can appeal to the sequence of the different words. On the one hand, as the nouns 'God' and 'Son' are put together and precede the participle 'having sent',[32] the sonship of the Son is literally affirmed before mention is made of his being sent for our salvation. In other words, it is not *the sending* that determines *the being-son* of the Son.

On the other hand, as we have already pointed out, the prepositional clauses 'in the likeness of sinful flesh and for sin', etc. are not directly attached to the complement 'Son', but to the participle 'having sent' which they modify and from which they are inseparable. That is why it is difficult for the Christian to read this participle without seeing in it an allusion to the incarnation. But what is the meaning of 'in the likeness of sinful flesh and for sin'?[33] Without repeating the commentaries that furnish detailed information on the different words, in particular on the noun 'likeness' ($\delta\mu o\acute{\iota}\omega\mu a$),[34] we can affirm that the expression aims to insist on the fact that the Son was fully human and received a body scarred like our own by the effects of sin—temptation, suffering, and death.[35] But when did

---

[32] Let us not forget that this syntactical trait differentiates Gal. 4: 4 from Rom. 8: 3.

[33] It is a question of a hypallage which commentators generally set out as follows: 'having sent with/in the body similar to that of sin', or, if we follow the *TOB*: 'in the condition of our sinful body'. Paul already used this figure with the same noun $\delta\mu o\acute{\iota}\omega\mu a$ in Rom. 1: 23; 5: 14; 6: 5.

[34] Why does Paul not only say 'in the sinful flesh' but also use the noun 'likeness'? Moo, *Romans*, 479–80, gives an explanation which reflects well the common exegetical opinion: 'Paul cannot mean that Christ had only the "appearance" of flesh. . . . [T]he word does not suggest superficial or outward similarity, but inward and real participation or "expression". It may be, then, that Paul wants simply to say that Christ really took on "sinful flesh". But this may be going too far in the other direction . . . On the one hand, [Paul] wants to insist that Christ fully entered into the human condition, became "in-fleshed" (*in-carnis*) [!], and, as such, exposed himself to the power of sin (cf. 6: 8–10). On the other hand, he must avoid suggesting that Christ so participated in this realm that he became imprisoned "in the flesh" and became, thus, so subject to sin that he could be personally guilty of it. *Homoiōma* rights the balances that the addition of "sinful" to "flesh" might have tipped a bit too far in one direction.'

[35] In Rom. 8: 3, as Moo seems to have perceived (see the end of the last note) the juxtaposition of the words 'body' and 'sin' is obviously pleonastic, inasmuch as Rom. 7: 14–25 amply shows that the 'body', partly linked with sin, is even totally dominated by it. But the pleonasm has the function of insisting on the fact that the Son of God experienced human fragility, in bearing and suffering all the effects of sin. See also the interpretation that Dunn makes of the phrase in *Romans*, 4: 21: '*sarx hamartias* is an effective summary statement of Paul's view of the fallen human condition, *not* as a dualistic denunciation of the flesh as in itself sinful, but as a sober recognition that man as flesh can never escape the enticing, perverting power of sin.'

that happen? Since when did the Son fully share our human condition, if not from his conception, *from the womb of the mother*, as the Prophet says? Should we not then conclude that Romans 8: 3 makes *the sending* correspond with the very beginning of the life of Jesus, with the becoming man of the Son of God?

The phraseology therefore clearly indicates that *the being-son* of the Son is not determined by *the sending*, and that this *sending* coincides with the very beginning of his human existence, is co-extensive with his human life, and characterizes him thus. These two particularities authorize us to conclude that even if he does not treat explicitly the question of a heavenly pre-existence, Paul highlights in Romans 8: 3 what was subsequently called the doctrine of the incarnation. But his formulation is sufficiently clear to avoid any ambiguity about monotheism![36] In brief, to read in Romans 8: 3 an inchoative expression of the incarnation does no violence to the precise phraseology of the Apostle, even if we have to admit with Dunn that the Apostle offers a functional Christology in which 'the ontological corollaries' are not yet fully clear or explicitly stated.[37]

III ROMANS 8: 1–17 AND THE IMPACT OF THE INCARNATION

1. Issues at stake with regard to the Incarnation

Supposing it is admitted that in Romans 8: 3 the *sending of the Son* indicates his *becoming-man* for our salvation, we return to the beginning of the verse because the finesse of its formulation stresses one of the essential ideas of Pauline soteriology. In effect, if the Apostle says that where the Law failed, God was successful, he does not add that God had to send his own Son *in order to* remedy the salvific incapacity of the Law: the incarnation does not open an economy that is an alternative to the Law. The Son does not come *to replace* a Law that is incapable of stamping out sin, as if God first

---

[36] On the manner in which Paul expresses at the same time the proximity of Christ to God while maintaining their distinction by their respective roles, and so forth., see J.-N. Aletti, *Jésus-Christ fait-il l'unité du Nouveau Testament?* (Paris: Desclée 1994), 50–6.

[37] Cf. J. D. G. Dunn, *The Theology of Paul the Apostle* (Grand Rapids, Mich.; Eerdmans 1998), 292–3. Paul does not say what *the Son's sending* from heaven means to him in terms of pre-existence. Further, he does not explicitly say that the Son enjoyed an actual (or personal) and not merely an ideal (or intentional) pre-existence.

tried in vain to overcome sin by means of the Law and then decided
on a more efficacious solution. Along the lines of Romans 7: 7–25,
the Apostle recognizes only the incapacity of the Law[38] and, in
comparison, the means by which God overcame sin.

If Paul does not say that the Son was sent *to* replace the economy
of the Law, he does not say either that he was sent *so that* God could
'condemn sin in the body'. He only affirms that in sending his Son
'in the likeness of sinful flesh and for sin', God *in fact* condemned sin
in the flesh. The two utterances[39] are merely affirmative. The
purpose of the incarnation is expressed only in the following verse
and in an entirely positive way: 'in order that the requirement of the
Law might be fulfilled in us'. Such is the redemptive impact of the
incarnation, and we will return to this decisive point. But first, let us
consider the modalities of *the sending of the Son of God* and their
importance for the subject under discussion.

We already saw that God does not send his Son in glory but in the
humble condition of a body wounded by sin: the Son of God will
experience temptation, suffering, and death like all humans. And it
is precisely this that must surprise the reader. If the Law was
incapable of overcoming sin, why was the Son of God (who
shared the fragility of all humans, because he was *in the likeness of
sinful flesh*) not weaker than the Law, *through the flesh?* We find here
a paradox that Paul likes to express in diverse passages and in
diverse ways: it is not by making his Son escape our human
condition that God accomplished his work of salvation but by
making him live that condition in all its dimensions—except sin.
Far from rendering the salvific plan of God weak or even incapable,
the passage of the Son through the fragility of the human condition
rendered him, on the contrary, fully efficacious and effective.

That Paul highlights this kind of paradox elsewhere, and in a
strong manner, is remarkably demonstrated by 2 Corinthians 5: 21
and Galatians 3: 13:[40] 'The one who did not know sin, God made
him to be sin, so that in/by him we might become the righteousness

---

[38] Dunn, *Romans*, 419, notes rightly that the phrase *to adynaton tou nomou* 'leaves
unclear what it is of which the powerlessness of the law consists'. But the following
verses (Rom. 8: 3b–4a) allow us to elucidate the ellipsis. By its affirmative nature,
Rom. 8: 3 indirectly confirms the interpretation of Rom. 10: 5, where Paul does not
affirm in any way, whatever commentators may say, the salvific nature of the Law
before the coming of Christ.

[39] That of the incapacity of the Law and that of the condemnation of sin.

[40] See again 2 Cor. 8: 9, where the same movement is discernible.

of God'; 'Christ redeemed us from the curse of the Law, having become himself a curse for us.' Certainly, Paul does not say that Christ was a sinner. But thanks to a metonymy,[41] he shows that all the effects of sin were in a certain way fixed on him, and adds: that is why we have become the righteousness[42] of God in Christ. It was in suffering to the extreme—by the death of a criminal—the consequences and effects of sin that the Son of God could obtain justification and blessing. Exegetes need to examine the *rationale* behind such paradoxical expressions, especially those similar to Romans 8: 3, where God is the subject of the verbs (he sent his Son, he handed him over,[43] etc.), because they indicate well that for Paul the 'excess' is in God himself. For if God loved us to the point of 'handing over his Son', to reconcile us with himself at the very time when all of us as enemies of God rejected this beloved Son, and if he made of us his children forever through the human existence and death of his Son, then at that point everything has been given to us. God could not, and will never be able to go any further. In brief, by these paradoxes, Paul wanted to express the real excess of divine ways, because for him, this excess can be expressed only by paradox. The difficulty comes from the fact that the Apostle never seeks to clarify or explain the paradoxes that he highlights, as if he is afraid of taking the edge off them. He insists on the contrasts, in order that his reader should not forget the extraordinary ways desired by God to obtain salvation for us.

Romans 8: 3 therefore stresses the human condition of the Son of God and indicates well what one is to understand in pronouncing the words of the Creed that relate to the incarnation—'he took flesh'. But the 'in the likeness of sinful flesh' is not the only phrase to qualify *the sending of the Son of God*. Paul adds that this *sending* was περὶ ἁμαρτίας, an apparently elliptical expression which commentators translate in two different ways: 'for sin' or 'as a sin offering'.[44]

---

[41] Unlike metaphor, metonymy does not necessarily imply that the two realities placed in a relationship of contiguity have some resemblance, but only that one be the cause or effect of the other, its container or content, and so forth.

[42] Again a metonymy, but one that determines, this time, a status where there is not only a resemblance but a community of nature between cause and effect.

[43] See Rom. 8: 32.

[44] NEB ('as a sacrifice for sin') and NJB ('to be a sacrifice for sin') converge. These English translations rightly avoided 'because of sin', since the 'because of' renders the Greek phrase *dia* + accusative, which Paul used a lot elsewhere. Apart from the well known *dia touto*, see for instance Rom. 2: 24; 4: 23, 24; 8: 10 (2 ×); 9: 32; 11: 28; 14: 15; 1 Cor. 4: 6, 10; 6: 7 (2 ×); 8: 11; 9: 10; 10: 28; etc. Moreover, the English phrase 'for sin' cannot mean that the Son of God was sent for the benefit of sin; another phrase would have been used (a 'dative of advantage' or εἰς ἁμαρτίαν).

The first translation is so generic that it becomes elliptical. Some see expressed in it a purpose, as the preposition περί suggests: the Son was sent to [condemn] sin. But if the Apostle meant that, he repeats himself heavily and contradicts himself, since the following verb, 'condemned', expresses precisely this idea but has God as subject. Would the Son have been sent in order to [wipe off or expiate] sin?[45] Although the notion of expiation is in accord with other Pauline passages, the formulation of the second part of the phrase seems to exclude this hypothesis, since it is not said that God wiped off but condemned sin (Rom. 8: 3c). Would the Son, in effect, have been sent in order to [become himself] sin? The idea would thus be close to the one expressed in 2 Corinthians 5: 21. But such a negative meaning threatens the whole phrase: would not the condemnation of sin amount to the condemnation of the Son (who was made or became himself sin)? It is to avoid these difficulties that other exegetes prefer to give to περὶ ἁμαρτίας the precise meaning that it has in its Old Testament occurrences:[46] 'sin offering'. According to these commentators, it is improbable that Paul, who was well acquainted with the Greek Bible, did not notice the ambiguity of his formulation. If in the Scriptures the phrase περὶ ἁμαρτίας designates a sin offering, Paul would have led his readers astray if he had not used it here with the same sacrificial connotation.[47] The phrase is therefore the attribute of the direct complement υἱόν and can be paraphrased as: 'God, having sent his own Son in the condition of our flesh wounded by sin, and having made of him a *sacrificial offering for sin* . . .'. The logic of the sentence becomes immediately clear, as J. D. G. Dunn notes:

[45] One can also translate περί, as meaning 'concerning': 'concerning sin [to expiate]'. The passage would then be close to Rom. 3: 25, even if in this latter verse the purpose is theological (the manifestation and recognition of the righteousness *of God*) and not ethical as here (the fulfilment of the requirement of the Law in believers).

[46] The phrase *peri harmartias* is used 64 times in the LXX, mostly in Leviticus and Numbers, to translate the Hebrew *hata't* and *l'hata't*. It is an abbreviation, as is indicated by the complete expression used in Heb. 10: 18 (offering for sin). The LXX itself at times introduces the phrase *peri harmartias* with a neutral article in the singular or in the plural (τὸ/τὰ περὶ ἁμαρτίας).

[47] If the περὶ ἁμαρτίας is not to refer to 'sin offering', the context must provide the desired precisions, as in John 8: 46; 16: 8, 9. According to Dunn, *Romans*, 422, 'such a sacrificial allusion would be wholly natural and unremarkable in a first-century context. Paul can merely allude to it since this way of thinking of Jesus' death was already well established in the Christian congregations.' He refers to Rom. 3: 25–6 of which the formulation, according to him, is pre-Pauline.

[T]he death of the sin offering effects God's condemnation of sin by the destruction of the sinful flesh; the only remedy for flesh's incorrigible weakness in the hands of sin is its death. Here it functions as part of Paul's Adam Christology: Christ's death, in its identity with sinful flesh, breaks the power of sin by destroying its base in the flesh (the new humanity beyond death is not of flesh, and so also not under sin). 'It is the death of sinners which he dies' (Althaus).[48]

We can thus grasp the soteriological issues at stake in the two clauses that go with the participle 'having sent' and constitute the two modalities of *the sending of the Son*—in the condition that is ours, which is determined by the effects of sin, and as an offering for sin. By this sending, God condemned sin *in the flesh*. If Paul uses only one participle, it is because he does not distinguish here two successive *sendings*: a first, in the flesh, and a second, towards the sacrificial death. This is because it is the entire human existence of the Son, from his birth to his death, which defines and realizes *the sending* in the totality of his movement. The formulation of Romans 8: 3 makes it clear that *the becoming-man* of the Son of God is at the same time a *becoming-an-offering* for sin: *the sending* or the incarnation of the Son of God includes these two dimensions, human and sacrificial.

The first issue at stake with regards to the incarnation is therefore the condemnation of sin. It is sin and the power of its domination that are intended here and they are both dramatically brought to light in Romans 7: 7–25. But why did Paul insist on adding 'in the flesh'? Moreover, the sentence can be understood in several ways: 'God condemned sin [which was or which was prevailing] in the flesh', or 'God condemned sin [at the very place where it was acting ruthlessly or was prevailing, that is] in the flesh', or again 'God condemned sin in the flesh'.[49] In order to respect the order of the Greek words, we shall limit ourselves to the first two interpretations, all the more so because the third agrees with the second. As regards the first, it cannot be excluded, because it is in the line of Romans 7: 14 and 18, where it was said that sin prevailed in the flesh of humanity not yet justified by faith in Christ, in the sense that carnal humanity is inhabited by sin and delivered to its power. Does Paul go further than this minimal affirmation—that is: God condemned[50]

---

[48] Dunn, *Romans*, 422.

[49] Paul would have used the figure of speech called hyperbaton.

[50] As many commentaries stress, one should take the verb 'condemn' in all its extension and performative dimension, as a strong condemnation, which has also been carried out. For what salvific value would a condemnation have had if it would

sin which was in the flesh and prevailed over it? Or does he insist on
the fact that sin was condemned and eliminated precisely where it
prevailed, in the flesh? But the condemnation of sin 'in the flesh' is
understandable only from the previous occurrences of the same
term 'flesh'. The passage from Dunn quoted above showed, I hope,
the rationale behind the choice of terms. It is therefore by following
this author and many others that we interpret 'in the flesh'. In
accord with him, let us add that

[t]he phrase must describe where and how God gave the decisive verdict
against sin—'in the flesh'. That could suggest a divine strategy whereby the
enticingness of the flesh's weakness was used to draw sin to the flesh and so
to engage sin's power that the destruction of the flesh became also the
destruction of that power. In the most dramatic reversal of all time (quite
literally), death is transformed from sin's ally and final triumph (Rom. 5: 21)
into sin's own defeat and destruction. At all events the decisive enactment
by God was clearly the death of Jesus; the death of Christ brought that whole
epoch characterized by sin's domination of the flesh to an end.[51]

The first issue at stake with regards to *the sending*—the incarnation—is therefore well stressed by the lexical repetitions and their
paradoxical arrangement: the defeat of sin has been embedded in the
flesh itself, that is to say, there where it has always been victorious
until now! The intentions of Romans 8: 3, eminently paradoxical as
we just recalled, evidently requested long explanations, but we also
observed that Paul never explains his paradoxical highlights, thus
leaving them all their enigmatic weight. In Romans 8: 3 the
terseness is also explained rhetorically: according to his habit,
when he develops an argument, the Apostle does not develop the
pisteis or the proofs that recall the past salvific events,[52] for that
would be to recall things already known. And since it is v. 4 that
indicates the impact of the incarnation, which Paul will progressively set out, we must focus on this verse.

---

not have been followed by an execution? But for what and to what was sin
condemned? Not to disappear immediately—Paul admits himself that this was not
yet so—but to be deprived of all power over all believers inhabited by the Spirit (cf. the
developments of Rom. 8 in its entirety).

[51] Dunn, *Romans*, 422.
[52] On the development of the argument in Rom. 8 (and Rom. 5–8), and the
function of vv. 3–4, see above.

2. *The Reason for the Sending of the Son*

That God sent his Son *in order* to condemn sin is affirmed by many texts of the NT. But, let us repeat, Romans 8: 3c does not make the condemnation of sin the motivation for the incarnation—the statement is simply affirmative. The only explicit motivation provided is expressed in the following verse: 'in order that the requirement of the Law might be fulfilled in us who walk not in accordance with the flesh but in accordance with the Spirit'. It is certainly to this motivation that Paul wants to draw attention, because he will develop various consequences and implications (Rom. 8: 5–17). For what would a condemnation of sin mean that leaves human beings in their miserable condition? Without their interior transformation, would the condemnation of sin have changed anything in the situation described by Romans 7: 7–25?

Such was the plan, well defined by God when he sent his Son: that the requirements of the Law find in us believers their accomplishment. But the reader must be surprised by such a formulation. In subordinating *the sending of the Son* to the accomplishment of the 'righteous requirement' of the Law, does Paul want to say that the baptized remain in the economy of the Law? Certainly not! Let us not forget that in effect v. 4 has to be understood in relation to the whole section, where it was explicitly repeated that those who are in Christ are no longer 'under the Law' (Rom. 6: 14; 7: 4 and 6).[53] The expression of Romans 8: 4 is nevertheless eminently paradoxical. While the subjects of the Law cannot obey it (Rom. 7: 7–25), the baptized, precisely because they are no longer under the Law, see 'the fulfillment of the righteous requirements of the Law in [themselves]'. But the paradox intensifies because the baptized do not bring about the fulfilment that goes on or took place in them: Paul uses a passive ('might be fulfilled' $\pi\lambda\eta\rho\omega\theta\tilde{\eta}$) which is theological. It is God himself who brought about the fulfilment of the requirements of the Law in the baptized.[54] Why did God want the righteous requirements of the Law to be accomplished in the baptized, when they are no longer under the power of the Law? Is it because this righteous requirement is the *agapè* itself? Paul does not say so, but

---

[53] A similar declaration can be found in Gal. 5: 18.

[54] The theological passive would be explained only in the following verses, by the developments on the Spirit, who, by indwelling the baptized, allows them to live the existence that God expects of them.

we may think so when we recall what he affirmed in Galatians 5: 14 and Romans 5: 5.

If Paul recognizes the weakness of the Law and gives the reasons for it, he does not thereby reject either its purpose or its value. The requirements of righteousness and *agapè* must be more than ever obeyed by those who are no longer under the power of sin. We can even affirm with Dunn that 'Paul here deliberately and provocatively insists on the continuity of God's purpose in the law and through the Spirit'.[55] That Paul wants to provoke a surprise is the least we can say. Although the believers are no longer under the power of the Law, he returns to that theme in Romans 8: 4 and in a paradoxical form, as we saw. But it was necessary to go beyond the situation described by Romans 7, in which even the faithful Jew, who desires to carry out the required righteousness of the Law cannot do so. If this is so for the pious Jew, is not the non-Jew disqualified *a fortiori*? Will the righteousness and *agapè* demanded by the Law remain unrealizable? That would mean that the situation described in Romans 7: 7–25 would not have changed, that it would even be universal, and that sin would not have been either condemned or deprived of its supremacy. Romans 8: 4 does not then function to express exhaustively the new situation of the baptized; its function is to develop the essential components that allowed the situation described in Romans 7 to be gone beyond. Nevertheless, the affirmation of Romans 8: 4 will be gradually amplified and completed by the verses which follow and show what the fulfillment of the righteous requirement of the Law implies in those who walk according to the Spirit.

Romans 8: 3–4 also allows us to understand the manner in which the Apostle proceeds. He starts by presenting the Law as entirely used by sin despite its holiness (Rom. 5: 20–1 and 7: 7–25); then he declares that it finds its *raison d'être* and its spirit in the ethical behaviour of the believers. Right from the promulgation of the Law, the will of God for humanity was formulated: God always called for righteousness and *agapè*. The Law manifested directly the will of God for humanity, and his will has to be accomplished. The incapacity of the Law to dominate sin was overcome thanks to *the sending of the Son*. Even if Romans 8: 3–4 expresses only in a summary way the dynamics of the divine project for salvation, it indicates well that

---

[55] Dunn, *Romans*, 423.

ethical transformation is the consequence of *the sending* and incarnation of the Son, through whom the Spirit was given in abundance. In brief, the impact of the incarnation—with the two modalities indicated by the prepositional phrases of Romans 8: 3—is significant. Thanks to it, in effect, not only the ethical conduct of human beings but their present and future status have been renewed. The Spirit not only gives the power to live as God wants, but also brings life and resurrection to those who become daughters and sons of God. The dynamics of the argument which goes from Romans 8: 1 to 17 shows well how *the sending* of the Son made possible the sonship of all those who believe. Their status is not only passive: Paul describes it as a relation or an attitude of closeness and total confidence, like that of the little child who says: 'Daddy!'.

IV Conclusion

Romans 8 is without doubt one of the most appropriate texts to help us determine how Paul understands the decisive role that *the sending of the Son of God* has for the situation of the entire human race. My chapter first showed that, by the disposition of the syntactic elements, Romans 8: 3 invites us not to limit *the sending* merely to the sacrificial death, but to see its maximal extension. *The sending*, as Paul speaks of it here, is oriented towards what it brings, that is, not only the defeat of sin and the ethical transformation of believers, but also the future glorious resurrection of those who are already sons and daughters of God.

If we have not analysed in detail all the consequences of the incarnation or *the sending* of the Son, it is because they are only indirect consequences and because Paul does not linger on *the sending* itself. But we needed to indicate the two modalities that he considers essential to his argument. This is because Romans 8 considers first and foremost the situation of believers and the moral transformation that it entails. Incidentally, we would not find elsewhere, either in Romans or in other letters of the Apostle, a coherent reflection on what has subsequently been called the doctrine of the incarnation. But it is in this perspective that Romans 8: 3 should be interpreted, despite its sparing and precise style.

6

The Incarnation: The Jewish Milieu

ALAN F. SEGAL

It has been my pleasure to attend each of the three seminars which have taken place at Dunwoodie. My task has been to survey the Jewish background to each of the Christian doctrines that we have explored together. By comparison to *incarnation*, the Jewish background to *resurrection* and *trinity* is much easier to find. Even the *trinity* can be shown to have some precedents in Judaism because, although the Christian notion of the Trinity is precisely formulated to fit Christian experience, it is possible to find Jewish writers who propounded that God could be perceived in many different forms, even at once. In fact, there were several important Jewish philosophical or mystical thinkers who speculated about the differences between the descriptions of God as a young warrior as opposed to an old man (e.g. Dan. 7: 9–13). So it is at least possible to find a clear precedent of hypostases within the Hebrew Godhead.

The *incarnation*, on the other hand, seems more puzzling because Jewish thinking, even Hellenistic Jewish philosophical thinking, avoided explicitly discussing the conception of incarnation; indeed they were perplexed to discover how matter and spirit could interact at all. *Incarnation* is a much later, much more refined notion of how matter and spirit relate. Indeed, it is hard not to put *incarnation* somehow in the same category as *avatar* as a strange and interesting but *different* notion of the Godhead which is at best comparable to some Jewish notions of Godhead.[1] Yet with allowance as for the Christian perspective, interesting precedents can be found.

Since the Christian concept of incarnation results from the inter-

[1] For an interesting comparison between the Christian and the Hindu notions of descent of the deity—incarnation and avatar—see J. B. Carman, *Majesty and Meekness: A Comparative Study of Contrast and Harmony in the Concept of God* (Grand Rapids, Mich.: Eerdmans, 1994). Also see Jon L. Berquist, *Incarnation* (St Louis: Chalice, 1999).

play of Greek philosophy with Hebrew thought and since it is a later and more refined concept, neither the Hebrew Bible, nor the Apocrypha, nor the New Testament contain the word. There are, of course, some interesting general precedents for the notion of incarnation. Like the Trinity, the best possible precedents come from the hypostasization of the Hebrew God or sometimes the figuring of Israel's God in angelic form. The Hebrew Bible, at best, contains a few reports which describe the LORD (YHWH) as an angel (Exod. 23: 21–2), speak of his Glory (Exod. 33), or discuss his Wisdom as a separate creature, as in Proverbs 8: 22: 'The LORD created me at the beginning of his work, the first of his acts of old; יְהוָה קָנָנִי רֵאשִׁית דַּרְכּוֹ קֶדֶם מִפְעָלָיו מֵאָז'. In this passage Wisdom speaks as a separate entity created by God, and though incarnation would technically entail an uncreated participation in the essence of God. The New Testament is much more explicit but even it barely outlines the conception. At best there are but two important passages which discuss the incarnation of the Christ. The New Testament seems to promote the notion in order to express the worthiness of Jesus to be appointed the Christ in his fleshly manifestation:

And the Word became flesh and dwelt among us, full of grace and truth; we have beheld his glory, glory as of the only Son from the Father (John 1: 14).

. . .who, though he was in the form of God, did not count equality with God a thing to be grasped, but emptied himself, taking the form of a servant, being born in the likeness of men (Phil. 2: 6–7).

One further passage seems to me to be relevant. In Luke 1: 26–35 when the angel tells Mary about the child she will bear, he reassures her with the following prophecy: 'The Holy Spirit will come upon you, and the power of the Most High will overshadow you; therefore the child to be born will be called holy, the Son of God'. This last describes the birth of Jesus as saviour, suggests that the birth was special in process as well as promise, but does not necessarily articulate a doctrine of the incarnation. Each of these three passages, while not directly discussing incarnation, expresses the relationship between Jesus and divinity in terms of how God acted to put himself in flesh. Not all discuss the fleshly character of the incarnation. They talk instead about Jesus' divine likeness and his human likeness.

In the early post-biblical period there is also no consensus on how this divine action is to be understood. In the *Shepherd of Hermas*, for example, God is understood to have made himself evident through the son, who is also an angel of the Lord. Nevertheless, later church Fathers, basing themselves on the explicit statement in John, concentrated on the notion of *logos*, Word or Wisdom of God, who, though divine, became flesh (John 1: 14: ὁ λόγος σὰρξ ἐγένετο). Equally important, as we shall see, will be the second part of the verse: 'and dwelt among us, full of grace and truth; we have beheld his glory, glory as of the only Son from the Father' (John 1: 14).

There is nothing that explicitly states anything this radical in Judaism. Yet, there are some partial precedents to be explored. When examining the *milieu* or *Umwelt* of this Christian concept, the most profitable place to start would seem to be the dialogue between Judaism and Hellenistic philosophy. That would mean beginning with Plato and his primary Jewish reader, Philo. For Plato was very concerned with the way matter and spirit, the divine and the material, interacted and that concern goes over into Philo's thinking as well.

There is a way in which incarnation is a commonplace, the way in which matter and form interact to form the visible world. And there is another way in which it is so special a thing for the divine and the human to interact that it is impossible. It appears that before Christianity Judaism was caught on one or other horn of this dilemma and never desired to resolve the impasse.

I Plato's Understanding of Matter and Soul

The writings of Plato and Aristotle settled the issue of the relationship between mortal matter and immortal soul by demonstrating that the soul and body are two separable entities and the soul, being rational, is the only immortal one. Indeed, as Plato developed his thinking, the one thing that most characterizes the relationship between the divine and matter is that only divinity can be immortal. Those that followed this philosophy accepted the immortality of the human soul in one form or another as the way in which divinity and non-divinity interact, though they did not all necessarily grant the survival of our individual personalities. The most important documents in this context are Plato's *Phaedo* and *Apology*. In the

Apology we have Socrates' legal defence against the charges brought against him, and in the *Phaedo* we must witness Socrates' execution but not before he demonstrates to us the reality of the soul's immortality.

Plato uses the figure of Socrates, his real-life teacher, as a literary convention to speak Platonic philosophy. How closely Plato's Socrates resembles the Socrates of history we cannot tell. It is clear in both the *Crito* and the *Phaedo* that Socrates has deliberately refused several chances to escape (with the tacit approval of his captors) to a disgraced life in exile, rather than drink the hemlock which is the sentence passed upon him by the court. The subject of the dialogue then becomes not just martyrdom and justice but a discourse on the issue of the immortality of the soul. In some ways, Socrates has already lost the battle for the preservation of his body, though he was certainly unjustly accused and convicted by his political enemies, at least in Plato's eyes. In the *Apology* he argues that one should concentrate one's efforts on the good of the soul over against the body (*Apology* 30a–b). Likewise in the *Laws*, Socrates states that the soul is completely superior to the body because the soul is the principle of life while the body is merely a resemblance of it. In the *Symposium*, Diotima gives a clear presentation of the way to achieve postmortem survival. The mortal nature seeks the immortal by reproduction, a vain and impossible effort, though a necessary one, but the soul is already immortal (207d, 208a–b).

In the *Phaedo*, Socrates undertakes to demonstrate that the soul is immortal, so that his execution is but a momentary inconvenience which will allow him soon to join the company of superior humans and gods. The proof is so important it is worth reviewing in a little more detail. Socrates begins his conversation with the observation that opposites seem to be related—like the pain of his bonds and the pleasure of their removal. No one can have both at once (60b). (This seemingly casual observation becomes the assumption on which all further arguments are built but that does not emerge until much later in the dialogue.) This leads to further musings on the relationship between life and death and on the fact that ordinary persons are afraid of death because they are going from life to an imagined end. Actually, continues Socrates, when viewed properly, a philosopher is not afraid of death because it is the opportunity to live as a soul without a body: 'They are not aware of the way true philosophers are nearly dead, nor of the way they deserve to be, nor of the sort of death they deserve' (64b–c).[2]

Indeed, much can be learned by thinking about death. Philosophers are encouraged to spend their lives doing it. For Socrates, death itself is the separation of the body from the soul: 'Is it anything else than the separation of the soul from the body? Do we believe that death is this, namely, that the body comes to be separated by itself apart from the soul, and the soul comes to be separated by itself apart from the body? Is death anything else than that?' (64c). Philosophers seek something very similar to death, separation from the bondage of the body and passions.

The proof of the immortality of the soul depends on Plato's notion that there are entities called the *forms* or *ideas* of all the material bodies on earth:

If those realities we are always talking about exist, the Beautiful and the Good and all that kind of reality, and we refer all the things we perceive to that reality, discovering that it existed before and is ours, and we compare these things with it, then, just as they exist, so our soul must exist before we are born. If these realities do not exist, then this argument is altogether futile. Is this the position, that there is an equal necessity for those realities to exist, and for our souls to exist before we were born? If the former do not exist, neither do the latter? (77d–e)

Socrates does not try to demonstrate the forms here. He merely suggests that if the soul exists, it must be one of the forms or ideas. It would follow that what Socrates attempts to demonstrate for the soul would be true for all the forms, although that is not explicitly discussed. Socrates is not purposely excluding arguments. He attempts to address a further, plaguing issue: perhaps souls exist, but it is also possible that while they pre-exist our bodies, they do not continue to exist after death or after a series of lives. It is also possible that the soul is a harmony, not a being in itself but a relationship between the parts: ' "Well then, since this is the case, is it not natural for the body to meet with speedy dissolution and for the soul, on the contrary to be entirely indissoluble, or nearly so?" "Of course" ' (80b).

Thus, it is still possible that the soul could dissolve after death or, stranger yet, wear out after having inhabited several bodies. Socrates therefore goes on to describe the relationship between the soul and the body:

[2] This translation is taken from Plato's *Phaedo*, trans. G. M. A. Grube (Indianapolis: Hackett, 1977).

But the soul, the invisible, which departs into another part which is, like itself, noble and pure and invisible, to the realm of the god of the other world in truth, to the good and wise god, whither if God will, my soul is soon to go—is this soul, which has such qualities and such a nature, straightway scattered and destroyed when it departs from the body, as most men say? Far from it, dear Cebes and Simias, but the truth is much rather this:—if it departs pure, dragging with it nothing of the body, because it never willingly associated with the body in life but avoided it, and gathers itself into itself alone (συνεφέλκουσα), since this has always been its constant study—but this means nothing else than that it pursued philosophy rightly and really practised being in a state of death: or is not this the practice of death? (80e)

Socrates even uses 'clouded together' or 'clumped together' to describe the relationship between the soul and the body. They are not willing companions and he articulates no exact way in which they can interact, though he thinks that the flesh has an effect on the soul. And this is the problem for Platonic thought thereafter. Matter either has an effect on the soul or it does not. But it cannot both have an effect and not have one. In fact, it is this problem which must be solved if Christianity's notion of incarnation is to be sensible.

To demonstrate that the soul is indissoluble at death, just as he has previously demonstrated that it pre-exists us, Socrates again has to return to the issue of the forms—the good, the beautiful, and so forth (100b). Socrates distinguishes between the properties and the form of a thing by showing that *cold* is not the same as the *snow*, nor *fire* as the *heat*. He then essentially defines the soul is the very thing that brings the property of life to an object. It is nothing else than its life and is the total opposition of death (105d). He states that life and death come from the same thing, follow each other, but cannot exist at the same time. What makes something alive is the presence of a soul; what kills it is the departure of the soul. But the soul itself remains alive, indeed must remain alive by definition, and is proven both to precede the body and outlive it. Thus we wind up with a definition of soul as the form or idea of life, something which is immortal by definition and by the prior assumption that the forms or ideas of everything on earth are the immortal plans for producing them. Yet it is not clear that the soul that survives death is a 'personal' soul in our sense of the word. Aristotle seems even less sure that the immortal aspects of the soul contain our 'personality'.

It is on this demonstration that Plato's Socrates stakes his life; he goes to his death willingly and calmly, though his proof has been halting and diffident. And indeed, the Western notion of the soul, even as mediated by Christianity, eventually depends on this dialogue of Plato, with all its attendant strengths and weaknesses.

There are, however, some aspects of the proof, which both Judaism and Christianity have understandably forgotten. Socrates suggests that we all have several incarnations. Only when we successfully learn how to separate the soul from the body are we granted rest from the tired cycle of incarnation and reincarnation—a notion which sounds very much like the ideas of *karma* and *samsara*, the religious insight of another great Indo-European civilization. For Socrates we can even be reincarnated as an animal: 'Those, for example, who have carelessly practised gluttony, violence, and drunkenness are likely to join the company of donkeys or of similar animals' (81e). Surely Apuleius' *Metamorphosis*, which relates such a transformation in detail, was partly inspired by these lines. Yet, all church Fathers but Origen denied that the soul has more than one life to live.

The issue of justice is very much the central concern in the last part of this dialogue. But it is a justice that operates as a pure mechanism of nature—a moral universe, in which human reward and punishment are built in. The doctrine of *metempsychosis*, or transmigration of the soul, is obviously a penalty which must be paid. It does not necessarily imply after-death suffering. Indeed, Plato appears to be somewhat ambivalent on the notion of retribution. In the *Republic*, he represents a kind of Orphic doctrine of retribution by means of Adeimantus:

> Musaeus and his son [Eumolpus] endow the just with gifts from heaven of an even more spirited sort. They take the righteous to another world and provide them with a banquet of the saints, where they sit for all time drinking with garlands on their heads, as if virtue could not be more nobly rewarded than by an eternity of intoxication. . . . When they have sung the praises of justice in that strain, with more to the same effect, they proceed to plunge the sinners and unrighteous men into a sort of mud-pool (εἰς πηλόν τινα) in the other world, and they set them to carry water in a sieve (κοσκίνῳ). (2. 363 c–d)[3]

Although this is obviously a satire on the teaching of Musaeus and Eumolpus, who were the legendary teachers of Orphism, one

---

[3] See S. G. F. Brandon, *The Judgment of the Dead: The Idea of Life After Death in the Major Religions* (New York: Scribners, 1967), 88.

must not think that Plato completely denied any rewards and punishments after death. On the contrary, he continually suggests that justice and retribution do exist, although he cannot demonstrate this in the same way that he attempts to demonstrate the immortality of the soul. Rather the particularly graphic notion of being immersed in mud seems to be the specific point of his satire.

At the end of the *Phaedo*, Socrates offers his own understanding of how humans can come to this wider perspective on life, through a heavenly ascent to the outer limit of our world:

Our experience is the same: living in a certain hollow of the earth, we believe that we live upon its surface; the air we call the heaven, as if the stars made their way through it; this too is the same; because of our weakness and slowness we are not able to make our way to the upper limit of the air; if anyone got to this upper limit, if anyone came to it or reached it on wings and his head rose above it, then just as fish on rising from the sea see things in our region, he would see things there, and, if his nature could endure to contemplate them, he would know that there is the true heaven, the true light and the true earth, for the earth here, these stones and the whole region, are spoiled and eaten away, just as things in the sea are by the salt water. (109d–e)

His description is truer than he could possibly have imagined, as we would be like fish out of water if we were to stick our heads above the atmosphere. And we would see worlds beyond our imaginings; but most likely they would impress on us the endangered, tiny environment in which we live our precarious existence, no bigger than a speck of dust when placed in the astronomical distances that characterize our universe. Plato's universe was a small, cosy place. But that is not exactly what Plato saw when he rose to these heights. From the perspective of the eternal heavens where the ideas reside, the corruptible earth is a puny failure and deserves nothing but our fond farewell. Indeed, the Hellenistic world was convinced that the hereafter would be far happier than the world we live in. As a result we see that even Plato's sense of the way in which body and soul interact is not an adequate basis for the Christian concept of incarnation.

II PHILO

It is hard to say that Philo is typical of anyone; his enormous wealth and power would suggest that he represents rather the cynosure of Jewish Hellenism, not a typical example of it. We also have more of his work than any other Hellenistic Jewish writer and perhaps any other writer of the period, with the exception of Plato and Aristotle. This privilege of material and intellectual wealth automatically catapults Philo to a position of great privilege, power, and authority. His enormous corpus of writing is unique in the Hellenistic Jewish world; he is unique in his attempt to synthesize Greek with Hebrew thought. His apologetic technique is very sophisticated, showing that the Hebrew Bible both clearly illustrates Greek philosophical truths in *allegory* (as do the *Iliad* and *Odyssey*, according to the Greek commentators) while morally surpassing them. Philo has been called both philosopher and mystic.[4] But when reading Philo, one meets quintessentially an exegete, a philosopher and mystic writing commentaries on the biblical works. He rarely indulges in systematic philosophical exposition. So it is difficult to find a short and full exposition of his ideas on any subject; they must be gleaned from many different sources. All these characteristics mean that we have to be satisfied with a characterization of his writing on incarnation rather than an extensive treatment of it.

Philo was born to a very wealthy Alexandrian family a fraction of a century before Jesus. He was a contemporary of both Jesus and Paul, probably outliving both of them. Unlike Jesus, however, he was born in a major centre of Hellenistic culture and brought up in one of the wealthiest families in the city. He presumably received private tutoring, probably also a gymnasium education and participated in Greek athletics. At the same time, he saw nothing in these activities to detract from his perfect observance of Jewish law, though he evidently did not practice the Jewish law in conformity with his contemporaries in the Land of Israel, the Pharisees. His life and writing make clear that Jewish observance and Pharisaism are not to be equated. There were many legitimate yet opposing ways to carry out the commandments which God had given Israel in this

---

[4] H. A. Wolfson, *Philo: Foundations of Religious Philosophy in Judaism, Christianity, and Islam*, 2 vols. (Cambridge: Harvard University Press, 1947), 4th edn., 1968; and E. R. Goodenough, *By Light, Light. . . : The Mystic Gospel of Hellenistic Judaism*, (New Haven: Yale University Press, 1935).

period. He lived long enough to accompany the Jewish legation to intercede with Gaius Caligula to rescind the law to put up the Emperor's statue in all public places in the mid-first century.

In terms of his ways of dealing with life after death, Philo is typical of the new Jewish intellectual class, well attuned to Greek philosophical traditions, and explaining the Bible and Judaism by means of philosophical notions. Being a good Platonist, Philo discusses the immortality of the soul without ever broaching the resurrection of the body. Since the Septuagint evinces a distinct interest in resurrection but no obviously clear statement of the immortality of the soul, Philo is forced to interpret the Septuagint against the grain. He has no problem doing this with his finely honed tool of allegory. No doubt his Bible had no book of Daniel in it or, if it did, he interpreted it allegorically.

Why should a good Platonist even want a resurrection of flesh, when flesh corrupts like all matter? Philo believes that the perfection of the intellectual and moral faculties is what leads to immortality of the soul, in a non-material way. It is the continuity of consciousness that most attracts Philo's observations.

Philo does not use the word *anastasis* (ἀνάστασις) or its derived verb forms which signify *resurrection* in the Septuagint and New Testament. He does not use any forms derived from *egeiro* (ἐγείρω) to signify post-mortem existence, as Paul likes to do. He either does not know or does not like the notion of a fleshly rising from the dead.

But it would be a mistake to consider him one of the Sadducees, who are universally described as eschewing any conception of beatific afterlife. Instead he almost exclusively uses the term *athanasia*, immortality. He scarcely attributes any messianic hopes to the Jews, defusing a political issue between pagans and Jews. Philo does valorize Jewish martyrdom, saying that Jews accept death as if it were *immortality* (*Legat.* 117. 2) and conversely saying that when threatened by death Jews are given *immortality* (*Legat.* 369. 2). He brags that Jewish youth seek liberty as eagerly as *immortality* (*Prob.* 117. 4). It is clear then that Philo is partly accessing his Jewish knowledge, explaining, privileging, and valorizing it, and explicitly describing a Jewish notion of martyrdom, although he describes it in Platonic garb.

Philo also makes central to his notion of the Bible's message an ascent to see God. In fact for Philo, the name 'Israel' designates ascent and philosophical contemplation. For Philo, Israel means 'the

person who saw God': אִישׁ שְׂרָאֶה אֵל in Hebrew. This refers both
to Jacob's wrestling with the angel (*el*) and to the people's quest for
God in their religious writings. It is also applicable to any who
pursue philosophy to its correct conclusion, a vision of God, and
therefore functions in a universalistic way in Plato's writing.[5] Philo
outlines a clear mysticism based on the mystical ascent to heaven
for prophecy and immortalization.

Philo does not so much demonstrate that the soul is immortal as
assume it. It is implicit in his anthropology, which is quite consistent
throughout:

Divine breath ($\pi\nu\epsilon\hat{\upsilon}\mu\alpha$ $\theta\epsilon\hat{\iota}ον$) migrated hither from that blissful and happy
existence for the benefit of our race, to that end that, even if it is mortal in
respect of its visible part, it may in respect of the part that is invisible be
rendered immortal. Hence it may with propriety be said that man is the
borderland between mortal and immortal nature ($\theta\nu\eta\tau\hat{\eta}s$ $\kappa\alpha\iota$ $\dot{\alpha}\theta\alpha\nu\dot{\alpha}\tauου$
$\phi\dot{υ}σεωs$ . . . $\mu\epsilon\theta\dot{ο}ριον$) partaking of each so far as is needful, and that he
was created at once mortal and immortal in respect of the body, but in
respect of the mind immortal. (Philo, *De opificio mundi* 135)[6]

Man is made of flesh and spirit: the body is dust ($\chiοῦs$) which is
animated by divine spirit ($\pi\nu\epsilon\hat{\upsilon}\mu\alpha$, $\psi\upsilon\chi\acute{\eta}$); the spirit is not created ($\dot{\alpha}\pi$'
$ο\dot{υ}δενός$ $γεν\eta\tauο\hat{υ}$ $\tauὸ$ $\piα\rhoά\pi\omegaν$) but originates directly from the Lord, the
Father, and Ruler of the Universe. This *spirit* or *soul* he breathed into
humanity. Notice that Philo would rather cede some of the Lord's
power as creator than cede any of his immutability. Anything that
the Lord directly created would imply change and therefore imperfection in him; hence the soul, like all the ideas, must be uncreated,
while the material creation is the product of an artisan angel, the
demiurge. The mind ($\deltaιάνοια$ or frequently $νοῦs$) is the soul of the
soul ($\psi\upsilon\chi\acute{\eta}$ $\psi\upsilon\chi\hat{\eta}s$; *Opif.* 66; *Heres.* 55). These terms seem to designate
the centre of the personality, the personal and individual aspects of
spiritual life. For Philo they must do so, as he believes strictly in
individual reward and punishment for individual moral decisions.

For Plato, immortality must also be an inherent quality of the
mind, which is the very nature of the human being. Mortality,

---

[5] See E. Birnbaum, *The Place of Judaism in Philo's Thought: Israel, Jews, and Proselytes*
(Atlanta: Scholars, 1996).

[6] *Philo* in 10 vols, Loeb Classical Library, trans. F. H. Colson and C. H. Whitaker
(Cambridge, Mass.: Harvard University Press, 1929–62). Discussion is taken from
H. C. C. Cavallin, *Life After Death: Paul's Argument for the Resurrection of the Dead in I
Cor 15* (Lund: CWK Gleerup, 1974), i. 135–46.

conversely, is directly related to our bodily nature. In direct opposition to Plato, Philo believes that the soul is immortalized by moral behaviour, so that those who do not act morally are condemned to non-existence at death. In other words, the immortality of the soul does not necessarily mean its indestructibility. Does this mean that Philo was not so impressed with Plato's proof of the soul's immortality? Maybe. It is not terribly convincing. But, if so, he remains silent. Rather he is at pains to make the Platonic doctrine coincide with his biblical faith and he uses the biblical text to demonstrate the full truth. For instance, he allegorizes the exile of Adam and Eve and later Cain:

(10) Accordingly God banished Adam; but Cain went forth from his presence of his own accord; Moses is here showing to us the manner of each sort of absence from God, both the voluntary and the involuntary sort; but the involuntary sort, as not existing in consequence of any intention on our part, will subsequently have such a remedy applied to it as the case admits of; for God will raise up another offspring in the place of Abel, whom Cain slew, a male offspring for the soul which has not turned by its own intention, by name Seth, which name being interpreted means irrigation; (11) but the voluntary flight from God, as one that has taken place by deliberate purpose and intention, will await an irremediable punishment in all eternity; for as good deeds that are done in consequence of forethought and design, are better than unintentional ones, so also among offences those that are undesigned are of less heinousness than those that are premeditated. (*Post.* 10–11)[7]

Clearly Philo takes great exception to the philosophy of Plato in order to bring it more into line with his reading of biblical faith. Even more interestingly, he seems more preoccupied by the issue of why Cain's sin is so little punished, while Adam and Eve's is so greatly punished. This shows, I think, that Philo is at least as much an exegete as a philosopher. Indeed, for Philo these precepts are primarily demonstrable from allegorized scripture and not logical proofs, which is partly where the wit and cleverness of Philo's writings come. Arguably, the Hebrew Bible has nothing like immortality of the soul, indeed except for Daniel no real beatific afterlife at all to teach. But that is not in Philo's purview. Instead he wants to show that the path to the soul's perfection is to seek an audience or vision of God, to become 'Israel', for God is the source of

---

[7] *The Works of Philo: Complete and Unabridged*, new edn., trans. C. D. Yonge, foreword by D. M. Scholer (Peabody, Mass.: Hendrickson, 1993).

all existence. This makes Philo one of the most important representatives of Jewish mysticism in the Hellenistic period.[8] For example,

The knowledge (ἐπιστήμη) of him is true consummation of happiness. It is also age-long life. The law tells us that all who 'cleave to God live,' and herein it lays down a vital doctrine . . . For in very truth the godless are dead in soul, but those who have taken service in the ranks of the God who only is alive, and that life can never die (οἱ δὲ τὴν παρὰ τῷ ὄντι Θεῷ τεταγμένοι τάξιν ἀθάνατον βίον ζῶσιν). (*Spec. Leg.* 1, 345)

Philo supports his equation of immortality and knowledge of God with a reference to Deuteronomy 4: 4: 'but you who held fast to the LORD your God are all alive this day'. The Greek for 'you who held fast' (οἱ προσκείμενοι) follows fairly literally the Hebrew (וְאַתֶּם הַדְּבֵקִים); so Philo allegorizes the term to mean those who have 'conceived of' or 'known' God.[9]

Platonic influence obviously contributed to Philo's identifying immortality with moral behaviour, although Philo's reading of the Bible is far more important in understanding his thinking here. Certainly Plato notes that moral behaviour is what perfects the soul for its intellectual adventure. However, for Plato all souls are immortal no matter how heinously they may act. The very sinful may be given special punishment in Hades but they will eventually be reincarnated for further progress (see e.g. *Republic* 10 [610a]). Philo's Jewish and religious commitment to a personal relationship between God and each human who seeks him is what makes necessary his further development on the Platonic notion—a totally individual and personal disposition of the soul, strictly dependent on its earthly behaviour. In any event, it is unclear how personal is the immortality that Plato outlined: the soul is forced to forget everything personal when it is reincarnated, leaving only some basic innate categories as the continuity between lives. Furthermore, personal immortality certainly falls by the wayside in Aristotle's thinking. All this is central to Philo's understanding of biblical ethics, and so he corrects the philosophical error.

---

[8] See E. R. Goodenough, 'Psychopomps', *Jewish Symbols in the Greco-Roman Period* (Lawrenceville, NJ: Princeton University Press, 1987), ch. 11; id., *An Introduction to Philo Judaeus*, introd. Jacob Neusner (Lanham, Md.: University Press of America, 1940); and id., *By Light, Light* . . .

[9] See Cavallin, *Life After Death*, 135–6.

And reincarnation too must fall by the wayside in Philo's adaptation of Plato's thinking. Thus, we face for the first time in Jewish life an explicitly and fully personal, immortal soul whose centre is the intellectual faculties. This is illustrated most clearly in Philo's notions of the reward and punishment of sinners. Although he sometimes interprets biblical passages to mean that the dead merely cease to exist, as the text itself seems to imply (*Posterit.* 39), when asked for his own opinion, he says that they will be punished: 'Men think that death is the termination of punishment but in the divine court it is hardly the beginning' (*Praem.* 60).

In other words, though Philo adopts the notion of the immortal soul from Plato, he equates moral living with the practice of philosophy and gives primacy to the kind of ethical behaviour which is outlined by the Bible: 'The souls of those who have given themselves to genuine philosophy . . . study to die to the life in the body, that a higher existence immortal and incorporeal in the presence of Him who is himself immortal and uncreated, may be their portion (μελετῶσαι τὸν μετὰ σωμάτων ἀποθνῄσκειν βίον, ἵνα τῆς ἀσωμάτου καὶ ἀφθάρτον παρὰ τῷ ἀγενήτῳ καὶ ἀφθάρτῳ ζωῆς μεταλάχωσιν)' (*Gig.* 14). Some of this sounds just like Plato, whose Socrates says that the truly philosophical live as already dead. But for Philo it is the process of moral education itself which brings us into the presence of God and transforms us into immortal creatures. There may be a hint of our previously discussed resurrection and transformation motifs in these doctrines but, if so, they are highly refined.

Philo thinks of the soul as a perfected body, sometimes implicitly described as made out of the same stuff as stars. He is therefore able to identify the righteous dead with the stars themselves, and hence as angels, as we have seen in the apocalyptic literature: 'When Abraham left this mortal life, "he is added to the people of God" (Gen. 25: 8), in that he inherited incorruption and became equal to the angels, for angels—those unbodied and blessed souls—are the host [and people] of God (καρπούμενος ἀφθαρσίαν, ἴσος ἀγγέλοις γεγονώς. ἄγγελοι γὰρ στρατός εἰσι θεοῦ, ἀσώματοι καὶ εὐδαίμονες ψυχαί)' (*Sacr.* 5). It seems here as if Philo is giving us his own interpretation of the various apocalyptic traditions we have already seen. But he styles them not in terms of resurrection (they are unbodied souls) but in terms of incorporeal intelligences. Thus we learn that the stars and the angels are both incorporeal and intelligent:

The men of God are priests and prophets who have refused to accept membership in the commonwealth of the world and to become citizens therein, but have risen (ὑπερκυψάντες) wholly above the sphere of sense-perception and have been translated (μετανέστησαν) into the world of the intelligible and dwell there registered as freemen of the commonwealth of ideas, which are imperishable and incorporeal (*Gig.* 61).

Notice that Philo does not use the standard vocabulary for resurrection in these passages, but rather makes up his own to distinguish his thinking from standard resurrection vocabulary in other Hellenistic Jewish writers. In most passages, however, Philo explicitly regards death as the soul's liberation from the prison of the body. Here he seems rather to be trying to accommodate post-biblical interpretations to his brand of Platonism.

III PHILO'S *LOGOS*

If Plato's sense of the way matter and spirit interact is not a likely precedent for the Christian notion of the incarnation, Plato's notion of *logos* and its interaction with matter is instructive in a different way from the Christian tradition. Philo also codes his philosophy according to gender. Matter is feminine (ὑλή) and passive to the masculine *logos* and *nous*. Unbridled sexuality is also a distraction and a detraction. The influence of women must be limited by human rules and regulation for the good of both sexes. Women, though theoretically the equal of men and equally responsible for their actions, are simply not treated as the equal of men, and certainly their will is viewed as weaker and their sexuality degraded. This is a judgement typical of Platonism but Philo seems more zealous than most. Philo points out the sexual abstinence and even celibacy of the Therapeutai, whom he admires and who are so similar to the Qumran group. As sexuality is such an important aspect of human life, gender coding is indeed quite frequent in other groups as well—including complete celibacy, which is characteristic of some Essenes, some Christians, and Manichaeans.[10]

Philosophically at least, Philo is committed to an equal and yet loftier view of the soul, which is resident in all humanity and hence

---

[10] See e.g. R. Baer, *Philo's Use of the Categories Male and Female* (Leiden: Brill, 1970); also D. Sly, *Philo's Perception of Women* (Atlanta: Scholars Press, 1990).

transcends gender. Some particularly moral souls can go beyond the angels and stars to be with God himself. In *De Somniis* 1. 4 and 23, Philo refuses to commit himself on the issue of whether the celestial bodies have souls and minds. This appears to be a further example of Philo's sensitive Bible reading. For him, as for the Genesis text itself, the heavenly bodies are but creations of God, not entities in themselves as in Plato. Furthermore, souls do not descend into non-human bodies, as they may in Hindu or Platonic thought. The highest expression of Philo's thought is, as usual, best expressed by the systematic treatment of Harry A. Wolfson:

> While encased in the human body, the rational soul affects the life of the body and is affected by it. On the one hand, it helps the process of sensation induced into the body by the irrational soul within it, and, on the other hand, it utilizes the data of sensation for the formation of intellectual concepts. More especially does it exercise control over the body by its power of free will, with which it was endowed by God. But still, even while in the body, it never loses its character as a distinct entity, so that when the body with its inseparable irrational soul dies, the rational soul departs and enters upon its bodiless, eternal and immortal life. The place where rational souls abide during their immortal life varies. Some of them go up to heaven, by which is meant the astronomical heaven, to abide among the angels; some of them go up to the intelligible world, to abide among the ideas; some of them go up even higher, to abide in the presence of God. Immortality, however, is not due to rational souls by their own nature; it is a gift from God, and God who created them can also destroy them; consequently only the souls of the righteous who have earned the gift of immortality survive, while those of the wicked may be destroyed.[11]

Philo notes that philosophical meditation is transformative in itself. It does not need to end in a right vision of the Existent One:

> Therefore we sympathize in joy with those who love God and seek to understand the nature of the living, even if they fail to discover it; for the vague investigation of what is good is sufficient by itself to cheer the heart, even if it fail to attain the end that it desires. But we participate in indignation against that lover of himself, Cain; because he has left his soul without any conception whatever of the living God, having of deliberate purpose mutilated himself of that faculty by which alone he might have been able to see him. (*Post.* 21)

Philo speaks of Moses as being made into a divinity (*koinonon*) in

[11] H. A. Wolfson, *Philo: Foundations of Religious Philosophy in Judaism, Christianity, and Islam* (Cambridge, Mass.: Harvard University Press, 1968), 415–16.

several places (e. g. *Sacrifices* 1–10; *Moses* 1. 155–8). In exegeting Moses' receiving the Ten Commandments, Philo envisions an ascent, not merely up the mountain but to the heavens, possibly describing a mystical identification between this manifestation of God and Moses by suggesting that Moses attained to a divine nature through contact with the *logos*. In *Questions and Answers on Exodus* 1. 29 and 40, Philo writes that on Sinai Moses was changed into a divinity. In *Life of Moses* 1. 155–8, he says that God placed the entire universe in Moses' hands and that all the elements obeyed him as their master; then God rewarded Moses by appointing him a 'partner' (*koinonon*) of his own possessions and put into his hand the world as a portion well fitted for his heir (155). In the *Sacrifices of Cain and Abel* 8–10, Philo refers to Deuteronomy 5: 31 as proof that certain people are distinguished by God to be stationed 'beside himself'. Moses is pre-eminent among these people for his grave is not known, which for Philo apparently means that Moses was transported to heaven.

Of course, all of this moves contrary to incarnation; indeed, Philo explicitly says that flesh and spirit are not permanently together. Like Plato he holds their combination to be both commonplace and a sign of earthly imperfection, not perfection. But it is important to see how divinity and mortality interact in Philo. Philo can also talk about ways in which God emanates through the world to make himself known. In this regard, we need to take a closer look at his notion of God's principal mediator, the mind itself, or as Philo constantly calls it, the *logos*. Philo also makes use of this important tradition in describing the *logos*, his name for God's demiurge in creation and the name for pattern for the world. Philo describes the creation of the heavenly man in Genesis 1: 26, while he took Genesis 2: 7 to refer to the creation of the earthly man (*On the Creation* 134; *Allegory* 1. 31, 53 ff, 88–9; *Questions on Gen.* 1. 4; 2. 56). He calls the heavenly man the image of man *(ho kat' eikona anthropos)*. He calls the logos 'a second God', a *deuteros theos*: 'Why does he say, as if of another god: "in the image of God he made man" and not "in His own image?"' The answer is: 'It is because nothing can be made in the likeness of God but only in that of the second God *deuteros theos*, who is His *logos*' (*QG* 2. 62). On the basis of the divine likeness, Philo can call the visible embodiment of God a second God. The heavenly man shares his image with mankind as well, since he is the Platonic form of man.

In fact, Philo can allegorize any reference to God's human features in the Hebrew Bible as the *logos*. Moses and the elders see the 'Lord', who is the *logos* (*Of Flight and Finding* 164–5). The 'Lord' whom Jacob saw on the heavenly ladder (Gen. 28: 13) was the 'archangel', i. e. the *logos*, in whose form God reveals himself (*On Dreams* 1. 157; *On the Change of Names* 87, 126; *On the Migration of Abraham* 168; *Allegory* 3. 177; *Who is Heir* 205). They are all anthropomorphic because they symbolize the likeness humanity shares with God.

As a result it seems unlikely that any notion of incarnation could have made it into Christianity directly from Platonism or Philonic Judaism. The reason is not hard to see. For Plato *incarnation* is either a commonplace—describing the way matter and spirit interact—or an impossibility, depending on whether you take the simple meaning or the miraculous meaning. Beyond the latter's implausibility in Philo's estimation, there is also his distinct lack of interest in matter as a physical phenomenon. To say that divinity became flesh and 'encamped' among us, as does John 1, Philo would have thought a disparaging statement about God or at best a statement that needs to be understood allegorically. After all it was the challenge to God's immutability which stimulated Philo's use of the term *deuteros theos*. It is more proper for humans to ascend and perfect themselves where the transubstantiation takes place.

On the other hand, both the normal process of the emanation of ideas into our world and the divinization of special mortals like Moses are so close to what the Christian community will later call *incarnation* that it is hard not to see in Philo a preparation for the later idea.

IV OTHER PRECEDENTS EMANATING FROM JOHN 1: 14: 'WE HAVE BEHELD HIS GLORY'

Although Philo would have balked at the idea of anyone actually becoming God through identification with the *logos* or the *logos* being made flesh, there are perhaps other examples where the distinction between human and divine was more ambiguous. These have been collected by Larry W. Hurtado in his *One God, One Lord: Early Christian Devotion and Ancient Jewish Monotheism*[12]

---

[12] Philadelphia: Fortress, 1988. See the 2nd edn. (Edinburgh: T. & T. Clark, 1998).

and by other members of the so-called 'New History of Religions School', in which I also consider myself. Briefly, Hurtado's main hypothesis is that while many groups in the history of Judaism cherished traditions of mediation or the primacy of a particular angel or patriarch, Christianity was the first group ever to give *devotion* to the mediating figure, praying to him as God. This, Hurtado maintains, is a distinct 'mutation' in the history of Judaism and explains why Christianity had such a distinctly different history from the other Jewish sects. Indeed, this entirely corresponds with our understanding of the philosophical problems inherent in the notion of incarnation.

But this is only the beginning of the phenomenon. Perhaps we ought to ask instead: why would Christians seek to go beyond the boundaries normally invoked by Platonic philosophical analysis within Judaism? The answer is not to be found within philosophy itself but in the various models available to early Christians within Judaism for understanding who Jesus was as Christ and how he could be rightfully understood as divine.

Let us look at the various precedents and see where and why Christianity has surpassed them in its formulation. To do so will entail a brief review of the material which is better developed by Hurtado himself, as he devotes an entire monograph to the subject. Of all the kinds of mediation that are discussed by the New History of Religions School, the ones most relevant in this context are those where the deity emanates through mediational forms. These would include the *logos* doctrine, which Philo used so effectively to explain God's special providence to the world in the Angel of the Lord.

Exalted patriarchs must be noted as a possibility for Christian modelling of the divinity of Jesus, especially when the patriarchs are assumed to have a heavenly existence before their earthly one. For instance, Enoch is sometimes esteemed as divine because of his heavenly voyage; indeed, his exploits form an enormous body of material, conventionally taken to be second only to Moses. According to *Jubilees*, Enoch receives a night vision in which he sees the entire future until the judgement day (4: 18–19). He spends six jubilees of years with the angels of God, learning everything about the earth and heavens, from their composition and motion and to the locations of hell and heaven (4: 21). When he finally ascends, he takes up residence in the garden of Eden 'in majesty and honour', recording the deeds of humanity and serving in the sanctuary as priest (4: 23–6); he writes many books (21: 20) and there are indeed references to his writings in many other pseudepigrapha,[13] where Enoch's revelations are made known. Other personal angelic creatures would include the Angel of the Lord, who deigns to show himself to human beings. This Angel of the Lord may be known by a bewildering number of names, depending on the tradition: Michael, Melchizedek, Taxo, Metatron, Yahoel, and probably also the Son of Man, which would be the source of its application to Jesus, as his resurrection was throughout the New Testament understood as the fulfilment of the prophecy in Daniel 7: 13–14 that a 'son of man' would be enthroned in heaven with God.

Jewish interpreters evidently also understood the Genesis story of the naming of Jacob as another case of angelic transformation. In a document quoted by Origen as *The Prayer of Joseph*, Jacob says he is 'an angel of God and a ruling spirit', and thereafter one 'whom God called Israel, a man seeing God', and the 'firstborn of every living thing', the first 'minister of the presence of God'. With these phrases the narrator equates the patriarch Jacob with the primary angelic manifestation of God, the equivalent of Philo's *logos*. Jacob/Israel descends to earth and becomes incarnate, as it were, in the patriarch, probably at the moment when he wrestles with the angel.

Of course, most famously, the way God emanates and incarnates himself is through his unnamed or personified divine agencies as the *logos*, applied in the Gospel of John to Jesus. Other such agencies are also important to Christianity and even earlier—such as the Glory, the Yekara (Aramaic for Glory), the Angel of the Lord, or the 'Wisdom'. These traditions have been so well traced into Pauline thought by Carey Newman in his book.[14] David Capes has shown that already in the writings of Paul the term Lord refers both to the tetragrammaton and to the risen Christ.[15] So both in the Gospel of John and in the first-generation writings of Paul, the mediation traditions find early and important use in Christianity. Basically, they serve to express why the person of Christ is worth devotion as to a God.

---

[13] See e.g. T. Sim. 5: 4; T. Levi 10: 5; 14: 1; T. Judah 18: 1; T. Zeb. 3: 4; Dan. 5: 6; T. Naph. 4: 1; T. Benj. 9: 1; and L. W. Hurtado, 'Exalted Patriarchs', in *One God*, 51–69.

[14] *Paul's Glory Christology: Tradition and Rhetoric*, NovTSup 69 (Leiden: Brill, 1992).

[15] *Old Testament Yahweh Texts in Paul's Christology*, WUNT 2: 47 (Tübingen: Mohr, 1992).

Any theophany text and the various traditions tied to the *imago dei* motif are clearly also precedents for these traditions. These have been traced in many places by Hurtado and by Andrew Dearman in this volume; so there is no need to go over the material already listed there. It is just worthwhile noting that this material is all related in one way or another. The divine image, which Adam bore but lost as a result of the expulsion from the Garden of Eden, can also be identified with any manshaped figure in heaven—including the Glory which appeared to Moses, the so-called 'son of man' in Daniel, or even any one of the human-shaped angelophanies of the Bible.

Indeed, to say that Christianity ceded devotion to the second power may be another way of saying what Hurtado has outlined for us so well—that Christianity worshipped the Christ as God and then sought to express why that response was necessary. The response of faith came before the intellectual formulation. In this respect, it may be that the exact formulation of the doctrine of incarnation is deliberately constructed to emphasize and underline the differences between Christianity and its Jewish past, as well as internally to distinguish between later warring factions. The doctrine of the incarnation is certainly one of the biggest differences between Judaism and Christianity. The exact formulation of the incarnation was a creation and accomplishment of later times.

V John 1: 14: 'And Dwelt Among Us': The Shekhina and the Presence of God

As we have already seen quite clearly, the presence of the Lord is not described in any one way in the Hebrew Bible but in a number of ways. None of them precisely fits the Christian use of the term incarnation. And often they overlap with what in Christianity is called pneumatology, as in the famous example of Elijah's theophany:

And he said, 'Go forth, and stand upon the mount before the LORD.' And behold, the LORD passed by, and a great and strong wind rent the mountains, and broke in pieces the rocks before the LORD, but the LORD was not in the wind; and after the wind an earthquake, but the LORD was not in the earthquake; and after the earthquake a fire, but the LORD was not in the fire, and after the fire a still small voice. And when Eli'jah heard it, he wrapped his face in his mantle and went out and stood at the entrance of the cave. And behold there came a voice to him, and said, 'What are you doing here, Eli'jah?'. (1 Kgs 19: 11–13)

In looking at the presence of the Lord at the Temple, we shall see that it partakes of pneumatology as well as of all the notions mentioned previously. It is significant that the word that the Gospel of John uses to describe incarnation is *eskenosen* signifying encampment. Its Hebrew equivalent is the root sh-k-n which designates both setting up a tent and dwelling. It is the same as the normal Arabic root for 'residing'. This word is obviously being used very specifically to suggest the presence of God that the Hebrew Bible associates with the Tabernacle and the Temple, everything from the pillar of fire and the cloud that children of Israel followed while wandering in the desert to the presence of God in the Jerusalem Temple. This is closely associated with the Glory and the Angel of the LORD, already discussed in the previous section. Jewish tradition will call this divine presence the Shekhina, the 'Indwelling'. Later mystical Judaism will even identify this figure with the lowest of the spheroth, the metaphysical divine emanations; this one is the spiritual Israel, the way in which God normally makes his presence known to the world.

The presence of the Lord is most closely associated with the Temple in the time of Jesus. This has been aptly pointed out by N. T. Wright in several places, but it is worth discussing at least briefly in several respects before concluding.[16] Wright's argument has basically two parts. He suggests that (1) the Temple provided the presence of God to the Jews but also demonstrated what was wrong with Judaism, and that (2) Jesus offered the corrective presence of God in one man. Now, obviously these statements are heavily tinged by Wright's own faith statements, typical of the Christian critique of most of Judaism in general. But the notion that the Temple represented the presence of God to Jews in Second Temple times is not wrong:

The Temple was of course, in this period, the heart and center of Judaism, the vital symbol around which everything else circled. It was supposed to be where YHWH himself dwelt, or at least had dwelt and would do so again. It was the place of sacrifice, not only the place where sins were forgiven but

---

[16] See e.g. N. T. Wright, *The Challenge of Jesus: Rediscovering Who Jesus Was and Is* (Downers Grove, Ill.: InterVarsity Press, 1999), 62–7.

also the place where the union and fellowship between Israel and her God was endlessly and tirelessly consummated. It was, not least because of these two things, the center of Israel's national and political life: the chief priests who were in charge of it were also, in company with the shaky Herodian dynasty and under Roman supervision, in charge of the whole nation.[17]

Wright suggests that this situation was also in need of reform. At the same time, the Christian critique was not unique. Virtually everyone but the Sadducees had a critique of the Temple, including the Pharisees and the Dead Sea Scroll sectarians. Along with the critique of the Temple came a unique exegesis of the purity regulations which supported the holiness of the Temple.[18] Each provided a substitute for the physical building of the Temple and its administration. The Dead Sea Scrolls sectarians along with the Christians appear to have believed that the Temple was beyond repair and needed a substitute. Qumran suggested that God's presence through his angels could be felt in their liturgy. The Christian critique was focused on Jesus' actions at the money-lenders' tables, but it grew in the early Christian period as the antagonism between Christians and Jews grew.

The Pharisees were able to resolve their problems with the Temple administration, for they continued to respect it in spite of their criticism of the Sadducees and their administration. When it ceased to exist, however, they forbade excessive asceticism or mourning and began to legislate substitutes for its rituals and services. They too suggested that prayer and acts of kindness would serve as atonement in place of the Temple. Jesus' own position was quite as complex, for he went there to observe the Passover; yet if the money-lenders' episode is historical (and the reasons to believe it outweigh the reasons not to, in my estimation), he had his own critique of the Temple administration. It seems in line with rural critique of the new moneyed economy in Jerusalem. It was not so thorough as the Christian critique of the Temple afterwards, which is what N. T. Wright is giving us.

The point, however, is that the Temple demonstrated that Jews felt the presence of God in their lives. As opposed to the various angelophanies mentioned in Jewish literature, they did not particularly ascribe human qualities to this presence. Nor did they say that

[17] Wright, *Challenge of Jesus*, 62–3.
[18] See e.g. the important new work by J. Klawans, *Impurity and Sin in Ancient Judaism* (New York: Oxford University Press, 2000).

God's presence adhered to the material building itself. The building was but the dwelling place for the presence of God. None of this was incarnation in the Christian sense of the term. Any full-scale study of the concept yields both an appreciation for the traditions that fed into Christianity and an equally strong appreciation for the unique-ness and inventiveness of the Christian response to the historical circumstances that formed it.

PATRISTIC AND MEDIEVAL WITNESS

What Does Chalcedon Solve and What Does it Not? Some Reflections on the Status and Meaning of the Chalcedonian 'Definition'

SARAH COAKLEY

Following, then, the holy Fathers, we all with one voice teach that it should be confessed that our Lord Jesus Christ is one and same Son, the Same perfect in Godhead, the Same perfect in manhood, truly God and truly man, the Same [consisting] of a rational soul and a body; *homoousios* with the Father as to his Godhead, and the Same *homoousios* with us as to his manhood; in all things like unto us, sin only excepted; begotten of the Father before ages as to his Godhead, and in the last days, the Same, for us and for our salvation, of Mary the Virgin *Theotokos* as to his manhood;

One and the same Christ, Son, Lord, Only begotten, made known in two natures [which exist] without confusion, without change, without division, without separation; the difference of the natures having been in no wise taken away by reason of the union, but rather the properties of each being preserved, and [both] concurring into one Person (*prosopon*) and one *hypostasis*—not parted or divided into two persons (*prosopa*), but one and the same Son and Only-begotten, the divine Logos, the Lord Jesus Christ; even as the prophets from of old [have spoken] concerning him, as the Lord Jesus Christ has taught us, and as the Symbol of the Fathers has delivered to us.

The purpose of this chapter is to examine a question of some subtlety and importance which is nonetheless often overlooked in the contemporary Anglo-American philosophical debates about the Chalcedonian 'Definition' of 451. I shall be asking, in the main body of the chapter, what *sort* of statement this statement about

Christ is; and this apparently innocent and simple question will be discovered to be capable of a wide range of possible answers. In particular, I shall focus on three answers to this question that are all current and influential, but which strike me as rather far from the properly understood intentions of the original authors of the document. These are the views: (1) that the 'Definition' is *linguistically regulatory* rather than ontological in intent; (2) that its language is rightly understood today as *metaphorical*; and (3) that its purpose is to 'define' the personal identity of Christ (as God-man) in a '*literal*' manner leaving as little room as possible for further ambiguity. It will be immediately obvious that these three approaches arise from very different schools of theological and philosophical understanding, all of which are worthy of close and sympathetic reflection, but none of which, in my view, probes to the heart of the document's simultaneous richness and elusiveness.

My second undertaking, in closing, will be to indicate a properly *apophatic* reading of the Definition (in a sense of 'apophatic' to be carefully defined). It will be underscored that this approach in no way excuses laxity of thinking, nor does it invite a glorying in the irrational or incoherent, but rather involves a form of precision exactly at the 'horizon' (*horos*) of defining what can, and cannot, be said. It will be underscored that this view is not novel; indeed there is some reason to think that it was what was in (at least some of) the minds of those shaping the document, and certainly in the minds of important later Eastern defenders of it. The closeness to (and slight difference from) a famous reading of Chalcedon by Rahner will also be noted. I shall end by enumerating a list of pressing christological questions that were *not* 'solved' by Chalcedon, and indeed could not be, given the sort of document I have shown that it was (and is). The effect of this explication will, I trust, be to pre-empt a significant range of responses to Chalcedon that simply miss the mark by misreading its intent.

Let us now turn, first, to the task of explicating the recent views that I find in different ways defective. It is perhaps a nice mimetic touch that by proceeding in this way (that is, by ruling out erroneous interpretations in order to leave room for a more creative and expansive alternative), we shall be following precisely the means of argument that Chalcedon itself also employs.

I CHALCEDON AS 'LINGUISTIC REGULATION'

The circumstances of the summoning of the Council of Chalcedon (451) are well-known and do not here need another rehearsal.[1] The immediate crisis was an attempt to find a way through the tortured debate between the rival Alexandrian and Antiochene schools of Christology. Whether we should see the resultant 'Definition' as an *effective* 'compromise' between the two is a moot point: the hostile, and secessionist, response of the Monophysite churches of the East thereafter painfully demonstrated the lack of balance that some felt was manifest in it. Nonetheless its aim to reconcile warring parties (whilst ruling out decisively three unacceptable understandings of Christ's person in the form of Apollinarianism, Eutychianism, and extreme Nestorianism) was clear. What is less commonly remembered in contemporary textbooks and commentaries (given the regrettable tendency to reprint the 'Definition' in isolation from the surrounding text), is that the assembled bishops were deeply reluctant to come up with any new formulas at all, their preference being to reaffirm—as they now did—the faith of Nicaea, itself grounded and founded in the biblical narratives of salvation.[2] Close attention to the *Acta*, therefore, gives the lie to the suggestion (associated with a critique of Henry Chadwick)[3] that the 'Definition' lifts away abstractly from the events of salvation and the biblical economy. On the contrary, the 'Definition', set in context, can be seen precisely to presume and reaffirm those events and then to provide a regulatory *grid* through which to pass them interpretatively. The special committee group which, under pressure, honed the linguistic terms for this grid were mainly concerned with finding an acceptable solution to the Alexandrian/Antiochene problem:

[1] See *inter alios*: A Grillmeier, *Christ in Christian Tradition*, i (London: Mowbrays, 1975), esp. 443–557; A. Grillmeier and H. Bacht (eds.), *Das Konzil von Chalkedon*, 3 vols. (Würzburg: Echter-Verlag, 1951–4); A. de Halleux, 'La Définition christologique à Chalcédoine', *Revue théologique de Louvain*, 7 (1976), 3–23, 155–70; V. Sellars, *The Council of Chalcedon* (London: SPCK, 1961); M. Slusser, 'The Issues in the 'Definition' of the Council of Chalcedon', *Toronto Journal of Theology*, 6 (1990), 63–9; and L. R. Wickham, 'Chalkedon', *Theologische Realenzyklopädie*, vii. 668–75.

[2] E. Schwartz (ed.), *Acta Conciliorum Oecumenicorum*, 4 vols. (Berlin: de Gruyter, 1914–84); vol. ii, *Concilium Universale Chalcedonense* (1932–8) is devoted to the Council of Chalcedon. I am aware of the irony of having myself quoted the 'Definition' in isolation at the opening of this chapter: such can only be a point of departure.

[3] In André-Jean Festugière (trans.), Henry Chadwick (preface), *Actes du Concile de Chalcédoine* (Genève: Patrick Cramer, 1983), 7–16, at 15–16.

cherished terminology from both sides of the debate was craftily pasted into the collage, along with inputs from Leo's *Tome*, but this is not to say that the result was a bodged or incoherent compromise.[4]

But was then the goal and achievement of Chalcedon *only* linguistic and regulatory? Such, at any rate, is the sophisticated thesis of Richard Norris in an important article for John Meyendorff's memorial volume, entitled 'Chalcedon Revisited: A Historical and Theological Reflection'.[5] Norris's thesis is complex and subtle, and deserves a full rehearsal.

First, he points out that the bishops assembled at Chalcedon were not 'professional philosophers' or even 'professional theologians'. They were not pronouncing a 'theoretically devised "christology"' (a modernist term with which they were in any case not familiar). Rather, they were weaving together a 'pastiche of allusions and quotations'—tidbits from Leo's *Tome* and from Cyril's letters, fragments or terms from the *Formulary of Reunion*, from Flavian, and from Proclus.[6] Their central question was how Christ (the 'one and the same', repeated five times) could be simultaneously God and human, an issue 'solved' by the crucial distinction between *physis* and *hypostasis*. Yet the 'solution' here, as Norris emphasizes, was actually a form of evasion: the terms were *linguistically distinguished* but never given substantial content. Hence 'The Chalcedonian *Definition* . . . offers little more than a paradigm. It does not explicitly explain or define what "nature" and "hypostasis" mean, save by tacit reference to the way in which the Nicene symbol *speaks* of Christ; . . . what it provides is essentially a transcription and an account of a pattern of predication.'[7]

Norris then argues that this merely 'paradigmatic' gesturing of the 'Definition' has to be sharply distinguished from the approach of contributors to the debate that *surrounded* Chalcedon, who in contrast saw the two sets of predicates as referring to things or substances of the ordinary sort; and hence the 'natures' become, as

---

[4] See Slusser, 'Issues in the Definition', 67.

[5] In B. Nassif (ed.), *New Perspectives on Historical Theology* (Grand Rapids, Mich.: Eerdmans, 1996), 140–58. A related argument is mounted by Norris in an earlier volume: R. A. Norris (ed.), *Lux in Lumine* (New York: Seabury Press, 1966); here I concentrate on the most recent essay. (I am grateful to my Oriel and Harvard pupil, Paul D. Jones, for an excellent term paper for my Harvard Christology seminar on Norris ('Christological "Rules", Theological "Commentaries" and Chalcedon: A Response to Richard Norris's Reading of the "Definition of Faith"'), from which I have learned much).

[6] Norris, 'Chalcedon Revisited', 141–2.   [7] Ibid. 151.

he puts it, 'reified'. (Norris cites, as instances of this 'reification',
Severus of Antioch's comparison of the union of natures to the
wedding of soul and body in the human individual; or John of
Damascus' later identification of the human intellect as the
'medium' through which the Word united with flesh.)[8] Driving a
wedge between Chalcedon's supposedly merely regulatory agenda
and this 'reification' via 'analogies' and 'metaphors' which others
applied to it, Norris concludes that the latter 'appears to insist upon
a synthesis or union of *incompatibles*—precisely because it takes its
physical models too seriously'.[9] In other words, the concretization of
thought about the 'natures' leads, he avers, to the supposition of
their 'incompatibility'. And whereas in the patristic debate this false
disjunction resulted in an overemphasis (claims Norris) on Christ's
divinity, the modern form of this aberrant perception of Chalcedon's
intent has been the opposite: 'a new type of Monophysitism—a
tendency, in the face of its own strong sense of the incompatibility of
divine and human agencies, to reduce the Christ not to a God fitted
out with the vestiges of humanity but to a human being adorned
with the vestiges of divinity.'[10]

Both these alternatives, however, suffer from a misconception of
the 'natures' as 'interchangeable contraries'—as 'differing items of
the *same* order',[11] competing against one another for the same
space. If we could counter this misconception, says Norris, we
would see that Chalcedon merely presents us with a 'rule of
predication'; it is non-committal on the 'logical relations' between
the divine and human natures, and it makes no attempt to give an
account of what those two natures consist in. Thus, finally, we need
a 'negative theology' here in a particular sense, one that *denies* that
the difference between God and humanity is a matter either of
'contrariety' or of 'contradiction'. It is not an issue of 'how to fit two
logical contraries together into one, as its ancient and modern
interpreters have all but uniformly supposed, but how to dispense
with a binary logic in figuring the relation between God and
creatures'.[12]

Norris's exposition is refreshingly direct and suitably challenging
to much current writing on Chalcedon. It appears to this writer to be
correct about several matters.[13] First, his underscoring of the

---

[8] Ibid. 149–51.   [9] Ibid. 154.
[10] Ibid. 155.   [11] Ibid. 155, 158; my emphasis.
[12] Ibid. 158.   [13] Here I largely concur with Paul D. Jones's assessment.

relatively *undefined* state of the key terms 'nature' (*physis*) and 'person' (*hypostasis*) in the so-called Definition rightly draws attention to the open-endedness of the document, its unclarity about the precise meaning of key terms. If anything is 'defined' in the 'Definition' it is not these crucial concepts. To be sure, these terms had a pre-history, but it was an ambiguous one and the 'Definition' does not clear up the ambiguity. This is a point to which we shall return in due course; for we are left wondering whether this feature 'looks like carelessness' (to reapply a phrase of Oscar Wilde) or whether it is a subtle and intentional ploy. Norris implies, though does not fully document, the latter. He also correctly notes that not only the *content* of these key terms ('person' and 'nature'), but also their 'logical relation' to one another is left undefined.

Second, we may agree with Norris that to gloss the human and divine 'natures' as inherently two of the same kind, and/or in 'contradiction' with one another, is not implied by the text of the 'Definition' *per se*. However, it has to be said that the text does not rule out that interpretation either; we have to probe into the debates that preceded and succeeded Chalcedon, especially over the human sufferings of Christ, to discover how 'divinity' and 'humanity' were deemed to constitute different, and mutually exclusive, ranges of characteristics.[14] There is a certain *fiat* on Norris' part, it seems, in attempting to rule out *any* logical incompatibility between the 'natures': this too goes beyond the (skimpy) evidence before us in the 'Definition' and depends on him successfully driving his wedge between 'regulatory' and 'reified' readings of the document.

Third, however, Norris is certainly right to claim that the major achievement of Chaldedon is its 'regulatory' vocabulary, on which semantic grid the events of salvation are now plotted. As with Nicaea, so here, unbiblical 'substance' language of ill-defined reference is wielded in order to 'settle' a set of problems that have their roots in the less consistent witness of the scriptural narratives. The 'rules' of predication are now that duality resides in the *physeis* and unity in

---

[14] See e.g. Grillmeier, 'Die theologische und sprachliche Vorbereitung der christo-logischen Formel von Chalkedon', in *Das Konzil von Chalkedon*, i. 5–202; and for a particularly sympathetic reading of Cyril, J. A. McGuckin, *St Cyril of Alexandria: The Christological Controversy* (Leiden: Brill, 1994), esp. on the vexed question of Christ's human sufferings. Norris's own important contribution to an understanding of Cyril's Christology as essentially founded in a *narrative* of *kenosis* can be found in R. A. Norris, 'Christological Models in Cyril of Alexandria', *Studia Patristica* XIII 2, in *Texte und Untersuchungen*, 116 (1971), 255–68.

the *hypostasis*. Yet what does this imply ontologically? And why is Norris so evidently coy about the metaphysics of incarnation?

It is here that we must turn the tables on Norris and enquire whether his own agenda, illuminating as it is, is not also driven by contemporary (but less than explicit) theological assumptions. First, and perhaps most obviously, Norris's insistence that Chalcedon is attempting not an ontological *proposition* but a more modest set of linguistic 'rules of predication' smacks immediately of a Lindbeckian 'post-liberal' programme. We recall the main themes of Lindbeck's *The Nature of Doctrine*,[15] which fit exactly with Norris's strong disjunction between 'regulatory' and ontological ascriptions; for Lindbeck in that book identifies three basic models for theological work, the 'cognitivist', the 'experiential-expressive', and the 'cultural-linguistic', and opts strongly for the last whilst eschewing the other two.[16] 'Cognitivist' theories according to Lindbeck understand doctrines as veridical truths, informative 'propositions' about objective realities; 'experiential-expressive' theories see religion as linking with 'pre-reflective experiential depths of the self';[17] whereas 'cultural-linguistic' theories, clearly favoured by Lindbeck, are set carefully apart from the other two, since here doctrines provide merely the 'grammar' for comprehensive interpretative schemes. On this view, doctrines do not even *attempt* to convey first-order beliefs, since 'their communally authoritative use hinders or prevents them from specifiying positively what is to be affirmed'.[18]

Lindbeck's highly influential work owes much to a non-realist reading of the late Wittgenstein which now, incidentally, seems questionable to an increasing body of philosophers.[19] But only thus can it drive so significant a wedge between 'ontological' and 'linguistic' claims, the (dubious?) apologetic advantage being a bashful 'recession from reality'[20] and into the buffering 'hermeneutical

---

[15] G. A. Lindbeck, *The Nature of Doctrine: Religion and Theology in a Postliberal Age* (Philadelphia: Westminster Press, 1984), 16–19.

[16] Ibid. 30–45.

[17] Ibid. 21.

[18] Ibid. 19. It is, however, debatable whether Linbeck can keep up this line consistently; see e.g. ibid. 68–9.

[19] See esp. H. Putnam, *Renewing Philosophy* (Cambridge, Mass.: Harvard University Press, 1992), chs. 7 and 8.

[20] The phrase is used by Nicholas Wolterstorff in his so-far unpublished Gifford Lectures: 'From Presence to Practice: Mind, Word, and Entitlement to Believe', ch. 1; see also the critique of G. Kaufman, in A. Plantinga (ed.), *Warranted Christian Belief* (New York: Oxford University Press, 2000), ch. 2, esp. 31–42.

circle' of the church community. Thus Lindbeck, like Norris after
him, can dub the efforts of Nicaea and Chalcedon mere 'second-
order guidelines', not 'first-order affirmations about the inner being
of God or of Jesus Christ'.[21] The trouble with this assertion, of
course (even if it proves suitable as a somewhat defensive post-
modern apologetic ploy, which this writer would question), is
whether it bears any relation to what the writers of the Chalcedonian 'Definition' and their sources thought they were up to
themselves. And in this area there appears to be no confirming
evidence whatsoever. Indeed the very disjunction between 'ontological', 'experiential', and 'linguistic' appears anachronistic in the
fifth-century *milieu*. Whereas writers like Augustine certainly
discourse lengthily on language's relation to reality,[22] they do
not make this fine-tuned Lindbeckian distinction between 'doctrinal' assertions as merely regulatory and other (separable)
propositional claims. And later, when (in the sixth-century material
covered by Brian Daley in this volume), fine-tuning about very
particular linguistic uses applied to Christ became a focus of intense
debate, this was done 'precisely with the understanding that these
[uses] refer to realities, and that the realities rather than our
language about them are what is important'.[23] In short, I can
find no evidence from either Aristotelian or Platonist-inspired
circles of the patristic period that linguistic terms for 'Christ'
could be divorced from ontological commitment, or indeed from
'experience' (despite the notable dearth of discussion of that latter
category); for why else would this matter have evinced such
intense and passionate controversy, if it were not about the very
reality of experienced salvation?

   If I am right, then, Norris's thesis is propelled by an anachronistic
Lindbeckian engine. Oddly, too (again, if I am right), it contains two
other covert strands of contemporary theological commitment, in
somewhat paradoxical relation to this first one. The second, which
emerges in Norris's allusions to the need for a form of 'negative
theology' in relation to an appropriate reading of Chalcedon,
suggests a slippage—even on his own terms—into a more 'cognitive' claim than his own 'regulatory' approach would allow; for here
he insists that God is no part of the natural order and that therefore

[21] Lindbeck, *Nature of Doctrine*, 94.
[22] Augustine, *De doctrina christiana*, bks. II and III.
[23] Brian Daley, in private correspondence.

all language used to speak of God is radically improper.[24] The claim sits oddly, we note, alongside his non-propositional interpretation of the 'Definition'; but it helps to explain the puzzling features of his theory, already mentioned, that 'metaphorical' and 'analogical' explications of Chalcedon's abstract terms *all* fall equally short of the mark and result in inappropriate 'reification'. What I suspect is obtruding into Norris's text at this point is a post-Kantian understanding of God's 'ineffability' (associated in the North American theological scene with the work of Gordon Kaufman and Sallie McFague[25]), where an insistence on God's *noumenal* unavailability is conjoined with a non-cognitive understanding of 'metaphor' and a tendency to smudge altogether the distinction between 'metaphorical' and 'analogical' speech for God. Since God *in se* is assumed to be completely off-limits epistemologically, then figurative speech about him/her is all at the same level of 'reified' inappropriateness: it is (paradoxically) *both* harmlessly ornamental *and* simultaneously 'radically improper'. Consequently it is not clear, on Norris's view, how anyone *could* apply the 'rules' of Chalcedon appropriately except by repeating its empty-sounding phrases. This form of 'apophaticism' is a far cry, we note, from the 'negative theology' of the pseudo-Dionysius, for whom even negations about God's nature must be negated linguistically, yet where a vision of ecstatic *encounter* with the 'dazzling darkness' of the divine is promised *hyper noun* ('beyond the mind');[26] and it is perhaps yet further still from Aquinas' sophisticated appropriation of Dionysius, which results in a theory of 'analogical' speech for God intentionally distinguished (by its 'appropriateness') from 'metaphor', and sustained by an ontology of participation.[27] Norris, however, does not even explore these more ancient theories of 'negative' religious language; instead it seems that the shadow of Kant falls upon his path.

Finally, we once again suspect a modern dogmatic commitment when Norris insists (again, more fervently than his 'regulatory'

---

[24] Norris, 'Chalcedon Revisited', 153.

[25] G. Kaufman, *In Face of Mystery* (Cambridge, Mass.: Harvard University Press, 1993); S. McFague, *Metaphorical Theology* (Philadelphia: Fortress Press, 1982).

[26] Pseudo-Dionysius, 'Mystical Theology', in *Pseudo-Dionysius: The Compete Works* (New York: Paulist Press, 1987), 133–41.

[27] See David Burrell's most recent reconsideration of 'analogy', 'From Analogy of "Being" to the Analogy of Being', in T. Hibbs and J. O'Callaghan (eds.), *Recovering Nature: Essays in Natural Philosophy, Ethics, and Metaphysics in Honor of Ralph McInerny* (Notre Dame, Ind.: University of Notre Dame Press, 1999), 253–66.

approach would seem to vindicate) that the divine and human 'natures' must be read without any possibility of 'contrariety' between them. How, we may ask, does Norris know this, when he has rightly pointed out that the term *physis* in itself imparts no clear description of the attributes of each—the human and the divine? In principle, on this (supposedly) 'contentless' reading of the linguistic 'rules', contrariety or non-contrariety between the natures could surely equally well apply. In a lightly footnoted article such as Norris's we are again left guessing at influence for his own *penchant* here; but it seems likely this time that Rahner is in the background, Rahner in a justly famous article in *Theological Investigations* (to which we shall return later) urges that God should be thought of as capable of creating in distinction from God-self a humanity 'abso-lutely open upwards',[28] not by definition therefore set in 'contra-riety' to the divine nature, nor competing for space over against it. That this reading might indeed commend itself to us (as an adjunct to Rahner's developed 'transcendental anthropology', and as a particular exposition of Chalcedon) is a matter here to be left open. All that we have established, however, is that Norris's thesis at this point technically extends beyond the 'regulatory' reading of Chalcedon that he himself has set up.

To sum up on Norris's important and challenging article: we have shown that he rightly identifies the regulatory force of the 'Defini-tion' as technical-cum-linguistic; but he also shows that the very terms that are proposed as solutions to the christological dispute are left deliberately undefined (an ostensibly surprising state of affairs for a 'Definition'). Where he errs is in suggesting that the 'Definition' required no concomitant ontological commitment, and in implying a theory of 'negative theology' that looks suspiciously, and ana-chronistically, modern. Let us now take these points forward in examination of the theory that 'incarnation' language *tout court* should be read as 'metaphorical'. Since we have already cleared some of the philosophical ground here, this theory can be considered rather more summarily.

---

[28] K. Rahner, 'Current Problems in Theology', *Theological Investigations*, trans. and introd. Cornelius Ernst, i (London: Darton, Longman & Todd, 1961), 183.

II INCARNATION LANGUAGE AS 'METAPHORICAL'

John Hick's famous (or notorious) assertion in *The Myth of God Incarnate* that the idea of a God/man is 'as devoid of meaning as to say that this circle drawn with a pencil on paper is also a square'[29] drew an immediate storm of defensive protest.[30] The most obvious riposte was that we cannot *know* that the notion of a God/man is incoherent unless we antecedently and exhaustively know what divinity and humanity consist in (which evidently we do not). However, it is ironic that Hick points precisely to those elements of indeterminacy in the Chalcedonian Definition which Norris also highlights, but uses them to insist that the God–Man formula makes no sense: 'orthodoxy insisted upon the two natures, human and divine, coinhering in the one historical Jesus Christ. But orthodoxy has never been able to give this idea any content. . . . The Chacedonian formula, in which the attempt rested, merely reiterated that Jesus was both God and man, but made no attempt to interpret the formula.'[31]

Rather oddly, the effect on Hick of his views about Chalcedon's supposed incoherence is to object (in his later book, *The Metaphor of God Incarnate*) that 'incarnation' language must therefore be seen as 'metaphorical' in nature rather than 'literal'. More usually, he agrees, such a linguistic process moves in the opposite direction: speech originally coined as metaphor settles into literalness over time. But here, with the claim of 'incarnation', what was once thought to be 'literal' (God becoming human in Christ) must now be seen to have failed as literal speech: 'in the case of divine incarnation the initial idea has proved to be devoid of literal meaning and *accordingly* identified as metaphor. . . .'[32] The effect of this attribution of 'metaphorical' status thus seems to imply a 'recession from reality' of the sort that Norris also entertained: unable to perceive 'metaphor' as cognitive, as precisely giving us a new purchase on reality, Hick instead assumes that to use 'metaphorical' speech is to say something with *less* firm ontological commitment than if one

---

[29] 'Jesus and the World Religions', in J. Hick (ed.), *The Myth of God Incarnate* (London: SCM Press, 1977), 167–85, at 178.

[30] Most immediately in M. Green (ed.), *The Truth of God Incarnate* (Grand Rapids, Mich.: Eerdmans, 1997).

[31] Hick, *Myth*, 178.

[32] *The Metaphor of God Incarnate* (London: SCM Press, 1993), 104; my emphasis.

spoke literally. But it should immediately be responded that this conclusion by no means follows: it is often by the means of a freshly minted metaphor that one can make the most intense claims on the real. As Soskice well illustrates, the coinage of new and striking metaphor ('speaking of one thing in terms suggestive of another')[33] has more often sprung in Christian tradition from a realist commitment, especially amongst mystical theologians,[34] than from a coyness such as Hick's about realist claims. Again, as we suggested with Norris, but here more explicitly, it is Hick's post-Kantian appeal to the *noumenal* that dictates his understanding of how 'metaphor' should remove us from reality rather than engaging it.[35]

So it seems that Hick has created a confusion here. He is right to imply that 'metaphorical' speech has an *oddness* characterized by a novel conjunction of ideas. But the oddness of the idea of 'incarnation' (or for that matter of the 'Definition' of Chalcedon) cannot be assumed to be the same oddness as that of the metaphorical *trope*; nor can its oddness be alleviated simply by asserting that 'God/man' talk is *outré* and empty, or that it is time we acknowledged religious claims other than the Christian one.[36] Indeed the whole attempt to dub 'incarnation' 'metaphorical' *tout court* at this second-order level looks misguided when compared with a close attempt to discern, in the terms of the 'Definition' of Chalcedon, how particular terms and words are being used. There, in comparison, it is surprisingly hard to clarify whether the key terms *physis* and *hypostasis* are being applied 'literally', 'metaphorically', or 'analogically', since these are 'substance' words with a bewildering range of uses elsewhere and, as we have already underlined, a non-specified use in this case.[37]

If the oddness of the claims of the 'Definition' is not the oddness of metaphor, then is it perhaps more truly the oddness of 'paradox' or 'riddle'? It is worth considering these two alternatives before passing on to our final (and very different) contemporary assessment of how to read Chalcedon.

In a broadly accepted sense, the Chalcedonian 'Definition' does

---

[33] J. M. Soskice, *Metaphor and Religious Language* (Oxford: Oxford University Press, 1985), 54.

[34] Ibid. 152.

[35] See esp. J. Hick, *The Interpretation of Religion* (New Haven: Yale University Press, 1989).

[36] Hick, *Myth*, 177–84.

[37] See G. C. Stead, *Divine Substance* (Oxford: Clarendon Press, 1977), who charts the different evocation of 'substance' terms in the formative patristic period.

indeed involve a 'paradoxical' claim—the claim that 'God' and 'man', normally perceived as strikingly different in defining characteristics, find in Christ a unique intersection. Here 'paradox' simply means 'contrary to expectation', and the mind is led on from there to eke out an explanation that can satisfy both logic and tradition. However, we should be careful to distinguish this meaning of 'paradox' from a tighter one in which not merely something 'contrary to expectation' is suggested, but something actually 'self-contradictory' or incoherent. In this latter sense, of course, Hick could most happily apply the term 'paradoxical' to the incarnation (and indeed less confusingly in my view than his chosen epithet 'metaphorical'); but it has to be said that, again, the 'Definition' of Chalcedon does not tell us, in and of itself, how to read its 'paradoxical' claim. The overwhelming impression from following the debate leading up to Chalcedon, however, as well as that which succeeds it, is that the 'paradoxical' nature of the incarnation in the first sense is embraced (with greater or lesser degrees of enthusiasm), but that 'paradox' in the latter sense is vigorously warded off.[38] The 'Definition' is propelled by an assumption of coherence, not by a glorying in incoherence.

The question of whether Chalcedon may be read as a 'riddle' is perhaps even more subtle. A playful case could be made, I think, for reading the famous negative epithets ('without confusion', 'without change', 'without division', 'without separation') in the form of a riddle. (*Q*: What is 'without confusion', 'without change', 'without division', 'without separation'? *A*: Two natures in one person, Christ.) But this is not just any riddle, for riddles can take various forms. Some, notoriously the Mad Hatter's ('Why is a raven like a writing desk?') have no answer; whereas others play on words to indicate a disjunction. (*Q*: What is the difference between God and Ninian Smart? *A*: God is everywhere, but Ninian is everywhere but *here*.) The sort encoded in the 'Definition', by contrast, is more truly the kind analysed by Wittgenstein in relation to a mathematical problem whose solution one cannot yet guess, but where one drives between the horns of a dilemma:

[it is] like the problem set by the king in the fairy tale who told the princess to come neither naked nor dressed, and she came wearing fishnet. That

---

[38] See Grillmeier, 'Vorbereitung', 199–202, but also the discussion of paradox in O'Collins's and Daley's chapters of this book.

might have been called not naked and not dressed either. He didn't really know what he wanted her to do, but when she came thus he was forced to accept it. It was of the form 'Do something which I shall be inclined to call neither naked or dressed'. It's the same with the mathematical problem. 'Do something which I shall be inclined to accept as a solution, though I don't know now what it will be like.'[39]

In a justly famous article applying this understanding of 'riddle' to Anselm's ontological argument, Cora Diamond clarifies this particular use of riddle thus: 'that reality may surprise us, not only by showing us what *is* the case, when we had not suspected it was, but also by showing us something beyond what we had ever taken to be possible, beyond anything we had thought of at all.'[40] By pointing disjunctively to what is *not* the case, one moves through to a novel level of perception: 'We express and do not express a thing, see and do not see a thing, when we express it in riddles . . .'[41] Now this seems to me a particularly apt way of describing what is going on in the Chalcedonian 'Definition' in the ruling out of disjunctive possibilities: a new, and surprising, reality which we could not previously have thought possible is being gestured towards, in this case the reality of Christ's *hypostasis*. And this seems to me infinitely more illuminating of the 'Definition's intent than a focus on metaphor. To this point we shall return in our last section, when we consider the status of the 'Definition' as an 'apophatic' document. Let us now look at the other end of the spectrum of contemporary debate and briefly chart the responses to Hick amongst the 'literalists'.

III INCARNATION LANGUAGE AS 'LITERAL'

The tactics of both Norris and Hick, as we have seen, involve a loosening of the relation between language and reality in the case of the Chalcedonian 'Definition': their distrust of 'literalism' (Hick) or 'reification' (Norris) has roots in a post-Kantian withdrawal from

---

[39] Margaret MacDonald's notes to Wittgenstein's lectures in 1935, cited in C. Diamond, 'Riddles and Anselm's Riddle', *The Realistic Spirit* (Cambridge, Mass.: MIT Press, 1991), 267.

[40] Ibid. 279–80.

[41] Ibid. 288. I do not see this reading of the negative epithets as necessarily in competition with the careful study of the terms in L. Abramowski, '$\Sigma YNA\Phi EIA$ und $A\Sigma Y\Gamma XYTO\Sigma$ $EN\Omega\Sigma I\Sigma$ als Bezeichnung für trinitarische und christologische Einheit', in *Drei christologische Untersuchungen* (Berlin: de Gruyter, 1981), 63–109.

'things-in-themselves'. In stark contrast, the analytic philosophers of religion who of late have leapt to the defence of incarnationalism in general, and Chalcedonianism in particular, affirm both the possibility, and indeed the necessity, of asserting the 'literal' truth of the incarnation. It is worth now enquiring a little more closely what they mean by this.

Let us take here two celebrated instances of this embracing of the claim of 'literalism' and then probe a little further what it implies for the philosophers concerned. Thomas V. Morris, first, opens his book on *The Logic of God Incarnate* thus: 'The core claim of the traditional Christian doctrine of the Incarnation, the fundamental and most distinctive tenet of the Christian faith as defined at the Council of Chalcedon (A.D. 451), is the claim that the person who was and is Jesus of Nazareth is one and the same individual as God the Son, the Second Person of the divine Trinity—a *literal* statement of absolute, numerical identity.'[42] Or again, David Brown, in his *The Divine Trinity* stresses that Jesus was 'in some *literal* sense God', and according to the 'Chalcedonian model' of that view, 'simultaneously God and man'.[43] But what exactly is meant in each of these cases by 'literal'? Both authors are explicitly writing to rebuff the views of the contributors to *The Myth of God Incarnate*, and in particular replying to Hick's charge of the incoherence of the doctrine of the incarnation in that volume: they obviously, and minimally, aspire to demonstrate the doctrine's logical *coherence*. But this is probably not the only, or even the prime evocation of 'literal' for them. It is worth clarifying further, with the aid of some thoughts from an essay of William Alston,[44] what *range* of meanings can be applied to the term 'literal', because this makes a great difference to how we assess the supposedly 'literal' status of the language of the Chalcedonian 'Definition'.

In the course of an illuminating discussion on the nature of metaphor in *Divine Nature and Human Language*, Alston insists that the primary and obvious meaning of the term 'literal' is that when I speak thus I mean what I say to be *true*.[45] The trouble, however, is that the word 'literal' has become, as Alston puts it, 'adventitiously'

---

[42] T. V. Morris, *The Logic of God Incarnate* (Ithaca, NY: Cornell University Press, 1986), 17–18, my emphasis.
[43] D. Brown, *The Divine Trinity* (London: Duckworth, 1985), 102–3; my emphasis.
[44] W. Alston, *Divine Nature and Human Language* (Ithaca, NY: Cornell University Press, 1989), 17–38.
[45] Ibid. 21.

associated with other synonyms, and herein lies the trouble and
confusion for theology when wondering what it means by 'literal'
statements about God (or Christ). These 'adventitious associations'
with the word 'literal' include: 'precise', 'univocal', 'specific', 'factual', 'empirical', and 'ordinary'.[46]

Now this list of Alston's is extraordinarily illuminating for pin-
pointing potential areas of conflict and misunderstanding between
parties in the debate about Chalcedon. For instance, Morris and
Brown (unlike Norris, it seems, and certainly unlike Hick) want to
insist that Chalcedon 'literally' makes a true, ontological statement
about Christ's person. This I take to be their prime meaning of 'literal'
in the statements by them I have quoted. Therein lies their main
bulwark against the 'recession from reality' school, and therein too
lies, as we have already argued, their clear continuity with the
intentions of the Fathers of Chalcedon. But when it comes to the
other 'associations' with literalness which they may be harbouring,
our analytic defenders of Chalcedon may prove not always to have
the same set of intentions as the writers of the Chalcedonian
'Definition'. For instance, whereas Morris's and Brown's re-evalu-
ation of the Chalcedonian heritage clearly reflects their primary
commitment, as those skilled in analytic philosophy, to the goals of
'precision' and 'specification', we may question whether the sort of
precision they have in mind is the *same* as that of the bishops who
penned the 'Definition'. In Morris's case, for instance (as in different
ways in Brown and Swinburne[47]), the Chalcedonian heritage is
subjected to an analytic going-over that leaves far less room for
equivocation or mystery than the 'Definition' itself.[48] It is worth
reminding ourselves here that the group of bishops initially charged
with producing a formula at the Council were *resistant* to the
Emperor's pressure for greater precision, a point to which we shall
want to return in our conclusions.[49] However, the question of
'literalness' when glossed as 'univocity' raises another, different,
set of issues which we have already touched upon earlier: the uses of
physis and *hypostasis* are not obviously or clearly the same as in other

---

[46] Alston, *Divine Nature and Human Language*, 25.

[47] For Richard Swinburne's contribution see his *The Christian God* (Oxford: Oxford
University Press, 1994), 192–238. It is worth underscoring that Swinburne avoids
talking about 'literal' truth in the manner of T. Morris and Brown.

[48] See Brown, *Divine Trinity*, chs. 5, 6, esp. 224–8; Morris, *Logic of God*, esp. chs. 1,
3, 4, 6; Swinburne, *Christian God*, ch. 9.

[49] See Slusser, 'Issues in the Definition', 63–5.

uses of those terms elsewhere ('univocal' with them), since that very matter remains unexplained in the 'Definition'. Although it appears that the term *physis* is to be used univocally *within* the 'Definition' for both the human and the divine, even that is not actually prescribed. (A stronger case for the 'univocity' of the term *prosopon* with ordinary uses as applied to humans could I think however be made[50].) As for 'empirical' or 'factual (historical)' as other glosses of 'literal', here we have instances where the *modern* concerns of the analytic school of philosophy of religion diverge strongly from what we know of the participants in the fifth-century debate, since it was clearly not their interest, as it is the almost obsessive interest of the analytic philosophers of religion, to establish that the empirical evidence about the 'historical Jesus' could rationally be construed as either demanding, or allowing, the ascription of divinity. (Brown's and Swinburne's projects, however, are centrally concerned with this issue[51].) Rather, the Chalcedonian 'Definition'—as Nicaea and Constantinople before it—*takes for granted* the achievement of salvation in Christ and then asks what must be the case about that Christ if such salvation is possible. In that sense Chalcedon is much more like a 'transcendental argument' (to use an equally anachronistic Kantian term) for Christ's divinity and humanity than an empiricist investigation of the evidences of Jesus' historical life.

In sum, the interest in 'literalness' in the analytic defence of incarnationalism in general (and of Chalcedon in particular) has at its core an insistence on the ontological reality of what it describes that is fully in line with Chalcedon's intentions. But in other matters which it may associate with the ascription of 'literalness', it goes beyond, or goes even against, what the fifth-century debate appears to have enshrined as assumptions or goals.

IV CONCLUSIONS: CHALCEDON AS 'HOROS'

Let us now in closing gather the pieces we have assembled from an engagement with these three contemporary Western approaches to Chalcedon, and see if we can find our way through to a fourth

---

[50] See my discussion of the use of *prosopon* in the trinitarian context in ' "Persons" in the "Social" Doctrine of the Trinity', in S. Davis, D. Kendall, and G. O'Collins (eds.) *The Trinity* (Oxford: Oxford University Press, 1999), 123–44, at 139–40.

[51] See Brown, *Divine Trinity*, 101–58; Swinburne, *Christian God*, 216–38.

position that learns from them all but avoids the pitfalls we have highlighted along the way.

From our discussion of Norris, first, we gleaned the conclusion that a 'regulatory' reading of Chalcedon's terms is correct so long as we understand (*a*) that the terms themselves are not 'defined' in a precise way, and (*b*) that this approach in no way implies lack of ontological commitment (as Norris appeared to endorse). From our treatment of Hick, second, we concluded that his attempt to dub the language of incarnation 'metaphorical' is misleading, and distinctly out of the line with the original intentions of Chalcedon; but applying the categories of 'paradox' (without the stronger evocation of logical incoherence) and 'riddle' (in a particular sense we clarified) get us nearer the heart of Chalcedon's intents. From our brief analysis of Chalcedon's treatment at the hands of analytic philosophers of religion, finally, we discerned a commendable interest in defending the propositional dimensions of Chalcedon's claims, but also a danger of smuggling in under the rubric of 'literalness' a number of issues anachronistic from the perspective of Chalcedon itself.

Taking these insights forward, let us now consider the crucial systematic issue touched on earlier, namely, whether and in what sense the 'Definition' speaks 'kataphatically' or 'apophatically', and where the line is drawn between the two. Here we shall, perforce, have finally to clarify what *genre* of text this is, and what we may appropriately expect of it.

An important clue here, I suggest, is provided by the very word used in Greek for the 'Definition', that is, *horos*, or 'horizon'. The evocations are mostly not the same ones that are set off by the English 'Definition'—that is, semantic clarity, linguistic precision, or careful circumscription (and we have already seen how Chalcedon apparently fails to deliver all of these). Rather, as a survey of the uses of *horos* in Lampe's *Patristic Lexicon* displays, meanings of *horos* in Greek range from 'boundary', 'horizon', and 'limit', to 'standard', 'pattern', and (monastic) 'rule'. The word can also be used directly of Christ with the meaning of 'expression' (Christ as the '*horos* and *logos* of God', in Gregory of Nazianzen[52].) Thus, when it is also used of liturgical or dogmatic 'decisions' and 'decrees', it brings with it different semantic baggage from our English equivalent. In a

---

[52] *Theological Orations*, 38. 13.

remarkably revealing passage using a cognate term, Plotinus (*Enneads* 5. 5 [32]. 8) speaks of the Intellect's waiting on contemplation of the One as equivalent to watching the 'horizon' for the rising sun, but then finding that limit dissolved away as the One manifests itself as a light that will not be so confined.[53] In a much later passage from John Climacus (*The Ladder*, Step 28), a similar thought is entertained in the context of mental prayer:

Enclose your mind within the words of prayer . . . the mind, after all, is naturally unstable, but God can give all things firm endurance . . . he who sets a *boundary* to the sea of the mind will come to you during prayer and will say. 'Thus far you shall come, and no farther' (Job 38. 11). The spirit, though, cannot be bound, and where the Creator of Spirit is found, all things yield to him.[54]

Taking this semantic background into account, and remembering again that the assembled bishops at Chalcedon resisted at one point the Emperor's demand for greater 'precision', we may perhaps begin to see the true intentions of the document. It does not, that is, intend to provide a full systematic account of Christology, and even less a complete and precise metaphysics of Christ's makeup. Rather, it sets a 'boundary' on what can, and cannot, be said, by first ruling out three aberrant interpretations of Christ (Apollinarianism, Eutychianism, and extreme Nestorianism), second, providing an abstract rule of language (*physis* and *hypostasis*) for distinguishing duality and unity in Christ, and, third, presenting a 'riddle' of negatives by means of which a greater (though undefined) reality may be intimated. At the same time, it recapitulates and assumes (a point often forgotten in considering the *horos* in abstraction from the rest of the *Acta*) the acts of salvation detailed in Nicaea and Constantinople; and then it leaves us at that 'boundary', understood as the place now to which those salvific acts must be brought to avoid doctrinal error, but without any supposition that this linguistic regulation thereby *explains* or *grasps* the reality towards which it points. In this, rather particular sense, it is an 'apophatic' document.

What category or *genre* of text, then, is the Chalcedonian 'Definition'? If my interpretation is right, it is clearly regulatory and binding as a 'pattern' endorsed by an ecumenical council: reflections

---

[53] Trans. A. H. Armstrong, Loeb Classical Library (Cambridge, Mass.: Harvard University Press, 1984), v. 179–80.

[54] John Climacus, *The Ladder of Divine Assent*, Classics of Western Spirituality (London: SPCK, 1982), 276 (slightly corrected).

on Christ's person must henceforth pass through this 'grid', as I put it at the outset. But it would be a mistake to expect it to deliver more than it can in its own terms, given its 'apophatic' dimension. As Rahner puts it famously, it is 'not end but beginning', or (more properly) 'end *and* beginning'.[55] For the East, in any case, it has always represented one—albeit crucial—moment in a process of christological clarification that continued long afterwards, through the debates of the sixth and seventh centuries and up to and including the iconographical decrees of Nicaea II. From this per- spective even Rahner is not quite modest enough in his ascription: Chalcedon is strictly speaking *neither* end *nor* beginning, but rather a transitional (though still normative) 'horizon' to which we con- stantly return, but with equally constant forays backwards and forwards. Whereas the West has tended to 'stop' at Chalcedon, and to expect of it something more metaphysically and substantially precise than it can yield, the East has in contrast tended to turn its phrases into liturgical prayer (especially in the *Theotokia* for Satur- day Great Vespers[56]), to gesture with it in worship beyond the 'limit' that it sets. Endless ecumenical misunderstanding, of course, has resulted from this divergence.[57]

It is worth enumerating, finally and in closing, some of the vital christological issues that Chalcedon *per se* cannot and does not solve. Not only is this undertaking suitably chastening, it also invites the last ecumenical reflection: is Chalcedon's 'limit' regrettable or laudable?

Thus: (1) Chalcedon does not tell us in what the divine and human 'natures' consist; (2) it does not tell us what *hypostasis* means when applied to Christ; (3) it does not tell us how *hypostasis* and *physeis* are related, or how the *physeis* relate to one another (the problem of the *communicatio idiomatum*); (4) it does not tell us how many wills Christ has; (5) it does not tell us that the *hypostasis* is identical with the pre-existent Logos; (6) it does not tell us what happens to the *physeis* at Christ's death and in his resurrection; (7) it does not tell us whether the meaning of *hypostasis* in this christo- logical context is different, or the same, from the meaning in the

---

[55] Rahner, 'Current Problems in Theology', 149, 150.

[56] The *Theotokia* of the Saturday Great Vespers, for instance, uses language from Chalcedon to laud the Virgin.

[57] For a recent assessment of the significance of Chalcedon for ecumenical interchange, see D. Wendebourg, 'Chalcedon in Ecumenical Discourse', *Pro Ecclesia*, 7 (1998), 307–32.

trinitarian context; (8) it does not tell us whether the risen Christ is male.

If these are some of the 'limits' of Chalcedon, does this 'look like carelessness', or is it a *felix culpa*? The answer, of course, will depend on what *genre* of text one is hoping, or expecting, it to be. All the questions I have just enumerated were bound to become pressing at some point, and to find more-or-less official responses. Such attempts at greater precision are theologically inevitable, and indeed laudable as speculative endeavours. But if my analysis in the foregoing has been at all convincing, then we shall at least have shown that expecting Chalcedon to answer these further questions is a mistaken hope of some seriousness: there are many issues that Chalcedon cannot 'solve'. Finally, then, the intriguing question that presses ecclesiologically for today is this: should *Chalcedon* be the primary bar of ecumenical engagement and discernment in christological matters? If so, its 'apophatic' horizon (at least as I have propounded it) could shelter many more alternatives than later official clarifications, East and West, would appear to allow; and its character as *horos* could perhaps find greater understanding in circles of the West, a development that would chasten expectations in some analytic philosophical quarters, but (I suspect) release spiritual and theological creativity in others.[58]

[58] I am most grateful to Charles Hefling of Boston College, and especially to Nicholas Constas of Harvard Divinity School, for helpful discussion and bibliographical suggestions whilst I was writing this chapter; and to Brian Daley, SJ, Joseph Lienhard, SJ, Daniel Howard-Snyder, Richard Swinburne, and Anthony Baxter for critical comments on the conference version of it, which have resulted in some ameliorations and changes for the final version.

8

Nature and the 'Mode of Union': Late Patristic Models for the Personal Unity of Christ

BRIAN E. DALEY, SJ

One of the older colleges of the University of Oxford—the one which still, more than six centuries after its foundation, characteristically goes by the name of 'New College'—bears on its coat of arms a medieval English proverb which apparently was the motto of its fourteenth-century founder, Bishop William of Wykeham: 'Maners Makyth Man'. The bishop was surely not trying to remind future generations of undergraduates of the importance of writing thank-you notes promptly and passing the port to the left; 'manners', in this somewhat archaic usage, clearly means something closer to 'virtue' or 'good character', something akin to the Latin word *mores*—in the words of the *Oxford English Dictionary*, 'a person's habitual behaviour or conduct, especially in reference to its moral aspect'. It may not be too much of an exaggeration to say that behind this phrase lies a whole anthropology, a whole metaphysics of what it is to be human: as free and intelligent beings, we are not simply the products of instinct or of the mechanical forces of our nature, not fully definable by dispassionate observation or philosophical analysis; we are formed, made human, made *persons* in the fullest sense by our choices and habits, and by the patterns in our relationships to others that define moral character.

We have gathered in this 'summit' conference to reflect on the significance, for the church and for human thought, of the Christian doctrine of the incarnation: the fundamental conviction of Christian faith that in Jesus of Nazareth God's eternal, personally substantial

Parts of this chapter, in earlier versions, were given as a paper to the North American Patristic Society (Chicago: May, 1996), and to the Thirteenth International Conference on Patristic Studies (Oxford; August, 1999).

Word 'became flesh and dwelt among us, and we have seen his glory. . .' (John 1: 14). What I propose to consider here, as a student of early Christian theology, is thus not so much anthropology as Christology. More specifically, I want to call attention to a continuing pattern of reflection on the ontological makeup and identity of Christ, which developed in Greek theology during the four centuries after the Council of Nicaea and which seems to have rested on the assumption that the concrete being of any individual subject—what was called the *hypostasis*—is primarily to be defined not by nouns and verbs, but by adverbs: not in terms of the universal concept that identified its substance, in other words, or of the range of possible functioning that was called its 'nature', but rather in terms of its 'manner' or 'mode' of being, of the *way* it realized its natural potential, the source and style of its origin, the web of relationships it formed with others, and all the other particular, historically contingent characteristics that identified that individual unmistakably as itself. My point here is that as the mainstream Greek Fathers, from the Cappadocians to John of Damascus, came more and more to describe the mystery of the person of Christ, at once divine and human, in the same terms they had come to use to describe the three persons who comprise the divine Mystery itself—οὐσία and φύσις, ὑπόστασις and πρόσωπον—they came to realize that the characteristics that were seen to be the key for distinguishing the persons of the Trinity—not their nature as God, but their origin, their 'mode of existing' or of coming-to-be (τρόπος τῆς ὑπάξεως), their relationships to each other—could also usefully be employed for giving an account of the uniqueness and inner coherence of the person of Christ, in the 'mode of union' by which the reality of God and the human reality shaped, expressed and conditioned each other in the life and work, the concrete existence, of Jesus.

Admittedly, the technicalities of the ancient vocabulary for the Mystery of God's being, and of God's presence in the world through Jesus, can strike us today as impenetrably arcane. Still, a closer look at the formation and use of this ancient terminology can help us understand better, I think, that what these terms were meant to convey about Christ was less rigidly abstract, less schematic, and less far removed from our own experience of historical existence than is often supposed. To put this chapter's thesis simply: for at least a central strand in Greek patristic tradition, just as *who* Father, Son, and Holy Spirit are is grounded in *how* they take their origin

from each other and are related to each other, so it was the 'how' of
Jesus—how he came to be, how he acted—that revealed and even
grounded the reality of who he was and what he was, and that
serves for us as an efficacious model of how we are called to live and
what we are called to be. Let us try, in broad strokes at least, to
sketch out the meaning and development of this family of words and
phrases that came to assume a growing importance in the development of classical Christology.

I   Leontius and the Mode of Union

'The mode of union', writes Leontius of Byzantium about the person
of Christ, shortly before the middle of the sixth century, 'rather than
the intelligible structure (λόγος) of nature, contains the great
mystery of our religion.'[1] Here and in several other places throughout his six extant controversial treatises, Leontius insists that 'union
and nature are not the same thing',[2] and says that he will focus his
own reflections not on the two natures or substances themselves,
which Christian faith confesses to be joined in Christ, but on their
'mode of union' (τρόπος τῆς ἑνώσεως).[3] Although his reflections on
that union may seem, to a modern reader, to be immersed to the
point of unintelligibility in technical detail, Leontius himself is
passionately convinced that this is one of the crucial, overarching
issues in the christological disputes of his day. 'What is under
discussion', he writes, 'is not simply a matter of phrasing, but the
modality of the whole mystery revealed in Christ: a mode of union,
namely, that has come into being in a substantial, and not simply a
relational, way, so that the Word is, within a complete humanity,
what "the inner person", in the Apostle's words, is in each of us—
co-existing, and contributing after the union to the definition of the
whole person . . .'[4] The chief issue in Christology during that

---

[1] *Epilyseis* (henceforth *Epil*), 8 (PG 86. 1940B). In citing the works of Leontius here,
I have used my own critical edition, which I hope will be published soon in the *Corpus
Christianorum, Series Graeca*; I will give column-references, however, to the edition of
Angelo Mai—currently the only text available—in the Patrologia Graeca, vol. 86.

[2] *Contra Nestorianos et Eutychianos* (henceforth *CNE*). 5 (1293A): 'That which is
said to be one by union is not the same as that which is one by nature . . .';
Epaporemata (henceforth *Epap*), 26 (1909 D): '. . . union and nature are not the same'.

[3] *CNE* 7 (1297C); *Epil* 8 (1940A, D; 1944D); *Deprehensio et Triumphus super
Nestorianos* (henceforth *DTN*), 42 (1380C).

[4] *DTN* 42 (1380BC).

embattled century after Chalcedon, in other words, is for Leontius not the nature of the God who has appeared in Christ, nor the natural constitution of the human person as *capax Dei*, but the manner in which those utterly distinct realities, joined in the one we confess to be Son of God, work together to form a single, concrete, contingent, historical individual: 'Let us, then,' he writes, 'investigate the mode of union and the product (ἀποτέλεσμα) of it'.[5]

Leontius' method of christological inquiry, reduced to its elements, is to begin not with a consideration of divinity in itself and humanity in itself, or with the related problem of how divine being and divine generation might differ from their human analogues; rather, he insists, we must begin from the concrete, historical Christ, the product of the incarnation, and ask how one can conceive the 'mode of union' that brings to reality Christ's complex existence as a person.[6] In Leontius' view, the Chalcedonian formulation of the person of Christ as one hypostasis, one concrete individual, existing simultaneously in two real and fully operational natures, is the only way to avoid 'the way of division' and 'the way of confusion', and to follow instead 'the middle [and therefore correct!] way. . . [of] unconfused and inseparable union'.[7] 'This kind of union', he remarks a few lines later—in an unacknowledged paraphrase of a remark of Gregory Nazianzen's on the Trinity—'is more unitive than one of completely divided things, yet richer than one of completely confused things; it does not make the elements united completely the same as each other, nor completely different.'[8] In the very difference of the elements united in Christ, in fact—in the paradoxical and unique heterogeneity of Christ's single person—Leontius sees something central to the saving mystery of the incarnation; if there were not 'something incommunicable in the union, rooted in the very greatness of the divine nature', he writes, 'there would be no condescension in the divine love for humanity, but only a natural joining of what is lofty with what is humble'.[9] To be good

[5] *Epil* 8 (1940C). For a similar insistence that readers focus their attention not simply on the language used for Christ, but on Christ as a 'thing' (πρᾶγμα), see his anti-Chalcedonian contemporary, John Philoponus, *Diaetetes*, frag. 2, in Nicetas Choniates, *Panoplia Dogmatica* (PG 140. 56B).

[6] See especially *Epil* 8 (1940C, 1941B).

[7] *Epil* 8 (1941A).

[8] *Epil* 8 (1941B); cf. Gregory Nazianzen, *Or.* 34. 8 (SC cccviii, 213, lines 14–15): the reality of God 'is more united than beings which are totally divisible, but richer than things that are completely unitary'.

[9] *Epil* 8 (1940A). An ancient scholion in a 10th-cent. MS of Leontius' works at this

news, in other words, our language and our thoughts about Christ must convey the miraculous character, the wonder, of the way God has chosen to meet us in human terms.

Leontius' own approach to explaining the Chalcedonian paradox is to develop more fully the Cappadocian terminology of substance and individual, which had been designed to facilitate discourse on the Trinity: substance (οὐσία) and nature (φύσις) refer, he insists, to the being and operation of things at their universal or general level, to the intelligible perfection or form in which many individuals normally participate; 'hypostasis' and 'person' (πρόσωπον) refer to the being and perceptible role of a concrete, historically identifiable individual, who participates—in order to be intelligible and real—in one or more universal substances, but who is marked off as a particular being, made eligible for a proper name, by his or her (or even its) unique pattern of accidental characteristics.[10] In a painstaking exposition of the interlocking relationships that bind concrete individuals together within a generic substance, or link generic substances within a single individual, Leontius recasts the traditional use of the soul–body relationship in the human person as an analogy for the incarnation of the Word by suggesting, in effect, that *every* human being is a remarkable 'hypostatic union' of two irreducibly different natures,[11] joined by an act of divine power into a single historic, existential unity that allows its different levels of being to remain intact and operative in themselves.[12]

Leontius draws help here from the Neoplatonic understanding of

point underscores the importance accorded to this assertion by Byzantine scholars: 'We speak the truth when we say that the mode of union is not realized by the principle of natural necessity, but solely by the principle of [God's] love for humanity.' The fact that neither the nature of God nor the nature of humanity, taken in themselves, can give us a satisfactory explanation of how we are saved in Christ confirms the fact that it is not something 'natural', but is a free gift of divine love.

[10] See especially *CNE* 1 (1280A) In the first seven testimonia of the florilegium appended to this treatise, Leontius offers as his sources various well-known passages of the works of Basil and Gregory Nazianzen that defined these terms for use in talking about God from a Nicene perspective.

[11] See especially *CNE* 4 (1285C–9B); *CNE* 7 (1301C–4C). It is interesting, if puzzling, to note that Leontius generally avoids the term 'hypostatic union' (ἕνωσις καθ' ὑπόστασιν, ἕνωσις ὑποστατική), perhaps simply because it was favoured by the anti-Chalcedonian and 'neo-Chalcedonian' parties of his time. He only uses the phrase twice on his own (*CNE*, preface to florilegium [1308C]; *Contra Aphthartodocetas* (henceforth *CA*; 1384 D)), and prefers to speak of the union in Christ as 'substantial (οὐσιωδής)' or a 'union according to substance (ἕνωσις κατ' οὐσίαν)': see, for example, *CNE* 7 (1300A)).

[12] *Epil* 8 (1940A).

the Aristotelian category of relationship (τὸ πρός τι; σχέσις), especially as it is used by Porphyry and Nemesius of Emesa to explain how a soul can be dynamically and ontologically united with a body without loss of its own transcendence.[13] In doing so, he takes pains to insist that the union of natures or substances in Christ is something 'substantial' and not merely 'relational',[14] even though it is itself, ultimately, an ontological relationship between substances that are complete in themselves and incapable of confusion. The concept of *relationship* had generally been understood, in the Aristotelian tradition, as the most extrinsic kind of accident,[15] and was doubtless still freighted with overtones of metaphysical 'distance' in the minds of many, despite the efforts of some of the Neoplatonists to see in certain kinds of relationship, at least, a real sharing of being.[16] For Leontius, the 'substantial relationship' of union between the divine Logos and the human nature of Christ is precisely *not* a 'relationship that divides', like a union simply in grace or in will, or a mere expression of divine benevolence towards the man Jesus.[17] Hence the crucial importance for him, when explaining the Chalcedonian conception of Christ, to stress that a union of two different substances in one hypostasis, although not 'natural' in that it is not automatically produced by those substances' natural functioning, is nevertheless a union of real ontological value, resulting in a real personal identity. In such a composite hypostasis, the two separate

---

[13] See my article, 'A Richer Union: Leontius of Byzantium and the Relationship of Human and Divine in Christ', *Studia Patristica*, 24 (1992), 239–65.

[14] *Epil* 4 (1925C); *Epil* 8 (1940D). At the end of *CA* (1353A), he refers to the 'organic (συμφυσής) union' of the Word with the full humanity of Jesus; in *DTN* 42 (1380D); he insists that 'the Fathers' taught that the union 'came to be in a substantial way, but you [the Nestorians] speak of one that is relative and moral (σχετικὴν καὶ γνωμικήν)'.

[15] See Aristotle, *Categories* 7; Alexander of Aphrodisias, *Quaestiones naturales et morales*, 2. 9 (ed. I. Bruns, *Supplementum Aristotelicum*, ii/7 (Berlin: G. Reimer,1892), 54. 20–31); Olympiodorus, *In Cat.* 4: *Commentatores in Aristotelem Graeci* (henceforth *CAG*), xii/1 (ed. A. Busse; Berlin, G. Reimer, 1902) 54. 4–26; Elias, *Prolegomena* 11: *CAG* xviii/1 (ed. A. Busse; Berlin: G. Reimer, 1900), 29. 8–18.

[16] See esp. Simplicius, *In Cat.* 7: *CAG* viii (ed. C. Kalbfleisch: Berlin, G. Reimer,1907), 169. 1–173. 32. See also Plotinus, *Ennead* 6. 1. 6. Perhaps with this shift of meaning in mind, the Cappadocians were prepared to speak of the defining relationships between Father, Son, and Holy Spirit as σχέσεις, too: e.g. Gregory of Nazianzus, *Or.* 29. 16; *Or.* 31. 9; Gregory of Nyssa, *Ref. Conf. Eun.* (Werner Jaeger *et al.*, *Gregorii Nysseni Opera*, 10 vols. (Leiden: Brill, 1960–90), ii. 319. 1–3, hereafter *GNO*); cf. Ps.-Athanasius, *Dialogue on the Trinity*, 1. 25 (PG 28. 1156 A). For a brief discussion, see F. Heinzer, *Gottes Sohn als Mensch*, Paradosis 26 (Fribourg: Universitätsverlag, 1980), 47–8.

[17] *CNE* 7 (1305C).

natures 'receive/together, in one another, a common share in being (κοινωνία τοῦ εἶναι)',[18] since the hypostasis is itself created by 'their mutually inherent life' (ἡ ἀλληλοῦχος ζωή).[19] The twenty-sixth of Leontius' *Hypothetical Propositions* (*Epaporemata*) against Severus of Antioch and other early sixth-century opponents of Chalcedon puts his conception of the distinctive ontological structure of composite hypostases clearly:

> If all consubstantial beings (ὁμοούσια) are joined together by the category of nature, and therefore are called 'one nature,' while beings of different substance (ἑτερούσια) are habitually joined by union and *not* by nature, and if union and nature are not the same, then the product coming from both is not the same. But if what nature joins together is called 'one nature,' what is joined together by union will be said to be one in hypostasis, but *not* in nature and substance.[20]

In the person of Christ, in other words, as in all composite hypostases, it is precisely 'union, not nature', that serves as the foundation of the subject's inner identity.

II Mode of Union: Its Philosophical and Theological Background

Given the emphasis this sixth-century defender of the Chalcedonian definition places, then, on the distinction between union and nature and the importance of the 'mode of union' in the ontology of the person and in the constitution of Christ, as well as the continuing use of this phrase by such later orthodox figures as Maximus Confessor and John of Damascus, it seems reasonable to ask what background and context, if any, such language might have in earlier philo-

---

[18] *CNE* 1 (1280A); cf. *Epil* 1. (1917D). Late antique philosophers occasionally used κοινωνία, 'participation', 'communion', as a synonym for ἕνωσις: see Simplicius, *In Cat.* 7: *CAG* 8 (ed. Kalbfleisch), 169. 19–20; John Philoponus, *In De Anima*: *CAG* 15 (ed. M. Hayduck: Berlin: G. Reimer, 1897), 471. 28–9. Origen, however, in his *Contra Celsum*, contrasts the terms, saying that the soul of Christ was united to God 'not just by κοινωνία, but by union (ἕνωσις) and intermingling (ἀνάκρασις)': 3. 41 (SC cxxxvi, 96. 9).

[19] *CNE* 4 (1288D). Neoplatonic philosophers often used the word ἀλληλουχία, 'mutual inherence', to express intense organic unity. See Iamblichus, *In Nicomachi arithmeticam introductionem* (ed. Klein; Leipzig: Teubner, 1975), 7. 6–7; *Theologoumena arithmeticae* (ed. de Falco; Leipzig: Teubner, 1922), 20. 16–17; Dexippus, *In Aristotelis Categorias commentarium*: *CAG* iv/2 (ed. A. Busse; Berlin; G. Reimer, 1888), 66. 25–6; Simplicius, *In Cat.* viii: *CAG* viii (ed. Kalbfleisch) 127. 19–21.

[20] *Epap* 26 (1909D).

sophical and theological discussion. *Tropos*, which at its most general simply means 'manner', 'mode', or 'way', is used by Aristotle and Stoic writers to refer to the 'forms' or figures of syllogisms, and more generally to indicate the various possible types of demonstration.[21] Aristotle also uses the word more widely, to refer to the 'circumstances' of the natural behaviour of living things, 'the how and where and when',[22] as well as to character or habit, 'the condition of a soul brought about by custom'.[23] It seems to have been in the works of the fifth- and sixth-century Athenian Neoplatonist Damascius that *tropos* first acquired a more ontological shading for the philosophers, signifying the attributes of the ultimate principles of being or transcendent hypostases, such as the 'mode' of eternity or even the 'mode' of substance itself.[24] *Henōsis* or *union* was also not a term of major metaphysical or anthropological interest for most Hellenistic philosophers. Neoplatonic Aristotle-commentators like the fourth-century Dexippus[25] or the fifth-century Syrianus[26] occasionally spoke of union as a kind of substantial relationship distinct from simple homogeneity, but it was only in the later fifth and sixth centuries that it became a major term in the metaphysical vocabulary. Damascius uses *henōsis* in a variety of senses, ranging from the formal unity of a universal class or form to higher levels of metaphysical unity, which ground both sameness and distinction in the world of experience that is, in his system, contained within Being-as-One, 'the substance of all substances'.[27] For his pupil

---

[21] See e.g. Aristotle, *Pr. Anal.* 43ᵃ10; 45ᵃ4; 65ᵃ18; *Post. Anal.* 82ᵇ15; *De An.* 402ᵃ19; Chrysippus: H. von Arnim, *Stoicorum Veterum Fragmenta*, ii. 81. 19–25; 82. 20–83. 10; the school of Crinis: ibid., iii. 269. 12–23.

[22] *De Gen. Anim.* 740ᵇ22–3.

[23] *De An.* 361ᵇ. Damascius, in his *Life of Isidore*, frequently uses the word to denote a person's public 'style' or personality: e.g. 69. 3; 99. 5; 109. 17; 261. 15.

[24] *De Principiis*, 1. 115. 9; *In Parmenidem*, 32. 5; 177. 18; 316. 8–11; *In Phaedonem*, 8. 6; 123. 7.

[25] *In Cat.* 3, 1. 1 = *CAG* iv/2, 65. 25.

[26] *In Met.* B 4 = *CAG* vi/1 (ed. G. Kroll; Berlin: G. Reimer, 1902), 43. 18. See also *In Met.* B 2: *CAG* vi/1, 24. 12–14, where Syrianus says that the intellectual life of the stars enjoys an 'unconfused union' and a 'ceaseless sharing' with other intelligible substances.

[27] *De Principiis*, 1. 299 (ed. L. G. Westerink and J. Combès (Paris: Les Belles Lettres, 1989), iii. 17). For Damascius, the whole realm of actuality consists of entities formed by a constant tension between the opposed principles of the One and the Many (ibid. 1. 128: Westerink–Combès ii. 66); it is a 'mixed' realm, where unity and multiplicity form together a kind of descending metaphysical scale of reality, reaching from the relative unity of intelligible forms to a kind of unity 'which opens itself up, as it were, to distinction' (ibid. 1. 206: Westerink–Combès ii. 191).

Simplicius, *henōsis* always implies both a real, intelligible, single being shared by a number of elements, and an abiding distinction among them; to be recognized as such, a union must always bind together distinct realities.[28] This holds all the more true if the things united belong to wholly different levels of being; so in discussing Aristotle's category of 'relationship', Simplicius observes that the communion (κοινωνία) of what he calls 'primary' real substances with 'secondary' real substances—the soul with the body, for example, or God with the mind—must be understood as something real itself, even as 'hypostatic', yet not as bringing about the kind of union that exists between beings that share the same substance or nature (ὁμοούσια, ὁμοφυῆ).[29]

It was in Christian discussion of what we call the 'persons' of the Trinity and the person of Christ, beginning in the second half of the fourth century, that both these terms—*tropos* and *henōsis*—took on a range of ontological meanings that eventually made them both classical and problematic. Origen, it is true, in one fragment, already uses the phrase 'mode of union' to designate the ineffable mystery of 'the way God took on a human body',[30] and in the *Contra Celsum* he insists that Christ's soul and body were united with the Logos not merely by participation (*koinōnia*), but by union and mingling (*henōsei kai anakrasei*).[31] But the widespread, reflective theological use of these terms, separately and together, began only in the later stages of the fourth-century trinitarian debates, which were also the opening stages of debate over the unity of the person of Christ. It seems, in fact, to have been Apollinarius of Laodicea, that brilliant and innovative opponent of the idea of a human soul in Christ, who coined the phrase 'supreme union' (ἄκρα ἕνωσις)—later a standard christological term—to refer to the organic integrity of the Incarnate

[28] See e.g. his commentary on Epictetus' *Enchiridion* (ed. F. Dübner, *Theophrasti Characteres*, (Paris: Firmin Didot, 1840) ii. 100), lines 33–4: a unity comes to be 'not by way of contact nor continuity nor bodily mixture, but by the joining into one of separate and indivisible forms; while their distinction remains unmixed, the whole contains each part'.

[29] *In Cat.* 7 (viii, 169. 16–23). Simplicius believes that the life of the mind includes a constant, undivided union between the act of knowing and the intelligible object (*In De Anima*: *CAG* xi (ed. M. Hayduck), 11. 31–2; 191. 12–23; 237. 15–29; 243. 19–20); this means that contemplation, the highest kind of knowing, is a union of the mind with the unitive basis of intelligible *reality* itself that is only a step short of complete identity (ibid. 29. 2–3; 47. 20–1; 67. 3–7; 235. 17–21; 311. 36–8).

[30] This is a fragment dealing with John 1: 23–4, found in the catenae: E. Preuschen, GCS Origenes iv (Leipzig: J. C. Hinrichs, 1903), 498. 23–4.

[31] *Contra Celsum* 3. 41. 8–10 (SC cxxxvi, 96).

Word;[32] his disciple Timothy of Berytus further defined the phrase as meaning that the Logos and his flesh shared each other's titles and characteristics, while remaining unchanged within their own natures.[33] Apollinarius insists, in several passages of his work *Against Diodore*, that it was the union of Jesus' flesh to the Word, not the nature of his flesh itself, that allows us truly to call that flesh divine.[34] Because it is divine through union, and not itself consubstantial with the Word, the flesh of Christ can retain its own distinctive nature while joined to the Word, in Apollinarius' view,[35] since—as his disciple Valentinus insisted—'union does not mean consubstantiality, and if something is consubstantial there is no union; nothing is united or joined with itself, but one thing is united or joined with *another*'.[36]

It was doubtless the use of this terminology by Gregory of Nyssa, however, that gave it both a clearer range of meaning and lasting influence on the orthodox tradition. Gregory, as has often been pointed out, in his attempt to refute the neo-Arian or 'Eunomian' notion that the 'unbegottenness' of the Father and the 'begottenness' of the Son indicate two radically different beings, argued that the different 'modes' or 'forms of generation' predicated of the Son and the Spirit, and so implicitly of the ingenerateness of the Father, are simply three distinct 'modes of existing' ($\tau\rho\acute{o}\pi\omega\iota\ \tau\hat{\eta}\varsigma\ \acute{v}\pi\acute{a}\rho\xi\epsilon\omega\varsigma$), and do not imply ontological separation or division of activity within the single infinite, unknowable divine substance. In his first book *Against Eunomius*, Gregory draws on the analogy between human generation and divine generation, arguing that even among

[32] See e.g. fragments 140–2, from his *Contra Diodorum* in H. Lietzmann (ed.), *Apollinaris von Laodicea und seine Schule: Texte und Untersuchungen* (Tübingen: J. C. B. Mohr, 1904), 241, lines 3–26; also his *Professio fidei cum Jovio Episcopo* (ed. id., 286. 16–287. 9: flesh of Christ is $\dot{a}\kappa\rho\hat{\omega}\varsigma\ \dot{\epsilon}\nu\omega\mu\acute{\epsilon}\nu\eta$ with the Word); frag. 147 (ed. id., 246. 20–8: $\tau\epsilon\lambda\epsilon\omega\tau\acute{a}\tau\eta\ \acute{\epsilon}\nu\omega\sigma\iota\varsigma$ of God with his body). All these fragments are contained in Leontius of Byzantium's florilegium of passages from the Apollinarian school, *Adversus fraudes Apollinaristarum* (henceforth *AFA*)! The phrase is also used by Proclus of Constantinople—a christological 'moderate'—in his *Tomus ad Antiochenos* 14 (*ACO* iv/2, 190.8), to refer to the indivisible identity of Word and human 'flesh' signified by $\dot{\epsilon}\gamma\acute{\epsilon}\nu\epsilon\tau\omega$ in John 1: 14. It reappears frequently in controversial works of the 6th and 7th cents.
[33] Timothy of Berytus, *Ad Homonium*, in Leontius, *AFA* 2 (1960 D).
[34] Frag. 160 (ed. Lietzmann, 254. 5–6); frag. 161 (ed. id., 254. 19–26); this is echoed by his disciple Valentinus in his *Apologia* (ed. id., 287, 289; cited in Leontius, *AFA* (1953BC, 1956B)).
[35] Frag. 161 (ed. Lietzmann, 254. 25–6); frag. 112 (ed. id., 233. 30–234. 10).
[36] Valentinus, *Apologia*: ed. Lietzmann 288.

humans, different modes of coming into concrete existence—that of
Adam, for instance, who was formed from the earth, and that of his
son Abel, who was born in the normal way—do not mean the two
individuals in question possess different substances or natures:

> The first human being and the one begotten from him each had their being
> in different ways—the one from the coupling of parents, the other from the
> formation of earth—and they are thought to be two; yet they are not
> separated from each other in the structure of their substance . . . For the one
> and the other is each a human being, the structure of substance is common
> to the two of them: each is mortal, each also rational, each shares in mind
> and knowledge in the same way. But if the structure of humanity, in the
> case of Adam and Abel, is not changed by the variation in their begetting—
> since neither the sequence nor the mode of their coming-to-exist introduces
> any alteration to their nature, but it is affirmed to be the same by the
> common agreement of sober people, and no one would contradict it who is
> not badly in need of an anti-hallucinatory drug [lit.: hellebore]—why must
> this unreasonable notion be artificially forced onto the divine nature?[37]

The very names of 'Father' and 'Son', Gregory adds, which are used
by Jesus, 'teach us of the unity of nature in the two subjects, with
the relationship of the one to other signified both by the natural
meaning of the names and by the very language of the Lord'.[38]

In all his discussion of the 'relationships' and 'modes of existence'
implied by Father-Son language, in fact, Gregory of Nyssa seems
clearly to be thinking in terms of *origination*: of the particular
characteristics given to a person by the conditions of his or her
historical begetting. For Gregory, it seems, both 'existence' and
'hypostasis', as terms marking the particularity of individual
humans—and so applicable, by analogy, to the persons in the
Trinity—refer to the distinctive character that is rooted in the
particular *origin* of each individual: in a person's ancestry and
family relationships.[39] In a passage in his *Antirrhetikos against
Apollinarius*, in fact, Gregory confirms the fact that he conceives of

---

[37] *Contra Eunomium* 1. 496–7 = GNO i. 169. 20—170. 12. For references to the
different 'modes of begetting' in the Trinity, see *Ctr. Eun.* 3. 32 (*GNO* ii. 197. 7);
Refutatio Confessionis Eunomii 91 (GNO ii. 349. 18); 'forms of begetting': *Ctr. Eun.* 3. 37
(*GNO* ii. 199. 11); *Ref. Conf. Eun.* 94 (*GNO* ii. 351. 5).

[38] *Ctr. Eun.* 1. 498 (*GNO* i. 170. 13–17).

[39] See *Ctr. Eun.* 3. 36 (*GNO* ii. 198. 16–17). On the notion of ὕπαρξις in Stoic
philosophy, as suggesting not simply 'existence' but *caused* existence, 'the actuality of
an effect', see P. Hadot, 'Zur Vorgeschichte des Begriffs "Existenz", ὑπάρχειν bei den
Stoikern', *Archiv für Begriffsgeschichte*, 13 (1969), 115–27; cf. F. Heinzer, *Gottes Sohn
als Mensch*, 33–9.

'hypostatic' or individual being, in the case of humans, at least, primarily as being determined by one's origin; after reflecting on the unique way in which Jesus was conceived, by divine power in the womb of the Virgin, he concludes:

In this way the truly 'new human being' was created, the first and only one to reveal such a mode of hypostasis (τὸν τοιτοῦτον τρόπον τῆς ὑποστάσεως)in his own case: created according to God and not in the human way, with the divine power pervading the whole nature of the mixture on an equal basis [with the human], so that neither part (I mean, soul and body) lacks a share in divinity, but it is, in all likelihood, present in both in the way that is suitable and appropriate.[40]

Each of us is a unique person in human history, Gregory seems to be saying, because we have each come into existence in a unique way; in Christ's case, that mode of origin—birth from a virgin, by the power of the Holy Spirit—is both human and divine.

As for union, *henōsis*, Gregory of Nyssa shows a tendency similar to that of the authors we have already discussed, taking it always to signify both oneness and abiding distinction. Defending his own tendency, in speaking of the Mystery of Christ, to equate the two phrases 'union [of the Word] with flesh' and 'assumption of a human being', Gregory argues: '"Union", after all, is *with* something, and "assumption", surely, is *of* something; each signifies a relation (*schesis*) to something else—the one who assumes is united to what is assumed, and that which is united is united by the act of assumption.'[41] In a fragment of a lost letter, Gregory even anticipates Leontius' analysis of the difference between the unity of a natural or universal essence, an οὐσία, and the existential unity of a concrete individual who may be composed of more than one such essence: 'Things which are of the same substance (*homoousia*) have achieved identity, but it is the opposite with things of different substances. For if both are one by an ineffable union, still they are not so by nature, for they remain unchanged. Christ, then, who exists as two natures, is truly recognized in them, but possesses a single *persona* of sonship.'[42]

---

[40] *Antirrh. Adv. Apol.*: GNO iii/1. 223. 20–224. 5. This is precisely a line of approach to the distinctive character of the person of Christ that Leontius later argues we must avoid: see above, p. 169.

[41] *Antirrh. Adv. Apol.*: GNO iii/1. 184. 27–30. For other statements of a similar nature, see *Contra Eunomium*, 3. 63 (GNO ii. 130. 11–18); 3. 69 (= GNO ii. 133. 5–7).

[42] *Letter to the Monk Philip*, quoted by John of Damascus, *Contra Jacobitas*, 112 (ed. B. Kotter, *Die Schriften des Johannes von Damaskos*, (Berlin: de Gruyter, 1981), iv. 149. 3–6). One might even translate the final phrase, 'plays a single role of Sonship'.

In one passage of his *Catechetical Discourse*, Gregory actually anticipates Leontius' phrase, 'mode of union' (τρόπος τῆς ἑνώσεως), when trying to explain the constitution of the person of Christ. It is no more absurd, he argues, to think of the transcendent spiritual substance of God being naturally united to a limited, circumscribed creature who is both spirit and matter than it is to consider the union of the human soul with its body. He writes:

If the manner in which your soul is joined to your body is a mystery, you must certainly not imagine this former question is within your grasp. In the one case, while we believe the soul to be something different from the body because on leaving the flesh it renders it dead and inactive, we are ignorant of the manner of the union. Similarly, in the other case we realize that the divine nature, by its greater majesty, differs from that which is mortal and perishable; but we are unable to detect the manner of the mixture.[43]

Gregory's description, in this passage, of the soul's union with the body yields unmistakable resonances with contemporary Neoplatonic accounts of the human composite, particularly that in Porphyry's *Sentences*.[44] The comparison of this union of spiritual and material to the 'manner of union' in the incarnation, however, was also explicitly made by Gregory's Christian contemporary, Nemesius of Emesa—whom Gregory may have known personally—in his treatise *On Human Nature*.[45] In an oft-cited passage in the third chapter of this work, Nemesius develops his description

---

[43] *Oratio Catechetica* 11 = GNO iii/4. 39. 13–22; trans. Cyril G. Richardson, in E. R. Hardy (ed.), *The Christology of the Later Fathers*, Library of Christian Classics, ii (London: SCM Press, 1954), 288 (trans. corrected). Later on in the work, Gregory uses the language of physical 'mixture' to contrast the unique unity of God with the humanity of Christ, on the one hand, and God's general, sustaining presence in us and in all creation, on the other. Different as they are, both kinds of presence are real. 'For even if the manner of God's presence in us is not the same as this [the incarnation], it is at any rate admitted that he is equally present with us in both cases. In the one, he is united to us insofar as he sustains nature in being; in the other, he is mixed with what is ours, so that what is ours may become divine by being mixed in with the divine . . .' (ibid. 25 = GNO iii/4. 64. 3–9; trans. mine).

[44] See *Sententiae ad intelligibilia ducentes*, 27–9 (ed. E. Lamberz (Leipzig: Teubner, 1975), 16–20).

[45] On possible contacts between Nemesius and Gregory Nazianzen, see L. Le Nain de Tillemont, *Mémoires pour servir à l'histoire ecclésiastique des six premiers siècles* (2nd edn.; Paris: Charles Robustel, 1714), ix. 541, 607. In fact, chs. two and three of his *De natura hominis* were at times attributed to Gregory of Nyssa in the early Byzantine period: see J. Dräseke, 'Ein Testimonium Ignatianum', *Zeitschrift für wissenschaftliche Theologie*, 46 (1903), 505–12, esp. 506–8. For a description of the Neoplatonic theory of the transcendent union of spiritual and material substances in a single subject, as represented in the works of Porphyry and Nemesius, see Daley 'A Richer Union', 254–6.

of the soul's union with the body much more fully than Gregory had needed to do, yet along similar lines. Rejecting all the forms of physical 'mixture', previously classified by the Stoics, as inadequate models for conceiving how the spiritual soul and the material body can organically comprise a single person, Nemesius argues that the two are united

in a kind of relationship, and by presence, as God is said to be present in us. For we say that the soul is bound by the body in a kind of relationship, and by a relative inclination and attitude, just as we say the lover is bound by the beloved: not in a bodily or spatial way, but by way of relationship (κατὰ σχέσιν).[46]

This model of body–soul unity, Nemesius goes on to say, can be seen 'in a purer form' in the relationship of the divine Word to the human being Jesus—'purer', perhaps, because while the soul is enhanced in its powers, yet also made to suffer new limitations and passions, through its union with the body, the Word in the incarnation remains unchanged and unlimited, giving the man Jesus a share in its divinity but itself remaining untouched by his bodily variability weaknesses.[47] So 'this mode of mixture or union is something new', Nemesius observes; yet it is not simply a matter of God's 'good pleasure, as some respected people believe, but *nature* is its cause', since the fact that the two substances preserve their integrity as they do is due to the 'proper nature of God'.[48]

Nemesius' way of conceiving the 'manner of union' of the incarnation in terms of relationship and causal operation, rather than physical presence or spatial mixture, seems itself to have played a role, as we have already mentioned, in shaping Leontius' explanation of how two different natures can be united without amalgamation or hybridization in a single hypostasis; in this way, this explanation entered the later tradition of orthodox Christology.[49] Leontius' explicit insistence, however, against Nemesius,

---

[46] *De natura hominis*, 3. I have used here the edition of B. Einarson, which is to appear in the *Corpus medicorum Graecorum*, as it is presently available in the databank *Thesaurus linguae Graecae*. See also the annotated and corrected text of this ch. in R. Arnou, *De 'Platonismo' Patrum*, Textus et documenta, ser. theol. xxi (Rome: Gregorian University Press, 1935), 54–5; trans W. Telfer, *Cyril of Jerusalem and Nemesius of Emesa*, Library of Christian Classics iv (Philadelphia: Westminster Press, 1955), 299. See also Alberto Siclari, *L'Antropologia di Nemesio di Emesa* (Padua: La Garangola, 1974), 115–37.

[47] Nemesius of Emesa, *De natura hominis*, 3.   [48] Ibid.

[49] For Leontius' use of an argument of Porphyry's, summarized in this ch. of

that 'union and nature are *not* the same thing', and that the internal cohesion of the person of Christ is due to union *rather than* to nature, seems to have been more directly influenced by the controversies between the Antiochene theologians and Cyril of Alexandria that surrounded the great synods of the early fifth century.

In his *Eighth Catechetical Homily*, for instance, Theodore of Mopsuestia takes great pains to distinguish in Christ between the natures of the 'assuming' divine Son and of the 'assumed man', the 'form of a servant' in which the Son worked our salvation. Theodore continues:

The distinction between the natures does not annul the exact conjunction[50] nor does the exact conjunction destroy the distinction between the natures, but the natures remain in their respective existence while separated, and the conjunction remains intact because the one who was assumed is united in honour and glory with the one who assumed, according to the will of the one who assumed him . . . The fact that a husband and wife are 'one flesh' does not impede them from being two. Indeed, they will remain two because they are two, but they are one because they are also one and not two. In this same way here [in the incarnation] they are two by nature and one by conjunction: two by nature, because there is a great difference between the natures, and one by conjunction because the adoration offered to the one who has been assumed is not divided from that offered to the one who assumed him, since he [the one assumed] is the temple, from which it is not possible for the one who dwells in it to depart.[51]

Nemesius' work, see A. Grillmeier, 'Die anthropologische-christologische Sprache des Leontius von Byzanz und ihre Beziehung zu den *Symmikta Zetemata* des Neuplatonikers Porphyrius', in H. Eisenberger (ed.), *Hermeneumata: Festschrift für Hadwig Hörner zum sechszigten Geburtstag* (Heidelberg: Winter, 1990), 61–72 (= id., *Fragmente zur Christologie* (Freiburg: Herder, 1997), 264–76); see also id., *Jesus der Christus* (Freiburg im Breisgau, Basle, Vienna: Herder, 1979), ii/2. 211–12. For the parallelism between Nemesius' christological argument and the definition of Chalcedon, see E. Fortin, 'The *Definitio Fidei* of Chalcedon and its Philosophical Sources', *Studia Patristica*, v (= *TU* xxc; Berlin: Akademie-Verlag, 1962), 489–98, esp. 493; and L. Abramowski, '*Ἐννά-φεια* und *ἀσύγχυτος ἔνωσις* als Bezeichnung für trinitarische und christologische Einheit', *Drei christologische Untersuchungen* (Berlin and New York: de Gruyter, 1981), 63–109, esp. 63–70.

[50] In the Syriac text, *naqiputha hatittha*; this was a standard expression used in the later 'Nestorian' tradition to express the union of natures in Christ, and probably translates the Greek *ἄκρα συνάφεια*, a self-consciously diphysite alternative to Apollinarius' *ἄκρα ἕνωσις*.

[51] Theodore of Mopsuestia, *Catechetical Homily*, 8. 13–14 (ed. Raymond Tonneau and Robert Devreesse, Studi e Testi (Vatican City: Vatican Apostolic Library, 1949), 204–7; trans. A. Mingana, *Woodbrooke Studies* (Cambridge: Heffer, 1933), v. 89–90 (altered)).

Anyone familiar with the christological controversies of the early fifth century will easily hear in the passage the tinkling of the Antiochene bells that were to alarm Cyril of Alexandria, with his more organic and integrated understanding of Christ: the seemingly weak term 'conjunction' (*synapheia*); union explained primarily in terms of will; union attested simply by our common honour and adoration; the analogy of the union of husband and wife. So Cyril's famous 'Third Letter' to the Patriarch Nestorius, written in the autumn of 430, explicitly rejects terminology that presents the union of God and humanity in Christ primarily in terms of dignity, authority, or an extrinsically conceived 'indwelling', parallel to the way in which Christ or the Spirit dwells in the hearts of the saints.[52] Nothing short of 'union by nature' (ἕνωσις φυσική, ἕνωσις κατὰ φύσιν) can express for Cyril the inner bond between the Word and his own humanity.

For equality of honour does not unite the natures. Peter and John, for instance, are of equal honour with each other, as both apostles and holy disciples, but the two are not made into one. Nor do we think of the mode of conjunction as being by association, for this is not enough for a natural union, nor as being by a relationship of participation, in the way that we, being 'joined to the Lord,' as it is written, are 'one spirit' with him (I Cor 6. 17). Indeed, we reject the term 'conjunction' (*synapheian*) altogether, as not sufficiently indicating the union.[53]

In the third of the celebrated anathemas which end this forceful letter, Cyril makes this point more emphatically: 'If anyone divides the hypostases in the one Christ after the union, joining them only by a conjunction in dignity, or authority or power, and not rather by a coming-together in a natural union, let him be anathema.'[54] A *natural* union', in the terms of this letter and of many of Cyril's writings that poured out during the years of controversy that followed Nestorius' deposition in 431, seems to signify above all a *true* union, a union realized in ontological terms, in contrast with a merely 'relational conjunction', such as each of us enjoys with God by the grace of adoptive sonship.[55]

---

[52] Ep. 17. 5 (ed. Eduard Schwartz, *ACO* i/1. 1. 36. 15–20).
[53] Ibid.; trans. adapted from that of Hardy, *Christology of the Later Fathers*, 351.
[54] Ibid., anathema, 3; Hardy, 353.
[55] See *Apol. adv. Theodoretum* 3 in Philip E. Pusey (ed.), *Sancti Patris Nostri Cyrilii Archiepiscopi Alexandriae Epistolae Tres Oecumenicae* (Oxford: Clarendon Press, 1975), vi. 412. 23–414. 2); cf. ibid. 414. 4: ἕνωσις κατὰ φύσιν means ἕνωσις οὐ σχετικὴ, ἀλλὰ

Cyril is clearly groping for terms to mark off the metaphysical uniqueness of the incarnation.

Yet it is crucial to recognize that Theodore of Mopsuestia also saw the united natures in Christ as in some way genuinely forming one reality, and that Cyril, too, remained far from asserting that union, in the case of the incarnation, means either a confusion of godhead and humanity without distinction, or the hybridization of two transcendentally different beings by some natural mechanism proper to either or both of them. In the eighth of his *Scholia on the Incarnation*, Cyril muses on the utterly mysterious nature of the union of God and an individual humanity in Emmanuel, and concludes that although 'the mode of the union' is beyond our understanding, still it is not entirely 'off the mark' to conceive of it in terms analogous to the union of body and soul in each of us, by which the soul 'owns' the body and experiences its physical sensations and its suffering, without itself becoming body in the process.[56] In his second letter to Succensus, written perhaps somewhat earlier, between 433 and 435, Cyril affirms the dialectical character of this mode of unified being more simply:

Understanding, then, as I said, the manner of his becoming human, we see that two natures come together with each other, without confusion and without separation, in the way of an indivisible union. For the flesh is flesh and not divinity, even though it became God's flesh. Similarly, the Word is God and not flesh, even though, in a way fitting the economy, he made the flesh his own.[57]

In his attacks on Cyril, Theodoret of Cyrus generally ignored passages such as these, and focused instead on the strongly unitive Christology of Cyril's third letter to Nestorius and its anathemas, in giving voice to all the misgivings the Antiochene tradition felt about the Alexandrian approach to the Mystery of Christ. The natural union (ἕνωσις κατὰ φύσιν) of two different things, such as the union

κατὰ ἀλήθειαν: also ibid. 416. 16–17, 24–5; 418. 3–7. See also *Expl. XII Cap.* (ed. Pusey, 246. 16–17); *Apol. Adv. Orientales* 3 (ed. Pusey, 286. 23–4; 287. 21–2; 288. 3–5).

[56] *Scholia de incarnatione Unigeniti*, 8 (ed. Pusey, vi. 510–14, esp. 512. 3–15). Cyril explains the analogy in terms that, if anything, emphasize the distinction of the elements: 'Just as the body is naturally different with regard to the soul, but one human being is formed from both, and is called such, so from the perfect hypostasis of God the Word, and from a humanity that is also perfect, according to its own structure, there is one Christ, himself existing at the same time as God and a human being' (ibid. 514. 2–8).

[57] Ep. 45. 6 (Ep. I to Succensus): *ACO* i/1. 6. 153. 12–20.

of soul and body, which Cyril and his followers offer as a model for the incarnation, Theodoret argues in his doggedly anti-Cyrillian dialogue, *Eranistes*, is a mutual fusion of equal ingredients, which may leave the characteristics of both elements still recognizable, but which by definition allows neither the guiding role.[58] Theodoret even has his Cyrillian character assert, in the course of the discussion, that the 'supreme union' realized in the incarnation is what the philosophers call a 'complete mixture' (κρᾶσις δἰ ὅλων), the Stoic term for an irreversible physical compound.[59] Theodoret is willing to allow the continued use of the body–soul analogy in discussions of the incarnation, insofar as it represents a real unity in the midst of abiding distinction,[60] but he stresses (as Cyril himself did) that the union of natures found in Christ is also significantly different from that of body and soul, in that it is *not* a union of equal elements and is *not* forced into reality by the nature of either element (as our human union is),[61] but is rather due solely to divine grace and favour.[62] Clearly, he argues, the incarnation is a 'conjunction' (*synapheia*),[63] a 'union of natures' (*henōsis tōn physeōn*);[64] but while it produces a single, indivisible, dynamic external form or *prosōpon*,[65] it leaves the natures of divinity and humanity in Christ 'unmixed' and 'unconfused'.[66] Interestingly, Theodoret does not take up the more relational understanding of *hypostasis* developed by Gregory of Nyssa, as a useful point of departure for talking about the person of Christ. At times he seems to assume *hypostasis* is a synonym for 'nature', at other times he uses it—without further explanation—as the apparent equivalent of *prosōpon*, his preferred term for speaking about Christ as a single agent.[67] In the *Eranistes*, his main contribution to christological controversy, Theodoret himself uses hypostasis-language only with reference to the persons of the Trinity.[68] And even in his discussions of the Trinity, while he uses the Cappadocian

---

[58] *Eranistes*, 2 (ed. G. Ettlinger; Oxford: Clarendon Press, 1975), 116. 11–13; 137. 31–138. 3.

[59] Ibid. 2 (144. 35–6; 145. 19); 3 (200. 1–2).

[60] Ibid. 2 (137. 31–138. 3).

[61] Cyril presents this as Theodoret's critique of his own third anathema, in *Apologia contra Theodoretum* 3 (ed. Pusey, vi. 408–12).

[62] *Eranistes*, 2 (137. 31–138. 3).   [63] Ibid. 3 (190. 21).

[64] Ibid. 2 (122. 10; 133. 11–24).   [65] Ibid. 3 (209. 26–30).

[66] Ibid. 3, syllogism 2 (257. 18–28); syllogism 12 (261. 1–2.).

[67] For a discussion of Theodoret's use of 'hypostasis' language, see A. Grillmeier, *Christ in Christian Tradition* (Oxford: Mowbrays, 1975), i. 489–91.

[68] See *Eranistes*, 1 (64. 11–13; 65. 11–16, 23–4; 66. 3–5); 2 (116. 23–4; 117. 7–10).

language of one *ousia* and three *hypostaseis* unreflectively, as something already canonized by use, his interest is less in the characteristics and relationships of origin that distinguish the persons in God, than in a philosophical discussion of the attributes that mark God, as a single Mystery, off from creation.[69]

During his long years of exile, the embattled Nestorius himself struggled to give systematic form and argument to a christological position not radically different from that of his more moderate Antiochene colleagues, such as Theodoret. Although the collection of his late essays, in what is now known as the *Book of Heracleides*, remains, for literary as well as philosophical reasons, confusing and difficult to interpret, it is clear that Nestorius, too, rejected the language of 'natural union' for the person of Christ as failing to do justice to the full richness of the divine initiative in the mystery of redemption. The key to Cyril's mistakes, Nestorius observes, is that his approach to the constitution of Christ's person is narrative or diachronic—'economic', a modern theologian might say—rather than analytical; it is focused on the divine initiative in salvation and on the origins and operations of the radically different components of the 'person' in which God the Son historically carries out his work, rather than on the paradoxical structure of Christ's being— what Leontius would later call the *apotelesma* or 'end-product' of the incarnation:[70] 'You take as the starting-point of your narrative the Maker of the natures and not the *prosōpon* of union.'[71] For Nestorius, as for Theodoret, what is *one* in the actual, concrete Christ is not the substance of God or the substance of humanity, let alone the natural functioning of either, but the concrete, intelligible, visible *form* in which Christ meets us: in Christ, God the Son, whose substance radiates its own set of identifying divine characteristics—exhibits its own *prosōpon* or *persona*—has 'taken up' the human characteristics, qualities and behavioural potentialities of the man Jesus by freely identifying himself with him, freely assuming through Jesus 'the

---

[69] See especially S.-P. Bergjan, *Theodoret von Cyrus und der Neunizänismus* (Berlin: de Gruyter, 1993), 192–5.

[70] CNE 7 (1297C–1305C); *Epil* 8 (1937A–1945C).

[71] *Book of Heracleides*, 2. 1 (ed. P. Bedjan; Paris and Leipzig: Letouzey et Ané, 1910), 225; trans. G. R. Driver and L. Hodgson, *The Bazaar of Heracleides* (Oxford: Clarendon Press, 1925), 153 (modernized). For a description of Nestorius' understanding of the 'natural union' of the human person, and for parallels in Stoic texts, see L. I. Scipioni, *Ricerche sulla Christologia del 'Libro di Eraclide' di Nestorio*, Paradosis 11 (Fribourg: Edizioni Universitarie, 1956), 25–31.

form of a servant'. The result is a new, combined '*prosōpon* of union', which leaves the underlying substances intact and distinct, while permanently creating a new, unified, divine and human face for God.[72]

III MAXIMUS THE CONFESSOR AND JOHN OF DAMASCUS

Writing in defence of the christological formula of Chalcedon in the 530s and 540s, Leontius of Byzantium, of course, faced a somewhat different situation from that of Gregory of Nyssa and Cyril of Alexandria, Theodoret of Cyrus, and Nestorius—a situation in which the fluid, often ambiguous terms of the previous century's polemics had become hardened by caricature and by repeated use as slogans of battle. The mood of the Byzantine Church during Justinian's reign was certainly in favour of reinterpreting, or at least clarifying, the language of the definition of Chalcedon in terms less ambivalent in themselves, and more congenial to Cyril's Christology. The canons of the Second Council of Constantinople in 553, while reaffirming the Chalcedonian definition as a binding codicil to the Nicene faith, were aimed primarily at excluding any interpretation of Chalcedon that seemed sympathetic to the language or concerns of Theodore, Nestorius, or even the more centrist Theodoret. So Constantinople II rejected the idea of a 'relational union' (*henōsis schetikē*) in Christ as Nestorian, even though its conceptual roots really lay with Gregory of Nyssa, and it condemned explicitly those who say that the union of natures in the incarnation is achieved by grace, combined operation, equality of honour, relationship, power, unity of name or divine good pleasure—who formulate the Mystery of Christ, in other words, in any terms other than that of a union 'by synthesis or by hypostasis'.[73] In this strongly unitive climate, it was the supreme achievement of Leontius of Byzantium to have upheld some of the more complex nuances of what such a 'hypostatic' union actually implied, and to have argued—however modestly and abstractly—for a more relational

---

[72] See Scipioni, *Ricerche*, 80–8 for texts and interpretation.

[73] Second Council of Constantinople, Anathema 4: in G. Alberigo *et al.* (eds.), *Conciliorum Oecumenicorum Decreta* (Bologna: Istituto per le scienze religiose, 1973), 114–15; trans. N. P. Tanner (ed.), *Decrees of the Ecumenical Councils* (Washington, DC: Georgetown University Press, 1990), 114–15.

understanding of the Chalcedonian Christology, an approach which more fully represented all the interests and voices in the debates of the previous two centuries, yet carried rich theological and anthropological implications of its own.

As one who had studied and excerpted the writings of the Apollinarian school first-hand, Leontius emphasized once again, without mentioning Apollinarius' name, the important insight of that controversial writer: it is union, *henōsis*, and *not* the nature of either God or Jesus' humanity that allows us to call his flesh divine. Speaking again of Christ, as Gregory of Nyssa and Nemesius had done, as *one* in 'the mode of union' rather than by the 'principle of nature', Leontius revived the metaphysical distinction between *tropos* and *logos*, mode of origin and structure of being, that had been forged in Gregory's trinitarian theology; and he preserved it, in the christological context, for the use of later synthetic thinkers like Maximus the Confessor and John of Damascus. Remaining sympathetic to Cyril's concern that the personal unity of Christ be understood in real, intrinsic terms as forming a single ontological whole, Leontius treated the traditional analogy of the human body and soul for the incarnation in a positive way, while recognizing its limitations, and sharply criticized the 'proponents of division' in the Antiochene tradition for rejecting it.[74] Yet his constant concern to emphasize the continuing, substantial, and natural distinction between God and humanity in Christ, and to stress the historical, contingent, unpredictably providential character of the 'mode of union' that forms Christ's unique hypostasis, was itself a serious reespousal of one of the Antiochenes' underlying christological concerns: that God's presence and saving action in Christ not be reduced to a part of the world's natural process.

Our considerations up to now have pointed to Leontius' role, in the middle of the contentious sixth century, as preserver and systematizer of crucial elements in earlier Greek philosophical and theological vocabulary that seemed to open promising ways of seeing the church's mainstream doctrines of the Trinity of God and the Mystery of Christ, the dogmas of Nicaea and Constantinople and Chalcedon, as a continuous whole. What remains for us is to cast a brief, summary glance at two of the dominant figures in Greek theology in the centuries after the Council of 553—Maximus the

[74] *CNE* 2 (1280C–1284A).

Confessor and John of Damascus—to see how their own use of this vocabulary of the 'mode of union' in Christ deepened and enriched, in significant and promising ways, earlier patristic reflection on God, Christ, and salvation.

Writing a hundred years after the sixth-century struggles over the reception of Chalcedonian Christology, Maximus the Confessor remains deeply indebted to Leontius' analysis of the language and concepts of trinitarian and christological debate. His *Epistle 15*, especially, written in his 'middle period' of activity sometime between 634 and 640, is a masterful and synthetic summary of the issues of substance and nature, hypostasis and persona, with regard to the Triune God and to Christ, that without a doubt draws heavily and directly on Leontius' anti-Severan writings, even if Maximus never mentions the earlier monk by name.[75] Maximus' use of the terminology of nature, union, and modality in a trinitarian context is evident in many of his works; in the *Mystagogia*, for example, written early in his career (probably around 630),[76] Maximus summarizes the classical Christian understanding of God as being

one substance, three hypostases; a tri-hypostatic singleness of substance and a consubstantial triad of hypostases; a monad in a triad and a triad in a monad; . . . a monad by its structure of substance (*kata ton tēs ousias logon*) or being, but not by synthesis or conflation or confusion of any kind; a triad by the structure of how it exists and concretely comes to be, but not by separation or alienation or any kind of division. For the monad is not divided up by the hypostases, nor is it in them by relation and seen in them

[75] On the structure of the person of Christ, as analysed in this letter, see especially PG xci, 557A–560D. The best recent survey of Maximus' use of the terms 'nature' and 'hypostasis' is Nicholas Madden, 'Composite Hypostasis in Maximus Confessor', *Studia Patristica*, 27 (1993), 175–97.

[76] See P. Sherwood, *An Annotated Date-List of the Works of Maximus the Confessor*, Studia Anselmiana 30 (Rome: Orbis Catholicus, Herder, 1952), 32; I.-H. Dalmais, 'Mystère liturgique et divinisation dans la "Mystagogie" de saint Maxime le Confesseur', in C. Kannengiesser and J. Fontaine (eds.), *Epektasis*, Mélanges Daniélou (Paris: Beauchesne, 1972), 55; cf. the introduction to the critical edition of the *Mystagogia* by C. Sotiropoulos (Athens: s.n., 1978), 87. For a discussion of Maximus' use of the λόγος–τρόπος distinction in trinitarian theology and Christology, see P. Sherwood, *The Earlier Ambigua of St. Maximus the Confessor*, Studia Anselmiana 36 (Rome: Orbis Catholicus, Herder, 1955), 154–64; A. Riou, *Le Monde et l'église selon Maxime le Confesseur*, Théologie Historique 22 (Paris: Beauchesne, 1973), 80–91; Heinzer, *Gottes Sohn als Mensch*, 117–45. Riou observes (p. 80) that he has not found a thorough study of the patristic use of the word τρόπος in connection with the incarnation—a gap that the present study is intended, in some degree, to fill.

by contemplative thought, nor are the hypostases compounded into the monad, nor do they fill it out by a process of combination; rather, it is identical with itself, yet in different ways.[77]

In other early works, also dating from the late 620s or early 630s, Maximus applies this same language of sameness of substance and difference in manner of subsisting to the unity of Christ's person, with a clarity and thoroughness seldom found in the earlier tradition we have been examining. In the brief *Difficulty* 36, for instance, Maximus comments on a remark in Gregory Nazianzen's celebrated *Christmas Oration*,[78] that 'the second communion' of God with humanity, in the incarnation, is 'more amazing' than the original communion enjoyed by an unspoiled creation before the fall. Maximus writes:

Formerly nature possessed no union with God in any mode or structure (τρόπον ἢ λόγον) of substance or hypostasis, those categories in which all beings are generally understood; but now it has received a union in hypostasis with him, through the ineffable union, preserving unchanged its own different structure of substance in relation to the divine substance, towards which it is hypostatically one and yet different, through the union. As a result, in the structure of its being (τῷ τοῦ εἶναι λόγῳ), according to which it has come into existence and continues to be, it [Christ's humanity] remains in unquestionable possession of its own being, preserving it undiminished in every way; but in the structure of *how* it is (τῷ τοῦ πῶς εἶναι λόγῳ), it receives existence in a divine way, and neither knows nor accepts at all the urge towards movement centred on any other thing. In this fashion, then, the Logos has brought into being a communion with human nature that is much more wonderful than the first one was, uniting the very nature to himself hypostatically, in a substantial way.[79]

In this thicket of technical terms and interlocking grammatical connections, Maximus lays out what will be a main theme of his Christology throughout his career: the point that in the person of Christ, a complete and fully functioning humanity has been brought into existence, which realizes and even goes beyond God's original design in creating the human person, precisely because the union of Jesus the man with the divine Logos is a union that preserves the substantial and natural differences of God and the human completely, and yet totally alters (at least as far as created history is

---

[77] *Mystagogia*, 25 (ed. Sotiropoulos, 239. 57–240. 72).
[78] *Or.* 38. 13.
[79] *Ambigua*, 36 (PG 91, 1289C3–D5).

concerned) the 'how' of their relationship and their common action—the kind of 'how' that makes concrete individuals or hypostases just what they are.[80] Jesus is Jesus by being, in every respect and at every moment, Son of God, Word made flesh; yet the intimacy and ontological absoluteness of this identification of the man from Nazareth with the second hypostasis of the Trinity does not make Jesus in any way less human than any other member of Adam's race. Rather, it changes the 'manner' of his being human, in a way that sets out before us the new 'manner of being' that is the pattern of our redemption.

Another important passage developing this terminology in the context of both Christology and theological anthropology is Maximus' long *Difficulty 42*, commenting on a passage in Gregory Nazianzen's oration *On Holy Baptism* that speaks of the three 'births' of the redeemed—birth of the flesh, rebirth in baptism, and the coming new birth of the resurrection.[81] Towards the end of the discussion, Maximus makes the point that *renewal* (καινοτομία), which is what the Gospel of salvation really proclaims to us, is primarily a renewal of the 'mode' of our being, rather than of the formal structure or *logos* of its nature,

because if the *structure* [of Christ's humanity] is renewed, that would destroy the nature, in that it would not have preserved unaltered the structure by which it is; but if the *mode* [of being] is renewed, while its structure with respect to nature is preserved, it reveals miraculous power, showing its nature as enlivened and enlivening beyond its own normal limits. The *structure* of human nature is the fact that it is soul and body, and that its nature is constituted by soul and body; but its *mode* is the order found in this natural give-and-take of activity, something often varied and altered, yet not altering the nature at all along with itself.[82]

Maximus then gives examples from the Old Testament of people enabled by God to do and experience wonderful things—to act and be acted upon in a divine way—without undergoing any basic alteration in their humanity. He continues:

Along with all these events, as well as after them, [God] brought to completion what was truly the newest of all mysteries, through which and because of which all these had occurred: his humanization for our sake;

---

[80] Nicholas Madden remarks, à propos Maximus' *Opusculum*, 25 (PG 91, 272B): 'The *ousia* exists as "what," the *hypostasis* as "how" or "who"' ('Composite Hypostasis', 190).

[81] *Or.* 40. 2.   [82] *Amb.* 42 (PG 91, 1341D4–14.

in doing this, he renewed our nature not in its structure, but in its mode, by taking up flesh through the mediation of a rational soul, having been ineffably conceived without seed, and having truly become a perfect human being, free of all corruption, possessing a rational soul with its body as a result of precisely that indescribable conception.[83]

The distinction between a natural structure and its mode of being is a centrally important one for Maximus, because, in his view, the underlying structure or nature of each identifiable thing has permanent validity before God, is what it is because God has made it such, and cannot become something different in that respect without simply ceasing to be: 'Those features which their structures (*logoi*) perfectly possess before God, along with their very existence— of these their own growth and substantial development, according to their own structures—are utterly unable to receive any addition or diminution, beyond being whatever they are.'[84]

The mystery of renewal, then—redemption from sin and restoration to the fullness of the image of God, for which humanity was originally created—must be, in Maximus' view, a fundamental transformation of the *way* we exist, which leaves intact the inner character of *what* we have been made to be. For one thing, it consists in the renewal of the particular way humans exercise their habitual freedom of choice—γνώμη—which Maximus defines as 'a mode of living according to virtue or vice'.[85] And since, as Gregory of Nyssa had suggested two and a half centuries earlier, the fallen condition of human nature is above all reflected in our 'animal' mode of sexual conception and birth, through which God providentially surrounds our conflicted natures in a merciful mortality,[86] Maximus sees the renewal of our mode of being through Christ as taking place mainly through a renewal of *birth*, as well: first through the new and unprecedented manner of Christ's birth, of his origin as a human hypostasis, of his human *hyparxis* or existence; and then, through

---

[83] *Amb.* 42 (PG 91, 1344D10–1345A5).

[84] Ibid. (PG 91, 1345B12–C2). As Madden remarks ('Composite Hypostasis', 193), 'The λόγος φύσεως and the τρόπος ὑπάρξεως require each other as the two necessary dimensions of all existents. It is the existent alone that is in reality and that acts in reality.'

[85] *Dialogue with Pyrrhus* (PG 91, 308B8–12; see also 308D8–10).

[86] *On the Making of the Human Person*, 16–17. For a recent discussion of this passage, with a survey of the abundant literature on it, and an attempt to reinterpret it as suggesting the positive potential of even human animality, see J. Behr, 'The Rational Animal: A Rereading of Gregory of Nyssa's *De hominis opificio*', *Journal of Early Christian Studies*, 7 (1999), 219–47.

the rebirth of baptism, made available to all of us after the example and through the activity of Christ.

Maximus makes this point in several places: one is a little work dating from the late 630s, a treatise on the Mystery of Christ addressed to the higoumen George (*Opusculum 4*). The Word of God renewed and saved our nature, Maximus says, by reordering not the functioning of our nature in itself, but the way we use it. This means not only that God empowers our wills to choose his will, free of the passionate inclinations that put us at war with him;[87] it also means that he has begun to reform the very way in which we come to live out our natural identity and potential, a way now rooted in the manner of our conception and birth. To do this, the Word himself became perfectly and completely human, but by a new and divine way of birth, and so—as a result of that birth—he now acts with a divinely oriented human will.[88] Maximus writes:

Having the Logos himself as its own seed, renewing the manner of begetting that had been introduced [into human nature], [Christ's humanity] received in itself, along with its natural way of being, a divine way of concretely existing, so that it might confirm what is ours and give credibility to what is above us. For it is completely necessary that he [the Son] conserve both the nature of the Word of God, who became flesh and perfectly human for our sakes, and the additional nature he took on, with its natural qualities— without which it is, of course, no nature at all, but merely an empty fantasy—and also that he preserve the union. The first is preserved by natural difference, the second recognized in hypostatic identity. So we shall wisely and piously profess the whole structure of God's saving plan, without confusion and without separation.[89]

It is in the hypostatic union of the divine and the human in Christ that our human way of using our natural faculties, and thus of being ourselves, is made new: first in Christ, born of the Father and of the Virgin, and then through him, by a second birth 'not of blood, nor of the will of the flesh nor of human will, but of God' (John 1: 13), also in us.[90]

A century after Maximus, this Greek Christian tradition of

---

[87] *Opusc.* 4 (PG 91, 60A9–12).
[88] Ibid. (PG 91, 60C5–15).
[89] Ibid. (PG 91, 61B10–C11).
[90] Maximus discusses the peculiar 'mode of union' in Christ in a number of passages in his work: see, for example, Ep. 12, to John the Chamberlain (written towards the end of 641), esp. PG 91, 477B. For further discussion of the 'mode of existence' of the Word in his flesh, see also *Dialogue with Pyrrhus* (PG 91, 177AB).

speculation on the meaning of the 'mode of union' of two natures in Christ's single, composite hypostasis reached a further degree of synthetic maturity, as well as considerably greater clarity, in the writings of the great patristic systematician, John of Damascus.

John, like Maximus, takes over Leontius of Byzantium's analysis of the meanings of substance-, nature-, and hypostasis-language with reference to the Mystery of Christ—without acknowledgement, but also virtually without alteration—and he uses them often as he expounds the orthodox tradition of the faith against its various alternatives.[91] Arguing against the Apollinarian phrase, 'one nature of the Word of God, made flesh', used first by Cyril as a convenient christological formula and then by the opponents of Chalcedon as a kind of dogmatic emblem, John argues that the earlier Fathers were clearly speaking of 'nature' here in an inexact way (*katachrēstikōs*); in saying that 'the Word was made flesh'; after all, the Evangelist was clearly referring to a particular hypostasis within the divine being, and not to the whole divine nature. 'For the Logos did not have another nature alongside that of the divinity; the Logos is of the same nature as the Father and the Spirit, and all things are common to Father and Son and Holy Spirit except the manner of existence.'[92]

In his treatise usually entitled *On the Two Wills in Christ*—actually a full discussion of the person of Christ, directed against the 'mon-energist' and 'monothelite' brands of opposition to Chalcedonian Christology condemned at the Third Council of Constantinople in 681—John develops this understanding of classical terminology more fully:

One must realize that every human hypostasis receives from the Creator both its being and the fact that it has proceeded from non-being into being. That is, [it has received] its being a creature, alive and active; its possessing sensation and understanding and reason, and appetite according to sensation and reason—in other words, its having a self-determining will; and its concrete existence consisting of substance and accidents. All these things are essential and natural qualities; but the particular mode of motion, particularly chosen by the individual, is the distinguishing mark of the hypostasis (*hypostatikē diaphora*). For sharing in the former characteristics establishes the identity of nature; but the manner of existing (ὁ τρόπος τῆς

---

[91] See especially his *Dialectica*, 30, 43–5, 67; *Expositio fidei*, 47–55, 57, 91; *Contra Jacobitas* 52; *De duabus in Christo voluntatibus*, 7.

[92] *Ctr. Jac.* 52. 24–7 (ed. Kotter, iv. 126).

ὑπάρξεως) introduces the difference of hypostases, and the separate existence of each, their internal coherence, their peculiar mode of being and movement, and their different use of natural qualities, all make for separate hypostases and allow us to say there are many human beings.[93]

John immediately goes on to observe that the most fundamental difference between the three divine hypostases and any number of human hypostases is that the Trinity wills and acts as one—only their *hyparxis*, their way of existing determined by their respective origins, differs in any way, so that we may not speak of 'three gods' as we might speak of 'three human beings'.[94] More pointedly, perhaps, than his patristic predecessors who used these terms, John is aware of the inherent difficulty of using hypostasis-language for the persons in God, given the notions of independent subjectivity and self-conscious personhood forced upon us by our experience as human individuals. Unlike his predecessors, too, John sees the defining characteristics of hypostatic being not only in origin and in relationships with other hypostases of the same nature—not only in one's place in the family, one might say—but also in behaviour, which for intelligent beings is inseparably rooted in the *will*. So he adopts the distinction Maximus had elaborated, a century earlier, between the 'natural will', the innate dynamism towards self-preservation and self-fulfilment shared by every living being, and the particular, 'gnomic will'—the human 'mode of using the natural will' determined by the inclinations of the individual—which in the present world, after the fall, tends to be self-centred and determined by passion. He writes:

Willing (θέλησις) is a natural appetite which is rational and living, suited only to what is natural. Natural acts of the will (φυσικὰ θελήματα) include, first, [to will] to be subject to the law of God—for the human person is naturally a servant of God and subject to Him—and next [to will] the things

---

[93] *De duab. Volunt.* 7. 1–27 (corrected recension) (ed. Kotter iv, 183–4).

[94] Ibid. In the chapter of his *Dialectica* where he deals more generally with the problem of the hypostatic union in Christ, John also seems to be aware that 'hypostasis' must be used of the persons in the Trinity in a more restricted sense than what we understand when speaking of created individuals. Having emphasized that no hypostasis can ever have undergone a new beginning in its own concrete being, since a hypostasis is 'coming-into-existence for oneself', he adds: 'one must know that in the case of the holy Trinity, hypostasis is the mode of each one's eternal existence, which has no beginning' (*Dial.* 67: ed. Kotter, i. 34–8). The contextual sense of historical contingency, of source and relationship and circumstance, implied in the word *hypostasis*, must clearly be taken analogously if one is to use the term for the inner life of the eternal God.

that hold nature together, such as hunger, thirst, sleep and such things.
Hypostatic, gnomic willing, on the other hand, is an appetite determined by
pleasure and by the private opinion of the hypostasis making use of the will,
not by the law of God; it is a mode of using the natural will, according to the
individual choice (*gnōmē*) of the hypostasis using it.[95]

John Damascene's analysis of the person of Christ in terms of
nature and hypostasis follows generally the lines of earlier tradition.
Christ, as a person, is unique—'one cannot find a common form' of
Christ, such as would allow one to speak of him as being a single
nature or universal substance![96] There never was and never will be
another Christ; his coming, his very being, is not the product of the
natural functioning of things either divine or human, but something
much more mysterious and unpredictable, 'a mode of adaptation
planned by God (τρόπος οἰκονομικῆς συγκαταβάσεως)'.[97] Thus we
must speak, in the language of the Second Council of Constantinople, of a 'union of two perfect natures, the divine and the
human'—not a union by confusion, as the 'Monophysites' imply,
nor a union of a merely 'external or relational kind', as the
Nestorians suggest—but a union 'by composition or indeed by
hypostasis'.[98] Following the earlier tradition, John emphasizes that
this notion of a 'hypostatic union' allows us 'to confess that the two
natures are preserved in him after the union, not as if we suppose
each of them to be by itself or set apart, but [seeing them as] united
with each other in the one compound hypostasis'.[99] And we can call
the union 'essential' (*ousiōdes*), not in the sense that the two united
natures form a single essence, but 'in the sense that they are truly'—
in other words, ontologically—'joined to each other to make the one
composite hypostasis of the Son of God', even while their 'essential'
differences remain intact as well.[100]

In the treatise *Against the Jacobites*, too, John emphasizes that the
paradoxical end-product (*apotelesma*) of the incarnation is not
something that developed over time, 'for ἕνωσις is not like the
nature of things that are coming to be but do not yet exist, such
as time or dancing or things like that.'[101] 'Things that are in relation

---

[95] *De duab. volunt.* 25 (ed. Kotter, iv. 207–8). For further discussion of the kinds of
will and their relation to nature and hypostasis, see ibid. 28. 74–7, 82–4; 35. 16–19.
[96] *Exp. Fid.* 47 (ed. Kotter, ii 113. 50). Cf. Leontius of Byzantium, *CNE* 5 (1292A).
[97] *Ctr. Jac.* 52 (ed. Kotter, iv. 127. 54–5).
[98] *Exp. Fid.* 47 (ed. Kotter, ii. 114. 60).   [99] Ibid. (ii. 114. 65–6).
[100] Ibid. (ii. 114. 67–115. 70).
[101] *Ctr. Jac.* 45 (ed. Kotter, iv 124. 7–9).

[τὰ πρός τι—the Aristotelian category] are simultaneous and always remain simultaneous', he asserts a few chapters later; 'but *union* and the things united belong to the class of things that are in relation. Union and the things united, therefore, are simultaneous'.[102] As a result, any union of two naturally different entities that we can call hypostatic must be temporally co-extensive with their very existence together as a hypostasis; so even in the case of the ordinary human 'hypostatic union' of soul and body to form the distinctive human individual, union is complete from the first moment of soul's and body's existence, and does not even come to an end when death separates body from soul. 'For the body and the soul remain, always preserving the single principle of their existence and hypostatic being, even if they should be separated from one another.'[103] Unlike natures, hypostases are always unique and unrepeatable, and endure as long as their natural powers allow. Yet they are constituted in their being by the very particular way in which their natural parts are related to each other and to the rest of creation— as individuals they are, in a sense, the product and the sum of their ontological circumstances.

IV Conclusions on the 'Manner' of Christ's Mystery

At the end of this rapid survey of the Greek patristic christological vocabulary—more particularly, of the use of the terms 'nature', 'hypostasis', and the 'mode of union' that can constitute the latter, without essentially changing or annihilating its component natural parts—what conclusions might we draw of a more general, theological kind that might help us reflect for ourselves on the 'manner' of the Mystery of Christ? Let me suggest at least a few:

1. When Greek theologians in the early church speak of the 'hypostasis' of Christ, or of the three 'hypostases' of the Trinity, it is clear that they are not referring to what we moderns might call a 'person': an independent subject, constituted by a unique and unrepeatable focus of self-consciousness, practical autonomy, and

---

[102] Ibid. 63 (iv. 131. 1–3).

[103] *Dial.* 67 (ed. Kotter i. 139. 22–4). Gregory of Nyssa had emphasized just this point about the souls and bodies of the dead in his dialogue *On the Soul and the Resurrection*.

some measure of psychological freedom, and so able to enter into relationships with genuine commitment, to 'give oneself away'; a repository of indestructible value within a world populated by persons, and thus an object of irreducible moral obligation for others; an individual whose existence is constituted by a contingent, limited yet authentic 'act of being' in its own right. Even language in these works identifying a hypostasis as possessing τὸ καθ᾽ ἑαυτὸ εἶναι ('being by oneself') should not lead us, as it has led a number of twentieth-century readers, to understand this as equivalent to the *Für-sich-sein* of German idealism—as referring to an ontological core of any particular density. For the authors we have been considering, who developed their notion of hypostasis to meet the needs of clarifying the apostolic faith, with the aid of contemporary philosophy but not necessarily determined by its conclusions, a hypostasis was essentially a particular individual within a universal species, identifiable as such or such a thing by the qualities it (or he or she) shared with similar individuals, yet marked off as unique by a set of characteristics all its own. It was the kind of thing so unique and unrepeatable you could call it by name—not just 'horse', but 'Silver'; not just 'man', but Peter or Paul or John, or even Jesus. Beyond this, however, the Greek Fathers we have been considering rarely attempt to 'look inside' the hypostasis of Jesus or of anyone else, and offer us little clue as to the peculiar ontological status or psychological character of any hypostasis within itself, besides insisting—as we have tried to show here—that the principal distinguishing characteristic of any individual is its *origin*: where it (or he or she) comes from, how it is situated genetically within the larger field of similar individuals, what its family relations are. In addition to origin, as John of Damascus observes, *behaviour*—the actualization of freedom in 'movement'—is also an indispensable determinant of the identity of human hypostases: *who we are* is revealed and actualized not only in *where we come from*, but in *how we act*. But whether it is origin or action that serves as our leading clue, for Greek patristic theology 'hypostasis', and even *hyparxis*, 'existence', were words that referred to the *manner* of being rather than to its general denomination—every 'who' was defined in terms of 'how' it was what it was recognized to be, rather than simply in terms of its 'what', its definition and its intelligible characteristics.

2. To say that Christ is a single hypostasis who joins together two wholly distinct and unequal natures—the transcendent, infinite,

foundational reality of God and the limited reality of a historical human being—in a 'mode of union' which constitutes his present personal reality is to say that he is a living paradox. It is also to say that his person, his life, the event of his coming and working in our world, are all contingent things, not derivable from our knowledge of human nature or from our speculations about the divine reality that lies at the heart of things. We cannot guess from what we know about humanity, the world, or even absolute reality itself that God would speak to us in this way, let alone that God's Word should 'become flesh and dwell among us' as a Jew in the time of Caesar Augustus. The features and acts that enable us to recognize Jesus as the eternal Word made flesh are all accidental, contingent, historical things, reported to us by historical witnesses: for the Fathers, first of all the extraordinary manner of his birth, his descendence from God's holy people, the holiness of his mother; then his miracles, the moral purity of his teaching, the extraordinary generosity and fidelity of his passion and death, the glorious transformation of Mount Tabor and Easter morning. All these things, as Maximus the Confessor liked to observe, reveal him as 'divine in a human way, and human in a divine way'.[104] For the Fathers, Christ the Lord is made a person, a hypostasis, precisely by the way God the Word acts in the world through Jesus, and the way the human Jesus is related to the Father and the Holy Spirit. How he exists, how each 'part' of him shapes and expresses the other, makes him who he is.

3. The core of the Mystery of Christ, then, for the authors we have been considering, is a mystery of *relationship*: God's relationship to the created world, and especially to the human community, now renewed and transformed by the unique, utterly particular relationship of God the Word to the humanity of Jesus. This is a relationship like no other we have experienced: totally unequal, expressing the total dependence of the human on the divine for its personal as well as its generic being, yet at the same time (as Maximus and John of Damascus recognized) setting this human freer than any human before him to be what all of us are created to be—sons and daughters of God, created in God's image and likeness. The uniqueness of Jesus' relationship to God is that the creative and redeeming presence of God in him—the mission of the Father, the creative ordering and self-revealing illumination of the Logos, the

---

[104] See, for example, *Opusc.* 7, To Marinus (PG 91, 84B11–D3); *Dialogue with Pyrrhus* (297D13–298A4).

anointing of the Spirit—brings his very person, his hypostasis into being in human terms, makes him who he is. Yet the Mystery of Christ's unique person is also a Mystery that potentially, at least, includes us: the model and source of our own renovation, as Maximus reminds us, the sign of our vocation as human creatures. Our hypostases need to be perfected in their humanity through our relationship to God in Christ.

4. In Christ, the particular and contingent character of the 'mode of union' reveals and embodies ultimate and universal things, the eternal, unknowable substance and nature of God, and also reveals and embodies human reality, human nature in its fullest perfection. This, perhaps, is why Greek christological writers continued to insist that for all its relational and 'modal' character, the union of divinity and humanity in Christ is also, paradoxically, a *substantial* one. Despite Nestorius' arguments, it was not to be conceived of as *simply* relational, simply a ἕνωσις σχετική. Neither of the realities involved, the divine or the human, could be conceptually plumbed to their depths or delimited, let alone explained in their new, unique christological structure of coinherence. But the struggle over the reception of Chalcedon made it clearer than ever before that the faith of Christianity is quite simply that it is *God* who encounters us personally in Jesus, that the hypostasis formed by Jesus' origin and his relationships and his actions 'has its being in the Logos'.[105] In recognizing and imitating the human Jesus' 'mode of union' with the transcendent substance of God, we discover nothing less than the presence of God here in the human world, inviting us to accept a new origin, a new set of relationships, a new personal identity and 'mode of being' that does not destroy what is proper to ourselves, but unites it to him.

---

[105] Leontius of Byzantium, *Epil.* 1944C 2–4.

9

Aquinas' Metaphysics of the Incarnation

ELEONORE STUMP

I INTRODUCTION

Aquinas' interpretation of the metaphysics of the incarnation is an attempt to make sense out of a theological doctrine bequeathed to him as a traditional and central part of Christian belief. In this chapter, I want to explicate his interpretation of the doctrine and go some way towards defending it. It is *not* my intent to argue that the formulation of the doctrine he accepts as traditional is the only orthodox one, or that his interpretation of that formulation is the only appropriate interpretation of the doctrine, or that his interpretation is the best way to understand biblical statements about the nature of Christ. It is also *not* part of my purpose to show that Aquinas' interpretation is completely intelligible and coherent or philosophically defensible in every respect. Rather, my aim in this chapter is a limited one: to explicate Aquinas' interpretation of the doctrine of the incarnation in terms of his metaphysics in such a way as to clarify and support both his understanding of the doctrine and his metaphysics.

The formulation of the doctrine of the incarnation which Aquinas accepts and takes as binding on Christians is the one put forward at Chalcedon in AD 451: Christ is one hypostasis, one person, with two natures, one fully human and the other fully divine. Stating the Chalcedonian formulation is one thing; explaining what it means is another. Aquinas relies heavily on his general metaphysical theory to provide one interpretation of the Chalcedonian formulation. His interpretation is so thoroughly rooted in his general metaphysics that it is not possible to grasp this part of his philosophical theology without some understanding of his metaphysics.[1] On the other

---

[1] So e.g. I disagree with much of Richard Cross's otherwise excellent analysis of Aquinas' account of the incarnation because I understand the underlying metaphysics

hand, the doctrine of the incarnation stretches that metaphysics almost to breaking-point. Consequently, in the course of considering the incarnation, Aquinas is compelled to explain his metaphysics with some care, in order to argue that, contrary to appearances, the doctrine of the incarnation does not serve as a counterexample to any of his general metaphysical claims. Some of his most helpful explanations of various parts of his metaphysics can thus be found in his discussions of the incarnation.

I shall begin by laying out just the parts of Aquinas' metaphysics which in my view are particularly important with regard to the doctrine of the incarnation. After that, I shall turn to Aquinas' interpretation of the doctrine of the incarnation itself. I shall be concerned primarily with the way in which Aquinas understands the Chalcedonian formula, the resources his interpretation of the formula has for handling familiar objections to the doctrine of the incarnation, and the view of the mind of Christ to which his interpretation is committed.

II MATTER AND FORM

Aquinas thinks that a macro-level material thing is matter organized or configured in some way, where the organization or configuration is dynamic rather than static. That is, the organization of the matter comprises causal relations among the material components of the thing as well as such static features as shape and spatial location.[2] This dynamic configuration or organization is what Aquinas calls 'form'.[3] Furthermore, a thing has the properties it

differently from the way in which he does; see R. Cross, 'Aquinas on Nature, Hypostasis, and the Metaphysics of the Incarnation', *Thomist*, 60 (1996), 171–202.

[2] That is why Aquinas thinks that at the instant of death the form of a human being is replaced by a different form, even if the general shape and appearance of the body remain the same. Once a human being dies and the soul is gone, he says, we use such words as 'flesh' or 'eye' equivocally if we apply them to the corpse (*Quaestiones disputatae de anima*, 9 corpus). At death, the matter of the body is configured in a substantially different way and so has a form different from the one it had before death. See e.g. *In De anima*, 2. 1. 1, 226; see also *Sententia super Metaphysicam*, 7. 1. 11 (1519). For a helpful discussion of the relation of a thing's form to its nature, see also *ST* 3a. 2. 1 and *SCG* 4. 35 (3728–29).

[3] For a very helpful attempt to explicate a notion at least closely related to the Aristotelian concept of form which is at issue in this part of Aquinas' metaphysics, see K. Fine, 'Things and their Parts', *Midwest Studies in Philosophy*, 23 (1999), 61–74. Fine does an admirable job of discussing this notion in the context of contemporary

has, including its causal powers, in virtue of having the configuration it does; the proper operations and functions of a thing derive from its form.[4]

Prime matter is matter without any form at all, 'materiality' (as it were) apart from configuration. When it is a component in a matter-form composite, prime matter is the component of the configured composite which makes it the case that the configured thing can be extended in three dimensions and can occupy a particular place at a particular time. Prime matter does not by itself occupy a place or extend through dimensions; it needs to be configured by forms in order to do so. But prime matter is the component of the configured whole which allows the configured whole to be spatially extended; form alone cannot be spatially extended.[5]

Aquinas takes it that the forms of material objects can be divided into two sorts, substantial forms (that is, the substantial forms of things that are primary substances) and accidental forms. For present purposes we can understand his distinction between substantial and accidental forms in this way. A substantial form of a material thing configures prime matter.[6] For this reason, configuration by a substantial form brings it about that a thing which was not already in existence comes into existence. Since any thing that comes into existence exists as a member of a kind, the substantial form of a thing is thus also responsible for a thing's belonging to a particular primary kind or lowest species.[7] The change produced by the advent of a substantial form is consequently a generation of a thing.[8]

From Aquinas' claim that a substantial form configures prime matter, it follows that no part of a substance counts as a substance in its own right as long as it is a component of a larger whole that is

mereology and showing that the Aristotelian notion can do what cannot be done equally well with mereological schemes. He also makes a very helpful distinction between what he calls 'temporary' and 'timeless' parts. This distinction has some resemblance to the distinction I make later in the chapter between integral and metaphysical parts (though perhaps Fine himself might think the resemblance attenuated).

[4] See e.g. *SCG* 4. 36 (3740).
[5] Cf. *De principiis naturae*, 1–2.
[6] For the claims about what substantial and accidental forms configure, see e.g. *De principiis naturae*, 1.
[7] For the claims about what the forms bring into existence, see e.g. *De principiis naturae*, 1; see also *ST* 3a. 2. 6 objs. 2–3, the replies to the objections, and *ST* 3a 3. 7 ad 1.
[8] See e.g. *SCG* 4. 48 (3834).

a substance.[9] Otherwise, the substantial form of the whole would configure parts which have their own substantial form, and so the form of the whole would configure matter-form composites, rather than prime matter. Consequently, the substantial form, which a part of a whole would have if it existed on its own, is absent when it becomes part of a composite substance and is replaced instead by the one substantial form of the composite.[10] Or, to put the same point the other way around, if we divide a composite substance into its parts, we may turn what was one substance into several substances.[11]

So a substance comes into existence when prime matter is configured by a substantial form. If its constituents existed as things before being woven together by that configuration, they cease to exist as things in their own right when they are conjoined into the whole, and a new thing is generated.

III Individuation and Identity for Material Substances

Aquinas thinks that a substance is always individuated by its substantial form, which is unique to it.[12] A thing is *this* thing just in virtue of the fact that the form which conjoins the parts of it into one whole is *this* form. So, for example, a substance such as Socrates is this human being in virtue of having *this* substantial form of a human being; what is necessary and sufficient for something to be identical to Socrates is that its substantial form be identical to the substantial form of Socrates.[13]

But what makes something *this* substantial form rather than some other? For any species of material thing, there are many individuals within a species, and the species-conferring configuration, the substantial form, of each member of the species will

---

[9] Cf. *ST* 3a. 2. 1, *Compendium theologiae*, 210 (406) and 212 (418), and *SCG* 4. 35 (3733).

[10] See e.g. *Compendium theologiae*, 210 (406), where Aquinas explains this general point in connection with the composition of the incarnate Christ, and *SCG* 4. 49.

[11] See e.g. *Compendium theologiae*, 212 (418).

[12] I discuss below Aquinas' claim that in the special case of material objects substantial forms are individuated by matter, so that matter is the ultimate individuator for material objects.

[13] *Expositio super librum Boethii De trinitate*, 4. 2; see also *ST* 1a. 119. 1 and *Quaestiones disputatae de potentia*, 9. 1.

therefore be the same. Aquinas designates the collection of the species-conferring properties a thing has in virtue of having a substantial form of a certain sort with the Latin term translated 'nature'. The nature of a thing is what is signified by the species name of the thing, and a thing's nature is given by its substantial form.[14] The human nature of Socrates is the same as the human nature of Plato insofar as they are both human beings, and so the species-conferring configuration of Plato is the same as the species-conferring configuration of Socrates. How, then, are the substantial forms of material objects such as human beings individuated?

Aquinas' response to this worry is expressed succinctly in his well-known line that matter individuates.[15] When Aquinas attempts to explain the concept of matter relevant to individuation, he tends to speaks of it as signate matter[16] or as matter under indeterminate dimensions,[17] that is, matter which is extended in three dimensions but where the degree of extension in any dimension is left open or vague rather than being specified. Now any actually existing matter has determinate dimensions. But the particular degree of extension in a dimension is one thing; the materiality, as it were, of matter is another thing. The determinate dimensions of a material thing have to do with exactly what space that thing occupies at a given time; the materiality of the matter is responsible for the space-occupying feature itself. That is, matter is the sort of thing which is *here* now,[18] in a way that numbers, for example, are not. This feature of matter, however, can be considered without specifying the precise spatial locations that the matter occupies. When Aquinas talks of matter under indeterminate dimensions, it seems to me that he is attempting to call attention to this feature of matter.

No doubt, one could wish for a great deal more clarity and

[14] See e.g. *De unione verbi incarnati*, 1; see also ibid. 2 ad 6 where Aquinas explains that the name of a species signifies a nature.

[15] See *De ente et essentia*, 2. Perhaps the most detailed exposition of this view of his is in his *Expositio super librum Boethii De trinitate*, 4. 2; see also *ST* 3a. 3. 7 ad 1 and *SCG* 4. 30 (3780–1).

[16] *De ente et essentia*, 2.

[17] *Expositio super librum Boethii De trinitate*, 4. 2. Aquinas does not always describe his position on this score in the same way; e.g. in *De ente et essentia*, 2 he explains signate matter as matter under determinate dimensions. The variation in terminology suggests to some scholars either a development in his thought or a series of changes of mind. The issue is complicated, and so I am leaving it to one side here. Cf. *Sententia super Metaphysicam*, 7. 1. 2 (1283) for a helpful discussion of matter and its dimensions.

[18] Cf. *Expositio super librum Boethii De trinitate*, 4. 2.

precision with regard to the notion of matter Aquinas has in mind when he claims that matter individuates. But perhaps this is enough to point us in the right direction for making sense of his concept of substantial forms that are individual rather than universal. For Aquinas, what individuates Socrates is *this* substantial form of a human being; and a substantial form of a material substance such as a human being is *this* substantial form in virtue of the fact that it configures *this* matter.

IV CONSTITUTION AND IDENTITY

It is important to see that on Aquinas' views of matter and form constitution is not identity,[19] and a whole is something more than the sum of its parts. One might wonder whether Aquinas is entitled to this claim if, as I claimed above, he takes the form of the whole to include the properties of the parts, as well as the causal relations among those parts. What else could there be to the configuration of the whole? Some confusion arises in considering this question because we can understand the properties of the parts in more than one way. In particular, when we include under the properties of the parts the relations and causal interactions among those parts, we can be thinking of these properties either as (i) the properties the parts have when they are taken *singillatim* (as e.g. the properties including causal powers which the constituent atoms of a molecule have considered on their own, when they are not configured together into the molecule), or as (ii) the properties the parts in fact have when they are in the whole (as e.g. the properties the atoms of a molecule have when they are configured into the molecule). If we understand the properties of the parts in sense (i), it is true to say, as biochemists do, that the features of a whole protein (such as its folded shape) cannot always be derived from

---

[19] See, e.g. *Sententia super Metaphysicam*, 7. 1. 17 (1672–74). There Aquinas says that in cases in which the composite is one thing, the composite is not identical with its components; rather the composite is something over and above its components. See also *De unione verbi incarnati*, 1. For interesting contemporary arguments against the reduction of wholes to their parts, see M. Johnston, 'Constitution is not Identity', *Mind*, 101 (1992), 89–105, and L. Rudder Baker, 'Why Constitution is not Identity', *Journal of Philosophy*, 94 (1997), 599–621. For an excellent discussion of the constitution relation, see L. Rudder Baker, 'Unity Without Identity: A New Look at Material Constitution', *Midwest Studies in Philosophy*, 23 (1999), 144–165.

even perfect knowledge of the properties (including the causal powers) of the atoms which are constituents of the protein. This is so because a large protein achieves its biologically active form, including its folded shape, only with the help of certain enzymes acting on it; and so the properties of the whole are a function of something more than the properties of the parts taken *singillatim*. But if we understand the properties of the parts in sense (ii), then in effect we are smuggling the configuration, or the form of the whole, into the properties of the parts of the whole. In sense (ii), it would be very surprising if there were properties of the whole that were not a function of the properties of the parts of the whole. Nonetheless, in sense (ii), the properties of the whole are a function of the properties of the parts *in the configuration of the whole*. Consequently, in either sense (i) or sense (ii), the parts alone are not all there is to the whole; the configuration of the whole is also required. A whole is thus not identical to its constituents alone.

The general designation Aquinas uses for a thing which has a particular substantial form is the Latin 'supposit'[20] or the Greek term transliterated into Latin as '*hypostasis*'.[21] A supposit is a particular or individual just in the category of substance.[22] The Latin term translated 'person' is Aquinas' technical term for an individual substance of a rational nature.[23] For Aquinas, although the existence of *this* substantial form is necessary and sufficient for the

---

[20] In the case of the incarnate Christ, the thing which has a human substantial form is the whole composite, and not just the human nature. Or, to put the same point another way, the substantial form of a human being which is part of the human nature of Christ is *had* not by the nature of which it is one constituent but by the whole composed of all the constituents of Christ.

[21] See e.g. *Compendium theologiae* 1. 210 (405–6) and *SCG* 4. 49 (3846). The terms 'supposit' and 'hypostasis' are not synonymous for Aquinas, strictly speaking, because although they pick out the same thing in reality (for this point see e.g. *SCG* 4. 38 (3766)), they pick out under slightly different designations, because 'suppositum' is a term of second intention and 'hypostasis' is a term of first intention. For the distinction, see *De unione verbi incarnati*, 2. This complexity of medieval logic is one I will ignore here for the sake of brevity.

[22] Aquinas gives a helpful explanation of his use of these terms in *De unione verbi incarnati*, 2; see also *Quaestiones quodlibetales*, 5. 2. 1. Strictly speaking, because God is simple, God does not belong in any of the Aristotelian categories. Consequently, strictly speaking, God is not a substance, and the person of Christ is not a supposit in virtue of being the second person of the Trinity. On the doctrine of divine simplicity, however, it is not possible to give an appropriate formulation which is in accordance with the doctrine, and Aquinas himself is willing to use the relevant terms broadly, rather than strictly, in the case of Christ. I follow his lead here.

[23] *ST* 3a. 2. 2.

existence of a supposit, a supposit is not identical with its substantial form alone. The substantial form is only a constituent of the supposit.[24]

To begin with, any thing which has a substantial form necessarily also has accidents, even though it is not necessary that it have one accident rather than another. So a substantial form is not the only metaphysical constituent of a thing; any thing will also have accidents as metaphysical constituents. In addition, for material things, the matter which the substantial form configures is also a constituent of a supposit.[25] So a supposit has more metaphysical constituents than just the substantial form. If, however, a supposit were identical to its substantial form alone, then these other metaphysical constitutents would not be constitutents of the supposit itself.

If constitution is not identity, then we need to consider the relation of the composite whole to its parts. The constitution relation lets us make a distinction among the properties appropriately predicated of the composite whole. The whole can have a property

---

[24] Eric Olson argues that a human person is identical to a living organism but that the persistence of only a small, living biological part of the organism (a part of the brain, namely, the brainstem) is necessary and sufficient for the existence of that organism; see E. Olson, *The Human Animal* (Oxford: Oxford University Press, 1997). That is, although a human being is not identical to a living brainstem, what a human being is identical to—a living biological organism—is such that it can exist when it is composed only of a brainstem. Aquinas' views are similar. A human being is not identical to a soul. But what a human being is identical to—a particular in the species *mortal rational animal*—is something that in certain circumstances can exist when it is composed of nothing more than a soul. And so Aquinas' position can be thought of as the metaphysical analogue of Olson's: the persistence of a small, living metaphysical part of the whole human supposit is necessary and sufficient for the existence of that human being. It doesn't follow that a human being is identical to his soul any more than it follows from Olson's view that a human being is identical with a part of his brain. For Aquinas, a soul is not identical to a human being; but a human being—a mortal rational animal—is such that, although it is naturally embodied, it is also capable of persisting for a time in an unnatural disembodied condition. In the same way, a living biological organism which is a human being is naturally and ordinarily composed of more than just a part of the brain; but, if Olson is right, it is also capable of persisting for a time in an unnatural, severely reduced condition. I am grateful to Scott MacDonald, whose persistent questions on this score helped me to see this point.

[25] See e.g. *SCG* 4. 40 and *De unione verbi incarnati*, 1 where Aquinas says that a suppositum will not be the same as a nature in anything in which there is either accident or individual matter, because in that case the suppositum is related to the nature by means of an addition. See also *SCG* 4. 40 (3781) where Aquinas explains the distinction between a singular and its quiddity or nature, and goes on to explain that a supposit such as Socrates is not identical to his substantial form because he is also constituted of designated matter.

either in its own right or else in virtue of the fact that one of its constituents has that property in its own right.[26] Consider, for example, the molecule CAT/Enhancer-Binding Protein (C/EBP), which is important in regulating DNA transcription, is a dimer, each of whose subunits is a protein which is coiled with an alpha helix coil.[27] The molecule thus has the property of being coiled in the alpha helix manner, but it has that property in virtue of the fact that it has two parts which are coiled in that way. Each of these parts of the molecule, however, is coiled in the alpha helix manner in its own right. On the other hand, the whole molecule has the property of regulating DNA transcription, and this property it has in its own right, in consequence of the shape of the molecule as a whole, which allows it to fit into one of the grooves of DNA.

Adopting a term from Lynne Rudder Baker,[28] we can say that the whole molecule 'borrows' some of its properties from its constituents, and it has these properties only in virtue of the fact that the constituents have them in their own right. Baker emphasizes the fact that a property borrowed from a part is nonetheless genuinely to be attributed to the whole. She says,

Borrowing walks a fine line. On the one hand, if *x* borrows *H* from *y*, then *x* really has *H*—piggyback, so to speak . . . . if I cut my hand, then *I* really bleed . . . I borrow the property of bleeding from my body, but I really bleed. But the fact that I am bleeding is none other than the fact that I am constituted by a body that is bleeding. So, not only does *x* really have *H* by borrowing it, but also—and this is the other hand—if *x* borrows *H* from *y*, there are not two independent instances of *H*: if *x* borrows *H*, then *x*'s having *H* is entirely a matter of *x*'s having constitution relations to something that has *H* non-derivatively.[29]

Although Aquinas does not draw this distinction among properties explicitly, his metaphysical views about constitution provide for it, and he relies on it in one place after another. So, for example, he argues that whatever follows naturally on the accidents or the parts of a supposit is predicated of the whole supposit on account of the

---

[26] Baker speaks in this connection of something's having a property independently, rather than in its own right, and she gives a helpful analysis of what it is for anything to have a property independently. See Baker, 'Unity Without Identity', 151–60.

[27] A helpful discussion of this molecule and its properties can be found in S. L. McKnight, 'Molecular Zippers in Gene Regulation', *Scientific American*, 264 (1991), 54–64.

[28] See Baker, 'Unity Without Identity', 151–60.

[29] Ibid.

accident or part in question. A man is thus said to be curly on account of his hair or seeing on account of the function of the eye, on Aquinas' view.[30] Similarly, in discussing the powers of the soul, the substantial form of a human being, Aquinas says: 'We *can* say that the soul understands in the same way that we can say that the eye sees; but it would be more appropriate to say that *a human being* understands *by means of* the soul'[31] (emphasis added). Here a property (understanding) of a metaphysical part, the soul, and a property (seeing) of an integral part, the eye, are transferred to the whole, the person, which in effect borrows these properties from its parts.

V INCARNATION: THE DOCTRINAL CLAIMS

With this much work on Aquinas' metaphysics, we are now in a position to turn to his interpretation of the Chalcedonian formulation of the doctrine of the incarnation. The Chalcedonian formula says that Christ is one person with two natures. On Aquinas' understanding of the doctrine, the one person of Christ[32] is the second person of the triune God.

There is some ambiguity in the notion of person in the case of Christ, as Aquinas himself recognizes.[33] Because Christ is one and just one person, and a person is a substance of a particular sort, there is just substance in Christ. That substance is composite. It includes a human soul and body and the divine nature. So Christ is one composite person. On the other hand, the second person of the Trinity, who is identical with his divine nature, is a constituent of the composite Christ. So in the case of Christ 'person' can refer either to the substance which Christ is, or to the second person of the Trinity in his incarnate state. I shall use the expression 'the person of Christ' to refer to the incarnate second person of the Trinity; to refer to the composite person which the incarnate Christ is, I shall use the expression 'the person Christ'. Nonetheless, it does not follow that there are two persons or two substances in Christ. The human nature, body and soul, are assumed by the second person of the

---

[30] *SCG* 4. 48 (3835).
[31] *ST* 1a. 75. 2 ad 2.
[32] See e.g. *ST* 3a, 2. 3–4 and 17. 1; *De unione verbi incarnati*, 4.
[33] Cf. *ST* 3a. 2. 4.

Trinity and united to him in a union of person. Consequently, the new composite is the same person as before the incarnation. For some discussion of the metaphysical difficulties of this claim, see the discussion below regarding the notion of a union in person in the incarnation. Finally, it is worth noticing here that this ambiguity does not mean that the term 'person' is equivocal. In either of its ambiguous uses as regards Christ, it means *an individual substance of a rational nature*. The divine nature includes the cognition of reasons, and the deity is one thing; so the Boethian definition of person fits the persons of the Trinity, too, as long as we are careful not to define the terms in that definition in such a way as to make them incapable of applying to what is simple. When the second person of the Trinity assumes a human nature, it does so in a union of person, so that the resulting composite is still only one supposit. Since this supposit is an individual substance and one which is rational, the composite incarnate Christ is still an individual substance of a rational nature.

All that is true of deity is true of the person of Christ. He is outside time; his knowledge, power, and goodness are not limited, and so on. In short, because the person of Christ is the second person of the Trinity, divine nature is the nature of that person.[34]

At a certain moment in time, the second person of the Trinity assumed a human nature. That is to say, the second person added to himself another nature, in addition to the divine nature already his own.[35] As I said above, for Aquinas, the nature of a material substance is conferred by a substantial form which is an individual; and a substantial form is an individual in virtue of configuring matter. So when the second person of the Trinity assumes human nature, he assumes a particular substantial form and the matter it configures.[36]

Like every other human substantial form, the substantial form assumed by Christ configures matter into a human body and confers those properties essential to human beings, including rationality. In virtue of having two natures, Christ therefore has two operations.[37] In his divine nature, he has the operation proper to the deity. In his human nature, Christ has a complete and fully human mind, and he also has a rational appetite, that is to say, a complete and fully

---

[34] See e.g. *ST* 3a. 2. 4.
[35] See e.g. *ST* 3a. 2. 8.
[36] *ST* 3a. 2. 5 and *Compendium theologiae*, 209 (402–4).
[37] *De unione verbi incarnati*, 5.

human will. Since intellect and will also characterize the divine nature, in virtue of having two natures Christ also has two intellects[38] and two wills,[39] one human and one divine.[40]

Furthermore, different things can be true of these intellects and these wills. The human intellect can fail to know something that the divine intellect knows.[41] It is impossible that Christ sin, in either his divine or his human will.[42] But it is possible for the human will to be out of accord with the divine will, at least as regards desire, without sin. Consequently, Christ's human will can desire what the divine will rules out.[43] When the human will of Christ desires not to die, there is a non-sinful discord of this sort between the divine and the human wills.[44]

For these reasons, the multiplicity of the natures is preserved on Aquinas' interpretation. However the unity of Christ is to be explained, it is not a unity of nature.

Now for a subsisting thing to have a complete human nature is just for it to have a human soul and body and thus to be a human substance. But to be an individual human substance is to be a human person. Consequently, it seems as if there must be a human person as well as a divine person in Christ. Aquinas' response to this sort of worry is to grant that in general a human soul configuring a human body composes a human body but that in the special case of Christ there is a human soul and body but not a human person. Because the substantial form and the matter it configures are part of a larger composite, which includes the second person of the Trinity and the divine nature, in this one case, the substantial form of a human being and the matter it configures do not constitute a human person. If they existed on their own, outside the composite which is the incarnate Christ, the human soul and body of Christ would certainly constitute a human person. But conjoined in Christ,

---

[38] *ST* 3a. 9. 1.   [39] *ST* 3a. 18. 1.

[40] Strictly speaking, this locution is inaccurate. The divine nature is simple, and so it is not accurate to speak of the divine person as having an intellect and a will. But the locutions needed to try to speak accurately in accordance with the doctrine of divine simplicity are so clumsy that Aquinas himself does not always avoid the simpler but inaccurate locutions. Having noted the constraints of divine simplicity, in the rest of the chapter I shall avail myself of the simpler locutions such as that used here, which describes the person of Christ's having an intellect and will.

[41] See e.g. *QDV* 20. 1 and 4.

[42] *ST* 3a. 18. 4.

[43] *ST* 3a. 16. 5, but see the qualification in 6.

[44] See *ST* 3a. 15. 4–6.

they do not, in virtue of being subsumed into the larger whole.[45] There is therefore just one person in Christ, and that person is divine.

The two natures of Christ are united into one thing in this one person, so that the unity of the incarnate Christ is a unity in person. (Since the person is a supposit or a hypostasis, this unity is sometimes also referred to as 'a hypostatic union'.)

There are perhaps three main questions to ask of this, as of any other, interpretation of the Chalcedonian formula of the doctrine of the incarnation.

First, does the interpretation succeed in preserving the Chalcedonian formula, or does it instead alter the doctrine, overtly or by implication, in the process of interpreting it? An interpretation of the doctrine which explicitly or covertly multiplied the persons or conflated the natures of Christ into one, for example, would be an interpretation which was not successful in preserving the Chalcedonian formula.

Second, does the interpretation give us a logically coherent position? An interpretation which in effect predicates contradictory attributes of one and the same thing would not be a logically coherent position. Does the interpretation have the resources to show that in predicating the attributes of divinity and humanity of one and the same thing, it is not simply making inconsistent claims?

Finally, we ordinarily think of a person as an entity with a mind and a will. Even in the bizarre human cases we know of in which there seem to be multiple personalities in one organism, one personality at a time is present in a body, so that there is one will and one mind operative at a time. There are those rare cases of dicephalic twins where one physically indissoluble biological organism is governed by two minds and two wills, but just for that reason most of us suppose that such an organism is governed by *two* persons, not one. Apart from worries about the logical coherence of the doctrine of the incarnation, is there any way to explain the claim that there is one person with two minds and two wills which makes psychological sense? What would it be for one person to be split in this way and yet constitute one person? Or, to put the same point another way, how could two minds constitute one person without thereby collapsing into one mind? If one mind knows the date of the

[45] *ST* 3a. 2. 3 ad 2.

Last Judgement and the other mind does not, what are we to say about the mental or cognitive state of the one person?

If Aquinas' interpretation does not have the resources to answer this third question, it will in effect have multiplied the persons in Christ. If, as things are in this world, two minds cannot comprise one person even if both minds are in one organism, then however much Aquinas may insist on the Chalcedonian orthodoxy of his interpretation, his interpretation will deviate from the Chalcedonian formula in virtue of holding that there are two minds in the incarnate Christ. On the other hand, unless there is some way of making sense of the claim that one thing can have contradictory human and divine attributes, Aquinas' interpretation will not be successful in modelling the Chalcedonian distinction of the natures of Christ. If his attempt to keep the doctrine of the incarnation from logical incoherence by segregating the apparently incompatible attributes into distinct natures is nothing but a complicated way of predicating incompatible properties of the same thing, then on his interpretation there will in effect be just one complicated nature of Christ, a conjunctive nature having incompatible divine and human properties.[46] In effect, then, Aquinas' interpretation will have conflated the natures.[47]

---

[46] In correspondence, Brian Leftow has asked whether it is so much as possible to avoid attributing a conjunctive nature to Christ. If Christ is human and divine, then it seems as if he has one nature, namely, the nature of being human-and-divine. I think, however, that Aquinas' metaphysics rule out such a conjunctive nature, and I also think that Aquinas is concerned to make sure that his views do not conflate natures in Christ. On Aquinas' view, a nature is something conferred by a substantial form (or a form which is a substance in the case of immaterial things). If there were only one nature in Christ, then there would be only one substantial form, or one form which is a substance. But the substantial form of a human being does not configure all the components of the incarnate Christ, because it does not configure the second person of the deity; the substantial form of a human being configures matter. The form which is the second person of the Trinity does not configure all of the components of the incarnate Christ either, however, because the second person is not a form configuring matter. So there is not one substantial form (or one form which is a substance) which configures all the components in the incarnate Christ; rather there are two such forms. Consequently, there are two natures, not one. It is for this very reason that Aquinas has so much difficulty in explaining what kind of union of the components there is in the incarnate Christ, as I explain below.

[47] For an example of a contemporary interpretation of the Chalcedonian formula which suffers this sort of defect, see T. V. Morris, *The Logic of God Incarnate*, (Ithaca, NY: Cornell University Press, 1986). Morris attempts to keep the two natures of Christ distinct, but the nature of his attempt makes it seem as if he has in fact conflated the natures. So, Peter van Inwagen, commenting on Morris's interpretation, says, 'One might wonder whether it is not a form of monophysitism' ('Incarnation and Christo-

For these reasons, the question whether Aquinas' interpretation of the doctrine is faithful to the Chalcedonian formulation is best answered by considering whether or not Aquinas' interpretation has the resources to deal successfully with the second and third questions.

VI LOGICAL INCOHERENCE

There is certainly a *prima facie* case to be made for the objection that the doctrine of the incarnation attributes contradictory properties to one and the same thing. On the doctrine of the incarnation, one and the same thing is said to be limited in power and not limited in power, for example. Being limited in power and not being limited in power are contradictory properties, and both properties are attributed to Christ. So, on the face of it, it seems as if the objection is right.

One traditional way, employed also by Aquinas, of defending the Chalcedonian formula against this objection is by means of reduplicative propositions.[48] According to the reduplicative strategy, the fact that both limited and unlimited power are attributed to Christ does not show the Chalcedonian formula of the incarnation to be incoherent, because omnipotence is predicated of Christ in his divine nature and lack of omnipotence is predicated of him in his human nature.[49] Christ *qua* God is omnipotent; *qua* human, he is not. Consequently, on the reduplicative strategy, the attributes that are incompatible with each other are also segregated from each other in the incarnate Christ in virtue of inhering in different natures of his.

The reduplicative strategy is not much in favour in contemporary philosophical theology. One apparently plausible criticism of it runs along these lines. For any reduplicative proposition of the form 'x as A is N and x as B is not N', if 'the reduplication predicates being A of x and predicates being B of x' and if 'being N is entailed by being A,

---

logy', in *The Routledge Encyclopedia of Philosophy* (New York: Routledge: 1999, 725–32, at 730)). See also my review of Morris's book in *Faith and Philosophy*, 6 (1989), 218–23.

[48] Aquinas uses or discusses the reduplicative strategy in many places. See e.g. *ST* 3a 16. 10–12 and *Compendium theologiae*, 210 (407), 229, and 232.

[49] Cf. *ST* 3a 13. 1.

and not being N is entailed by being B',[50] then the reduplicative proposition is nothing more than a complicated way of predicating contradictory attributes of its subject, x.[51]

Aquinas' metaphysics, and especially his attitude towards constitution, give a response to this sort of objection to the reduplication strategy, however.[52] On Aquinas' view, there is a distinction between a property a whole has in its own right and a property it has in virtue of having a constituent that has that property in its own right; as I explained above, a whole can borrow a property from one of its constituents.

This distinction gives us one helpful way to analyse *qua* locutions of the form *x qua A is N*. In such a locution, the property of being N is predicated of *x*, but it is predicated of *x* just in virtue of the fact that *x* has a constituent *C* which has the property of being *N* in its own right. So, for example, 'C/EBP *qua* dimer with coiled subunits has the property of being coiled in the alpha helix manner' predicates a property of the whole molecule which it borrows from a part. C/EBP has a constituent C—in this case, a coiled subunit of the dimer—which has in its own right the property *being coiled in the alpha helix manner*. *Being coiled in the alpha helix manner* is thus predicated of C/EBP in virtue of the fact that the molecule's dimer subunit is coiled

---

[50] Morris, *Logic of God Incarnate*, 48.

[51] See van Inwagen, 'Incarnation and Christology', 730–1, for a helpful and succinct expression of the challenge to the reduplicative strategy, which he calls 'a predicative solution'. Van Inwagen says: 'A satisfactory predicative solution must supplement the abstract theses . . . [which give a reduplicative form to statements predicating attributes of Christ] with some sort of reply to the following challenge: Where *F* and *G* are incompatible properties, and *K1* and *K2* are "kinds", what does it mean to say of something that it is *F qua K1* but *G qua K2*?—or that it is *F qua K1* but is not *F qua K2*? And can any more or less uncontroversial examples of such pairs of statements be found?' This section of my chapter is an attempt to show that Aquinas' metaphysics has the resources to respond to this challenge, and the example of the borrowed properties of C/EBP is an attempt to provide a more ordinary and less controversial case of such pairs of statements.

[52] A different and elegant solution to the problem of the apparent logical incoherence of the doctrine of the incarnation can be found in P. van Inwagen, 'Not by Confusion of Substance, but by Unity of Person', in A. G. Padgett (ed.), *Reason and the Christian Religion: Essays in Honour of Richard Swinburne* (Oxford: Clarendon Press, 1994). Van Inwagen provides an analysis of reduplicative propositions in terms of relative identity. On this interpretation, God is the same person as the human being Jesus of Nazareth, but not the same substance or being. Aquinas considers a solution of this sort himself (see *ST* 3a. 2. 3 and *De unione verbi incarnati*, 2), but he rejects it, as he has to do. On his metaphysics, a person is an individual substance of a rational nature, and so for any individuals x and y, x is the same person as y only if x is the same substance as y.

in that way. On the other hand, C/EBP is a conglomerate of two such dimer subunits which bend away from each other in a limp Y-shape at one end of the molecule. So this is also true: 'C/EBP *qua* Y-shaped is not coiled in the alpha helix manner.' Here again a borrowed property is being attributed to the whole. C/EBP has a constituent C—in this case, the Y-shaped end of the molecule—which has in its own right the property *not being coiled in the alpha helix manner*.

Someone might suppose that when in a *qua* locution we attribute to the molecule C/EBP the property *being coiled*, we are in effect just attributing to it the property *having a coiled part*, and when we attribute to it the property *not being coiled*, we are just attributing to it the property *having a part that is not coiled*. Clearly, there is no incoherence here, but that is because these are not incompatible properties. But, then, on this way of analysing the relations of part to whole, the properties which really are incompatible—*being coiled* and *not being coiled*—are not attributes of the molecule; they are attributes only of its parts.

But this line of argument cannot be right. A thing which has a coiled part really is itself coiled in some respect or to some degree. Similarly, in virtue of having a part that is Y-shaped, the whole itself is really not coiled in that respect or to that degree. If a student, seeing a diagram of the molecule for the first time, were to try to describe it to someone unfamiliar with its shape, she might well say, 'Well, it's a sort of complicated coiled, Y-shaped molecule.' So the incompatible properties *being coiled* and *not being coiled* are attributes of the whole molecule, not just of different parts of the molecule. But because these are borrowed properties, since the molecule does not have these properties in its own right, there is no incoherence in the claims that the molecule is both coiled and not coiled.

As long as *qua* locutions are understood in this way, it is clear that both *qua* locutions—'x as A is N' and 'x as B is not N'—can be true without any violation of the laws of logic. The two *qua* claims taken together do not have the result that we are making inconsistent claims or that we are giving a logically incoherent account of x. Although contradictory attributes are being predicated of the same subject, they are not being predicated in the same respect. C/EBP is coiled in virtue of having a constituent which is coiled in the alpha helix manner, and it is not coiled in virtue of having a constituent which is Y-shaped.

Someone might suppose that we should simply reidentify the characteristics which are being attributed to the whole. Someone might hold, that is, that C/EBP has the properties *being coiled with respect to its alpha helix constituents* and *not being coiled with respect to its Y-shaped constituent*. On this way of understanding the characteristics in question, it is easier to see that the simultaneous predication of these attributes does not violate any laws of logic, and this feature of this way of specifying C/EBP's characteristics is no doubt an advantage. On the other hand, this formulation may make it seem as if the characteristics in question are in fact just characteristics of the constituents of the molecule and not characteristics of the whole molecule; and that is a significant disadvantage of this formulation. Some theological claims central to Christianity require attributing to the whole composite that is Christ properties had in their own right only by a constituent of the composite. So, for example, a central Christian claim is that Christ died on the cross. Here the property of dying on the cross is attributed to the whole. It is, however, not possible that immutable, eternal deity die. Human beings can die; God cannot. Therefore, it is true that Christ dies only in the case that a property had in its own right by a constituent of Christ, the human body and soul, is also properly attributed to the whole. For this reason, as well as for the metaphysical reasons given earlier, it seems to me better to say that a whole borrows properties of its parts, so that the whole can be said to be coiled, for example, in virtue of having a part that is coiled.[53]

Analogously, some of the properties attributed to Christ are properties borrowed from his constituent natures. So, for example, Christ is limited in power and not limited in power, but he borrows the first attribute from his human nature and the second from his divine nature. So he has the property of being limited in power just by virtue of having a constituent, namely, human nature, which has the property of being limited in power in its own right; he has the property of not being limited in power just in virtue of having a different constituent, divine nature, which has the property in its own right. Because the incompatible properties are borrowed properties, Christ does not have them in the same respect. And so it is no more incoherent to attribute both properties to Christ than it is to attribute being coiled and not being coiled to C/EBP.

---

[53] I am grateful to Scott MacDonald and Brian Leftow for making clear to me that this paragraph needed to be added.

In correspondence, Brian Leftow has suggested that some of Christ's divine properties, such as the property of being omnipotent, should be considered properties had in their own right by the whole Christ; on this view, a property such as being omnipotent is not a borrowed property for Christ. Leftow argues that a being having both a fast and a slow body would have the property *being fast* in its own right, because 'one is fast if one can run fast on some occasions (e.g. when using the right body)'. Analogous reasoning suggests that *being omnipotent* is a property the whole has in its own right also. My purpose in this chapter is only to show the way in which Aquinas' metaphysics supports the reduplicative strategy, and so it does not matter for my purposes exactly which properties of Christ's are borrowed and which are had by the whole Christ in their own right. But I am inclined to think that whether or not a property such as *being fast* is equivalent to a property had by a whole in its own right or to a borrowed property depends on the reasons for the ability in question. C/EBP has the property *able to reconfigure DNA on some occasions* in virtue of the shape of the molecule as a whole, and so the property in question is appropriately considered a property the whole has in its own right. But it has the property *being able to uncoil* only in virtue of the fact that it has a coiled part, and so this property is borrowed from a part. Because running fast for normal human beings requires a co-ordination of the whole body, from brain to toes, the property *being fast* does seem to be a property had in their own right by whole human beings. But in the case of Christ, who is a composite of one person and two natures, the property of being unlimited in power is a property had by the whole only in virtue of the fact that one constituent of the whole has this property. Furthermore, if all the constituents of Christ other than the divine nature were removed, what remained would still be omnipotent. By contrast, it is not the case that we could remove all but one constituent of a human body and still have a fast human being. For these reasons, it seems to me that *being fast* is disanalogous to *being omnipotent*, so that *being omnipotent* is a borrowed property of Christ's.

Someone who rejects the reduplicative strategy might repudiate this attempt to resuscitate it in connection with the Chalcedonian formula, on the grounds that the case of the C/EBP molecule and the case of the incarnate Christ are not suitably analogous. The molecule has integral or physical parts—the dimer subunit, the Y-shaped end of the molecule—which have certain properties, and we attribute those properties to the whole molecule only because the molecule has these integral parts. But in the case of Christ, the natures are not integral parts; insofar as they are any sort of part at all, they are metaphysical parts. Metaphysical parts aren't physically segregated bits of the whole, and so it seems that a whole cannot borrow properties from them. Consequently, it appears that the original objection to the reduplicative strategy still stands. The reduplicative strategy can be defended against that objection by the notion of borrowed properties only in the case the properties are borrowed from physical constituents of the whole.

This conclusion, however, and the line of thought that supports it seem to me mistaken. It is true that the case of Christ differs from the case of the molecule insofar as the parts in question in the case of Christ are not integral or physical parts. But it is false that a whole borrows properties from its parts only in the case the parts are physical parts. Consider, for example, Mark Twain's *Letters to the Earth*. This work is a passionate indictment of Christianity based largely on a dark and hard-hitting review of the suffering in the world and what Twain takes to be the insipid nature of Christian attempts to explain it away. As such, *Letters to the Earth* is a serious complaint against Christianity, and Twain meant it to be. On the other hand, the attack is carried out by means of Twain's characteristic biting humour. As such, *Letters to the Earth* is comic. So the work *qua* attack on Christianity is serious (and therefore not funny); *qua* work of satire, on the other hand, it is very funny. In fact, one might argue that a satire is a work which uses various forms of humour as a means to a sober end. Jokes and sarcasm are parts of the whole which are woven together by the configuring serious purpose. The comic bits and the overriding purpose are therefore some sort of constituents of the whole, but certainly not integral or physical constituents. Nonetheless, it is clear that the whole can borrow properties from these constituents, just as the molecule can borrow properties from its integral constituents. That is why Twain's work taken as a whole is correctly characterized both as a hilarious piece of satire and as a deadly earnest attack on religion. Because the properties of the whole are borrowed from the constituents in this way, there is no more incoherence in saying of the work that it is funny and not funny than there is in saying that C/EBP is coiled and not coiled. The work is funny in one respect and not funny in another, just as C/EBP is coiled in one part and not coiled in another.

So a whole can borrow properties from its constituents even if those constituents are not integral or physical parts of the whole. Consequently, there is no reason for denying that Christ can have properties borrowed from either his human nature or his divine nature, even if the natures are not integral parts of Christ and the properties are contradictories. Because each of the incompatible properties is had in its own right by a different constituent of the whole and because they attach to the whole only derivatively, in consequence of the fact that the whole has these constituents, there is no incoherence in attributing both otherwise incompatible properties to the whole.

Therefore, the objection to the reduplicative strategy fails. The objection would succeed if the attributes in question were attributes of the whole not borrowed from the parts. In that case, incompatible properties would be predicated of the same thing in the same respect, and that would be incoherent. But the point of the reduplicative strategy is to segregate the incompatible properties into different constituents of the whole and to attribute them to the whole derivatively, and Aquinas' metaphysics of composite things supports this use of the reduplicative strategy. Aquinas' metaphysics therefore provides a way to support his interpretation of the Chalcedonian formula against the charge of incoherence.

VII CONCLUSION: ONE PERSON AND TWO NATURES

The preceding considerations make clear, I think, that Aquinas' interpretation of the doctrine of the incarnation succeeds in remaining faithful to the Chalcedonian formula it wants to explain. Aquinas' metaphysics includes an understanding of constitution which supports the reduplicative strategy. It thus has the resources to ward off the charge that the doctrine of the incarnation is logically incoherent. Furthermore, it does so in virtue of keeping the natures separate, so that the distinct properties of the two natures are separated from each other and not joined together into one super-nature. In addition, the reduplicative strategy can be shown to work even for properties involving intellect and will, such as the properties of knowing and not knowing something. So

Aquinas' interpretation stays true to the Chalcedonian formula at least in this respect: Christ is *one* person, and there are *two* natures in Christ.

I conclude therefore that Aquinas' interpretation of the doctrine of the incarnation, as it is explained and supported by his metaphysics, is a philosophically sophisticated, rich and powerful account which is faithful to the Chalcedonian formula and successful in defending it against some of the formidable objections commonly levelled against it.[54]

[54] I am grateful to William Alston, Lawrence Dewan, Brian Leftow, Scott MacDonald, and Gerald O'Collins for comments on an earlier draft of this chapter on the metaphysics.

FOUNDATIONAL AND SYSTEMATIC ISSUES

10

Was Jesus Mad, Bad, or God?

STEPHEN T. DAVIS

I

The argument that Jesus was either 'mad, bad, or God' (let's call it the MBG argument) is sometimes used by popular Christian apologists as a way of defending the incarnation. Since Jesus claimed to be the divine Son of God—so the argument goes—then if he was not in fact divine, he must have been either a lunatic or a moral monster. No sane and righteous person can wrongly claim to be divine. But since Jesus was evidently neither a lunatic nor a moral monster—so the argument concludes—he must indeed have been divine.

Occasionally one encounters this argument in serious Christian literature as well. For example, C. S. Lewis wrote:

Then comes the real shock. Among these Jews there suddenly turns up a man who goes about talking as if he was God. He claims to forgive sins. He says He has always existed. He says he is coming to judge the world at the end of time. . . . I am trying here to prevent anyone saying the really foolish thing that people often say about Him: 'I'm ready to accept Jesus as a great moral teacher, but I don't accept his claim to be God.' That is the one thing we must not say. A man who was merely a man and said the sort of things Jesus said would not be a great moral teacher. He would be either a lunatic—on a level with the man who says he is a poached egg—or else he would be the Devil in Hell. You must make your choice. Either this man was, and is, the Son of God: or else a madman or something worse.[1]

And even J. A .T. Robinson, in the midst of a discussion of the Fourth Gospel in which he argues for its early dating and the

---

[1] C. S. Lewis, *Mere Christianity* (New York: Macmillan, 1960), 40–1. I have been unable to locate any published uses of the argument prior to the 20th cent. G. K. Chesterton does not state the argument as clearly or succinctly as does Lewis, but its premises can be found in *The Everlasting Man* (Garden City, NY: Doubleday, 1955 (1925)), 185–212.

general historical reliability of its picture of Jesus, can say: 'No sane person goes about saying "Before Abraham was I am" or "Whoever eats my flesh and drinks my blood shall live forever." These are theological interpretations, not literal utterances. Yet at the deepest level of faith they may indeed be the truth about the eternal Word of life, made flesh in this supremely individual and uniquely moral man of history.'[2]

On the other hand, the MBG argument is often severely criticized, both by people who do and by people who do not believe in the divinity of Jesus. For example, Donald MacKinnon criticized the argument on the grounds that it presupposes that we know what it is like to be God.[3] And John Hick makes critical reference to the MBG argument in *The Myth of God Incarnate*. He recalls that he was taught the argument in his childhood confirmation class and comments that it reflects a precritical attitude toward the Christian faith, one in which the idea of supernatural divine interventions in human history are acceptable and in which the Gospels are read as straightforward historical accounts of the life of Jesus.[4] Others object to the MBG argument on the grounds that the statements made by Jesus about himself in the Gospels that form the basis of the argument are being misinterpreted; properly understood, they do not constitute 'claims to divinity'. Finally, and doubtless most importantly, some argue that the statements about himself that are attributed to Jesus in the Gospels were not really said by him; they express the views not of Jesus but of the Christian church forty to sixty years later.

It is odd that the MBG argument is subject to such differing evaluations—all the way from people who endorse and use it, presumably because they consider it a good argument,[5] to people

---

[2] J. A. T. Robinson, *Can We Trust the New Testament?* (Grand Rapids, Mich.: Eerdmans, 1977), 91. See also R. H. Fuller and P. Perkins, *Who Is This Christ? Gospel Christology and Contemporary Faith* (Philadelphia: Fortress Press, 1983), 24: 'Therefore, the question of Jesus' identity, role, or relationship to the divine forced itself on those who came in contact with him. Either he was blasphemous, a fool, or he spoke with divine authority.'

[3] MacKinnon made this remark in a lecture attended by me at the Divinity School, Cambridge, in the Lent Term of 1978.

[4] John Hick (ed.), *The Myth of God Incarnate* (Philadelphia: Westminister Press, 1977), 4.

[5] Two contemporary apologists who make use of the argument are W. L. Craig and P. Kreeft. See W. L. Craig, *Reasonable Faith: Christian Truth and Apologetics* (Wheaton, Ill.: Crossway Books, 1984), 233–54, and P. Kreeft and R. K. Tacelli, *Handbook of Christian Apologetics* (Downers Grove, Ill.: InterVarsity Press, 1994), 150–74. For a

who dismiss it as unworthy of serious consideration.[6] Is it a good argument, or not?[7] Probably no central issue of Christian belief depends on the argument. Orthodox Christians could go on believing in the divinity of Jesus even if the argument fails. (On the other hand, if the argument succeeds, those who deny the incarnation at the very least have some explaining to do.) But the frequency with which the argument appears in popular defences of the divinity of Jesus, as well as its almost total absence from discussions about the status of Jesus by professional theologians and biblical scholars, makes one curious what to make of the argument.

The present paper constitutes a qualified defence of one version of the argument. I will claim that the MBG argument, properly understood, can establish the rationality of belief in the incarnation of Jesus. But a caveat is called for: I do not want to be interpreted as implying that any validation of Jesus' divinity must rest solely on what Jesus himself (explicitly or implicitly) claimed to be. Along with the memory of Jesus' sayings and doings, the post-Easter response to his death and resurrection (as well as the coming of the Holy Spirit) also played a crucial role in forming the early Christians' confession of Jesus as their divine Lord and Son of God. Even if it concentrates on what we know of Jesus' pre-Easter activity, the MBG argument should not be taken to belittle or

more extended discussion of the argument, see P. Kreeft, *Between Heaven and Hell: A Dialog Somewhere Beyond Death with John F. Kennedy, C. S. Lewis, and Aldous Huxley* (Downers Grove, Ill.: InterVarsity Press, 1982). See also J. M. Boice, *Foundations of Christian Faith* (Downers Grove, Ill: InterVarsity Press, 1986), 275–7.

[6] One such person is John Beversluis, who strongly criticizes C. S. Lewis's version of the MBG argument in *C. S. Lewis and the Search for Rational Religion* (Grand Rapids, Mich.: Eerdmans, 1985), 54–7. He calls the argument 'emotionally inflamatory' and claims it is based on a 'fallacious strategy', i.e. a 'false dilemma'. It is 'not a philosophical argument but a psychological spell'. Beversluis is correct that the truth and value of Jesus' moral teachings need not be affected by a judgement that he was mistaken in claiming to be divine; even if he was a lunatic, his moral teachings may still stand. But the major problem with Beversluis's critique is that he does not succeed in explaining how a sane person can be sincerely mistaken in claiming to be God. When Beversluis sets out to explain this point, he inexplicably switches from Jesus' claim to be divine to his claim to be the Messiah. These are two quite different things. Of course, there were sane people in ancient Judaism who mistakenly claimed to be the Messiah; indeed, that was almost commonplace. But how can a sane person—especially a 1st-cent. Jew—mistakenly claim to be *divine*?

[7] I am presupposing here the discussion of the nature of argument, proof, validity, soundness, and success for an argument in my *God, Reason, and Theistic Proofs* (Edinburgh: University of Edinburgh Press, 1997), 1–14, 188–93.

ignore the post-Easter developments. I am definitely not suggesting that the MBG argument is the only or even the best argument Christians can give for the divinity of Jesus.

II

It will facilitate matters if I lay out the argument in what I take to be its logical form:

(1) Jesus claimed, either explicitly or implicitly, to be divine.

(2) Jesus was either right or wrong in claiming to be divine.

(3) If Jesus was wrong in claiming to be divine, Jesus was either mad or bad.

(4) Jesus was not bad.

(5) Jesus was not mad.

(6) Therefore, Jesus was not wrong in claiming to be divine.

(7) Therefore Jesus was right in claiming to be divine.

(8) Therefore, Jesus was divine.

Let me now comment on each premise. Some will require more extended discussion than others.

Premise (1) will turn out to be crucial—indeed, it is probably the crux of the argument—so let us postpone extended comment on it till later. Suffice it for now simply to define its crucial term. Let us say that someone is *divine* if that person is in some strong sense identical with or equivalent to the omnipotent, omniscient, and loving creator of the heavens and the earth.

Now if (1) is true (as I will argue), then premise (2) follows from a substitution-instance of a well-recognized law of logic, namely, the law of excluded middle. Some philosophers have raised questions about this law (which says that every proposition is either true or, if not true, then false), but it nevertheless seems about as secure as any premise of any argument can be. The vast majority of philosophers will agree that (2) is true. The claim, 'Jesus was correct in claiming to be divine', is either true or, if not true, then false. The MBG argument cannot be successfully challenged here.

But premise (3) *can* be questioned. Let us say that the statement, 'Jesus was mad', means that he was insane or mentally deluded, just like those confused and frequently institutionalized people today who sincerely believe themselves to be the Virgin Mary or Napoleon.

Let us say that the statement, 'Jesus was bad', means that he was a liar, or was at least lying about who he was, just like someone today who intentionally deceives people by claiming to be someone else.

Perhaps Jesus claimed to be divine, was neither mad nor bad, but was merely *sincerely mistaken* about the matter, just as it is possible for a person to be sincerely mistaken about who her true parents are. Now the defender of the MBG argument will surely not want to claim that it is logically or even causally impossible[8] that Jesus was sincerely mistaken in claiming to be divine. If we tried hard enough, we probably could cook up a scenario in which a sane and moral person mistakenly took himself to be divine. But is it *probable* that Jesus was both sane and sincerely mistaken? Is it probable that

(9) Any good person who mistakenly claims to be divine is mad

is false? Or is it probable that

(10) Any sane person who mistakenly claims to be divine is bad[9]

is false?

These are obviously difficult questions. I am inclined to accept both (9) and (10) (and thus (3) as well), but I do not know how to prove them. Certainly a sane and good person could be sincerely mistaken about who her true parents are. Doubtless this very thing has occurred. But it is hard to see how a sane and good person could be sincerely mistaken in holding the extremely bizarre belief that she is divine (assuming she uses the word 'divine', as Christians normally do in this context, i.e. as indicating a robust identity with the omnipotent, omniscient, loving creator of the world). There *is* something extremely odd about the notion of a sincere, good, and sane person mistakenly claiming to be God. Nor do I consider it possible for an *otherwise* perfectly sane and good person mistakenly to consider herself to be God. Accordingly, (9) and (10) (and thus (3)), seem to have a high degree of plausibility. I conclude, then, that while (3) may be false, it is most probably true and can stand as a premise in a successful argument.

[8] Let us say that 'Jesus was sincerely mistaken in claiming to be divine' is logically impossible if the statement amounts to or entails a contradiction. Let us say that 'Jesus was sincerely mistaken in claiming to be divine' is causally impossible if its truth entails a violation of one or more of the laws of nature—gravity, thermodynamics, the speed of light, etc.

[9] The Revd Jim Jones, whose cult followers committed mass suicide in Guyana in 1978, is reported to have said to them: 'I'm the closest thing to God you'll ever see.'

One suspects that few will want to dispute (4) and (5). It is possible, however, that someone might want to use them against each other, so to speak, and argue either that:

(11) If Jesus mistakenly claimed to be divine and wasn't mad, then, improbable as it seems, he must have been bad,

or else:

(12) If Jesus mistakenly claimed to be divine and wasn't bad, then, improbable as it seems, he must have been mad.

But, again, I believe there is good reason to accept both (4) and (5). Unless the most radical of Gospel critics are correct—those who claim we can know virtually nothing about the historical Jesus[10]— there is precious little in the Gospels to suggest that Jesus was either a lunatic or a liar, and much to suggest strongly that he was neither.

Virtually everyone who reads the Gospels—whether committed to Christianity or not—comes away with the conviction that Jesus was a wise and good man. He was loving, compassionate, and caring, hardly the sort who tells lies for self-interested reasons. During his lifetime Jesus was apparently accused by his enemies of being demon-possessed and 'out of his mind' (cf. John 10: 20). And Jesus is certainly quoted as making what can seem to be bizarre claims, especially when taken outside the context of his life and the rest of his teachings: for example: 'Unless you eat the flesh of the Son of Man and drink his blood, you have no life in you' (John 6: 53).

But Peter Kreeft argues convincingly that Jesus shows none of the character traits usually associated with those who have delusions of grandeur or 'divinity complexes'. Such people are easily recognized by their egotism, narcissism, inflexibility, predictable behaviour, and inability to relate understandingly and lovingly to others.[11] Other seriously disturbed people show signs of extreme irritability, debilitating anxiety, or inappropriate beliefs and behaviour. This is not the sort of picture of Jesus that we form by reading the Gospels. We live in an age when all sorts of bizarre claims about the historical Jesus are confidently made. But few Scripture scholars of any theological stripe

---

[10] 'I do indeed think that we can now know almost nothing concerning the life and personality of Jesus', Rudolf Bultmann, *Jesus and the Word*, trans. L. P. Smith and E. H. Lantero (New York: Charles Scribner's Sons, 1958), 8.

[11] Kreeft and Tacelli, *Handbook of Christian Apologetics*, 159.

seriously entertain the possibility that Jesus was either a lunatic or a liar. When we return below to premise (1) we will have to enter more deeply into the question of the reliability of the New Testament picture of Jesus. Suffice it to say here that there seems every good reason to accept both (4) and (5).[12]

Premise (6) is entailed by premises (2), (3), (4), and (5). It is impossible for them to be true and (6) false. Premise (7) is entailed by premises (2) and (6). If they are true, it is true. Finally, step (8), the conclusion of the MBG argument, is entailed by premise (7). If (7) is true, then (8) must be true as well. What we have in the MBG argument, then, is a *valid* argument. That is, there are no mistakes in logic in the argument; it is logically impossible for its premises (i.e. (1)—(7)) to be true and its conclusion (i.e. step (8)) false.

But is the argument also *sound*? Let us say that a sound argument is a valid argument whose premises are all true. It appears thus far that while premises (3), (4), and (5) can be criticized, a plausible case can be made for their truth. Clearly the premise that will seem most vulnerable to criticism is premise (1).

Is it true that Jesus claimed, either explicitly or implicitly, to be divine? Before addressing this question directly, it will be helpful to consider the notion of an 'implicit claim', since my argument in the present paper is that Jesus *implicitly* claimed to be divine. First, what is a 'claim'? Let's say that a claim is an assertion or statement, the kind of linguistic utterance that has a truth value. That is, according to the principle of excluded middle, it is true or, if not true, then false. Now an *explicit* claim that a proposition p is true would be a statement like 'p is true' or 'Not-p is false'; or 'It is true that p is true' or even simply 'p'.

What then is an *implicit* claim that p is true? Well, there appear to be several ways of implicitly claiming that p is true. (1) One might implicitly claim that p is true by explicitly asserting that x, y, and z are true, where x, y, and z logically entail p. If one were explicitly to assert 'R. E. Lee was a Confederate general' and 'R. E. Lee was a famous general' and 'R. E. Lee was a great general', that could be

---

[12] For a fascinating argument against any claim that Jesus was mad, written by a practising clinical psychiatrist, see O. Q. Hyder, 'On the Mental Health of Jesus Christ', *Journal of Psychology and Theology*, 5: 1 (Winter 1977), 3–12. Hyder's argument falters at one or two places, but he skilfully shows that we find no convincing evidence in the biblical materials that Jesus was delusional, paranoid, schizoid, or manic depressive, and lots of convincing evidence that he was an emotionally sound and healthy person.

taken as an implicit claim to the effect that 'R. E. Lee was a great and famous Confederate general'. (2) Or one might implicitly claim that p is true by explicitly asserting x, y, and z, where only people who hold that p is true can hold that x, y, and z are true. If one were explicitly to assert that 'R. E. Lee was a Confederate general' and 'R. E. Lee was a famous general' and 'R. E. Lee was a great general', that could be taken as an implicit claim to the effect that 'R. E. Lee was a human being'.[13] (3) Most importantly, one might implicitly claim that p is true by *doing* action A, where the only people, or the only sensible people, who do A are people who believe p. Suppose that Jones, tired and perspiring at the end of a long run, bends over and drinks from a drinking fountain. This might be taken as an implicit claim on Jones's part to the effect that 'The liquid emanating from this drinking fountain is potable'.

We are now able to return to the question whether Jesus implicitly claimed to be divine. This is a good question, to say the least. Much ink has been spilled over it, especially in the past two centuries. (Before that it would have been taken as virtually axiomatic that the answer is yes—indeed, that he *explicitly* claimed as much.) What is clear, and I think is quite beyond dispute, is that a literalistic and ahistorical reading of the Gospels, and especially the Fourth Gospel, strongly supports premise (1). Notice, for example, the following statements that are attributed to Jesus there (as well as, in some cases, the reactions of those who heard him):

But Jesus answered them, 'My Father is still working, and I also am working.' For this reason the Jews were seeking all the more to kill him, because he was not only breaking the sabbath, but was also calling God his own Father, thereby making himself equal to God.   (John 5: 17--18)

The Father judges no one but has given all judgement to the Son, so that all may honour the Son just as they honour the Father.   (John 5: 22)

'Very truly, I tell you, before Abraham was, I am.' So they picked up stones to throw at him, but Jesus hid himself and went out of the temple.   (John 8: 58–9)

'The Father and I are one.' The Jews took up stones again to stone him.   (John 10: 30–1)

---

[13] The difference between (1) and (2) is perhaps not very great. In the case of (2), it is quite possible that the one who is making the implicit claim has never consciously formulated the belief, 'R. E. Lee was a human being', while that seems less probable for the one who is making the implicit claim that 'R. E. Lee was a great and famous Confederate general' in (1).

'The Father is in me and I am in the Father.' Then they tried to arrest him again, but he escaped from their hands.   (John 10: 38–9)

'Have I been with you all this time, Philip, and you still do not know me? Whoever has seen me has seen the Father'.   (John 14: 9)

Now there appear to be four main attitudes that might be taken towards claims such as these. First, perhaps Jesus explicitly taught his own divinity, that is, perhaps words such as these constitute the *ipsissima verba* of Jesus. Second, perhaps Jesus only implicitly taught his own divinity. Third, perhaps Jesus said the things, or some of them, that have been taken to imply his own divinity in John's Gospel and elsewhere, but this is not the proper interpretation of those sayings. Those who defend this option (which corresponds to the third objection to the MBG argument mentioned in Section I) might argue as follows: the words from Jesus like those just cited should be interpreted as indicating something less than robust identity with God; perhaps Jesus was only indicating unity of purpose or will with the Father, or something of that sort. What Jesus *really meant*, so it might be said, is that he had a very special place in God's redemptive plan, or he had an extraordinarily strong desire to do God's bidding, or he felt such an intimate closeness to God that it was almost as if God were his own father.[14] Fourth, perhaps Jesus said nothing about the matter, and the relevant statements attributed to him in the Gospels are inauthentic; they represent the beliefs not of Jesus but of the Christian church at the time that the Gospels were being written.

In the present chapter, I do not intend to defend the first option, but rather the second; thus I must argue against options three and four.

III

As noted in Section I, there appear to be four main criticisms that can be raised against the MBG argument. First, it presupposes that we know what it is like to be God. Second, it presupposes a naive world-view, one that allows for special divine acts in history. Third (the same point as the third option just discussed), it misinterprets

---

[14] This is certainly the route that must be taken by all those who, like Jehovah's Witnesses, claim to accept the full theological authority of the Bible but reject the idea that Jesus was God incarnate.

what Jesus meant by the statements about himself that we find in the Gospels. Fourth, it presupposes a precritical view of the Gospels (and especially John), one that views them (and it) as straightforward history. Let us consider these objections in turn. (When we get to the fourth objection, we will also be replying to the fourth option noted at the end of Section III—that the high christological statements attributed to Jesus in the Gospels are inauthentic.)

As to the first criticism, it is not easy to understand precisely what MacKinnon had in mind. What he said was that the MBG argument presupposes that we know what it is like to be God. Of course it is true that we do not know what it is like to be God. But it is hard to grasp exactly why the MBG arguer must presuppose that we have that knowledge. Let's make a distinction between *knowing what it is like to be God* and *knowing what God is like*. It is surely true that it would border on blasphemy for those who use the MBG argument—or anybody else, for that matter—to presuppose that they know what it is like to be God. In the fullest sense, we don't even know what it is like to be another human being, or what it is like to be a bat.[15]

But is it possible for human beings to know what God is like? The answer to this, at least from a Christian perspective, is surely yes. One of the defining ideas of the Christian faith (as well as other versions of theism) is that God has been revealed. God has chosen to show us and tell us what God is like. God is self-revealed. We learn in the Scriptures, for example, that God is the creator, that God is all-powerful, that God is all-knowing, that God is to be worshipped and obeyed, that God is loving, that God works for the salvation of humankind, that God forgives our sins, etc.

It is surely true that the MBG argument presupposes that we know something of what God is like. If a person is morally despicable, that person is not God. If a person makes insane claims, that person is not God. But, as noted, Christians hold that we *do* know what God is like (to the extent that it has been revealed to us by God),[16] and there seems to be nothing blasphemous or otherwise theologically untoward here. For the MBG argument to

[15] See Thomas Nagel's article, 'What is it Like to Be a Bat?', in Douglas Hofstadter and Daniel Dennett (eds.), *The Mind's I*, (Toronto: Bantam Books, 1981), 391–403.

[16] To avoid any hint of circularity (since Christians claim that the fullest revelation of God's nature is Christ), we could even limit our knowledge of God to what can be known about God apart from Christ. We could limit ourselves to what has been revealed about God in the natural order, or in the OT Law, or in the words of the prophets.

work, our knowledge of God need not be comprehensive; we need to know only a little about God. So the partialness of our knowledge of God need not constitute a problem for the MBG argument. But does the MBG argument presuppose that we know what it is like to be God? Certainly not. Or at least, it is not easy to see how. I conclude that MacKinnon's criticism does not damage the MBG argument.

As to the second criticism, Hick argues that the MBG argument presupposes a pre-critical world view, one in which special divine acts in human history are allowable. But there is something slightly off-target about this criticism: Hick's objection appears to be directed more against the idea of incarnation as such than against the MBG argument in favour of the incarnation. Hick is right that the very idea of incarnation—of God becoming a human being—presupposes divine interventions in human history. This is why Deists must deny not only all miracles, epiphanies, visions from God, and prophetic messages from God, but all incarnations as well.

And it is true that if the very idea of incarnation is discredited, then the MBG argument can hardly constitute a successful argument in favour of incarnation. Still, since Hick's criticism is not directed against the MBG argument *per se*, and especially since many contemporary Christian philosophers have defended the adequacy of theism versus Deism (i.e. of the possibility of special divine acts),[17] I will discuss this matter no further here. (An atheist could similarly argue that belief in incarnation is irrational because belief in *God* is outmoded, but again that would not count as an objection to the MBG argument itself.)

As to the third objection, the violent reactions of Jesus' enemies in the texts cited (and in many other texts where Jesus speaks about himself, some from the Synoptics) seem to preclude any such minimalist interpretation as, 'Jesus just meant that he felt extraordinarily close to God'. As well as the reactions mentioned in the above citations, note the argument of the chief priests at John's trial account: 'We have a law, and according to that law he ought to die because he has claimed to be the Son of God' (John 19: 7). It would hardly have constituted an offence worthy of arrest and execution had Jesus simply been declaring his own unity of purpose or will with the Father, or claiming to have a special place in God's plan. Odd, maybe; egotistical, maybe; but hardly blasphemous. Notice

---

[17] Including myself in ch. 1 of my *Risen Indeed: Making Sense of the Resurrection* (Grand Rapids, Mich.: Eerdmans, 1993).

further that Jesus did not step in to correct the impression his enemies apparently gained from hearing his words.

As noted earlier, the fourth criticism—that the MBG argument presupposes a precritical view of the Gospels and especially John as straightforward history—is the really important one. This criticism amounts to a denial of premise (1) of the MBG argument. Is premise (1) true?

It is a commonplace of much contemporary New Testament scholarship that words such as those cited above from the Fourth Gospel do not constitute the *ipsissima verba* of Jesus. These statements, it is said, and the many other statements in the New Testament that imply or seem to imply the divinity of Jesus, tell us more about the faith of the early church at the time the Gospels were being written or were receiving final form than they do about the actual teachings of Jesus. Later Christians wrongly attributed these words to Jesus as part of their theological programme. Thus— so a critic of the MBG argument will argue—the MGB argument for the incarnation cannot even get going. Its first premise is false; Jesus never claimed—explicitly or implicitly—to be divine.

IV

Is this a good objection? Well, there is much in the neighbourhood that is beyond reproach. It is true that the Gospels are statements of faith with definite theological agendas rather than 'facts-only' biographies of Jesus. (The writer of John even admits as much— see John 20: 31.) It is also almost certainly true that John's Gospel was the last canonical gospel written, and thus the furthest removed from the events it records. But it is a long way from these sensible admissions about the Gospels to the point that none of the sayings of Jesus that imply or seem to imply his own divinity can be authentic. Let us see what can be said on behalf of the historical reliability of some of the statements Jesus makes about himself in the Gospels, especially in the Synoptics. I will *not* presuppose the view that the evangelists were offering straightforward, theologically neutral history. Moreover, I take it as given that the church translated, edited, rearranged, recontextualised, paraphrased, abbreviated, and expanded the sayings of Jesus. Furthermore, since the NT was written in Greek, then assuming that Jesus spoke and taught in

Aramaic, precisely *none* of the sayings attributed to Jesus in the Gospels constitute his *ipsissima verba* (except possibly those few sayings that are cited in Aramaic).

Again, premise (1) of the MBG argument says:

> (1) Jesus claimed, either explicitly or implicitly, to be divine.

Is this true? I am going to argue that it is. But let me first note three things that I am not claiming. First, I am not claiming that Jesus went about saying 'I am God' or making any sort of *explicit* claim to status as deity. The radical monotheism to which first-century Judaism was committed, in all its various forms, made anything like that impossible. Second, I am not claiming that Jesus' consciousness of his divinity was expressed by him in the language of later creedal orthodoxy: for example, 'truly divine and truly human', 'of one substance with the Father', 'Second Person of the Blessed Trinity', etc. Third, I am not claiming to be able to psychoanalyse Jesus. As N. T. Wright points out, historians are frequently concerned with the motivation and self-understanding of the figures they write about, especially as they find expression in what these figures can sensibly be concluded to have said and done, and that is what I am doing here.[18]

My claim is that by his words and deeds, Jesus implicitly saw or experienced himself as divine, as having a unique relationship of divine sonship to God. This does not necessarily mean that Jesus, throughout his life or even throughout his ministry, ever formulated or expressed the idea precisely in language, although I hold that at some point he was able to do so. I suspect his sense of mission and identity was shaped and confirmed by various crucial events during his ministry, for example, the baptism, temptation, transfiguration, and passion. It is possible to have a vague and inchoate awareness of something that one is able only later to capture in words. So the question, 'Did Jesus know that he was God?' is ill-formed. Jesus surely did not confuse himself with God the Father to whom he prayed. But did he implicitly claim to be divine or to have divine prerogatives? Did he implicitly claim to have a unique relationship to the Father which in effect placed him on a par with God? I believe the answer to these questions is yes. (Again, my argument will not presuppose a naive and ahistorical reading of the Gospels.)

How do we go about deciding what someone believes or implicitly

---

[18] N. T. Wright, 'Jesus and the Identity of God', *Ex Auditu* 14 (1998), 51.

claims? Well, the most obvious way to find out whether Jones believes p is to ask her or wait till she expresses some sort of epistemic attitude toward p (assertion, denial, certainty, doubt, uncertainty, etc.). And in cases where there is no good reason to doubt Jones's word, this will normally be convincing evidence. In other cases, we might have to listen to other things that Jones says or watch things that she does in order to see if any of them constitute convincing evidence that Jones implicitly claims that p (or not-p) is true. It is possible, as noted above, for a person to believe that p is true without ever having formulated 'p' as a conscious belief. There are probably people who walk to work every day who believe, without ever having consciously formulated the belief, that 'the pavement will hold me up'.

I am going to present my argument in two stages. The first will presuppose the basic correctness of the methods and conclusions of some of the most radical of biblical critics.[19] Its aim is to open the door to the *possibility* of showing, even on the methods of people like Bultmann, Perrin, and the members of the Jesus Seminar, that Jesus implicitly taught his own divinity. The second stage (which contains five sub-arguments) will try to confirm the point that Jesus *actually did* this very thing. At this second stage, I will continue to eschew any naive or ahistorical view of the Gospels, but will no longer consider myself limited by the views of the radical critics.

In this first stage of my argument, I want simply (1) to point out a fact about early Christian history that is becoming clearer and clearer, even if radical methods of criticism are employed, namely, that *worship of Jesus* was a very ancient phenomenon in the Christian community; and (2) to ask why this fact is so. As to the fact that worship of Jesus was primitive in the Christian community, Richard Bauckham says: 'The prevalence and centrality of the worship of Jesus in early Christianity from an early date has frequently been underestimated. . . . In the earliest Christian community Jesus was already understood to be risen and exalted to God's right hand in heaven, active in the community by his Spirit, and coming in the future as ruler and judge of the world.'[20]

[19] Here I indicate my indebtedness to Royce Gordon Gruenler, who follows a similar methodology in his *New Approaches to Jesus and the Gospels: A Phenomenological and Exegetical Study of Synoptic Christology* (Grand Rapids, Mich.: Baker, 1982), esp. 19–108.

[20] R. Bauckham, 'Jesus, Worship of', *The Anchor Bible Dictionary* (New York: Doubleday, 1992), iii. 812. See also L. W. Hurtado, 'Pre-70 C.E. Jewish Opposition to Christ Devotion', *JTS* 50: 1 (April 1999), 36.

Notice that prayers addressed to Jesus can be found from the earliest times. It is significant that Greek-speaking churches preserved in Aramaic the cry *Maranatha* ('Our Lord, come!') (1 Cor. 16: 22; Didache 10: 6); this shows its primitive origin. Personal prayers to Jesus seem to have been commonplace (2 Cor. 12: 8; 1 Thess. 3: 11–13; 2 Thess. 2: 16–17; 3: 5, 16; Acts 1: 24; 7: 59–60). There were also doxologies addressed to Christ, or to Christ and the Father together, although most appear in relatively late NT texts (2 Tim. 4: 18; 2 Pet. 3: 18; Rev. 1: 5–6, 13; cf. 7: 10). In earlier texts, doxologies with the phrase 'through Jesus Christ' appear (Rom. 16: 27; cf. 2 Cor. 1: 20). Hymns of praise to Christ were also common (Phil. 2: 6–11; 1 Tim. 3: 16; cf. Eph. 5: 19; Col. 3: 16).[21]

In a recent paper, L. W. Hurtado argues that a careful reading of Matthew and Mark reveals that there was vigorous Jewish opposition in the pre-70 period to Jewish-Christian worship of Jesus.[22] Bauckham claims that the transition from prayers to Jesus, thanksgiving to Jesus, and reverence for Jesus to actual *worship* of Jesus (cf. Acts 13: 2) was a smooth and perhaps not even conscious process; there is no evidence, he says, of anybody in the earliest Christian community contesting it. He concludes that 'the role which Jesus played in the Christian religion from the beginning was such as to cause him to be treated as God in worship'.[23]

All this despite the fact that the earliest Christians were Jews, people whose rigid monotheism and antipathy to worship of any other gods besides the Lord was perhaps their defining religious characteristic. Indeed, the New Testament church did not see itself as backing away from monotheism; in 1 Corinthians 8: 4–6 Paul accepts the classic *Shema* of Judaism (Deut. 6: 4), but interprets the monotheism of the Christian community as including the lordship of Jesus. And in the Book of Revelation, Jesus is considered worthy of divine worship because worship of Jesus can be included in worship of the one God (Rev. 5: 8–12). Worship of Jesus *was* worship of (not a competitor to God but) God.

---

[21] The hymn from Phil. 2, in particular, witnesses to the way in which early Christians viewed the crucified and exalted Jesus as meriting the adoration of the universe. In *The Changing Faces of Jesus* (London: Penguin, 2000), Geza Vermes has recently suggested that a later, anonymous copyist inserted this hymn into the text of the letter (pp. 78–9)—a proposal which enjoys no support from the New Testament MS evidence.

[22] Hurtado, 'Pre-70 C.E. Jewish Opposition', 5–6, 10.

[23] 'Jesus, Worship of', 815.

Next, a question: if Bauckham is correct that worship of Jesus was primitive in the Christian community, *why* is this the case? There appear to be two main possibilities. First, perhaps the early church worshipped Jesus because social, economic, liturgical, polemical, or other sorts of needs and pressures that the early Christians faced pushed them in that direction. That is, the early church made up the idea that Jesus was divine. Second, perhaps they worshipped Jesus at least in part because Jesus himself implicitly encouraged, instructed, or allowed them to do so.[24] That is, Jesus himself was conscious of being divine and implicitly communicated that fact, by his words and deeds, to his followers.

Interestingly, the Synoptic Gospels, and especially Matthew, opt for the second alternative. That does not settle the case, because for now we are accepting the methodology and conclusions of some of the radical critics, and many of them regard Matthew's Gospel as an unreliable guide to the life of Jesus. Still, Matthew commonly uses one or another form of the word *proskynesis* (obeisance, prostration before someone in worship) in relation to Jesus. Jesus is worshipped by the wise men from the East (2: 2, 11), by the disciples in the boat (14: 33), by Mary Magdalene and the other Mary after the resurrection (28: 9), and by the eleven disciples on the mountain (28: 17). Bauckham argues that 'Matthew's consistent use of the word *proskynein* and his emphasis on the point show that he intends a kind of reverence which, paid to any other human, he would have regarded as idolatrous'.[25]

Let's now look at a few Synoptic texts that are accepted as authentic by people like Bultmann, Perrin, and the members of the Jesus Seminar. Even in limiting ourselves in that way, I believe a probable case can be made that Jesus implicitly taught his own divinity.

> But if it is by the finger of God that I cast out the demons, then the kingdom of God has come to you. (Luke 11: 20; par. Matt. 12: 28)

Bultmann enthusiastically accepted the authenticity of this statement from Jesus.[26] In it, Jesus is clearly claiming to be exhibiting in

---

[24] I say 'at least in part' since Jesus' resurrection from the dead and the outpouring of the Holy Spirit (both of which need, of course, to be independently investigated) also fed into the new faith and practice of early Christians.

[25] 'Jesus, Worship of', 813.

[26] R. Bultmann, *History of the Synoptic Tradition*, trans. John Marsh (New York: Harper & Row, 1976), 162.

his exorcisms the eschatological power of the finger of God. Note the parallel to Exodus 8: 19, where the Egyptian magicians confess their inability to duplicate the plague of gnats, and declare, 'This is the finger of God.' Jesus is claiming to be acting as the agent through which the reign of God, with all God's power, enters history.

On a different vein, notice:

Listen to me, all of you, and understand; there is nothing outside a person that by going in can defile, but the things that come out are what defile. (Mark 7: 14–15; par. Matt. 15: 10–11; Thomas 14: 5)

This text, which Perrin accepts as authentic[27] and which the Jesus Seminar rates pink ('Jesus probably said something like this'[28]), is remarkable in the authority that Jesus is taking upon himself to relativize and de-emphasize Jewish dietary law. Jesus is in effect abolishing the divinely given food laws, that is, he is dismantling one of the major barriers between Jews and Gentiles that God was understood to have erected. Jesus is saying that in the light of his own presence in the world, a radically new attitude toward religion is required. Along the same lines, notice this statement (again coloured pink by the Jesus Seminar):

The sabbath was made for humankind, and not humankind for the sabbath; so the Son of Man is Lord even of the sabbath. (Mark 2: 27–8; par. Matt. 12: 8; Luke 6: 5)

Here again Jesus is taking upon himself the authority to reinterpret the teachings of Moses in a radically new way. Even more dramatically, notice this text (accepted as authentic by Perrin and coloured pink by the Jesus Seminar):

Follow me, and let the dead bury their own dead   (Matt. 8: 22; par. Luke 9: 59)

where Jesus is clearly opposing and correcting the Mosaic Law. Proper burial, especially of one's relatives, was one of the most sacred duties in Palestinian Judaism (cf. Gen. 50: 5–6; Lev. 21: 2–3;

---

[27] N. Perrin, *Rediscovering the Teaching of Jesus* (London: SCM Press; New York: Harper & Row, 1967), 149–50.

[28] Robert Funk *et al.*, *The Five Gospels: The Search for the Authentic Words of Jesus* (San Francisco: HarperSanFrancisco, 1993), 36, 69. This work in collaboration came from the Jesus Seminar, a group of biblical scholars led by R. Funk and J. D. Crossan, who met mainly in Sonoma (California) and voted on the authenticity of the Gospel material: a red bead for what sounded to them 'Definitely from Jesus', a pink bead for 'May well be', a grey for 'Doubtful', and a black for 'Definitely not'.

Tobit 4: 3); this duty took precedence over study of the Torah, Temple service, circumcision rites, and even reciting the *Shema* (Megillah, 3b; Berakath 3: 1). Accordingly, Jesus was declaring that the need for people immediately and unconditionally to become his disciples took precedence even over the solemn responsibility to bury one's own father.

It would be helpful to ask at this point what sort of first-century Jew would take upon himself the authority to set aside requirements of the Mosaic law and replace them with his own teachings? It seems that Jesus' view of his own authority was such that he took the duty to follow him as a far more urgent task than burying one's father. Gruenler pointedly asks, 'Who could possibly make such an offensive and insensitive statement except one who is absolutely convinced that following him is worth more than anything else in the world?'[29] In other words, it is probable that Jesus considered himself to be divinely authoritative.

Notice also the new attitude toward enemies, sins, and the forgiveness of sins that Jesus introduced. (I am not here speaking of Jesus' taking upon himself the authority to forgive sins; we shall discuss that point later.) Most famously, note:

You have heard that it was said, 'you shall love your neighbour and hate your enemy.' But I say to you, 'Love your enemies and pray for those who persecute you'. (Matt. 5: 43–4; par. Luke 6: 27, 35)

The 'love your enemies' piece of this text is coloured red by the Jesus Seminar; they are suspicious of the rest of it (it is either black or gray); but Perrin accepts the whole antithesis as authentic. The point is that those who were once considered unforgivable enemies (Gentiles, outcasts, sinners, etc.) are now, in the light of the inbreaking of the Kingdom of God in Jesus, seen as recipients of God's love and forgiveness, and as worthy participants in table-fellowship in the kingdom of God. Jesus is again apparently taking upon himself the authority to reorder religious life, in this case around the principles of love and forgiveness. We see this same point more fully and dramatically in the parable of the Prodigal Son (Luke 15: 11–32; coloured pink by the Jesus Seminar). Gruenler comments: 'Only one who is conscious of exercising divine privileges (or is mad) could assume the right to proclaim the eschatological presence of the forgiveness of sins with such authority. . . . [Jesus]

---

[29] *New Approaches to Jesus and the Gospels*, 61.

is consciously speaking as the voice of God on matters that belong only to God, and accordingly is creating a new and decisive Christology which far exceeds in claim to authority the messianic models of Judaism.'[30] Jesus' idea seems to have been that salvation has arrived in his own person and ministry, that salvation for humans is to be understood in terms of his own person and mission, and that he can speak with divine authority. Jesus had an extraordinarily high opinion of himself and his mission.

Notice finally the parable of the wicked tenants in Mark 12: 1–9 (coloured gray by the Jesus Seminar but pink in the *Gospel of Thomas* (65: 1–7)).[31] The owner of the vineyard unsuccessfully sends two employees to collect the harvest, and then finally sends his son, whom the tenants recognize as the son and heir, and then murder him. Clearly, the son in the parable allegorically stands for Jesus himself, who is different from and superior to God's previous emissaries (the prophets), and who is indeed God's son and heir.

Now I am not claiming that Bultmann, Perrin, Funk, Crossan, *et al.* accept my interpretations of these texts. Doubtless they do not. My claim is simply that they consider these statements from Jesus to be authentic or probably authentic, and that from these texts alone a very high Christology can be inferred.[32] That is, a probable case can be made that Jesus implicitly taught his own divinity. Perhaps then one reason for the existence of worship of Jesus in the primitive Christian community is that Jesus himself expected and accepted it.

---

[30] Ibid. 46.

[31] As they themselves admit in their commentary on this text, the members of the Seminar were bothered by the allegorical aspect of the parable in its Synoptic versions, with its obvious application to Jesus (= the son) himself. Funk *et al. Five Gospels*, 101.

[32] Beyond question, the interpretation of all these texts, especially those that bear on the Jewish law, is controversial. Vermes for example interprets the sayings about the sabbath, the dietary laws, and the antitheses ('but I say to you . . .') as entailing no high claims for Jesus' personal identity; they are, he says, the kinds of statements that could have been made by Jewish teachers of his time (*Changing Faces of Jesus*, 196–7). Yet some of the evidence to which Vermes points comes from rabbis who lived one or two centuries later. Besides, the more one portrays Jesus as religiously 'normal' and not scandalously offensive, the more puzzling becomes the opposition that led to his crucifixion. The present chapter attempts to sketch the various steps in the MBG argument. For a full discussion of the key texts about Jesus and the Jewish law, see the work of such scholars as J. D. G. Dunn, E. P. Sanders, and the earlier Vermes, as well as the data supplied by commentaries on Matthew, Mark, and Luke from such writers as J. A. Fitzmyer, R. A. Guelich, D. Hagner, and J. Nolland.

V

Let me now proceed to the second stage of my argument that premise (1) is true, that Jesus implicitly taught his own divinity. By the use of five sub-arguments, I will try to prove not just the possibility that Jesus implicitly taught his own divinity, but its actuality. Again, I will strive to avoid ahistorical use of the Gospel texts, but I will no longer limit myself to texts accepted as authentic by radical critics. Some of the sub-arguments will at this point sound familiar, but the slightly more relaxed methodology just mentioned will allow some new points to be made.

Let me then discuss five reasons why Jesus can be said to have implicitly claimed to be divine. No one reason constitutes, in and of itself, a convincing argument. There is no 'smoking gun' on this issue. What we do find are various considerations which together, and together with points already made, constitute a powerful cumulative case argument in favour of premise (1). The best interpretation of the five considerations that I am about to dis-cuss—so I am arguing—is that Jesus did indeed implicitly view himself as divine.

First, Jesus assumed for himself the divine prerogative to forgive sins (see Mark 2: 5, 10; Luke 7: 48). Now, all human beings as moral agents own the prerogative to forgive sins *that have been committed against them*, but only God (or God incarnate) can *forgive sins*. Some have objected to this point. John Hick, for example, argues that Jesus did not usurp God's prerogatives, but only 'pronounced forgiveness, which is not the prerogative of God, but of the priesthood'.[33] But this is hardly a convincing argument. For one thing, it concedes part of the point at issue, namely, that Jesus was usurping prerogatives that were not his. He was a layman, not of the priestly tribe, and was forgiving sins outside what were understood to be the divinely established means of obtaining forgiveness. More importantly, there are several texts that cannot be reconciled with Hick's argument. Note the story of the healing of the paralytic in Mark 2: 1–12. There is no evidence here on the part of the paralytic of any of the religious acts normally requisite for forgiveness—no sorrow for his sins, confession, repentance, sacrifi-

---

[33] J. Hick, *The Metaphor of God Incarnate* (London: SCM Press, 1993), 32. Here Hick quotes E. P. Sanders, *Jesus and Judaism* (Philadelphia: Fortress Press, 1985), 240.

cial acts at the temple, etc. This is surely the reason the scribes were so incensed when Jesus said to the paralytic, 'Your sins are forgiven'. They said: 'Why does this fellow speak in this way? Who can forgive sins but God alone?' In other words, the violent reaction of the scribes belies Hick's interpretation of such texts.

Second, the intimate, almost blasphemous way Jesus addressed God (usually translated '*Abba*, Father!'—something analogous to our English expression 'Papa') indicates at least a uniquely close relationship to God. I suspect the amazement caused by this novel way of speaking to God—whose name was sacred to first-century Jews—was the reason that the church remembered and imitated it (Rom. 8: 15; Gal. 4: 6). Hick also objects to this point. '*Abba*' was fairly commonly used of God in first-century Judaism, he claims, and simply meant 'father'; while Jesus certainly sensed that God was his Heavenly Father, this had nothing to do with incarnation.[34] But other scholars deny that there are any Jewish parallels to referring to God in prayer the way Jesus does; nobody has ever produced a convincing example of *Abba* being used of God in pre-Christian, first-century Judaism.[35] The argument that Jesus' use of *Abba* shows a consciousness on his part of a unique position in relation to God stands. Jesus very probably thought of himself as God's special son.[36]

Third, Jesus spoke 'with authority', not citing sources or precedents of famous rabbis. He was no mere prophet or religious teacher (as is so often asserted about him today); no such person would have acted and spoken with such independence of the Mosaic law as Jesus did. Note the way he quotes, and then corrects, the Mosaic teaching about divorce in the Sermon on the Mount

---

[34] *Metaphor of God Incarnate*, 31. Hick is following the lead of James Barr at this point. See Barr's 'Abba Isn't "Daddy"', *JTS* 39 (1988), 28–47, and 'Abba, Father', *Theology*, 91 (1988), 173–9. For a response to Barr, see G. D. Fee, *God's Empowering Presence: The Holy Spirit in the Letters of Paul* (Peabody, Mass.: Hendrickson, 1995), 408–12.

[35] Thus Joachim Jeremias: 'Nowhere in the literature of the prayers of ancient Judaism . . . is this invocation of God as *Abba* to be found, neither in the liturgical nor in the informal prayers' J. Jeremias, *The Central Message of the New Testament* (London: SCM Press, 1965), 19. See also G. O'Collins, *Christology: A Biblical, Historical, and Systematic Study of Jesus* (Oxford: Oxford University Press, 1995), 60–2, and J. P. Meier, *A Marginal Jew: Rethinking the Historical Jesus* (New York: Doubleday, 1994), ii. 358–9, both of whom support Jeremias's conclusion.

[36] Ben Witherington sensibly discusses all the arguments and evidence, and supports the notion that Jesus' use of *Abba* in prayer was unique and indicated a relationship of intimacy with the Father. See his *Christology of Jesus* (Minneapolis: Fortress Press, 1990), 215–21.

(Matt. 5: 31–2; cf. Mark 10: 2–12). Jesus spoke, not as if he were speaking *on behalf of God* (he did not say, as the prophets had done, 'Thus says the Lord'), but *as if he were divine*, delivering the truth to human beings. As J. A. T. Robinson said, 'This is epitomized in his characteristic and distinctive form of address, "Amen, I say to you" . . . While a pious Jew concluded his prayer with an "Amen", . . . Jesus prefaces his words with an "Amen", thus identifying God with what he would say.'[37] As Raymond Brown points out, nowhere in the Gospels does it say anything like, 'The word of God came to Jesus.' The idea instead seems to have been that he already had or even (in John's terminology) *was* the word.[38] His words are true and binding because of his own personal position and authority; he is in a position to give the Law's true meaning, to reveal God's will.

Ernst Käsemann argues that Jesus' 'but I say to you' language 'embodies a claim to an authority which rivals and challenges that of Moses'.[39] The fact that Jesus claimed Moses-like authority, an authority to supervene all other authorities, has been noticed, and reacted to negatively, by contemporary Jewish scholars who write about Jesus. For example, Schalom Ben-Chorin says: 'The sense of the unique, absolute authority that is evident from [Jesus'] way of acting remains deeply problematic for the Jewish view of Jesus.'[40] And Jacob Neusner states[41] that Jesus' attitude toward the Torah makes him want to ask: 'Who do you think you are? God?'[42] It is highly significant that Jesus assumed for himself the authority to reinterpret and even overrule the OT Law (see Matt. 5: 21–48; Mark 2: 23–8), again something no mere human being could do. Jesus considered his words as permanent and indestructible (Mark 13: 31). In short, Jesus did not think of himself as just another prophetic spokesperson for God; he spoke as if he were divine.

Fourth, even in the Synoptic Gospels, Jesus said things that can sensibly be interpreted as implicit claims to divinity. I see no way of

[37] Robinson, *Can We Trust the New Testament?*, 104.
[38] R. Brown, 'Did Jesus Know He Was God?', *Biblical Theology Bulletin*, 15 (1988), 77.
[39] E. Käsemann, 'The Problem of the Historical Jesus', in id., *Essays on New Testament Themes* (Naperville, Ill.: Allenson, 1964), 37.
[40] S. Ben-Chorin, *Jesus in Judenthum* (Wuppertal: R. Brockhaus, 1970), 41, cited in Craig, *Reasonable Faith*, 241.
[41] In an interview about his book, *A Rabbi Talks With Jesus: An Intermillenial, Interfaith Exchange* (New York: Doubleday, 1993).
[42] Cited in Wright, 'Jesus and the Identity of God', 22.

ruling out as inauthentic Jesus' claim to be 'the Christ, the Son of the Blessed' (Mark 14: 61–2), which the high priest took to be blasphemy. Notice finally this claim, the so-called 'Johannine thunderbolt', which seems a kind of bridge from the Christology of the Synoptics to the Christology of the Fourth Gospel: 'All things have been delivered to me by my Father; and no one knows the Son except the Father, and no one knows the Father except the Son and anyone to whom the Son chooses to reveal him' (Matt. 11: 27).[43] Here Jesus seems to be claiming to be the Son of God in a unique and exclusive sense, the only true and authoritative revelation of the Father.

Fifth, Jesus, the coming 'Son of Man', implicitly made two dramatic claims: first, that our relationship to him would determine our final status before God; second, that he himself would be the judge of all human beings at the end of history.[44] Both seem clearly to be claims to be standing in a divine role.[45]

So Jesus apparently saw himself as having the right to act as God and do what God appropriately does. The argument in favour of this point does not depend on ahistorical readings of the Gospels, nor on the claim that the sayings cited from the Fourth Gospel above come directly from Jesus (though I believe that in substance they do).[46] Jesus implicitly claimed divine status. That is the best interpretation of the four considerations I have been citing. Accordingly, a strong case can be made that premise (1) of the MBG argument is true.

---

[43] Witherington argues convincingly that these words are authentic. See *Christology of Jesus*, 221–8.

[44] See O'Collins, *Christology*, 60–2.

[45] There is a curious tribute to this argument from an unexpected source in George W. E. Nickelsburg's entry, 'Son of Man', in the *Anchor Bible Dictionary* (New York: Doubleday, 1992), vi. 149. He argues that Jesus could not have implied that he was the 'Son of Man', because that would mean (what Nickelsburg cannot accept) that he went around claiming to be the eschatological judge of all.

[46] A brief note about the Christology of the Fourth Gospel: it is often pointed out that alongside the texts such as those cited above that seem to indicate Jesus' oneness with God and equality with the Father, there are texts that point toward Jesus' dependence on the Father, who is greater than he (see 7: 16; 5: 19, 30–31; 14: 28). My only comment is that the best way to keep both sorts of texts theologically in view is the classic doctrine of the incarnation, where Jesus is both 'fully divine' and 'begotten of the Father'.

VI

Where then do we stand? Is the MBG argument a successful argument, or not? Can it be used as a convincing piece of Christian apologetics (as Lewis clearly thought it could), or not? The conclusion we reached earlier is that the argument, as outlined in steps (1)–(8), is valid. But of course that does not show much. The argument:

(13) Everybody in Tibet believes in Jesus;
(14) Bertrand Russell lives in Tibet;
(15) Therefore Bertrand Russell believes in Jesus

is also a valid argument, but is obviously a rhetorically useless device for providing rational support for its conclusion.

But is the argument *sound* (i.e. valid plus true premises)? Well, as we have seen, premise (2) is virtually beyond reproach; and while premises (3), (4), and (5) can be disputed, an excellent case can also be made for their truth. But premise (1), which I take to be the crux of the argument, not only can be but frequently is disputed, even by some who believe in the incarnation. I take it that the perceived weakness of premise (1) is the most important reason why the MBG argument has not often been used or defended by Christian theologians and exegetes (as opposed to a few apologists) since Lewis. But, as we have also seen, a strong (and, in my view, convincing) case can also be made in favour of premise (1), a case that does not depend on viewing the Gospels ahistorically. The MBG argument also seems immune to such informal fallacies as equivocation, question-begging, arguing in a circle, etc.

Whether the MBG argument is a successful argument accordingly depends on what 'success' for an argument amounts to. That is, it depends on what is taken to be the goal, purpose, or aim of the argument. And of course there are many quite different ways of envisioning the goal or purpose of the MBG argument (or indeed of any deductive argument). Suppose the goal of the MBG argument were *to convince all nonbelievers in the incarnation of Jesus to believe in it* or *to constitute an argument that rationally should convince all nonbelievers in the incarnation of Jesus to believe in it*. Then one must doubt that the MBG argument can count as successful. Few nonbelievers will be converted by it; no matter how hard we argue for the truth of premise (1) (or even premises (3), (4), or (5)), the nonbeliever can go on disputing it (or them). Indeed, it seems a nonbeliever in the incarnation can always say something like this: 'I do not know whether Jesus was mad, bad, honestly mistaken, or never said or implied that he was divine—after all, that was twenty centuries ago, and by now it's hard to tell—but one thing I do know is that he was not divine.'

But suppose the aim of the MBG argument is *to demonstrate the truth of the incarnation of Jesus* or (see the very end of Section I, above) *to demonstrate the rationality of belief in the incarnation of Jesus*. If one of these constitutes the true aim or goal of the MBG argument, then it will not matter whether nonbelievers in the incarnation can rationally reject one or another of the argument's premises.

My own view is that the last goal mentioned—to demonstrate the rationality of belief in the incarnation of Jesus—is the proper goal or aim of the MBG argument. And given what we have concluded in this chapter, I believe it succeeds in doing that very thing. Accordingly, the MBG argument can constitute a powerful piece of Christian apologetics.[47]

[47] I would like to thank C. Stephen Evans, Daniel Howard-Snyder, Brian Leftow, Carey Newman, Gerald O'Collins, SJ, Alan Padgett, Dale Tuggy, and an anonymous referee from Oxford University Press for their helpful comments on earlier versions of this chapter.

11

The Self-Emptying of Love:
Some Thoughts on Kenotic Christology

C. STEPHEN EVANS

Kenotic Christology is an attempt to understand how Jesus can be both human and divine by taking seriously the idea that the incarnation involved some kind of self-limitation or 'self-emptying' on the part of the Son of God. Such theories, inspired by Philippians 2: 6–11 as well as other New Testament passages, are regularly attacked, though the reasons given by different critics are often incompatible. Some reject kenotic Christology because they believe it is unorthodox, incompatible with the classical Chalcedonian statement about the status of Jesus as a single person with both a human and a divine nature.[1] Others reject kenotic Christology because it is *too* orthodox, since it clearly presupposes the pre-existence of Christ as the second person of the Trinity, the One who emptied himself of divine prerogatives to suffer and die as a human for the human race.[2] One suspects that some of this second class of critics worry that a viable kenotic Christology would perhaps make orthodox beliefs about Jesus more intellectually credible by doing full justice to the humanness of Jesus, which contemporary New Testament scholarship has emphasized, without being forced thereby to compromise Jesus' divinity.

In this chapter I shall try to make some progress toward the development of a kenotic account of the incarnation, building on recent work of others. Let me first delimit my task, then highlight some assumptions. First, I need to make it clear that I shall defend a

---

[1] For examples see D. MacLeod, *The Person of Christ* (Downers Grove, Ill.: InterVarsity Press, 1998), 205–20; and R. Swinburne, *The Christian God* (Oxford: Oxford University Press, 1994), 230–3.

[2] For good examples see the 'Critiques' of Stephen Davis offered by James Robinson and John Hick in S. T. Davis (ed.), *Encountering Jesus: A Debate on Christology*, (Atlanta: John Knox Press, 1988), 59–64 and 66–9.

kenotic view of the incarnation, rather than a kenotic view of God. I am not without sympathy for the latter; in fact, I would argue that if the incarnation is revelatory of God and involves a *kenosis*, then this must reflect something deeply true of the nature of God. However, I think the order of discovery here requires that one first understand the incarnation kenotically before extending these insights so as to throw light on the character of the Godhead.

Also, in this chapter I shall not attempt to defend the truth of the doctrine of the incarnation, either in a general or in a kenotic form, except insofar as making sense of a kenotic version of the doctrine contributes to the intelligibility of the doctrine. I shall assume the standpoint of someone committed to the truth of orthodox Christology, taking Chalcedon as defining the boundaries of orthodoxy on this question.[3] The question is whether a kenotic theory can be developed that helps makes sense of the doctrine. I do not argue here that a kenotic theory is the only viable account of the incarnation, or even that it is the best account, but only that it is a coherent, viable view.

So this chapter should not be viewed as an attempt to give evidence for the incarnation or any particular theory of the incarnation. I do in fact believe that one can give evidence or reasons for belief in the incarnation, but that is not my purpose in this essay. (I should note in passing that I also think that reasonable belief—and even knowledge about—the incarnation is possible without propositional evidence.[4])

I shall also assume that some form of the doctrine of the Trinity that preserves real distinctions between the persons of the Trinity is viable. A moderate form of Social Trinitarianism would be a good example of the kind of account I have in mind.[5] Although

---

[3] It should be obvious that those boundaries provide space for a variety of theories. For an excellent treatment of the diverse ways the concept of *kenosis* has been treated in the Christian tradition, see S. Coakley, '*Kenosis* and Subversion', in D. Hampson (ed.), *Swallowing A Fishbone? Feminist Theologians Debate Christianity* (London: SPCK, 1996), 82–111.

[4] See ch. 11 of my book, *The Historical Christ and the Jesus of Faith: The Incarnational Narrative as History* (Oxford: Oxford University Press, 1996), 259–82.

[5] For examples of Social Trinitarianism, see C. Plantinga, Jr., 'Social Trinity and Tritheism', and D. Brown, 'Trinitarian Personhood and Individuality', in R. J. Feenstra and C. Plantinga (eds.), *Trinity, Incarnation, and Atonement: Philosophical and Theological Essays* (Notre Dame, Ind.: University of Notre Dame Press, 1989), 21–47, 48–78. For a vigorous critique of Social Trinitarianism see B. Leftow, 'Anti Social Trinitarianism', in S. Davis, D. Kendall, and G. O'Collins (eds.), *The Trinity* (Oxford: Oxford University Press, 1999), 203–49.

historically Christology certainly preceded the development of the doctrine of the Trinity, once the latter doctrine is formulated it is proper to take full account of its resources in developing an understanding of the incarnation. I think it would be impossible to develop any coherent account of the incarnation understood in an orthodox manner that does not presuppose the doctrine of the Trinity. David Brown has claimed that kenotic accounts of the incarnation are committed to some form of Social Trinitarianism. I am inclined to think that this is right, though I do not want to commit myself to the claim that a kenotic theory rests on Social Trinitarianism. The important point is that the real distinctions between the persons of the Trinity must be respected. If God the Son (but not the Father or the Spirit) empties himself of some qualities to become incarnate as a human being, this will require that we take seriously the differences between the persons of the Trinity.[6]

Since my purpose is to develop a kenotic theory that is consistent with Chalcedonian orthodoxy, I shall not consider theories in which the *kenosis* is understood as God emptying himself of divinity. Critics of kenotic theory often consider the theory to be an alternative to Chalcedon and criticize it in that light. Richard Swinburne, for example, says of a kenotic theory that '[w]here it differs from Chalcedon is in supposing that [God humbling himself and living a human life] could only be achieved by God the Son ceasing in some way to have the divine properties'.[7] Swinburne claims to argue 'in defence of Chalcedon, that God cannot cease to be God . . .'.[8] Donald MacLeod, representing a reaction typical among evangelical theologians, is even more explicit in claiming that a kenotic theory is one in which God the Son empties himself of deity.[9] It hardly needs to be said that any theory that can be described 'God ceasing to be God' or 'God relinquishing divinity' will not count as a kenotic theory that is attempting to make Chalcedonian orthodoxy intelligible. An

---

[6] Several theologian have urged that a kenotic theory, at least as I develop it, also assumes that God should be understood as being everlasting rather than being atemporal. This is probably correct. In any case, I do not regard it as an objection to a kenotic theory if it is true, since it seems to me that the claim that God is everlasting is a defensible one. My attitude towards the claim that God is everlasting is similar to my attitude towards a kenotic theory: it seems a viable view of God and I am inclined to hold it but with some tentativeness. The debate between defenders of an atemporal view of God and an everlasting God is a vigorous one and both sides can make reasonable cases for their positions.

[7] Swinburne, *Christian God*, 233.   [8] Ibid.
[9] D. MacLeod, *Person of Christ*, 205.

orthodox kenotic theory of the incarnation cannot deny the truth of the incarnation, and an orthodox kenotic theory should say something about what God the Son retains in his incarnation as well as what is relinquished. What is retained will chiefly be the self-giving love that is regarded as lying at the heart of divinity and which is exhibited precisely in God's willingness to empty himself for the sake of his creatures.

It is important to note that a kenotic theory should not be identified with an approach to Jesus that denies any possibility of the miraculous or supernatural. To say that the incarnate Son emptied himself of such properties as omnipotence and omniscience is not at all the same thing as saying that Jesus was incapable of miracles or possessed no supernatural knowledge that ordinarily a human would not possess. A kenotic theory can recognize supernatural power in the life of Jesus. Even if Jesus is not omnipotent and omniscient as a human being, he might well possess supernatural abilities. It is possible though probably not necessary for the kenoticist to attribute Jesus' possession of any such powers to his dependence on the Father and the Spirit who might endow him with these powers.

I THE APPEAL OF KENOTIC THEORIES

Before proceeding to the main issues that confront a kenotic theory, I would like to say some things about the motivation for such a theory. The motivation as I see it is partly intrinsic and partly consists in problems in the main rival type of theory. The intrinsic motivation itself consists of two different kinds of factors that make a kenotic theory appealing.

The first and most powerful source of the appeal of a kenotic theory is the great religious power and meaning that is intrinsic to the idea of a God who sacrifices and suffers with and on behalf of his creatures. If I am caught up in terrible suffering it is one thing to be assured of the love and kindness of another person. It is quite another thing for that other person to give the assurance by entering into my situation and suffering with me or even for me. A God who empties himself out of love for human beings, who recklessly as it were gives up divine privileges to endure all the hard realities of human life, is a God whose love is credible and inspires love in return.

It is worth noting that such a love on the part of God does not necessarily imply any intrinsic need or emptiness in God. Rather, any 'need' that God may have as a human being is one he has chosen to assume. The following passage from W. H. Vanstone expresses this thought quite powerfully:

Trinitarian theology asserts that God's love for his creation is not the love that is born of 'emptiness'. . . . It is the love which overflows from fullness. Its analogue is the love of a family who, united in mutual love, take an orphan into the home. They do so not out of need but in the pure spontaneity of their own triumphant love. Nevertheless, in the weeks that follow, the family, once complete in itself, comes to need the newcomer. Without him the circle is now incomplete; his absence now causes anxiety; his waywardness brings concern; his goodness and happiness are necessary to those who have come to love him; upon his response depends the triumph or the tragedy of the family's love. . . . Love has surrendered its triumphant self-sufficiency and created its own need. This is the supreme illustration of love's self-giving or self-emptying—that it should surrender its fullness and create in itself the emptiness of need. Of such a nature is the Kenosis of God—the self-emptying of Him Who is already in every way fulfilled.[10]

The second source of appeal that kenotic Christologies possess is an ability to deal without embarrassment with the very human portrait of Jesus that is seen in the Gospels. An honest reading of the NT reveals a Jesus who is in many respects clearly human and who possesses at least to a degree the normal limitations all humans experience. Thus, Jesus reveals ignorance at times (Mark 13: 31–2). He grows in his wisdom and knowledge in the way that all children do (Luke 2: 52). Jesus seems to be able to experience hunger, to feel weary, even deep frustration (the latter in John 11: 23). The writer of Hebrews says that Jesus was tempted in the same way as other humans, which seems, to some people at least, to imply the possibility of moral failure (Heb. 4: 15). This sketch of the very human qualities of Jesus in the NT could easily be expanded of course.[11]

I do not wish to claim that the humanness of the portrait of Jesus in the NT entails or requires a kenotic theory of the incarnation. I think,

---

[10] W. H. Vanstone, *Love's Endeavour Love's Expense: The Response of Being to the Love of God* (London: Darton, Longman, and Todd, 1977), 69.

[11] Some other NT passages that seem to support a kenotic view would include 2 Cor. 8: 9, Acts 10: 38, Luke 2: 52, and Heb. 5: 7–9.

for example, that the 'two minds' theory (to be explained below), which I see as the chief rival to a kenotic account, can account for this data. However, I do think that a kenotic theory can handle this data in a more natural and convincing manner than does a two minds theory. It is easy to understand how a divine being who has divested himself, at least temporarily, of omnipotence and omniscience could be ignorant and weak. It is not so easy to see how this could be true of a being who remains omnipotent and omniscient.

In addition to the intrinsic appeal of a kenotic theory, I believe that some of the appeal of the theory is due to difficulties faced by the two minds view. By the 'two minds view' I mean to speak about the kind of theory defended by Thomas Morris, in which the incarnate Son of God is regarded as having both a divine and a human mind.[12] A somewhat similar view is defended by Richard Swinburne who speaks not of two minds but of a 'divided mind' in which an agent has 'two systems of belief to some extent independent of each other'.[13] On this kind of view, the limitations that the NT seems to attribute to Jesus are regarded as pertaining to his human mind, which is indeed limited in knowledge and power, but these limitations do not affect his divine mind.

I do not wish to attack such an account of the incarnation. Indeed, I have argued elsewhere that it is intellectually viable and coherent.[14] Nevertheless, the account faces an obvious difficulty that will be clear to anyone who has ever attempted to teach this theory to students. There are many *desiderata* for a theory of the incarnation. A good theory should not undermine the divinity of Jesus, should not compromise his humanity, and should not compromise his unity as a single person. It is this last item that presents at least a *prima facie* difficulty for the two minds theory. I do not wish to claim too much here. It is probably the case that every theory of the incarnation will be subject to difficulties, and difficulties can often be resolved in a satisfactory manner. Nevertheless, the presence of a difficulty provides at least some motivation for exploring an alternative account, to see if the difficulties it faces are less, or if it resolves those difficulties in a more satisfying manner.

[12] See T. Morris, 'The Metaphysics of God Incarnate', in *Trinity, Incarnation, and Atonement*, 110–27, for a brief statement. For a longer account see id., *The Logic of God Incarnate* (Ithaca, NY: Cornell University Press, 1986).
[13] Swinburne, *Christian God*, 201.
[14] See Evans, *Historical Christ and the Jesus of Faith*, 128–32.

In this case the difficulty is not hard to discern. If we take a case of Jesus manifesting ignorance or being subject to temptation, the two minds theory will say that it is with respect to his human mind that Jesus was ignorant or tempted, and that his divine mind had an entirely different perspective on the situation. In such a situation, it is difficult to understand Jesus as a unified single person. Swinburne appeals to Freud in order to claim that such a divided mind can still be the mind of a single person, while Morris actually goes so far as to rely on the analogy of a person who is afflicted with multiple personality disorder in order to make sense of this 'doubleness'.[15] These strategies may be acceptable, but they produce enough discomfort to make us look to see if a more natural way of safeguarding the unity of Jesus as divine-human person can be found.

II Review of Some Recent Discussions

Without attempting to be comprehensive, it will be helpful to situate my defence of a kenotic account of the incarnation in the context of some recent discussions. Stephen Davis has been a prominent advocate of kenotic theories, first in *Logic and the Nature of God* and more recently in *Encountering Jesus*, in which Davis discusses and debates Christological issues with a number of other thinkers, including John Hick. In both works Davis defends the claim that Jesus as a divine-human being has all of the properties essential to divinity and humanity even though in his earthly life he shared in the limitations of human life.

I shall begin with an issue from the later work. In *Encountering Jesus*, Davis deals with a special type of property that makes the idea of divine-human being problematic. It would seem that a divine being would have essential properties such as 'being uncreated' or 'having had no beginning', while one might think that a human being would have properties incompatible with these, such as 'being created', or 'being conceived at a particular time'. In both cases, such properties would seem to be properties that a being could not lose; they are, in Davis's word, 'ungiveupable'. Hence, with respect to this kind of property, a kenotic account makes no sense.[16] Davis

---

[15] See Swinburne, *Christian God*, 201, and Morris, 'Metaphysics of God Incarnate', 122–4.

[16] It seems to me that John Hick unfairly characterizes the two types of arguments

therefore makes a different kind of response for this kind of property, one used by more traditional Christologies, by arguing that such properties are 'reduplicative'. If one wishes to be precise one should say that Jesus *as* a human being was born at a particular time and that Jesus *as* God was uncreated. Despite the air of paradox, it is not a logical contradiction to say that Jesus possesses both properties, because he does not possess them both in the same manner. I agree with Davis that some divine properties must be treated by the kenotic theorist in this reduplicative way, and not seen as having been relinquished. Insofar as non-kenotic theories make use of such a reduplicative strategy, there is at least some common ground between kenotic theories of the incarnation and other theories.

Leaving aside these 'ungiveupable' properties, let us look at Davis's kenotic theory. In *Logic and the Nature of God* Davis explains a kenotic theory along the following lines. Jesus is fully divine and fully human. As incarnate, he lacks some divine properties and some human properties, but he has all the properties essential to divinity and all the properties essential to humanity.[17]

What about such divine properties as omnipotence and omniscience? Here Davis attempts to have his cake and eat it too. He agrees that such properties are essential for a divine being, and thus Jesus must possess them to be divine. However, he wants to say that Jesus was as a human being both ignorant and weak in various respects. How is this possible? Davis makes a distinction between possessing a property such as omniscience *simpliciter* and possessing such a property 'in some way'. He thinks it is possible for a divine being who is omnipotent and omniscient to choose to divest himself temporarily of these properties. If the being in question retains the

employed by Davis when he says that Davis's view is similar to a defence attorney who argues that 'my client did not do it', but also 'if my client did it, it was not a crime'. (See Hick's 'Critique' of Davis in *Encountering Jesus*, 66.) Hick seems to think that Davis is arguing that the essential divine and human properties are consistent (compossible, to use a more precise logical term), but also that if they are not, then they can be understood in this reduplicative manner. However, it seems clear to me that Davis means to employ these two strategies for two different types of properties. Properties, whose 'reduplication' would require 'two minds' or a divided consciousness, are treated as kenotically given up, while properties possessed by something in virtue of its history or status and which cannot therefore be lost, are treated reduplicatively. These latter propositions do not imply any division or duality in the mind of the bearer.

[17] S. T. Davis, *Logic and the Nature of God* (Grand Rapids, Mich.: Eerdmans, 1983), 127.

power to reassume these properties, then in a sense the being remains omnipotent and omniscient.

In what sense? One might think that a more natural description of the sequence Davis portrays would be that such a being was omnipotent and omniscient, temporarily lost these properties, and then regained them. However, one might argue that an essential property cannot be lost, even temporarily. Can we make sense of Davis's view here?

I believe that we can. One possibility is to interpret Davis as suggesting that such properties as omnipotence and omniscience might be understood as *powers*. An omnipotent being has the power to do all things that are logically coherent; a being who chooses not to exercise this power continues to be omnipotent. Similarly, perhaps, an omniscient being might be a being who has the power to know all things. If a being chooses not to exercise this power by willing to limit itself in some way, we could reasonably say that such a being remains omniscient even though for a time the being might be ignorant in various respects. So if the second person of the Trinity decided to become incarnate as a human being and thereby assumed certain limitations associated with being human, this would not imply that this divine being was no longer divine, so long as the limitations were freely willed by the divine being. I shall return to this idea of self-limitation later. Here I wish only to say that it seems to me that a genuine kenotic account of such a willed self-limitation must recognize that self-limitation of this sort amounts to divestiture, at least for a period of time. If we (perhaps unconsciously) imagine God the Son as continuously willing a self-limitation, we have really not departed from a two-minds model.

In his essay 'Jesus Christ: Savior or Guru?', in *Encountering Jesus*, Davis defends a similar kenotic view with respect to such properties as omnipotence and omniscience but does so in what appears to me to be a slightly different way. He continues to claim that Jesus has those properties that are essential to divinity and humanity.[18] However, appealing to a type of consideration employed by Brian Hebblethwaite, he points out that it is often very difficult to know what properties are indeed essential to an actual being. If we have good reason to believe that Jesus is divine and that as a human being Jesus was not omnipotent or omniscient, then we have good reasons to think that these properties are not in fact essential to divinity. Perhaps they would be essential to a God who could not become incarnate and who consequently never does become incarnate, a type of God that Davis calls 'God *simpliciter*', but Christians believe that no God of that type exists.[19] The only God we have knowledge of is a God who did become incarnate. Such a God is doubtless omnipotent and omniscient when not incarnate, but these properties turn out to be contingent properties and not essential ones for God.

There appears to be a contradiction between these two accounts, for on the first view omnipotence and omniscience are essential properties of a divine being but on the second they are not. However, as I have interpreted Davis, there is no real contradiction, because 'omnipotence' and 'omniscience' are not understood in the same way in the two accounts. If we take these terms as referring to powers that one might temporarily choose not to exercise, then they may be properties essential to divinity. However, if we understand omniscience, for example, as referring to actual knowledge of all true propositions, then this property is possessed by God contingently.

It seems that the two types of argument employed by Davis, as I have interpreted them, each have characteristic strengths and weaknesses. The first view allows one to claim that omniscience and omnipotence are essential properties of a divine being and that Jesus has those properties. The price to be paid is of course that those properties are understood in a somewhat unusual way, as powers. One might think that for omnipotence, this would not be odd, since omnipotence surely must be understood as the power to do things, and a power does not have to be exercised to be possessed. It is unusual to understand omniscience as a power, however, since it has usually been thought that an omniscient being possesses actual knowledge of all truths and not merely an ability to have such knowledge.

Is it satisfactory to understand Jesus' self-emptying to consist merely in a failure to exercise a power he continues to possess in some sense? It might seem that a being who has truly 'emptied himself' does not merely choose not to exercise powers he continues to possess but has in some sense given up such powers. A committed

---

[19] Ibid.

kenoticist might argue that a Jesus who is omnipotent at every moment, but chooses not to exercise this power, would surely not fit well with the Chalcedonian description of Jesus as 'like us in all respects, apart from sin'. This critic could argue that since it is one of the strengths of a kenotic theory that it does a better job of fitting this description of Jesus as like other humans than other Christologies, the 'emptying' involved in the incarnation must be something more radical than merely a continuous choice not to exercise divine power.

There is a sound point behind this criticism. A continuous choice not to exercise a power does seem to assume, as I noted above, 'two minds'. This is so because the choice not to exercise the power would seem to imply a kind of divine consciousness of that power, a consciousness that would not be present in the human consciousness of the one who is limited. Perhaps then a choice not to exercise divine power must be understood not merely as a continuous self-limitation but rather as a kind of 'binding' choice. This kind of choice would be a true emptying.

Nevertheless, we should not rush too quickly past the idea of a continuous divine act of self-limitation. It is important to see that even a theory that is not properly described as a kenotic theory can and should include a kenotic element, something like a continuous act of self-limitation. If I choose to spend a period of time in a homeless shelter, one could argue that I have indeed chosen to give up the privileges of living at home, even though I retain the power of doing that. The fact that even a theory that does not see itself as kenotic must somehow incorporate this element of self-limitation may show that the differences between kenotic and non-kenotic theories may not be so great as we might imagine.

To understand the nature of what we might call the kenotic element of the incarnation places us at the boundary of very difficult questions about the nature of omnipotence and omniscience. If omnipotence is a power, could it or must it include the power to relinquish or limit that power? Could such a self-limitation be a 'one-time' choice, so to speak, or could it be a continuously exercised self-restraint? If it is possible for omnipotence to restrict itself, would an omnipotent being also necessarily have the power to relinquish or limit his knowledge? I shall return to these questions in due course.

The strategy Davis employs in his later book, as I have interpreted it, which involves giving up the claim that omnipotence, omniscience, and other divine properties are really essential to divinity, is subject to a different type of worry. John Hick worries that if properties such as omnipotence, omniscience, and (especially) moral perfection are not essential to God, and are therefore merely contingent, this makes for a religiously inadequate concept of God.[20] The same kind of point is made from the other end of the theological spectrum by Tom Morris, who argues that we ought to think of God as Anselm does, as a 'greatest possible being' or a being who is 'maximally perfect'.[21] Morris argues that a being who is not essentially omnipotent or omniscient would fail to satisfy our 'Anselmian intuitions' about God.

Morris actually makes a significant contribution to kenotic theory, even though he ultimately rejects this type of theory, by suggesting that what the kenotic theologian might hold is that it is not omnipotence and omniscience that are essential properties of divinity. Rather, he says, the kenotic theologian might hold that the properties essential to God are properties like 'being-omniscient-unless-freely-and-temporarily-choosing-to-be-otherwise'. Such properties are both plausibly thought to be essentially divine and such that an incarnate God who is not omnipotent or omniscient during his earthly career might possess them. Morris gives several reasons for not accepting his own proposal for a revised kenotic Christology. Of these, I think the most important is that he holds that a being who possessed only attributes such as 'omniscient-unless-freely-choosing-not-to-be' would not be as perfect as a being who was simply omniscient, and that we should think of God as supremely perfect.[22]

Ronald Feenstra has, I believe, given a convincing response to Morris's objections.[23] First, Feenstra notes, Morris himself admits that Anselmian intuitions are defeasible. I would add that they can also vary. It is not at all self-evident that a being who is incapable of self-limitation is superior to a being who is capable of such limitation.[24] In fact, my intuitions are just the reverse on this

[20] Critique by John Hick, in *Encountering Jesus*, 68.
[21] For an explanation of Morris's 'Anselmian' or 'perfect-being' theology, see his *Our Idea of God: An Introduction to Philosophical Theology* (Downers Grove, Ill.: InterVarsity Press, 1991), 35–40. The criticism of a kenotic theory based on this method can be found in Morris, *Logic of God Incarnate*, 76.
[22] Morris, *Our Idea of God*, 167.
[23] See R. J. Feenstra, 'Reconsidering Kenotic Christology', in *Trinity, Incarnation, and Atonement*, 128–52.   [24] Ibid. 143.

issue. However, even if we share Morris's intuitions, do we have any real ground for being confident of their validity? It might appear (to some people at least) that a being incapable of divesting itself of omniscience and omnipotence is more perfect than a being who is able to divest himself of these properties. But surely such intuitions could be wrong, and are subject to correction. A defender of a kenotic theory of the incarnation could say, as Davis does in *Encountering Jesus*, that we have discovered facts that suggest that these properties are not necessary to divinity and are therefore not required in a supremely perfect being.

This first argument seems quite adequate to me as a response to Morris's objection. However, Feenstra advances another argument that seems to me to be even more decisive. Any 'Anselmian intuitions' we have about divine perfections surely are intuitions about God and not intuitions about the properties of the individual persons that compose the Trinity. We have no reliable *a priori* intuitions about what properties the individual persons of the Trinity might possess, because our natural reason, unenlightened by special revelation, would never have discovered the idea of God as three-in-one, and has no 'natural' conception as to what the persons of the Trinity would be like.[25]

Even if we have reliable 'Anselmian' intuitions about divine perfection, and even if such intuitions support a non-kenotic theory of the incarnation (both questionable, as we have seen), from the perspective of trinitarian theology, such intuitions would only apply to the Godhead, to God as the unified being who is in fact composed of three persons. It may be quite reasonable to think that the Godhead as a unity would indeed possess such properties as omnipotence and omniscience, but this does not necessarily imply that the individual persons of the Godhead must all possess these properties at any given time. Presumably there are properties which the individual persons of the Trinity possess essentially, but it may

---

[25] Recently, Richard Swinburne has creatively (some might say audaciously) attempted to give rational arguments that God would be expected to exist in three persons. Swinburne apparently thinks that even apart from the Christian revelation, we would have good reasons to think of God as existing in three persons. See his *Christian God*, 170–91. However, Swinburne's view is certainly not the traditional Christian position, which has held that the Trinity is a mystery revealed to faith, and is not something that reason could know apart from faith in God's revelation. I have been informed that a few other thinkers support Swinburne's view here, notably Richard of St Victor.

be beyond our powers to know all of them, especially from an *a priori* perspective.

This proposal has the added bonus that it suggests an answer to a famous criticism of a kenotic theory, posed by Archbishop William Temple in the form of a rhetorical question: 'What was happening to the rest of the universe during the period of our Lord's earthly life?'[26] Temple's implied point is that one of the functions of the second person of the Trinity, the Divine Word through whom all things were created and are upheld, could not be carried on by a divine being who had emptied himself of omnipotence and omniscience. Davis replies to this charge with the suggestion that Christ could have 'planned ahead, made arrangements, settled matters ahead of time', a reply that John Cobb finds 'excessively anthropomorphic'.[27]

I do not claim that Davis's view here is necessarily wrong, though I confess that his reply could be taken as suggesting a vaguely deistic view of the divine ordering of creation that is somewhat worrying. However, if someone does not care for this 'pre-arrangement' theory, the defender of the kenotic theory can reply in another fashion. The Divine Trinity of Persons must in some way constitute a profound unity. In some way the activity of each person of the Trinity must involve the activity of each of the others. I see no reason why, if the second person of the Trinity became incarnate and divested himself of omnipotence and omniscience, what we might call the sustaining work of this person in creation could not be carried on by the other persons. Furthermore, if some kind of real unity remains between the Son and the Spirit and the Father (and if this is not the case, the doctrine of the Trinity must be false), then the Son could still be said to carry on this work by virtue of his unity with Father and Spirit.[28]

---

[26] W. Temple, *Christus Veritas* (London: Macmillan, 1924), 142.

[27] See Davis, 'Jesus Christ: Savior or Guru?', in *Encountering Jesus*, 54, and 'Critique by John Cobb', ibid. 65.

[28] Someone might object that this would mean the Son would be dependent on the Father and the Spirit to carry out his work, and that this would imply some kind of inequality. However, there must be asymmetries in the relations of the Trinity if there is to be any real distinction of persons. Each must depend on the other in various ways. One could also say that the Father and the Spirit depend on the incarnate Son to accomplish their redemptive aims. In any case, the biblical picture of Jesus constantly portrays him as both unified with and completely dependent on the Father.

III OMNIPOTENCE, THE PARADOX OF THE STONE, AND THE CONSEQUENCES OF EMBODIMENT

As I see things, Feenstra has adequately answered one of the strongest objections to Davis' view. However, an unfriendly critic might still worry about this response. The property of 'being-omnipotent-unless-freely-wishing-to-limit-one's-power' (or some similar property) may have an artificial 'cooked-up' feel to it. Attributing such a property to a divine being may seem to be an *ad hoc* move to save a theory, and even someone inclined to think our 'Anselmian intuitions' are fallible might well think that it would be better to have plain old omnipotence.

However, an argument can be mounted that there is no such thing as 'plain old omnipotence' and that the only coherent account of omnipotence is one that includes the ability of an omnipotent being to limit its power. Oddly enough, the materials for such an argument are provided by Richard Swinburne, a critic of kenotic theories. As noted above, Swinburne treats the kenotic theory as an alternative to Chalcedon rather than as a way of making Chalcedon intelligible, and he argues, in *The Christian God*, that a divine being must have the properties of omnipotence and omniscience essentially.[29] However, in an earlier book, *The Coherence of Theism*, Swinburne argues that an omnipotent being necessarily must have the power to limit his own omnipotence.[30]

Swinburne's argument here is rooted in his attempt to resolve what has come to be called 'the paradox of the stone'. Critics of the concept of omnipotence have employed this paradox as part of an argument that the concept of omnipotence is incoherent. Roughly, the paradox is as follows: the concept of an omnipotent being is that of a being who can do any action that is logically possible. Suppose a being to be omnipotent. Can that being make a stone which that being cannot move? If the being can make such a stone, then there is something that being cannot do, namely lift the stone (or, more felicitously, cause the stone to rise). However, if the being cannot make the stone, it would seem that there is still something the being cannot do, which is of course to make the stone.

There are a number of ways philosophers have attempted to

[29] Swinburne, *Christian God*, 232–3.
[30] R. Swinburne, *The Coherence of Theism* (Oxford: Oxford University Press, 1994), 157–8.

resolve this paradox, and space does not permit a critical discussion of the alternatives. Swinburne himself discusses and criticizes several of these alternatives, and argues that the key to the resolution of the paradox is the recognition that an omnipotent being must indeed have the power to limit its own omnipotence. Thus, an omnipotent being does indeed have the power to create a stone that this being cannot move, but the being remains omnipotent so long as he does not exercise that power. 'True, if an omnipotent being actually exercises (as opposed to merely possessing) his ability to bring about the existence of a stone too heavy for him subsequently to bring about its rising, then he will cease to be omnipotent.'[31] Swinburne goes on to say that an omnipotent being may (and presumably will) remain omnipotent for ever, 'because he never exercises his power to create stones too heavy to lift, forces too strong to resist, or universes too wayward to control'.[32]

The point I wish to emphasize is that omnipotence, as Swinburne conceives it, entails the power to limit omnipotence. If this account of omnipotence is correct, then there cannot be an omnipotent being who does not have the ability to limit omnipotence. The kind of omnipotence that a kenotic theory attributes to the pre-incarnate Christ would not be a second-best, inferior kind of omnipotence, but the only possible kind. At the very least I would argue that it is epistemically possible that the only kind of omnipotence there could be is omnipotence that includes the power to limit itself.

What about Swinburne's obvious assumption that a divine, omnipotent being would not choose to exercise this power to limit himself? I do not believe this assumption can be safely made in the context of trinitarian theology. Perhaps if God were not three-in-one, such a view would be reasonable. The God who creates and controls the universe for loving purposes would not cede ultimate power to achieve his ends. However, it is not at all clear that the same assumption can be made for the individual persons of the Trinity. Perhaps the pre-incarnate Christ could and did willingly choose to divest himself of omnipotence, secure in his faith and trust and love in the other persons of the Trinity, confident that the creative and providential work of the Godhead would be maintained, and that he himself could accomplish his divine work through dependence on the Father and the Spirit.

---

[31] Ibid. 157.   [32] Ibid. 158.

What about other properties traditionally attributed to God? I shall take omniscience as a test case, though one could certainly consider other properties, such as omnipresence as well. If the above argument is sound for omnipotence, then surely it would hold for omniscience as well. If an omnipotent being must be able to limit its own power, surely it must be able to limit its knowledge as well. One might object that it would be impossible to limit one's knowledge. After all, I cannot forget something I know simply by willing to forget it, at least not without allowing some time for the forgetting to occur, and one might think this would be even harder for a divine being. However, it is clearly logically possible for a being to choose to do things that would impair or destroy knowledge. I might, for example, choose to have a brain operation that I know might eliminate a particular type of knowledge.

One might think that such a possibility might be open to a finite being, but not to a divine being. However, if one goes down this road, the paradox of the stone seems close at hand, since self-limitation of this type seems to be logically possible. In any case, if we ask *how* it might be possible for a divine being to limit itself, the analogy of the brain operation suggests a type of answer. We humans can choose to limit our power and our knowledge because we are bodily beings. If it is possible for God to become incarnate, to take on life as a bodily spirit, then it seems possible for God to assume the limitations of being embodied as well. In fact, the choice to become embodied would be, among other things, the choice to assume certain limitations.

Obviously, we cannot explain *how* God became an embodied being. That is part of the mystery of the incarnation, and the explanation of how it came about must be simply that it was willed by an omnipotent being. However, a decision by God to live as an embodied being would be analogous in some ways to a decision by a human being to undergo a brain operation that would limit his mental functioning in some way.

We human beings are bodily spirits. Even without adopting any form of materialism (I am myself a dualist), it is evident that humans are dependent on their bodies in all kinds of ways. In this life, at least, our ability to think depends on an intact and healthy brain, and the ways in which we think are shaped by physical states of the brain. We do not fully understand all the ways that mental life and bodily life are related, but it seems reasonable to think that a being whose mental life is thus dependent on the physical will necessarily be finite and limited in various respects. Insofar as what is physical is finite and limited, it would seem reasonable to think that what is dependent on the physical is also finite and limited. A decision by God to become incarnate would thus be a decision to assume these limitations. In willing to begin to exist as a human infant, Christ would also be willing to enter a condition in which he would divest himself of omnipotence and omniscience, just as I might clear-headedly will to accept some limitation on my mental life by deciding to undergo a particular kind of brain operation.

Plato is well known for his view that each human soul pre-existed its birth in a human body, and that at birth the immortal soul, because of the limitations of bodily existence, 'forgets' the eternal Truths it previously clearly knew. Christians have generally held that this Platonic view was mistaken, because human persons do not exist prior to their conception. However, on the orthodox view of the incarnation, the individual who was Jesus of Nazareth did indeed pre-exist as the second person of the Trinity. It does not seem too unreasonable to think that something like a Platonic 'forgetting' would be entailed by a divine incarnation, and that a divine decision to become embodied would be a voluntary embrace of this condition.

Orthodox defenders of Chalcedon who wish to attack the above line of thought should be careful about how they do so. In particular, they must be wary of denying the possibility of divine self-limitation, I think. If we wish to acknowledge Jesus' full humanity, and recognize that as a human he was finite in knowledge and that he could be tempted, and if there is any real unity of the person of Jesus, then it seems that this requires the divine mind at every moment to limit itself in some way. A divine power is possessed, but its exercise is willingly prevented. God chooses to limit himself. It is hard to see how something *like* a kenosis can be avoided, even on a two-minds account.

IV Glorification

I should next like to address a different type of difficulty that is often thought to beset kenotic theories. This type of difficulty concerns the state of the glorified, post-risen Christ. Many theologians, including some kenotic ones, seem to think of the glorified Christ as reassuming the properties of omnipotence and omniscience. The difficulty for a kenotic theory, as I understand it, could be put in the form of a dilemma. Either the glorified Christ reassumes these properties or he does not. If he does not, then the kenotic theory has an inadequate account of the glorified Christ, and the loss of omnipotence and omniscience is no longer merely a temporary divestiture but a permanent loss. If the glorified Christ does reassume these properties, however, then it appears that there is no reason why an incarnate God cannot be omnipotent and omniscient (on the assumption that the incarnation and embodiment of Jesus is permanent and not merely temporary). If a glorified, bodily Christ who is fully human can be omniscient and omnipotent, then one cannot claim that a being must divest himself of these properties to become human.

Ronald Feenstra has suggested two lines of response on the part of the kenotic theologian to this problem. The first suggestion is that omnipotence and omniscience are compatible with *being* incarnate but not with *becoming* incarnate.[33] On this view, it was necessary for Christ to empty himself of omnipotence and omniscience in order to assume a bodily existence as a human being. Having become a human being, however, it is possible for him to have those qualities restored to him by the power of God the Father.

Feenstra's line of thought here seems problematic to me, though a view that is similar in some respects seems plausible. In his defence, one might argue that it is hard to see how a decision to become embodied could lead to a genuine embodiment if it did not include a decision to assume the limitations of embodied existence. So it seems reasonable that becoming incarnate might require a *kenosis*. However, Feenstra also seems to think that it is possible for the power of God to grant a human being who is fully embodied the qualities of omnipotence and omniscience.[34] However, if it is possible to *be* embodied and have these qualities, it is hard to see

---

[33] Feenstra, 'Reconsidering Kenotic Christology', in *Trinity, Incarnation, and Atonement*, 147.

[34] There is a well-known objection to the idea of two omnipotent beings. How can there be two such beings without one limiting the power of the other? However, I believe Swinburne has answered this objection in a satisfactory manner. If we assume the two beings in question are completely united in their wills and joined by love, then their wills cannot come into conflict and so cannot be said to limit each other. See Swinburne, *Christian God*, 170–5.

why it would not be possible to *become* embodied with these qualities.

I think a more plausible version of Feenstra's view here can be developed if we take note of the fact that the biblical picture of the risen Christ as glorified and exalted includes the claim that Jesus now has a new type of body, a spiritual body that has properties that our current bodies do not have. The risen Jesus, for example, suddenly appears in a room with locked doors, indicating an ability not to be limited by solid objects in the way that normal bodies are. Since we do not know very much about such a body, we cannot rule out the possibility that such a body could be granted omniscience and omnipotence by the power of the Father and the Son. Perhaps the relevant difference is not between becoming embodied and being embodied, but between having a physical body like those humans now possess and having a spiritual body such as that possessed by the risen Christ. It is possible that someone whose mental life is mediated through the brains of our current type of bodies cannot be omniscient and omnipotent, but we do not know that this would necessarily be true of Christ's resurrected body.

The second option Feenstra offers to the kenotic theologian is to distinguish between the *kenosis* of God and the incarnation.[35] Though the two began at the same time, *kenosis* is not necessary for incarnation, but reflects the particular way Christ chose to become incarnate. God can be and could have become incarnate without emptying himself. Christ chose to become incarnate in a kenotic manner in order to fully share in our human lot or condition while on earth. On this view, God's self-emptying is not necessary for incarnation, though it might be necessary for some other purpose, such as redemption.

As a response to the objection, this second reply of Feenstra's seems satisfactory to me, as does the first response as I have amended it. However, I would like to consider a more radical alternative by grasping firmly one horn of the dilemma. The whole problem is generated by the assumption that the exalted or glorified Christ must be omnipotent and omniscient. Is this assumption really necessary?

Feenstra implies at one point that the view that the exalted Christ is omniscient and omnipotent is necessary for 'Christian orthodoxy'.[36]

---

[35] Feenstra, 'Reconsidering Kenotic Christology', 148–9.   [36] Ibid., 146.

Perhaps he is right about this, but I am inclined to doubt it. I am
hardly an expert on such matters, but it does not appear to me to be
something that is required either by the biblical revelation or by the
central creeds of the Church. The risen Christ is in some way exalted
or glorified, united with Father and Spirit. However, it seems to me
that the nature of this glorified state is left somewhat open. Hebrews
2: 17, a passage that strongly supports a kenotic account of the
incarnation, says that Christ 'had to become like his brothers and
sisters in every respect, so that he might be a merciful and faithful
high priest in the service of God' (NRSV). This passage suggests that
Christ, who is now 'crowned with glory and honour because of the
suffering of death' (Heb. 2: 9), continues in his priestly work to
experience solidarity with the creatures for whom he makes intercession. It also suggests that the glorification and exaltation of Christ
is not something he acquired simply by virtue of being divine, but is
rather something earned and bestowed upon him by virtue of his
human suffering. The 'kenotic hymn' passage in Philippians 2 carries
the same idea when it affirms, after recounting Jesus' work in
humbling and emptying himself 'to the point of death', that '*therefore*
God also highly exalted him'.

  1 John also gives us some reason to affirm that our understanding
of the status of the exalted Christ is somewhat indeterminate. The
writer affirms of the Christian's own future destiny: 'What we will be
has not yet been revealed. What we do know is this: when he is
revealed, we shall be like him, for we shall see him as he is' (1 John
3: 2).[37] This passage clearly suggests some ignorance about the
actual state of the risen Christ, since it affirms that we do not yet
know what our future condition will be, but that whatever it is, it
will be 'like him'. Even more significantly, it seems to me that this
passage suggests that whatever the exalted state of Christ is, that it
does not include being omniscient and omnipotent. At least this
follows if we take seriously the notion that we will be 'like him' and
also assume that this does not mean that all followers of Jesus will be
made to be omniscient and omnipotent.

  It is important to note that there is no hint of 'adoptionism' in this
account of the glorified Christ. Christ is not here 'receiving his
divinity back' because his divinity was never relinquished, only
some of the prerogatives he enjoyed in his pre-incarnate state. Nor

---

[37] [The 'he' of 'when he is revealed' could well be Christ, but it might refer rather to
God the Father. Eds.]

does such an account of glorification threaten the perfect equality enjoyed by the members of the Trinity. It is true that there will be asymmetries in the relations enjoyed by the persons of the Trinity. However, this will be true even of the Trinity apart from the incarnation. The Father begets the Son; the Son does not beget the Father. The incarnate Son, both in his earthly career and in his glorified state, may depend on the Father and the Spirit in fundamental ways. However, it seems equally true that they depend on him as well to accomplish some of the divine ends, for he is the one who became incarnate and died and rose again for our sins, and he is the one who makes intercession for the saints. There can I think be equality of divinity even where there are differences in roles that require other differences.

It seems to me that the defender of a kenotic theory can then respond in one of two ways to the charge that such an account does not do justice to the glorified status of the ascended Christ. One may argue that the ascended Christ is omniscient and omnipotent and that this is quite consistent with his emptying himself of those qualities to become incarnate. *Kenosis* is not necessary for incarnation, but is necessary either to become incarnate in our present type of body or necessary only for other redemptive purposes. Alternatively, the kenotic theorist may hold that the ascended Christ, though glorified and exalted in ways we do not fully understand, has received whatever supernatural power and insight he possesses from the Father. The self-emptying of the incarnation is not in this case a temporary loss but an irrevocable decision that is rewarded by God with glory, and provides us with a model of our own intended destiny.

V   KENOSIS AND PERSONAL IDENTITY

In conclusion I should like to address a problem that may be suggested by the type of kenotic theory I have defended. If the choice to become an embodied spirit and be born as a human being was a self-conscious choice on the part of Christ to empty himself of the attributes of omnipotence and omniscience, one might think that a change of this magnitude would threaten the self-identity of Christ. A worry along these lines is articulated by Donald MacLeod:

[T]he Kenotic Theory makes it difficult to maintain continuity between the pre-existent and the incarnate Son. Up to the moment of his enfleshment, according to this theory, the Son was omniscient. At that fateful moment, however, his knowledge suddenly contracts: from infinity to that of a first-century Jew. That represents a degree of amnesia to which there can be no parallel. He forgot virtually everything he knew. . . . At the very least, after an eternity of divine self-awareness he would suddenly not know who he was. Indeed considering the importance of memory to personal identity, he would not even be who he was.[38]

In this last claim MacLeod seems to presuppose something like John Locke's theory of personal identity, in which identity is constituted by memory. Roughly, I am who I am conscious of having been on this view.

Certainly a kenotic theory must maintain that Jesus as the incarnate Son of God maintains his identity with the pre-incarnate Son. What is in fact necessary for such identity? Many Christian thinkers have followed Thomas Aquinas in holding that in this life we cannot know the divine essence. Since questions about the identity of something are closely linked to questions about the nature of that thing, we may not be able to know all that we would like about the conditions for divine identity. Nevertheless, I think we can make some headway by thinking about the question of what is necessary for personal identity for ordinary human persons.

Of course the philosophical debate about the nature of personal identity is complicated with a large literature. There are a number of ways to categorize the various positions. Richard Swinburne divides theories of personal identity into three types: bodily continuity theories, psychological theories stressing memory, and what he terms 'simple theories', following Derek Parfit.[39]

Bodily continuity theories are perhaps the most natural theories. However, these theories contradict an intuition that many people find attractive, by making the idea that a person could acquire a new body not merely scientifically or naturally impossible, but logically impossible. The idea that a person might acquire a new body does not appear to be logically impossible. Many religions have supposed that a person could be re-embodied or could even exist in a disembodied form. A movie such as *All of Me*, starring Steve Martin

---

[38] MacLeod, *Person of Christ*, 210.

[39] See Swinburne, 'The Dualist Theory', in S. Shoemaker and R. Swinburne, *Personal Identity* (Oxford: Blackwell, 1984), 3–66.

and Lily Tomlin, works despite or perhaps because of a plot involving body-switching. (For a large part of the movie, the character played by Lily Tomlin actually shares a body with the character played by Steve Martin.)

Another grave objection to bodily theories is that they appear to be subject to 'duplication' problems. The part of the body that seems most crucial for personal identity is the brain. However, the brain exists in two hemispheres. If one hemisphere is transplanted into a new body, and the hemisphere seems to function, a bodily continuity theory seems to imply that the transplant recipient (person A) would be identical to the donor. But what if the other hemisphere is also successfully transplanted into person B? Persons A and B cannot both be identical to the donor, since they are obviously not identical to each other. Perhaps in such a case we would say neither recipient is identical to the donor. However, that would mean that whether A is identical to the donor would depend on whether B survives, but it seems bizarre to claim that a person's identity might depend on what happens to someone else who is clearly independent of that person. Hence, bodily theories are subject to major difficulties, although of course defenders of this type of theory are aware of the difficulties and have developed various ingenious ways to resolve them.

It seems to me, however, that the most important point to make about a bodily continuity theory in this case is as follows. Even if such a theory were plausible for humans in general, it is patently obvious that it is a non-starter as an account of how personal identity is maintained in the incarnation. A traditional theory of the incarnation here is no different from a kenotic theory; neither can say that the identity of Jesus as the Son of God is grounded in bodily continuity, since the incarnation is a change from a bodiless state to an embodied state on both theories.

The second type of theory, psychological or memory-type theories, may seem more plausible as an account of how identity is maintained through the incarnation, and it is clearly this type of theory that MacLeod seems to presuppose when he objects that a kenotic theory undermines identity in this case. However, it is important to see that memory theories are subject to grave difficulties even for ordinary human persons.[40]

[40] Ronald Feenstra has addressed the issue of personal identity in the case of the incarnation and criticized 'empiricist theories' of personal identity (bodily continuity

It is obvious that it is what we might call personal memory that is relevant here, not memory of facts learned but memory of what one has personally experienced. A distinction must be made between actual (or true) personal memory and apparent personal memories. If the memory theory holds that identity is constituted by actual memory, then the theory is circular, since it is a necessary condition for actual memory that the person having the apparent memory be identical to the person he or she is remembering having been. The theory must therefore be stated in terms of apparent memory. However, in this case a 'duplication' objection can be mounted. Apparent memories can be mistaken. There seems no reason why two or more different individuals could not have apparent memories of having been the same person, having performed particular actions at particular times, and so on. Yet it is obvious that different persons who are not identical with each other cannot all be identical with one person, since identity is a transitive relation.

To resolve such problems Swinburne and others defend the 'simple' view, which holds that personal identity is something distinct from both bodily continuity and psychological continuity. Though bodily continuity and psychological continuity are fallible evidence of personal identity, personal identity is not constituted by either or even both together. Such a view can be developed simply as a claim that personal identity is something simple, ultimate, and unanalysable.[41] Alternatively, if one wishes to endorse a dualistic metaphysic, one can say that a person is identical with a non-material substance that bears psychological properties without being identical to those properties, as does Swinburne himself. In the latter case, the non-physical substance is usually regarded as a 'simple' (non-divisible) entity and as the bearer of personal identity, with the assumption that this reality is not reducible either to a physical substance or a complex of psychological properties or states.

The latter type of theory appears to me to be the strongest by far, and I take its current lack of popularity among philosophers to be

and psychological continuity theories) in ways that parallel some of the arguments that follow. See his 'Pre-Existence and Personal Identity', *Logos: Philosophical Issues in Christian Perspective*, 9 (1990), 127–42.

[41] Roderick Chisholm, following Reid and Butler, has developed this view. See his 'The Loose and Popular and the Strict and Philosophical Senses of Identity', in N. S. Care and R. H. Grimm (eds.), *Perception and Personal Identity* (Cleveland: Press of Case Western Reserve University, 1969), 82–106.

explicable by materialistic and naturalistic prejudices. It does seem difficult to square this latter kind of account of personal identity with the view that persons are simply natural, bodily entities to be explained purely by scientific processes. However, no one who takes the incarnation as a serious possibility should be attracted to such a materialistic, naturalistic worldview, and hence no one who takes the incarnation as a serious possibility should have a strong aversion to theories that are hard to square with philosophical naturalism.

If we accept a theory in this 'simple' category, I see no reason why a kenotic theory is incompatible with an affirmation that the incarnation preserved the identity of Christ as the second person of the Trinity. If personal identity is an ultimate, unanalysable fact, then there is no reason why it cannot simply be a fact that the baby born in Bethlehem is in fact identical with the Word of God. If we say that the bearer of identity is the soul or spirit, we simply must affirm that the Word of God as a spiritual being united himself with material reality and assumed those properties necessary to become a human soul. An individual with a divine nature assumed human nature without ceasing to be divine.[42]

Actually, I believe that a kenotic theory is even compatible with a reasonable version of a psychological theory. No one who holds that personal identity is constituted by memory can hold that a person must remember his or her past at every moment. Because I cannot remember signing a cheque last month, it does not follow that I am not the person who signed the cheque. A reasonable theory must surely hold to a weaker claim, that it is possible for a person to remember his or her past at some time or other under the right conditions. Even if a kenotic incarnation required a profound forgetting, I see no reason why Jesus, as his mind developed and as he experienced the illumination of the Father and Spirit, could not at some point have gained a consciousness of his own pre-existence as the Son of God.

Of course such a view of Jesus' consciousness will seem far-fetched to many biblical scholars today. I would not wish to see the case for

[42] Of course it is crucial here *not* to say that Jesus had a 'divine soul in a human body'. Rather, I would say that as a divine being the Word became a human soul and was enfleshed without ceasing to be the divine being he was. It should be obvious that I am here thinking of 'human nature' as a set of properties, not as a concrete individual. On the kind of view I here defend, God the Son acquires a new set of properties by becoming human but does not become a different individual.

the divinity of Jesus dependent on such claims about his consciousness of his divinity, since it seems at least logically possible that Jesus
could have been divine without realizing this (at least at some points
in his earthly career). Nevertheless, I do not believe that a serious
historical portrait of Jesus rules out his having such a consciousness
of divinity, and such a consciousness on the part of Jesus seems just
as possible on a kenotic theory as any other. However, obviously a
kenotic theory is no more dependent on such a supposition than any
other theory of the incarnation.

I personally find memory theories of personal identity far-fetched;
they confuse evidence of identity with the ontological conditions of
identity. However, someone attracted to such a theory does not have
to reject a kenotic view. It seems to me that, on the most plausible
account of personal identity we have, the kenotic account of the
incarnation can do full justice to the identity that holds between the
pre-incarnate and incarnate Christ.

Of course we know little about the conditions for ensouling a
body. The last thing I would want to claim is that the incarnation is
unsurprising. It is a profound mystery, and I believe that Kierkegaard was right to insist that the incarnation was paradoxical,
contrary to our human expectations about what God could do and
would do. However, I think he was also right to insist that this
paradoxicality is actually a mark of its truth: 'Comedies and novels
and lies must be probable', but one mark of the transcendence of
God's revelation in Jesus Christ is precisely that it is something that
'could not have arisen in any human heart'.[43] That God should
empty himself and become a human being is beyond surprising.
However, for those who are convinced of the truth of the incarnation, I believe that a kenotic theory is a viable means of making
sense of that truth, one that does justice to the Chalcedonian claims.

---

[43] Søren Kierkegaard, *Philosophical Fragments*, ed. and trans. H. V. Hong and
E. H. Hong (Princeton: Princeton University Press, 1985), 52. Kierkegaard is here
loosely quoting Johann Georg Hamann. According to the Hongs, the reference is to
Hamann's Schriften, by F. Roth and G. A. Wiener (Berlin and Leipzig: G. Reimer,
1821), i. 497. The scriptural allusion is to 1 Cor. 2: 9, one of the most frequently
quoted verses in Kierkegaard's writings.

12

A Timeless God Incarnate

BRIAN LEFTOW

Christians hold that God became incarnate—somehow became the man Jesus of Nazareth. Many Christians have also held that God is timeless, that is, that though he is eternal, his life does not last through any stretch of time, long or short. The doctrine of divine timelessness has found many critics of late, and one line of attack has been that it is not compatible with the claim that God became incarnate. If this is true, of course, Christians must jettison it. For the incarnation lies at the core of Christian belief. Divine timelessness does not.

This chapter argues that divine timelessness and the incarnation are compatible. I begin by sketching what it means to say that God is timeless. I then present two plausible arguments that this claim is not compatible with the doctrine of the incarnation. With this done, I sketch enough of the orthodox doctrine of the incarnation to let me address the arguments. Finally, I use this material to show that the arguments fail. If they do, it is *prima facie* plausible that God can be both timeless and incarnate, for the arguments present perhaps the strongest reasons to doubt this.

I A Non-temporal God

The orthodox view of the incarnation was hammered out in the theological debates culminating in the Council of Chalcedon (AD 451). In this period 'classical theism' ruled the theological roost. The church Fathers who worked out incarnational orthodoxy were those very Greeks (and Latins) whose fondness for such doctrines as God's simplicity and atemporality so many now chide. Thus it is a simple historical fact that those who defined orthodox Christian belief about the incarnation universally held that God is non-temporal.

To see what this meant for them, we can consult Augustine:

In . . . an eternity which is always in the present . . . Your 'years' neither go nor come. Ours come and go so that all may come in succession. All your 'years' subsist in simultaneity . . . Your 'years' are 'one day' and your 'day' is . . . today, because your today does not yield to a tomorrow, nor did it follow a yesterday. Your today is eternity.[1]

Temporal lives lasting more than an instant always have tomorrows or yesterdays, parts coming or going: future or past parts.[2] Not so God, for Augustine: rather, no part of his life is ever past or future. God lives his life in a single present, no 'part' succeeding any other. God's life simply does not have temporal parts.

Eternality, for Augustine, is a matter of how God lives his life, not 'where'. For Augustine, 'God is eternal' ascribes a mode of being, not a location 'in' or 'outside' time. All the same, God's being eternal in Augustine's sense entails that his existence has no temporal location, at least if there has been more than one moment of time. For suppose that God's existence is located at times t_1 and t_2. If God's existence has no temporal parts, only the whole of it can be located at either time. So if God's existence is located at times t_1 and t_2,

the time of God's whole existence is t_1, and
the time of God's whole existence is t_2,

whence it follows that $t_1 = t_2$. To make this a bit clearer, if God's whole existence is located at times t_1 and t_2, then

God's whole existence is at the same time as t_1,
God's whole existence is at the same time as t_2, and of course God's whole existence is at the same time as God's whole existence,

whence it follows that t_1 is at the same time as t_2—which is to say that t_1 and t_2 *are* one single time. Now if God exists in time and exists at only some times, God exists temporally, not eternally. So if God is eternal and exists in time, he exists at all times. So if God is Augustine-eternal and exists in time, all times collapse into a single time: there has been just one instant of time. And so, as

---

[1] Augustine, *Confessions*, 11 (13). 16, trans. Henry Chadwick, *St Augustine: Confessions* (Oxford: Oxford University Press, 1991), 230.

[2] Once over, they have only past parts. While still to come, if they have parts at all, they have only future parts.

there has been more than one instant of time, if God is Augustine-eternal, God's existence has no temporal location. If God is Augustine-eternal, God exists and it is (say) Monday, but God does not exist *while* it is Monday, that is, *during* the stretch of time we call Monday. There is no paradox in this, for 'and' does not entail 'while'. Leftow was born before 1960 and Plantinga was born before 1950, but it does not follow from this that Leftow was born before 1960 *while* Plantinga was born before 1950. The latter claim makes dubious sense.[3]

Atemporalists agree with other Western theists that God exists forever. But they give a more complex account of this than temporalists do. For atemporalists, 'God exists forever' asserts only that at every time, it is true to say that God exists. But this is not (they say) because God exists *at* these times. If I am here and you are there, it is true here to say that you exist, but not because you are located here. I, here, say that you exist (over there). So too, say atemporalists, when I say truly that God exists, I, here (in time), say truly that God exists (over there, outside time).[4]

II A CHARGE OF CONTRADICTION

Thus the Chalcedonian age on God and time. Given this history, it is surprising to read one recent author's claim that 'if one is committed to an orthodox Christology, one shall have to reject (at least with respect to the Second Person of the Trinity) the doctrine of [divine] timelessness'.[5] For it implies that those who worked out Chalcedonian Christology somehow overlooked a glaring contradiction at the heart of their thinking. Yet it is not hard to see why the claim of contradiction can seem plausible. Jesus walked in the Temple before his arrest. Thus the event, Jesus' walking in the Temple, was before

---

[3] At least with 'while' read as a temporal connective.

[4] I would like to explore just why the classical age's theists thought God timeless. Nelson Pike suggests that 'the doctrine of God's timelessness was introduced into Christian theology because Platonic thought was stylish at the time and because . . . of (its) systematic elegance' (N. Pike, *God and Timelessness* (New York: Schocken Books, 1970), 189–90). I disagree; Augustine and Boethius, at least, have reasons with nothing essential to do with Platonism. But space constraints keep me from taking up this matter. I can only say: here is the timelessness-doctrine. Whatever the reasons one might have to adopt it, let us see whether one can hold both this and that God became incarnate in Christ.

[5] T. Senor, 'Incarnation and Timelessness', *Faith and Philosophy* 7 (1990), 161.

another event, Jesus' arrest. Events before or after other events are temporal—occur 'in time'. Those to whom such events happen are also *ipso facto* 'in time'. If so,

(1) Jesus Christ existed in time.

But (one would think)

(2) Jesus Christ = God the Son,

the second person of the Trinity. So it seems to follow that

(3) God the Son existed in time.[6]

Strictly, (1)–(3) license just a claim that the Son existed in time while Christ did. But this is enough to create a problem for the claim that God is timeless, if the God the Son is God and an item is timeless only if its existence is not located at any time.

Again, in the incarnation,

(4) God the Son began to be human.

Beginning to be human sounds like some sort of intrinsic change. That is, seemingly

(5) whatever begins to be human changes intrinsically.

So it seems to follow that in becoming incarnate,

(6) God the Son changed intrinsically.

But

(7) whatever changes intrinsically exists in time.

For to change intrinsically is to have different intrinsic attributes at different times. So it seems to follow that

(8) God the Son exists in time.[7]

I now argue that the doctrine of the incarnation is compatible with the claim that God exists timelessly. I do so by contending that the two arguments I have just sketched fail. I begin by briefly sketching the doctrine of the incarnation.

---

[6] Senor, 'Incarnation and Timelessness' 152.   [7] Ibid. 157.

III THE INCARNATION: ABSTRACT AND CONCRETE NATURES

Christian orthodoxy holds that in Christ, the Son takes on human nature while retaining his divine nature. But there have been two accounts of what a 'nature' is in this context. Aquinas deploys both. He writes in *Summa Contra Gentiles* that 'the nature of a thing is . . . the essence the definition signifies. In this way . . . we say that there is in Christ human and divine nature.'[8] Here a nature is an 'essence'—an attribute, an abstract entity. But just a few sentences earlier, Aquinas wrote that

there was in Christ Jesus a body, a rational soul and divinity. It is clear that the body of Christ, after the union, was not identical with the divinity of the Word . . . Similarly Christ's soul, after the union, was other than the divinity of the Word . . . a human soul and body constitute a human nature. So therefore after the union, the human nature of Christ was other than the divinity of the Word.[9]

Here a nature is composed of a body and a soul—two concrete objects. So here a nature is some sort of concrete object itself.

Plantinga contrasts 'concrete nature' and 'abstract nature' accounts of the incarnation.[10] Plantinga has it that in 'concrete nature' accounts, the Son

assumed *a* human nature, a specific human being. What happened when he became incarnate is that he adopted a particularly close and intimate relation to a certain concrete human being . . . a creature with will and intellect (so that) in the incarnate Christ there were two wills, one human and one divine, and two intellects, one human and one divine.[11]

On the 'abstract nature' view, Plantinga writes, 'when the second person of the Trinity became incarnate and assumed human nature . . . he . . . acquired the property of being human . . . '. The human nature he assumed, then, was a property.[12] Thenceforth one being, with one intellect and will, had those faculties count as both human and divine.[13] As Plantinga sees it, the cash value of the difference is that 'abstractists' do and 'concretists' do not accept that 'the second Person of the Trinity became a human being'.[14] Others might say

---

[8] *SCG* 4. 35. [9] Ibid.
[10] A. Plantinga, 'On Heresy, Mind and Truth', *Faith and Philosophy*, 16 (1999), 184.
[11] Ibid. 183–4. [12] Ibid. 183. [13] Ibid. 185. [14] Ibid. 186–7.

that the difference is over whether Christ includes two immaterial
particulars, a human soul and God the Son, or only one, or over
whether Christ has two minds and wills or only one.

Plantinga's description of 'concrete nature' incarnation is near
the mark, but just slightly and importantly off it. A human being is a
person and an animal. The Son did not in the incarnation join with
another person. To say that he did is the heresy attributed to
Nestorius. This *is* a heresy precisely because all Christians should
hold that 'the second Person of the Trinity became a human being',
and if in the incarnation the Son merely teamed up with an already
existing person, he did not. Nor did the Son 'take over' the body of
an independently existing animal: incarnation is not possession. So
it is not the case that on a 'concrete nature' view, the Son assumes a
human being. Aquinas suggests that what the Son assumes *would*
on its own—i.e. if unassumed—have been a human being.[15] But
even if it would have, the fact is that it was not on its own, even for a
moment. (Of this more anon.) So it never actually *was* a human
being. It was always something slightly but dramatically different,
the human nature of the Son of God.

On the concrete nature view, the 'human nature' the Son
assumes is a full natural endowment of a human being, that is, a
human body and (if such there be)[16] soul, 'carrying' a human mind
and will. On the concrete nature view, then, to take on human
nature is to acquire such an endowment; what the Son assumed is
not a human being, but the natural endowment of one. Usually, as
soon as there is such an endowment—i.e. a human body and soul—
it constitutes a human person who 'owns' it, and whose human soul
is his/her sole immaterial part. In the incarnation, so soon as such
an endowment exists, it constitutes a human person who 'owns' it,
whose human soul is his *created* immaterial part but not his sole
immaterial part. For this person includes a further immaterial part,
the Son. And the created parts of this human person 'constitute' him
not in the sense that they metaphysically account on their own for
his existence, but in the sense that they compose with a pre-existing
person a human being including them.

To be a human being is surely to be a person 'owning' a human
body, soul, mind and will.[17] If this is right, then someone acquires

---

[15] *ST* 3a. 4. 2 ad 3.

[16] From here on, please read in this qualification where I speak of a soul.

[17] Even a 'two-parter' would grant this, adding only that in the incarnation, this

the property of being human only if that person comes to 'own' the full human natural endowment: that is, abstract-nature incarnation takes place only if concrete-nature incarnation does. Equally, concrete nature incarnation takes place only if abstract nature incarnation does: God has not done what he wanted to do by taking on a human natural endowment unless by doing so he comes to exemplify the property of being human. So one could not believe in abstract-nature incarnation without also believing in concrete, and vice versa. But the symmetry ends there. One does not usually interact directly with properties, 'assuming' or 'exemplifying' them. Concrete things act, and in virtue of their activities, they come to exemplify properties. Abstract-nature incarnation can take place only *by* concrete-nature incarnation. In this sense, the concrete-nature view of the incarnation has to be basic.

Given that concrete-nature incarnation takes place if abstract-nature incarnation does, Plantinga's real point has to concern the difference between two- and one-mind theories of Christ's makeup, or what we might call three-part and two-part theories, the two parts being Jesus' body and God the Son, and the third being a human soul paired with Jesus' body. Three-part theorists certainly do not mean to deny that the second person became human. Aquinas, for one, is explicit about this.[18] They just give a particular account of how God the Son acquires and 'owns' the human natural endowment. But Plantinga's point above may be polemical. He may want to suggest that whether they mean to or not, 'three-part' theorists *do* deny that the second person became human. Plantinga may really be challenging 'three-partists' thus:

all the rest of us exist as soon as our bodies and souls are conjoined: given soul and body, there we are. If every other appropriately paired human body and soul compose something on their own, surely Christ's soul and body compose something on their own. They have a sum, whether or not the sum is also included in a larger whole including God the Son. If they do, surely this sum is or on its own constitutes a person and a human being. For how could the recipe (soul + body) that produces a person and a human in all other cases fail to do so in this one? What's missing, or what stops them? But if they do compose a person and a human, three-parters are Nestorians. On the two-part view, all the rest of us consist of a soul and a body, and

comes about because the Son comes to count as a human soul (the soul of a human body), and his mind and will as a human mind and will.

[18] *ST* 3a. 16. 1.

Jesus Christ does too—only his soul is God the Son. There is no second soul to complicate matters. Christ's body is the only part of his natural endowment that is not God the Son, and it is not enough on its own to compose a human being. So abstractism is not Nestorian. Hence three-parters must either explain how Christ's soul and body fail to compose a human being on their own, or explain how they can avoid Nestorianism if Christ's soul and body do compose a human being.

If this is the challenge, the 'three-parter' must make two replies.

One is that the Son assumes Christ's body (henceforth B) and soul (henceforth S) before S and B can on their own compose or constitute a human being or person. (S and B compose on their own a human being just in case their sum, S + B, is identical with a human being. S and B 'constitute' a human on their own if the sum S + B is not identical with a human, but a human's existence supervenes on S + B's. 'On their own' here has the sense: S + B is identical with or is a supervenience-base for a human being *whether or not* S + B is part of some larger whole, such as one consisting of S, B, and God the Son.) For if he does not, then either concretism *is* Nestorian, or the Son's assumption destroys the person to whom S + B previously belonged—turning the incarnation into a bizarre form of human sacrifice. Just when S + B *would* on their own constitute or compose a person or a human being is a knotty issue. Those who want their Christology orthodox had best not hold that every human zygote constitutes or composes a person or a human being on its own.[19] For if every human zygote composes or constitutes a person on its own, and so Christ's does too, then Nestorianism follows. But Christ's full humanity demands that he receive a standard human nature. If every other human zygote composes or constitutes a person on its own, and Christ's does not, he *ipso facto* does not receive a standard-issue human nature, and so is not fully one in nature with us. Further, it does not seem plausible that in general, some zygotes do and others do not count as or constitute humans on their own. (What would make the difference between the two types?) So if it is not the case that every human zygote constitutes or composes a person or a human being on its own, the most reasonable view to hold is that none does. If one rules it out that zygotes are or constitute persons, one can assume that

---

[19] One way not to hold this: say with Aquinas that while a zygote grows into a human body, it lacks a human soul till some time after conception (*QD de Potentia*, 3. 9 ad 9).

the Son 'gets to' S + B before S + B are or constitute persons by holding that Christ assumes S + B as a zygote, at the moment of conception.[20]

The three-parter's second reply must be that it is coherent to suppose that after the Son assumes S + B, the sum of S, B, and the Son contains just one person (and so just one human being). Avoiding Nestorianism requires us to say that even if the created parts of the incarnate Christ would on their own have constituted a person, they instead only joined with a pre-existing person to constitute a 'larger' person.[21] But one can make a decent case for this. Geach puts forward this paradox: suppose that a cat, Tibbles, is sitting on a mat. It has at least 1,000 hairs. Now

let c be the largest continuous mass of feline tissue on the mat. Then for any of our 1000 cat-hairs, say h_n, there is a proper part c_n of c which contains precisely all of c except the hair h_n; and every such part c_n differs in a describable way . . . from any other such part . . . and from c as a whole. Moreover . . . not only is c a cat, but also any part c_n is a cat: c_n would clearly be a cat were the hair h_n plucked out, and we cannot reasonably suppose that plucking out a hair generates a cat, so c_n must already have been a cat. So . . . there was not just one cat . . . on the mat; there were at least 1001 . . . [22]

One wants to avoid the 1,001 cats, of course. (Among other reasons: plucking out a hair does not kill a cat. So if 1,001 cats with differing complements of hair are on the mat, then if we pluck all the hairs from c, 1,001 cats will occupy precisely the same space at once.) The way to do so is clearly to adopt some principle ruling it out that cats have cats as proper parts. Surely this is true: there is just one cat, Tibbles, on the mat. As it is, c composes or constitutes Tibbles. Were h_n plucked out, c_n would compose Tibbles. But c_n does not actually

[20] An alternate approach: say that God designed human bodies and souls, and so it is up to him what they by nature compose or constitute on their own. Perhaps human bodies and souls are not such by nature that when conjoined, they compose or constitute on their own a human being. Perhaps their natures include not the property of composing or constituting on their own, when conjoined, a human being, but the property of composing or constituting on their own when conjoined a human being *unless assumed by a divine person*. Perhaps God (as it were) built a slot for his incarnation into human nature. If one is willing to jigger with human nature in this way, one can allow that every other zygote on its own composes or constitutes a human being, but the zygote S + B did not.

[21] As Aquinas notes, *ST* 3a. 2. 5 ad 1.

[22] P. T. Geach, *Reference and Generality*, 3rd edn. (Ithaca, NY: Cornell University Press, 1980), 215.

compose a cat, even if c_n would compose a cat were c_n not a proper part of c. There is no cat composed by just c_n. More generally, given a set of parts composing at time t a member of a natural kind (e.g. cat), no subset of that set composes at t a member of the same natural kind. Well, then: persons are a natural kind. So if at t S, B, and the Son compose a person, no subset of {S, B, the Son} does so. And so even if the created parts of the incarnate Christ would on their own have constituted a person, a human being, they actually only join with the Son to constitute a 'larger' person and human, just as c_n only joins with h_n to compose a larger Tibbles than c_n would on its own.

If the Son did assume S and B at B's conception, S + B did not get the chance on its own to compose or constitute a person or human being. S + B does either on its own only if at some point S + B (or what S and B constitute) lives a life of its own, a life which is not just one more part of the life of someone already living when B is conceived.[23] Ordinary human conception satisfies this condition. For the zygote lives its own life from the moment of conception, though the mother biologically supports it.[24] But S + B's was no ordinary human conception. So soon as Mary's egg began to live the life that would be Jesus', the life being lived in that tissue was God the Son's life. Any soul/body composite lives just one life. The life S + B live, from B's conception on, is just a phase of God the Son's life, not a life of its own. What now comes to live this life (S + B) was created. The life itself is uncreated. A life is a sequence of events of certain sorts, causally linked in the right ways.[25] To say that God the Son was incarnate in S + B (or in B, on two-part views) is to say that the life lived in S + B (or B) has the right sort of causal and other ties to the Son's life to count as simply an extension of it.

It is as if God the Son were a bit of 'super-DNA' implanted in Mary's zygote at conception. This DNA controls the workings of the rest of the zgyote's DNA, determining the biological development of

---

[23] If God is timeless, the life lived in S + B is not a temporal part of God's life. A timeless life has no temporal parts. So 'one more part', with its implication of succession, speaks with the vulgar. If we think with the learned, God's incarnate life is some sort of non-temporal part of his life.

[24] The sperm too lives its own life—ceases to be part of or draw on the biological processes constituting the father's life—not later than its ejaculation. I do not know what biologists say about eggs.

[25] For a careful treatment of the concept of a life, see P. van Inwagen, *Material Beings* (Ithaca, NY: Cornell University Press, 1990), 145–65.

the zygote, and the further development of the fetus, infant and child Jesus. It thus determines the identity of the resulting person, at least as much as our DNA determines who we are. But the zygote etc. never has more than one DNA sequence, which includes this special addition. So it is never going to develop into any but a single person whose DNA includes this. DNA-codes do not normally fully determine the identity of the person who embodies them: twins and clones can be distinct persons despite sharing the same DNA. But we have no problem with the general concept of an identity-determining body-part. Many of us would grant, for instance, that if A's brain is transplanted into B's body, the resulting person is A. If we do so, we take the brain as the identity-determining body-part for A. And if we demur, we nonetheless fully understand the claim brain-based theories of personal identity make, that where the brain goes, the person goes. If we understand this, we can also understand the following claim: the super-DNA God the Son is an identity-determining part for God the Son incarnate. Where this DNA is implanted, the resulting person *must* be God the Son incarnate, and nobody else.

To come at this from another direction, any soul-body composite lives, from its moment of conception, the life its components determine that it lives. Whose life this is depends on just what those components are, and what the facts are about persons' identity over time. Suppose that who a person is depends on the identity of his/her soul, and suppose that reincarnation actually occurs. Then whose life a soul-body composite lives depends on whether its soul is new or re-used. Suppose that who a person is depends on some complex condition involving the ancestry of its psychology: that a person P is identical with an earlier person P* if (say) P*'s psychological state causally conditions P's in an appropriate way.[26] Then there is no person in a particular soul-body composite until it develops a psychology, and whose life that composite lives depends on whether its psychology is or is not conditioned in the right way by a prior person's psychology. I claim that the Son assumed S + B at conception, and so S + B live the Son's life as soon as they begin living, and this is *why* they do not on their own compose a human being. This is no stranger a

---

[26] For a recent version of such a broadly Lockean view, see S. Shoemaker's 'Personal Identity: A Materialist's Account', in S. Shoemaker and R. Swinburne, *Personal Identity* (Oxford: Blackwell, 1984), 67–132.

claim than that whose soul or psychology are in S + B determines whose life it lives, and whether that life is the beginning of a new one or a continuation of an old one.

'Three-part' Christian orthodoxy is compatible with many but not all theories of personal identity. One can sort these theories into three broad types. Some base persons' identity over time on the continuity or identity of their live bodies or some portion thereof (e.g. the brain). Others base persons' identity over time on the identity of their souls. Still others (broadly Lockean/Humean views) base persons' identity over time on causal and other relations among their psychological states.

Under body-based theories, let us first consider 'animalism', which holds that as soon as one has a live human body, one has a person, and as long as one has the same live human body, one has the same person.[27] On the one hand, as just noted, the body just *is* the person. On this version, the Son owns B only if the Son *becomes* B: only if an immaterial item becomes material. This does not seem possible.[28] On the other hand, the body *constitutes* the person, who is an item distinct from it. The 'constitution' animalist holds that a person's existence *supervenes* on a live human body's, which means only that necessarily, given a live body, there is also a person. On this version of animalism, the orthodox can say: we accept the 1 : 1 correlation between live human bodies and persons. But in this one case, the person is God the Son, and the body 'constitutes' the human person not by bringing it to be but by humanizing it. The orthodox must also of course give a suitable account of what it is for the Son to 'own' that body, and how the Son can 'beat' the body to the constitution of a person. (Hint: the Son is there before the body is, and as its creating/conserving cause determines its nature and purpose as a potter determines the nature and purpose of an artefact he/she designs and produces. If the potter means it to be a paperweight, that's what it is—even if its shape also fits it to serve as (say) a coffee mug. So if the potter means the zygote into which he is about to turn a virgin's egg to be his body, that is what it is. For that matter, given God's power over what things' natures are, God might simply have decreed from all eternity that what supervenes on the existence of a new live human body is not that of a new person, but either the existence of a new person or a union with the Son of God.

[27] See e.g. E. Olson, *The Human Animal* (New York: Oxford University Press, 1997).
[28] So Plantinga, 'On Heresy', 186, though without the tie to animalism.

If he did this, then the ordinary case—new body, new person—is ordinary only because the Son ordinarily turns down his chance to be incarnate.) What I say of animalism can apply (suitably altered) to views which base personal identity on the continuity of a whole brain, or of enough of a brain to support a suitable mental life: orthodoxy must balk at the claim that a person just *is* (say) a brain, but can allow that persons correlate 1 : 1 with brains.

Soul-theories sort into Platonist views, on which souls just *are* persons, and what I would call broadly Thomist views, on which souls are not persons but are the identity-conferring constituents of persons, which (say) do their thinking for them: a status materialists do not hesitate to ascribe to brains. If human souls just are persons, the orthodox must deny Christ a distinct human soul, moving instead to Plantinga's 'two-part' view. But orthodoxy and three-partism can cohere with a Thomist view, on which souls are sub-personal constituents of persons.

Psychological continuity ('Locke/Hume style') theories hold that one has a person as soon as one has a psyche of a certain sort, and that identity of that person follows the continuity of that psyche. How the orthodox handle this may depend on how the psyche is generated. If mental life causally depends on the brain—as even dualists concede[29]—then whose the mental life is depends on whose the brain is. If the brain is the Son's, because he assumed its body at the moment of conception, the mental life that brain generates is also his. But psychological continuity theories usually do not ask how the psychological states they discuss are generated. They instead just speak of causal or memory-relations among the states.[30] Now on a three-part (and eternalist) view, in the incarnate Christ are two minds, one a timeless complex of mental states in the timeless Son, one a temporal series of mental states in S. For orthodoxy, these must belong to just one person. So the orthodox who also hold psychological continuity theories of personal identity cannot allow the series in S an independence that would let it constitute a new person. They must hold that the S-series branches

[29] So e.g. H. Robinson, 'A Dualist Theory of Embodiment', in J. Smythies and J. Beloff (eds.), *The Case for Dualism* (Charlottesville, Va.: University Press of Virginia, 1989), 43–57; and R. Swinburne, *The Evolution of the Soul* (New York: Oxford University Press, 1986), 310.

[30] See e.g. J. Locke, *Essay Concerning Human Understanding*, 1, 27, and the chapters by A. Quinton, H. P. Grice, S. Shoemaker, and J. Perry in J. Perry (ed.), *Personal Identity* (Berkeley: University of California Press, 1975).

out of the Son's mind in some way sufficient to count as a second mind, but not with such independence as to constitute a second person. But this seems possible in principle. One person's having first one mind and then two, the second branching off from the first psychologically, is in fact a legitimate description of what goes on in cases of cerebral commissurotomy.[31] So the best psychological continuity theory will be one which allows this to be possible. Suppose that the right account of personal identity in us is something like this:

> person P = person P* if an identity-preserving chain of overall psychological states (OPSs) links P's OPS at some time t with P*'s at some time t*, and a chain of OPSs linking OPS s at t and OPS s* at t* is identity-preserving if any two adjacent OPSs s_1 at $\leq <_1$ and s_2 from t_1 on in the chain are such that s_2's psychological and cognitive content depend causally *and* counterfactually only on influences transmitted through
> a. s_1's psychological and cognitive content,
> b. the non-psychological state up to t_1 of the body in which s_1 occurs, and
> c. the input of that body's senses up to t_1 [32]

this the 'chokepoint' version of the psychological continuity theory. The intuitive idea here is that you have the same person as long as you have the same mind developing through time, and s_2 belongs to the same mind as adjacent state s_1 just if s_1 is the sole chokepoint for s_2, where a chokepoint is an OPS directly linked causally to s_2 such that the decisive impacts on that s_2's psychological content are just the earlier content of the mind including that chokepoint-state and the new stimuli s_2's environment provides.[33] Given some such theory, the application to the incarnation goes thus: the influence of the Son's mind on S + B's first OPS suffices to make the sequence of OPS' in S + B his, but the content of the sequence of OPS' in S + B is so related to the content of the Son's mind before the S + B series

---

[31] See e.g. T. Nagel, 'Brain Bisection and the Unity of Consciousness', in Perry (ed.), *Personal Identity*, 227–45.

[32] I do not doubt that further clauses would be needed to render this account even roughly adequate. This account is *only* for illustration. I am not committed to it or any like it.

[33] Having (d) as a separate clause allows e.g. that the body's having a limb cut off without sensation during a certain period might alter the mind which then becomes aware of this.

began that they constitute two minds, not one. I will not try to spell this latter relation out; Swinburne and Morris offer suggestive accounts.[34]

So the 'tally' on personal identity and incarnational orthodoxy comes to this. If a body, brain, or brain-part on its own is identical with a human person, Nestorius wins, whether one is a two- or a three-parter: created parts of the incarnate Christ actually do on their own constitute a person. If a soul on its own is identical with a human person, only Plantinga's 'two-part' view can hold Nestorius at bay. If persons are distinct from but supervene upon or are constituted by bodies, body-parts, souls, or conjunctions of these, three-parters can steer clear of Nestorius, as they can on Lockean/ Humean views. Thus 'three partism' can cohere with a wide variety of personal-identity theories, and (I would argue) with the more plausible ones. This is good reason to think that 'three-partism' can give a viable, non-Nestorian theory of the incarnation.

IV Incarnation: Mereology

Perhaps the most formal, abstract thing one can say about the incarnation is this (following such as Aquinas):[35] for the Son to become incarnate is at least for there to come to be a whole consisting of certain parts. Let 'the Son' name the Trinity's second person and 'Jesus Christ' name the whole consisting of the Son + B + S. Then for the incarnation to take place is for Jesus Christ to come to be, by the joining of the Son, S and B. But even at this formal, abstract level, divine timelessness can raise a worry.[36]

There is (we think) no such thing as a whole consisting of a number and a proton. How *can* some one thing have a timeless and a temporal part? How can a timeless and a temporal thing compose something? But timeless and temporal things clearly do compose some items. Even if God is timeless, God and I compose a pair, which is a set, and a mereological sum, which is something concrete. Perhaps, then, the question should be of how a timeless and a temporal thing can compose a *substance*, something (we think) more

[34] T. Morris, *The Logic of God Incarnate* (Ithaca, NY: Cornell University Press, 1986) 102–7; R. Swinburne, *The Christian God* (Oxford: Oxford University Press, 1994), 194–209.

[35] *ST* 3a. 2. 4.   [36] Stephen Davis has had it.

really one than a mereological sum. Here my reply rests on two points. One is that in many cases, causal relations are what unite parts into substances. Quarks form protons, protons and neutrons nuclei, nuclei and electrons atoms, atoms molecules, molecules larger items animate or inanimate, just in case appropriate causal relations bind them together. The other is that even if God is timeless, God can have causal relations with temporal things, for example in creating and sustaining them. This is a rather large claim, but I defend it elsewhere.[37] I now simply pose a question: given that causal relations unite parts into substances and a timeless God can have causal relations to a temporal being, is there any good reason *a priori* to think that a timeless God's causal relations to some temporal being(s) could not be such as to form with them a single substance? I cannot think of one.

If we allow talk of a timeless Son and temporal beings forming a whole, part/whole considerations can disarm well-known objections to moves in Christology. Wholes often have attributes because their parts do. Apples are red because their skins are—that is, because their parts include red skins. Nothing else about an apple makes it red; peel off the skin, and what is left is no longer red. Apples are nutritious because their parts include certain molecules (e.g. carbohydrates). Nothing else about apples makes them nutritious. In particular, it is not because their parts include skins that they are nutritious, even if their skins contain nutrients. (Plastic fruit also has skin, of a sort.) One can use the term '*qua*' to indicate just which parts give an item certain of its attributes. Apples are red *qua* skinned, that is, because they include skins. Apples are nutritious *qua* containing (e.g.) carbohydrates, i.e. because they include carbohydrates.

Christologists often say things like

(C) Christ died *qua* human but not *qua* divine.

I think the best reading of claims like (C) is mereological: we ought to read them as we just read my claims about apples. If (C) is true, I suggest, Christ did die: for a person including a human body and soul dies if his body dies and his soul is parted from it. What (C) asserts is that Christ died because his human part died, not because his divine part did. In fact, his divine part did not die. But this does

[37] B. Leftow, *Time and Eternity* (Ithaca, NY: Cornell University Press, 1991), 290–5.

not alter the fact that Christ did. So too, an apple's skin is not nutritious, but this does not alter the fact that the apple is.

Reading the christological '*qua*' this way disarms Morris's well-known objections to it. Morris asks us to consider any conjunctive reduplicative proposition of the form 'x as A is N and x as B is not N'. 'If the subjects of both conjuncts are the same and the substituends of N are univocal across the conjunction, then as long as the reduplication predicates being A of x and predicates being B of x, and being N is entailed by being A and not being N is entailed by being B, then . . . the contradiction stands of A being characterized as both N and not N.'[38]

Morris has in mind a recasting of (C) as

(C*) Christ as human died but as God did not die.

Since Christ is both human and divine, Morris reasons, it seems to follow that Christ did and did not die. But on the mereological reading, (C*) does not entail this. On such a reading, Christ died, period. (C*) merely tells us that Christ died because S + B died, and despite the fact that the Son did not die. It is not in general true that if a whole consists of two parts, one F and one non-F, it follows that the whole is both F and non-F. An apple consists of two parts, its nutrients and its non-nutrients. Its nutrients nourish. Its non-nutrients do not. But it does not follow from this that an apple both nourishes and does not. Any whole including nutrients and no poisons nourishes, period.

Morris again asks us to consider . . . the christological proposition (that)

(H') Christ as God is uncreated but as a man is a created being . . .

The property of being created does seem to be the sort of metaphysical property individuals have *simpliciter*, rather than only in virtue of having other properties.[39] This *is* a reasonable cavil with a reading of (H') involving abstract natures, i.e. taking 'as God' to indicate not a *part* but a *property* in virtue of which Christ has a property. But it fails absolutely against a mereological reading of (H'). On such a reading, (H') tells us that Christ has one part which is created and one which is uncreated. Each part has this property *simpliciter*, not in virtue of other properties. And again, no

---

[38] Morris, *Logic of God Incarnate*, 48–9.   [39] Ibid. 54.

contradiction emerges here. We do not have to say that Christ is both created and uncreated. The worst we might have to settle for is a claim that Christ has a created part and an uncreated part, and neither 'created' nor 'uncreated' applies *simpliciter* to a whole consisting of such parts. (Consider a sphere whose surface is half-white, half-black: it has a white part and a black part, and neither 'white' nor 'black' applies to it *as a whole*, for the way we use colour-words requires [something like] that a thing be called [say] black only if the *majority* of its surface is black.) But we need not settle. On a mereological account, Jesus Christ—the Incarnate Son—is created. For the whole, Jesus Christ, did not exist till all its parts existed, and so owes its existence to what brought its parts to be. S and B are created *ex nihilo*. So the whole, Son + S + B, owes its existence to the act of creation which brought S and B into existence. Any whole with created parts is a created whole, even if it also includes an uncreated part. But this does not entail that the *Son* is created. For as we are now using 'Jesus Christ', the Son is not identical with Jesus Christ. The Son is instead just part of Jesus Christ, the part which determines who Christ is. (Of this a bit more anon.)

Senor writes

'John *qua* citizen has the duty to vote' entails that 'John (*simpliciter*) has the duty to vote', since if it is true that John, in virtue of being a citizen, has the duty to vote, then it is true that John has the duty to vote . . . Why should we think that sentences predicating things of Christ are any different? It is true that Christ qua God is omnipotent; but why doesn't that just entail that Christ (*simpliciter*) is omnipotent?[40]

The answer, on a mereological reading of Christology's '*qua*', is that there is no entailment here because sometimes the attributes of one part become the attributes of the whole, and sometimes the attributes of another part do: the apple as a whole is nutritious because of some of its parts, though the rest are not nutritious, and the apple as a whole is red due to other of its parts, though the rest are not red. So the attributes of the apple's non-red and non-nutritious parts do not become attributes of the whole, and there is just no uniform rule by which to figure out which part's attributes will come to qualify its whole. Thus christologists and students of apples must work things out case by case. The Son is omnipotent.

---

[40] Senor, 'Incarnation and Timelessness', 153.

S + B is not. Here, probably, the whole counts as omnipotent, *simpliciter*. But divine attributes do not always become attributes of the whole: again, the whole Jesus Christ is created. Again, Jesus Christ was tempted due to including a part, B + S, which was tempted: here the attribute of the human nature becomes an attribute of the whole. Yet Jesus Christ was impeccable: in this case, the attribute of the divine part dominates. Jesus Christ can be both tempted and impeccable because the two attributes have their sources in different parts of this whole: here seemingly incompatible divine and human attributes *both* come to qualify the whole, and the mereological analysis explains why the incompatibility is only apparent. Now this *kind* of explanation can seem to block a contradiction only at the cost of fracturing the unity of Christ: how *could* parts of one single thing differ so radically? Well, parts of single things do have contradictory attributes: apple-skins are red, apple-flesh is not. Getting more specific, one can analyse Christ's being tempted in terms of psychological processes in B + S proceeding toward the commission of a sin in response to the tempter's wiles. Let the processes draw close enough, and this will constitute temptation: perhaps the processes can go about as far as they do in cases of *our* resisting temptation, if the mind in B + S is suitably insulated from the Son's mind. Even so, there will be a reason that Christ does not actually give in and sin, and this will lie in the Son's role in the actions of Christ, i.e. in the fact that the mind in B + S is in the end *his*. It is common enough to have parts of the same mind 'pull' in different directions, and nonetheless be parts of one mind. If we can make sense of two minds belonging to one person, it will take little more imagination to think of one mind—one part of the person's overall mental endowment—pulling toward sin and another, successfully, pulling Christ away from it. This may differ only in degree, not kind, from our ordinary experience of mental conflict, as a commissurotomy patient's having two minds may differ only in degree, not kind, from our ordinary experience of less-than-perfect mental integration.[41] I cannot here go into further detail; there is, again, a suggestive treatment in Swinburne.[42]

---

[41] For this approach to commissurotomy see K. V. Wilkes, *Real People* (New York: Oxford University Press, 1988), 132–67.

[42] Swinburne, *Christian God*, 203–9.

V   Mereology, Timelessness and the Incarnation

A part-whole account of the incarnation has the resources to deal with our first problem argument, (1)–(3). On a part-whole approach, one can at least question (1). For while S + B exist in time, it may not follow that Jesus Christ does. If part of me is in the room, it does not follow that I am. Suppose that I am seated in the living-room, with a foot extended so that just my left big toe passes through the adjacent door to the kitchen. I do not think that anyone would say that in this case, Leftow is in the kitchen. Most of Leftow is in the living-room, and so we say instead that Leftow is in the living-room, but his big toe is in the kitchen. The Son is in a non-spatial sense 'most' of Jesus Christ. (For that matter, if one wants to speak spatially, the Son is always in some sense everywhere, while S + B never is.) S + B are merely the fleshy curtain which bring the Son into space and time—his instruments to walk about the world, as my big toe is mine. So perhaps not the Son, but only S + B is in time, even if the Son is incarnate in S + B.

Still, what seems most accurate in the kitchen case is that Leftow is part in one place, part in another. Strictly speaking, then, neither 'Leftow is in the kitchen' nor 'Leftow is in the living-room' is true, if each purports to give a location containing all of Leftow.[43] In parallel, if Jesus Christ is part in time and part without, neither 'Jesus Christ is in time' nor 'Jesus Christ is outside time' should come out true, if each purports to give a location containing all of Jesus Christ. It is not clear that

> (1a) Jesus Christ has a part in time

can cause the same trouble (1) does. For (1a) leaves the way clear to claim that Jesus Christ also has a part who is not in time, namely God the Son. This reply might seem to endanger the intimacy of the connection between S + B and the Son. It should not. Scuba gear is intimately connected to the diver's body. Yet it keeps the diver disconnected from the water it touches: scuba gear lets one swim without getting one's feet wet. S + B is the Son's environment suit, letting him manoeuvre in time yet stay dry.[44]

[43] That Leftow has a part in the kitchen may imply that in some sense, Leftow is in the kitchen: but the 'some sense' is just that Leftow has a part in the kitchen. A validly inferred conclusion cannot say more than its premises do, after all.

[44] Sarah Coakley reminds me that some late-patristic christologists like to speak of

On my account, God the Son is part of a partly temporal whole. Some might reply: there is no such thing as a partly temporal whole. Whatever has a temporal part is a temporal whole. Being temporal is not like being red (an apple is red not through and through, but only by having a red skin). It is like being nutritious. An apple is nutritious through and through by containing nutrients. Every part of an apple containing some of its nutrients counts as nutritious, even if it also contains non-nutrients: thus a mouthful of apple containing some skin (which is pure cellulose) is a nutritious mouthful if it also contains apple-flesh.

But at the least, this reply requires further supporting argument, and so one who has recourse to it gives up on (1)–(3) as an *independent* case that the incarnation is incompatible with divine timelessness. The support might well come from some such argument as this:

> if part of a whole changes intrinsically, the whole *ipso facto* changes intrinsically. Whatever changes intrinsically is in time. So if part of a whole changes intrinsically, the whole is in time, and not just partly in time. S + B changes intrinsically. So Jesus Christ is in time. So God the Son is in time.

But changing wholes can have unchanging parts. Imagine a rotating sphere whose parts do not change their relations to one another (e.g. there is no Brownian motion within it) and which is not changing its place as a whole. This sphere rotates about an axis at its centre. The part of the sphere which just overlaps this axis is point-thick, as the axis is, and so cannot spin: points have no circumference, and only items with circumferences can have their circumferences in motion. Nor does this part have parts moving relative to each other or the rest of the sphere. In a universe consisting solely of this sphere, then, the axis-overlapping part of the sphere would be wholly motionless, absolutely and relatively— and if in this universe all physical change supervenes on motion of wholes or parts, this part would be physically changeless. Such a

the Son's divine and human parts somehow interpenetrating. (My thanks to her for a relevant article.) The present metaphor can allow for this: think of the scuba suit as permeable (though not wholly) in one direction, or lit from within, suffused by the glow of the diver. (Thus Christ's deity 'deifies' his humanity.) We could also speak of the suit as rubbing off on the diver. (Thus—if we wish—Christ's humanity 'humanizes' his deity.) The important thing is that in neither case do we imply that any water gets through the suit.

sphere in such a universe seems so clearly conceivable that we strongly think it possible. So (again) it seems that changing wholes can have unchanging parts.

So even if it is true that if part of a whole changes, the whole *ipso facto* changes, the way it is true that the whole changes does not preclude the whole's having unchanging parts, even as the way it is true that a whole apple is nutritious does not preclude the apple's having non-nutritious parts. But if God the Son can be the unchanging axis-part about which Jesus Christ spins, one can maintain despite the above argument that God the Son is not in time even if Jesus Christ is.

Thus part-whole considerations can make a case against (1). They also cut against (2). For (2) appears to identify a proper part (God the Son) with its containing whole (Jesus Christ). If it does, (2) is not just false, but necessarily so. What is true is that

(2a) the person who is Jesus Christ = God the Son.

But the 'is' in (2a) is not that of identity. The person who 'is' Jesus Christ is Jesus Christ's psychological core, the ultimate determiner of his attitudes and actions, the one whose character Jesus Christ reveals and the ultimate subject of some of Jesus Christ's attributes.[45] But this person is not identical with Jesus Christ. Jesus Christ has a part which is a human body. God the Son does not. He has instead, immaterially, the attribute of being part of a whole which includes a body. (So too, if we have souls, our bodies are parts of us, but not parts of our souls. Our souls have, immaterially, the attribute of being part of a whole which includes a body.) Again, Jesus Christ has a temporal part. God the Son does not. Instead, he has atemporally the corresponding attribute of being part of a partly temporal whole.

Denying (2) may seem unorthodox. After all, if the Son is divine and Jesus Christ is divine, and both are persons, then if the Son = Jesus Christ, there are (it seems) four divine persons, not three. I reply that Jesus Christ is divine only because Jesus Christ includes the Son; to worship Christ is to worship the Son. What would be unorthodox would be to add a person to the Trinity. The incarnation does not do this. Jesus Christ is just the sum of one person of the Trinity and two non-divine things. Christ's deity and personhood *are* the Son's.

---

[45] Jesus Christ is created. The Son is not. So the Son is not the ultimate subject of the attributed *being created*. The Son has the attribute of belonging to a whole with a created part.

VI The Second Argument

Our second argument hinges on two premises,

(4) God the Son began to be human, and
(5) whatever begins to be human changes intrinsically.

It seems to me that (4) is false. If God the Son is timeless, he nonetheless has properties due to events in time. If God the Son is timeless, he nonetheless knows (say) that I wrote this chapter in 1999–2000. This last is true solely due to events in those two years. So if God the Son is timeless, he has the property of knowing that I wrote this chapter in 1999–2000 due partly to events in those two years.[46] If a timeless Son could *not* know such truths, then since God the Son *does* know such truths, what follows is simply that God the Son is not timeless. So, again: *if* God the Son is timeless, he timelessly has properties due to events in time. Why not, then, the property of being human? But if the Son does have this property timelessly, he never began to have it, and so indeed (4) is false.

Let us ask just why we are supposed to accept (4). The answer, surely, is that

(9) S + B began to exist,

and we are supposed to accept that

(10) before S + B existed, God the Son was not human.

Now taken at face value, (10) just begs the question against divine timelessness. To a timeless God, there *is* no 'before' S + B appear. If any event in God's life (say, God's knowing that he is God) is before any other (e.g. S + B's appearing), God *ipso facto* is temporal. If God is timeless and is incarnate, then he just is timelessly incarnate: the whole of his timeless life is spent so. But this implies that

(11) before S + B existed, it was timelessly the case that God the Son was human.

And so one can restate the thought behind (10) as a denial of this, a claim that

---

[46] Note that I do not claim that these events *cause* God's cognitive state to be as it is. The 'due partly' claim would be true even if its only basis were that God's cognitive state is knowledge only if what God believes is true, and the events account for the truth of God's belief.

(12) before S + B existed, it was not timelessly the case that God the Son was human.

(12), then, will appeal to our intuitions that before S + B appear, it just is not appropriate to call God human, or incarnate. And the objection to divine timelessness will be that it would require us to speak so, to talk as if there were some period before S + B appeared, during which God existed and was human.

But even if we speak as if God existed for some period before S + B appeared, I am not sure there is a real problem here. Earlier items can have properties due to later events. I believed yesterday that the next Pope will be Catholic. This belief was (say) true, and so had the property of being true; if we hesitate to say that it was true, we do so not due to any doubt that it has a truth-value, but because there is a slight chance that the College of Cardinals might do something really surprising, or that the world might end before there *is* a next Pope. My belief had the property of being true due to a later event, one which has not yet occurred. So too, God the Son could have been human before (say) 4 BC in virtue of what was to happen in 4 BC. My belief is true due to its relations to a future event. Similarly, God the Son could have been human due to his relations to a future event. With this sort of case in view, even a temporalist might want to deny (10). Temporalists (e.g. Ockham) often hold that God has foreknowledge—that, for example, God has always known that the next Pope will be Catholic. Such temporalists allow God to have a property (knowing that the next Pope will be Catholic) through all time prior to an event (the enthronement) because the event *will* occur. Such temporalists could equally well hold it proper to say that the Son was always human, given that S + B *were* going to appear.

Here is a rationale for this. If the Son is human, he, S, and B compose a whole. For the Son to be human is for him to be part of this whole. The Son is the first part of this whole to exist. But the first part of a whole *is* part of that whole. The first brick laid in a certain place is the beginning of a wall. The beginning of a wall is part of a wall, the first part of a wall to be built. The brick is the first part of a wall as soon as it is laid. It does not wait to become so until there are enough bricks to count as a wall of which it is part. The brick is not a wall by itself, but it is *part* of a wall by itself.[47] If only one brick of a

---

[47] One might object: if it is part of a wall, and the only part, then it is an *improper* part of a wall, and so identical with a wall, and so a wall. If so, then if one brick is not

projected Memorial Wall were ever laid, a tour guide might point it out and saying, 'there it is, folks—all of the Memorial Wall that ever got built'. This might be funny, but it would not (it seems to me) be *false*. For the builder's intent was enough to make it the first part of a wall. And even if the rest of the wall is never built, the brick is still the beginnings of a wall, the only part of a wall there ever is in that place: which is to say that it is *still* the first part of a wall, and also the last. I suggest similarly that the Son is part of a human composite as soon as the Son exists, even if the rest of the composite does not yet exist—for the rest of the composite *is* surely coming, and the builder's intent makes the Son so. If the Son is part of a human composite, the Son is human. So if we speak as if God existed before 4 BC, we can also say this: God the Son was human before 4 BC because S + B was to exist and he was to join with it, and this would be so because God intended that it would.

One might reply: if S + B do not appear until (say) 4 BC, does it not at least follow that the Son is not incarnate till then? Surely the Son cannot take on the flesh of Christ before that flesh exists. Well, a defender of divine timelessness will certainly agree that God did not take on B before 4 BC. For again, to a timeless God, nothing occurs before anything else. But it does not follow that when God became incarnate was 4 BC. The event of God's becoming incarnate is not *complete* until 4 BC. But this is a different matter.

Some events have scattered temporal locations. When did Booth kill Lincoln? Booth shot Lincoln at t_1. Lincoln died at t_2. Surely Booth's shooting Lincoln is part of his killing Lincoln. The killing was completed at t_2, when Lincoln died. But it does not seem right to say that Booth was gradually killing Lincoln the whole time Lincoln lay dying: the killing was not a *continuous* event stretching from the shooting to t_2. Rather, it was a 'scattered' event, consisting of the shooting and Lincoln's finally becoming dead. The incarnation, I submit, is another event with a scattered location. It consists of God's taking on flesh and the flesh's being taken on. God performs the action of taking on Christ's flesh timelessly, as Booth shot Lincoln at t_1. The flesh God takes on comes to be in 4 BC, at

---

a wall, one brick is not part of a wall either. I reply that we have the phrase 'the beginnings of a wall' to deal with this case and others like it (two bricks, three, etc.). Parts of a wall not yet built which do not add up to a wall add up to the beginnings of a wall. Similarly, parts of a wall once built which no longer add up to a wall add up to the remains of a wall.

which point the flesh *is* taken on, and the event of taking on flesh is complete—as Lincoln's dying at a later time makes Booth's action complete. Booth did not have to be there for his killing to become complete. He could well have been killed himself before it was. Nor then need Booth have changed intrinsically for the event he put in motion to become complete. So too, then, the completion of the event of becoming incarnate need involve no intrinsic change in God. The incarnation, I submit, is not complete until 4 BC, but its completion involves changes only in temporal things, not in God.

Thus I claim that we have no good reason to accept (10), and so none to accept (4). I also question (5). For one thing, beginning to be human is arguably *not* an intrinsic change in any ordinary individual who becomes human. For arguably being human is among any ordinary human's essential properties: arguably I, for instance, cannot exist unless I am human. If this is so, then when what was in my mother's womb became human, I did not exist until that change was complete. But in a genuine change, one single thing exists both when the change begins and when it is over. Turning from green to brown is a change in a leaf only because the same thing, a leaf, is first green, then brown. If I did not exist before what was in my mother's womb was human, there was no prior state from which becoming human changed me, and so I did not change in becoming human (or in coming to exist, either). (5) seems flatly false.

But being human is not an essential property of God the Son—he could have existed unincarnate. And God the Son did exist before he became human, if we speak of him as if he were in time. So even if (5) is false in ordinary cases, the reasons for this do not apply to the Son, and so one might wonder if despite (5)'s falsity

> (5a) any divine Person who begins to be human changes intrinsically.

I think not. For God the Son, becoming human consists in becoming part of a whole also including S and B. This in turn consists in beginning to have certain relations to S and B. One can begin to have relations without changing intrinsically: I can begin to bear to you the shorter-than relation purely due to your growing. So at the least, before conceding (5), we need to hear some story about what relations are involved in the Son's forming a whole with S and B, and why the Son cannot begin to have these unless he changes intrinsically.

Senor writes that

any deeply orthodox account of the Incarnation . . . will include the idea of the word becoming, or taking on, flesh . . . the second Person of the Trinity . . . is co-eternal with the Father and Spirit . . . only in his divine nature. The human nature is something Christ adopted for his earthly mission . . . Perhaps the only plausible way of understanding the 'taking on' aspect of the doctrine of the Incarnation is as the claim that the assumption of human nature involves a change in the intrinsic . . . attributes of God the Son . . . how can (one) deny that one's taking on a nature entails that one has changed [or] that Christ's assuming a human nature entails that his human nature is not co-eternal with . . . his divine nature?[48]

But if the Son is timeless and incarnate, it does not follow that his human nature is co-eternal with his divine nature. There were times when S + B did not exist, and during those times, it was true to say that God timelessly exists. But the import of the 'taking on' claim on God's side is modal, not temporal. That God took on flesh does not entail that he changed. It entails only that he could have been God without being incarnate, and that if he could have refrained from becoming incarnate, he could have not had a body. Here I simply bat the ball back onto the temporalist's side of the net: why *isn't* this enough to make orthodox sense of the claim that God the Son took on flesh?

Just what relations God has to S + B in virtue of being incarnate— taking on flesh—is a large topic, one I cannot broach here. Certainly God has certain thoughts and sensations due to this which he would not have had otherwise. And if God is timelessly incarnate, he always had these, timelessly, even at times before S + B appeared. One might ask whether this implies that

(13) In 900 BC, the Son was tasting the wine at Cana.

But (13) is false. The timeless Son's relations to these events are only causal, not temporal. It would be as wrong to say that he tasted the wine literally while he drank it as to say that he tasted it literally beforehand. He simply tasted it *because* he drank it. Why need one tack on a temporal 'while' or 'before' for this to make sense?

Temporalists will doubtless have more arguments to offer. Still, I suggest that if I have dealt adequately with those I have treated, it is *prima facie* plausible that God can be both timeless and incarnate.[49]

---

[48] Senor, 'Incarnation and Timelessness', 156, 157, 158.

[49] My thanks to my commentator Steve Davis and other members of the Summit (including William Alston *in absentia*) for their comments on this chapter.

The Incarnation Practised and Proclaimed

13

A Word Made Flesh:
Incarnational Language and the Writer

KATHLEEN NORRIS

The words of God, expressed in the words of men, are in every way like human language, just as the Word of the eternal Father, when he took on himself the flesh of human weakness, became like men.

> The Second Vatican Council,'Dogmatic Constitution of Divine Revelation'[1]

The substance, the means of art, is an incarnation: not reference but phenomena.

> Denise Levertov, 'Origins of a Poem'[2]

The incarnation contains within it a little joke on writers. For we discover that when we want to evoke religious experience, merely piling on the etherous superlatives—*holy, mysterious, wondrous, glorious*—does not work. In fact, it is decidedly counterproductive. Only when we are willing to get down to the nitty-gritty, returning to that manger stall, as it were, with its earthy smells, chill air, and a baby's cry, is it possible for our words to incarnate religious faith. Only then can our words invite the reader to discover, not ideas about the holy, but an experience of it.

I WRITING LESSONS

The primary maxim of the contemporary writing workshop— 'Show, do not tell'—has its correlative in the incarnation itself. If

---

[1] A. Flannery (ed.), *The Conciliar and PostConciliar Documents* (Grand Rapids, Mich.: Eerdmans, 1975), 758.

[2] D. Levertov, 'Origins of a Poem', in D. Hall (ed.), *Claims for Poetry* (Ann Arbor: University of Michigan Press, 1982), 260.

Mary had wanted to 'tell', she might have come forth with a treatise, or a book of theology. Instead, she had a baby, and that has made all the difference.

For the writer intent on writing incarnational literature—and by that I don't mean writing centred on the life of Christ or the theology of the church, but simply literature that 'shows' in such a way that it comes to life for the reader—one of the first lessons is that you must give up the illusion of control. Adjectives are dangerous, for example, and must be used with care, as they tend to tell the reader how to feel. A copy editor once caused me to rethink a phrase in which I had described something as a 'shocking lie', by commenting 'Don't you think you should let the reader decide that for herself?'

The poet W. H. Auden puts this into theological terms in his essay, 'Words and the Word', stating that the analogy of creation 'by the Word of God implies a belief that creation is an act of power, or authority, not of force or violence, one in which the role of the created is as essential as that of the creator'.[3] In a well-realized poem, the poet is invisible behind the words, but in more amateurish work the poet seeks to force the reader to adopt his or her point of view. In sentimental verse about the incarnation of Jesus Christ, for example, one might encounter a surfeit of statements replete with adjectives, the words 'wonderful', 'glorious', 'miraculous', used to emphasize that a momentous event has occurred. Christmas cards are often overloaded with such words, words that preach to the converted, in that they reassure believers who are already convinced of the miracle. But they are incapable of quickening the hearts of those who stand outside, who doubt, or who find words such as 'miraculous' devoid of meaning. And even for believers, in a culture laden with too much talk, religious words and images can rapidly turn dull, calcifying into jargon that has lost its power to surprise or move us.

Religious language seems especially vulnerable to being taken for granted and turned into mindless slogans, and yet Christian poets and pastors alike must employ the language and imagery of faith. The 'lamb of God', for example, is an image, a phrase with a rich history in the tradition, but today tends to remain submerged in the

---

[3] W. H. Auden, 'Words and the Word', in J. Greenhaigh and E. Russell (eds.), *If Christ Be Not Risen: Essays in Resurrection and Survival* (San Francisco: Collins Liturgical, 1988), 69.

Roman Catholic Mass. In that context it is heard in passing and quickly passed over, not much examined or discussed. But the poet Denise Levertov makes it come alive again in her 'Mass for the Day of St. Thomas Didymus'. In the 'Agnus Dei' the poet wonders at a God who would appear as defenseless as a lamb, whose omnipotence has been '. . . tossed away | reduced to a wisp of damp wool'. The poet asks if we must 'hold to our icy hearts | a shivering God'?, and concludes: 'Come, rag of pungent | quiverings, dim star. | Let's try | if something human still | can shield you, | spark | of remote light'.[4]

The adjectives Levertov employs tend to be those that speak directly to our senses: 'icy', 'shivering', 'pungent'. And yet she manages to evoke not only the wonder of the Bethlehem star, but the smells of the manger, and the incarnation of Jesus Christ that takes hold in the human heart. Her language might spark a renewed sense of awe in a Christian reader, and for an atheist or a reader of another faith, might well provide a better understanding of what the incarnation means for a Christian. Her poem has done the work of poetry, which is not argument, but revelation. Not reference, but incarnation.

II Incarnational Language

I use the term 'incarnational language' with poetic licence, as I generally mean it in a literary sense, rather than an exclusively theological one.[5] There is a great distinction between language that is incarnational, and that which is not, and it is usually easy for people to tell the difference, especially to hear the difference when listening to a speech, or a literary work read out loud.

Incarnational language engages our senses, but mere verbiage serves to dis-incarnate us, asking us to pretend that we live in a

---

[4] D. Levertov, 'Mass for the Day of St. Thomas Didymus', *Candles in Babylon* (New York: New Directions, 1982), 114–15.

[5] [The other chapters of this book persistently use 'incarnation' in its precise, theological sense. But that is not to belittle various 'extended', literary meanings: for example a writer may describe some character as 'affability incarnate' or 'the incarnation of affability'. Naturally David Brown's chapter on the incarnation in 20th-cent. art at times also introduces 'wider' religious impulses. The creative freedom of literature and art calls for such an 'extended' use of the language and symbols for the incarnation. Eds.]

world of abstractions. A brief passage from George Orwell's essay, 'Politics and the English Language', vividly illustrates this point. Orwell first cites Ecclesiastes 9: 11 (KJV): 'I saw under the sun, that the race is not to the swift, nor the battle to the strong, nor yet bread to the wise, nor yet riches to those of understanding, nor yet favour to those of skill; but time and chance happeneth to them all.'[6]

This language reflects the world we know from our senses: we can smell the bread, and feel the sunlight on our faces as we see the racers running swiftly, with all their strength and skill. We can almost feel the whoosh of air on our skins as they pass by. Even the abstractions here—time and chance—have some incarnational weight, because they cause us to brood on our own mortality. Once 'time' and 'chance' enter the picture, we can be more realistic about both hope and failure, and the vulnerability to happenstance that is the common human lot.

Just as we are savouring the wisdom incarnated in the rich language of the seventeenth century, however, Orwell translates the passage into a twentieth-century tongue with which we are all too familiar: 'Objective considerations of contemporary phenomena compel the conclusion that success and failure in competitive activities exhibits no tendency to be commensurate with innate capacity, but that a considerable element of the unpredictable must invariably be taken into account.'[7]

The language of the King James Version speaks to us incarnationally, revealing a truth about human experience. Its words can engage anyone, literate or not, as participants in that experience. But Orwell's version talks at us in the jargon of the professions, and self-perpetuating bureaucracies. Its words are hot, dead air, engineered so as to make the person using it feel capable and important, while keeping the underlings being addressed in their place. It is an abuse of language that we know all too well, from the worlds of education, business, sociology, psychology, the military, and politics. In distancing itself from human experience, disincarnating it, if you will, such verbiage allows the speaker to disguise or otherwise manipulate the truth, and even to turn a truth into a lie.

George Orwell was a prophet of language, the inventer of the term 'double-speak', and we can hear, in the words of this spoof that he

---

[6] Quoted in George Orwell, 'Politics and the English Language', in *The Orwell Reader* (New York: Harcourt, Brace, Jovanovich, 1956), 360.   [7] Ibid.

wrote in the 1920s, something we take for granted at the start of the twenty-first century, that a military operation in another country is not an 'invasion' but only an 'incursion', that an accident at a nuclear power plant is merely an 'event', that a company calling itself 'Natural Solutions' may be disposing of hazardous chemical waste in short-sighted and irresponsible ways. It is the language of dis-incarnation, which asks us to distrust the experience of our senses, that makes such manipulation possible. Its sole purpose is to conceal, or hoodwink, or offer palliatives. In an environment in which language has been so debased, I would like to suggest that the use of incarnational language is a theological imperative.

III LANGUAGE FOR THE CHRISTIAN CHURCH: SHOWING AND TELLING

The Jesus revealed in the Gospels speaks in the language of 'showing', the language of story. Most of his words are readily comprehensible to his listeners, not only the fishermen and labourers who became his disciples, but also the more educated religious authorities of his day. And even when Jesus employs the oblique and mysterious methods of parable, his metaphors tend to come from the natural world: yeast, a mustard seed, sandy or rocky ground, fertile soil.

The language of Christian theology has tended to be the language of 'telling', a philosophical language speaking from a presumed vantage point of objectivity and distance. The religion needs both the language of 'showing' and of 'telling', but since the earliest days of the religion Christians have experienced considerable tension between a dual heritage of Semitic storytelling, which tends to allow for a great diversity of voices and perspectives, and Greek philosophy, which opts for abstraction, categorizing, and paring down what is admitted into the tradition. This tension says to me that presence of God in the world—God's incarnation into our everyday life—is too multifarious to be contained by the precise terminology of theology, but must also be expressed in the language of poetry and story.

When Christian language is weighted too much toward the abstract philosophical and theological terminology of the academy and the seminary, more incarnational language is often drowned

out. It can leave Christians wondering, as Emily Dickinson did after
one church service in her Amherst congregation, 'What confusion
would cover the innocent Jesus | to meet so enabled a Man!'[8] In
the twentieth century, theology, like sociology and psychology,
seems driven to prove itself as science, a discipline, a genuine
profession. Unfortunately, in terms of language, the result has been
what the poet Czesław Milosz describes in his recent book, *Road-side
Dog*, in a prose poem entitled 'Theology, Poetry': 'What is deepest
and most deeply felt in life, the transitoriness of human beings,
illness, death, the vanity of opinions and convictions, cannot be
expressed in the language of theology, which for centuries has
responded by turning out perfectly rounded balls, easy to roll but
impenetrable.'[9]

Incarnational language is not only impenetrable, it permeates. It
evokes a reality that is far more than the sum of the mere words that
are its parts.

IV THEOLOGY, POETRY, WORSHIP

Ideally, worship is the ground on which the two great traditions of
theology and story might come together on good terms, with
hymns, prayers, and preaching solidly grounded in the theology of
the creeds, but also reflecting the experience of a lived and living
faith. Unfortunately, the dead jargon of the professions all too often
creeps into contemporary worship, along with therapeutic language
that reduces the deep wisdom of religion into the superficial slogans
of pop psychology. Hence, a banner above the altar reading, 'You
can fly, but that cocoon has to go.'

The liturgical scholar Gail Ramshaw makes a useful distinction
between the vernacular, which the church needs if its worship is to
remain in a living tongue, and the colloquial, which is too flimsy to
sustain the experience of worship. I make a habit of collecting
prayers that fail to take this crucial distinction into account. A
communal prayer of confession reads: 'God of active love, we confess

---

[8] E. Dickinson, 'He preached upon "Breadth" till it argued him narrow—', Poem
no. 1207 in *The Complete Poems of Emily Dickinson*, ed. T. H. Johnson (Boston: Little
Brown, 1960), 533.
[9] C. Milosz, *Road-side Dog*, trans. by the author and Robert Hass (New York : Farrar,
Straus, and Giroux, 1998), 21.

our tendency to pay lip-service to your Gospel. Sow in us a deep discontent with a rhetorical faith that is all talk and no action.' Another that confesses: 'Our communication with Jesus tends to be too infrequent to experience the transformation in our lives You want us to have.'[10]

This is not a prayer so much as a memo from one professional to another. And perhaps that is the point. At religious conferences I have attended, 'worship facilitators' hand out booklets entitled 'worship resources' that include our hymns, scripture passages, and prayers. The effect of all this is to reassure everyone that we are not merely praying here, but are engaged in something more substantial, useful, and professional. All too often, the experience of worship in such settings feels oddly dis-incarnational. It becomes as heady and passive as watching several videos in a row in the motel room because you cannot sleep.

People come to church to be reminded of God's presence, to have the hope they know in Jesus Christ reincarnated in their lives. They come seeking peace in a world of violence. They come seeking healing in a world of hurt. They come seeking consolation in a world of despair. And they come seeking language in a world of verbiage, language that will make them more fully present to God, and to each other. And that is a real trick in today's talk culture. The monk Thomas Merton, like Orwell a prophet of language, summed up the preacher's predicament way back in 1968 by saying: 'People don't want to hear any more words. In our mechanical age, all words have become alike. These days, to say "God is love" is like saying "Eat Wheaties".'[11]

But it is not comfortable to be fully present to others, and preachers have many ways to avoid it. One can choose to become just another talking head, putting up a wall of excess verbiage, as in an offertory prayer I recently experienced that ended, 'Let the love behind every gift find expression in deeds of mercy and kindness before all people towards the end that suffering might be alleviated and your name be praised.' 'Love', 'gift', 'mercy', 'kindness', 'suffering', 'praise', and the name of God

---

[10] These are not quotations but my paraphrase of a central theme in several of Ramshaw's books on liturgy, notably *Searching for Language* (Washington, DC: Pastoral Press, 1988).

[11] T. Merton, *New Springs of Contemplation* (New York: Farrar, Straus, and Giroux, 1992), 9.

remain abstractions here, and worship becomes as dis-incarnate an experience as watching TV. Eat Wheaties.

People come to church to hear potent, truth-telling language, in a world full of talk that manipulates, trivializes, and generally evades the truth. They come to have the Word of God wash over them in a way that makes them whole. I was certainly in need of that when I returned to church after a hiatus of twenty years, and was dismayed to find that I often experienced worship as a kind of assault, a bombardment of heavy-duty words. I was not surprised to hear recently a pastor with forty years in the ministry say that when he had retired after being diagnosed with cancer, he had a very hard time finding a church service that spoke to him, that offered any meaningful words of consolation and hope. Perhaps he was less than moved by vague talk of 'enriching the whole person', or prayers in which we 'offer ourselves as facilitators of a unity in which we all know each other through Christ'.

That pastor might have been better served by simple language, simple truth. There's a story in a recent *New Yorker*—in an article about the exceptionally dull orations of the current American Presidential campaign—in which the Revd Jesse Jackson recalls a childhood experience, the visit of a singing group to his church in South Carolina. 'Before they sang that day,' Jackson said, their tenor, 'Archie Brownlee, said "This is my last tour through the South. And I hope you'll forgive me if there's a little liquor on my breath"—now this was in a church, and so there was some rustling in the pews—"but I'm not using it for pleasure. I have the cancer, and I need it to ease the pain. . . . But don't worry about me, because I'm going across the river. I hear there's a man on the other side who cures cancer, and can make the blind to see."' 'Well,' Jackson said, 'the place just went crazy. The power of a simple truth.'[12] Simple. And profound, because it is an incarnation, a person engaged in the pastoral endeavour of rendering his life as a story to benefit other suffering people.

---

[12] J. Klein, 'Where's the Music?', *New Yorker*, 27 Sept., 1999, 38.

V A WORD THAT BREATHES

A Word that breathes distinctly
has not the power to die[13]

Poets and novelists are usually far from pastoral in how they conceive of their work. The poet begins a poem with only the pleasure of word-play in mind. Donald Hall, in an essay on poetry, asserts that 'poems are pleasure first: bodily pleasure, a deliciousness of the senses'. He sees the 'body [as] poetry's door', finding the origin of poetic metre in the rhythms of human walking.[14]

If a poem begins for the poet in the body, it quickly takes on a life of its own, incarnating itself in the bodies, minds, and experiences of others in ways that the poet could not have imagined. This incarnational quality may constitute literature's greatest gift to us, in a time when we are over-saturated with both ideology and information. For when a well-realized poem or story does its work as literature, it has the power to nudge people past the ideologies that polarize them. In a 1998 essay in the *Atlantic Monthly* the writer Cynthia Ozick stated:

An essay is a thing of the imagination. If there is information in an essay, it is by-the-by, and if there is an opinion, one need not trust it for the long run. A genuine essay rarely has an educational, polemical, or sociopolitical use; it is the movement of a free mind at play. Though it is written in prose, it is closer in kind to poetry than to any other form. Like a poem, a genuine essay is made of language and character and mood and temperament and pluck and chance.[15]

The poem or story succeeds by sounding like a real person speaking; by breathing. And insofar as it provides a real experience for the reader, something that could not have taken place without the encounter with the poem, the words do become flesh. They offer what cannot be offered or received in any other way, not in a 'meaning' that can be separated from the words themselves, but in these very words. For both poet and reader, as the poet William Stafford has said, the poem 'will always be a wild animal . . . there is

---

[13] E. Dickinson, 'A Word Made Flesh', Poem no. 1651 in *Complete Poems*, 675.
[14] D. Hall, *The Unsayable Said* (Port Townsend, Wash.: Copper Canyon Press, 1993), 1.
[15] C. Ozick, 'She: Portrait of the Essay as a Warm Body', *Atlantic Monthly*, 282: 3 (Sept. 1998), 114.

something about it that won't yield to ordinary learning. When a poem catches you, it overwhelms, it surprises, it shakes you up. And often you can't provide any usual explanation for its power.'[16]

The job of the poet is to draw up out of the unconscious an awareness of something that is greater than anything that can be expressed in words. It might even be called a revealing of God's presence, or God's incarnating in a particular way to this particular poet, whose task it is to articulate the experience and pass it on. To surprise you. To shake you up. To renew your sense of wonder at your being, and God's being, and the mystery of creation.

[16] W. Stafford, 'You Must Revise Your Life', in *You Must Revise Your Life*, Poets on Poetry Series (Ann Arbor: University of Michigan Press, 1986), 99–100.

14

The Incarnation and Virtue Ethics

LINDA ZAGZEBSKI

I. CAN THERE BE A DISTINCTIVELY CHRISTIAN ETHICAL THEORY?

Christian ethics purports to centre on the life of Christ, but little of it actually does so. Perhaps the approach that comes the closest in recent years is narrative ethics.[1] This technique is easily adapted to the use of the Gospels as vehicles of moral instruction, but it has usually been offered as an alternative to theory, an outgrowth of the anti-theory movement in philosophical ethics.[2] In my view ethical theory serves an important purpose and it is premature to reject it. Nonetheless, it is difficult to harmonize any kind of theory with a Christocentric ethics. That is because theories are systems of concepts, not descriptions of persons or stories about them. Christian thinkers no doubt agree that Jesus Christ was paradigmatically good, but when this belief is incorporated into a theory, it too often amounts to nothing more than secular ethics plus an example. Even when Christian philosophers promote an explicitly theistic theory, they have traditionally adopted either a form of Divine Command theory or a form of Natural Law theory. In both of these theories the incarnation is at best peripheral and neither is distinctively Christian. Both are simply monotheistic.[3] If the

[1] For an overview of the use of narrative ethics in religious philosophy see R. C. Roberts, 'Narrative Ethics', in P. L. Quinn and C. Taliaferro (eds.), *Companion to Philosophy of Religion* (Cambridge, Mass.: Blackwell, 1997).

[2] For a good but somewhat out-of-date anthology on anti-theory in ethics see S. G. Clarke and E. Simpson (eds.), *Anti-Theory in Ethics and Moral Conservatism* (Albany, NY: SUNY Press, 1989). B. Williams is perhaps the leading anti-theorist.

[3] Theologians have also been criticized for failing to make their moral theologies Christocentric. Edward Vacek points out that James Gustafson has passionately and rightly criticized theologians for their failure to provide a theocentric ethic, yet his own critics argue that he does not provide a sufficiently Christian understanding of God. See E. Vacek, *Love, Human and Divine: The Heart of Christian Ethics* (Washington, DC: Georgetown University Press, 1994), p. xvii.

incarnation had a moral purpose other than the atonement, one would expect it to be given a central place in Christian ethics, and indeed, in Christian ethical theory. But it appears that we are caught in a dilemma: if a Christian ethical theory is really Christian it is not really a theory; if a Christian ethical theory is really a theory it is not really Christian.

In this chapter I shall propose a formal framework for an ethical theory that makes the incarnation central to the theory and the imitation of Christ the basic normative idea. The formal framework may be called exemplarism. I shall then give a sketch of a particular form of exemplarist virtue theory that I call Divine Motivation theory.

Before proceeding further there are two matters that need to be addressed, at least briefly. First, why not go the way of the anti-theorists and embrace a form of narrative ethics that eschews theory? Second, why think that the incarnation had a moral purpose other than atonement for the Fall? And even if it did, why think that that purpose should be given a central place in Christian ethics?

To begin, it should be admitted that while most human beings care about living an ethical life, the theorizing urge is far from universal. A theory is an abstract structure that aims to simplify and systematize a complex area of life or field of inquiry. Ethical theory attempts to impose order on the moral life, but moral phenomena are so complicated and diverse and have so many different purposes, that the price we pay for the order we get from theory is bound to be a certain amount of distortion. Our moral beliefs and practices are simply not as rational and coherent as we would like to think, and any attempt to pretend otherwise is bound to miss some important subtleties in our practices. For example, Bernard Williams and Thomas Nagel have illustrated the ways in which we both tolerate and do not tolerate moral luck.[4] Some moral intuitions move us to

---

[4] T. Nagel, 'Moral Luck', in id. *Moral Questions* (Cambridge and New York: Cambridge University Press, 1979); B. Williams, 'Moral Luck', in id., *Moral Luck and Other Essays* (Cambridge: Cambridge University Press, 1981), 20–39. In my paper ('Religious Luck', *Faith and Philosophy*, 11: 3 (July 1994), 397–413), I argue that some Christian doctrines magnify the problem of moral luck, whereas others make it easier to handle. One of the attractions of Kant is his clear attempt to eliminate luck in the moral realm. Many Christian philosophers have found Kantian ethics appealing partly for this reason, yet John Hare has argued that a Kantian view of the moral demand combined with a Christian view of human moral ineptitude produces a gap that is irreparable without Christian doctrines of grace and salvation. See Hare, *The Moral Gap* (Oxford: Clarendon Press, 1996).

attempt to eliminate luck from the moral realm, but a theory that eliminates luck entirely will be incompatible with important intuitions undergirding our practices. Equally important is the work of moral particularists who argue that what the abstraction necessary for theory leaves behind is often what is most important. What makes one particular person or set of circumstances different from any other can sometimes make a moral difference. When that difference is abstracted, we lose what we might better have preserved. The cost of theoretical purity may therefore be a certain degree of error, and a certain kind of subtlety. It is very hard to retain that subtlety without stories. That is the advantage of narrative ethics.

There is no doubt, then, that theory has its limitations, but it also has some impressive advantages. Theory compensates for the finitude of the human mind. We are not capable of comprehending the whole of reality, and we are not even capable of comprehending very much at any one time. Abstraction sacrifices detail in order to give us greater scope. Theory leaves behind the richness of detail, but it reveals structures that the details cover up. It is not necessary to understand these structures to be a morally good person; the purpose of theory is not moral training. Rather, the philosophical theorist's aim is to satisfy a purely intellectual desire, the desire to understand. Understanding is greater the more extensive the grasp. What we aim to achieve in ethical understanding is the grasp of the whole of value and everything related to it. But we can never achieve that state if all we have to work with is stories. There is a reason why metaphysics was invented, and philosophical ethics was invented for the same reason. We want a map of ethical reality.

Theory is valuable, but I believe that a moral theory which is Christian in any important way must refer to the person of Jesus Christ and the stories about his life, particularly as they are found in the Gospels. And the reference to Christ ought to be an essential aspect of the theory. Christ is not just the instantiation of a set of virtues and his life an illustration of a set of general principles. If that were the case, someone else could have filled the role instead. This raises the second preliminary issue mentioned above. Should Christians think of the incarnation as a central event in human moral awakening, or was its purpose limited to the atonement for sin?

For Anselm the incarnation was a drastic move in response to human sin. It was not part of the original divine plan and its primary purpose was the atonement. In the thirteenth century Robert Grosseteste rejected Anselm's view, contending that God would have become incarnate even if the human race had not fallen. The incarnation would have perfected the human race and all creation because it would have been a manifestation of divine goodness, wisdom, and power.[5] Notice that the aims Grosseteste identifies are not moral ones. God would have become incarnate for the sake of the order and excellence of the universe, not for the purpose of being a moral exemplar. (Presumably the latter purpose is not as lofty as metaphysical order.) Bonaventure was sympathetic with both positions and declared both to be defensible, but decided it was more consonant with piety to regard the incarnation mainly as a remedy for sin.[6] Aquinas concurred.[7] However, Scotus enthusiastically adopted the view that God would have become incarnate even if Adam had not sinned. The hypostatic union is a proximate means for enlarging the trinitarian community of co-lovers, and this was settled by God prior (in the explanatory order) to the Fall and God's foreknowledge of the Fall. Scotus' reason for rejecting the Anselmian/Thomistic position is particularly interesting. If the incarnation were motivated only by the sin of Adam, he said, then the best thing God does in creation would be motivated by the worst thing creatures do, and that would be irrational.[8]

In the Hebrew Bible it is clear that humans are made in the image of the one God, and the basic moral doctrine is the *imitatio Dei*, to become as much like God as is humanly possible. 'You shall be holy, for I the Lord your God am holy' (Lev. 19: 2). In the Hebrew Scriptures we do not become like God by modelling ourselves on him, which we cannot do, but by following his commandments. The incarnation shifts the ethical direction. Christ is the Word made flesh, the perfect revelation of the Father, which means that, to the Christian, God is most perfectly revealed in a person, not in a set of commandments or any written or spoken words, although Jesus says he comes to fulfil the law, not to destroy it (Matt. 5: 17). Through him we have access to the Father and come to share in the divine nature

---

[5] See M. McCord Adams, 'What Sort of Human Nature? Medieval Philosophy and the Systematics of Christology', *Aquinas Lecture 1999* (Milwaukee: Marquette University Press), 24.

[6] Ibid. 27.

[7] *ST* 3a 1. 3. See Adams, 'What Sort', 51.

[8] Ibid. 69–70.

(Eph. 1: 9). In the Letter to the Philippians Paul says, 'In your minds you must be the same as Christ Jesus' (2: 5). Throughout the New Testament the motive for imitation is that what we are imitating is the love which we have already received. Love is naturally imitative. 'We love because he first loved us' (1 John 4: 18).

In the second century Irenaeus tells us how the image of God is shown through the incarnation, so that the *imitatio Dei* of the Hebrew Scriptures is dramatically deepened:

The truth of this was shown when the Word of God became man, assimilating Himself, so that, by His resemblance to the Son, man might become precious to the Father. For in times past it was *said* that man was made in the image of God, but not *shown*, because the Word, in whose image man was made, was still invisible. That is why man lost the likeness so easily. But when the Word of God was made flesh, He confirmed both things: He showed the true image, when He Himself became what His image was; and He restored and made fast the likeness, making man like the invisible Father through the visible Word. (*Adversus Haereses* 5. 16. 2)[9]

Irenaeus may have been the first Christian theologian to propose a moral purpose for the incarnation in addition to the atonement:

There was no other way by which we could learn the things of God than for our Teacher, who is the Word, to become man. No other could have revealed to us the secrets of the Father, none but the Father's very own Word. 'For who (else) has known the mind of the Lord, or who has been His counsellor?' (cf. Rom. 11: 34). Again, there was no other way for us to learn than to see our Teacher and hear His voice with our own ears. It is by becoming imitators of His actions and doers of His words that we have communion with Him. It is from Him who has been perfect from before all creation that we, so lately made, receive fulfilment. (*Adversus Haereses* 5. 1. 1)[10]

At the other end of the spectrum of Christian history, Dietrich Bonhoeffer argues that our primary task is to recognize that we are reconciled with God. We need a metamorphosis, a complete inward transmutation of our previous form, a 'renewing of mind' (Rom. 12: 2), a 'walking as children of light' (Eph. 5: 8). This metamorphosis of man can only be the overcoming of the form of the fallen man, Adam, and conformation with the form of the new man, Christ:

---

[9] Quoted in H. U. von Balthasar (ed.), *The Scandal of the Incarnation*, trans. John Saward (San Francisco: Ignatius Press, 1990), 56.
[10] Ibid. 57.

The will of God, therefore, is not an idea, still demanding to become real; it is itself a reality already in the self-revelation of God in Jesus Christ. . . . After Christ has appeared, ethics can have but one purpose, namely, the achievement of participation in the reality of the fulfilled will of God. But this participation, too, is possible only in virtue of the fact that I myself am already included in the fulfilment of the will of God in Christ, which means that I am reconciled with God.[11]

Bonhoeffer does not speak of the 'imitation' of Christ, but of 'conforming' to Christ since Christ is the one who initiates our metamorphosis. This difference is important, but for my purpose here it suffices to notice that Bonhoeffer's view shares the fundamental point of the imitation literature: The Christian's primary moral aim is to be like a certain person.

I find it reasonable to conclude that the purpose of the incarnation was not only to atone for the sin of Adam and Eve, but was also to give us a perfect moral exemplar. It is arguable whether there would have been an incarnation in the absence of the Fall, but even if there would not have been, it does not follow that the purpose of the actual incarnation was limited to the atonement. Furthermore, even if the revelation of the perfect human in God incarnate was not part of the *purpose* of the incarnation, it nonetheless did have that effect, and the effect is powerful and significant. The imitation of Christ is therefore not just an accidental feature of Christian piety, but is central to the Christian's attempt to live a moral life.

II Exemplarism

There are not many ways to go about defining something when we do not pretend to know what it really is. However, there is one way of doing so that has become important in contemporary philosophy of language. In fact, a similar technique was arguably used by Aristotle. In the 1970s, Saul Kripke, Hilary Putnam, Keith Donnellan, and others proposed a way of defining natural kind terms that became known as the theory of direct reference.[12] Leaving aside

---

[11] D. Bonhoeffer, *Ethics* (New York: Simon & Schuster, 1995), 42.

[12] This theory originated with S. Kripke's *Naming and Necessity* (Oxford: Blackwell, 1980), and H. Putnam's paper, 'The Meaning of "Meaning"', in his *Mind, Language, and Reality* (New York: Cambridge University Press, 1975); first published in K. Gunderson (ed.), *Language, Mind, and Knowledge* (Minneapolis: University of Minnesota Press, 1975).

differences among the versions of the theory, the idea was that a natural kind such as *water* or *gold* or *human* should be defined as whatever is the same kind of thing or stuff as some indexically identified instance. For example, they proposed that gold is, roughly, whatever is the same element as *that*, water is whatever is the same liquid as *that*, a human is whatever is a member of the same species as *that*, and so on. In each case the demonstrative term 'that' refers to an entity to which the person doing the defining refers directly, typically by pointing. Subsequently, the theory was applied to terms other than natural kind terms, including terms for theoretical entities.[13]

One of the main reasons for proposing definitions like this was that Kripke and Putnam believed that often we do not know the nature of the thing we are defining, and yet we know how to construct a definition that links up with its nature. We may not know the nature of gold, and for millennia nobody knew its nature, but that did not prevent people from defining 'gold' in a way that fixed the reference of the term and continued to do so after its nature was discovered. In fact, the discovery of the nature of gold implies that modern speakers are knowledgeable about the nature of the same stuff of which pre-modern speakers were ignorant. The theory of direct reference permits the referent of the word 'gold' to remain invariant after it was discovered what makes gold what it is. If 'gold' did not refer to the same thing both before and after such a discovery, it is hard to see how we could claim that there is *something* about which the discovery was made.

This proposal began a revolution in semantics because it meant that competent speakers of the language can use terms to success-fully refer to the right things without going through a descriptive meaning. Gold is not whatever satisfies a certain description, nor is water. A natural kind term is associated with a descriptive *stereo-type*, but the stereotype is not part of the meaning of the term, and it can be mistaken. It is important that the stereotype be revisable, whereas the referent of the terms remains invariant. An important consequence of this theory is that it is not necessary that speakers associate descriptions with natural kind terms and it is even possible that they succeed in referring to water and gold even when they

---

[13] Initial discussion focused on natural kind terms and proper names, but later the theory was applied to a broader class of terms. The extent of the class of terms which can refer directly is not important for my purpose in this chapter.

associate the wrong descriptions with terms like 'water' and 'gold'.[14] What is required instead is that they be related by a chain of communication to the actual stuff: water and gold.[15] It is not even necessary that every speaker be able to identify water and gold reliably themselves as long as some speakers in the community can do so and the other speakers rely on the judgement of the experts. This point leads to an important feature of Putnam's theory: the division of linguistic labour. According to Putnam, non-specialists can successfully refer to the kind in question because they are part of a linguistic community some of whose members can reliably pick out instances of the kind. Obviously, this is not as important for a kind like water, but for kinds like diamond and uranium it is crucial.

The theory of direct reference assumes that nature can be carved at the joints (to use Putnam's phrase), which means that nature must *have* joints at which it can be carved. The theory also assumes that human minds are naturally suited to notice the joints of nature, and when we make a demonstrative reference to a natural kind in the above definitions of natural kind terms, it is to those kinds that we intend to refer. This is important because reference is in principle indeterminate with respect to indefinitely many objects. When we point to the water in a glass, for instance, our pointing gesture could be variously construed as referring to the surface of the water, the water plus the glass, the water and a portion of the air above it, the water at this moment only, and so on. Demonstrative reference to a natural kind is successful, provided that it is natural for speakers to have the idea of a natural kind and to intend to refer to such a kind, and for others in the linguistic community to understand the intention and to interpret the ostensive reference appropriately.

A widely discussed consequence of the theory of direct reference is that there can be necessary, *a posteriori* truths. Kripke argued that since the reference of 'water' is fixed by ostension, scientists can

---

[14] On one version of the theory, natural kind terms have no meaning; they are purely denotative (like John Stuart Mill's theory of proper names). On another version of the theory, natural kind terms have a meaning, but meanings are not in the head. That is, they are not something a speaker grasps and through which he finds the referent. See Putnam, 'Meaning of "Meaning"'.

[15] In some later versions of the theory the chain is thought to be causal, hence the term 'causal theory of reference', but the idea that the use of a term by many speakers is causally connected was not part of the original theory and in fact was explicitly rejected by Kripke.

then discover the nature of water empirically. Since the nature of water is essential to it, it follows that certain necessary truths such as 'Water is H_2O' are known *a posteriori*. The process would proceed roughly as follows: (1) We know *a priori* that the deep structure of water is essential to it. (2) We discover *a posteriori* that the deep structure of water is its chemical constitution, H_2O. We conclude: (3) It is essential to anything that is water that it is H_2O. We know (3) *a posteriori* because we cannot know (3) without empirical observation. If this is right, it means that the connection philosophers had accepted for centuries between the modal status of propositions and the way in which we know them is mistaken.

Let us now look carefully at the way Aristotle defined *phronesis*, or practical wisdom. I think we find a remarkably similar demonstrative procedure, but without the well-developed semantics of the theory of direct reference. Aristotle has quite a bit to say about what the virtue of *phronesis* consists in, but he clearly is not confident that he can give a full account of it. And what is more important for my purposes here, he thinks that, fundamentally, this does not matter because we can pick out persons who are phronetic in advance of investigating the nature of *phronesis*. The *phronimos* can be defined, roughly, as a person *like that*, where we make a demonstrative reference to a paradigmatically good person. So Aristotle assumes that we can pick out paradigmatic instances of good persons in advance of our theorizing. Aristotle does not even think it necessary that every competent speaker of Greek be able to reliably identify the *phronimoi*, as long as some speakers in the community can do so and the rest of the speakers defer to their judgement.[16]

I suggest that Aristotle was basically right about this. Just as competent speakers of English can successfully refer to water or gold and make assertions about it whether or not they know any chemistry, so can competent speakers successfully talk about practically wise persons. They can do this even though they can neither describe the properties in virtue of which somebody is a *phronimos* or even reliably identify the *phronimoi* in their community. But, like 'water', '*phronesis*' (or the English 'practical wisdom') is a term that each speaker associates with paradigm instances. The *phronimos* is a person *like that*, just as water is a substance *like that*.

---

[16] Since Aristotle thinks that the virtue of *phronesis* is both a necessary and sufficient condition for having the moral virtues, the truly phronetic person will always be paradigmatically good as well as paradigmatically practically wise.

If I am right about this, the traditional charge against Aristotle that his definition of '*phronesis*' is circular is misplaced. I suspect that Aristotle was attempting a way of defining '*phronesis*' directly, parallel to the way of defining 'water' in the theory of direct reference. Perhaps Aristotle did not actually have this in mind, but he might have. At least, it seems to me to be consistent with Aristotle's exposition of *phronesis*, and, in any case, this interpretation aids his theory.

Like the use of direct reference in defining natural kind terms, the use of direct reference in defining 'good person' or 'practically wise person' makes certain assumptions. It assumes that what is good is natural, not conventional, and that our minds are equipped to notice the division of persons and things into good and bad. Like the stereotypes of natural kinds, there are no doubt also stereotypes of good persons which are subject to revision. There is also probably some room for a division of linguistic labour, in that some people are better at identifying good persons than others (although it is unlikely that people will be as quick to defer to the 'experts' on moral matters as they are on scientific matters).

Let us now return to the issue of what a moral theory is and how it should be constructed. A moral theory is a system of concepts. Some concepts in the theory are defined in terms of others. But unless we are willing to accept conceptual circularity, some concept or concepts will either be undefined or will refer to something outside the domain. Most moral philosophers have done the latter. The basic evaluative concept in their theory is defined in terms of something non-evaluative, typically human nature, rationality, or the will of God. The alternative I am suggesting is to anchor moral concepts in an exemplar. Good persons are persons like that, just as gold is stuff like that. The function of an exemplar is to fix the reference of the term 'good person' or 'practically wise person' without the use of any concepts, whether descriptive or non-descriptive. The exemplar therefore allows the series of conceptual definitions to get started. The circle of conceptual definitions of the most important concepts in a moral theory—*virtue, right act, duty, good outcome*, etc.—is broken by an indexical reference to a paradigmatically good person.

Making the exemplar a person has an even more important advantage than its aid to theory. If all the concepts in a formal ethical theory are rooted in a person, then narratives and descriptions of that person are morally significant. It is an open question what it is about the person that makes him or her good. When we say that water is whatever is the same liquid as the stuff in this glass, we are implicitly leaving open the question of what properties of the stuff in this glass are essential to its being water. For the same reason, when we say that a good person is a person like that, and we directly refer to St Francis of Assisi, or to Mahatma Gandhi, or to Jesus Christ, we are implicitly leaving open the question of what properties of St Francis, Gandhi, or Christ are essential to their goodness. Perhaps there are non-evaluative descriptions of these persons that are sufficient to determine their moral goodness; perhaps not. Perhaps their goodness is not determined by any descriptive properties we know how to apply, and we need to resort to narratives.[17] Perhaps the distinction between evaluative and non-evaluative properties is itself problematic.[18] The exemplarist approach has the advantage that none of these matters need be settled at the outset. We need to observe the exemplar carefully to find out what the relevant properties are. Since narratives can be considered detailed and temporally extended observations of persons,[19] exemplarism gives narrative an important place within the theory itself. If I am right, then, we do not need to choose between theory and narrative ethics. This view commits me to the position that ethics is not purely *a priori*, but that is a reasonable view in any case. At least, I see no reason to think that ethics is any more *a priori* than the metaphysics of natural kinds. I find it fascinating to consider the possibility that if propositions such as 'Water is H_2O' are necessary *a posteriori*, there are also necessary *a posteriori* truths in ethics and that some of them are discovered in a way that parallels the discovery of the nature of water. Perhaps narratives serve a purpose in ethics analogous to scientific observation about natural kinds. Narratives might reveal necessary features of value by uncovering the deep properties of a good person.

---

[17] 'Resort' may be an unfair word because it suggests that narratives are something we appeal to as a last resort, and I do not mean to imply that. But I do think that narratives are harder to handle than descriptions. There is a good reason why our language developed thick descriptive terms like 'courageous' or 'haughty'. It saves a lot of time.

[18] I have argued for this in 'Emotion and Moral Judgment', unpublished.

[19] The narrative of internal consciousness is, of course, a modern invention, and one we could not expect to get out of Gospel narratives. The latter are closer to third-person observations.

III Exemplarist Virtue Theory and the Imitation of Christ

Ethical theory is concerned with at least three general objects of moral evaluation and the relations among them: acts (right, wrong, duty), persons (virtues and vices), and states of affairs (good and bad).[20] Usually one of these categories is taken as basic and the others evaluated in terms of the basic one. For example, some theorists maintain that persons have traits of character, like kindness or unkindness, because of their propensity to perform acts of a certain description. These theories make the moral properties of acts more basic than the moral properties of persons. Some of them also make the evaluation of acts more basic than that of states of affairs; others do not. So they may define the concepts of a right and wrong act in terms of the goodness and badness of the states of affairs those acts bring about (consequence-based), or they may instead treat the concepts of act evaluation as basic (act-based). Both kinds of theory differ from the type of theory according to which acts have moral properties in virtue of the fact that they are the sort of act that good or bad persons do. This kind of theory makes the moral properties of persons more basic than the moral properties of acts. That is what I mean by a virtue theory. In the most radical form of virtue theory all moral properties derive from the property of being a good person or having a good personal trait, including the moral properties of states of affairs. There are, of course, many ways to structure a theory of this kind.[21]

In introducing exemplarism in the last section I assumed that the moral exemplar is a person, but that is not actually required by the logic of exemplarism. If the only purpose of an exemplar is to break the circle of concepts in a moral theory, that can be done in any

---

[20] John Rawls proposes something similar to this as a way of classifying ethical theories in 'The Independence of Moral Theory', *Proceedings of the American Philosophical Association* 48 (1974–5), 5–22. In the attempt to show what virtue theory would have to be like in order to be a distinctively different kind of theory, Gary Watson pursues the idea in 'On the Primacy of Character', in O. Flanagan and A. O. Rorty (eds.), *Identity, Character, and Morality* (Cambridge, Mass.: MIT Press, 1990), 449–83. I examine Watson's argument in *Divine Motivation Theory*, ch. 1, manuscript in progress.

[21] I examine some alternatives in *Divine Motivation Theory*, chapter. 1. In *Virtues of the Mind* (New York: Cambridge University Press, 1996) I outline two forms of pure virtue theory, one happiness-based, the other motivation-based.

number of ways. If the theory is not foundationalist in structure and has no basic concept, then the circle can in principle be broken anywhere. If the theory does have a basic concept, as in the kinds of theory mentioned in the preceding paragraph, then the basic concept is the one that we would want to define by ostensive reference to an exemplar. An act-based or consequence-based theory could in principle use the exemplarist procedure I have described, but if we want the exemplarist approach to give a theoretical basis to the Christian idea of the imitation of Christ, the exemplar should be a person and the resulting theory will be a form of virtue theory.

There is another reason why we would want the exemplar to be a person apart from theological considerations. It is an advantage of a theory if it is practically useful. For that purpose we need to take into consideration the facts of human behavioural learning. There is significant evidence in developmental psychology that human infants are born to learn through imitation.[22] The imitation mechanism appears to be innate and phylogenetically old, although only humans have it in its complete form.[23] It is critical during development and remains an important aspect of social interaction throughout life, and most behaviour is acquired in this way.[24] Moreover, there is evidence that humans model not only overt behaviour, but the attitudes and emotional reactions of others. These features of human learning make it desirable that the paradigmatic instance used in exemplarist moral theory be a person who can be imitated. Humans naturally imitate other persons, particularly admired other persons.[25] There is plenty of evidence, then, that the Christian idea of the imitation of Christ is based on good behavioural psychology.

In an exemplarist virtue theory all three of the categories of moral evaluation mentioned above—personal traits, acts, and the states of affairs brought about by acts—would be defined by reference to the exemplar or exemplars identified by the theory. Good and bad traits of character are defined in terms of the traits of character of the

---

[22] See, among others, the research programme of Andrew N. Meltzoff, University of Washington.

[23] See ongoing research by Maja J. Mataric, Brandeis University.

[24] A. Bandura, *Social Learning Theory* (Morristown, NJ: General Learning Press, 1971), and *Social Foundations of Thought and Action* (Englewood Cliffs, NJ: Prentice-Hall, 1986).

[25] Bandura, *Social Learning Theory* and *Social Foundations*.

exemplar. The moral properties of acts are defined in terms of the actual or hypothetical acts of the exemplar. Good and bad outcomes are defined in terms of the states of affairs the exemplar aims to bring about or to prevent. Clearly, this is a very general schema and it can be adapted to a number of different approaches to virtue ethics.

Traditional Aristotelian virtue ethics makes the concept of virtue dependent upon the more basic concept of *eudaimonia*—happiness or flourishing. *Eudaimonia* is in turn dependent upon the idea of human nature, understood as teleological. It is well known that one of the stumbling blocks to the acceptance of virtue ethics among modern philosophers is the worry that we shall never get agreement on what constitutes *eudaimonia*, as well as doubts that human nature is teleological, and even more radical doubts that there is any such thing as human nature at all.[26] Exemplarist virtue theory has an advantage since it is not teleological in structure and does not refer to either *eudaimonia* or human nature. It is consistent with exemplarism that *what makes* an exemplar good is that he or she has traits that are constitutive of *eudaimonia* or that lead to the fulfilment of human nature, but the theory does not require that that be the case. To return to the analogue of natural kinds, we have discovered that what makes something water is that it is H_2O, but that has been settled by scientific investigation, not by the way 'water' is defined. Similarly, it may turn out that what makes the exemplar good are certain descriptive properties or the fact that he or she leads a life of a certain kind or the fact that he or she fulfills the potentialities of human nature, but that need not be settled in advance of the construction of the theory. We need not refer to any of these features of the exemplar in defining 'good person'.

I have been working on a particular form of exemplarist virtue theory that I call Divine Motivation theory. This theory is a form of a non-teleological virtue theory I call motivation-based, but it has a foundation in God's motives. The main idea of motivation-based virtue theory is to derive all moral concepts from the concept of a good motive, where what I mean by a motive is an emotional state that initiates and directs action towards an end. A virtue is defined as an enduring trait consisting of a good motive-disposition and reliable success in reaching the end (if any) of the good motive. Moral properties of acts (right, wrong, duty) in a set of circum-

---

[26] For recent discussion of this issue see L. S. Rouner (ed.), *Is There a Human Nature?* (Notre Dame, Ind.: University of Notre Dame Press, 1997).

stances are defined in terms of what virtuous persons would characteristically do, would characteristically not do, or might do in relevantly similar circumstances. Good outcomes are defined in terms of the aims of good motives. The theory is exemplarist because the basic concept in the theory, that of a good motive, is defined via reference to the motives of a paradigmatically good person.

The structure of motivation-based virtue theory is quite general and it can have religious or secular forms, depending upon the identity of the paradigms. Divine Motivation Theory is the Christian form of motivation-based virtue theory. It is motivation-based virtue theory with a foundation in God's motives. God is the paradigmatically good person in the theory. Value in all forms derives from God's motives. A very brief outline of the theory is as follows: the paradigmatically good person is God. Value in all forms derives from God's motives. God's motives are perfectly good and human motives are good, insofar as they are like the divine motives as those motives would be expressed in finite and embodied beings.[27] Motive-dispositions are constituents of virtues. God's virtues are paradigmatically good personal traits. Human virtues are those traits that imitate God's virtues as they would be expressed by human beings in human circumstances. The goodness of a state of affairs is derivative from the goodness of the divine motive, not the other way around. So outcomes get their moral value by their relation to good and bad motivations. For example, a state of affairs is a merciful one or a compassionate one or a just one, because the divine motives that are constituents of mercy, compassion, and justice respectively aim at bringing them about. Finally, acts get their moral value from the acts that would, would not, or might be done by God in the relevant circumstances.

What can it mean to say that a human virtue is a trait God would have if he were human? What can it mean to say that a wrong act is an act God would never do if he were human and were in relevantly similar circumstances? What can it mean to say that a good state of affairs is one God would be motivated to bring about? We cannot expect a procedure for determining the answers to these questions,

---

[27] In my view a motive is an emotional state and God has emotions. But Divine Motivation theory does not require accepting the controversial position that God has emotions. It suffices to say that God's motives are related to human emotions analogously. God has emotions in the same sense in which he has beliefs. I explore the issue of God's emotions and virtues in 'The Virtues of God and the Foundations of Ethics', *Faith and Philosophy*, 15: 4 (Oct. 1998), 538–53.

but we have a revelation of value in the incarnation. The life of Christ is a narrative that illuminates a point of view from which we can see a number of exemplary acts, and especially exemplary motives and the virtues of which they are constituents. The message of the Sermon on the Mount is a call to us to do the same, to transform our motives into a life of love and compassion.

Many Christian theologians and ethicists have written penetrating discussions of the Gospel narratives for the ethical viewpoint they reveal. I will not try to add anything to that work. My purpose here is to show that an ethics centred in Gospel narratives can be given a viable theoretical foundation that would be desirable even apart from the needs of Christian ethics. An exemplarist virtue theory is the only form of ethical theory I can think of that harmonizes well with an ethic of the imitation of Christ. The ultimate ground of moral value for all human motives, traits, acts, and aims is the motives, traits, acts, and aims of Christ. Divine Motivation theory requires the doctrine of the incarnation, because the theory needs both a human exemplar to whom we can refer in moral discourse and a divine metaphysical ground for value. The theory needs a God-man to serve both roles.

In the last section I raised the possibility that we could find out necessary truths about the nature of good persons empirically for the same reason that we can find out necessary truths about the nature of water and gold empirically. In Divine Motivation Theory (and in motivation-based virtue theory in general) the motivational structure of a good person is parallel to the chemical structure of water. It is a necessary truth that the motivational structure of a good person is the motivational structure of Christ, just as it is a necessary truth that the chemical structure of water is H_2O. Clearly, however, there are disanalogies between water and a good person that make my theory more complicated than a theory of natural kinds, since motivational structure is much more complex than chemical structure, and we permit many variations in the motivational structure of a good person, whereas we permit no variation at all in the chemical structure of water. That means that to imitate Christ is not to aim to be an exact copy of Christ. Another reason why imitation is not copying is that Jesus had a distinctive mission which the rest of us do not have. But each of us does have a mission and each of us should be as faithful to it as Jesus was to his.

There are many ways to imitate Christ, and that is why there are so many different kinds of saints. Some saints exemplify one moral trait in an extraordinary degree, such as Mother Teresa. Others excel because of the overall quality of their character. They possess the full complement of virtues in a uniformly admirable life. These saints may not stand out for any particular admirable quality, but they are morally worthy in the whole of their lives. Others, such as St Thomas More or Oskar Schindler, are exemplary because of a single noble decision. Which saints a person should imitate is probably determined partly by his or her life circumstances and partly by his or her individual moral personality. Of course, there are also exemplars in other religions, such as the Buddhist arahant, the Confucian sage, and the Jewish tzaddik.[28] I will not attempt here a discussion of moral pluralism and its challenge to Christian ethics, which is a problem no matter what kind of theory the Christian chooses, but it is worth pointing out that exemplarist virtue theory can have either an inclusivist or an exclusivist form. There is nothing in the structure of the theory itself that requires one rather than the other.

In traditional Christian philosophy it is taken for granted that in a very important sense God is the foundation of all value. God is good and everything that is good or bad is good or bad because of something about God. Acts derive their rightness or wrongness from God. This has most often been interpreted to mean that something is right or wrong because God commands it or forbids it. Divine Command theory has a very long history in Western ethics. In fact, its only serious rival among those who think ethics should have a theological foundation is Natural Law theory. But from what has already been said about the structure of a moral theory, I think we can see that both Divine Command theory and Natural Law theory presuppose something about ethical theory that is arguable: they assume that an ethical theory is a way of system-atizing rules or principles for human action that have a law-like form. Both are act-based, not virtue-based theories. To return to the observations of Bonhoeffer, the will of God is not an idea waiting to become real; an ethic of law is that of the OT. The law is fulfilled in the incarnation and after Christ ethics has the purpose of achieving participation in the reality of the fulfilled will of God. That leads to an ethic of imitation rather than law.

[28] See R. Adams, 'Saints', *Journal of Philosophy*, 81 (1984), 392–401.

This is not to deny the place of law in Christian virtue ethics. The place of divine commands in Divine Motivation theory is parallel to the place of laws and principles in any form of pure virtue theory: they are derivative. One of the things we see in imitating Christ is that Jesus was obedient to the Father; Jesus followed his Father's commandments. But the moral life of Jesus was not exhausted by the following of divine commands. He taught that the entire moral law can be summed up in the two great commandments of love—to love God with our whole hearts and to love our neighbour as ourselves, but even here the law is subsumed under the motive of love.

IV THE SELF VS. THE EXEMPLAR

Human beings have an innate propensity for imitation, but that does not mean imitation has been unchallenged as a method for learning the most important human behaviour. Even if we can identify the morally best persons, some of us hesitate to model ourselves on them. The complaint is not that we do not want to be good and even as good as we can be, but that we want to be ourselves. In modern philosophy being oneself usually means making one's own decisions, making up one's own mind about what to do, perhaps even making up one's own mind about the kind of person one wants to be. That might mean consulting reason, but even then, it is one's own reason that one wants to consult. Iris Murdoch reminds us how riveting Kant is when he says that even when confronted with Christ, a man still consults his own reason:

How recognizable, how familiar to us, is the man so beautifully portrayed in the *Grundlegung*, who confronted even with Christ turns away to consider the judgement of his own conscience and to hear the voice of his own reason. Stripped of the exiguous metaphysical background which Kant was prepared to allow him, this man is with us still, free, independent, lonely, powerful, rational, responsible, brave, the hero of so many novels and books of moral philosophy.[29]

Is the man who consults his own reason when confronted with Christ a hero or an anti-hero? Dostoevsky's Grand Inquisitor is just

---

[29] I. Murdoch, 'The Sovereignty of Good', in id., *The Sovereignty of Good and Other Essays* (London: Routledge & Kegan Paul, 1970), 101.

such a man.[30] Murdoch believes that the centre of this way of looking at ethics is the notion of the will as the creator of value. When a society that once embraced Divine Command theory gives up belief in God, values collapse into the human will. I am proposing the reverse move: keep God in value theory but give up the idea that values are rooted in a will. Nonetheless, I want it to be clear that I know what the alternative is . . . and how attractive it is in its own way. But that way has been tried, and Murdoch's assessment of its subsequent history may temper our enthusiasm. Here is the continuation of the passage just quoted:

The *raison d'être* of this attractive but misleading creature is not far to seek. He is the offspring of the age of science, confidently rational and yet increasingly aware of his alienation from the material universe which his discoveries reveal; and since he is not a Hegelian (Kant, not Hegel, has provided Western ethics with its dominating image), his alienation is without cure. He is the ideal citizen of the liberal state, a warning held up to tyrants. He has the virtue which the age requires and admires, courage. It is not such a very long step from Kant to Nietzsche, and from Nietzsche to existentialism and the Anglo-Saxon ethical doctrines which in some ways closely resemble it. In fact Kant's man had already received a glorious incarnation nearly a century earlier in the work of Milton: his proper name is Lucifer.

I suggest we heed Murdoch's warning. Perhaps she overstates the consequences of adopting the Kantian imperative of making the will the centre of value. But better to be like Christ than Lucifer.

[30] I thank Eberhard Hermann for reminding me how the Grand Inquisitor fits Kant's description of the autonomous man in the passage mentioned above.

15

The Incarnation in Twentieth-Century Art

DAVID BROWN

The choice of title is deliberate. My focus will be doctrinal. At the heart of Christianity lies the assertion that Jesus Christ was (and is) at once divine and human. So in what follows I want to examine which particular aspects of that humanity or divinity the artists selected have chosen to focus on, the means they have employed to achieve their purpose (particularly in respect of divinity), and finally what the Christian viewer might learn from them. Immediately, though, the objection must be answered that great Christian art is now firmly in the past. Certainly, there is no denying that the twentieth century witnessed a great decline in the quantity and quality of art with explicit Christian reference. Not only has the church long since ceased to be the artist's principal patron, but also the general retreat from representational art and unfamiliarity with the details of Christ's story has meant that, insofar as Christ's life is treated at all, reference is now largely confined to his birth, death, and resurrection. Even so, this has still produced some great art, and we need also to recall that, although the amount of explicitly Christian art is in decline, there is no shortage of Western artists who have seen their main objective in spiritual or religious terms. One thinks, for instance, of Brancusi in sculpture or in painting of Kandinsky, Klee, and Mondrian in Europe or of Newman and Rothko in the United States. One other factor that needs to be borne in mind is that the use of Christian symbols has been by no means confined to artists with an explicit Christian faith. In some cases, as we shall see, their art succeeds in capturing important aspects of that faith, but, even where the intention was hostile, such art can still sometimes present a pertinent critique that the church needs to face. So, in what follows I shall survey art of both kinds. To avoid too much subjectivity, I shall focus on those who have achieved wide public recognition in the art world, thus ignoring at the one extreme more popular forms of representation and at the other artists whose religious work in my view deserves a better evaluation than it has hitherto received.[1] Also, to make my task manageable, I shall exclude at one end of the century all artists who had already achieved distinction before the end of the First World War and at the other any who may still be among us. Sculpture will be treated briefly at the end of this essay. I begin with painting.

I PAINTING

Later I shall look at the work of some artists without Christian belief, among them Bacon and Picasso, but I begin with those who saw themselves as practising Christians. Here the range of approach is much larger than might initially have been anticipated, but this perhaps becomes less surprising to the reader when reminded that the list must include Dalí and Warhol as well as more obvious cases such as Rouault and Spencer.

Georges Rouault (d. 1958) is often regarded as the greatest religious painter of the twentieth century. Reasons for singling him out can be both good and bad. Among the bad, it seems to me, must be put the moral quality of his life and his extensive contacts with the theology and spirituality of his time. No doubt these helped shape his intentions, but it puts matters the wrong way round if we suppose that artistic creativity of the appropriate kind is only an appendage to such qualities. These can enhance already existing gifts, but are no substitute for them.[2] Again, to draw attention to the iconic character of his painting explains little, except perhaps its accessibility as religious art. It is surely because

---

[1] The former qualification is intended to exclude the work of someone like Warner Sallman (d. 1968), who despite the art critics became the most reproduced religious artist in 20th-cent. America, estimates suggesting more than 50 m. reproductions; for a serious examination of the reasons for such popularity (see D. Morgan (ed.), *Icons of American Protestantism: The Art of Warner Sallman* (New Haven: Yale University Press, 1996). An example of the latter would be the Expressionist religious paintings of Emil Nolde, unjustly neglected in my view in favour of his landscapes; for an interesting attempt to redress the balance see M. Reuther, *Emile Nolde: naturaleza y religión* (Madrid: Fundación Juan, 1997).

[2] For understanding the intellectual and spiritual influences on him, particularly helpful is W. A. Dyrness, *Rouault: A Vision of Suffering and Salvation* (Grand Rapids, Mich.: Eerdmans, 1971). In my view, though, he wrongly finds in the paintings an emphasis on evil, and suffering as punishment for sin, e.g. pp. 108, 144–5.

he is so much more than just a traditional icon painter that his painting can speak so powerfully to our own age.[3] But how exactly? As pupil of Gustave Moreau and custodian of the museum eventually founded in Moreau's honour, Rouault was used to the question of how symbolism might best be employed in painting.[4] Where part of his originality lies is in his combining of conventional iconic techniques (such as the elongated face) with his own distinctive symbolism, a symbolism that draws from us a recognition of Christ's transcendent identity without us always being aware that this is what has happened.

Part of the reason for that success is that Christ's humanity is not made fundamentally different from our own. It was not until 1914 that religious painting began to bulk large in Rouault's oeuvre, and by then he had already established a distinctive style in portraying the human figure, one seen clearly in his series on prostitutes and circus acts.[5] There is no sense of condemnation, but an empathetic entering into the sadness of their lot, and this is then what we are offered in his presentations of Christ. Christ is seen as entering into the sadness of the human condition, but to make that point Rouault finds no need to accentuate Christ's sufferings. It is enough to know that he is one of us. But were that all, there would of course be no message of hope. Sometimes that other side is shown quite conventionally in the traditional halo, but more commonly one finds techniques such as the range of colours surrounding his head or, more dramatically, the sun or moon either on its own or as a complement to light or colour round Christ's himself suggesting that wider transcendent significance.[6] It is only as one becomes familiar with a number of his paintings that one notices what an important role the sky has played in arousing in the viewer some sense of cosmic significance.

---

[3] Yet to my mind he remained too firmly locked into past tradition, and so failed to become as great a painter as he might have been.

[4] His earliest paintings in fact closely follow Moreau in style, as in his *Dead Christ Mourned* of 1895 in which obscure light and a lengthy body are used to give a supernatural significance to Christ that the women present lack.

[5] One of the finest is *Prostitute at her Mirror* of 1906: for an illustration, no. 5 in J. M. Faerna, *Georges Rouault* (New York: Abrams, 1996), 14.

[6] For use of colour, including band of red, note two *Heads of Christ*, ibid. 58, 59 (nos. 66, 67); for illustrations of sun or moon acting on its own, his autumn miracle paintings of 1952, ibid. 52, 53 (nos. 58, 59), also Plate 1; for acting in combination with a reflected radiance round Christ, R. Chiappini, *Georges Rouault* (Milan: Skira, 1997), illus. 64, 73–5. In *Christ in the Suburbs*, the moon reflects the whiteness of Christ's robes.

One criticism that could be made, though, is that it is hard to point to a painting by him that speaks of unqualified joy. It is perhaps significant that he chooses to represent Jesus' early life with the flight into Egypt,[7] while a rare Virgin and Child has the infant holding an apple with an infinitely sad expression.[8] Equally, use of resurrection appearances is rare and not at all as hopeful as one might have expected. Perhaps he found the image of the crucified Christ too evocative of suffering easily to speak another message. At all events, the significance of the living Christ emerges much more clearly when transferred to a modern context such as in his well-known *Christ in the Suburbs*.[9] There his cosmic symbolism is once more to be found, though a little surprisingly not the church tower that is so familiar from some of his other paintings.

Overall, though, such contemporary allusions are not all that frequent in Rouault, whereas with Stanley Spencer (d. 1959) they become dominant. Although highly regarded in England, it has taken a recent exhibition in Washington to begin to establish for him a comparable reputation in the United States.[10] If the iconic character of Rouault's work sometimes gives the strong impression that one is being drawn into an alternative world, with Spencer's religious painting the experience is quite different. Here the sense is of this world transformed. That sensation corresponds with Spencer's own experience, for from childhood onwards he had a very lively awareness of the presence of God in the everyday life of the village in which he was brought up, Cookham in Berkshire.[11]

When one turns to consider the impact of such experience on his painting, one observes the humanity of Christ very firmly set in Spencer's own contemporary setting. One observes too that he is not always even the most prominent figure in the picture, as indeed

---

[7] Chiappini, *Georges Rouault*, illus. 60 (105).

[8] No. 56 in the *Miserere* engraving series. 'Presque jamais traité ailleurs'; so B. Dorival in *Le Miserere* (Montréal: Musée de l'oratoire Saint-Joseph, 1979), 15.

[9] Another example would be his *Stella Vespertina* (1946), in which Christ watches over a sleeping child: Chiappini, *Georges Rouault*, illus. 66 (121); or his *Judges* (1912), where a crucifix is used to bring under judgement all systems of merely human justice.

[10] The exhibition in 1997 at the Hirshhorn in Washington was a great critical success.

[11] He talks of his experience of the 'Wesleyan heaven' in childhood chapel worship: F. MacCarthy, *Stanley Spencer: An English Vision* (New Haven: Yale University Press, 1998), 8–9. Again, as an adult he declares: 'Everything I see is manifestly religious': ibid. 49.

must sometimes have been the case for Jesus in real life. So he sometimes appears ignored or almost forgotten, as in *Christ's Entry into Jerusalem* (1921) or *Christ Preaching at Cookham Regatta* (1955).[12] Sometimes, though, such apparent reduction of significance adds eventually to the overall impact. This is particularly true of the central panel of his major commission at Burghclere Chapel. Granted the prominence given at the front of the painting to men rising from their graves and the collapsed wagon at its centre, initially one could easily fail to notice Christ at all. But the eye is eventually drawn up through both scenes to a small Christ presiding over the whole. Medieval and Renaissance conventions for such portrayals of the resurrection of the dead would have led one to expect a large and imposing figure, but it is arguable that Spencer's small figure is all the more effective, precisely because the eye only finds him after it has observed the attendant consequences of Christ's own resurrection.[13]

In these paintings there is little or nothing to suggest divinity in the figure himself. One has thus to look elsewhere for an effective presentation of Christ's dual nature. In Spencer's *Nativity* of 1912 this is achieved through the traditional means of light surrounding the infant, though an unfortunate consequence follows: Mary, his mother, is given a dark, almost forbidding presence.[14] Light is also used in Spencer's portrayal of the Arrest. But the more common method is perhaps one of scale, with Christ's physical size and presence dominating a particular painting. This is true of the Wilderness series, where the result is, as Spencer intended, a strong sense of God's care for all creation.[15] In portraying Christ's careful attention to scorpions and lilies, Spencer comments that 'in Christ, God again beholds his creation'.[16] One notes too the scale of

---

[12] For illustration of former, no. 11 in MacCarthy, *Stanley Spencer*; for latter, D. Robinson, *Stanley Spencer* (London: Phaidon, 2nd edn., 1992), 114–19.

[13] Illustrated, MacCarthy, *Stanley Spencer*, 30. It has led some commentators to find a self-created 'resurrection': e. g. K. Pople, *Stanley Spencer: A Biography* (London: Collins, 1991), 269–70. But this is contradicted both by Spencer himself and by his brother, Gilbert, also a painter; for former, Pople, 274; for brother, G. Spencer, *Stanley Spencer by his Brother, Gilbert* (Bristol: Redcliffe, 1961), 147.

[14] For illustration, Robinson, *Stanley Spencer*, no. 2.

[15] For illustration, *The Scorpion* in MacCarthy, *Stanley Spencer*, no. 42.

[16] Quoted in Pople, *Stanley Spencer*, 399. There is also a splendid pencil drawing of the *Baptism of Christ* from the 1940s that portrays Christ seated in the water with fish happily swimming around him: C. Leder, *Barbara Karmel Bequest* (Cookham: Stanley Spencer Gallery, 1996), no. 12.

his Jesus in *The Last Supper* (1920), where Christ's head alone rises above the line of the surrounding brick wall. But no less important in that painting is the way in which all the disciples have their legs raised in the air. Although Spencer gave a flippant answer when asked why this was so, and in part the explanation must lie in an allusion to John's Gospel and the washing of the disciples' feet, it is perhaps not too fanciful to see the device as a means of suggesting that Christ by his presence exalts his disciples onto an altogether different and higher plane.[17] In a similar way in his portrayal of Christ praying in the wilderness, a bursting shell and Christ's upper gaze are used very effectively to indicate the birth of a new world.[18]

One unusual aspect of Spencer's approach is the great variety of different facial features he is prepared to give to Christ. So, for example, he fails to adopt any consistent iconography in respect of whether he was bearded or not, round or square-faced, and so on. Thus, in marked contrast with Rouault, it is impossible immediately to identify the face of a Spencer Christ. Instead, we find constant experimentation.[19] Another contrast with Rouault is his attitude to evil and suffering. Spencer's life was by no means free of suffering. A favourite brother died in the First World War, another of alcoholism.[20] There was also the tragic consequences of his love for two women, Hilda and Patricia, involving as it did two sets of divorce proceedings, loss of home, and the eventual confinement of Hilda to a mental hospital, where Spencer visited her each week despite their divorce and the difficulties of war-time travel.[21] Even so, the mood of his paintings is overwhelmingly optimistic. Only in *Christ Delivered to the People* of 1950 and *The Crucifixion* of 1958 does he imply Christ's need to confront real evil.[22] So it is perhaps not surprising that none of his various general resurrections alludes to the punishment of the

[17] The flippant answer given to a child was that the disciples were a bit bored and so stretching their legs: Pople, *Stanley Spencer*, 196. For illustration, Plate 2.

[18] MacCarthy, *Stanley Spencer*, no. 43.

[19] In his *Cookham Resurrection* of 1924–6 we even find Christ treated as a maternal figure, shown nursing two babies close to his bosom, and looking distinctly more female than male, for illustration, K. Bell, *Stanley Spencer* (London: Phaidon, 1999 edn.), 70–1.

[20] Sydney, an intending ordinand, was killed during the First World War, while Horace became an alcoholic and died while under the influence in a tragic accident in 1941.

[21] More accurately, annulment in the case of Patricia Preece, whose real love was Dorothy Hepworth.

[22] For latter, MacCarthy, *Stanley Spencer*, no. 62.

wicked, nor that when asked to paint angels of the Apocalypse he modified Scripture to remove their more negative role.[23] In defending one of his own paintings he was moved to observe how frequently in earlier Christian tradition the crucifixion had been portrayed as a joyful event, with stress on its positive and redemptive character brought to the fore.[24] That kind of perspective helps to make sense of one of his more unusual crucifixion scenes, where the crosses are placed in three separate ravines and the observers on the ridge above. His intention appears to have been to recall his own earlier experience of facing three such ravines in war-time Macedonia when his spirits were at a low ebb only to have them exalted by a sense of divine presence.[25] The emphasis thus falls on God pulling us out of the ravine rather than on what we must endure while there. Again, though the outstretched arms in *The Coming of the Wise Men* (1940) seem clearly to allude to the crucifixion, as possibly also the three mirrors behind, it is an allusion that has almost already become a paean of praise, so prominent are the exalted arms.   Perhaps most surprising of all is his depiction of the Deposition where we find Christ already fully awake.[26]

One generalization that is still commonly made in comparing Catholic and Protestant approaches to the world is to declare that the former is more world-affirming than the latter. The contrast between Rouault and Spencer demonstrates that any plausibility such a contrast may have is likely to be heavily dependent on specific contexts, for certainly with these two artists matters are the other way round. Spencer is much the more world-affirming of the two, yet his background and religious practice, though nominally Anglican, was really more Protestant still.[27] Admittedly, in later life

[23]   The story of how the angels of Rev. 16 moved from distributing vials of wrath to pouring out fresh seed on the earth is told in Pople, *Stanley Spencer*, 468–9.

[24]   He makes the comment when defending the contented and hopeful character of his painting of 1919, *Travoys with Wounded Soldiers*: for illustration and Spencer's comments, MacCarthy, *Stanley Spencer*, no. 7.

[25]   For illustration of 1921 painting, MacCarthy, *Stanley Spencer*, no. 10; for the connection with Macedonia, Pople, *Stanley Spencer*, 205.

[26]   For illustration of *Coming of Wise Men* (1940), Bell, *Stanley Spencer*, 163; for illustration of *Deposition* (1956), ibid. 234; for perceptive discussion of the latter, Pople, *Stanley Spencer*, 487–91.

[27]   Initially he attended a Methodist chapel with his mother, but when this acquired a new building, they moved to the local parish church. But his brother notes that this was just as low-church, and that their father refused to have the boys confirmed, despite continuing in weekly church attendance: G. Spencer, *Stanley Spencer*, 55, 76, 82–4, 154.

he had some important Catholic contacts,[28] but long before these his view of the world as thoroughly imbued with the divine presence had already been formed. Not only should this fact warn us against facile contrasts, it might also be taken as support for the need to complement artistic visions with one another rather than see them as necessarily opposed. This is emphatically not to suggest that none should be excluded. Criteria are still obviously necessary, but it is unwise to pre-empt any such decisions, as indeed the case of Spencer's own wife, Hilda, illustrates. Her commitment to Christian Science with its denial of the reality of the physical world might be thought to preclude any religious worth to her painting, but in fact, despite this, they display as much engagement with the reality of the world as any other competent or serious painter. Spencer seems to have seen this, and so found no difficulty in valuing her art, despite their in theory quite opposed motivations.[29]

The dangers in confusing motivation and content are even better illustrated in the next artist whom I wish to consider, Salvador Dalí (d. 1989). Although his father was at the time an atheist, Dalí did receive a religious education,[30] but this he rejected and became quite virulent in his endorsement of atheism, particularly during the Surrealist period that generated some of his most famous paintings. Indeed, the content of some is most naturally interpreted as blasphemous.[31] Even so, in early middle age he announced his conversion to Catholicism,[32] and the result was a quite different form of art. Many art critics insist upon seeing this period as significantly less creative, some even talking of 'repetitive

---

[28] Desmond Chute, who eventually became a Roman Catholic priest, was for some years a close friend, and introduced him to Eric Gill (not a success). Gilbert mentions as an aberration he and Stanley as children making paper nuns (*Stanley Spencer*, 37).

[29] For an excellent discussion of their relationship, and some illustrations of her paintings, A. Thomas, *The Art of Hilda Carline* (London: Lund Humphries, 1999).

[30] After an unsuccessful attempt at secular education, he was entrusted to a school of the Christian Brothers.

[31] As in two paintings of 1929, *The Lugubrious Game* and *The Profanation of the Host*. For illustration and commentary, I. Gibson, *The Shameful Life of Salvador Dalí* (London: Faber & Faber, 1997), 215–16, 282, and illus. XV and XVIII. There was also his sexual reading of Millet's *Angelus* of 1859 that resulted in quite a number of paintings of his own, as well as a monograph on the subject that he eventually published in 1962. For some examples, R. Descharnes and G. Néret, *Salvador Dalí* (Cologne: Taschen, 1993), 76–83.

[32] The first hints were in his closing pages of his autobiography *The Secret Life*, published in 1942 when he was still only 38, but it was only with his return to Europe in 1948 and his meeting with Pius XII the subsequent year that definitive signs begin to emerge in his art.

kitsch'.[33] One complication in its assessment is that it also went with enthusiasm for Franco's Spain, and in consequence some have suggested that his endorsement of fascism and Catholicism were alike inspired by purely pragmatic considerations, his desire to live in Spain.[34] But, so far as fascism is concerned, a more plausible interpretation seems to me to lie in the deep psychological need that he appears to have had throughout his life for authority figures, as is witnessed also at a more personal level by his relations with friends such as Lorca and James, and more especially with his wife, Gala.[35] Indeed, if this does not sound too patronizing, much of his outrageous conduct can be glossed as the acts of a spoilt but insecure child who never quite reached adulthood.[36] As for the sincerity of his religious conversion, that too went with some absurd acts of self-ostentation, but there were also moments when a humbler seeker after faith came through.[37] My point in summarizing this complex history and arguing for a more sympathetic interpretation than is customary is not to turn Dalí into a conventional Catholic, but rather to note that, however strange some of his ideas and behaviour were at this time, the motivation does seem to have been ultimately religious.

Although Dalí's religious corpus is a large one, most of it is not directly relevant to our theme here, but concern such topics as the Assumption of Mary, an ecumenical council, Mary Magdalene, or the role of the church in the discovery of America.[38] Here I shall focus on seven of his presentations of Christ's significance, including

---

[33] So Gibson, *Shameful Life*, 463. Paintings from the years before his conversion, 1926–38 are described as 'his real claim to our admiration': ibid. 629.

[34] The view of Gibson, but also of other biographers, e.g. M. Etherington-Smith, *Dalí* (London: Sinclair-Stevenson, 1992), 305. It was also the interpretation given by some of his friends, such as Edward James: ibid. 249, 383.

[35] As Etherington-Smith herself seems to admit at one point, when she talks of his need for 'another benevolent bully:' *Dalí*, 143. All are agreed that Gala certainly fulfilled that role.

[36] His published autobiography is so obviously designed to shock and mislead that biographers have rightly focused on some unusual features in his childhood: e.g. M. Secrest, *Salvador Dalí* (New York: Dutton, 1986), 7–69.

[37] Gibson doubts his regular attendance at mass, but, uncharacteristically, his religious marriage was done without ostentation as were his prayers for Franco's recovery: pp. 466, 492, 563. One should also note his repeated anxious expression of a lack of sufficient faith: various admissions quoted in Etherington-Smith, *Dalí*, 324; Secrest, *Salvador Dalí*, 253.

[38] *Lapis-lazuli Corpuscular Assumption* (1952), *Discovery of America* (1959), *Life of Mary Magdalene* (1960), *The Ecumenical Council* (1960): for illustrations, R. Descharnes and G. Néret, *Dalí* (Cologne: Taschen, 1997), 454, 510, 525, 530.

some of the best-known. Probably the most familiar is his *Last Supper* of 1955. Notoriously, Tillich objected to it on the grounds that not only was it sentimental and trite but also that Jesus resembled a 'very good athlete on an American baseball team'.[39] But in response one wants to ask whether, just as artists in the past employed suitable models from those around them, Dalí was not right to do this also, as a way of underlying the ordinariness of Christ's humanity. His decision to use a common tumbler for the wine also adds point to the contemporary relevance of the scene. If we then ask how the divinity is conveyed, one notes not only the use of light and Christ pointing to a large human frame stretching like a vast cruciform body above him, but also a small boat swimming in front of his chest as though already initiating a journey that will endorse his final status as exalted to heaven. If one objects that there is little or nothing in the painting to suggest suffering, it is important to note that Dalí was consciously rebelling against the tradition of Christian art that had taken its inspiration from Grünewald as its norm.[40] In his view the famous Isenheim altarpiece went too far in materializing Christ, whereas what he thought contemporary physics was showing is the ultimate dissolution of matter, and this indeed he sought to portray in a series of paintings, not directly relevant here.[41] One can see the effect, though, in one of his crucifixions, the *Corpus Hypercubus* of 1954.[42] Here he goes back to much earlier theories, but the effect is the same. There is no obvious sign of suffering, and one of the cubes seems in effect already to be pushing Christ off the cross and heavenward.

Does that mean that we should accuse Dalí of a Gnostic approach that fails to take suffering seriously? In part one might be justified, but again it needs to be balanced by his non-religious paintings which had already identified many of the more gruesome elements

---

[39] Quoted in Secrest, *Salvador Dalí*, 216.

[40] In his *Mystical Manifesto* of 1951 Dalí writes: 'I want my next Christ to be the painting containing the most beauty and joy that has ever been painted up to today. I want to paint a Christ who will be absolutely the contrary in everything from the materialistic and savagely anti-mystic Christ of Grünewald': quoted in Descharnes and Néret, *Dalí* (1997), 471.

[41] For some examples, Descharnes and Néret, *Dalí* (1993), 160–1; id., *Dalí* (1997), 444–5, 458–9. One might also note his absurd lunch with Crick and Watson, Etherington-Smith, *Dalí*, 408.

[42] For illustration and commentary, R. Descharnes, *Dalí* (New York: Abrams, 1993), 154–5. The cubic theories he employs go back ultimately to Raymond Lull (d. 1315).

in the world. So it might perhaps be more accurate to speak of a lack of integration between the two types of reality, the earthly and the divine, rather than any failure to acknowledge how awful the world can sometimes be. The kind of tensions he may have felt are to be observed in some of the contrasts one finds between an earlier sketch and the final version of his *Nativity of a New World* (1942).[43] In the earlier version Coca-Cola and other obvious modern artefacts are among the Magi's gifts, whereas in the later a shepherd's gift of a lamb is substituted. On the other hand, whereas in the earlier version the infant Christ is portrayed as happily playing within the large globe that represents at once a womb and the world to which he is the key, with the later version we find the newly born infant lying by the bubble's side, looking distinctly frail and uncertain of its future. Similarly, in the better-known *Madonna of Port Lligat* of 1950 we again find two versions.[44] It is only in the later and better-known version that finally not only does Mary reveal the child in her womb but also that the child discloses the bread and wine within itself. Future pain is not made explicit but there seems little doubt that an allusion is intended, with the eucharistic elements meant also to point to the crucifixion, not least because in the egg suspended above Mary we have a reference to the third key element in the story of Jesus, his resurrection.[45]

So it is perhaps fairer to suggest that Dalí preferred allusions to the whole story of Christ, suffering and all, rather than specific identifications with the less pleasant aspects of life, which he found difficult to detach from the sordid. There is, however, one exception to this pattern that is worth noting, and that is his *Debris Christ* of 1969, created on a Spanish hillside. Ordinary detritus, including an old boat, are here used to create a suffering Christ laid flat out, presumably in death, and with the crown of thorns still upon him.[46] Even so, it is interesting to observe that the colour of the branches and roof tiles used naturally reflect the light, and so can easily be taken to imply that not all is in fact lost. Similarly, his late *Pietà*, based though it is on Michelangelo's famous version, refuses to leave us with a picture of sorrow, but instead allows the

---

[43] For illustrations of both, Descharnes and Néret, *Dalí* (1997), 354.

[44] The earlier version dates from 1949; for illustrations of both, ibid. 426, 443.

[45] A piece of symbolism not used arbitrarily by Dalí, but rather in conscious awareness of its central role in Piero della Francesca's famous painting, *Madonna with the Duke of Urbino as Donor*.

[46] Illustrated in Descharnes and Néret, *Dalí* (1997), 607.

yellow of Christ's skin to suggest a light to come, just as the land and seascapes that replace Mary's breasts imply a hope for the future, even if it can no longer come through the milk of a mother's breasts.[47] So perhaps we should view what seems to me his finest religious painting as also his most typical, his famous *Christ of St John of the Cross* of 1951, now in Glasgow. Here a tiny figure in a bright dawn gazes up to a vast figure of Christ on the cross looking down upon us. The mood is overwhelmingly one of confidence and hope and of mystical identification with the glorified Christ, which is perhaps not surprising since it was modelled on the only drawing of one of his visions St John ever did. That saint and mystic was far from being unaware of the importance of the suffering Christ. Dalí, though, only allows this element to emerge indirectly, in the fact that Christ looks down to earth, with face concealed and head bowed.[48] The hint is there, but it remains a hint, since the angle of the cross continues to pull our vision heavenward.[49] So generally we look in vain for the complete integration of the Christian message in Dalí's work, however powerfully he succeeded in capturing its more positive aspects.

If some recoil from Dalí's religious art, with Andy Warhol (d. 1987) art in general is often viewed as at its most shallow and frivolous. Not only does his version of Pop Art appear to celebrate consumerism and the exaltation of the purely ephemeral, it is also hard to detect any clear moral content, when pop stars and politicians, car crashes and murderers are all subjected to essentially the same kind of treatment. Yet the eulogy at the memorial service in St Patrick's Cathedral in New York went so far as to describe him as a sort of saint,[50] while the last few years of his life did result in a number of memorable religious paintings. As it now turns out, he continued to attend church throughout his life, regularly carried with him the symbols of his

---

[47] From 1982. Illustrated, ibid. 698.

[48] By way of justification, Dalí noted that this was how John had also portrayed Christ, the angle being the same as that at which a crucifix might be presented for a dying person to kiss, but, significantly, the weight on Christ's arms is more pronounced in John's case: to compare the two images, see illustrations ibid. 450–1, also Plate 3.

[49] Once strongly underlined by its hanging at the head of the principal staircase in the Kelvingrove Art Gallery in Glasgow, but now diminished by its rather crowded presentation in another of the city's museums, the new St Mungo Museum of Religious Life and Art.

[50] John Richardson described him as 'one of those saintly simpletons who haunt Russian fiction and Slavic villages'.

religion, and also in later years volunteered to help in serving meals to the poor.[51] But some caution is necessary, for this went with a number of practices that suggest someone who, if not an unbeliever, had scarcely an integrated view of his faith. Perhaps these can all be found to be rooted in an inability to commit himself to others, since biographers repeatedly detect a meanness in dealing with friends and colleagues when down on their luck, as also a preference for voyeurism in sexual relations.[52] A well-known remark of his described the telephone as his best friend;[53] one way to read his art is that it too projected an essential loneliness, its very impersonality helping to make him impervious to possible hurt. Certainly, it would be hard to establish that any deep social comment was intended, since he himself was so much a reflection of his own times, as, for example, in his love of possessions and fame.[54]

From the previous paragraph it might be deduced that my objective is simply to rubbish Warhol's potential significance as an artist, but this is very far from being the case. In fact it is precisely that background that gives his art much of its strength: his deep immersion in American society, combined with his attempt to maintain a protective shell for himself from it, enabled him to reflect more accurately social values of the second half of the twentieth century than perhaps any other artist. The advertising images of the age were, for example, also Warhol's own.[55] Again, his *Marilyn Monroe Diptych* of 1962 succeeds in my view precisely because it was not intended as a critique. The repeated image progressively smudged spoke very effectively of her status as a modern icon, worn through frequent attention in the way that travelling religious diptychs would once have been. It is his images of the incarnation, however, that must be our focus here, and in particular his adaptations of

[51] Ironically, as an alternative to a holiday: so V. Bockris, *The Life and Death of Andy Warhol* (London: Fourth Estate, 1998), 478–9. For his carrying of crucifix, rosary, and missal: D. Bourdon, *Warhol* (New York: Abrams, 1991), 38, 225. Bockris speculates that his father's early death and near death of his mother were decisive in shaping his religious belief, p. 48.

[52] For examples of the former, Bourdon, *Warhol*, 54, 216, 307; one notes also, despite having lived with her most of his life, his failure to visit his mother when confined to a home or even attend her funeral. For examples of his voyeurism, Bockris, *Life and Death of Andy Warhol*, 196, 325, 441.

[53] In a *Stern* interview in 1981 he responded to the question, 'do you have real friends?': 'My friend is the telephone' (Bockris, *Life and Death of Andy Warhol*, 442).

[54] He loved to be asked for his signature, and left a house full of purchases, mostly unpacked: ibid. 234, 495–6.

[55] As in the *Campbell's Soup* acrylics of the early 1960s.

Leonardo's *Last Supper* from 1985 and 1986. Not all work. His attempt to make the divinity more explicit through new symbols, for example, I find somewhat crass. Advertising signs are employed to represent the presence of the other two members of the Trinity, the dove of Dove Soap being used to represent the Holy Spirit and, less obviously, the emblem of GE (General Electric) the Father as creator of light. More effective in my view is the version that introduces motor cycles on either side, with 'the Big C' at the bottom and a 6. 99 dollar sign at the top, framing two images of Christ. If the motor cycles suggest youthful vitality, the big C speaks of the modern fear of death ('The Big C' as cancer), but also of the ability of Christ (another 'Big C') to overcome that fear in the equivalent of a cheap (6. 99 dollar) meal.[56] For those, however, who find the attempt at contemporary relevance too forced, more poignant may be his re-creation of Leonardo's image in a pink hue. Whereas in most of his other versions Leonardo's painting is simplified and the table brought closer to us, here its basic pattern is retained and the pink used to give viewers a strong sense of them being drawn into another dimension.[57] That sense of another dimension is also strongly present in his adaptation of Leonardo's earlier painting of the *Annunciation*, the only one of Warhol's treatments of other ancient masterpieces which I find truly effective. Only the hands of Mary and the angel remain, but their significance is left in no doubt for us by the way in which Warhol highlights, in the space between their hands, the mountain that had been scarcely visible in the background of the original painting. The downward thrust of the divinity in the forthcoming birth is thus very effectively underlined.[58]

Warhol also experimented with images of Virgin and Child, attempting to give them a modern look. Mostly they come across as a purely human couple, but in one he does give the child an interrogating look that harks back to the imagery of previous centuries, while at the same time looking thoroughly modern.[59]

[56] Both paintings are illustrated in J. D. Dillenberger, *The Religious Art of Andy Warhol* (New York: Continuum, 1998), 93, 90–1. Dillenberger offers a valuable study, but I have often found myself in disagreement with her interpretations and evaluations, partly because she credits Warhol with a greater critical distance than I think plausible and partly because she wants to give a positive estimate to all his work.

[57] Illustrated in Dillenberger, *Religious Art*, 104–5. I am unpersuaded by her view that 'baby pink' is used to indicate life and the black elements death.

[58] For illustration, ibid. 51. The screenprint dates from 1984.

[59] His pencil drawing of a *Modern Madonna* of 1981: ibid. 58. Contrast e.g. his *Mother and Child* (ibid. 64).

More commonly praised are his various renderings of the Cross, bare of the human figure but done in a range of colours and sometimes in multiples. One commentator, for instance, finds in them a 'spiritual resonance' that makes for 'a joyous and breathtaking painting'.[60] But to my mind it is the colouring and patterning that appeals rather than some deeper religious meaning. This is perhaps particularly true of the multiple crosses now in Cologne,[61] but even the single exemplar I suspect elicits a positive response from the viewer more in the manner of Warhol's coloured cats of the 1950s rather than by virtue of any inherent religious dimension.[62] To see why this is so, we might compare them with the work of my first representative non-Christian artist, Georgia O'Keeffe (d. 1986). She also uses the same simple image but, I think, to quite different effect.

O'Keeffe is typical of that large band of painters (whom I mentioned earlier) who saw their work in essentially spiritual terms but without any direct influence from Christianity. O'Keeffe had been brought up in a Christian home, but she was to end up refusing any form of religious observance after her death, whether funeral or memorial service. Instead, her ashes were to be spread over the New Mexico desert, and that tribute to nature does indeed represent the source of her inspiration. Both her flowers and animal skull paintings were misunderstood during her lifetime. Her intention seems not to have been sexual or funereal but rather to celebrate nature, and in particular the way in which the microcosm can reflect the mystery of the macrocosm.[63] One might recall Walt Whitman's words: 'I believe that a leaf of grass is no less than the journey-work of the stars.'[64]

Seldom did she find the need to resort to explicit symbolism.[65] A discriminatory choice of subject and use of colour to reflect what she

---

[60] Dillenberger, *Religious Art*, 45.

[61] For illustration of the series of multiples of twelve in various colours, and a comparison with the dissemination of the True Cross in the Middle Ages: R. Rosenblum *et al.*, *Andy Warhol's Crosses* (Cologne: Diocesan Museum, 1999), esp. 21.

[62] For his *Lavender Sam* and *Pink Sam* of 1955, Bourdon, *Warhol*, 58, 59.

[63] For her denial of common readings, R. Robinson, *Georgia O'Keeffe* (London: Bloomsbury, 1990), 282, 368, 421. For a good illustration of the macrocosm/microcosm theme, with painting of a rose also capable of being read as a cloud formation, E. H. Turner, *Georgia O'Keeffe: The Poetry of Things* (New Haven: Yale University Press, 1990), 56, 83.

[64] From *Leaves of Grass* (1855): *Song of Myself*, 31, line 662.

[65] Contrast her use of Indian religious symbolism in her *Ladder to the Moon* of 1958, with the less artificial *Lawrence Tree* of 1929 and the intermediate *From the Faraway Nearby* of 1937: B. Bebke, *Georgia O'Keeffe* (Cologne: Taschen, 1995), 57, 60, 76, 81.

saw were usually enough. However, in 1929 she was confronted by a number of crosses already in the landscape, first in the New Mexican desert and then on the Canadian coast, and these led her into a number of powerful paintings, where landscape and cross interact, and in which, despite her lack of explicit belief, the theme of crucifixion and resurrection seem clearly present. In the Mexican series the crosses were raised as part of the flagellation ritual of the native Indians, and the blackness of the cross reflects this self-imposed suffering, but the colour and pounding life in the mountain behind indicates that such suffering is not to be allowed the last word.[66] The Canadian situation was quite different. There the crosses had been erected to welcome home sailors from long journeys at sea. So, the contrast here is less stark. Even so, one notes the way in which the subtle play of light is used to indicate that hope is not simply confined to the cross itself. Something more can be expected.[67] My point is not that this turns O'Keeffe into a Christian after all. Rather, it is that Christians are entitled to appropriate such art as, however differently conceived, in effect it actually embodies what we already believe.

Not that this will always be so. The twentieth century's most famous artist also turned his hand to images of the crucifixion, but in a way that demeaned its significance. Although Pablo Picasso (d. 1973) had an uncle who was a priest and his two earliest paintings were on religious themes, thereafter there is little to suggest any awareness of the transcendent and indeed these two paintings are entirely conventional and of cloying sentimentality, almost as though he were more concerned to evoke a response than express any convictions of his own.[68] Certainly, not long thereafter we find a crucified Christ with a dog's head and in later years the use of the image in contexts that are most naturally seen as blasphemous, such as obscene relations with Mary Magdalene

---

[66] For illustration of *Black Cross with Red Sky* of 1929: C. C. Eldredge, *Georgia O'Keeffe: American and Modern* (New Haven: Yale University Press, 1993), illus. 61. Note also the hint of the rising sun, which like the life in the mountains is made more explicit in another version from the same year, ibid. 200.

[67] My description of what I regard as the most successful version *Gray Cross with Blue* (Turner, *Georgia O'Keefe*, 125). *Black Cross with Stars and Blue* (Eldredge, *Georgia O'Keeffe*, no. 60) strikes me as too obvious in its symbolism.

[68] *First Communion* of 1896 and *Science and Charity* of 1897; illustrated in C.-P. Warncke and I. F. Walther, *Pablo Picasso* (Cologne: Taschen, 1997), 38, 50–1. One commentator speaks of 'sugary emotionalism': I. F. Walther, *Picasso* (Cologne: Taschen, 1993), 10.

or Christ taking one arm from the cross in order to play the matador.[69] Yet one face from 1959 is tender and genuinely moving,[70] while a whole series of experiments in the 1930s at adapting Grünewald's famous painting to a more cubist or abstract type of representation suggests some real engagement with the image. Yet what remains most significant in these adaptations is the reduction of the event to the purely human. The suggestion of divinity in the upward thrust of the arms in Grünewald's Christ is removed, and in its place comes a figure entirely weighed down by what is happening to him.[71] One surprising development is the introduction of a safety-pin in some later versions, as though Picasso was toying with a new way of effecting traditional attempts to link nativity and crucifixion.[72] Noting similarities to his *Three Dancers* of 1925, however, others have suggested that his ideas were really moving in a quite different direction, that the crucifixion has become part of the ritual 'dance' of sacrificial patterns that are found throughout history.[73] I doubt whether there is the evidence to decide either way. What, however, is worth noting is the possible influence of such experiments on his famous *Guernica* of 1937. There an agonized horse and a glowing sun are used to indicate an event of more than merely domestic significance.[74] Picasso may have discounted the crucifixion, but he could not finally escape its symbolism, however muted this might now appear.

Like Dalí, Max Ernst (d. 1976) and René Magritte (d. 1967) were part of the Surrealist movement, but, unlike Dalí, both remained without any religious affiliation. Nonetheless, both had religious connections, and so it is fascinating to observe the quite different impact this had on their work. In Ernst's case he came from a devout

[69] The complete range of images is usefully gathered in G. Régnier (ed.), *The Body on the Cross* (Montreal: Museum of Fine Arts, 1992), esp. 14–43, 63. For the more controversial, pp. 15, 33 and 43, dating from, respectively, 1897, 1938, and 1959.
[70] Ibid. 63.
[71] For a detailed study of the 1932 series, S. G. Galassi, *Picasso's Variations on the Masters* (New York: Abrams, 1996), 60–87.
[72] Ibid. 82–3. She surely goes too far, though, in deducing 'a vital, if deeply ambivalent, religious faith'.
[73] So Ruth Kaufmann in Régnier (ed.), *Body on the Cross*, 74–83.
[74] Among others who note the connection with the crucifixion is W. Rubin, *Dada and Surrealist Art* (New York: Abrams, 1968), 294–5. One intriguing question is why Picasso turned the sun into artificial light (this only happened in his seventh version). Could it be that he thought that the sun implied too objective a hope? For the various versions, Warncke and Walther, *Pablo Picasso*, 397–401.

Catholic home, and an early painting survives of his father using the features of the young Ernst to represent the infant Saviour.[75] However, in later life he rebelled and became strongly hostile. Such hostility, though, seldom makes itself explicitly felt in his painting, where religious or metaphysical themes are almost wholly absent. He did win a prize for his *Temptation of St Anthony*, but even here gruesome monsters replace any real sense of moral struggle, in marked contrast to Dalí's version which in my view is the better painting.[76] However, in the 1920s he produced two works concerned with the early stages of Christ's life. In his *Chaste Joseph* of 1928, Mary's husband is presented as a neglected and almost vanishing bird as the two figures of the annunciation assume central stage. If the element of critique here is subdued, it is more prominent in *The Blessed Virgin Chastising the Infant Jesus* of 1926, a painting which on first showing at Cologne had to be removed from display, so widespread was public protest.[77] Yet, both could be read as legitimate challenges to Christian belief. One notes the reluctance of many Christians to offer a realistic account of the childhood of Jesus, supposing, as they do, that his conduct could never have generated the kinds of conflicts that accompany the rest of us as we grow to adulthood. But does not taking the incarnation seriously force us to the recognition that Jesus may sometimes have rebelled against his parents' authority in ways that merited reprimand, and in the context of first-century Palestine might that not almost inevitably have meant corporal punishment?[78]

If Ernst illustrates how we might learn even from those who are hostile, Magritte provides an example of how those outside who are more sympathetic can offer new ways of viewing familiar themes. In this Magritte might have been helped by his practising wife, whom he defended in a famous confrontation with that doyen of Surrealists,

---

[75] Illustrated in U. Bischoff, *Max Ernst* (Cologne: Taschen, 1994), 7.

[76] Ibid. 75. The painting dates from 1945. For the piece Dalí entered and some of the competition details, Descharnes, *Dalí* (1993), 144–5.

[77] For illustrations, W. Spies (ed.), *Max Ernst: A Retrospective* (Munich: Prestel, 1991), 176, 301, also Plate 4. His hostility to Christianity at the time is well illustrated by the comments he makes in his *Biographical Notes*: ibid. 307.

[78] This is not to deny the perfection of Christ, but different standards of conduct surely apply in respect of a child, where testing the limits of parental authority seems an inevitable accompaniment to forging self-identity. For the argument pursued in more detail with further illustrations, see the opening section of my essay, 'Mary's Discipleship and the Artistic Imagination', in M. Warner (ed.), *Say Yes To God* (London: Tufton, 1999), 69–82.

André Breton.[79] At all events, although he was officially indifferent
and for many years an active member of the Communist Party,[80]
commentators have noted various remarks in his writings that
show some sympathy towards a religious view.[81] In his own self-
understanding he certainly saw himself as disclosing the 'mystery'
that lies at the heart of the world, and, although in most of his
paintings there is no obvious religious element, some do, quite
naturally, invite a transcendent reading.[82] Only occasionally,
though, does this spill over into treatments of Christ's life. For
example, in *Taste of Tears* (1948) it is not too fanciful to see in the
dead bird an allusion to the crucifixion.[83] The angle of its head
reminds one of many a crucifixion scene, while the destructive
caterpillar could easily be read as an allusion to the destructive
snake, the sin that was responsible for Christ's death. Although the
colours are sombre, the luxuriant leaves hint that the bird's death
might not after all be the end of the story. Such hope is more
prominent in Magritte's *Annunciation* where the white lattice work
emerging from a dark solid mass suggests that its confrontation
with the chessman angel is about to bear fruit.[84] It is of course
possible to take both paintings as intended to offer a purely secular
message of hope, but the fact that elements in the imagery are
borrowed from Christianity allows the church to reclaim the power
of the message in these paintings and make it its own.

Whereas the reputation of Picasso, Ernst, and Magritte was
already firmly established before the Second World War, because
he destroyed almost all his pre-war works the reputation of Francis
Bacon (d. 1992) was only effectively established in 1944, with his
Three Studies for Figures at the Base of a Crucifixion.[85] Three
unpleasant creatures recalling the Greek Furies are represented as
part of what would originally have apparently included a central
crucifixion scene, with these figures on an armature round the base

[79] Breton was virulently anti-religious. In 1930 Magritte left Paris and the other
Surrealists, the final straw apparently having been an offensive remark made by
Breton to Georgette Magritte because she was wearing a crucifix at the time.

[80] He left in 1947.

[81] Jacques Meuris observes that 'he never lost the latent idea of the existence of an
immanent deity'; for some evidence, cf. his *Magritte* (Cologne: Taschen, 1994), 70.

[82] Such as *The Beyond* of 1938; illustrated, ibid. 67.

[83] For illustration, ibid. 118.

[84] The painting dates from 1929, and is now in Tate Modern, London.

[85] Illustrated in M. Leiris, *Francis Bacon* (Barcelona: Ediciones Polígrafa, 1987),
no. 1.

of its cross.[86] That the indefinite article was used to refer to 'a crucifixion' was clearly deliberate on the artist's part. The language and metaphor of crucifixion was being used, not to recall Christ's own suffering, but rather to comment upon all the horrors that Europe had so recently endured.[87] Equally, his famous reworking of Velásquez's portrait of Pope Innocent X seems to reflect less the character of that particular pope or corruption within the church as the suspicion that now became widespread throughout society of power and its misuse.[88] A major reason for Bacon's reputation was thus the way in which he reflected so accurately the pessimism of the time about the human condition and its potential. Even so, it would seem to me a mistake to use this fact as an excuse for denying the relevance of his art to religion.

Of course, one could easily use Bacon himself in support of such a rejection. Throughout his life he refused to give explicit meanings to his works,[89] while his explicit comments on religion indicate an unqualified atheism. Yet it was an atheism that still conceded the loss of something worthwhile, not only in terms of hope but also in terms of commitment.[90] So we shall not go far amiss if we find religious meaning in his work to this degree, both in its stark recognition of the extent of human evil and in Bacon's recognition of the inadequacy of atheism to surmount it, however inescapable he felt that atheism to be. However, this much, I believe, takes us only part of the way in coming to terms with Bacon's full significance.[91] For the frequency of his allusion to the crucifixion in one way or another surely indicates a deeper wrestling with religion

---

[86] So Bacon himself in D. Sylvester, *Interviews with Bacon* (London: Thames & Hudson, 1993), 112.

[87] Note the comments of the then Director of the Tate, Sir John Rothenstein; quoted in A. Sinclair, *Francis Bacon* (London: Sinclair-Stevenson, 1993), 164.

[88] The 1953 version is perhaps best known (Leiris, *Francis Bacon*, no. 12), but he began the series several years earlier. For a similar interpretation of the significance of Bacon's treatment, J. Russell, *Francis Bacon* (London: Thames & Hudson, 2nd edn., 1979), 41–3.

[89] 'I'm not really trying to say anything': quoted in Sylvester, *Interviews with Bacon*, 198.

[90] See ibid. 134.

[91] A helpful analysis of Bacon's treatment of evil is W. Yates's article, 'Francis Bacon: The Iconography of Crucifixion, Grotesque Imagery and Religious Meaning', in J. L. Adams and W. Yates, *The Grotesque in Art and Literature* (Grand Rapids, Mich.: Eerdmans, 1997), 143–91. Less convincing, though, is his support for the view that such portrayals were primarily intended as cathartic or purgative, pp. 160–1, 187, 190–1.

than his admirers generally suppose. His pre-1944 output had
already included at least three crucifixions, while subsequently it
was not only a format to which he returned directly a number of
times but also allusively in his numerous triptychs, quite a few of
which deal with not unrelated themes. Early in his career he had
been impressed by the way Poussin had represented the scream of a
mother in his *Massacre of the Innocents*,[92] and that scream one finds
reflected in his *Crucifixion* of 1950.[93] The strange creature on the
cross might be taken to represent all of creation in pain and not just
humanity, while the more kindly dog at the top (in the position
normally reserved for those helping with the deposition) is clearly
shown as powerless to help.[94] The work's unrelieved suffering could
easily be read as an indictment of the Christian God, but Bacon did
not in fact share the now common critique of a God who fails to
intervene; for him suffering and unfairness were essential as a spur
to human creativity.[95] Rather, the point seems to be that traditional
crucifixions had failed to take the awfulness of human evil and
suffering with sufficient seriousness. If so, it was a point that was
reinforced in his *Three Studies for a Crucifixion* of 1962 and, more
importantly, his *Crucifixion* of 1965.[96] Various forms of conflict
(emotional, physical, and sexual) are shown in both, and both are
made to culminate in a bloody carcass. The later painting, though,
is better at making his point. For looking on at the central carcass
are two men at a bench, so portrayed that they can easily be read
either as kneeling at an altar rail or else as hunched over a drink in
an American bar while watching a television screen. Indifference to
the evil all around us could scarcely have been more effectively
shown.

It is the tradition of Grünewald taken to its ultimate extreme. We
are made to face the starkness of evil, but an evil no longer confined

[92] The other image that affected him was the scream of the nurse in Eisenstein's
film *Battleship Potemkin*.

[93] For illustration (black and white only), Russell, *Francis Bacon*, 77, also Plate 5.
More commonly illustrated is the related 1946 work simply entitled *Painting*; e.g.
Leiris, *Francis Bacon*, no. 5.

[94] Here I disagree with Russell who speaks of 'the dog bending down to savour the
fresh meat' (p. 82), for, if this were so, the obvious allusion to Depositions such as that
of Rubens would seem misplaced.

[95] See Sylvester, *Interviews with Bacon*, 124–5.

[96] For illustrations, Leiris, *Francis Bacon*, nos. 21 and 30. According to Bacon
himself, the carcass in the earlier painting is an inverted form of Cimabue's *Crucifixion*
of 1272: for a visual comparison, Sylvester, *Interviews with Bacon*, 14–15.

to such an unusual context as Christ's own crucifixion. It is there, we are being told, even in the most ordinary of human relations such as a drink at a bar or in sexual relations. As is well known, both of these activities played a large part in shaping Bacon's own life. His drinking and sexual partners were to provide material for some of his best-known portraits. Indeed, his sexual masochism may well have helped generate one reason for his interest in the brutality of the crucifixion.[97] Yet a positive contribution from his homosexuality should also not be discounted. For it seems to me likely that his long and tumultuous affair with George Dyer did in the end force upon him a more positive crucifixion image. Dyer was the sort of apparently tough East-Ender to whom Bacon was attracted, but, as a previous suicide attempt had already indicated, he could easily be hurt by Bacon's waspish comments to his more conventional friends. A successful suicide finally occurred in Paris in 1973. Of the fact that Bacon loved Dyer, we are left in no doubt through the spate of posthumous portraits that followed.[98] But that fact is also to be seen, I believe, in the triptych that records the suicide. Although the side-panels may seem brutal in their stark depiction of Dyer first being sick into a basin and then dying on a toilet seat, the central panel suggests a quite different verdict. For, if the sheer bulk of his body still casts a shadow like that of a bird of prey, above there is shining a bright yellow bulb that hangs not directly from the ceiling but by means of two wires that are made to form the traditional shape of Christ's arms hanging from the cross. I find it hard to believe that this is an accident. Not that Bacon had somehow come to believe in the Christian doctrine of resurrection after all, but the general colour and lightness of this part of the painting do suggest to me that Bacon's love for Dyer has elicited a probably unconscious use of earlier Christian symbolism, there to indicate Bacon's commitment to allow Dyer at the very least to continue to live in the artist's memory. This is not to suggest that George Dyer has in some way become a Christ-figure, but it is to note that even where the crucifixion was usurped to deliver an apparently purely secular critique of twentieth-century humanity, its own distinctive message does in fact come through, both in identifying the extent of

---

[97] For his masochism, D. Farson, *The Gilded Gutter Life of Francis Bacon* (London: Random House, 1994), 116, 128–9, 161; for the possible influence of another painter (Roy de Maistre) in seeing the crucifixion in this light, ibid. 28.

[98] See Sinclair, *Francis Bacon*, 219–25.

humanity's problem and what is for the Christian its only possible solution, in the love that refuses to allow evil the last word.

That same refusal to allow evil the last word emerges with conspicuous clarity in what might initially seem a surprising context, given the terrible sufferings to which his people have been subject this century: namely in the paintings of the Russian Jew, Marc Chagall (d. 1985). More surprising still is his use of Christian symbolism, particularly the crucifixion, to express that hope. Admittedly, in some paintings completed not long after the Second World War the element of hope has become rather muted, and probably implies an implicit critique of Christianity. So, for instance, in *Flayed Ox* (1947) all the faces are sad, a candle at top right almost extinguished and a cockerel at bottom left fleeing in terror. The central image, the flayed ox, looks suspiciously like a crucified figure, while the voracious way in which it drinks its own blood seems to suggest that the reason for the terror and the Jew's candle going out derives from a thirst for blood that is part of the inheritance of Christianity. Even so, the ox, strung up like a crucified figure, still tenaciously holds on to life, drinking his own blood from the vat below.[99] Likewise, the initial impression one gains from *Falling Angel*, another painting completed that same year, is overwhelmingly one of gloom. Dark colours give a brooding aspect to the picture, while the implicit threat in the angel like Lucifer hurtling to the earth is reinforced by a rabbi hastily racing off the canvas with Torah scrolls in hand. Yet a bright yellow innocent looking lamb is juxtaposed with a bright blue violin, suggesting that all hope is perhaps not after all lost. Nonetheless, the crucified Christ, though associated with a burning candle, is placed behind the falling angel, probably thereby indicating an ambiguous inheritance.[100]

However, this was not Chagall's normal attitude, and in fact, he was the object of much criticism from some of his fellow Jews for employing Christian symbolism so often in a positive way. Art historians sometimes attempt to blunt the force of these criticisms by suggesting that no more was at stake than the employment of a ready-made image to indicate Jewish martyrdom, and indeed even his most famous use has been interpreted in this way as an

---

[99] For illustration and some discussion, W. Haftmann, *Chagall* (New York: Abrams, 1998), 130–1.

[100] Ibid. 128–9. Although completed in 1947, Chagall took a quarter of a century over the painting, beginning in 1922; so its theme was clearly important to him.

'unredemptive symbol'.[101] But this will not do. The use extends throughout his long career, and is perhaps to be explained by Jewish reflection at the turn of the nineteenth and twentieth centuries when a positive role for Jesus within Judaism was being actively canvassed. Thus, Chagall was by no means alone among Jewish painters in associating Christ with specifically Jewish imagery, while some poetry of the time does not hesitate to see in Jesus a true prophet and legitimate aspect of the Jewish hope, as in these words by Uri Zvi Greenberg:

> What happened to Jesus our brother crucified . . . ?
> . . .
> He hangs in the middle of the world
> and looks out to the end of all times.
> Deep is his longing.
> He will return with a prayer shawl
> around his shoulder
> on the day of redemption
> at the end of time.[102]

Although it would be absurd to attach too much significance to the fact that Chagall was buried in a Catholic and not a Jewish cemetery, there seems little doubt that his acceptance in later life of various Christian commissions, so far from indicating opportunism, in fact represented a real and deep love for the Christian story.[103] To me this seems clearly indicated by the gratuitous way in which he sometimes introduces the crucifixion into contexts where even Christian artists might hesitate to follow, as in the story of the Creation.[104]

The nature of that commitment can perhaps best be explored by examining one representative example of his work from different

---

[101] So Gill Polonsky interpreting his 1938 *White Crucifixion* in *Chagall* (London: Phaidon, 1998), 94. For the general tenor of the criticisms, and a possible response from a sympathetic fellow-Jew, J. Baal-Teshuva, *Chagall* (Cologne: Taschen, 1998), 265–9.

[102] Quoted in A. Kampf, *Chagall to Kitaj: Jewish Experience in 20th-Century Art* (London: Lund Humphries, 1990), 13; for examples from visual art, p. 164 n. 2.

[103] Despite the best efforts of the chief rabbi in Nice, the choice of cemetery was determined by his second wife, Vava, so Baal-Teshuva, *Chagall*, 266. That no opportunism was involved is confirmed by the fact that, if it was a church commission, he refused payment: ibid. 244.

[104] In his *Creation of Man* (illustrated in Baal-Teshuva, *Chagall*, 207) of 1958 an angel holds Adam while in the background there is a crucifixion (as well as a divine hand delivering the tablets of the Law).

epochs of his long life. His 1912 *Golgotha* is one of the most startlingly original of his compositions. A bearded figure and a woman with bared breast look up at a crucified figure but the figure is of a child. Meanwhile another young person rows away from the scene towards some idyllic islands in the distance, watching with distrust, as he does so, a man retreating with a ladder. The image is perhaps suggesting that despite the youth's hopes such islands cannot be successfully reached without some innocent suffering.[105] By 1938 and his *White Crucifixion* the extent of such suffering was no longer in doubt, with Nazi persecution now in full swing, and that is reflected in the tearful and fleeing people and the burning village. Centrally placed, though, is Christ crucified, draped in a Jewish prayer shawl. Although his eyes are closed, the lit candle beneath and the great shaft of white light in which Christ is bathed both suggest that his death cannot possibly have the last word.[106] That for Chagall it was not so is clearly demonstrated in his 1950 *Christ*, where the crucified one seems almost to smile, while the person starting to take his body down from the cross, together with bright moon and stars behind alike all add up to some sense of positive impact.[107] Finally, one might mention his 1972 *Village* in which the artist with his palette surveys some hamlet from his Russian youth with the crucified Christ behind and in front a cow gaily leaping with Jewish candelabra in hand.[108]

Such a meeting of Jewish and Christian symbols takes us back to a painting contemporary with his 1912 *Golgotha*, where Jewish prayer cap and Christian church literally meet as the *Holy Coachman* flies down, as it were, into the canvas.[109] It would be pleasant were we able to say that through such mysterious encounters Chagall laid the foundations for a potential reconciliation between Judaism and Christianity, but it is highly unlikely that Chagall valued in the story of Jesus anything more than its symbolic content. The claim of orthodox Christianity to an actual resurrection was for him a stage too far. Nonetheless, this does not mean that Christians are precluded from reading his art in this way. Chagall himself refused

---

[105] Illustrated and discussed in Haftmann, *Chagall*, 84–5.
[106] Illustrated and discussed in Polonsky, *Chagall*, 94–5, see also Plate 6.
[107] Illustrated in R. Cogniat, *Chagall* (Naefels, Switzerland: Bonfini, 1978), 61.
[108] Illustrated in Baal-Teshuva, *Chagall*, 267.
[109] Illustrated and discussed in Haftmann, *Chagall*, 76–7. Ironically, the painting was originally intended to hang what would now be seen as upside down, but Chagall himself came to prefer the implications of an original wrong hanging.

to offer any overarching explanations of his art: 'I did not try to follow any theory. God created man without a theory and art is best created without a theory. All I can do is work for art. The rest is done by God.'[110] Christians may therefore, it seems to me, without impropriety speak of Chagall's art as conveying not merely the involvement of God in the life of Christ but also even some sense of the divinity present in that life. That emphatically does not make Chagall a crypto-Christian, nor does it prevent Jews (or atheists) from interpreting him quite differently. What it does assert is that because the meaning of any image is in part formed by context, sometimes, as here with Chagall, what has been shaped outside explicitly Christian belief can, nevertheless, quite naturally and without any sense of being forced, legitimately acquire a Christian meaning, even where this is an implied critique of Christianity, as in the two painting considered earlier that reflected Chagall's immediate post-war pessimism. The Christian may want to speak of the providence of God in all of this, but even the secularist could accept such a general theory of artistic meanings. If so, that could help with interpretation of the work of another Jew, Jacob Epstein, and his use of Christian symbolism in sculpture, the subject to which we now turn.

II SCULPTURE

In sculpture, as with painting, the spiritual in art will be seen to be much less in retreat, once due account is taken of instances where Western sculpture is not specifically Christian in its inspiration. An obvious example would be the work of Constantin Brancusi, many of whose sculptures resonate with religious themes even though he did not turn directly to Christianity for his inspiration, despite his Orthodox upbringing in Romania.[111] Here, however, the incarnation is our concern, and to reflect on how it has been treated in twentieth-century sculpture, I shall take as representative examples one practising Christian, one sympathetic agnostic, and one non-practising Jew, namely Gill, Moore, and Epstein.

The Christian reputation of Eric Gill (d. 1940) has suffered much

[110] Quoted without reference in Baal-Teshuva, *Chagall*, 248.
[111] *Prayer* and *Endless Column* are obvious explicit examples, but many others such as *Bird in Space* point one in the same direction: for illustrations, E. Shanes, *Brancusi* (New York: Abbeville, 1989), 14, 41, 82.

of late, and there have even been calls for the removal of his *Stations of the Cross* from Westminster Cathedral in London. Certainly, very little seems to have been out of bounds in his sexual behaviour, but even here this was combined with a genuine and mutually deep love for his wife.[112] One must also not discount the seriousness of his attempts to revitalize among artists a distinctively Christian working tradition, under which his successive foundations were bound together by a strong sense of community and a daily habit of corporate prayer.[113] He himself had become a member of the Third Order of St Dominic after his conversion to Rome, and there were a number of Catholic priests who strongly supported the positive sides of his contribution, even though they appear to have had some knowledge of his sexual licence. It would be a pity, therefore, if the sensational side of his life was allowed wholly to define his overall achievement.

One commentator ends his survey of Gill's work by pronouncing him the end of a line, the last major attempt to maintain a distinctively Christian tradition in sculpture in the face of an increasingly secular culture.[114] By contemporary standards much of his work does indeed seem conventional, and so does little more than remind one of the glories of an earlier age, but this is by no means true of all. The very sexuality that has caused so many problems for his modern reputation also in fact led him to produce some of his most distinctive and original work in representing the Christian story. If the use of the archaic and monumental was one source of inspiration, Hindu and Buddhist art was another.[115] To my mind his monumental figures of the Madonna or Mother and Child succeed less well than those of Moore,[116] whereas there is a

---

[112] The most explicit biography notes as well as numerous affairs sexual relations with his daughters, homosexuality, and bestiality: F. MacCarthy, *Eric Gill* (London: Faber & Faber, 1989), 155–6, 191, 239. Yet 'Mary remained the life-long focus of his deepest love': so M. Yorke, *Eric Gill: Man of Flesh and Spirit* (London: Constable, 1981), 38.

[113] His best-known and longest lasting community was at Ditchling Common in Sussex which had 41 members by 1922: MacCarthy, *Eric Gill*, 148.

[114] Yorke, *Eric Gill*, 274.

[115] For the influence of Coomaraswamy, J. Collins, *Eric Gill the Sculpture* (London: Herbert, 1998), 33–4; for an example, Plate 7.

[116] He produced several versions of his naked *Madonna and Child* in 1910, while his *Mulier BVM* from the following year (now in the Sculpture Garden of the University of California, Los Angeles) which shows a naked Mary offering her breast had to be modified to suit even the tastes of the critic, Roger Fry: for illustrations, Collins, *Eric Gill*, 62, 66, 72–4.

figure of Christ sleeping from 1925, influenced by Buddhist art, that captures magnificently some sense of Christ as more than merely human, while the very sensuality of his *Deposition* (1924) with its idealized human figure compels from us a different meaning for the dead figure than the immediately obvious.[117] Not that all his successes were achieved through the sensual; far from it. One of the most astonishing is the mock-up for his *Prospero and Ariel* (1933) now on the front of Broadcasting House, London. As he himself admitted, despite the precise nature of the commission, he decided to make the model as a study of God the Father and his Son. Christ is presented as a naked young boy displaying his wounds with a huge Father above, holding him tenderly.[118] It reminds one of the work of the Romanesque sculptor, Gislibertus at Autun, but with a warmth that Gislibertus never quite achieved.

Where the parallel does hold is in the general Romanesque style, for one of the surprises in Gill's work is how seldom his inspiration comes from Gothic and how frequently he turned to the Byzantine or Romanesque. His most obviously Gothic-looking sculpture is perhaps his *Spoil Bank Crucifix* of 1922, where Christ's pain is emphasized both in his face and tensed body, but the body's length and its upstretched arms used to suggest divinity.[119] However, normally for Gill the cross is to be portrayed as a triumph, and to do this he resorts to conventional devices of the past, such as Christ crowned or with no sign of wounds. Now and then, though, some new piece of symbolism emerges. So, for instance, in his 1910 *Weltschmerz* splindly legs combine with unmarked hands, or in his *Armless Crucifix* of 1922 chopped-off arms with a brilliant sheen, to raise the question of the true identity of the crucified figure, while in his last sculpture (for Guildford Cathedral) two hands (obviously those of the Father) exalt the figure on the Cross.[120] Yet, ironically, in the end one must, I think, pronounce Gill too restrained by earlier tradition. In his *Leeds University War Memorial*, for instance, it was a fine idea to highlight the role of business interests in bringing about the war, but his contrast between a conventional first-century Christ and men in modern business suits merely strikes one as incongruous, whereas had he sought a different way of presenting Christ

---

[117] For illustrations, ibid. 145, 147. Gill considered the *Deposition* his best work: E. Gill, *Autobiography* (London: Cape, 1940), 219.

[118] For the model, final version, and later adaptation as Abraham and Isaac, Collins, *Eric Gill*, 171–2, 181, 204.   [119] Ibid. 127.   [120] Ibid. 63, 130, 229.

(both modern and obviously divine), the result might have been quite different.[121]

Henry Moore (d. 1986) also turned his hand to an archaic Mother and Child, but, perhaps because he experimented with the image more often, it is with him, I believe, that we find the better portrayal of the Christian faith, when he was commissioned to turn his secular image into a sacred one. Although some critics have detected no significant difference,[122] Moore himself certainly recognized the importance of distinguishing between the two. In considering how he should respond to a commission in 1943 from Walter Hussey for a *Madonna and Child* for St Matthew's church, Northampton, he specifically records how he sought to give Mary a certain 'hieratic aloofness' and the child a look that suggested a more than ordinary human destiny.[123] The latter might be held to undermine the kenotic character of the incarnation, but in defence of Moore one might note that not only has he tradition on his side, but also the need for any form of art inevitably to simplify in order to provoke reflection upon its underlying point. 'Provoke' seems the right word, for Moore himself is clear that any art worthy of the name should not yield its meaning immediately, but rather require sustained reflection from the viewer in order fully to elicit its meaning.[124]

Yet it is not immediately obvious that all his secular versions of Mother and Child should in fact always be viewed in such terms. Moore found his inspiration primarily in pre-Columbian and African art,[125] and he himself was the first to acknowledge that in those cultures no sharp distinction existed between sacred and secular. Instead, sculpture was used to evoke mystery and power, and that is why expression and presence took precedence over beauty.[126] That too was why monumentality was sought (though not necessarily of scale).[127] No doubt, even with these facts acknowledged, many of

---

[121] Collins, *Eric Gill*, 134–5.

[122] Julian Stallabrass, for example, argues that because the Virgin Birth is ignored, his Northampton sculpture is no more than an idealized version of his other works: D. Mitchinson (ed.), *Mutter und Kind* (Cologne: Käthe Kollowitz Museum, 1992), 14–15.

[123] P. James (ed.), *Henry Moore on Sculpture* (New York: Da Capo, 1992), 235–9.

[124] All good art demands an effort from the observer': ibid. 80.

[125] His 1929 *Reclining Figure in Leeds*, modelled as it is closely on the Mayan Chacmool figure, provides perhaps the clearest illustration of such influence: A. G. Wilkinson, *Henry Moore Remembered* (Toronto: Key Porter, 1987), 66–7.

[126] e.g. James, *Henry Moore*, 96, 191.

[127] As more recent examples of this point, Moore draws our attention to Masaccio's *Tribute Money* and Cézanne's *Bathers*; James, *Henry Moore*, 129.

his sculptures on this topic will still remain unsuitable to speak to us today of incarnation. To take an extreme case, one could scarcely use his vivid (and shocking) image of mother and child in conflict.[128] Nonetheless, there remain several others that might be usurped for just such a role.[129] Indeed, given the pressing issue of abortion, his image of the child still in the womb might seem an obvious candidate.[130]

However that may be, we need also to note his other major religious work, the *Glenkiln Cross*, magnificently set against the Scottish countryside.[131] Those familiar with ancient weather-beaten Celtic crosses left out in the open to face (and survive) wind and rain alike will immediately respond to this particular creation. The symbolism, though, is significantly different. The customary bare cross is replaced by a crucifix but one in which body and cross are completely moulded into one, while it is only on the base that we observe more traditional symbolism, with a ladder, the moon, and an eye. The eye is an ancient way of portraying the Father, while moon and sun used regularly to appear in paintings of the crucifixion in pre-Reformation times and occasionally later.[132] The reference is of course to the darkening of the old order and the emerging of the new. So setting and imagery combine to suggest an ultimately positive message.

While a young man Moore had been encouraged in his career by Jacob Epstein (d. 1959). It is, therefore, rather sad to note his grudging praise for Epstein's male portraits, quite to the neglect of his religious art, which in my view (and most others') would deserve a far more favourable estimation.[133] Epstein was the product of an Orthodox Jewish immigrant home in New York, but as an adult he too changed nations, first living in France before eventually settling permanently in England. His Jewishness undoubtedly contributed to

---

[128] His *Mother and Child* of 1953, now in Tate Modern: illustrated Wilkinson, *Henry Moore*, 141.

[129] Among my favoured candidates would be three from the 1980s: illustrated in Mitchinson, *Mutter und Kind*, 67, 91, 93.

[130] Known as *Internal and External Forms* (1953–4); for illustration, James, *Henry Moore*, 265.

[131] The cross was erected in 1956 on Sir William Keswick's Glenkiln Farm, Shawcross, Dumfries. It is described by Wilkinson as one of Moore's greatest achievements (*Henry Moore*, 159).

[132] All ultimately based on Mark 15: 33. For a late example, Raphael's 1502 *Crucifixion*, now in the National Gallery, London.

[133] For Moore's views on Epstein, James, *Henry Moore*, 209–12.

the animosity with which some of his sculptures were received.[134] The surprise is how very few of them were in fact Jewish in inspiration. Among the best-known is *Jacob and the Angel* (1940), but perhaps the most relevant, had it survived, might have been his poignant anticipation of the Holocaust in his representation of Jewish persecution through the ages, *Cursed Be the Day wherein I was Born* (1914).[135] The official biography describes Epstein as not religious, and this is true if by that one means attendance at synagogue or church, but we know that he read the Old Testament to his children every night, and was also well versed in the New Testament.[136] Not only that, the great collection of primitive art that he began to amass from the age of 32 onwards he himself saw as essentially religious, and so other commentators have not been slow to see a spiritual motivation in the sculptures he did of the life of Christ.[137] What perhaps also makes this more likely is the fact that many of them were done of his own volition, prior to any commission.

Whatever his intentions, though, these should not be given the last word. The more important issue for us here is whether they succeed or not in conveying the doctrine of the incarnation. With his final work *Christ in Majesty* there seems general agreement that he was unlucky in its precise setting in the restored Llandaff Cathedral, the architect George Pace's concrete arch weighing down a sculpture which had been intended to soar and which would have been better suspended from the ceiling. Yet perhaps Pace thought that he was simply reflecting Epstein's own preference for Romanesque monumentality, well illustrated by *Behold the Man* which like his more familiar *St Michael and the Devil* is now at Coventry Cathedral. The bulk of the former was no doubt intended to indicate Christ's exalted status but, unfortunately, instead the sculpture simply weighs us down with its monumentality.[138] More promising is his *Madonna and Child* (1952) in Cavendish Square,

---

[134] Though the question of nudity also played its part, as in the sculptures on the British Medical Association Building, Father Vaughan being his most vociferous opponent and the future Archbishop of Canterbury, Cosmo Gordon Lang, one of his defendants: S. Gardiner, *Epstein* (New York: Viking, 1993), 64–5.

[135] Both illustrated in R. Cork, *Jacob Epstein* (London: Tate, 1999), 29, 61.

[136] Contrast Gardiner's comment (*Epstein*, 200) with his admissions elsewhere: e.g. pp. 207, 330.

[137] So various writers in E. Silber *et al.*, *Jacob Epstein: Sculpture and Drawings* (Leeds: Maney and Son, 1989), 19, 32. By his death he had about a thousand items.

[138] Illustrated Cork, *Jacob Epstein*, 54.

London. Here a thoughtful Mary holds up her son, clearly already perplexed by the suffering that is to come. Yet a subtle indicator is offered of the ability of them both to rise above it: both sets of feet point downwards, as though they could take flight at any moment.[139]

However, for me the best of his works are now both to be found in the Scottish National Gallery of Modern Art in Edinburgh. His *Risen Christ* was done as his own personal memorial for the victims of the First World War.[140] So, not surprisingly, Christ points accusingly at his wounds, but one notes how easily the angle of the hand might turn towards a blessing, and the elongated body too makes the theme of resurrection clear. The other work is his *Consummatum Est* (1936). One commentator strangely protests that 'the meaning of the title . . . does not match the sculpture's sense of residual strength', but 'it is finished' in St John's Gospel is of course a great cry of triumph and not of mere completion, still less despair.[141] Epstein brings this out well with the corpse's head and hands already elevated from the ground where it lies, as also in the raised feet, strangely reminiscent of Spencer's *Last Supper*. Epstein tells us that the idea for the form of presentation came to him quite suddenly while he was listening to the 'Crucifixus' from Bach's *B minor Mass*, and that section does seem to have a mood of quiet expectancy before the riot of joy in the 'Et resurrexit' that follows.[142]

III CONCLUSION

What I think my brief survey indicates is that the religious impulse in art during the twentieth century was in fact much healthier than commonly supposed. If relatively few artists who have been practising Christians achieved international fame and recognition, this is not because the symbols of Christ's life ceased to engage the human imagination. Indeed, we have observed such engagement in some surprising places. The danger for the church is that it refuses the relevance unless done with an explicit religious motivation or at

[139] For illustrations, Silber, *Jacob Epstein*, 264–5; for a perceptive detailed analysis by nuns in the neighbouring convent, ibid. 262.

[140] Illustrated Cork, *Jacob Epstein*, 42; for the story of its genesis, Gardiner, *Epstein*, 199–200.

[141] Cork, *Jacob Epstein*, 54. The Latin is from the Vulgate of John 19: 30.

[142] For Epstein's own comments, Silber, *Jacob Epstein*, 32; for illustration, Plate 8.

least under ecclesiastical supervision. But in fact, as I have tried to indicate, some personal work from non-Christians can easily be usurped to speak the Christian message powerfully to our own age. Among the examples I gave were works by O'Keeffe, Magritte, and Epstein. But even where the intention was hostile, relevance should not always be denied. Bacon and Ernst offered powerful critiques which require addressing, while hostility in one particular painting should not make us assume its universality in that artist's work, as the case of Picasso himself well illustrated.

The Christian artists I selected were themselves a mixed bunch. Roualt and Gill have had little impact outside the church, because, it seems to me, they failed to be sufficiently innovative. Byzantine and Romanesque models held too powerful a sway over them, and they were at their best when they also allowed influences from elsewhere. Even Dalí was less imaginative than Magritte in his exploration of alternative symbolism, while Warhol could only juxtapose modern and traditional symbols in creative tension. As we embark upon a new century, Christian artists are faced with a real difficulty. The divinity of Christ can still be proclaimed through art, but if that proclamation is to be made effective beyond the confines of the church, such artists will need to be more ready to break with tradition and take seriously the experiments of non-Christians with that same imagery. That does not mean rejecting the art of the past, but it does mean acknowledging that the Christian tradition in art has always been in the process of development and should not stand still, as though there had only ever been one golden age. If the church enters the new millennium with that spirit, then it seems to me that it can continue to expect much from the work of artists, whether one thinks of established figures or of a rising generation.[143]

---

[143] Obviously too large a question to deal with here except cursorily, but, somewhat arbitrarily chosen, as an innovative example of the former one might consider the *Crucifixions* of Craigie Aitchison (b. 1926), in which armless Christs are combined with landscapes of great lyrical beauty to suggest powerlessness and acute suffering caught up into something much larger, and of the latter, some of the more novel devices tried by younger artists exhibiting in Suffolk churches over Easter 2000. For the former, A. G. Williams, *The Art of Craigie Aitchison* (Edinburgh: Canongate, 1996), 104–17, 148–9, 158; for the latter, R. Davey (ed.), *Stations: The New Sacred Art* (Bury St Edmunds: Art Gallery, 2000).

1. George Rouault, *Nazareth* (1948). Vatican Museum. SCALA © ADAGP, Paris and DACS, London 2002.

A rural and humble Nazareth is set in an autumnal landscape. Christ's open humanity is underlined by the way in which all the human figures seem enveloped by a mandorla of which he is the apex. As is common in many of Rouault's other paintings, the heavens are made to echo Christ's divinity, with the same colour range in and around Christ as we find in and around the sun, and the road linking them.

2. Stanley Spencer, *The Last Supper* (1920). Stanley Spencer gallery, Cookham, Berkshire. Bridgeman Art Library © Estate of Stanley Spencer 2002. All Rights Reserved, DACS.

Here Christ's washing of his disciples' feet and the last Supper are effectively linked by the prominence given to the disciples' feet. If the setting in a local brewery gives an obvious human touch, the outstretched feet help to draw attention to the central figure of Christ, significantly exalted above the rest both by the light catching his garment and by the way in which his head rises beyond the line of the brick wall.

3. Salvador Dalí, *Christ of St John of the Cross* (1951). St Mungo Museum of Religious Life and Art, Glasgow Galleries, Glasgow.

Dalí disliked representations of the crucifixion inspired by Grünewald. For him the crucifixion should essentially speak of hope and joy, and so it is not surprising that in this painting it is the divine side of that joy that is being emphasized: Christ having overcome suffering now looks with compassion on the world. Still, the human Christ is not absent, and can be seen, for instance, in his workman's hands, or in his concern for the particular, in this case the fishermen of Port Lligat.

4. Max Ernst, *The Infant Jesus Chastised by the Virgin Mary before Witnesses* (1926). Museum Ludwig, Cologne. © ADAGP, Paris and DACS, London 2002.

Ernst had been brought up in a devout Roman Catholic family, and so the force of his critique in this painting of too unqualifiedly divine a reading of the incarnation is well made. If an amusing side is provided by the child's loss of his halo and Ernst's fellow surrealists looking on like the elders in the story of Susanna, the serious issue is also raised of whether the taking on of humanity would not also inevitably involve an element of naughtiness as the child grew up.

5. Francis Bacon, *Fragment of a Crucifixion* (1950). Stedelijk van Abbe Museum, Eindhoven, Netherlands. © Estate of Francis Bacon / ARS, NY and DACS, London 2002.

Here, as one might expect from a convinced atheist, any suggestion of divinity has been removed from the story, and the crucifixion has become a symbol for the hopelessness of the human condition. Even though for the religious believer that must remain unacceptable as a final message, there is still surely something to learn, in the need to take the awfulness of suffering in the interim with full seriousness.

6. Marc Chagall, *White Crucifixion* (1938). Art Institute of Chicago.
© ADAGP, Paris and DACS, London 2002.

Given the extent of Jewish suffering in the twentieth century, it is truly astonishing that it is from a Jew tht some of the most powerful expressions of Christian incarnational belief should come. So here, as in several of Chagall's other paintings, an element of hope is introduced into human suffering through the crucifixion, in this case by means of the great shaft of light by which it is illuminated, as by the lighted menorah beneath. For Chagall himself, though, the cross remains essentially a universal symbol, a mythic story of hope, not an incarnational reality.

7. Eric Gill, *The Holy Face of Christ* (1925). Manchester City Art Gallery.

The influence of Buddhist art here is unmistakble. As with heads of Buddha, the closed eyes are used to suggest divine or semi-divine strength and peace gained through inner meditation. At the same time the jaggedness of the stone at its edges and the hint of sensuality in the figure emphasize his materialty and humanness.

8. Jacob Epstein, *Consummatum Est* (1936). Scottish National Gallery of Modern Art, Edinburgh © The Artist's Estate.

The title comes from the Latin version of John 19: 30, and is ironically a more accurate translation of the Greek than most modern English translations, which talk merely of 'it is finished' rather than the great shout of triumph and consummation that John intended: 'all has been accomplished.' Epstein brilliantly captures that wider meaning by making the dead Christ already point heavenwards, in his feet, hands, and uplifted head. As in John, death and resurrection are one.

16

The Incarnation in Selected Christmas Sermons

MARGUERITE SHUSTER

Anyone who has worked with the various formal categories of Christian theology knows that, in theology, everything is so tied to everything else that it is a continual challenge to find a way to speak without stumbling over oneself by trying to say everything at once. And what is true of theology generally is perhaps supremely true when the incarnation is at stake. After all, *Christian* theology gains its particularity precisely through the Person and Work of Jesus Christ; so it would be odd if one's views on these central matters did not significantly shape one's other positions, from the way one conceives the purpose of creation to the way one construes one's final hope for oneself and the created order.

What is true for Christian theology is, if anything, even more true for Christian preaching, for it is the coming of Christ that gives us good news to proclaim. Even those of us who do not insist that every sermon (particularly every OT sermon) must explicitly name Christ, usually expect that all sermons will be moulded at least implicitly by the hope we have in him alone. Thus, one would anticipate finding remarks that in one way or another assume the incarnation almost everywhere in sermons. In fact, given the intrinsic difficulty as well as the centrality of the idea, one might expect to find much more material that simply *assumes* a vaguely conceived incarnation than that tackles the incarnation conceptually. Intellectual puzzles are not in themselves good preaching material. It follows that a paper on preaching the incarnation could readily be derailed by too much data with too little specificity.

To circumvent these problems, I have chosen to look at selected Christmas sermons (including a few advent and epiphany sermons

based on the birth narratives) preached by four Roman Catholic
and three Protestant theologians: Hans Urs von Balthasar, Gustavo
Gutiérrez, Karl Rahner, Edward Schillebeeckx, Karl Barth, Harry
Emerson Fosdick, and Helmut Thielicke. (Fosdick is more noted as
a preacher than as a theologian; but he was reasonably knowledgeable and thoughtful theologically.) These men were chosen
somewhat, but not entirely, arbitrarily: I was looking for theologically sophisticated, twentieth-century preachers who would
manifest at least a moderate range in theological position and
who had published enough Christmas sermons to provide what
might be considered a representative sample of their work.[1] I have
chosen Christmas sermons for the obvious reason that Christmas
pushes one to articulate at least something of what we believe we
are celebrating on that occasion. (This choice also means, though,
that certain themes are likely to get short shrift: Jesus' sinlessness,
to take a single example, is not so likely to come up at Christmas
as it would be in sermons dealing more directly with his adult
life.[2])

As I examined these sermons, I was struck by the broad range of
issues related to the incarnation that were touched upon at least
implicitly: of course, these theologians are by no means one's
average preacher; but even someone like Gutiérrez, who is
certainly not intending to address an elite audience, takes up as
many theological themes as those preaching in a more academic
context. And Barth, in the one sermon to a university crowd
contained in his *Deliverance to the Captives*, does not sound very
different than he does in the remaining sermons, addressing
prisoners. These observations support my general conviction (and
agenda, as a teacher of homiletics) that theological issues are
issues of broad human interest and concern, which can and

---

[1] I have not intended to look exhaustively at all the Christmas sermons preached by
these men, but at a large enough number to suggest their usual approaches. Some (e.g.
Barth) had Christmas sermons in only one of several volumes of sermons available in
English: these other volumes are not cited because they do not contain Christmas
sermons. I did not use Paul Tillich—seemingly an obvious choice—because of the lack
of published Christmas sermons by him (which may or may not be significant in itself).
For details of sermons consulted, see the note at the end of the chapter.

[2] This seemingly obvious supposition cannot be taken as completely safe, however:
Schleiermacher—not treated here because of his earlier time frame—did in fact
specifically emphasize Jesus' sinlessness in a Christmas sermon. See 'Jesus Born the
Son of God', *Selected Sermons of Schleiermacher*, ed. W. R. Nicoll, trans. M. F. Wilson
(London: Hodder and Stoughton, 1890), 279–94.

should be broached in the ordinary preaching of the church.[3] As a sort of test of how far that proposition might be taken, I have chosen in this paper to see how (if at all) the various issues Gerald O'Collins, in his introductory chapter, identifies as key for the current christological discussion, come up in the preaching of my exemplars. I hope to show not only that almost all of them do come up, but also that they frequently come up in ways that take the form not of bare theological assertion but rather of truths consequential for Christian living (consequences being read differently dependent on differing theological positions of the preachers, of course). That is, I hope to illustrate (for the most part) meaningful ways of speaking of these issues in the pulpit, whether or not one agrees with a particular formulation. Naturally, my preachers were not intending specifically to deal with the questions O'Collins has laid out; so it is to be expected not only that some approaches will be oblique, but also that there will be a certain amount of overlap: some of their remarks could be used with respect to more than one category.

Of O'Collins's categories, I shall deal sequentially with all except numbers 10 and 11, incarnation as possible only for the Word and incarnation as once and for all (his number 12 therefore appearing as number 10 in this paper). These latter categories, more than the others, tend to come up (and they *do* come up) only as they overlap with others, especially with the historical union of divinity and humanity in Jesus and with the question of the 'unfairness' of the incarnation (the scandal of particularity): despite their importance, taken alone they still push toward the speculative in ways that make them awkward preaching material.

---

[3] It does not follow, of course, that preachers are thereby given licence to indulge in vast obscurities and abstractions, as certain of my examples on occasion did. To give a single example, surely it is not helpful to say in the pulpit, 'This nearness of God . . . is not to be conceived as existing in Jesus' consciousness as a given and uniform situation; it is not an already universally given human existential which can at most be forgotten and suppressed, and for that reason only has to be preached anew. For Jesus that nearness of God is with him and his preaching in a new, unique and henceforth insurpassable way' (Rahner, 'Power of Birth', 45–6). I do not deny that these sentences can be understood by a reader, but I do deny that they are useful for an ordinary listener.

I THE *HISTORICAL* UNION OF DIVINITY AND
HUMANITY IN JESUS (INCLUDING THE IDEA
OF THE UNIQUENESS OF THE EVENT)

As might be anticipated by the fact that they are preaching
Christmas sermons, my seven theologians all speak to this issue,
and all of them do so in more than one sermon. All except Fosdick
and Schillebeeckx insist upon the historical particularity and
uniqueness of the Christmas event, and all affirm that it is somehow
God who comes to us in Jesus. A primary conclusion drawn is that
we must turn nowhere else, for God has acted in a definite and final
way:

Christmas does not describe a state of general transfiguration but rather an
event at a specific historical point to which we must go if we are to stand in
this light.   (Thielicke, 'Redeeming Light', 64)

*He who was born in the stable is he who stands by you, stands by me and stands
by us all.* I do not say *one* who stands by you, but *he* who stands by you. For
only One, only he who was born on the first Christmas Day, can stand by us
in utter unselfishness and with ultimate authority and power.   (Barth, 'He
Stands By Us', 137)

[T]his coming of God, his action in us, was intended to be tangible and
irrevocable, irrevocably and tangibly historical . . .   (Rahner, 'Human
Abyss', 56)

While Barth, Balthasar, and Gutiérrez also affirm that there is a
sort of 'Christmas' when Christ takes up residence in his people,[4]
Gutiérrez and Rahner caution against allowing this idea to take
precedence over the actual Christmas event, for example:

During this period of Christmas, people often say that Jesus is born in every
family and every Christian heart. But these 'births' must not bypass the
primary and undeniable reality: Jesus was born of Mary in the midst of a
people dominated at the time by the greatest empire of those days. If we forget
this, Jesus' coming into the world can become an abstraction. For Christians,

---

[4] 'The Saviour does not need to be born again. He was born once for all. But he
would like to take up quarters among us, by whom he stands so faithfully and so
powerfully, whose Saviour he is' (Barth, 'He Stands By Us', 140); 'If we live out our
lively faith in the God who wants to become man on earth, we are already "pregnant"
with him, empowered to carry him until he is born—and that will be a Christmas'
(Balthasar, 'Waiting for God', 256; while this statement might seem to suggest a lack
of particularity to the incarnation, Balthasar is clear elsewhere that he intends no
such interpretation).

Christmas manifests God's irruption into human history.   (Gutiérrez, 'Joy for All', 23)

This warning would seem to be particularly important in the face of the common sentimental assertion—common even among preachers who may not intend to be demythologizing—that Christmas 'really' occurs when Christ is born in your heart, a statement that subtly empties the incarnation itself of content. Balthasar also remarks that the incarnation is an event of such a stupendous character that it 'explodes all categories, so much so that in the future [one who reflects on it] will be much more cautious in speaking about human progress' ('Fullness', 288)—quite a different tack from that taken by those who see in Jesus an example of a supreme but human possibility.

Fosdick often seems to speak in the latter way, not unwilling to call Jesus divine, nor unwilling to affirm the importance of the historical reality of Christ, yet not granting him a status different in kind from that possible for us through 'the indwelling, transforming presence of the Divine' ('Christ of Experience', 44).[5] Uniqueness is at least implicitly denied: 'we humans believe at last, not in isms but in incarnations' ('Christ Is Christianity', 192). Thus, Jesus' import is exemplary: 'religion is a realm of personal, spiritual values which always must be incarnate to be seen and understood. If it is to be real, the word must become flesh and dwell among us' ('Christ Is Christianity', 191); 'If he reveals the universal it is inside of us' ('Christ of Experience', 41); 'What if, when saviors come in any realm, we did not meet them with this obdurate, impassive refusal of a welcome! . . . This puts the world's salvation squarely upon us' ('Hospitality', 280). This conclusion will, in its own way, preach; yet the tenor and content could hardly be farther from an orthodox view.

Schillebeeckx seems to struggle, caught intellectually between what he cannot affirm (e.g. he avers that we can know nothing historically about the circumstances of Jesus' birth;[6] most homileticians would say that dwelling much on what we do not or cannot know does not make for strong preaching); what one can say in

---

[5] '[T]he Christ of history is real. . . . His coming was the most significant event in the spiritual history of man and we do well to celebrate it in this radiant festival of the Christian year . . .' ('Christ of Experience', 35). 'They crowded Christ completely out because they never guessed who he *would be*' ('Hospitality', 276, emphasis added).

[6] 'God Who Visits', 8; 'Authentic Humanity', 61.

general about human beings ('The birth of a human being is always
the beginning of a new possibility in our history' ('God Who Visits',
8)—a point often made by Fosdick as well); and his conviction that
there was indeed something of particular importance about Jesus
('God had indeed visited his people, as the Semites put it: the *kabod* of
God himself, his invisible glory and splendour, shone out visibly on
Jesus' countenance for anyone who looked to Jesus in trust, who
actively saw and listened to him [II Cor. 4. 6]' ('God Who Visits',
11)). These sermons seem to reveal an honest and believing
intellectual who is, nonetheless, afraid to believe too much; and
while the hesitation is sometimes disarming, it does not make for
bold proclamation.

II THE PERSONAL PRE-EXISTENCE OF THE WORD

Thielicke, Barth, Gutiérrez, and Balthasar all speak of the pre-
existence of the Word in ways that imply the personal quality of
the pre-existence, although the matter is not taken up in precisely
those terms. The homiletical goal appears to be both to emphasize
the divinity of Jesus and to impress upon hearers the magnitude of
the divine condescension—an appeal, in this latter regard, to the
heart and the conscience. Thus,

Christmas tells of one who left his base in heaven . . .   (Thielicke,
'Conceived by the Holy Ghost', 83)

What is the kingdom of God save himself—the Son of the Father, descending
from heaven to earth so that we may be God's children as his brothers and
sisters?   (Barth, 'Gospel of God', 73)

The Word is not created; it is creating . . . the Word was with God in the
beginning, he *enters* into history to bring life, and he *returns* to the
Father.   (Gutiérrez, 'Coming of the Lord', 27, 28)

'This day is born the Savior', that is, he who, as the Son of God and Son of the
Father, has traveled (in obedience to the Father) the path that leads away from
the Father and into the darkness of the world. Behind him omnipotence and
freedom; before, powerlessness, bonds and obedience. Behind him the
comprehensive divine vision; before him the prospect of the meaninglessness
of death on the Cross between two criminals. Behind him the bliss of life with
the Father; before him, grievous solidarity with all who do not know the
Father, do not want to know him and deny his existence. Rejoice then, for God
himself has passed this way!   (Balthasar, 'Setting Out', 279; elsewhere, in a

non-Christmas radio broadcast, he says, 'No one can *become* God if he is not
God *already*' ('Interpretation', 314))

Rahner is theologically precise on this subject in ways that do not
go very far with respect to the sermonic, 'So what?':

> Using an authentic 'descent Christology', we can say that the Word that
> pre-existed from God in eternity became flesh; that the eternal Word of God
> descended into our history. We can call that Word the eternal Son of the
> Father, even though we must not deny that the biblical Word of the Son of
> the Father (at least in the oldest layers of the New Testament) refers
> primarily to the Man Jesus. . . . ('Made Man', 63)[7]

Schillebeeckx says nothing in his sermons bearing directly on the
question. Fosdick's assertion that people 'never guessed who Jesus
would be' ('Hospitality', 276) implicitly denies the personal pre-
existence of the Word. And while it is easy enough to imagine strong
and orthodox preaching that would never concern itself directly
with the idea of the personal pre-existence of the Word, it is at least
interesting, and further evidence that one's theology and preaching
are of a piece, that the more liberal of the theologians discussed here
are those less likely to say anything affirming it, while more
conservative theologians at least point in its direction.

III Paradox of the Hypostatic Union, and the Presence of God in History

That there is an immense mystery to Jesus' person is a theme
common to most of these sermons, sometimes momentarily
obscured by plain, orthodox assertions like, 'The one person is
there in whom God and man are one, without detriment to one or
the other' (Rahner, 'Human Abyss', 56); 'no theologian who intends
to interpret what is attested by faith, by the Church and by Scripture
will ever be able to dissolve the unity of Jesus Christ's human and
divine being' (Balthasar, 'Waiting for God', 255). All emphasize the
vital importance of Jesus' presence, as meaning God's presence, in
history. From that presence, some derive a message of comfort based
upon *God's solidarity* with humankind:

---

[7] The 'meditations' in this volume are allegedly aimed at a general audience, but
they vary enormously from straightforward homilies to pieces that would seem more
at home in a volume of theology proper.

God has become man and . . . now I am no longer alone in the darkness.   (Thielicke, 'Festival', 29)

[T]he Lord, the High God, has taken the same path as they have: he has left his glory behind him and gone into the dark world, into the child's apparent insignificance, into the unfreedom of human restrictions and bonds, into the poverty of the crib.   (Balthasar, 'Setting Out', 277)

The Word enters into history, taking on our human condition including its most fragile aspect.   (Gutiérrez, 'Coming of the Lord', 28)

That the infinity of God should take upon itself human narrowness, that bliss should accept the mortal sorrow of the earth, that life should take on death—this is the most unlikely truth.   (Rahner, 'I Became Your Brother', 49)

Sometimes, it seems to be Jesus' *humanity* itself that is significant, whether as dignifying ours or as revealing something about God (see also section VIII, below):

Jesus was a man, a true man without reservation, and without anything left out, a man like us.   (Rahner, 'Power of Birth', 38)[8]

In Matthew's Christmas story it becomes clear that Jesus becomes truly man, without any condition, without any claim to even a suspicion of divine attributes for his humanity. God discloses *his being in the humanity* of Jesus. . . . Through his message and his way of life Jesus redefines in word and deed what being human is and what being God means. And he does this by declaring humanity to be the nature of God. According to Jesus there is no difference between what scholars call 'God in himself' and 'God for us'. He is God for us in his own being.   (Schillebeeckx, 'Being Made Man', 47, 48)

For Barth, the decisive thing is the presence of *God's power* to help:

But now, the good news of Christmas! He who was born on Christmas Day is not only the son of Mary; he is also the son of God. If he stands by you, he does so in full power, in the power to help you at any cost, to shield you against each and everyone, above all against your worst enemy, yourself. He stands by you in the power to help you effectively, to carry you, to save you.   ('He Stands By Us', 139)

In Fosdick alone is the tone of mystery almost wholly lacking, turning his message into one of human potential:

---

[8] Rahner, for all his emphasis on the true humanity of Jesus, is clear that while 'God is man' does indeed say something about God, it does not mean that he has ceased to be God ('Answer of Silence', 65). Furthermore, 'the traditional doctrinal formulations of the Church on Christology do prevent us from reducing Jesus to the level of a religious genius . . .' ('God Made Man', 60).

There are many questions about Christianity and about Christ which we cannot answer. But Jesus himself, the essence of his character, the quality of his spirit, the core of his teaching, we do know. And we know that those areas of life where his spirit has been welcomed and enthroned, as we have seen it in some genuinely Christian friendships and families and in some genuinely Christian social attitudes, are the loveliest results our civilization has to show for its centuries of struggle.   ('Hospitality', 277)

[C]onsider what it is that makes a baby decisive. It is not the baby alone. . . . Of all decisive lives this is true—they are concentration points where multitudes of hopes, thoughts, faiths, and aspirations of common men and women are drawn together and focused.   ('Decisive Babies', 227)

Long ago in Palestine [Christ] played the gospel on his own life. But you cannot adequately play the gospel even on his life; it takes an orchestra; it requires a chorus. It takes communities, cities, nations, the world. Jesus has never heard how his gospel would really sound.   ('Christ of Experience', 45)

He was not trying to be a gigantic individual; he was trying to reveal eternal truth . . .   ('Christ of Experience', 38)

For Fosdick, it would seem, to attribute uniqueness and mystery to the incarnation would deprive it of its universal and inspirational value.

IV THE 'UNFAIRNESS' OF THE INCARNATION

While many of the theologians in this group are very clear about the historical particularity of the incarnation,[9] their remarks are striking in that they are all, insofar as they say anything about the matter, very concerned to keep this particularity from being scandalous. That is, they struggle mightily to find ways to speak good news to people of all times, places, and faiths:

No one is first, no one is last, no one gets preference, no one gets short-changed, and most important, not a single one goes wanting. He who was born in Bethlehem is the eldest brother of us all.   (Barth, 'Unto You Is Born', 24)

[9] e.g.: 'Jesus was born in a determined place and time: under Augustus and Quirinius and at the time of King Herod, a traitor to his people' (Gutiérrez, 'Joy for All', 23); 'He is the last call of God after which no other is to come or can come on account of the definitive nature of the self-communication of God (who represents himself in no other way)' (Rahner, 'Power of Birth', 47–8).

If he is not welcome, he is nevertheless present as a silent guest and listener, and as a silent yet impartial judge as well. (Barth, 'Gospel of God', 68)[10]

The incarnation of the Son of God is the heart of a message of solidarity with everyone, especially with the marginalized and the oppressed. (Gutiérrez, 'Joy for All,' 24)

As a mystery, [Jesus] is therefore never the exclusive possession of Christians. He is 'common property'. (Schillebeeckx, 'All Jerusalem', 18)

Even when someone who is still far from any explicit and verbally formulated revelation accepts his human reality in silent patience, or rather in faith, hope, and love (however these may be named), as a mystery which loses itself in the mystery of eternal love and bears life in the very midst of death, that person says yes to Jesus Christ even if he does not realize it. (Rahner, 'Human Abyss', 56)

We read in scripture that those who love their neighbor have fulfilled the law. This is the ultimate truth because God himself has become that neighbor, and so in every neighbor it is always he, one who is nearest and most distant, who is accepted and loved.   (Rahner, 'Human Abyss', 57; Rahner goes on to speak explicitly of 'anonymous Christians')

If there is unfairness here, it is not in the nature and impact of the incarnation as these men describe it. It might instead be seen in the often-remarked danger of imperialism—the bringing of those into the Christian fold who explicitly do not wish to be there. Or it might, ironically, be in giving short shrift to the more exclusivistic strands of Scripture. But surely it is not these theologians' intention to deprive anyone of the benefits of the incarnation. A broad inclusivism makes for more inviting preaching on the surface than does a sharp particularism; but it of course reduces the necessity for preaching at all.

---

[10] Note also this moving paragraph: 'And, thanks be to God, as we now consider the Saviour's coming into our own midst, there are not only the various inns where he stands outside, knocking and asking. There is quite another place where he simply enters, indeed has already secretly entered, and waits until we gladly recognize his presence. What kind of a place in our life is this? Do not suggest some presumably noble, beautiful or at least decent compartment of your life and work, where you could give the Saviour a respectable reception. Not so, my friends! The place where the Saviour enters in looks rather like the stable of Bethlehem. It is not beautiful, but quite ugly; not at all cosy, but really frightening; not at all decently human, but right beside the animals. You see, the proud or modest inns, and our behaviour as their inhabitants, are but the surface of our lives. Beneath there lurks the depth, even the abyss. Down below, we are, without exception, but each in his own way, only poor beggars, lost sinners, moaning creatures on the threshold of death, only people who have lost their way. Down there Jesus Christ sets up quarters' (Barth, 'He Stands By Us', 142).

V The Sinless Harmony of the Divine and Human Wills and Minds of Christ

Several interrelated matters come together here: the sinlessness of Jesus; that, as church councils have affirmed, the hypostatic union entails Christ having two minds and two wills; and the harmony of these minds and wills. Rahner speaks explicitly of the Monophysite and Monothelite controversies[11]—not language that will go over well in most sermons. He also allows for 'error', carefully construed, on Jesus' part, even in so important a matter as his expectation of an imminent End, though not in the significance of that expectation as meaning that God is indeed near and calls for unconditional decision.[12] What he seems most to want to convey, though, is the significance of the human mind and will of Jesus for the whole concept of human freedom: 'God's word has to be issued to us in the free obedience of a man to God, in which, in one man, God's promise is also perceptible for us; the promise, in other words, that God's mercy includes our freedom despite the ambivalent attitude of our freedom to its own salvation' ('Obedient unto Death', 53). Human freedom is also entailed in Thielicke's assertion that, 'When guilt, suffering, and death began their painful encirclement, he could have broken out, he could have been spared all that humiliation just by a wave of his hand. But, although it was possible for him to do it, that hand never moved' ('Conceived by the Holy Ghost', 84).

For Balthasar, Mary's immaculate conception comes importantly to bear here, particularly as regards the possibility of Jesus' sinlessness:

A mother does not only give her flesh and blood to the child but also something of her soul and spirit. . . . Jesus has to learn from his Mother how a man devotes himself totally to God and utters a limitless 'Yes' to him. He learns this from her not only by what she says but also in the only way children really learn anything: by example. . . . Just as Jesus erects no barriers of distrust between himself and God, he sets up none between himself and his Mother; and in this way he learns in human terms that the restrictions of man under original sin, erecting ultimate barriers between men, really can fall down. He needs this human experience in order to be able to fulfill his Father's great commission of destroying the world's sin . . . ('Boundaries', 268)

[11] 'Power of Birth', 42–3; 'God Made Man', 60.
[12] 'Power of Birth', 44.

This paragraph would be meaningless if Jesus had no truly human mind and will.

For Schillebeeckx, a key issue is Jesus' messianic consciousness, or rather lack thereof:

> [W]as he so filled with the one whom he called the Father that he was never concerned about his own person and only thought of his calling and his mission for others? 'Why do you call me good? Only the Father is good'. That can be said only by someone who is so obviously good that he is not even conscious of being good. And precisely that will betray his identity. ('God Who Visits', 9--10)

> I am struck by the fact that in the New Testament Jesus' identity is not a problem for Jesus himself but only for his followers. Perhaps that is not so much because his identity was crystal clear to himself, but because he simply did not think about it. ('All Jerusalem', 17)

A significant point for preaching may be that to be sinless is not intrinsically opposed to being human. Orthodox theologians, of course, affirm that point as a sort of reflex, but it is hardly the reflex of those hearers for whom any and all failings are 'merely human', a little wickedness is a lot more interesting than presumably bland and sticky 'goodness', and fears of loss of freedom threaten every significant commitment.

VI THE VIRGINAL CONCEPTION OF JESUS

The Protestants in my sample—none of whom was a biblical literalist—are not greatly concerned with the virginal conception. Thielicke, who weakly affirmed it, puts his conviction thus: 'When confronted with this ultimate mystery, who could say where reality leaves off and symbol begins? Who would assert that God couldn't also have come to us through the *normal* processes we know as conception and birth . . .?' ('Conceived by the Holy Ghost', 87). Barth did not speak to the issue in these Christmas sermons. Nor did Fosdick, but elsewhere, Fosdick explicitly denied the virginal conception and did not want it identified with affirmation of Jesus' divinity.[13]

---

[13] In his preaching related to the Fundamentalist/Modernist Controversy, he said, 'I am not deeply concerned whether you believe the virgin birth as a historic fact or not, although, as you know, I cannot believe it. But I am concerned that no one should tie up in one bundle the virgin birth and divinity of Jesus. The divinity of Jesus

The Roman Catholic theologians (excepting Schillebeeckx, who does not take up the issue in these sermons), by contrast, rather uniformly speak in a way that assumes or asserts the virginal conception.[14] The homiletical conclusions, however, tend to focus not on the meaning of the virginal conception as it relates to the incarnation (which, as a unique event, does not lend itself to general application), but rather on the human response of Joseph or, more usually, Mary.[15] Insofar as one does not tie the virginal conception *necessarily* to the divinity of Jesus, it would seem that its place in the preaching of the church would be likely to have to do more with such responses, or with one's anthropology,[16] or with one's teaching with Scripture and tradition, than with the incarnation as such.

VII   God's Reasons for the Incarnation

Almost all these theologians, with the very striking exception of Fosdick, put heavy emphasis on the divine love as the fundamental reason for the incarnation. (Rahner, interestingly enough, gives it less prominence than any of the others except Fosdick, but does not utterly neglect it.) But what should a supreme love offer to a world like ours? What is most required and most truly loving? Here my exemplars differ significantly from one another.

For Thielicke, the divine love takes the initiative, enters into the lowest, gives of itself, and so becomes a source of hope seemingly by its very presence:

was not physical. That is absurd. It was spiritual. It was the inner quality of his life in which his divinity consisted. . . . No, the divinity of Jesus was a convinced and singing faith that God can come into human life because God had come into human life' ('What Does the Divinity of Jesus Mean?' *Living Under Tension*, 157).

[14] e.g. Balthasar: '[Mary] knows what the Holy Spirit of God—he and no other— has done to her' ('Waiting for God', 253); or again, '[W]ithout the intervention of earthly seed, Mary conceives, carries and gives birth to him who will be the incarnate Word of God' ('Uniting the Disparate', 296); or Rahner's 'No Angel', which obviously assumes the virginal conception throughout.

[15] Thielicke goes this way as well: '[T]he husband, the symbol of "what makes history" or what creatively masters life, doesn't enter the picture. Rather, the focus is on the virgin, the symbol of silence, listening, and acquiescence' ('Conceived by the Holy Ghost', 87).

[16] Gutiérrez, for instance, refers to it as manifesting 'the greatness of [Mary's] condition as a woman' ('Blessed', 18).

[T]he love of God is so big that it gives itself in what is smallest, where the eternity of God is so mighty that it enters a feeble and despised body. For its strength is not in size and greatness. It is its ability to give itself, to become small, in order to draw near to those who are poor and needy and who can never storm heaven of themselves.   ('Redeeming Light', 63)

Long before they began to ask whether there was still any hope and meaning in their lives, Someone was already on his way to them. Christmas tells us that God comes to find us no matter where we are.   ('Reflection', 23)

[I]f this Child exists, then he is the heart and center of the world, then, to put it in philosophical terms, he is the hermeneutical principle which unlocks the mystery of the world. Then I see in the Child that in the background of this world there is a Father. I see that love reigns above and in the world, even when I cannot understand this governance . . .   ('Festival', 28)

Barth emphasizes the wholly free and sovereign quality of God's self-giving, which is explicitly for our salvation:

[H]e emptied himself that you may be exalted; for you he gave himself that you may be lifted up and drawn unto him. The wondrous deed brought him no gain, fulfilled no need of his. It was accomplished only for you, for us.   ('Unto You Is Born', 23)

This is the very heart of the Christmas story. To you this day is born a *Saviour* . . .   ('Unto You Is Born', 26)

He who loves us infinitely more than we love ourselves saw the misery in which we engulf ourselves by thinking we know how to love and understand ourselves. He saw the hardships, the atrocities, the injustice and the disorder, he saw our false securities and our breakdowns. He could not stand it any more. He could not bear any longer being God on high without being God on earth, our helper, saviour and redeemer.   ('Gospel of God', 70–1)

Gutiérrez focuses on *life* as 'the purpose of creation and of salvation' ('Coming of the Lord', 270): '[Jesus] expresses the love of the Father: "all things came into being" through him (Jn 1: 3). This marks the meaning of all that exists; the key word is "life"' ('Before Creation', 35).

Rahner avers that God gives 'himself to us ultimately as forgiveness, liberation and deification' ('Power of Birth', 42). Schillebeeckx says Jesus is 'someone who as a human being wants to bring order to things; he wants to remove our chaos in word and deed by radical humanity in our world as a visible form of the all-embracing love of God' ('Being Made Man', 49). Balthasar speaks of the quality of God's love itself, but particularly what it means for the future:

[I]n this event, Love has appeared on earth, absolute, unsurpassable Love, so great that it causes every lover to catch his breath . . .   ('Fullness', 290)

[O]ne man has loved all other men unto the end that has no end, winning for all, through his living and dying, both access to the Father and the seal of the Holy Spirit of God. But if this act, in itself, contains and dispenses all the fullness of grace, it necessarily puts itself 'before' each man, presents itself as a model: what has been done, if it is to become the meaning of existence, is what is to be done . . .   ('Future Already Come', 244)

It is evident, then, that to specify 'love' or 'salvation' as the reason for the incarnation is both to say something critical and not to say quite enough; for while these terms evoke an emotional reaction for most people, that reaction does not in itself specify the *content* of these terms. And it would seem evident that cultural and theological location, and not only the biblical narratives themselves, bear very importantly on what that content is perceived to be. What is true for preachers is surely equally true for hearers: we do not all need to be loved in exactly the same way or delivered from exactly the same thing, unless these too are construed so broadly as also to lose identifiable content.

VIII THE REVELATORY AND REDEMPTIVE IMPACT OF THE INCARNATION

With respect to the revelatory and redemptive impact of the incarnation, Thielicke and Barth add little beyond what has already been reported of their ways of focusing on God's presence with us— in the little things of life (Thielicke); in the fullness of his authority and power (Barth). Besides repeating that God abides forever with those he loves, and especially with the poorest and most insignificant, Gutiérrez adds: 'By becoming human, the Son of God transforms every human face into the expression of God's presence and exigency' ('Mother of Jesus', 34).[17]

Fosdick, Balthasar, and Schillebeeckx all give a great deal of weight to the power of Jesus' example, though in very different ways. For Fosdick, it appears to be mainly a matter of ideas revealed by concrete example and hence brought to life, joined to the conviction that world-changing ideas, like babies, are born

---

[17] See also 'God with Us', 16, and 'Coming of the Lord', 29.

small.[18] Christ's character becomes the standard of judgement for character;[19] Christ 'let loose in this world a kind of life that mankind never has been able to escape . . . [g]reatness measured by usefulness . . .' ('Christ of Experience', 39). 'Somebody incarnates goodness until it becomes fascinating and transforming—that works the consequence' ('Christ of Experience', 43). Fosdick obviously implies that what starts small has potential at last to change everything; Christ is the pioneer.[20]

By contrast, Balthasar asserts that 'in a hundred thousand years mankind will not be a finger's breadth nearer the prototype, Christ, than it is today' ('Future Already Come', 247). Nonetheless, 'world history after Christ can never be the same . . . [U]ltimately it comes down to the attitude adopted by Jesus in his living and dying: the attitude of perfect, selfless love, service to the very last and the fruitfulness that comes from it. This is the innermost meaning and core of all mankind's questions . . .' ('Waiting for God', 255). The Christian must always keep what Christ has done before him and move toward it: 'It depends on him [the Christian] whether or not it will be embodied, incarnated, now' ('Future Already Come', 245). The model is of final importance, but its importance is intrinsic, not established or threatened by greater or lesser human progress.

As might not be surprising, given Schillebeeckx's emphasis on the radical humanity of Jesus and yet his desire to affirm something about his uniqueness, it is not entirely clear how he sees Jesus' example as actually functioning, though he clearly says that Jesus has brought something new:

For the believing Christian, the birth of Jesus is the real beginning of salvation, that is, of a concern to bring renewal to the bloody course of our history, coming to life and taking personal form in that history. The birth of this man is a first great step towards what the Bible calls the coming 'commonwealth of God' . . .   ('All Jerusalem', 14)

[T]he incarnation of Jesus is fundamental opposition to this world. But in the coming of Jesus the fundamental, open yes becomes a clear message; only more humanity, to the end, can save the world. . . . He gives perspective on how the human face of the world can look; he treads the way to it before us. From this it emerges that he believes in a God who

---

[18] 'Decisive Babies', 223–35.
[19] 'Light', 216.
[20] e.g. 'Christ Is Christianity', 187.

wholly accepts human beings as they are and tries to renew them, on the basis of this unmerited acceptance . . . ('Being Made Man', 48)

One senses, in any case, a certain reserve about the renewing power of Christ and the likelihood that people will seize upon the salvation—defined as 'man's well-being, disclosed in Jesus' ('All Jerusalem', 16)—that he offers.

In the midst of these somewhat limited offerings, the breadth of Rahner's treatment is refreshing, and the passion with which he speaks, moving. The incarnation gives humans significance and meaning; Jesus' relationship to the Father had an exemplary aspect that opened up new possibilities for all; Jesus' passing 'along our path of fate' has 'opened it up into the unending spaces of God'; since the incarnation is permanent and eternity is now linked to a piece of history, the world is united to God in Christ; so 'no longer can God allow the world as a whole to fall out of his love and grace'; it will not at last be 'burned to nothing by his consuming fire of holiness and righteousness'.[21] Many of these ideas are captured in the following long paragraph:

It must be worthwhile being a human being, if God was not satisfied to be in himself but also willed in addition to be one of these human beings, and if that was not too dangerous or too trivial for him. Humankind is not a herd, but a sacred family, if God himself is a member of it as a brother. The tragedy of its history must after all have a blessed outcome, if God does not just observe this hardly divine comedy unmoved from the throne of his infinity but takes part in it himself, as seriously as all the rest of us, who have to do so whether we want to or not. The so-called genuine reality both of the embittered and disillusioned and of the superficial bon vivant is reduced to a mere semblance which only unbelieving fools take in deadly earnest or with greedy seriousness, now that God himself has become the true reality behind and in the midst of this appearance. Eternity is already in the heart of time, life is at the center of death, truth is stronger than lies, love more powerful than hatred, the wickedness of human beings already irrevocably conquered by God's grace. ('Great Joy', 62)[22]

Surely such a paragraph is a sermon in itself.

---

[21] See 'Advent', 8; 'I Became Your Brother', 48, 50; 'Power of Birth', 49; 'Lighten Our Darkness', 73.

[22] Note, in addition, these remarks: 'If, therefore, I, as a creature, want to prove in me and in you, my brothers and sisters, that I, as creator, have not made a hopeless experiment with the human race, who then shall tear my hand away from you?' ('I Became Your Brother', 51); 'Now we no longer need to seek him in the endlessness of heaven, where our spirit and our heart get lost' ('I Became Your Brother', 49).

IX The Relationship of the Incarnation to the Resurrection

I recall from childhood a pastor preaching an Easter sermon on Christmas, on the grounds that apart from cross and resurrection, we would not be celebrating Christmas at all. None of the sermons I analysed took that tack as a whole, though Rahner several times made that essential point.[23] Many other sermons also explicitly linked the beginning and the end of Jesus' earthly life. Sometimes the emphasis was on the depth of the divine condescension, not reached until the cross: 'the descent of the Christmas child did not reach its lowest point on Christmas night' (Thielicke, 'Redeeming Light', 63); 'Crib and cross are both of the same wood' (Thielicke, 'Reflection', 23). Sometimes the emphasis was on the resurrection: 'True, he once lived and then died—and how he died!—but he also rose from the dead; he lives and is present among us now, much closer to each one of us than we are to ourselves' (Barth, 'He Stands by Us', 137). Sometimes, as in Fosdick's exemplary approach, the emphasis was on the whole course of Jesus' life and death. Balthasar says that 'the point of departure and the destination point match one another' ('Waiting for God', 254): it is in the whole that we learn who Jesus really is. Since Schillebeeckx understands the birth narratives to have been radically shaped by the resurrection from a literary point of view, and does not believe we can get behind the telling to the history, he obviously sees all that we glean in Scripture of Jesus' life to be governed by the Gospel writers' understanding of its end.[24] He also notes, however, that it is the crucifixion that gives us a whole new view of how God's love, power, and splendour manifest themselves.[25]

All of these approaches, it would seem, have positive homiletical potential and help to guard against a merely sentimental approach to Christmas, without robbing it of its importance.

---

[23] 'Power of Birth', 35, 39; 'Obedient Unto Death', 55.

[24] 'All doors are closed to him; he is born in a manger. Matthew makes Jesus' end, as one who is outcast and rejected, already begin at his birth' ('Being Made Man', 47). 'The angels in fact made their appearance when after the resurrection of Jesus believers celebrated in their assemblies their trust in Jesus and thus as it were mobilized all that was real to them, to present it to God with their praise and thanks for the gift which had been given to them in Jesus. Then nothing was too much. Angels, stars, wise men from the east, "astrologers", but also simple people and shepherds, everyone was summoned to offer praise to God' ('God Who Visits', 11).

[25] 'God Who Visits', 11.

X The Credibility of the Incarnation

Lay theologian Dorothy Sayers, who held generally orthodox opinions herself on matters theological, once said that it was not too surprising if people claimed not to believe the doctrine of the church, since it does take some believing.[26] Fosdick reduces what one needs to believe essentially to the eventual 'triumph of Christ's way of life' in our world; and for that he thought, at least in many cases, 'the crux of the matter was not simply faith, but intelligence and insight' ('Christ Is Christianity', 187; at the beginning of the twenty-first century, many would suppose that such a triumph—if one relies on human capacity alone, at least—takes a good deal more believing than the most recondite orthodox doctrines). Most of the others, though, refer to difficulties of quite another kind.

Thielicke and Rahner both refer explicitly to the intellectual problems attached to the idea of incarnation; to these Thielicke adds the *risk* of believing something so implausible, should it turn out to be a fairy tale; and Rahner notes that even if we came up with a solution that satisfied us intellectually, it wouldn't matter if the event merely occurred and ended in the remote past.[27] Barth and Balthasar put the fault implicitly or explicitly on the human side as regards the difficulty of belief, Barth speaking of the need to 'accept [the gospel] as told by God, to make it our own' ('Gospel of God', 72); and Balthasar noting the obstacles imposed by riches, whether material or those of 'neat and tidy concepts, opinions, perspectives, experiences and world views', from which people must extricate themselves 'until they finally stand on the naked earth where the Child lies in the crib' ('Uniting the Disparate', 292). For Schillebeeckx, the problem of evil tests the plausibility of Christian faith as a whole: it would be a fault *not* to struggle with it.[28] But in a similar context Thielicke says, 'The highest love is almost always incognito and therefore we must trust it' ('Festival', 28). Perhaps yet more significantly, Gutiérrez—who surely knows as much about suffering as the others—does not in these sermons make of the incarnation an intellectual obstacle to belief at all, but simply affirms: 'Faith and trust always entail a journey' ('My Father's Interests', 33). One

---

[26] *The Whimsical Christian* (New York: Macmillan, 1978), 24.

[27] 'Conceived by the Holy Ghost', 82–3, and 'Power of Birth', 36–7, respectively.

[28] e.g. 'Being Made Man', 47, 49.

wonders if his stance might be related to what certainly appears to be a much franker acceptance of the supernatural, in its power as well as its mystery, than Schillebeeckx shows.

However they may pose the problems, all of my exemplars affirm the human journey, not supposing that a fully formed faith somehow drops on one's head with everything doctrinally intact.[29] They at least imply, and most say rather directly, that belief grows by experience, most particularly by the experience of 'living with' as much of Jesus as one can honestly grasp at the moment. Even Fosdick obviously goes this way: 'Identify yourself with the Christ life, until the Christ of history becomes the Christ of experience' ('Christ of Experience', 45). Thielicke puts it quite fully:

We should quietly leave aside everything that appears dogmatic and mythological to us and hold on to what we understand: that here is someone who has spoken words about sorrow, anxiety, and freedom that get under our skin; that here is someone who is totally identified with his life's work; that here is a man who loved until it killed him, because he took love seriously and did not hold back any reserves for his own safety. If I held on to all of that, it would still be only a *hem* of his garment. That wouldn't be Jesus *himself* at all. Perhaps it would only be the ideal picture of a noble man and therefore somewhat deceptive. If I grasped him at *this* point and held on—if I tried to understand him from my point of view as if he were like me—then I would soon come to the place where he mysteriously eluded my grasp and simply could not fit into my psychological and ethical table of values. But I would have come to the key point precisely when I made that discovery. I must start by walking this road of natural, human togetherness with him . . . ('Conceived by the Holy Ghost', 93–4)

Schillebeeckx adds that to become more human (his view being, again, that Jesus reveals the fully human[30]), we 'must first become aware of the nagging experience of suffering humanity and consequently also go through the school of *docta ignorantia*: learning to doubt with the doubters, searching with those who search, suffering

[29] Even Barth, whose advocacy of simple 'acceptance' of the Gospel as God's word can sound rather bald, goes on to say that one must 'let it take root in our hearts and grow and bring forth fruit'. Furthermore, 'to believe in the gospel in the deepest sense means, quite simply, *to stand by the messenger who brought us the gospel of God, to stand by Jesus Christ*' ('Gospel of God', 72, emphasis his).

[30] But he does not want to be tied down: 'This mystery of the man Jesus, God's parable and man's paradigm, cannot be summed up in one formula. The church did what it could given the historically-conditioned questions that were posed. But the mystery can never be eliminated nor can it ever be put fully into words' ('All Jerusalem', 18).

with those who suffer, being open to "the unknown" and not keeping the free Holy Spirit in its own sovereign care' ('Being Made Man', 49).

It is not just a matter of will and effort and clear thinking, though. Sometimes grace simply surprises us, meets us in our human experience in a compelling and unanticipated way. Maybe it is a moment of meaning and happiness (Schillebeeckx, 'Being Made Man', 47), a flash of transforming joy (Thielicke, 'Conceived by the Holy Ghost', 87), a 'music of the soul' that reaches out to the God who has already reached down to us (Rahner, 'Lighten Our Darkness', 75). And we may at some odd moment discover that, in our heart of hearts, we believe a great deal more than we thought we did (Rahner, 'Human Abyss', 55)—an affirmation that could grant a glimpse of Christmas hope to many anxious, doubting hearts.

Two contrary risks beset the preacher who undertakes to proclaim Christian doctrine. On the one side, he or she may make it all too easy, too tidy—perhaps mouthing formulas as if swallowing a certain number of unlikely assertions before breakfast were the key to spiritual health. The questions the thoughtful or sceptical hearer might have are either ignored or are dismissed in such a way that it might seem as if having such questions were a proof of spiritual failure. Or, on the other side, he or she may make it all so complicated, so demanding of erudition, or simply so mysterious, that one wonders in the end if we can affirm anything at all that we could claim makes a difference—or even has a chance of making sense. Either way—by saying too much or too little—the preacher can maintain a sort of safe distance and control. And either approach, ironically enough, can leave listeners shut up in their subjectivity: either they have some experience or *feeling* that validates Christian belief for them, or they don't; they are thwarted at the level of thoughtful, believing intellectual engagement. It seems to me that the latter outcome is dismayingly common in ordinary congregations today, contributing seriously to disengagement on the part of lay people, and even of many pastors, from the content of Christian belief.

I would judge that the preachers in my sample did, in the sermons I reviewed, sometimes err in one direction or the other, not asking questions that begged to be asked or falling into a disastrous muddle of theological jargon and convoluted existential angst. However, I was struck not only that almost all the areas O'Collins identifies as key for the current discussion did come up one way or another, but also that the homiletical 'so what' could usually be identified. More, it was often conveyed in a moving and compelling way that might provide inspiration for other preachers, demonstrating once again that one need not bypass the human head in order to reach the human heart.[31] True, the taking up of complex issues was often implicit, without the technical jargon and careful hedging theologians use among themselves. Sermons, at least as preached, do not have footnotes. But surely that is as it should be; and the preacher should not take lightly the fact that very much of the knowledge we humans rely upon in a pinch, we have gained implicitly: it has become part of the fabric of our thinking almost without our realizing it. And if ordinary preachers were less fearful of exploring doctrinal matters and of doing a bit of teaching to help people understand something of what is at stake at various points, their hearers would have an easier time giving a reason for the hope that is in them (1 Pet. 3: 15). At least in this sense, then—the sense in which the content and consequences of Christian doctrine are set forth in practical terms as well as being intrinsic to the preacher's thinking about all he or she declares—Christian doctrine can and should be proclaimed from the Christian pulpit.

Note: Sermons consulted include the following (where no short title is given, either the sermon was not quoted directly in the chapter, or the title is later given in full): Hans Urs von Balthasar, *You Crown the Year with Your Goodness*, trans. Graham Harrison (San Francisco: Ignatius Press, 1982)—'The Future Has Already Come' (pp. 243–51, henceforth 'Future Already Come'); 'Waiting for God' (pp. 251–7); 'Abolishing the Boundaries' (pp. 264–9, 'Boundaries'); 'Defenseless and Fruitful' (pp. 269–74); 'Setting Out into the Dark with God' (pp. 275–80, 'Setting Out'); 'Fullness Creates History' (pp. 280–91, 'Fullness'); 'Leveling Downward' (pp. 291–4); 'Uniting the Disparate' (pp. 295–9); also a radio broadcast entitled 'The Church's Interpretation of Jesus' (pp. 311–15, 'Interpretation'); Gustavo Gutiérrez,

---

[31] In the words of Scottish preacher James Stewart, 'There is a type of preaching which apparently regards it as more important to generate heat than to supply light. . . . Some preachers have the fixed idea that the way to reach the human heart is to by-pass the human understanding. It is emphatically mistaken strategy' (*Heralds of God* (London: Hodder & Stoughton, 1946), 152–3).

Sharing the Word Through the Liturgical Year, trans. Colette Joly Dees (Maryknoll, NY: Orbis, 1997)—'God with Us' (pp. 15–16); 'Mary' (pp. 16–17); 'Blessed among Women' (pp. 18–19, 'Blessed'); 'Joy for All the People' (pp. 23–4, 'Joy for All'); 'One More Christmas, One Less Christmas' (pp. 25–6, 'One More Christmas'); 'The Coming of the Lord' (pp. 26–9); 'My Father's Interests' (pp. 32–3); 'The Mother of Jesus' (pp. 33–4); 'Before the Creation of the World' (pp. 35–6, 'Before Creation'); Karl Rahner, in *Biblical Homilies*, trans. D. Forristal and R. Strachan (New York: Herder and Herder, 1966), 'For Us No Angel from Heaven' (pp. 9–12, 'No Angel'); in *Meditations on Hope and Love*, trans. V. Green (London: Burns & Oates, 1976), 'God Is with Us' (pp. 27–32); 'The Power of Birth' (pp. 35–51); 'Obedient unto Death' (pp. 52–6); 'God Made Man' (pp. 57–64); 'Lighten Our Darkness' (pp. 65–75); in *The Great Church Year: The Best of Karl Rahner's Homilies, Sermons, and Meditations*, ed. A. Raffelt, trans. H. D. Egan (New York: Crossroad, 1995), 'The Advent of the World and Our Advent' (pp. 7–10, 'Advent'); 'Christmas: "Every Since I Became Your Brother. . ."' (pp. 47–52, 'I Became Your Brother'); 'Christmas: The Feast of History' (pp. 52–4); 'Grace in the Human Abyss' (pp. 54–7, 'Human Abyss'); 'Holy Night' (pp. 57–61); 'Christmas: The Great Joy' (pp. 61–3, 'Great Joy'); 'Christmas: The Answer of Silence' (pp. 63–6, 'Answer of Silence'); Edward Schillebeeckx, in *God Among Us: The Gospel Proclaimed*, trans. John Bowden (New York: Crossroad, 1983), 'God "Who Visits His People"' (pp. 8–12, 'God Who Visits'); '"All Jerusalem was Afraid"' (pp. 13–19, 'All Jerusalem'); in *For the Sake of the Gospel*, trans. John Bowden (New York: Crossroad, 1990), '"Being Made Man"' (pp. 46–9); 'Epiphany: God, but in Authentic Humanity' (pp. 59–63, 'Authentic Humanity'); Karl Barth, *Deliverance to the Captives*, trans. Marguerite Weiser (London: SCM Press, 1959), 'Unto You Is Born This Day a Saviour' (pp. 20–7, 'Unto You Is Born'); 'The Gospel of God' (pp. 67–74); 'The Great Dispensation' (pp. 101–8); 'He Stands By Us' (pp. 136–43); Harry Emerson Fosdick, in *Living Under Tension* (New York and London: Harper & Bros., 1941), 'The Decisive Babies of the World' (pp. 222–32, 'Decisive Babies'); in *A Great Time To Be Alive* (New York and London: Harper & Bros., 1944), 'The Light that No Darkness Can Put Out' (pp. 209–17, 'Light'); in *On Being Fit To Live With* (New York and London: Harper & Bros., 1946), 'Christ Himself Is Christianity' (pp. 185–93, 'Christ Is Christianity'); in *What is Vital in Religion* (New York: Harper & Bros., 1955), 'The Christ of History and the Christ of Experience' (pp. 34–45, 'Christ of Experience'); in *Riverside Sermons* (New York: Harper & Bros., 1958), 'Hospitality to the Highest' (pp. 275–83, 'Hospitality'); Helmut Thielicke, in *Christ and the Meaning of Life*, trans. John W. Doberstein (New York and Evanston: Harper & Row, 1962), 'Reflection in a Dark Glass' (pp. 20–3, 'Reflection'); 'The Festival of Light' (pp. 24–9, 'Festival'); in *The Silence of God*, trans. G. W. Bromiley (Grand Rapids, Mich.: Eerdmans, 1962), 'The

Message of Redeeming Light' (pp. 61–6, 'Redeeming Light'); in *I Believe: The Christian's Creed*, trans. J. W. Doberstein and H. G. Anderson (Philadelphia: Fortress, 1968), 'Conceived by the Holy Ghost, Born of the Virgin Mary' (pp. 82–94, 'Conceived by the Holy Ghost').

Index of Names

Abraham, W. J. 18 n.
Abramowski, L. 156 n., 178 n.
Adams, J. L. 351 n.
Adams, M. McCord 316 n.
Adams, R. 329 n.
Adeimantus 122
Aitchison, C. 364 n.
Alberigo, G. 183 n.
Aletti, J.-N. 5, 52 n., 86 n., 93–115
Alexander of Aphrodisias 169 n.
Alston, W. 157–8, 218 n., 299 n.
Alsup, J. E. 37 n.
Anderson, H. G. 396 n.
Angerstorfer, A. 39 n.
Anselm (of Canterbury), St 4, 16, 18,
    156, 257, 315–16
Apollinarius of Laodicaea 145, 161,
    172–3, 178 n., 184, 190
Apuleius, L. 122
Aquinas, St Thomas 12 n., 19
  on incarnation 10 n., 14 n., 52,
    197–219, 277–81, 287
  on knowledge of God 268
  on language for God 151
  on motive of incarnation 17–18,
    22 n., 316
Aristides 99 n.
Aristotle 10, 26 n., 124
  on accidents 169
  on body and soul 118, 121, 128
  on practical wisdom 321–2
  on relationship 171–2
Arius 5, 24, 70 n.
Armstrong, A. H. 161 n.
Arnim, H. von 171 n.
Arnold, C. E. 70 n.
Arnou, R. 177 n.
Athanasius of Alexandria, St 16
Auden, W. H. 304
Augustine (of Hippo), St 4, 24 n., 150,
    274–5

Baal-Teshuva, J. 355 n., 356 n., 357 n.
Bach, J. S. 363
Bacht, H. 145 n.
Bacon, F. 333, 350–3, 364
Baer, R. 130 n.
Baker, L. R. 202 n., 205
Balthasar, H. U. von 24 n., 317 n.,
    374–94
Bandura, A. 325 n.
Barr, J. 42, 43–4, 241 n.
Barth, K. 20 n., 374–95
Basil of Caesarea, St 168 n.
Bauckham, R. 234, 235, 236
Baxter, A. 163 n.
Beasley-Murray, P. 70 n.
Bebke, B. 346 n.
Bedjan, P. 182 n.
Behr, J. 188 n.
Bell, K. 337 n., 338 n.
Beloff, J. 285 n.
Ben-Chorin, S. 242
Benoit, P. 3 n.
Bergjan, S.-P. 182 n.
Berquist, J. 116 n.
Beversluis, J. 223 n.
Birnbaum, E. 126 n.
Bischoff, U. 349 n.
Bloom, A. 12 n.
Blowers, P. 32 n.
Bockris, V. 344 n.
Boethius 200 n., 201 n., 207 n., 275 n.
Boice, J. M. 223 n.
Bonaventure, St 316
Bonhoeffer, D. 317–18, 329
Booth, J. W. 297–8
Bordreuil, P. 40 n.
Borg, M. J. 47 n., 58, 59 n.
Borland, J. 37 n.
Bourdon, D. 344 n., 346 n.
Bouyer, L. 3 n.
Bowden, J. 63 n., 395 n.

Brancusi, C. 332, 357
Brandon, S. G. F. 122 n.
Breton, A. 350
Bromiley, G. W. 20 n., 395 n.
Brown, R. E. 15, 16 n., 242
Brown, D. W. 18 n., 24 n., 27 n.,
    157–9, 247 n., 305 n., 332–64
Brownlee, A. 310
Bruce, F. F. 71 n., 85 n.
Bruns, I. 169 n.
Bultmann, R. 24, 226 n., 234, 236,
    238
Burghardt, W. J. 38 n.
Burrell, D. 151 n.
Busse, A. 169 n., 170 n.
Butler, J. 270 n.
Byrne, B. 63 n., 67 n.

Caesar, Augustus 195, 381 n.
Caird, G. B. 55
Caligula, Emperor Gaius 125
Calvin, J. 52
Campbell, J. 1, 2 n., 3
Capes, D. 32 n., 135
Capra, F. 27 n.
Care, N. S. 270 n.
Carline, H. 337, 339
Carman, J. B. 117 n.
Casey, P. M. 45 n.
Cavallin, H. C. C. 126 n., 128 n.
Celsus 3, 7
Cézanne, P. 360 n.
Chadwick, H. 145, 274 n.
Chagall, M. 354–7
Chester, A. 37 n.
Chesterton, G. K. 221 n.
Chiappini, R. 334 n., 335 n.
Chisholm, R. 270 n.
Choniates, N. 167 n.
Chrysippus 171 n.
Chute, D. 339 n.
Cicero 90 n.
Cimabue, G. 352 n.
Clarke, S. G. 313 n.
Coakley, S. 10, 27 n., 143–63, 247 n.,
    292 n.
Cobb, J. 259
Cogniat, R. 356 n.
Collins, J. 358 n., 359 n., 360 n.
Colson, F. H. 126 n.
Combès, J. 171 n.
Confucius 10
Connolly, M. 26–7

Constas, N. 163 n.
Coomaraswamy, A. K. 358 n.
Cork, R. 362 n., 363 n.
Craig, W. L. 222 n.
Crick, F. 341 n.
Cross, R. 197 n.
Crossan, J. D. 237 n., 239
Crouzel, H. 39 n.
Cupitt, D. 7–8
Cyril of Alexandria, St 38 n., 146,
    148 n., 178–83
Cyril of Jerusalem, St 177 n.

Daley, B. 3 n., 10, 150, 155 n., 163 n.,
    164–96
Dalí, G. 340
Dalí, S. 333, 339–43, 348, 349, 364
Dalmais, I.-H. 185 n.
Damascius 171
Daniélou, J. 185 n.
Davey, R. 364 n.
Davila, J. R. 55 n.
Davis, S. T. 27 n., 63 n., 159 n., 247 n.,
    299 n.
    on divine timelessness 287 n.
    on Jesus as 'mad, bad, or God' 24 n.,
    221–45
    on kenotic Christology 246 n.,
    252–6, 258, 259–60
Day, J. 31 n.
Dearman, J. A. 6 n., 31–46, 136
Dees, C. J. 395 n.
Dennett, D. 230 n.
Descharnes, R. 339 n., 340 n., 341 n.,
    342 n., 349 n.
Devresse, R. 178 n.
Dewan, L. 218 n.
Dexippus 170 n., 171
Diamond, C. 156
Dickinson, E. 308, 311
Dillenberger, J. D. 345 n., 346 n.
Diodore 173
Dionysius the Pseudo-Areopagite 151
Diotima 119
Doberstein, J. W. 395 n., 396 n.
Dohmen, C. 43 n.
Donnellan, K. 318
Dorival, B. 335 n.
Dostoevsky, F. 330
Dräseke, J. 176 n.
Driver, G. R. 182 n.
Dübner, F. 172 n.

Dunn, J. D. G. 49–50, 51, 52 n., 67 n.,
 90 n., 107
 on Adam-Christology 87 n., 88 n.
 on Christ's pre-existence 63 n., 70 n.,
  73 n., 80 n., 84 n., 85 n., 91 n.
 on incarnation 5, 31 n., 88 n., 99 n.,
  103–5
 on Judaism 45 n., 69 n.
 on the law 108 n., 239 n.
 on Romans 98, 106 n.
 on salvation 38 n., 110–12, 114
 on wisdom 7, 77 n.
Duns Scotus, Blessed John 16, 17,
 316
Dupuis, J. 11 n.
Dyer, G. 353
Dyrness, W. A. 333 n.

Edelman, D. V. 36 n.
Egan, H. D. 395 n.
Eichrodt, W. 33 n., 37 n.
Einarson, B. 177 n.
Eisenberger, H. 178 n.
Eisenstein, S. M. 352 n.
Eldredge, C. C. 347 n.
Elias of Jerusalem 169 n.
Eliot, T. S. 19
Epictetus 172 n.
Epp, E. J. 69 n.
Epstein, J. 357, 361–3, 364
Ernst, C. 152 n.
Ernst, M. 348–9, 350, 364
Etherington-Smith, M. 340 n., 341 n.
Ettlinger, G. 181 n.
Eumolpus 122
Eunomius 173, 174 n.
Eutyches 145, 161
Evans, C. A. 31 n., 37 n., 55 n.
Evans, C. S. 245 n.
 on incarnation 1, 8–9, 12–13, 19,
  25 n.
 on kenotic Christology 3, 246–72
 on special acts of God 11
Everitt, N. 6 n.

Faerna, J. M. 334 n.
Falco, V. de 170 n.
Fantino, J. 39 n.
Farson, D. 353 n.
Fee, G. D. 3, 62–92, 241 n.
Feenstra, R. J. 247 n., 257–8, 260,
 264–6, 269 n.
Festugière, A.-J. 145 n.

Fine, K. 198 n.
Fisk, B. 66 n.
Fitzmyer, J. A. 15–16, 239 n.
Flanagan, O. 324 n.
Flannery, A. 303 n.
Flavian of Constantinpole, St 146
Fontaine, J. 185 n.
Forristal, D. 395 n.
Fortin, E. 178 n.
Fosdick, H. E. 374–95
Francis of Assisi, St 323
Franco, F. 340
Frend, W. H. C. 21 n.
Freud, S. 252
Fry, R. 358 n.
Fuller, R. H. 31 n., 222 n.
Funk, R. 48, 237 n., 239

Galassi, S. G. 348 n.
Gandhi, M. 323
Gardiner, S. 362 n., 363 n.
Geach, P. T. 8, 281
Gibson, I. 339 n., 340 n.
Gieschen, C. 37 n., 38 n.
Gill, E. 339 n., 357–60, 364
Gislibertus 359
Goodenough, E. R. 124 n., 128 n.
Green, J. B. 45 n.
Green, M. 153 n.
Green, V. 395 n.
Greenberg, U. Z. 355
Greenhaigh, J. 304 n.
Gregory of Nazianzus, St 160, 167,
 168 n., 169 n., 186, 187
Gregory of Nyssa, St:
 on human fallenness 188
 on hypostasis 181
 on image of God 38 n.
 on incarnation 25
 on relationships 169 n., 173–7, 183,
  193
Grice, H. P. 285 n.
Grillmeier, A. 145 n., 148 n., 155 n.,
 181 n.
Grimm, R. H. 270 n.
Grosseteste, R. 316
Grube, G. M. A. 120 n.
Gruenler, R. G. 234 n., 238
Grünewald, M. 341, 348, 352
Guelich, R. A. 239 n.
Gunderson, K. 318 n.
Gunton, C. E. 45 n.
Gustafson, J. 313 n.

Gutiérrez, G. 374–95
Gwynne, P. 11

Habermann, J. 37 n.
Hadad-Yithi, King 39
Hadot, P. 174 n.
Haftmann, W. 354 n., 356 n.
Hagner, D. A. 70 n., 239 n.
Hall, C. 32 n.
Hall, D. 303 n., 311
Halleux, A. de 145 n.
Hamann, J. G. 272 n.
Hampson, D. 247 n.
Handy, L. K. 35 n.
Hanson, A. T. 32 n.
Hardy, E. R. 176 n., 179 n.
Hare, J. 314 n.
Harnack, A. von 32 n.
Harris, M. J. 70 n.
Harrison, C. 24 n.
Harrison, G. 394 n.
Hass, R. 308 n.
Hastings, J. 22 n.
Hawthorne, G. 37 n., 62 n.
Hayduck, M. 170 n., 172 n.
Hebblethwaite, B. 9, 11, 254
Heckel, U. 37 n.
Hefling, C. 163 n.
Hegel, G. W. F. 2 n., 17, 331
Heidt, W. 35 n.
Heinzer, F. 169 n., 174 n., 185 n.
Helyer, L. L. 70 n.
Hengel, M. 37 n., 73 n.
Hepworth, D. 337 n.
Heraclides (of Damascus) 182
Herod the Great, King 381 n.
Hermann, E. 331 n.
Hermas, Shepherd of 118
Hibbs, T. 151 n.
Hick, J.:
    on divine intervention 222, 231
    on Jesus forgiving sin 240–1
    on kenotic Christology 246 n., 252,
        257
    on metaphorical incarnation 2–4,
        12, 153–4, 156–8, 160
Hodgson, L. 182 n.
Hofstadter, D. 230 n.
Holmgren, F. C. 31 n.
Holtzer, S. W. 18 n.
Hong, E. H. 272 n.
Hong, H. V. 272 n.
Horbury, W. 32 n.

Hörner, H. 178 n.
Howard-Snyder, D. 27 n., 163 n.,
    245 n.
Hume, D. 285, 287
Hunter, A. M. 65 n.
Hurtado, L. W. 45 n., 62 n., 67 n.,
    133–6, 234 n., 235
Hussey, W. 360
Huxley, A. 223 n.
Hyder, O. Q. 227 n.

Iamblichus 170 n.
Ignatius of Antioch, St 99 n.
Ignatius of Loyola, St 19
Innocent X, Pope 351
Inwagen, P. van 210 n., 212 n., 282 n.
Irenaeus, St 16, 17, 19, 39 n., 317
Isidore 171 n.

Jackson, J. 310
Jaeger, W. 169 n.
James, E. 340
James, P. 360 n., 361 n.
Jamros, D. P. 2 n.
Jeremias, J 33 n., 241 n.
John Climacus, St 161
John of the Cross, St 22, 343
John of Damascus, St 147, 165, 170,
    175 n., 184–5, 190–6
John Paul II, Pope 13 n., 48
John Philoponus 167 n., 170 n.
Johnson, A. R. 37 n.
Johnson, D. 47 n.
Johnson, E. 73 n.
Johnson, T. H. 308 n.
Johnston, M. 202 n.
Jones, J. 225 n.
Jones, P. D. 146 n., 147 n.
Jónsson, G. A. 39 n.
Jossua, J.-P. 19 n.
Justin Martyr, St 7, 32, 99
Justinian, Emperor 183

Kalbfleisch, C. 169 n., 170 n.
Kampf, A. 355 n.
Kandinsky, W. 332
Kannengiesser, C. 185 n.
Kant, I. 151, 154, 156, 159, 314 n.,
    330–1
Karmel, B. 336 n.
Käsemann, E. 65 n., 87 n., 242
Kasper, W. 84 n.
Kaufman, G. 149 n., 151

Kaufmann, R. 348 n.
Kendall, D. 4 n., 13 n., 14 n., 24 n., 63 n., 159 n., 247 n.
Kennedy, J. F. 223 n.
Keswick, W. 361 n.
Kierkegaard, S. 12, 25, 272 n.
Kim, S. 73 n.
Kitaj, R. B. 355 n.
Klawans, J. 138 n.
Klee, P. 332
Klein, J. 310 n.
Klein, U. 170 n.
Kominiak, B. 32 n.
Kotter, B. 175 n., 190 n., 191 n., 192 n., 193 n.
Kreeft, P. 222 n., 226
Kripke, S. 318–19, 320
Kroll, G. 171 n.
Kuntz, J. K. 33 n.
Kuschel, K.-J. 63 n., 67 n.

Lamberz, E. 176 n.
Lampe, G. W. H. 160
Lang, C. 362 n.
Lantero, E. 226 n.
Lawrence, D. H. 1 n.
Leder, C. 336 n.
Lee, A. 22 n.
Lee, R. E. 227–8
Leftow, B. 27 n., 210 n., 214 n., 218 n., 245 n.
  on divine properties 215
  on divine timelessness 6 n., 273–99
  on social trinitarianism 247 n.
Leiris, M. 350 n., 351 n., 352 n.
Leo the Great, St 19 n., 146
Leonardo da Vinci 345
Leontius of Byzantium 166–70, 173 n., 175–8, 182–5, 190, 192 n., 196 n.
Levertov, D. 303, 305
Lewis, C. S. 221, 223 n., 244
Lewis, G. S. 55 n.
Leys, R. 38 n.
Lienhard, J. T. 163 n.
Lietzmann, H. 173 n.
Lincoln, A. 297–8
Lindars, B. 91 n.
Lindbeck, G. 149–50
Locke, J. 268, 283 n., 285, 287
Lohse, E. 71 n.
Lorca, F. 340
Lovering, E. H. 45 n.
Lull, R. 341 n.

MacCarthy, F. 335 n., 336 n., 337 n., 338 n., 358 n.
MacDonald, M. 156 n.
MacDonald, S. 204 n., 214 n., 218 n.
MacDonald, W. G. 37 n.
Mach, M. 36 n.
MacKinnon, D. M. 222, 230
MacLeod, D. 246 n., 248, 267–8, 269
Macquarrie, J. 49 n.
Madden, N. 185 n., 187 n., 188 n.
Magritte, G. 349–50, 364
Magritte, R. 348, 349–50
Mai, A. 166 n.
Maimonides, M. 43 n.
Maistre, R. de 353 n.
Marchesi, G. 24 n.
Marinus 195 n.
Marsh, J. 236 n.
Martin, R. P. 62 n.
Martin, S. 268–9
Masaccio (Tommaso di Giovanni di Simone Guidi) 360 n.
Mataric, M. J. 325 n.
Mauser, U. 44 n.
Maximilla 21 n.
Maximus Confessor, St 170, 184–91, 195
McFague, S. 151
McGuckin, J. A. 148 n.
McInerny, R. 151 n.
McKnight, S. L. 205 n.
McLeod, F. G. 39 n.
Meier, J. P. 241 n.
Meier, S. 36 n.
Melito of Sardis, St 7
Meltzoff, A. 325 n.
Mercadante, L. A. 22 n.
Merton, T. 309
Mettinger, T. 43 n.
Metzger, B. M. 70 n., 91
Meuris, J. 350 n.
Meyendorff, J. 146
Michelangelo Buonarroti 342
Mill, J. S. 320 n.
Millard, A. 39 n.
Millet, J. F. 339 n.
Milosz, C. 308
Milton, J. 331
Mingana, A. 178 n.
Mitchinson, D. 360 n., 361 n.
Moltmann, J. 49 n.
Mondrian, P. 332
Monroe, M. 344

Montanus 21 n.
Moo, D. 87 n., 105 n., 106 n.
Moore, H. 357, 360–1, 358
More, St Thomas 329
Moreau, G. 334
Morgan, D. 333 n.
Morris, T. V. 212 n.
    on Christ's sinlessness 14–15
    on Christ's two minds 251–2, 287
    on Council of Chalcedon 157–8,
        210 n.
    on kenotic Christology 257–8
    on reduplicative propositions 212 n.,
        289
Morrison, J. T. 47 n.
Murdoch, I. 330–1
Murphy-O'Connor, J. 63 n., 65 n., 67 n.
Musaeus 122

Nagel, T. 230 n., 286 n., 314
Napoleon Bonaparte, Emperor 224
Nassif, B. 146 n.
Nemesius of Emesa 169, 176–7, 184
Néret, G. 339 n., 340 n., 341 n., 342 n.
Nestorius 145, 161
    on divine and human in Christ
        179–83, 196, 278
    on human person 280–1, 287
Neuner, J. 11 n.
Neusner, J. 46 n., 128 n., 242
Newman, A. 332
Newman, C. C. 55 n., 56 n., 59 n., 135,
        245 n.
Newman, J. H. 11–12
Newsom, C. A. 35 n., 36 n.
Nickelsburg, G. W. E. 243 n.
Nicoll, W. R. 374 n.
Nietzsche, F. W. 331
Nolde, E. 333 n.
Nolland, J. 239 n.
Norris, K. 24 n., 303–12
Norris, R. 146–53, 156, 158, 160

O'Brien, P. T. 71 n.
O'Callaghan, J. 151 n.
Ockham, W. 296
Ockinga, B. 39 n.
O'Collins, G. 48 n., 63 n., 155 n., 159,
        218 n., 245 n., 247 n.
    on Christ as judge 243 n.
    on God as *Abba* 241 n.
    on incarnation issues 1–27, 375, 394
O'Keeffe, G. 346–7, 364

Olson, E. 204 n., 284 n.
Olyan, S. M. 36 n.
Olympiodorus 169 n.
Origen 7, 39 n., 122, 135, 170 n., 172
Orwell, G. 306, 309
Osburn, C. D. 69 n.
Ozick, C. 311

Pace, G. 362
Packer, J. I. 73 n.
Padgett, A. 2 n., 5 n., 8 n., 24 n., 27 n.,
        212 n., 245 n.
Parfit, D. 268
Paul VI, Pope 11
Peers, E. A. 22 n.
Perkins, P. 222 n.
Perrin, N. 234, 236–9
Perry, J. 285 n., 286 n.
Philip the Monk 175 n.
Philo 43, 118, 124–34, 135
Philoponus, *see* John Philoponus
Picasso, P. 333, 347–8, 350, 364
Piero della Francesca 342 n.
Pike, N. 275 n.
Pilate, Pontius 2, 22
Pius XII, Pope 339 n.
Plantinga, A. 149 n., 275, 277–9,
        284 n., 285, 287
Plantinga, C. 247 n.
Plato 118–33, 201, 263
Plotinus 161, 169 n.
Polonsky, G. 355 n., 356 n.
Pople, K. 336 n., 337 n., 338 n.
Porphyry 169, 176, 177 n.
Porter, S. E. 12 n.
Poussin, N. 352
Preece, P. 337 n.
Preuschen, E. 172 n.
Prisca 21 n.
Proclus of Constantinople, St 146, 173 n.
Pseudo-Athanasius 169 n.
Pseudo-Dionysius, *see* Dionysius the
        Pseudo-Areopagite
Pusey, P. E. 179 n., 180 n.
Putnam, H. 149 n., 318–20
Pyrrhus 189 n., 195 n.

Quinn, P. L. 313 n.
Quinton, A. 285 n.
Quirinius, Publius Sulpicius 381 n.

Rad, G. von 40 n., 42, 44
Raffelt, A. 395 n.

Rahner, K.:
  on Council of Chalcedon 144, 162
  on Christmas 374–95
  on humanity 9 n., 152
  on incarnation 17, 19–21
  on trinitarian persons 4
Ramshaw, G. 308–9
Raphael (Raffaello Sanzio) 361 n.
Rawls, J. 324 n.
Régnier, G. 348 n.
Reid, T. 270 n.
Reimer, D. J. 31 n.
Reuther, M. 333 n.
Richard of St Victor 258 n.
Richardson, C. G. 176 n.
Richardson, J. 343 n.
Riou, A. 185 n.
Roberts, R. C. 313 n.
Robinson, D. 336 n.
Robinson, H. 285 n.
Robinson, J. A. T. 221–2, 242
Robinson, J. M. 246 n.
Robinson, R. 326 n.
Rorty, A. O. 324 n.
Rosenblum, R. 346 n.
Roth, F. 272 n.
Rothenstein, J. 351 n.
Rothko, M. 332
Rouault, G. 333–5, 337, 338, 364
Rouner, L. S. 326 n.
Rousseau, J. J. 12
Rowley, H. H. 43–4
Rubens, P. P. 352 n.
Rubin, W. 348 n.
Russell, B. 244
Russell, E. 304 n.
Russell, J. 351 n., 352 n.

Sallman, W. 333 n.
Sanders, E. P. 239 n., 240 n.
Sanders, J. A. 31
Sanna, I. 19 n.
Saward, J. 317 n.
Sayers, D. 391
Schillebeeckx, E. 374–95
Schindler, O. 329
Schleiermacher, F. D. E. 7–8, 374 n.
Schnabel, E. J. 73 n., 78 n.
Scholer, D. M. 127 n.
Schoonenberg, P. 4–5, 17
Schüssler Fiorenza, E. 59 n.
Schwartz, E. 145 n., 179 n.
Schweizer, E. 79

Schwöbel, C. 45 n.
Scipioni, L. I. 182 n., 183 n.
Scotus, *see* Duns Scotus, Blessed John
Secrest, M. 340 n., 341 n.
Segal, A. 3 n., 6 n., 50, 54, 116–39
Sellars, V. 145 n.
Senor, T. 275 n., 276 n., 290 n., 299
Severus of Antioch 147, 170
Shanes, E. 357 n.
Shenouda III, Pope 11
Sherwood, P. 185 n.
Shoemaker, S. 268 n., 283 n., 285 n.
Shuster, M. 24 n., 373–96
Siclari, A. 177 n.
Silber, E. 362 n., 363 n.
Simonetti, M. 32 n.
Simplicius 169 n., 170 n., 172
Simpson, E. 313 n.
Sinclair, A. 351 n., 353 n.
Slusser, M. 145 n., 146 n., 158
Sly, D. 130 n.
Smalley, S. S. 91 n.
Smart, N. 155
Smith, L. P. 226 n.
Smythies, J. 285 n.
Socrates 119–23, 129, 200–1, 204 n.
Söderblum, N. 22
Soderlund, S. K. 67 n., 73 n.
Soskice, J. M. 154
Sotiropoulos, C. 185 n., 186 n.
Spencer, G. 336 n., 338 n., 339 n.
Spencer H. 337 n.
Spencer, Stanley 333, 335–9, 363
Spencer, Sydney 337 n.
Spies, W. 349 n.
Stafford, W. 311–12
Stallabrass, J. 360 n.
Stead, G. C. 154 n.
Stewart, J. 394 n.
Strachan, R. 395 n.
Strauss, D. F. 1, 2 n., 3
Stump, E. 8 n., 10 n., 197–218
Sturch, R. 10
Successus 180
Swinburne, R. 8, 163 n., 212 n.
  on Council of Chalcedon 158–9
  on Christ's two minds 251 n., 252 n.,
    287, 291
  on kenotic Christology 246 n., 248,
    260–1
  on personal identity 268, 270,
    283 n., 285 n.
  on Trinity 258 n., 264 n.

Sylvester, D. 351 n., 352
Syrianus 171

Tacelli, R. K. 222 n., 226 n.
Taliaferro, C. 313 n.
Tanner, N. P. 183 n.
Teilhard de Chardin, P. 17, 27 n.
Telfer, W. 177 n.
Temple, W. 259
Teresa of Calcutta, Mother 329
Tertullian 4, 5, 25
Theodore of Mopsuestia 178, 180, 183
Theodoret of Cyrus 180–3
Theophrastus 172 n.
Thielicke, H. 374–96
Thomas, A. 339 n.
Tillemont, L. S. Le Nain de 176 n.
Tillich, P. 341, 374 n.
Timothy of Berytus 173
Tomlin, L. 269
Tonneau, R. 178 n.
Toorn, K. van der 36 n.
Trakatellis, D. C. 32 n.
Trypho 3, 7
Tuggy, D. 245 n.
Turner, M. 45 n.
Turner, E. H. 346 n., 347 n.
Twain, M. 216

Vacek, E. 313 n.
Valentinus 173
Vanstone, W. H. 250
Vaughan, B. 362 n.
Velásquez, D. 351
Vermes, G. 47–8, 50, 235 n., 239 n.

Walther, I. F. 347 n., 348 n.
Waltke, B. 73 n.
Warhol, A. 333, 343–6, 364

Warncke, C.-P. 347 n., 348 n.
Warne, G. J. 45 n.
Warner, M. 349 n.
Watson, G. 324 n.
Watson, J. D. 341 n.
Watts, R. 54 n.
Weiser, M. 395 n.
Wendebourg, D. 162 n.
Werther, D. 15 n.
Westerink, L. G. 171 n.
Whitaker, C. H. 126 n.
Wickham, L. R. 145 n.
Wiener, G. A. 272 n.
Wilde, O. 148
Wilkes, K. V. 291 n.
Wilkinson, A. G. 360 n., 361 n.
William of Wykeham, Bishop 164
Williams, A. G. 364 n.
Williams, B. 313 n., 314
Wilson, M. F. 374 n.
Wilson, R. 39 n.
Witherington, B. 59 n., 73 n., 74 n., 75 n., 77 n., 241 n., 243 n.
Wittgenstein, L. 149, 155
Wolfson, H. A. 124 n., 131 n.
Wolterstorff, N. 149 n.
Wright, N. T. 67 n., 70 n.
  on Jesus' self-understanding 24, 47–61, 233, 242 n.
  on precedents for incarnation 6 n., 137–8
  on wisdom 74 n.

Yates, W. 351 n.
Yonge, C. D. 127 n.
Yorke, M. 358 n.

Zagzebski, L. 18, 313–31
Zuntz, G. 70 n.